THE RISE OF MODERN EUROPE

*A SURVEY OF EUROPEAN HISTORY
IN ITS POLITICAL, ECONOMIC, AND CULTURAL ASPECTS
FROM THE END OF THE MIDDLE AGES
TO THE PRESENT*

———

FOUNDING EDITOR

WILLIAM L. LANGER

Harvard University

THE
PROTESTANT
REFORMATION

1517–1559

BY

LEWIS W. SPITZ
Stanford University

ILLUSTRATED

1817

HARPER & ROW, PUBLISHERS, New York
Cambridge, Philadelphia, San Francisco, London
Mexico City, São Paulo, Sydney

Grateful acknowledgment is made for permission to reprint the maps on pp. xiv, 284 and 318:

page xiv: *Atlas of World History*, ed. R. R. Palmer. © Rand McNally & Co., R.L. 84-S-3. Used by permission.

page 284: *A History of the Western World*, Bryce Lyon, Herbert H. Rowen, Theodore S. Hamerow. Copyright © 1969 Houghton Mifflin Company. Used by permission.

page 318: *Historical Maps On File*, © 1984 Martin Greenwald Associates. Reprinted by permission of Facts On File, Inc., New York.

FIRST EDITION

Library of Congress Cataloging in Publication Data

Spitz, Lewis William, 1922–
    The Protestant Reformation, 1517–1559.

    (The Rise of modern Europe)
    Bibliography: p.
    Includes index.
1. Reformation.   I. Title   II. Series.
BR305.2.S66   1985   270.6   83–48805
ISBN 0-06-013958-7

85 86 87 88 89 10 9 8 7 6 5 4 3 2 1

To
Stephen Andrew
and
Philip Mathew

CONTENTS

ILLUSTRATIONS

These photographs, grouped in a section, will be found following page 128.

MAPS

PREFACE

The appearance of this volume on the Reformation is a publishing event of special significance, for it is the final volume of the distinguished series *The Rise of Modern Europe*, founded and edited by William L. Langer, the renowned diplomatic historian and initiator of the psychohistory movement of recent times. To the very end Professor Langer continued to be interested in broad questions of historical interpretation and methodology. In his last letter to the present author he wrote: "Thus far the growing interest in the whole approach of psychohistory has continued to concentrate on biography, but within the last couple of years I sense a growing tendency among younger scholars to tackle the larger and more difficult problem. More difficult, because 'social psychology' has mighty little to tell us. You can learn how small groups and larger congregations act. But LeBon did that decades ago. What we want is help in establishing motivation." May this volume take motivation into account, and in other ways be worthy of Professor Langer's memory.

Three decades have passed by since my genial mentor and dear friend Myron P. Gilmore published his excellent work on the Renaissance, *The World of Humanism 1453–1517*, which precedes this volume in the series. Since that time historians have come to stress somewhat more strongly social history, economic factors, demographic data, even climatology, although there is currently a renewed interest in cultural, political, military, and diplomatic history. Good narrative history, with sound generalization and synthesis, is finally the historian's most serious task. It is that which distinguishes his work from that of the chronicler or the producer of monographs. Such general history moves along like a hydrofoil buoyed by the specialized research of thousands of scholars—many more than could be acknowledged in the footnotes—the "black snow" of the experts.

This book presents special problems, for it is intended on the one hand to relate the history of Europe during four critical decades, and on the other hand to do justice to the Reformation movement itself, the most striking and important development in those years. Moreover, its parameters are set by the chronological limits, the tone, and the approach of the preceding and succeeding volumes. Fernand Braudel spoke of ideal history as "the sum of all possible histories, a collection of occupational skills and points of view—those of yesterday, today, and tomorrow." This volume offers a modest response to his challenging view of history.

The author owes much to many colleagues both at Stanford and throughout the historical profession. Their example, collegiality, and goodwill have proved an inspiration through the years. Special thanks are due to Christiane Andersson for preparing the album of illustrations; to Robert Kingdon, who read and improved upon Chapter 4; to Helen Defosses, who brought her demographic expertise to bear on the sections dealing with population; to Robert Rosin, who gave a close reading to the initial draft of the manuscript; to Marilyn J. Harran, who gave the final manuscript a critical reading; to Colleen Redmond for her work on the bibliography; and to Mark Edwards, who contributed substantially to the growth of the book and gave the bibliography careful scrutiny. Dr. Edna Spitz once again read the typescript, galleys, and page proofs with skill and patience. I am indebted to Hugh Van Dusen and Janet Goldstein of Harper & Row for their encouragement and for their editorial assistance in the publication of this book.

The author benefited greatly from a year at the Institute for Advanced Study, Princeton, which provided the sustained time needed for writing a good portion of this book. For that invitation I am indebted mostly to John H. Elliott and Felix Gilbert of the School of Historical Studies. While at Princeton I enjoyed the company of Natalie Davis, Theodore Rabb, Donald Queller, Kenneth Setton, Randolph Starn, Robert Somerville, J. Russell Major, Lawrence Stone, and others. The generous award of a fellowship by the National Endowment for the Humanities and a summer grant from the Pew Foundation administered by Stanford facilitated the research and writing for this volume.

"History is the mother of truth!" Luther exclaimed after the Leipzig Debate of 1519 brought home to him the power of historical knowledge. The English Catholic biographer of Luther, John Todd, writes: "A major part of the phenomenon of Luther is the extraordinary corpus of writings, over one hundred volumes in the Weimar edition. In most big libraries, books by and about Luther occupy more shelf room than those concerned with any other human being except Jesus of Nazareth." The year 1983, the quincentennial of Luther's birth, inspired the publication of dozens of new biographies and monographs as well as hundreds of articles on the great reformer. At the Heidelberg meetings of the Verein für Reformationsgeschichte G. R. Elton, Regius Professor at the University of Cambridge, sounded a cautionary note: "Luther and the Reformation are naturally linked, but they are not in fact identical. The history of the Reformation in Europe is not the same as the history of Luther in Germany. But in the quincentennial year of Luther's birth it is a bit much to expect people to make that distinction." Perhaps the most significant tribute that can be paid to Luther, he added, would not be yet another biography, but a new history of the Reformation. The reader may consider this present volume a modest tribute of that kind.

In 1984 historians commemorate the five hundredth anniversary of the Swiss reformer Huldrych Zwingli's birth, and so the celebrations continue. In the words of Pericles: "The whole earth is the sepulcher of famous men and their story is not graven only on stone over their native earth, but lives on far away, without visible symbol, woven into the stuff of other men's lives." This history of the Reformation era, however, is concerned not only with uncommon men and women, but with the common people, those millions whose lives and destinies were changed by historical forces they but dimly perceived and could scarcely understand. On June 20, 1543, Luther wrote to Wenceslas Link, who had requested a foreword for his book on the first part of the Old Testament: "But, anyway, here you have the preface, however it turned out. If you do not like it, you can either change it, if you wish, or throw it out."

Reformation Day, 1984
LEWIS W. SPITZ
STANFORD UNIVERSITY

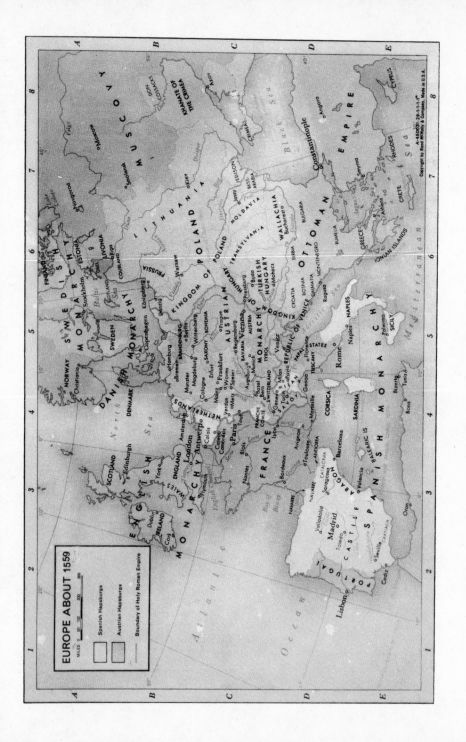

THE PROTESTANT REFORMATION
1517–1559

Chapter One

REFORMATION EUROPE

1. REFORMATION AND RENAISSANCE

FEW periods in the long history of Europe have had such a momentous impact upon the western world as the four decades lying between the years 1517 and 1559. It began when a very personal matter, Luther's struggle for a right relationship to God, became a popular cause. Its end was marked by an auspicious public event, for Europe entered one of its rare interludes of peace.

The year 1517 was notable for nothing more than the festive close by Pope Leo X of the ineffectual Fifth Lateran Council and the nailing of ninety-five theses for a university disputation by a lowly Augustinian monk. The year 1559 saw the signing of the Treaty of Cateau-Cambrésis, which formalized the relations between France, Spain, and the Holy Roman Empire for decades to come. That same year witnessed yet other events of telling importance: the opening of the third session of the Council of Trent, the murder of Henry II in France, the death of Pope Paul IV, the demise of Christian III (who had established Lutheranism in Denmark), the English Parliament's Acts of Supremacy and Act of Uniformity, the publication of the definitive edition of Calvin's *Institutes,* a revolt and the return of John Knox to Scotland. A year before, Queen Mary and her Catholic counselor Cardinal Reginald Pole had died on the same November day. In 1560 Gustavus I, who established Lutheranism in Sweden, died. These four decades corresponded roughly to the reign of Emperor Charles V in the West and of Suleiman the Magnificent in the East. Charles V became king of Spain in 1516 and Holy Roman Emperor in 1519 and abdicated soon after the Peace of Augsburg in 1555. Suleiman succeeded his father Selim I in 1520 and died in 1566. The other two most colorful kings had preceded him, Henry VIII of England dying in January of 1547 and Francis I of France in March of the same year. There are, then, historical events of critical importance or of symbolic value that justify the parameters of this volume between the two fixed dates. But essentially the coherence of this period rests on the fact that the Protestant

Reformation was on the offensive, enjoying rapid success and expansion during the forty years that lay between the world of humanism and the Counter-Reformation.

The historian who describes and analyzes the events of a narrowly defined span of time must remain conscious of the long-term developments consuming centuries or millennia in their unfolding. Fernand Braudel, nestor of the influential *Annales* school, distinguishes between the conspicuous history that holds our attention by its continual and dramatic changes and that other, submerged history, almost silent and always discreet, virtually unsuspected either by its observers or its participants, which is almost untouched by the obstinate erosion of time.[1] He describes the history dealing with short-term realities as *conjuncture* (ten-, twenty-, or fifty-year periods) and that dealing with long-term realities as *structure.* If it is no longer fashionable to describe the Reformation in the words of the Whig historian James Froude as "the hinge on which all modern history turns," it remains true that the Protestant Reformation was one of those highly significant conjunctures that have determined the course of Western history. Of course, one must remain aware of long-term realities and the glacial pace of some basic developments. In a brief span of time only very little can occur that detectably alters the basic climatic, geographic, and demographic features of that appendage to the Asian landmass known in modern times as Europe. Economic forces and social institutions are patently less volatile and subject to rapid change than are political, religious, and intellectual forces. But social historians who are disdainful of all but statistical evidence and the condition of the masses are in grave danger of producing hoministic rather than humanistic history (reminding one of Disraeli's comment that there are three kinds of lies —lies, more lies, and statistics). The intellectual and spiritual aspects of life, those that grip the heart and mind, are subject to spectacular change. The historian Sir Lewis Namier, who once observed that fifty men do not make one centipede, believed that history can never be anything else than the story of men in action. Many of the eventmakers in history have been uncommon men, the world's most persistent minority group. History is the story of *homo sapiens* gifted with a capacity for thought and spiritual aspirations. The nineteenth-century English historian Thomas Carlyle, who lionized Luther as a religious *Wundermann,* in his *Essays* quite rightly

1. Fernand Braudel, "History and the Social Sciences," in Peter Burke, ed., *Economy and Society in Early Modern Europe: Essays from Annales* (New York, 1972), pp. 11–39, 12–13.

asked: "What is all knowledge, too, but recorded experience, and a product of history; of which, therefore, reasoning and belief, no less than action and passion, are essential materials?" Acknowledgment of this elementary fact is a necessary first step toward an authentic appreciation of Reformation history.

It is possible to write the history of this period exclusively as the story of the Protestant religious movement. It is also possible simply to chronicle the history of all of Europe at the time of the Protestant Reformation. But yet another approach, more in keeping with the purpose and tenor of this series, commends itself, namely, to emphasize the account of the religious Reformation as the most characteristic and dominant achievement of the time, but to include also the most significant developments in other areas of life throughout the European world. "Better fifty years of Europe than a cycle of Cathay," penned Tennyson, but to portray even a half century of European history is a formidable task, so complex is that history and so enormous the mountain of scholarly literature that looms above it. More has been written about Luther, it has been said, than about any other person in the history of the world with the exception of Christ.

The term "Protestant Reformation" has become so much a part of everyman's conceptual scheme of history that its source and original connotation are sometimes forgotten. It was at the Diet of Speyer in 1529, which revoked the recess of 1526 favorable to the Lutherans, that the term "Protestant" was born. For there the Lutheran estates protested that the recess could be revoked only by the mutual consent of both Lutherans and Catholics and that they could not be forced to act against faith and conscience. So they came to be called "the Protesting Estates" or "Protestants." The word from the very beginning had both a negative and a positive connotation, for the Protestants not only objected to illegal action but also affirmed their evangelical faith. The word "Reformation" has a much longer and complex history, and its relation to the term "Renaissance" sheds interesting light on the historical assessment of the period.

The idea of reformation in Western intellectual history was essentially a Judeo-Christian conception, although it had antecedents in pre-Christian literature, in Greco-Roman and even in preliterate religious belief. In the Christian tradition it was basically associated with personal spiritual regeneration and individual reform. During the medieval period it was used to describe the restoration of an ideal monastic community life and it was applied also to the Gregorian reform of the eleventh and twelfth centuries to restore "the right order of things in the world," establishing the independence of the church from control by secular rulers. Even though the cosmological, vitalistic, millennarian, and conversion ideologies were out of phase with the Christian linear view of history, some aspects of renewal ideologies were adapted to and fused with the medieval ideas of reformation. During the sixteenth century the call for individual, ecclesiastical, and social reform became louder, more strident and insistent than ever before. The term eventually came to be associated almost exclusively with the sixteenth-century development within church history and applied to an entire era of general European history.

It comes as a surprise to learn that Luther did not apply the word "reformation" to his movement as a whole. He used the term in the legal sense of the restoration of the old state of affairs, not in an apocalyptic or utopian sense. Only in connection with the reform of the university did he use the word to describe the creation of something new, a new liberal arts and theological curriculum. As the organization of territorial churches emerged, the concept of a re-formation of the church in Protestant lands developed. The first serious, self-conscious, and consistent use of the term "reformation" for the evangelical movement came only in the seventeenth century with the histories of the famed Lutheran Veit Ludwig von Seckendorf. Like Luther, Calvin viewed his cause only as an evangelizing of the one church, the *una sancta,* not as a separatist movement. Zwingli differed in emphasis, for his conception of a "restoration of Christendom" in a city-state context had more explicit social as well as spiritual implications. By the eighteenth century historians quite generally acknowledged the Reformation as an independent and separable period of Western history. The word "Reformation" was applied to a wide variety of reforms in Enlightenment society.

The idea of Reformation, then, differed from the concept of Renaissance with its renewal imagery, cyclical and vitalistic connotations. Classical culture had borrowed from the renewal myths of the ancient Near East. The Romans associated the longing for a rebirth of culture and advent of better fortunes with the hope for a return of the Golden Age under the aegis of Saturn. The term *restitutio* gained currency with the revival of Roman law from the twelfth century on. In the fourteenth century Cola di Rienzo's abortive attempt to restore the Roman republic awakened the desire for political rebirth and the fifteenth century witnessed a broad humanist and artistic effort toward cultural renewal. The term *rinascita* (rebirth), in the sense in which historians have come to use it, however, was first introduced and gradually adopted only during the sixteenth century. In 1553 the natural philosopher Pierre Belon substituted the French word *renaissance* for *rinascita* to describe a new cultural epoch which began in Florence and spread through Italy and Europe in the sixteenth century. The concepts of the Renaissance as a cultural rebirth and the Reformation as a religious restoration were clearly distinguishable. But they were so closely related that Renaissance and Reformation have become forever linked in the mind of Western man. The thrust of much recent research has been to stress the affinity and close interior ties of the two historical epochs. Their genuine cultural cohesiveness is most obvious in the continuance of Christian humanism into the seventeenth century. In the matter of religious intensity and the evangelical direction of religious concern, in contrast to the metaphysical and ethical emphasis of the Renaissance, there developed an essential difference which proves the impossibility of completely identifying the two. Taken together, it has been argued, they constitute the twin cradle of modernity.

But historical concepts are empty and meaningless unless they are filled with the rich and near infinite subject matter of history from which they themselves were derived, history as past actuality as reflected in narrative and analysis. Edward Gibbon near the end of his monumental *Decline and Fall of the Roman Empire* observed: "After a fair discussion we shall rather be surprised by the timidity than scandalized by the freedom of our first reformers." The account that follows, however, will reveal that the Reformation, for all its conservative overtones and its intensely religious drive, was a more radical historical movement than the Renaissance. It provoked the breakup of the unity of Christendom and the breakthrough of modern Europe with the introduction of religious pluralism, the development of the national churches, the further growth of national monarchies, and the dramatic expansion and eventual ascendancy of Europe in the world. With the seventeenth-century additions in the natural sciences, the advances in mathematics, and the continuous development of a more comprehensive rationalism, all the ingredients were present for the rise of modern technological and industrial culture and national liberal states or totalitarian societies. The Protestant Reformation was a conjuncture of critical importance for the whole course of modern history.

2. POPULATION: FIGURES AND TRENDS

Historians have in recent decades evolved a new way of examining the past: from the bottom up rather than from the top down. Great men and great events are today viewed as less significant clues to an age than was true in the heroic days of nineteenth-century historiography when Thomas Carlyle wrote: "Universal History, the history of what man has accomplished in this world, is at bottom the history of great men who have worked here." Influenced by the positivist sociological strain and the *Annalistes* historical school, the "new" history emphasizes economic processes, social and cultural facts, the ordinary as well as the uncommon events in the lives and perceptions of common people. While regrettably some naive historians, often with a blare of trumpets, proclaim that the two approaches are mutually exclusive, or that social history on a quantifying basis possesses a monopoly on real history, demographic data subject to statistical methodology clearly do supply the necessary quantified base for prosopography or group biography. The sources for such data are not state documents but parish registries, tax returns, local census reports, estate financial records, and military manpower requisitions. Unfortunately the sources for demographic studies are far less reliable for the early sixteenth century than they became with the eighteenth century and especially after the modernization of the state with the French Revolution and Napoleon. Nevertheless, while fully recognizing the limitations of the sources and the necessarily tentative nature of the highly speculative estimates, it will prove useful to survey the demographic profile of Europe in these decades, collating the soundest research of primarily English, French, and German demographers.

The intellectuals of the fifteenth and sixteenth centuries commented on birthrates and population in a way that reflected conditions and requirements of their time. Leon Battista Alberti in his *Della Famiglia,* 1432, reflecting a period of low population following the Great Plague of 1348, alluded unfavorably to the limitation of births, and urged the state to honor those who have the most children. Dour Francesco Guicciardini, living during Italy's time of troubles under Spanish dominance, commented that it is a kind of good fortune not to have any children. Machiavelli pointed to the risk of overpopulation and attributed to it plague and famine. Thomas More in his *Utopia,* 1516, argued that the state must know its population since that is what guarantees its resources and furnishes its armies. Jean Bodin in his *Six Books of the Republic*, 1576, wrote that "there is neither riches nor power, but only men." He argued that the state should know the number of people in each social category—nobles, bourgeois, common people—taking note of the professions and of vagabonds, for only if the state is informed statistically can it act consequentially. Near the end of the sixteenth century, after a dramatic population expansion, Giovanni Botero in 1589 urged the necessity of achieving a balance between births and resources, the *virtus generativa et virtus nutritiva*. He found historical evidence, ancient and modern, for the fact that overpopulation produces epidemics, famines, wars, slavery, brigandage, and cannibalism.[2] Concerns about overpopulation, then, were already expressed in the sixteenth century, although such fears are commonly associated with the Rev. Thomas Robert Malthus's *An Essay on the Principle of Population*, 1798, in which he warned that "the power of population is indefinitely greater than the power in the earth to produce subsistence for man!"

In his programmatic article on "History" in the *Dictionnaire philosophique*, 1764, Voltaire admonished historians to give greater attention to details, precise dates, and population. But in the sixteenth century Guicciardini had already pointed to the administrative skill of the Romans, who had carried out a systematic census of people and properties. The practice of regular enumerations of the population was introduced to Europe by that most serene city Venice, which learned the procedure from the Byzantine Empire. In 1268 the Grand Council initiated an extensive statistical inquiry and by the end of the thirteenth century the Venetians had developed a complete statistical service. Sicily rivaled Venice in the antiquity of its population census, which may have been learned from the Moslems. In subsequent centuries Naples, the Papal States, Tuscany, Genoa, Milan, and other cities produced demographic documentation, often in connection with tax assessments. In the north the German states of Prussia, Brandenburg, and Saxony were precocious, developing population records in the fifteenth century, and the Swiss followed along.

The parish records perhaps provide the most universal source of demographic information, despite their many failings. There are discrepancies in the records between births and baptisms, deaths and burials, lacunae in

2. Marcel R. Reinhard and André Armengaud, *Histoire Générale de la Population Mondiale* (Paris, 1961), pp. 81–83.

the records, chronological confusion of the series of registries, and instability of parish boundaries and discordance with city limits. Frequently, no proper distinction is made between the legally recognized population and the actual number of inhabitants, and there is the inconvenience resulting from a conventional chronological division.[3] All this is to say that the population statistics of the early sixteenth century are highly speculative and in general can afford us little more than a rough demographic estimate. Moreover, the reliability of the figures becomes increasingly tentative the farther east one moves.

It is thought that from 1100 to 1650 the overall world population of possibly 500,000,000 people probably increased very little, but that the population of Europe had grown steadily until the middle of the fourteenth century when the Black Death wiped out as much as 25 to 30 percent or in some localities even more of the population of central and western Europe. Losses due to war, famine, and the plague continued sporadically, so that during the remainder of the fourteenth century and throughout the fifteenth, Europe barely maintained its population level and only gradually recovered the total number it had achieved before the disaster struck. Though less dramatic than the bubonic plague, malaria took a continuous and steady toll throughout the Mediterranean world, leaving people weak and enervated, if not dead. The sixteenth century, however, witnessed a dramatic population expansion which provided an enlarged base for the so-called vitalistic revolution of the ensuing centuries. The first half of the sixteenth century, then, was one of growing population pressure, with all the economic implications resulting in terms of higher food and land prices, relatively lower wages, and popular unrest.

A number of variable factors contributed to this population growth. Just as in the high Middle Ages (from the eleventh to the fourteenth century), there was an increase of births over deaths. But there was a marked difference in the birthrate between cities and country. It has been estimated that for a German city of 20,000 or more in the fourteenth and fifteenth centuries, only half of the population was generated by city dwellers, so that the population level could be maintained and new growth achieved only by the immigration of country folk. The limited housing and employment opportunities in the crafts and guilds contributed to the difficulty of early marriage in the city, and families produced small num-

3. Roger Mols, S.J., *Introduction à la Démographie Historique des Villes d'Europe du XIVᵉ au XVIIIᵉ Siècle*, I (Louvain, 1954), pp. 18–19, 261–290.

bers of children. One factor that contributed to the overall increase of population in the sixteenth century was the lowering of the marriage age for women. In England, for example, the marriage age dropped from twenty-four at the time of Edward I (1272–1307) to twenty at the beginning of the sixteenth century. In the high Middle Ages the migration of people from central and to a lesser extent from western Europe into eastern Europe or into sparsely inhabited newly cleared areas led to colonization predominantly by the peasant population in contrast to the transient migrations of nomadic peoples in Asia. This eastward migration and expansion contributed to the overall geographical biological base of the European population. Moreover, the sixteenth century witnessed a second such surge of population movement and growth, although on a scale much more limited in number and duration. While it is impossible to be statistically precise, the fact of an impressive demographic growth from 1450 to 1550 continuing on to 1600 is well established. This was accompanied by economic expansion, increased production and exchange. There were great regional variations, of course, such as the geographical expansion of Russia, in contrast to the supposed static popular state of southeast Europe under the Turkish hegemony. Emigration to the New World, largely of peasants, was small but as a mark of population growth not a negligible index. Because of the variations it will serve a useful purpose to examine European demography by cities, countries, or regions. In the telling phrase of A. L. Schlözer, "History is a statistic in movement; the statistic is history in repose."

This rapid demographic survey begins in the south with Italy and Spain, moving up through central Europe, then to western, northern, and eastern Europe to Russia. Estimates for the population of Italy as a whole vary greatly, but a reasonably fair approximation suggests that in the mid-fourteenth century, just before the Black Death struck, the total population was about 10.5 million. After the decimation by the plague—which may have claimed 25 to 30 percent of the population in most cities; evidence for rural areas is less certain—the population gradually rose nearly to that figure again by the early sixteenth century and then advanced slowly to 11 million by the end of the sixteenth century. Italy held its own in terms of population and wealth during that century longer than historians have supposed and yielded its traditional commercial leadership only in the latter half and especially toward the end of the century.

The regional differences within Italy are striking though perfectly understandable in view of its geographic fragmentation and political divisions. Both Sicily and Naples were under Spanish kings from 1504 to 1713 and during the sixteenth century enjoyed a long period of peace disturbed only by occasional raids of Turkish pirates from North Africa. Spanish census figures show nearly a doubling of the population of Sicily during the course of the sixteenth century, from 600,000 at the start of the century to 1,100,000 at the end of the century. Sicilian cities registered a lively growth, quadrupling in size from a total of 25,000 to 100,000. At the end of the century Catania stood at 18,000 and Messina at 42,000. The kingdom of Naples experienced a similar increase, with a rise from 1,500,000 to 2,000,000 between 1443 and 1518. The capital city grew dramatically during the early sixteenth century, requiring the building of new city walls in 1533, and by 1547 it had reached 225,000 inhabitants, although some of the smaller towns around lost some population, perhaps through emigration to Naples.

Demographic statistics on the Papal States are very sparse and unreliable, but we are better informed on the city of Rome itself. Rome experienced a growth from around 30,000 in 1393, 36,000 in 1458, 55,000 in 1520, to nearly 100,000 at the end of the sixteenth century. The region around Rome, which developed a new resurgence of feudalism under the pope's patronage system, had a population of a quarter of a million people, mostly centered in such towns as Viterbo, with about 15,000 inhabitants. Bologna had some 70,000 inhabitants in 1527. Umbria may have had as many as 300,000 inhabitants, but they were spread throughout smaller settlements, such as Perugia and lesser towns.

Tuscany progressed relatively slowly and in the subsequent century seems even to have lost ground. We are somewhat better informed on the second half of the century, when the statistics indicate a slight growth from 913,000 inhabitants in 1550 to 980,000 in 1600, with a drop to 920,000 by 1650. Another estimate, however, is more modest, citing 525,000 for 1551 and 570,000 for 1622. The city of Florence had a population of approximately 70,000 in 1527. Siena had some 20,000, but declined somewhat after its conquest by Florence. In northern Italy two great cities, Milan and Venice, were dominant. The population of Milan exceeded 100,000 by 1592. Venice, which had a population of 163,000 in 1563, grew to 170,000 in 1576, the apogee, and fell off after the plague of 1577 to 120,000, where it stabilized. It is thought that some four to five thousand Venetian families lived in the Venetian imperial outposts in the eastern Mediterranean during the later sixteenth century.

During the greater part of the sixteenth century Spain experienced a very striking increase in population, although the final decades seem to have witnessed a population decline which accompanied major economic dislocations. Galicia in the northwest had a population of approximately 600,000 around 1490, and about 900,000 a century later. The population of Castile doubled in six decades, from 3,000,000 in 1530 to 6,000,000 in 1594. The region around Salamanca increased by a third, and the area around Toledo doubled. Valencia experienced a moderate increase between 1527 and 1563, but then there was a major growth. The peasant population tended to emigrate to the emerging coastal cities, escaping the latifundia of the Spanish feudal system. Seville grew to be a city of 100,-000, thanks to its commercial importance, but Madrid was a mere village until Philip II made it his capital, when it grew to some 60,000 people. The total Spanish population may have increased to 11,000,000 in the earlier sixteenth century only to fall off to 8,400,000 at the end of the century; an even more disastrous decline in the seventeenth century to 5,000,000 or 5,700,000 followed, with a return to the sixteenth-century maximum only in the eighteenth century.

Like Spain's, the population pattern in Portugal reflected the contrast between the semiarid zones and the burgeoning maritime areas. By the middle of the sixteenth century Lisbon had passed the 65,000 population mark. At the start of the century the total population was 800,000 to 850,000, and by the end of the century it was around a million. According to Fernand Braudel, the effects of overseas emigration from the Iberian peninsula did not produce significant population decreases until the seventeenth century.

The population of Germany experienced a dramatic increase during the course of the sixteenth century, and a substantial part of that growth took place during the first half of the century. There is still a debate as to the advance in numbers in western Germany, but there is some agreement that the population rose from 12,000,000 to 20,000,000 during the century. Because of the recent emphasis upon the role of the cities in the Reformation, note should be taken of the multiplying of the urban population, the growth of many small cities without the development of any huge cities comparable to Milan or Venice. There were some sixty-five free imperial cities *(Reichsstädten)*, subject only to the emperor and summoned to the Diet, and over 2,000 territorial cities or towns *(Landstädten)* subject to princes, some of them larger than many imperial cities and a considerable number of them proudly and justly calling themselves free cities *(Freistädten)*. The city of Cologne was the largest, with over 40,000 inhabitants. The list of cities exceeding 20,000 in population includes Nuremberg, Augsburg, Ulm, Strasbourg, and Metz, as well as Vienna and Prague. In the north, Erfurt, Lübeck, Magdeburg, and Danzig exceeded 20,000. There were possibly ten cities between the 10,000 and 20,000 size, such as Frankfurt-am-Main, Rostock, Breslau, and Brunswick, and perhaps as many as 200 small or medium-sized cities of 2,000 to 10,000. The vast majority were very limited in size—from 500 to 2,000 or smaller. Whereas some cities such as Worms, Speyer, Mainz, and Freiburg remained fairly static, others such as Lübeck, Danzig, Hamburg, Leipzig, Ulm, Augsburg, and Nuremberg blossomed and in some cases more than doubled their size during the course of the century. At the time of the Reformation possibly 10 to 15 percent of the population lived in sizable towns or cities. The colonization of the east, which had played such an important role in the medieval eastward expansion, began anew in the 1520s and 1530s, and reached a high point of expansion in 1550, especially in the territories of Brandenburg and Pomerania. New clearings were made along the Warta River, in the Neumark, and the lower Silesia areas, new deforestation of the wooded belt between German and Polish settlements. Dutch and Friesian settlers cleared the marshy lands along the Vistula for settlements. Where the new mining operations were undertaken in the Erzgebirge, for example, population centers developed to the end of the sixteenth century. As the large land holdings in the east coalesced and peasants were reduced to a feudal status, many eastern cities withered as market centers for the landed economy and experienced a decline in population.

The Swiss population grew during the sixteenth century despite the constant drain of mercenaries leaving to serve in foreign armies. With births outstripping deaths, the forest cantons were the great reservoir of population growth, sending country folk to fill the cities in the plains below. A marked population increase is noticeable after the religious war of 1531–32. The canton of Bern grew from 40,000 in 1499 to 65,000 people in 1558. From 1529 to 1785 the canton of Zurich grew from 50,000 to 70,000. There was a gradual retreat from serfdom in the sixteenth century and a dropping off from feudally prescribed marriages. But a large class of daily wage earners without any landholding developed. From the fifteenth century to the eighteenth there were constant emigrations, and it is estimated that between 100,000 and 120,000 people left the country permanently, some 20,000 to 25,000 during the sixteenth century. Swiss mercenary service began in the thirteenth century, and despite Zwingli's strong opposition it continued down to the time of the French Revolution, when in 1792 the French Swiss regiment disbanded and the day of the national army had arrived. The Swiss may have lost 900,000 to 1,000,000 men through mercenary service, some 250,000 to 300,000 during the course of the sixteenth century. Most of the emigrants came from the inner Swiss cantons such as Graubünden and Bern, so that despite a high birthrate, the Alpine population remained constant, whereas the midlands increased three- or fourfold.

Records for the Netherlands in our period are poor, but there is evidence of demographic growth. One rather unreliable estimate is that a total of 3,000,000 people lived in all the Netherlands. The medieval process of building dikes and filling land continued in North Holland during the sixteenth century. In 1556 the Netherlands came to Spain by inheritance, and in the latter part of the century Spanish oppression drove many people into the northern provinces. The medieval cities of Ypres and Bruges, after the silting up of its port, yielded leadership to Antwerp, which before its destruction by the Duke of Alba in 1567 had reached 100,000 inhabitants. During the latter half of the century Amsterdam replaced Antwerp as the leading commercial city, and between 1578 and 1658 it was enlarged seven times.

Spoiled by post-Napoleonic precision in such matters, historians are impatient with the vagueness of French demographic data for the sixteenth century. Although King Francis I ordered a study of the population of his realm, the documents are missing. A reasonable modern estimate is that of R. Mousnier, who proposes the figure of 16,518,000 for the countryside, to which he adds 10 percent for the city population, arriving at a total of 18,000,000. This comes close to a very old tradition which preserved the number of 20,000,000, which seems to go back to a numeration done under Charles IX, although that manuscript is precise only for men and not for women and children. Local research dependent upon parish records reveals some interesting developments. In many regions there was a powerful population increase in the first half of the sixteenth century.

In the area south of Paris, for example, from the end of the fifteenth to
the mid-sixteenth century the population doubled in places, tripled, sextu-
pled, and even increased tenfold or more in others. Natality was high but
so was mortality, and the levels of population that preceded the Black
Death were frequently not achieved. Local records also reveal a steady
emigration from the Massif Central and Languedoc toward northern
Spain. Moreover, a comparison of the number of parishes in 1568 and in
1585 shows a great increase (in the number of parishes), data that run
counter to the earlier assumption that the wars of religion and civil disorder produced severe losses in population. Paris grew from 100,000 to
200,000 during the course of the sixteenth century and then doubled its
size to 400,000 by 1730.

Tudor England experienced a dramatic population growth during the
sixteenth century, so much so that Englishmen complained loudly of overpopulation. Part of the increase was absolute, but in part the pressure
reflected migration from the countryside to overcrowded cities. The
growth was not evenly distributed over the century, however, for the first
half saw modest gains, with a much more powerful surge in the last half
century. The population in 1500 was approximately 2,700,000, in 1550
it was about 3,300,000, in 1577 it was some 4,400,000, and in 1600 it
was roughly 5,000,000. The explanation of Malthus that high real earnings made earlier marriages possible and thus increased birthrates is weak,
for those earnings would have to have been sustained for over ninety
years, whereas in actual fact real wages declined during that period.
Rather, a lower mortality rate may have been of greater importance. This
lower mortality rate was due in part to the loss of bubonic bacterial
virulence. Some historians attribute this lower mortality rate to a better
diet due to an increase in food production, though in fact agricultural
efforts could hardly keep up with the population nor was there any new
staple to feed hungry mouths, such as the potato which came to the rescue
during the so-called vital revolution of the eighteenth century. The population growth of the fifteenth century did not aid the cities, but cities
showed a marked growth during the course of the sixteenth century.
London grew to a population of 80,000 by 1545, of 120,000 by 1582,
and of 674,000 by 1700. Rough current estimates provide a figure of
700,000 or 800,000 inhabitants for Ireland in 1545, 260,000 for Wales,
and 690,000 for Scotland.

For northern Europe demographic estimates are extremely tentative and are arrived at by the highly suspect method of piecing together fragmentary information on the seventeenth and eighteenth centuries and by extrapolation making some assumptions about the early sixteenth. The most heavily settled part of Scandinavia until the middle of the fifteenth century was Denmark, and the most populous areas of Sweden and Norway were under Danish domination. Early in the sixteenth century the Swedes of the northern valleys won their independence. Sweden embraced the coastal area of north Sweden and Finland, dominating the Baltic. In the Union of Kalmar, in 1397, Norway was united with Denmark and remained so until 1814. What can be said by way of sweeping generalization is that by the seventeenth century the population of Scandinavia had reached the level previously attained in the Middle Ages after the decimation of the Black Death, which hit Norway especially hard. Denmark, it is said on a folklore level, reached its old population only in the eighteenth century. The demographers tell us that around the beginning of the sixteenth century Norway had a population of 250,000, Denmark had a population of 800,000 around the year 1300 and 660,000 in mid-seventeenth century, and Sweden had a population of 1,786,000 in 1751. As to the first half of the sixteenth century, one is tempted to say one may draw one's own conclusions.

The demographic uncertainty regarding eastern Europe makes northern Europe look like an open invitation to a positivist celebration, for our dependable information on the East is even more meagre. The population of southeastern Europe including Greece has been estimated for 1600 at 15,000,000, and the reader is free to make imaginative subtractions to arrive at the period 1517–1559. The population of the lands of the crown of Bohemia amounted to some 4,000,000, of the Austrian Alps to 2,000,000, and of upper Austria and the part of Hungary not occupied by the Turks to some 1,000,000. The lands under Ottoman Turkish occupation totaled possibly 5,600,000, a figure that includes an estimated 700,000 for the city of Constantinople. In 1526 Bohemia, Moravia, Hungary, and Croatia were joined by a personal union under the Habsburgs, a combination that played a critical role in European history, of course, until the time of the First World War in the twentieth century. All that can safely be ventured about the lands under Turkish rule is that an economic improvement and cultural upswing are evident under Turkish rule and that this development was probably accompanied by a population rise. Balkan urban centers were growing, and most likely the rural population was also increasing. As for Poland, the population expansion provides a confused picture; while the Slavs were notable for their reproductive power, nonetheless from the time of Casimir the Great (1333–1370), who settled Germans on the edge of the Carpathians, many rulers and Polish overlords invited Germans to settle in their sparsely populated lands and to bring with them the agricultural techniques developed in the west. The towns in the later Middle Ages had been largely settled by Germans; Cracow, 1257, on the plan of Breslau, and Warsaw, 1334, founded on the basis of German law. It is difficult in a period of renewed German emigration to the east—the region between the Elbe and Vistula—to be specific regarding Polish or German demographic developments.

The story of Russia during these decades is one of impressive territorial expansion and a steady but relatively modest population growth, given the vast expanse of arable land. At the beginning of the reign of Ivan III in 1462, the Muscovite principality scarcely extended to more than 430,000 square kilometers. Around 1533 the Russian state totaled 2,800,000 square kilometers and at the end of the sixteenth century it comprised more than 5,400,000 square kilometers. Just as the establishment of permanent settlements had characterized European migrations such as the German move into the east, so the territorial expansion of Russia combined with demographic growth led to colonization toward the east and south. At the same time old Russia in the basin of the Volga River experienced an intensification of cultivation and settlement. Once again the data available for the sixteenth century are insufficient to allow assured conclusions, so that it is necessary to work backward from the more reliable information available from the late seventeenth and the eighteenth centuries. Some registries of various districts provide information on the number of hamlets or settlements, though not a census of the population. The survey of the district of Tver made in 1539 mentions 2,542 hamlets, 327 new localities, and only 187 abandoned settlements; the survey made in 1548 indicates 4,224 hamlets, 653 new localities, and 278 deserted settlements. The regions around Moscow and Rostov similarly show an abundance of new villages and few deserted localities. The Novgorod region shows similar growth, as much as 50 percent in some parishes and cities. The territory of Novgorod had some 800,000 inhabitants at the beginning of the sixteenth century. The density averages out to five people per square kilometer. The Kazan district also grew, although much more tentatively, due to the political instability of the area.

Within the Muscovite state at the beginning of the sixteenth century there were approximately 96 cities, and at the middle of the century about 160, if one can glorify with the name of city those governmental and military administrative centers with their small commercial quarter. In the mid-sixteenth century Moscow was the only major city with a population of 100,000, which grew to over 200,000 by 1630. Novgorod had 27,000 inhabitants, and the other cities had populations of 1,000 or 2,000, a few as many as 8,000. The aggregate urban population was obviously minuscule for so vast a territory. The most heavily populated area lay between the Oka and the Volga rivers east of Moscow and around Novgorod. East of the Volga, the population was very thin. Toward the north the population pattern stretched out along the rivers flowing into the White Sea and Arctic Ocean. The population of European Russia has been estimated at 10,000,000 to 11,500,000 around the year 1550. To see this figure in dynamic terms one needs to add that the population at the end of the sixteenth century has been estimated at 15,000,000, and for the outgoing seventeenth century at 17,000,000 to 18,000,000, again with the greatest increases in the old area of Novgorod and Moscow. In the second half of the sixteenth century the advance to the east continued, but there was some population thinning in the center.[4]

Demography without the benefit of historical narration and analysis remains enigmatic. A historian given to unilateral causal explanations could easily be tempted to leap from such data as population increases in Germany in the last half of the century and heavy population pressure in England from mid-century on to conclusions about the early popular Reformation in Germany and the gradual Protestantizing of the English Reformation as the century advances. But such connections and correlations, if they can be established at all, are much more complex and can be plausibly sustained only insofar as the economic and sociopsychological

4. This discussion of European demography is dependent upon various authorities, most directly upon Chapter VIII, "Un nouvel essor: le XVIe siècle en Europe," in Reinhard and Armengaud, *Histoire Générale*, pp. 82–95; Ernst Wolfgang Buchholz, *Vom Mittelalter zur Neuzeit*, III, *Raum and Bevölkerung in der Weltgeschichte. Bevölkerungs-Ploetz*, 4 vols. (Würzburg, 1966), pp. 8–77; Carlo M. Cipolla, *The Economic History of World Population* (Baltimore, 1962); Karl F. Helleiner, "The Population of Europe from the Black Death to the Eve of the Vital Revolution," in E. E. Rich and C. H. Wilson, eds., *The Cambridge Economic History of Europe*, IV, *The Economy of Expanding Europe in the Sixteenth and Seventeenth Centuries* (Cambridge, 1967), pp. 1–95. William L. Langer, "Europe's Initial Population Explosion," *American Historical Review*, 69 (1963), 1–17, discusses diet and disease, the importance of the lowly potato for the "vital" demographic revolution.

effects of population pressure are taken into account. In all of this one needs to draw what comfort one can from H. R. Trevor-Roper's maxim, "Better fruitful error than sterile truth."

3. ECONOMIC DEVELOPMENTS

During the sixteenth century the European economy was dynamic in contrast to the century and a half preceding and the one succeeding. The captains of commerce, the international merchants and financiers, led the way. Only in a tertiary sense did industrial development play a major role. The most striking secular economic trend was toward a high rate of inflation which was not to be matched again until the twentieth century. This so-called price revolution arrived at different places at different times and proceeded at a varying pace. It began just before 1500 and persisted throughout a "long sixteenth century" to about 1620, some decades experiencing a 3 to 5 percent annual price rise, especially at mid-century and again toward the end of the century.

The causes of this prolonged inflation are not fully understood, but it is usually attributed to the influx of American silver and to a lesser extent gold, or to the population pressure and the attendant demand for a relatively constant supply of foodstuffs; to an increased velocity of monetary circulation resulting from a feverish mercantile activity; to monopolistic manipulation by financiers of the prices of basic commodities; and to government deficit spending and debasement of coinage. The effects of this prolonged inflation are more easily discerned than its causes, for it disrupted traditional price and wage structures, worked acute hardship on people with a fixed wage or rent income, and opened the way for aggressive profiteers to take advantage of rapidly changing economic conditions. The study of the European economy in this century underlines the fact that despite the diversification of many regimes and the natural grouping together of some of them, there was a growing tendency toward a complex economic interrelationship and a common economic destiny touching all parts of the continent.

The impact of the price revolution was not the same for all parts of Europe, for it expressed itself differently in western and eastern Europe, a classic instance of economic dualism. In the west, it contributed toward accelerated economic growth and the speedier development of the capitalist economy. In the east, along with other causes, it strengthened and prolonged the feudal system by encouraging the unilateral development of agriculture; extended the manorial system; encouraged the "second serfdom" of the *Gutsherrschaft* system; impeded the development of trade and industry in the towns; and hastened the establishment of a home market. Finally, one of the great paradoxes of the century is that despite the increased economic activity and the influx of new wealth in the form of precious metals from the New World, there was a persistent trend toward a greater impoverishment of the population, wage laborers and agricultural workers alike, with all of the social problems that implies. Many problems of interpretation remain, such as the relation of government finance to the activity of the international bankers and to mercantile policy, but the most highly controverted question is that of the fundamental cause or causes for the enormous price rise in that century.

Two great political economists, to use the old-style term, served as protagonists for the quantity theory of the price rise and for the demographic theory respectively, two explanations that in a statistically refined form still dominate the historical literature. Adam Smith in *The Wealth of Nations* (1776) wrote with respect to the impact of American silver and gold upon the price rise in the sixteenth and seventeenth centuries: "The discovery of the abundant mines of America seems to have been the sole cause of the diminution in the value of silver in proportion to that of corn. It is accounted for accordingly in the same manner by everybody; and there has never been any dispute either about the fact itself or about the cause of it." Adam Smith was not the first to offer this "quantity of bullion" explanation for the inflation, for half a century earlier Richard Cantillon had written in his *Essai sur la nature du commerce en général:* "Everybody agrees that an abundance of money or an increase in the exchange of money, raises the price of everything. The quantity of money brought from America to Europe in the last two centuries bears out the truth of this statement."[5] Indeed, the quantity theory of money goes back to the sixteenth century itself, when Jean Bodin argued it in his controversy with Malestroit in 1568. Recent studies have undertaken to give this theory statistical and historical confirmation.

Another major political economist, who proposed an alternative explanation, was Malthus, who in his *An Essay on the Principle of Population,* 1798, wrote: "From the end of the reign of Henry VII to the end of the

5. Alexandre R. E. Chabert, "More about the Sixteenth-century Price Revolution," in *Economy and Society,* p. 47.

reign of Elizabeth . . . it is an unquestionable fact that the corn wages of labor fell in an extraordinary degree, and towards the latter end of the century they would not command much above one-third of the quantity of wheat which they did at the beginning of it" (Chapter IV, sec. 4). Malthus thought it to be more difficult to explain the high wages and the high purchasing power of those wages in the fifteenth century than the relatively low wages and weak purchasing power of the sixteenth, since it seemed obvious to him that the growing population of the sixteenth century produced an excess of manpower on the one hand and drove up the prices of the relatively stable supply of foodstuffs and other commodities on the other. This assertion has emerged in recent literature as the realistic explanation, which is frequently contrasted to the quantity theory in analyzing the price rise of the sixteenth century.

most widely accepted explanation

Clearly the causal nexus is complex, and the historian is not necessarily reduced to an either/or choice in the matter. The pattern that best accommodates the facts seems to involve a shift in causation without a change in direction. During the four decades with which this volume is concerned the realistic explanation seems to be the most cogent, with the inflationary trend given some additional impetus by the increase of bullion through growing domestic mining and some small beginnings of mineral wealth from the New World. The cost of the wars in parts of Europe, the profligacy of governments and princes, mid-century debasement of coinage, as in England, and other factors accelerated the inflation.

Economic historians have amassed a great deal of evidence pointing to a price evolution in all of Europe and a price revolution in many parts of Europe. Inflation was accompanied by a serious loss of real wages or purchasing power on the part of wage earners over the course of the century, with attendant social malaise. In fiscal terms the problem can be described as a critical devaluation of the money of account, or the raising of the face value of real money, which became the crux of every currency and price problem throughout the century. Fernand Braudel in his famous work on *The Mediterranean and the Mediterranean World in the Age of Philip II* has given the concept of a price revolution his blessing, speaking of the "violence and length of this revolution" and asserting that there can be no possible doubt about the effect of the influx of gold and silver from the New World, for the coincidence of the curve of influx of precious metals from America and the curve of prices throughout the sixteenth century is so clear that there seems to be a physical, mechanical link between the two.

He accepts the traditional view that everything was governed by the increase in stocks of precious metals. With respect to the economy of the Mediterranean world he sees two sixteenth centuries, one running roughly from about 1450 to about 1550 marked by an economic upswing followed by a downswing, and another from about 1550 to 1630 or 1650 characterized by a revival of the economy and then its final plunge and exit from the center of the stage, yielding its leading role to the Atlantic powers. A substantial number of monographic studies have given us a clearer picture of the price rise and its impact upon real wages of the common laborers in western and central Europe.[6]

The evidence in the case of England indicates that during the course of the sixteenth century the wages of agricultural workers merely doubled whereas the price of food increased sixfold. The figures for the building craftsmen, the masons, carpenters, painters, tilers, and plasterers, suggest that in England and even more sharply in France and Alsace, where detailed studies have been made, a day's wages at the end of the sixteenth century would buy less than half of what it would buy during the second half of the preceding century. A careful study of the peasants of Languedoc documents the same pattern. A rapid demographic growth began in about 1490–1500 and continued throughout the century, but whether because of technological conservatism, paucity of capital, absence of initiative, or preoccupation with religious life and otherworldly concerns, agricultural production failed to respond by providing sufficient foodstuffs to meet the growing demand. By 1530 the disparity between supply and demand had become serious, and signs of austerity such as forms of "rationing" developed; wage rationing through the reduction of real wages and the pauperization of hired hands and day laborers; land rationing through the accelerated subdivision of tenures. So despite the rise of entrepreneurial profits, agrarian capitalism on a large scale failed to develop, and the production of food per person did not increase.

6. The great pioneering work in this field was Georg Wiebe, *Zur Geschichte der Preisrevolution des XVI. und XVII. Jahrhunderts* (Leipzig, 1895). Representative recent studies reflected in these pages are E. H. Phelps Brown and Sheila V. Hopkins, "Wage Rates and Prices: Evidence for Population Pressure in the Sixteenth Century," *Economica,* XXIV (November, 1957), 289–306; "Seven Centuries of the Prices of Consumables, Compared with Builders' Wage-Rates," *Economica,* XXIII (November, 1956), 296–314; Peter H. Ramsey, ed., *The Price Revolution in Sixteenth Century England* (London, 1971); F. P. Braudel and F. Spooner, "Prices in Europe from 1450 to 1750," in *Cambridge Economic History of Europe,* IV, 374–486; Peter Earle, ed., *Essays in European History 1500–1800* (Oxford, 1974).

People seem to have been but dimly aware of what was happening and responded with surprising patience. After 1560 they were deeply involved in the religious struggle. Social protest late in the century took the innocuous form of an antitax movement or was diverted into witch-hunting.[7] The same pattern of population growth and static resources resulting in a deteriorating level of real income for both agricultural workers and urban laborers is evident in western Europe in the north as well as the south. The realistic theory seems to provide the best primary explanation for the price rise at least during the first half of the sixteenth century.

The quantitative theory postulates a fairly simple or even rudimentary economic structure with a limited or rigidly defined productive capacity, so that an increase in the stock of monetary materials or an acceleration in the rate of circulation would necessarily produce an inflationary situation. The economy of Europe in the sixteenth century fits that definition, but only with reservations, especially with respect to the first half of the sixteenth century. According to Earl J. Hamilton, roughly 181 tons of gold and 16,000 tons of silver flowed in from America between 1500 and 1650.[8] But prior to 1550 the influx of gold and silver may be described as moderate, with a great increase in the second half of the century, especially from 1570 on. It must be remembered that impressive as the stream of bullion from the New World was, the new monetary resources were simply added to a reserve that had been built up over twenty centuries, so that with all the wear and tear, the losses of two millennia, the gold stock of Europe in 1500 has been estimated at still roughly 3,000 tons. The new mining techniques of the late fifteenth and sixteenth centuries had increased European production. Even on a very generous estimate, the influx of precious metals from America did not reach one half of the gold stock of existing European resources.

The pattern of distribution of the new bullion and the consequent depreciation of the currency have not yet been defined by comprehensive and detailed research, but enough work has been done to allow a sketch of the overall European scene. Seville was the main port of entry for the American bullion. The Spaniards, due to their conservative social struc-

---

7. Emmanuel Le Roy Ladurie, *Les Paysans de Languedoc* (Paris, 1969); "A Long Agrarian Cycle: Languedoc, 1500–1700," in *Essays in European History*, pp. 143–164.

8. Earl J. Hamilton, *American Treasure and the Price Revolution in Spain, 1501–1650* (Cambridge, Mass., 1934); *Money, Prices and Wages in Valencia, Aragon and Navarre, 1351–1500* (Cambridge, Mass., 1936).

ture, ponderous governmental system, the loss through exile of some of the most enterprising elements in the population—the Jews (1492)—and the activity of foreign bankers and commercial agents, failed to use their new wealth for their own economic development. Thanks to the European bankers, primarily German, Dutch, and Italian, the new gold and silver reserves found their way to the Netherlands and the adjacent area, where a medieval industrial base, essentially textile manufacture, served as the nucleus for a newly financed industrial expansion. Antwerp and later Amsterdam served as the new centers of a stimulated commercial activity with an attendant sharp price rise. A subsidiary stream was directed toward traditional north Italian commercial centers such as Milan and Genoa. The years 1552 to 1560 witnessed an unusually rapid rate of inflation in Italy, reaching 5.2 percent a year. The effects of new monetary resources on investments were reflected in turn in general prices. In Italy the wars and the requirements of reconstruction surely played an important role in the price rise. In the Germanies a very noticeable price rise characterized the decades of 1520 and 1540, attributable in small part to domestic mining, but predominantly to realistic causes such as population pressure. The story in Poland and eastern Europe was similar and tended to reinforce the feudal agrarian trend.

In England the effects of the New World bullion and the quantitative theory have been seriously questioned. The rise of agricultural prices in England began very gently perhaps as early as 1480, but prices rose markedly only in the 1520s, accompanied by agricultural wage-rate rises near London. The sharp acceleration of prices and laborer's wages did not develop until the 1540s and 1550s. In the case of England, excessive government spending and the "Great Debasement" of the currency, 1542 to 1551, escalated prices. This adulteration of the coinage for fiscal ends, reducing the purities and weights of gold and silver coins, during the final years of Henry VIII and the reign of Edward VI, was a unique event in English history, but it came at a time of the general European price rise and added impetus to the overall trend.[9] The debasement was credited by contemporaries with being the chief cause for the rise in prices, which was the main argument of the Doctor in the *Discourse of the Common Weal,* the major burden of some of Latimer's sermons, and the subject of various

9. J. D. Gould, *The Great Debasement: Currency and the Economy in Mid-Tudor England* (Oxford, 1970), a study of the mints, in the Tower and new mints, and the effect of debasement on exports, especially wool cloth, which increased markedly after 1548.

learned treatises on coinage. The fall of the exchange rate and greater exports were also blamed for producing a "wonderful dearth and extreame pryses" in the land. Occasionally contemporaries observed that demands on limited resources were growing because of a rising population. Although many preachers and moralists attributed much of the price rise to monopolists as obvious and concrete targets, they were by no means a major factor. They might contribute to a short-term rise in prices sometimes just in local markets, but their manipulations had a general and lasting effect only insofar as prices, once artificially forced up, never seemed to return to the previous low.

The sensible conclusion to be drawn so far as England is concerned is that over the period as a whole such "real" factors as the increasing imbalance between the growth of population and agricultural output offer the most satisfactory general explanation of the price rise, although the great debasement sharply exacerbated its pace. Increases in the money supply and the improved efficiency of its use were necessary concomitants of the total process. The silver used by the mints for the greater output of coins seems to have been largely domestic in origin, although the question of specie flow is as yet uncharted territory, and the debasement led to the influx of silver from abroad. The last word of explanation in all this remains to be spoken.[10]

It is clear that throughout Europe the rise in prices and the failure of real wages to keep pace contributed to social and political discontent as early as the first half of the sixteenth century. It is necessary to sound a cautionary note against making too facile a leap from the fact of a widespread decline in the standard of living to the advent of Protestantism or even to such patently social traumas as the Peasants' Revolt of 1525. The people of that century followed other stars and answered to different calls than that of economic rationalism. Religion and the church played such a dominant role in their lives that many were willing to give up their chattels and goods, their spouses and lives for the sake of their convictions. Moreover, one cannot superimpose a map of Protestant Europe upon a sketch of the inflationary pattern, for some Protestant areas were the last to be affected, while some that remained Catholic suffered economically most grievously. It was, all the same, a time of profound discontent, for

10. R. B. Outhwaite, *Inflation in Tudor and Early Stuart England* (London, 1969), pp. 49–55.

despite the dynamic nature of the economy, most people were worse off than their forebears had been during the century before.

European society has experienced two fundamental economic changes during the long millennia: the agricultural revolution, which transformed hunters and food gatherers into shepherds and farmers, and the industrial revolution, which transformed the population into machine operators. These fundamental economic revolutions were prepared for more by basic changes in the level of culture during the preceding centuries than by changes in the natural condition of the environment. The necessary precondition of the first was the "neolithic revolution," a change in man's consciousness of himself. The necessary preliminary to the second was the development of a mercantile mentality and a desire to dominate nature through scientific and technological mastery. The early modern period of European history played that preparatory role and made a modest contribution toward the development of industrial Europe.

In the first half of the sixteenth century Europe as a whole was still predominantly agricultural but, despite the fact that economic life displayed certain basic similarities throughout the continent, fundamental changes were under way. These changes occurred at a more rapid rate in some parts of Europe than in others, and a disjuncture of decades is obvious in terms of certain developments. Viewed in the large, two opposing tendencies were becoming increasingly evident between the areas to the west and to the east of the Elbe River. From the middle of the fifteenth century to the middle of the seventeenth in the west the manorial system lost much of its traditional force and structure, whereas in the east the manorial system became entrenched and the feudal system extended and deepened its hold.

In the west the subsistence level farming characteristic of feudal agrarian arrangements was gradually changed to capitalistic farming. There was a gradual commutation of feudal rents paid in kind, such as the corvée and tithes, into money payments. The landlords increasingly abandoned the traditional kind of estate organization. During the period following the Black Death, when there was a real shortage of farm labor, in order to forestall the departure of their tenants for new land or for the cities, the landlords granted greater individual and collective liberties. They also altered land leases as to length of contract and cost in rent. Moreover, landlords rented out a larger portion of their land rather than pay high

effect of Black Death.

wages to landless workers on their own alodial holdings. Some of the prosperous peasants took advantage of the situation in order to enlarge their own holdings, cutting into the demesne. These changes effectively undercut the personal or feudal basis of the manorial system.

This general development took place in broad areas of France, Germany, and England. In England the landholders regularly commuted their demesnes to wheat farms or to stock-graining, the sheep replacing the peasants, creating deserted villages. The "new English nobility" or gentry received feudal rents due them in the form of cash and were singularly successful in expropriating small farmers and peasants and farming the lands themselves.

It is virtually a misnomer to speak of a manorial system in Italy, for there was a lack of organizational structuring, ownership rights were so varied, land holdings so scattered. Besides, the early, rapid, and widespread development of a trade economy weakened the bonds of fealty. Cash rents were introduced early, and the movement of landowners to the cities and the purchase of land in the countryside by urban bourgeoisie introduced capitalistic agriculture early. The communes paid for the freedom of the peasants so that they could move to the cities as laborers in the textile and other industries. The traditional manorial arrangements persisted in southern Italy, in Naples, Sicily, Sardinia, and Corsica. Certain areas in western Europe, however, proved to be exceptional to the general development. Thus in Aragon and Castile, in the Tyrol, and in parts of France and the Holy Roman Empire real serfdom was strengthened and expanded.

East of the Elbe River the overall trend, which ran right through the sixteenth century, was toward the development of a more rigorous feudalism with a deeper entrenchment of the manorial system. The landed nobility in the east enlarged their demesnes further, encroaching on the rights of those peasants who had migrated eastward during the late Middle Ages, and on the native Slavic population. They renewed the exploitation of the serfs, intensified labor services, extended their legal power over the very persons of the serfs in what came to be known as the *Gutsherrschaft*, which contrasted with the less oppressive western *Grundherrschaft*. The bond between the demesne and forced labor was strengthened. The landholders also encroached upon the privileges and prosperity of the market towns and reversed what early moves toward urban development had been attained. In Poland, for example, with the subordination of the towns to the control of the landed nobility and the strengthening of the system of serfdom, there was no opportunity for the bourgeoisie or peasants to develop a vital economy, and the country slid into an economic decline that lasted from the sixteenth to the eighteenth century.

This development toward the *Gutsherrschaft* took place on a different timetable in various parts of eastern Europe. In Hungary, for example, the tendency of the landed nobility to show economic initiative and to assert themselves against the peasants came to dominate developments. The peasants had been the key figures, as cattle breeders, cereal and wine producers, in the expanding trade of the small market towns and villages. Now the growing participation of the nobility in commerce and subsequently in the production of commercial goods counteracted the tendency of the richer peasants to develop into small-scale bourgeois landowners and to expand their market production. The nobility sold wine, traded livestock, meat, wheat, cloth, lead, copper, and other products in a way reminiscent of the advances of the English gentry, which engaged in wool and wheat trade. They took over peasant holdings, used paid labor on their demesnes, and increasingly reestablished forms of the old feudal forced labor.[11]

The all-pervasive influence on agricultural production was climate, whether in the east or west. The Scandinavian historian Gustav Utterström argued that there was a general trend toward a milder climate in the late fifteenth and early sixteenth centuries, but unfortunately the proofs which he adduced are not compelling. The evidence of dendroclimatology, derived from the American southwest or the forests of Scotland, indicates that climate as such has been generally stable over the past thousand or even two thousand years. This was true of Scotland, for example, which experienced short cycles of ten years of cold and warmth within an overall regular climatic pattern. Climate, then, does not provide a simple causal explanation for the "crisis" of the sixteenth century. However, the phenological method of climate analysis, based upon the dates of the official harvest proclamations in areas with a highly developed viticulture such as France and Germany, offers some fairly dependable evidence as to the coldness and duration of winters, the warmth and extent of rainfall in the summers. Evidence compiled by O. J. Schove suggests that the decades

11. Z. P. Pach, "Sixteenth-century Hungary: Commercial Activity and Market Production by the Nobles," in *Economy and Society*, pp. 113–133. See also Ingemar Bog, ed., *Der Aussenhandel Ostmitteleuropas 1450–1650* (Cologne/Vienna, 1971); pp. 56–104, for Hungary.

from 1500 to 1550 enjoyed cool humid summers, with a peak in the 1520s when the Seine and Tiber reached new heights and there was a widespread fear of another deluge. Some climatologists assert that there was a period after 1540 dominated by a continental climate with cold winters and hot summers. In fact, the period from 1540 to 1890 has been termed a "little ice age," with milder winters returning in the twentieth century. Whatever effect the milder winters and cooler summers had on the historical developments of the first half of the sixteenth century is open to imaginative interpretation, but it is clear that the watershed year 1540 did not correspond to any marked change in the demographic curve or economic development, which continued unbroken through the sixteenth century.[12]

The continuing dominance of agriculture as the primary base of economic life should not obscure the fact that there was a persistent trend away from a nearly exclusively agrarian economy, characterized by manorial or village life supported at a near subsistence level, toward a growing urban life dependent upon a commercial and in small part upon an industrial base. Even though possibly no more than 10 to 15 percent of the population were "city" dwellers, towns and cities were growing rapidly all over central and western Europe; by this time no fewer than a dozen had topped 100,000 in population, while Paris, Venice, and Milan approached 200,000. No feudal restrictions or princely regulations could prevent the migration of thousands of serfs and peasants to the cities in search of economic opportunities and greater personal freedom. *Stadtluft macht frei!* was an old German saying—city air frees.

The most dramatic instance of urban growth during the first half of the sixteenth century was the city of Antwerp. Not only did it double in size from 50,000 to 100,000 population, plus a floating population of merchants and mariners, in five decades, but it became the financial and trade center of Europe and developed a vigorous industrial quarter of its own as well. It replaced medieval cities such as Bruges and, after the financial and political catastrophes of the late 1550s, was succeeded in turn by Amsterdam; but during the period of this study, it enjoyed a centrality in the economic activity of Europe that was nearly unique in history. A number of developments contributed to its rise: the freedom from re-

12. Emmanuel Le Roy Ladurie, "History and Climate," in *Economy and Society,* pp. 135–163.

straints allowed by the Burgundian ruling house; the deepening of the
channel up the Scheldt River and the excellence of the harbor; the establishment of the English "nation" dealing mainly in textiles but also in
some lead and tin; the activity of the Hanse; but, more than these, the
establishment of the German merchants from Augsburg, Nuremberg,
Frankfurt, and other cities dealing in such metals as copper and silver from
the south German mines. Antwerp also benefited from its good connection with the old major road running from the German Rhineland to the
delta and channel towns. Moreover, the Portuguese royal agent, who
directed the colonial spice trade and purchased goods for the royal monopoly in the year 1499, moved permanently from Bruges to Antwerp.
The wealth in pepper and other spices from the Far East and Lisbon
poured through Antwerp into the European markets for over half a century. The first shipload reached Antwerp in August, 1501, and in July,
1504, a thousand tons of spices were unloaded on contract between the
Portuguese royal agent and an Antwerp merchant. The Portuguese in turn
purchased grain, metals, and cloth for their own use but also as items to
trade for spices in Africa and Asia. The Italian banking houses dominated
financial affairs during the early years, for the Italians were the most
advanced in commercial techniques, insurance programs, and in banking
and finance, most skilled in managing credit transactions and foreign
currency exchange and in maximizing interest rates on loans; but the great
German merchant-banker families such as the Webers, Fuggers, Höchstät-
ters, Imhoffs, and Tuchers also came to play important roles.

Yet it was as the mart town of the English that Antwerp grew so
phenomenally to special prominence, for the English ships had access
through the western Scheldt and English merchants made Antwerp their
major continental port. Antwerp also developed an industrial sector devoted to spinning and weaving, cloth-finishing, dyeing, metalwork, armor
and weaponry, bell-founding, and other products. It continued to benefit
from an unusual amount of liberty under the Habsburg rule during that
half century. The changed political situation after the mid-century, with
the introduction of restrictive controls, the suspension of the Portuguese
royal factory in 1549, the declaration of bankruptcy by France and Spain
in 1557 and by Portugal in 1560, many private bankruptcies, a slowdown
of international trade, and a general financial crisis, undermined the prosperity and dominance of Antwerp. Leadership in trade shifted farther to

the north with the rise of Amsterdam after the 1560s as the great shipping center of continental Europe.[13]

City growth was firmly linked to the vitality and expansion of mercantile capitalism and industrial development. Antwerp was rivaled in the south by Lyons on the Rhône River, which was a major center of finance and of the new printing industry. But the two areas of greatest economic activity in this period remained Flanders and northern Italy, the most highly urbanized and industrialized regions on the continent. They served as the north and south hubs, connected by sea through the Mediterranean and Atlantic and by overland routes. The economic expansion which began picking up momentum in the fifteenth century continued in force throughout these decades, suffering a mid-century depression in certain regions of the continent, but making a reasonable recovery and progress later in the century.

One factor that increased the volume of trade during the two preceding centuries was the "democratization" of large-scale international commerce. This was especially obvious in the cloth trade, where textiles of ordinary or mediocre quality were traded in large quantities, particularly between Flanders and eastern, central, and southwestern Europe. From the fifteenth century on there was a marked increase of trade in cereals, furs, and timber from the old Hanse region in the Baltic to the western markets, in exchange for such items as salt and wines from France and Portugal. Spanish raw wool took over in the markets of Italy, the Lowlands, and even England, whose export of raw wool to the Netherlands yielded to the export of cloth still in need of finishing. Not only were textiles and metallic wares transported over long distances, but perishables such as salted fish, butter, cheese, wines, and beer. In addition there was an increase in local trade in tens of thousands of villages and towns and at the weekly markets as well as in regional commerce. This trend continued during the first half of the sixteenth century, with interesting economic and social results. The familiar domestic or "putting out" system of production *(Verlagsystem)* involved not only townsmen but many peas-

13. S. T. Bindoff, "The Greatness of Antwerp," in G. R. Elton, ed., *The New Cambridge Modern History,* II (Cambridge, 1958), pp. 50–69; Hermann van der Wee, *The Growth of the Antwerp Market and the European Economy,* 3 vols. (The Hague, 1963). An excellent popular picture of Antwerp in the sixteenth century is John J. Murray, *Antwerp in the Age of Plantin and Brueghel* (Norman, Okla., 1970), describing the city as the richest and perhaps most famous city of the century, with its harbors on the Scheldt teeming with ships and the Amsterdam Exchange as the Wall Street of the known world.

ant hearths. As more people had to purchase necessities, being unable to produce them in a self-sufficient way, a primitive division of labor evolved. Moreover, the growth in the volume of trade contributed to the velocity of the circulation of money and to the sixteenth-century inflationary spiral.

The "new towns" in Spain, Italy, and the north generally seemed to have an advantage over the old towns with their more traditional ways of regulating trade and production. It is often said that during the sixteenth century commerce shifted from the Mediterranean to the Atlantic sea lanes, but such grand generalizations need to be qualified. The definitive effects of that shift became crucial (and final) only in the seventeenth century. In our decades the Italian cities suffered only relative losses and showed real strength and staying power. Venice, for example, staged an exceptional comeback, for at the start of the sixteenth century it lost heavily in the Oriental spice trade to the new Portuguese competitors, but by mid-century regained its important position even though it could never again maintain the near monopoly on the Levant trade it had once enjoyed. It distributed its wares through its own merchants as well as through German merchants, who maintained a large warehouse and trading post, the *fonda dei Tedeschi* in Venice. Flanders and the cities of northern Italy competed in the production of high-quality woolen cloth, though Flanders was better known for its lace, linens, and tapestries while Italy still produced silks and other rich fabrics, though in reduced quantity. Shipbuilding continued to be a major enterprise for some Italian seaside cities, but developed rapidly in the Atlantic coastal ports. The Portuguese and Spanish built ever larger ships, while the Dutch and English preferred smaller, lighter, and more maneuverable types. The mining of alum, which served to fix the dye in cloth, developed further in the Papal States and elsewhere. The mining of iron, copper, tin, gold, and silver became an increasingly important enterprise. With the enlarged mining operations, a thriving metallic industry developed, especially in the southwest German cities and in Flanders. Metal was also imported from Sweden, where iron mines were in operation from the thirteenth century on. This little industrial revolution was dependent upon relatively primitive wooden machines, pumps with wooden parts, rope pulleys, animal or human treadmills, waterwheels, and other simple mechanical devices.

During the sixteenth century a "transcontinental economy" developed with an increase in the volume of trade on both maritime and overland routes. The overland routes picked up a much heavier traffic without cutting into the still expanding trade on the sea routes. <u>The truly sensational development in commerce during the sixteenth century was the emergence of the Spanish Atlantic trade,</u> which came into being during the two decades following the discovery of America. Historians have the trade figures for Spain thanks to the happy facts that the Spanish trade with America was concentrated in Seville and ancillary ports and that the Spanish state took such a proprietary interest and control over the trade with the New World. No comparable studies have as yet been made on Portugal, England, France, or Holland. We are at this point not even certain as to what proportion of all Atlantic trade in this period fell to the Spanish. To the end of the sixteenth century, however, the Spanish-American trade seems to have been dominant. From 1500 to 1580 the so-called Indies trade rose from between 3,000 and 4,000 tons at the outset to some 30,000 tons in the 1580s. Practically the total amount of the trade between the Old World and the New was at first in Spanish bottoms. There were ups and downs, of course, with the first plateau around 1530–1535 followed by a great increase of volume until the second plateau about 1560, followed by a steady ascent to the climax, marked by the debacle of the Armada.[14] Until 1630–40 this Spanish trade constituted more than half of the total.

For overland trade there is unfortunately no equivalent material or research available, and it is necessary to piece together a picture from fragments of data from "dry land ports," and to reconstruct a map of the road system. Some areas still had the use of old Roman roads, the most durable monument of Roman civil engineering. Within the Ottoman Empire the Turks constructed roads with a narrow hard surface of stone in the center, wide enough for horsemen, and with broad soft shoulders for pedestrians, foot soldiers, wagons, and herds being shepherded along to new pastures and to market. In central and western Europe roads were usually dusty or muddy dirt paths too narrow or uneven to allow passage to carriages, wagons, or sometimes even to the more numerous carts. Most of the long distance trade was consequently carried on with pack animals. Early in the century horses were used for that purpose, but as the century

14. P. and H. Chaunu, "Économie atlantique, Économie mondiale," *Cahiers d'histoire mondiale,* I (1953), 91–104; P. and H. Chaunu, *Seville et l'Atlantique,* 11 vols. (Paris, 1955–1959). In 2,500 pages the Chaunus provide a full reconstruction of the voyages of ships bound in and out of Seville between the years 1504 and 1650 as well as a partial one of the goods, a sensational achievement of historical research.

wore on they were replaced more and more by mules, a stronger and, except for their notorious stubborn streak, a more easily manageable animal. Governments, in fact, began to pass regulations against the use of horses for nonmilitary portage, since they were considered to be strategic natural resources for the military. People preferred the overland routes as being more dependable for letters, news, and the more precious goods, such as silk cloth, which were less bulky and lighter. For other purposes riverboats and barges or ships were preferred to the arduous and hazardous overland travel.

The north and south land routes carried a heavy commercial traffic from the fifteenth century on. It is impossible to describe here the total network of roads that crisscrossed Europe, but we may chart a few by way of example. For trade from Venice and other north Italian cities to central Germany, the Brenner Pass and the Danube crossing at Ulm and Regensburg were very important. The main trade routes ran through Swiss and Austrian Alpine passes, over Ulm or Basel, down the Rhine Valley to Cologne, Bruges, Antwerp, and Amsterdam, and westward toward the channel towns. There was a passageway between the two heavy forests, the Schwarzwald and the Odenwald. Along the left bank of the Rhine the old Roman road ran between Trier and Cologne. Two important east–west trade routes ran from Paris, Châlons, and Toul to Strasbourg, Worms, and Mainz.

It is difficult since the modern transport and communication revolution to think back to those days when travel took infinitely longer and was extremely uncertain due to the elements. A journey of a few days might take weeks during inclement weather, so there was a wide spread between the shortest possible travel time, the maximum recorded time, and the average time between two cities. A few examples of the "elasticity of news," drawn from a study of the travel times from Venice, will illustrate the point. Between Venice and Florence the minimum, maximum, and average travel times were 1 day, 13 days, and 3 days, respectively; between Venice and Rome they were 1.5, 9, and 4; Venice and Augsburg, 5, 21, and 12; Venice and Lyons, 4, 25, and 13; Venice and Antwerp, 17, 89, and 55; Venice and London, 9, 52, and 24; Venice and Alexandria, 17, 89, and 55; Venice and Constantinople, 15, 81, and 34.[15] The correspondence of

15. From Pierre Sardello's study of Marino Sanudo's record of the arrival of letters and news between 1497 and 1532, cited in Fernand Braudel, *The Mediterranean and the Mediterranean World in the Age of Phillip II*, I (New York, 1972), p. 362.

statesmen, churchmen, businessmen, and the literary figures of the time are replete with complaints and laments of delayed or lost dispatches, shipments, and letters. Natural disasters and the hazards of an unruly society combined to delay communication and plague the economy.

4. SOCIAL RELATIONS

The fundamental division in European society remained in the early sixteenth century what it had been in the late Middle Ages: that between the great mass of people living narrowly circumscribed lives near the subsistence level in villages, towns, and small cities; and a narrow stratum of society above with the requisite income and leisure for political and cultural activities, relieved as they were of the need to cope with immediate problems of survival. Among the common people there was a considerable variety of vocation and there were noteworthy differences between various parts of the continent in the range of privilege and freedom enjoyed. There were also tremendous variations in wealth and social status among those in the upper levels of society.

The array of social and political institutions defies easy classification, and yet certain generalizations about European society as a whole may be ventured. The social structure continued to be essentially pyramidal or hierarchical. The major reformers of all persuasions were social conservatives opposed to egalitarian tendencies. The Reformation was a very specialized revolt against the papal monarchy and the priesthood; it was not intended by its prime movers to overturn society or even to disrupt the church order. Political authorities made short shrift of radical movements that sought to overthrow traditional societal arrangements. The princes and nobility ruthlessly suppressed the peasants during the revolt of 1525; Protestant princes and a Catholic archbishop joined forces against the Anabaptists at Münster; and the Castilian grandees supported the despised young King Charles I from Burgundy in suppressing the native *communero* movement. There were no sudden dramatic or critical social changes during the sixteenth century.

Society's fundamental unit whether on the land or in the city continued to be the extended family. Family connections constituted the basic determinant of status and position in society. From free peasants who sought to combine small landholdings through marriages, up through the gentry to the great royal families, connections by blood were the essential means toward the end. The Habsburgs were clearly the great masters at arranging advantageous marriages that linked together Austria, Burgundy, the Spanish Netherlands, and Spain in one mighty dynastic chain. In the Italian city-states, the importance of the family—the Medici, Albizzi, Visconti, and the rest—is legendary. But the same kind of family cohesion characterized the German merchant cities, those of the Netherlands, France, England, and all parts of Europe. Even in London, during the earlier sixteenth century, the parish community remained very much a traditional familial society where all, even the sick or incompetent, were cared for by household or kinship ties or by extension through friendship or neighborly obligations. It was not until the late sixteenth century, especially during the 1570s and 1580s, that the stream of wage laborers from other municipalities, of vagrants and country migrants, overwhelmed the social order based on kinship and transformed it into one based on occupation or company membership. In this period one must beware of speaking of social classes, because of nineteenth- and twentieth-century connotations, but the growing mass of commoners, often unemployed, can best be thought of as a rootless class below the ranks of established families and people of status.

Urban social structure followed a similar pattern in most parts of Europe. A patrician class arose from diverse groups that dominated the city council and magistracies, an oligarchy based on wealth, business, family connections, monopolies, and political influence. Below it were the middle and lower strata of burghers, mostly organized in guilds to protect, control, and foster their economic interests. Beneath them were the artisans and craftsmen, the apprentices, and finally, the poor and the vagrants. The secular clergy, upper and lower, and the mendicant friars tended to identify on many issues with the social groups of their own origin. In university towns the academics and thousands of students also were to be reckoned with. Urban social grouping and social tensions were to play an important role in the introduction and promotion of the Reformation.

Early sixteenth-century society was bound together by strong bonds of personal obligations and a sense of duty which were not spelled out in law but were implicitly understood and acted upon. In eastern Europe, the *Gutsherrschaft* extended feudalism over a wide area and maintained it in some degree until the nineteenth century. In central and western Europe, where feudalism was yielding to a capitalist agriculture and growing urbanization, the gentry, nobility, aristocracy, monarchies, and by mimesis even the urban patriciate assumed quasi-chivalrous manners and half-feudal attitudes toward social obligations. This sense of duty and of mutual obligations, powerful unwritten laws of behavior, generally served to control people's attitudes and actions more effectively than specific prescriptions of law or even self-interest. Social relations were still closer to the personal fealties of feudalism than to the demands of an impersonal modern society, but the direction in which they were moving is clear.

5. POLITICAL STRUCTURES

The most striking political development of the early sixteenth century was the rise of the national monarchies in the west and of the territorial states within the Holy Roman Empire. The new monarchies did not set a pattern markedly different from the traditions of their medieval predecessors, but there was a notable difference in the degree of centralization in government; in the pervasiveness of the power of the state; and in the success of energetic monarchs in controlling noble opposition and enforcing their own will. They were not absolutist in any genuine sense, much less so than kings of the two centuries following. But compared with earlier monarchs and with the Holy Roman Emperor, they were clearly in the ascendancy. Although it is difficult to draw a line of demarcation between Louis XI and Francis I or between Henry VII and Henry VIII, there was clearly a heightened sense of royal authority. The number of government tasks multiplied; the state assumed new functions; the secular arm, both Catholic and Protestant, exercised even more proprietary control over the church than in earlier centuries; and the stage was set for those international rivalries at home and abroad which led to the long and bloody wars on land and sea that filled the sixteenth and succeeding centuries.

The reign of Charles V witnessed the last attempt of a Holy Roman Emperor to assert the universality of the medieval imperium. Historians have generally held that the Reformation broke up the unity of medieval civilization, fragmenting the universal church and undercutting the most Catholic emperor. The concept of the unity of the *corpus christianum* does not hold up, however, under close scrutiny, for religious diversity was expressed in a wide variety of heresies; secularism disputed the claims of popular religiosity of whatever sort; princely and monarchical ascendancy produced a political particularism which belied the imperial claims to universal authority long before the Reformation. One can properly speak of a late medieval political polycentrism that was irreversibly accentuated during the sixteenth century.

The Reformation began within the Holy Roman Empire. Perhaps it could not have arisen or survived in any other state of sixteenth-century Europe. The weakness of the emperor compared with the western monarchs and his many commitments elsewhere coupled with the relative strength of the German princes prevented adequate repressive reaction. Machiavelli once commented upon the contrast between the existence of great political powers within Germany and the impossibility of making use of them. A long history lay behind the condition of Germany in this period. For six or seven centuries German emperors had been engaged in a struggle for the centralization of power against the centrifugal forces of the territorial states of the dukes, princes, and independent cities. The elective nature of the imperial office meant that the emperors were regularly chosen for their relative impotence by the seven electors so that they would not pose a threat to other princes and would be unable to make their office hereditary. Under the emperor Maximilian I (1493–1519) the last attempts at constitutional reform prior to the Reformation were made. Berthold von Henneberg, archchancellor of the Empire, developed a plan for concentrating the federal powers into a corporation of the estates, and the Diet of Worms in 1495 addressed itself to this imperial reform. Maximilian, dubbed the "last knight," made a counterproposal: to modernize administration by strengthening the emperor's power. But neither reform plan had a future, for the estates were divided by a near infinite number of conflicting interests, and Maximilian was personally inadequate to the demands of the hour. Charles V (1519–1556) struggled in vain with these difficulties and acknowledged his failure toward the end of his reign by turning over what power remained to his brother Ferdinand to rule as king over the Austrian Habsburg lands and then withdrew to Spain. Luther in his *Table Talks* (5,57,35) observed: "Germany is a beautiful strong horse with food and everything she needs, but she lacks a rider."

The Holy Roman Empire has been the object of many historians' relentless ridicule, reading back into history its wretched final condition when Napoleon delivered the coup de grace in 1806, or reflecting Voltaire's famous witticism about its being neither holy, Roman, nor an empire. A revisionist view, however, holds that Germany's loose federal system actually provided an effective form of government attuned to the needs of its own society and to the wider requirements of early modern Europe. The

Empire was not a mere assemblage of territorial states, nor the ghost of a departed giant, but a federation of states and estates with certain central political and judicial institutions of great importance. The tremendous number of some 240 small states and the estates of the imperial knights cooperated in the management of the mundane affairs of government, and reasonably effective bodies were set up for that purpose at the imperial level. Federal bodies such as the *Reichstag* or diet and its committees, the *Reichskammergericht,* the imperial chamber or supreme court, the *Kreisdirektorien* or circuit directories, served well the limited purposes for which they were established. At the Diet of Cologne in 1512 ten circuits or circles called *Landfriedenskreisen* were established to aid in the maintenance of public peace. They comprised Austria, Bavaria, Swabia, Franconia, Upper Rhine, Lower Rhine, Burgundy (which was ceded to the Spanish line of the Habsburgs in 1556), Westphalia, Lower Saxony, and Upper Saxony. The territorial states within the Empire continued to develop institutions in their microcosm that in part paralleled the imperial institutions and in part imitated those of western monarchies. Thus territorial diets representing the various estates of clergy, nobility, and burghers supported and supplemented the governmental functions of the princes. Towns had either imperial or territorial status and enjoyed varying degrees of independence. The territorial states enjoyed a great deal of autonomy. One advantage of this two-tiered system was that there could be no real autocracy. In an age based solidly upon privilege and property, the more divided the political power and the administration, the less absolute the system. Moreover, in this complex system more people had an opportunity, largely through the study of the law, to gain positions of some power and responsibility. The Holy Roman Empire, then, was not a will-o'-the-wisp or a pale reflection of the medieval empire, but a unique federal solution to the problem of government in an age when federal solutions were neither fashionable nor effective in other countries. This very special political structure of the Empire must be appreciated if the flowering of the Reformation in Saxony is to be understood, despite the determined opposition of the emperor and the defensive leagues of Protestant and Catholic princes.[16]

16. G. Benecke, *Society and Politics in Germany 1500–1750* (London, 1974), bases a revisionist view upon a close archival examination of the state of Lippe in eastern Westphalia, an independent territory. A near classic study is that of F. L. Carsten, *Princes and Parliaments in Germany from the Fifteenth to the Eighteenth Century* (Oxford, 1959), with special attention paid to Württemberg.

The Habsburg dynastic domain in Austria took on increasingly the character of an independent territorial principality. Spain, on the other hand, even after the unification of the kingdoms in 1479, remained an assemblage of kingdoms united in the person of the Habsburg kings. Only gradually did a civil service attitude toward public office develop in the Spanish bureaucracy, replacing more personal traditional attachments. Geographical decentralization persisted in the form of regional councils. The Spanish viceroys were more like department heads. Only during the reign of Philip II in the latter half of the century did a more consistently autocratic approach to government evolve and even that was by no means absolute.

Spain systematically extended its control over the Italian peninsula following the defeats of France during the course of the Habsburg-Valois wars. The Italian city-states paid the price for their particularism and their inability to form a federation to repel the "barbarians." The Medici dukes of Florence became the tools of the Spaniards and the other states became virtually puppets of Spain. Only two states in Italy, Piedmont and Sicily, retained parliamentary institutions beyond the sixteenth century. But the Sicilian parliament was constantly on the defensive, seeking to protect the country's privileges from the encroachments of Castilian absolutism and the rapacity of the Spanish treasury. The estates of Piedmont, the only parliament functioning in an independent Italian state, remained effective until it was destroyed by Emmanuel Philibert in 1560.[17] Venice alone among the larger city-states retained its independence and oligarchical rule, but it was engaged in a fierce contest with the Turks to preserve something of its eastern Mediterranean empire.

The two strongest monarchies to develop, France and England, posed an interesting problem as to the advantages and disadvantages of representative institutions for the power of the ruler. On the surface it seemed that the kings of France had most nearly arrived at autocracy, whereas those of England had to deal with a powerful Parliament. Yet the events of the sixteenth century suggest that the answer to the question of representative institutions and monarchies is not so simple as it might at first seem. In France the activities of the royal administrative institutions had been expanded from about 1450 onward through the gradual extension of control by the crown over provinces formerly ruled

17. H. G. Koenigsberger, *Estates and Revolutions: Essays in Early Modern European History* (Ithaca, 1971), pp. 19–22, 91–93, on the parliaments of Piedmont and of Sicily.

by royal dukes. These administrative agencies developed a strong combination of institutional centralization and geographical decentralization. Francis I knew how to use able advisers to good effect and regularly consulted a small group of councillors in the *conseil des affaires* or *conseil étroit.* The legal system was made more uniform and more severe during and after his reign. The civil law was codified for the whole kingdom. In criminal cases procedures became more arbitrary: judges were given greater power of interrogation; there was even greater use of torture to obtain confessions; harsher penalties were imposed; and in the provinces the provost-marshals and other royal officials assumed harsh, summary jurisdiction.[18] It did indeed seem that France was well on the way to achieving a very strong and even absolutist monarchy, yet the power of the king was still hemmed in by the customary rights and ancient liberties of the nobility and other segments of society. With the rise of Calvinism and the civil war, it became painfully obvious that provincial independence, local loyalties, traditionally privileged and antimonarchical forces were still powerful.

The monarchy in England rested upon the sovereignty of the king in Parliament and was circumscribed by a largely unwritten constitution. Yet England developed a modernized consolidated monarchy. The changes under the Tudors were so extensive that Geoffrey Elton has ventured to speak of a "Tudor revolution" in government characterized by a shift from medieval "household" to "national" bureaucratic methods, with the initiative passing from royal to public administration.[19] Henry VIII's chief minister, the secretary of state Thomas Cromwell, created the Privy Council and reformed other councils in the 1530s. The Privy Council supervised closely all aspects of government, while the Court of the Star Chamber served as a separate court for important judicial hearings. The revenue courts effected financial reforms which offset in part the losses created by Henry's ill-advised wars. Parliament served the crown well during the most critical years of the Henrician Reformation. England, then, as another national monarchy, provided a different model from that of France. Through a mutually advantageous alliance with Parliament, a representa-

18. Henry J. Cohn, ed., *Government in Reformation Europe 1520–1560* (London, 1971), pp. 10, 27, 33.

19. G. R. Elton, *The Tudor Revolution in Government: Administrative Changes in the Reign of Henry VIII* (Cambridge, 1953), p. 415: "To say it once again, in every sphere of the central government, 'household' methods and instruments were replaced by national bureaucratic methods and instruments."

tive institution, the Tudor monarchs were enabled to reach heights of power transcending that of their medieval predecessors. At the same time, their very cooperation with and use of Parliament amounted to an implicit rejection of autocracy and set up the preconditions for the development of limited monarchy.

Compared with that in England, the situation in Scotland seemed chaotic. The ruling house of Scotland, descended from the heroic Robert Bruce (1306–1329), basically served as faction leaders among the Scottish clans, enjoying little of that "divinity which hedges 'round the king." James IV (1488–1513) was a strong but reckless ruler, who had rebelled against his own father and in the end was brutally pierced with arrows and hacked to death in the battle of Flodden (September 9, 1513), against the English army under Surrey. During his reign the houses of Hepburn of Hailes, the Huntly Gordons, Kers, and the Argylls rose among the fighting clans and aggrandized themselves at the expense of the Macdonalds, Camerons, Macleans, and Clan Chattan. The long minority of James V (1528–1542), who was born in 1513, undercut even further the power of the monarchy. The clans, divided between pro-French and pro-English sentiments, were further factionalized by their attitudes toward the old church and the Reformation. The burgesses were less developed than in more commercial and industrialized lands, but they antedated the Reformation and were to play a key role in the drama in which John Knox was to play the lead role.

The general tendency of the time toward the consolidation of territorial states was evident also in Scandinavia, but it led to the breakup of the Union of Kalmar, 1397, which had united Denmark, Norway, and Sweden "for all eternity" under a single ruler. Denmark had played the leading role in the union, with Sweden offering resistance throughout the fifteenth century in alliance with the Hanseatic League. Denmark in return favored the Dutch with many trading privileges, a policy that eventually undercut the Hanse even in the Baltic Sea. These inner rivalries put too great a strain upon the political union, which lacked an imperial ideal, and Sweden finally broke with Denmark in 1523. The drive toward stronger monarchy paralleled developments in the west and in the territorial states of the Holy Roman Empire, but the upper nobility and higher clergy in the councils retained much of their power. Erich of Pomerania, the first king under the Union, had worked energetically to repress the power of the aristocratic councils, but failed. The last king under the Union, Christian II, in the early sixteenth century also ran into the determined resistance of the council of upper nobility and bishops. In Sweden a diet representing all four estates developed during the sixteenth-century struggle against Denmark and the Reformation. The council remained powerful in Denmark and regained much of its power in Sweden later in the century.

A look at the map of eastern Europe at the start of the sixteenth century could be very deceptive, for it would reveal the vast kingdom of Lithuania-Poland reaching from the Baltic nearly to the Black Sea and from the Oder River to lands beyond the Dnieper River in the Ukraine, but it was a kingdom far less powerful than the new monarchies of the west. The two countries were bound together by a personal union under the Lithuanian Grand Duke Jagiello in 1386 after he received in marriage Hedwig, the young daughter of the Angevin King Louis, who had worn the crown of Poland and Hungary. Jagiello promised that he and his people would accept the Roman Catholic faith and pledged his landed wealth perpetually to the crown of the Kingdom of Poland, thereby more than tripling the size of Poland. Baptized, married, and crowned in Cracow, he took the Christian name Ladislav. He zealously Christianized his people, but stirred up conflict in certain areas that were already Orthodox Christian under Kievan Russia by promoting Roman Catholicism. The fifteenth century was one of territorial expansion. In 1410 at Tannenberg the Lithuanian-Polish forces virtually annihilated the Teutonic knights and, in 1466 in the second peace of Thorn, forced them to cede to Poland a large part of West Prussia including Danzig and Thorn, providing access to the Baltic Sea. The Teutonic Order kept East Prussia with its capital city Koenigsberg, but as a feudal dependency of Poland.

The Jagiellons also had designs on Bohemia and Hungary. Vladislav, son of Jagiello, became king of Hungary, but he was killed in the battle of Varna against the Turks in 1444. King Casimir of Poland made his son Ladislav king of Bohemia in 1471, and in 1490, in competition with the Habsburg Maximilian I of Austria, Ladislav won the St. Stephen's crown of Hungary. Toward the end of the fifteenth century the Jagiellons suffered some serious setbacks. Their attempt to take possession of Moldavia failed, and drew the Turks down on the Poles in 1498/99. The Muscovites took the offensive and seized substantial territories. The new Grand Master of the Order of the Teutonic Knights, Frederick of Saxony, chosen in 1498, refused to take the oath of fealty to Poland and repudiated the peace of Thorn. His successor, Albert of Brandenburg, with the support of Emperor Maximilian, continued this policy of resistance. Casimir's youngest son, Sigismund I, who ruled from 1506 on, decided upon a policy of reconciliation with the Habsburgs. In the summer of 1515 in Vienna he and his brother Ladislav, whose position in Bohemia and Hungary was weak due to the hostility of the nobles, agreed with Maximilian I that Ladislav's infant son Louis should be married to Maximilian's granddaughter Mary, and his daughter Anne should be married to Mary's brother Ferdinand, while Maximilian in turn promised not to support the Teutonic knights and the Muscovites against Poland. After Louis II was killed in the battle of Mohács against the Turks in 1526, these fortunate marriages enabled the Habsburgs to inherit Bohemia and Hungary.

The political structure of the Jagiellon kingdom was unique in that the nobility preserved controlling power. The burgesses were not represented in the diet as a third estate, and the king, even though relatively weak, lost further power during the subsequent period, in contrast to the western monarchs. The kings had sought to restrain the power of the great landed magnates by favoring the lower nobility or *szlachta*. Thereby they became dependent upon them. This development received formal recognition in the fundamental statute *Nihil novi* of 1505, which prohibited the king from promulgating any new law without the consent of representatives of particular noble diets or *sejmiki*. The Polish diet or *sejm,* as it developed from the fourteenth to the early sixteenth century, was made up of three orders, the first being the king, the second the senate, made up of the *ministri,* castellans, and bishops, and the third composed of representatives of the *szlachta*. The cities were not, except for Cracow, represented, for not only were they few in number and spread over a wide area, but the nobility formed a strong closed caste which considered itself a single body whether the members were large or small landholders and deliberately excluded the urban bourgeoisie. Laws of 1496 and 1538, for example, explicitly forbade the burghers to purchase land. Later in the century the diet legislated even against commerce. That the kings of Poland would be reduced to absolute impotence and subject eventually to the *liberum veto* was not entirely predictable in the early sixteenth century, but, in retrospect, their growing impotence foreshadowed the ultimate breakdown of the state in the eighteenth century. Moreover, the landed nobility exploited the peasantry in an unconscionable way. Because the lords needed the peasants to work their vast holdings, during the sixteenth century they made it illegal for a peasant to leave his village without the permission of the overlord. The production and export of grain increased appreciably, but it was at the cost of the peasantry, whose only escape was in flight to the Cossacks to the southeast.

The history of the grand principality of Moscow in early modern times was characterized by a dramatic territorial expansion and by the development of an autocratic structure lacking the representative institutions that characterized the states of western and central Europe. The divergent development of Russia has frequently been attributed to the two centuries of Asiatic Tatar domination, but this easy "scratch a Russian and you find a Tatar" explanation is not only inadequate, but actually mistaken. It is true that the princes of Moscow rose to prominence from the time of Ivan I (1325–1341), who served as the sole collector of tribute for an Ilkhan of the Golden Horde; that he and his successors took full advantage of this situation to increase their wealth, possessions, and power; and that they learned something of Oriental despotism from the Tatars. But other factors were more determinative, such as the sociopolitical realities of the Russian scene, the character of rulers such as Ivan III (1462–1505), the Byzantine ideology, and the unique relation of the Orthodox Church to the state. Except for Novgorod and Pskov, the cities served largely a military or administrative function, so that a genuine bourgeoisie which could have formed a third estate representation was lacking. In taking Novgorod, a commercial center in 1478, Ivan III established complete sovereignty over that city, eliminated the position of mayor (posadnik), confiscated the lands of the archbishops and of the six wealthiest monasteries, instigated mass executions, exiled eight thousand wealthy citizens to a region near Moscow, and in 1494 expelled the Hanseatic League from the city. Instead of cultivating a mercantile or industrial segment in society, which might have shaped a different political destiny for Russia, Ivan III destroyed its promise.

The ideology of the Byzantine inheritance contributed as well to the autocratic mentality of the Russian rulers. In 1453, upon the fall of Constantinople to the Turks, the grand prince declared Moscow to be the "third Rome," the true religious capital of the world. Ivan III married as his second wife Zoe, the niece of the last Paleolog emperor, used the title Caesar or Tsar (although it was not adopted officially until 1547 by Ivan IV), took over the Byzantine coronation and court ceremonial, and adopted the imperial double-headed eagle as his emblem. He brought in

Italian architects to help design the Kremlin as the royal residence and imported western foundrymen for making arms. Ivan was an impressive personality: tall, thin despite his gluttony, slightly stooped, and so striking in his bearing that women are reported to have fainted at the sight of him. He undercut the old aristocracy, built up a body of support among the lesser princes and boyars or warriors, and extended the *pomestye* system by granting to the service class lands *(pomestya)* for their lifetime, but not hereditary freehold estates. No real representative institutions developed, for the council of boyars had mainly advisory functions and was incapable of offering effective opposition.

The close tie between the Orthodox Church and the state, analogous to the Caesaropapism of Byzantium, further strengthened the Muscovite rulers. Ivan III's second wife had lived in Rome, and the Papal Curia expected her to work for the reunion of the Roman Catholic and Russian Orthodox churches, a step that Moscow had earlier refused to take following the declaration of unity at the Council of Florence in 1439. But in reality a sharpening of hostility toward Rome developed, and Ivan III let it be known that the true orthodox faith was to be found only in Moscow. Except for the confiscations of church properties at Novgorod, church lands were considered inviolable. At a Moscow church council in 1503, called to deal with abuses in the church, an elder, Nil Sorsky, urged that all monasteries be deprived of their lands in the interest of spirituality. He was opposed by Joseph Sanin of Volokolamsk (1440–1515), who argued that lands were necessary to attract and support the monks. The council decided in favor of the Josephians or "possessors," and the secular rulers from Ivan III on were obliged to respect the integrity of church lands. Joseph also led the campaign against a sect of Judaizers, which spread from Kiev to Moscow and infected even Ivan's daughter-in-law Elena and her son. In the struggle with these heretics, Joseph addressed the prince of Moscow as the "defender of the faith" and developed a theory of the supreme authority of the sovereign who is "by nature like unto all men, but in authority like unto God Almighty." Not without cause did Ivan III style himself the "autocrat of all Russia."

By the end of his reign Ivan III had completed the absorption of the neighboring princedoms, the "gathering together" of the Great Russian territories: Yaroslavl, Rostov, Novgorod, Tver, Pskov, and Ryazan. He had a natural instinct for diplomacy and timed his military campaigns well. He held off Ahmed, Khan of the Tatars of the Golden Horde to the south, he invaded Livonia and forced the Teutonic Knights to accept a ten-year truce, and he drove back the Lithuanians under Casimir Jagiellon and his weak successor, Alexander, taking a large section of eastern Lithuania and posing a threat to Smolensk and Kiev. By the time he died on October 27, 1505, he had made sensational progress toward becoming in actual fact the "Sovereign of all Russia." His eldest son, Vasily, who succeeded him on the throne, continued his father's foreign policy and rounded out the Russian territories, making Smolensk the key to Russia's defense system in the west and southwest. The link for Russia's future expansion had become clearly visible.

The other eastern power which pressed its expansion westward into Europe was the empire of the Ottoman Turks. With the accession of Mohammed II (1451–1481), the Turks began a new period of conquest, three decades of warfare comparable to that surge into the Balkans during the final third of the fourteenth century which had culminated in the defeat of Emperor Sigismund and his army of 10,000 men. The son of a non-Turkish mother, Mohammed II grew up in contact with westerners and knew the political and psychological terrain. A network of spies kept him well informed of western movements. He brought in a Transylvanian armament maker to forge the artillery needed to besiege Constantinople. He was a master strategist and military organizer. Despite the consternation and despair which news of the fall of Constantinople on May 29, 1453, brought to the West, no cooperative defense or plan for the liberation of the city could be realized. Mohammed II took Corinth in 1458, northern Serbia in 1459, Trebizond in 1461, then in the 1460s Bosnia and Albania, despite the resistance under Skanderbeg. Highly mobile Turkish units made demolition raids into Carinthia and Styria, foreshadowing an eventual push toward Vienna. Mohammed II also drove hard against the Venetians, who in 1479 were forced to abandon their resistance. In return for a payment of 10,000 ducats annually, they received the privilege of free export and import of goods in Ottoman ports and were given the right once again to have an ambassador in Constantinople. The Venetians had to leave Negroponte in the Aegean and the defense post at Scutari in the Adriatic. The sultan had long planned a foothold in Italy itself and in 1480 an expeditionary force landed at Otranto and maintained itself until the fall of the following year. Fortunately for Europe, Mohammed II died on May 3, 1481, at the age of forty-nine.

Bayezid II was of a less aggressive disposition and directed his attention

more to North Africa and the Near East. The Persians, who belonged to ⎤
the Shiite Moslem faith, opposed the Ottomans, who were Sunnite Mos- ⎟
lems, and posed a constant threat on the east. By the end of the fifteenth ⎦
century the Turks had added Syria, Arabia, and Egypt to their empire. The
Europeans did not use the peaceful interlude to their advantage, for they
were distracted by the wars in Italy and by overseas expansion and rivalries. Moreover, when Pope Innocent VIII could accept an annual payment
for keeping Bayezid II's brother Djem under arrest to prevent his return
to Turkey, how could mere Christian princes be expected to unite against
the infidel! Forty years after Mohammed II's death another great con-
queror, Suleiman the Magnificent (1520–1566), directed the full force of
the Ottoman Empire against the west and penetrated to the very gates of
Vienna in 1529.

The political and social structures which sustained this massive military
effort excited the fear and admiration of the Europeans. Historians are not
entirely agreed upon the extent to which the Turks borrowed from Byzantine institutions, but the main features of their administration antedate the
actual conquest of Constantinople. The Turkish government was a highly
organized military state with supreme power in the hands of the sultan.
Mohammed II created a legal statute authorizing the sultan to put his
younger brothers to death upon his assumption of power in order to
preclude civil war over succession to the throne. Despite his great power,
the sultan could not be completely arbitrary, for he was constrained by the
legal system, by religious considerations, and by the fact that the Ottoman
Empire stretched over areas with customs and local laws of great antiquity.
There was no nobility of birth, so that the highest military and civil offices
were open to men of ability, but all those who aspired to high places had
to bear in mind that the price paid for error or for failure was often death.
The grand vizier served as the sultan's deputy as head of state, while the
head of the armed forces served as minister of justice in that paramilitary
government, with a treasurer and a secretary serving as the other two of
the four leading officials. Anatolia and Rumalia, east and west of Istanbul,
were each under a vicar or governor who ruled through local officials.
Landholdings, somewhat like feudal fiefs, were given to Turks who in turn
owed military service to the overlord and, if their possessions were large,
had to provide a large contingent of cavalry and militiamen. These warriors together with the Janissaries, the elite shock troops consisting of Christian children abducted and trained for military service, made up the main

body of the Turkish armies. All public lands in conquered territories reverted automatically to the Ottoman state. The peasants on such lands were obliged to turn over a portion of their produce to the state.

The Turks were reasonably tolerant of local religions and customs in areas they had conquered, surprisingly so considering the ideological importance of Islam as an inspiration for conquest. There were always cases of local officials who were intolerant and repressive, but the attitude of the sultans was permissive. The Christian population was forbidden to build new churches or to ring church bells, some children were taken away to serve as Janissaries, people captured in raids were often sold into slavery, but very few were converted at the point of the sword. It has been suggested that the Turks did not wish to reduce the non-Moslem population, since Moslems were excused from paying the head tax. A weightier reason may have been the realization that the cultural differences between parts of their multilingual empire facilitated governing on the divide-and-conquer principle. A deeper reason may lie in a certain tolerance in Islam itself toward Judaism and Christianity as religions not unrelated to their own, despite the bitter legacy of the Crusades. Throughout western Europe the Turks were feared and abhorred and rumors of their cruelty and of mass murders stirred up the will to resist as it expressed itself in the battles along the Danube and during the siege of Vienna, where the Turks were finally obliged to turn back. The shadow of the crescent lay across central Europe on the eve of the Reformation, and the Turks were to play a critical role in the *Realpolitik* that determined the course that movement was to take.

Such was the European state system at the outset of the Reformation. Vast differences existed in the political structures and in the direction of political development between the western monarchies and the eastern states. Changes were taking place also in the art of diplomacy and the instruments of war, but these must be discussed later as the story of interstate relations unfolds.

6. CHURCH AND POPULAR RELIGION

On the eve of the Reformation the Roman Catholic Church was the most universal institution and the Christian religion the most pervasive spiritual and intellectual force in Europe. It shared its dominance only with the Orthodox Church and Islam in eastern Europe, and was soon to have missionaries at work in the New World as well as in Asia and Africa. As an institution the church had a hierarchical organization that reached into every parish, and a bureaucracy that rivaled that of kings and emperors. Church law affected public affairs and touched the private life of every individual. The church had great wealth acquired through the centuries by legacies, gifts, bequests, investments, and ecclesiastical dues and taxes. Possibly a third of the real estate in the Holy Roman Empire was held or controlled by the church and in many larger cities a fourth or more of the property in the business section was similarly held. But one must not exaggerate the unity or uniformity of Christendom, for great differences in structure and cultural niveau existed in various parts of Europe, as say between the church in Italy and England. In view of the multitudinous heresies and extremes in the perception of the faith, from the scholastic doctor down to the most superstitious peasant, it is a mistake to conceive of an all-encompassing cultural monism.

The Renaissance popes asserted the universal claims of the monarchical Roman episcopate, but in reality they increasingly took on the character of Italian Renaissance princes. They were concerned with their political and military control over the Papal States and with the enrichment of their families. The wickedness of popes such as Sixtus IV, Alexander VI, Innocent VIII, has often been exaggerated. There is no real proof, for example, of fornication by one of these popes after his elevation to the papal chair. They did, however, scandalize the faithful and failed to provide spiritual leadership, for their interests ran more to politics and war, art and literature, hunting and luxurious living than to their apostolic duties.

All too many bishops emulated the example of the pontiffs, for they were regularly chosen for political reasons, came from the upper nobility, and were in some cases as much feudal overlords as ecclesiastical leaders. In Germany especially the higher ecclesiastical positions were of great political importance. The archbishops of Mainz, Trier, and Cologne were three of the seven electors of the Holy Roman Empire. Cathedral chapters in cities such as Augsburg were the special preserve of the local aristocracy. At one time a Bavarian prince became Archbishop of Cologne and held four other sees without even being in priestly orders.

The Fifth Lateran Council (1512–1517) offered the final chance for a general reform before the Reformation cataclysm. Pope Julius II convoked the council only under considerable pressure. A French synod at Tours, called for September 14, 1510, at the insistence of King Louis XII, who was at loggerheads with the pope, demanded reform, condemned the pope's action against the king, and appealed to a general council. The following year a clique of dissident cardinals, led by the Spaniard Cardinal Carbajal, convoked a council at Pisa for September 1, 1511. As a counter-measure Julius II called the Fifth Lateran, which was to reform the church, heal schism, and support a crusade against the Turks. The council opened on May 3 with an eloquent sermon by Egidio da Viterbo, general of the Augustinian order, calling for an inner spiritual reform which would lead to outward change. The council, never numbering more than a hundred cardinals and bishops, mostly Italian, lacked the full force of a truly ecumenical conference. At its second session in May 1512, Cardinal Cajetan (Thomas de Vio), general of the Dominican order, in a sermon forcefully proclaimed the papal theory of authority. This was clearly the pope's council and no more hope for reform could be entertained under Leo X than under Julius II. The council called for perpetual peace among Christian rulers, demanded a levy on all states to finance a crusade against the Turks, allowed the taxation of the clergy in some lands, and granted bishops a little more control over the monastic and mendicant houses in their dioceses. But thorough reform of the church floundered on the resistance of the Curia and bishops. In the final session, which took place early in that fateful year 1517, the council reaffirmed the bull *Unam sanctam* (1302) in which Boniface VIII had claimed the *plenitudo potestatis* in spiritual matters and real, though indirect, authority over earthly rulers. The edicts of the council were received with widespread indifference and even cynicism. The Venetians, for example, suspected that Leo X would use the crusade money for his war against Urbino, where he planned to acquire territory for his Medici family. This was in important ways an age of demoralization, division, and dissolution. "If Christianity had remained what its Founder made it," wrote Machiavelli, "things would have gone differently, and mankind would have been far happier, but there is no plainer proof that this religion is falling to pieces than the fact that the people who live nearest to Rome are the least pious of any."

Problems of ignorance, immorality, and irregularities reached down through the lower levels of the secular and regular clergy whose hostility and rivalry were a disturbing element in many dioceses. There is some confusion as to who should be counted as clergy, since the word "cleric" was used to identify a great many men who were not fully ordained priests, such as students, canons, ancillary clergy, and teachers. The clergy constituted a significant part of the population, in many cities, such as Worms, comprising at least 10 percent of the population. Cologne with a population of 40,000 had more than 6,000 clerics, Hamburg with a population of 12,000 had 450 parish priests, and Breslau had more than 400 chantry priests. If the higher members of the hierarchy were drawn from the upper classes, the lesser clergy usually came from families of the lower classes who did not have a tradition of study and learning. Many clerics studied at some prominent church or cathedral or were apprenticed to some literate priest. In England 10 to 20 percent of the clergy with benefices had some university education. In South Germany some 30 to 50 percent had seen the towers of university towns. The Latin of many was poor, hardly adequate for liturgical purposes, but the laity in general did not seem to demand a high level of reading proficiency in Latin. Despite the jibes of the humanists, who mocked the ignorance of the clergy, there is evidence to indicate that, due in part to the advent of printing, the level of clerical learning was improving. There were some great preachers prior to the Reformation: John of Capistrano, Bernardino of Siena, Girolamo Savonarola, Geiler von Kaisersberg; and towns now began to endow preacherships, not unlike the Puritan lectureships in England at a later day. There were at least a dozen such positions in the Swiss cantons by the end of the fifteenth century. The evangelical service of the Reformation is related generically to the late medieval preaching service in South Germany and Switzerland. Since preaching requires higher intellectual gifts than rote performance of ritual, this development suggests an improvement in clerical education. Many of these preachers, the most alert and serious members of the clergy, were to join the Reformation movement.

The most obvious and to some laymen the most egregious abuse was that of clerical concubinage. In some parts of Europe as many as one-third of the clergy who had taken the vow of celibacy kept concubines. In Italy common-law wives for the clergy were widely accepted. Prominent churchmen even before the Reformation, including Pope Pius II, came out in favor of the marriage of the clergy in order to relieve the situation, but the church was not ready to move in that direction. All too many bishops preferred to collect the fines exacted of the clergy for wives and illegitimate children. The monks were derided as a special threat to the wives and daughters of burghers. A common witticism ran, "She entered a convent because she wanted a lover." A particularly sensational incident occurred in the Tyrol, where the daughters of the upper nobility turned their convent into a brothel and had to be evicted by force.

Many abuses related to ecclesiastical fiscalism or cupidity had reached down to the parish level, where they became obvious to all. The catalog of wrongdoing is familiar to any student of the period: simony, nepotism, pluralism, absenteeism. The payment of annates meant that the first year's income of a papal appointment went to the pope. If an appointment to a vacancy in a bishopric or abbacy could be deferred, the income would be appropriated during the interim through reservation by the papal fiscal officer. The sums involved were not insignificant: for Cologne, Mainz, Salzburg, and Trier the amount was 1,000 gulden; for Liège, 7,200 gulden; for Freising, 4,000 gulden; for Minden, 500; for Halberstadt, 100. For the archbishoprics the additional charge for the pallium was 10,000 gulden. These sums could not be paid from the regular income of the see, and so the burden was laid on the people. The parish priests in turn increased exactions on the laity, often charging for services which were part of their sacerdotal duties. Payments were required for dispensations from or the changing of vows for marriages, for annulments of marriages, for the administration of baptism, confession, extreme unction, or burial. Unfortunates caught up in legal processes in the ecclesiastical courts could be bankrupted paying fees and bribes in processes which could be carried by appeals all the way to Rome. Excommunication of an individual or the ban laid on an entire community could be ruinous. Special payments on feast days, charges to see relics, pilgrimages to shrines were frequently required of the faithful as spiritual obligations. In 1492 the Abbot of Deutz commanded Duke Wilhelm of Jülich to force the villagers to go on a pilgrimage and give the customary offerings, because they had refused to do so voluntarily. He threatened to apply "spiritual sanctions" if the duke did not cooperate.

The worst abuse, however, came to be the sale of indulgences, writs given on the payment of money excusing the recipient from deeds of satisfaction or suffering in purgatory upon repentance and confession of sins. While some indulgence preachers emphasized repentance and stirred the consciences of sinners, all too many gave the impression that they were selling the forgiveness of sins for a price. Chantry priests were an especially grievous problem, for they drew their salaries for celebrating the mass for the living or for the souls of the dead, but they usually had no other duties than to say the endowed masses and the office of the dead, so that the devil found work for their idle hands to do. There was little counseling or genuine cure of souls. A further source of hostility between the clergy and the laity was in the economic competition on the part of monasteries and religious brotherhoods. The peasants and the workers and merchants in the cities, who were in an economically difficult situation, were angered at monastic enterprises such as breweries, wineries, mills, tanneries, bakeries, printeries, taverns (often open on Sundays), for the monks could produce and market their wares more cheaply and generally enjoyed tax-free status. A German witticism which went back as far as the year 1200 told of the avaricious priest who read the lesson for the day in this way: "Here beginneth the holy gospel according to the Mark."

Lay people at the close of the Middle Ages were deeply involved in religious life. The proliferation of monastic establishments tapered off, as can be seen from the case of the Cistercians, since 694 of the 742 Cistercian houses in the year 1500 had been founded before 1300. Instead of building more cathedrals laymen directed their beneficences toward local parish churches, monastic houses and confraternities, brotherhoods for prayers or for sharing collectively the merits of good works. The evidence is nearly everywhere still present in European churches: side altars, memorial windows, statues of saints, organs, vestments, crucifers, reliquaries, chapels in hospitals, almshouses, workers' quarters, and schools. New hospitals, colleges, and professorships were endowed for the welfare of the donor's soul. New saint cults, such as the Fourteen Helpers in Time of Need, the rosary, pilgrimages to new shrines, immense new relic collections, and benefices or endowments for chantry priests or other church offices, all gave evidence of a marked increase in religiosity from the mid-fourteenth century, following the depredations of the Black Death. Laymen were regularly involved as elders in local churches and were responsible for managing endowments and controlling appointments to benefices, which put them outside the reach of papal provisions, but introduced lay interference with some deleterious effects. In the cities the councils asserted an increasingly thorough control over the religious establishments within their walls and territories, frequently in defiance of and against the armed resistance of the bishops.

Lay literacy was on the rise and a flood of new municipal schools were being founded, city councils struggling to keep them free of episcopal authority. In a city such as London basic literacy was necessary to participation in commerce and business. The spread of printed books was certainly a major factor in the rise of literacy. At least a thousand printers were at work before 1500 and they produced 30,000 titles for a total output of between nine and twelve million volumes. Nearly half of the books printed before 1500 (the incunabula) were religious in nature, including many devotional and sermon books. Three-fourths of them were in Latin, the number of books in the vernacular increasing gradually until the great explosion of vernacular books and treatises in the Reformation period. Moreover, the Bible appeared in the language of the people, at least twenty-nine vernacular Bibles having been printed before 1500, including those in German and even low German. The Archbishop Berthold of Mainz said of printing: "The clergy . . . hailed it as a divine art."

Advances in education are further evident in the founding of new universities. By 1500 there were some seventy-nine universities in Europe. In England new colleges were added to Oxford and Cambridge. Popes, prelates, princes, and cities established new universities. In some cases endowments originally intended for some strictly religious purpose such as the saying of masses were diverted to support new colleges and university foundations. Ironically this very rise in the literacy and learning of the laity became a source of the criticism directed against the deficiencies of the clergy. Moreover, just as the church had been the mother of the medieval universities, the university now became the mother of the Reformation.

The upsurge of frenetic religious activity does not prove the case for a renaissance of the pure Christian faith as such. There was, to be sure, a new mystical faith reflected in such movements as the Brethren of the Common Life, in individual mystics such as Catherine of Siena, the Englishwoman Margery Kempe, Brigitta of Sweden, Jean Gerson, or even Lefèvre d'Étaples, and in the work of artists such as Matthias Grünewald, whose portrayal of the crucifixion for the Isenheim altar was starkly realistic. The *Pietà,* Christ taken from the cross and held in the arms of his mother, as a new German art form reflected a genuine Christocentric piety. But there is also evidence in many parts of Europe and on all levels of society of a persistence of paganism, the survival of Germanic folklore, an inclination toward superstition, the practice of witchcraft, a substratum of materialism, and a failure to understand or appreciate the transcendent and otherworldly dimensions of the faith. The extent of popular theological understanding was not impressive, and the sense of sin was often fear of damnation rather than deprivation of God. The perception of grace was often distorted into a magical interpretation of the *ex opere operato* or mechanical and external operation of the sacraments. There was often more preoccupation with the devil than affection for God. One student of popular religion in Flanders has ventured the rather extreme judgment that 40 percent of the people were Christians of good character and 10 percent were fervent practitioners, while the rest were indifferent or negligent formal adherents. Catechisms were 80 percent morality, 15 percent dogma, and only 5 percent concerned with the sacraments. The Christian facade concealed an anemic concern with the supernatural.[20] Historical judgments in this area are difficult, dependent as they are upon subjective views of what constitutes pure Christianity. One might argue, for example, that the resurgence of Lollardy, the continuance of Waldensianism, the persistence of Hussitism, the vitality of the Beghards and Beguines, the appearance of flagellants, and other heresies revealed the strength of religious impulses. Certainly the credibility gap between the religious expectations of the people and the ability of the official church to meet those expectations promised little good for the future. But there was still a great deal of health and strength in the old church, and thousands of faithful priests and millions of devout believers sought a more intense religious experience and a pure form of Christianity. The church was perhaps in at least as sound a condition on the eve of the Reformation as it was when it entered the crises of the fourteenth century. But this time the forces against it proved to be even more powerful.

7. HUMANISM AND REFORM

Urban life was highly developed in the Italian home of Renaissance humanism. The social experience of the city dweller, who earned his living by his wits in a game in which he did not control or even fully understand the rules, was qualitatively different from that of the peasant or noble in an agricultural or forest setting. The eternal return of the seasons, the tie to a natural reality with patterns of regularity, the assumption regarding a natural hierarchy which was mirrored in the feudal and ecclesiastical structure, all gave way to a new world of calculation, energetic action, individual initiative, practical ingenuity, and personal aggressiveness. Minds moved away from the static cosmic order and the great verities of scholastic philosophy, to a humanist approach to reality that stressed moral philosophy as prudential virtue, history as change, political theory as a reflection of reality, poetry as an expression of feeling, and

20. Jacques Toussaert, *Le Sentiment religieux en Flandre à la fin du Moyen-Âge* (Paris, 1963), pp. 3–4, 67, 605–606.

above all rhetoric as the articulation of thought in action and of truth which did not convince merely by the rules of logic, but actually moved the will to action. Humanism rediscovered classical antiquity as a great reservoir of divine and human wisdom on which to draw in support of its program.[21]

The humanists paid a heavy price in a deeply rooted anxiety and sometimes even in dark melancholy, which may be attributed to the need to cope with broader horizons, their new independence, the conflict of classical with Christian cultural values, and the impact of pessimistic late classical literature and philosophy. The new lay culture which saw nonclerics writing theology was far less secure than the clerical culture of the preceding centuries, for all the debates and controversies in that more narrowly confined world. The Florentine Neoplatonic school of the late quattrocento represented a deviation from the norm of humanistic culture, almost a reversion to the medieval cosmic order and hierarchy. It proved to be very appealing to many northern humanists, possibly for that very reason.

Northern humanism was related generically to Italian humanism and received from that source its more powerful creative impulses in art, literature, philosophy, education, historical and political thought. There were indigenous roots, of course, particularly for French humanism in Provençal literature and the medieval classical tradition. German humanism had certain personalities such as Conrad Celtis, the first German poet laureate and archhumanist, who were Italianesque in character. But in general German humanists tended to be more serious and devout, concerned with history, philosophy, and education. They were inclined to be more schoolish if not more scholarly, and took philology so seriously that by the end of the century a knowledge of Hebrew as well as of Latin and Greek was commonplace among learned men. They shared Italian humanists' antipathy toward scholastic philosophy, although the battle against both *viae, antiqua* and *moderna,* often took the form of a struggle for chairs of rhetoric in the universities. Criticism frequently went no deeper than jibes at the barbarous Latin of the scholastics, their involuted dialectic, and their hostility to the new culture. The thrusts of Crotus Rubeanus and Ulrich von Hutten in the *Letters of Obscure Men* were of this kind, just as

21. See William J. Bouwsma, "Renaissance and Reformation: An Essay in Their Affinities and Connections," in Heiko Oberman, ed., *Luther and the Dawn of the Modern Era* (Leiden, 1974), pp. 127-149.

many of Hutten's diatribes, such as the *Trias Romana,* were aimed at the ignorance of the "sophists" and the Roman clergy. The controversy over Johannes Reuchlin's defense of Hebrew books was a classical affair of humanists against the "obscurantist" Cologne doctors, men such as Ortwin Gratius, who were really not, however, devoid of classical knowledge.

German humanism was characterized by two main themes, a form of patriotic cultural nationalism and a desire for religious enlightenment. The German humanists rediscovered German as well as classical antiquity, responding to Tacitus' flattering description of the noble barbarians. Their humanist sodalities in all parts of the Empire were engaged in a great topographical-historical project to be called *Germania illustrata* under the leadership of Celtis, who called them to cultural rivalry with the overbearing Italians. Inevitably the humanists turned their pens also against the Roman Catholic Church. Their criticisms of abuse and opposition to the exploitation of the Germans by the Italian churchmen—wagons of gold taken annually over the Alps to enrich the Curia and to enable the Roman conquerors to live in luxury—fused with the *gravamina* or grievances of the German nation as expressed in the imperial diets for nearly a century, and added to the general malaise.

The desire for religious enlightenment evolved naturally under the influence of German mysticism, the *Devotio moderna* of the Brethren of the Common Life, and the religious concerns of Italians such as Valla, Ficino, Pico, and Baptista Mantuanus, the four authors most popular with the German humanists. Rudolf Agricola, the "father of German humanism," emulated Petrarch in his criticism of scholasticism, in his cultivation of rhetoric, and his work for the reform of education and the clergy. Jakob Wimpfeling excoriated abuses, Reuchlin looked to the Cabala as yet another source of religious knowledge, useful for revitalizing Messianic Christianity, and Mutianus Rufus, who was intrigued by skepticism and arcane pagan lore, sought to spiritualize dogma and taught a kind of ethical Paulinism. The giant figure among the northern humanists, Desiderius Erasmus (c. 1469–1536), laid out a program for the *restitutio Christianismi.* He envisioned the restoration of that golden age of those first centuries of Christendom when, as he imagined, Christianity and classical antiquity were in harmony. In that age apologists such as Justin Martyr and church fathers such as St. Clement, Origen, St. Jerome, and St. Augustine achieved a perfect balance of Christian and ancient classical thought. Erasmus appreciated man's moral and intellectual faculties which, when rightly informed and activated, were able to achieve a God-pleasing life and a desirable level of human culture. He became not only the literary arbiter and dominant intellectual influence on northern humanism, but the very idol of the German humanists.

The limitations of northern humanism prevented it from becoming a world-changing elemental force. The humanists did not touch the institution of the church, the hierarchy, the sacramental-sacerdotal system, but only the abuses, the ignorance, immorality, and sloth of the priests and monks, the fiscal chicanery of the Curia and financial exploitation of the Germans. They did not question the position of the papacy as the absolutism of a single bishop but rather struck at the luxurious living, political involvement, and the wars of the vicar of Christ. They did not attack ecclesiastical law and legalism. They did not wrestle with basic articles of faith or the fundamentals of theology. Their critique and program of reform remained, therefore, superficial compared with the radical thrust of the Protestant Reformation.

Reformation Europe, then, was a dynamic continent undergoing powerful currents of change. The population was growing at a notable rate; the climate for several decades grew more benign; the economy was in motion with markedly rising prices accompanied by a lag in real wages and rents; commerce expanded with a wider diversity of commodities and markets; industrial production rose somewhat; political structures were evolving toward centralization of power in the national monarchies and territorial princedoms; a great shift was under way from a focus of economic and political action in central Europe to the Atlantic seaboard states; a significantly different social structure developed in eastern Europe; there were signs of discontent and disaffection within the church, and intellectual and cultural life was stirring anew. There were signs not only of increased criticism of the church but of actual resistance to the church. The German scene was particularly volatile, where the political and cultural situation was charged like the atmosphere with electrical tensions before a thunderstorm. With the advent of Martin Luther the lightning struck. Fire fell from heaven.

Chapter Two

THE LUTHERAN REFORMATION

1. LUTHER THE REFORMER

FRANCE, the "eldest daughter of the church," became in a special way the mother of high medieval culture. Italy with its ancient marble monuments gave birth to the golden age of the Renaissance. Germany, brought to Christianity by the monks, became the homeland of the Reformation, its first truly original contribution to European culture. It was, declared Leopold von Ranke, the most profound spiritual revolution ever experienced by a people in so short a period of time. Luther, the first reformer, an Augustinian monk, embodied in his own person all the driving forces and reformatory impulses of his generation. He cried out from the depths of his soul, he was pressed into becoming a spokesman of the German nation, and he served as the conscience of Christendom, for his call corresponded to a widely felt need for reform and spiritual renewal. The Reformation was born deep within a single individual but emerged to become a public matter and a powerful historical force. So many of the subsequent religious and political developments were conditioned and even determined by the nature of Luther's evangelical breakthrough and by the events of the brief period from 1517 to 1521 that a detailed examination is warranted. "The particular," Leopold von Ranke held, "contains the general within it." Nearly a millennium and a half had rolled by since Christ suffered under Pontius Pilate when Luther made his brave stand before the Holy Roman Emperor in one of the most magnificent scenes of human history. The road to Worms was for that earnest follower of Christ his very own *via dolorosa*.

"I was born in Eisleben and baptized in St. Peter's there," Luther once observed. "I do not remember this, but I believe my parents and fellow countrymen."[1] The date was November 10, 1483, St. Martin's Day, when Hans and Margarethe Luther's second son entered the world. His parents

1. *D. Martin Luthers Werke. Briefwechsel* (Weimar, 1930–), hereafter cited as *WA Br*, I, 610, 18 (Jan. 14, 1520), cited in Gordon Rupp, *Luther's Progress to the Diet of Worms* (New York, 1964), p. 9.

had moved to Eisleben from the ancestral home at Moehre, a small village of some fifty families on the western slope of the Thuringian forest. His forebears had emigrated to this colonial region from western Germany centuries before and were free peasants. His family was relatively well off, for his grandfather Heinrich owned a substantial house and a small estate. According to Saxon law, the youngest son inherited landed property—just the reverse of Norman primogeniture—and the eldest son, Hans, had to strike out on his own. The burgeoning mining industry offered the best opportunity, so Hans moved to Eisleben, and later to Mansfeld, where he worked as a miner, became a foreman, a renter, and by the time his son Martin was eight years old, he had become a member of a mining firm. Twenty years later he owned substantial shares in six pits and two smelting companies. He supported his family of eight children well and could afford to send Martin to the best schools in the region. Hans Luther was a solid, rugged, plain and honest man, hard-working, sober, and wholesomely ambitious. He was highly respected in the community, was elected city councillor, and served as a layman responsible for endowments in the parish church. He was a sensitive person, a highly religious man who enjoyed the company of clergymen and loved his family very much. Margarethe was an imaginative person, gifted with a beautiful voice for song, who worked hard for the children, though she could be overly severe, once spanking Martin until he bled for stealing a nut. Luther in later life remembered them both with great affection and observed that "they meant well by me." He inherited his father's physical and moral strength and his mother's musical and imaginative ways. He named two of his own children for them.

Martin attended the local school in Mansfeld to the age of fourteen, a school typical for its joyless pedagogy, the grinding of declensions, and flogging for minor offenses such as speaking German instead of Latin on the playground. His parents sent him for a year to a good secondary school at Magdeburg, where he encountered the Brethren of the Common Life, and then to Eisenach for three years, where he studied at St. George School with the well-known grammarian Trebonius. In April, 1501, he matriculated in the faculty of Arts at the University of Erfurt, as "Martinus Ludher ex Mansfeld" and was registered *in habendo,* having means and therefore ineligible for a scholarship. Erfurt University had been founded in 1397, enjoyed an outstanding reputation in arts and law, and was well attended with some 2,000 students. Luther took his A.B. degree in the fall of 1502 and an M.A. on January 7, 1505. He studied the traditional trivium and quadrivium, and his instruction in philosophy was in the *via moderna*, notably under the nominalist teachers Jodocus Trutvetter and Bartholomäus Arnoldi of Usingen, as well as in the natural, moral, and metaphysical philosophy of Aristotle. His father gave him an expensive *Corpus iuris* as a graduation present and on May 20 he entered law school, headed for the regal legal road to wealth and social preferment. But on July 16 Luther invited his student friends for a farewell meal, beer and song, for he loved to play the lute. The next day he greeted them with, "Today you see me, henceforth never more." The somber little group accompanied him to the door of the monastery of the <u>Eremites of St.</u> 1505- <u>Augustine</u> not far from the university. As the door closed behind him he entered upon a new monastic way of life, seeking, he said later, "my salvation."

A number of incidents may have served as a catalyst for his momentous decision. The death of a close friend affected him deeply. He once accidentally fell and cut his leg on his dagger and was in danger of bleeding to death. On July 2 he was returning from a visit home when he was overtaken by a thunderstorm near Stotternheim, a village about a mile north of Erfurt. When a bolt of lightning struck nearby he cried out in terror: "Help, dear [St.] Anne, I will become a monk!" Although we do not know his inner state of mind, it seems likely that he was oppressed with an acute sense of mortality, was driven by the fear-motivated piety and religious scruples characteristic of the time, and had been mulling over his own relationship with God, questioning whether his good works were sufficient to merit salvation. His pious family background, his encounter with the Brethren at Magdeburg—where he had been deeply moved to see Prince Wilhelm of Anhalt-Zerbst, patron of the Franciscans, begging in the streets—the religious devotions that were a regular part of life in the student bursa, and his own sensitive nature all combined to turn his reflections toward questions of eternal salvation.

The house he chose to enter had an impeccable reputation and belonged to the observantine or strict constructionist branch of the order. <u>Luther was an extraordinarily conscientious monk,</u> praying, fasting, begging, flagellating, confessing, outdoing himself and others in his attempt to lead a righteous life. A fellow monk who remained Catholic declared much later that "Luther lived a holy life among them, kept the Rule most exactly, and studied diligently." But having done all as a very good monk, he was left with a feeling of doubt and uncertainty as to whether he had done enough. In September, 1506, he left the novice state, took the irrevocable vows of poverty, chastity, and obedience, and prepared for ordination. He became a subdeacon in December, a deacon in February, 1507, and in April, 1507, was ordained priest. At the beginning of May Luther celebrated his first mass and he recalled later how his hand trembled as he held the sacred host. His father came for the occasion and brought two wagons of provisions for a banquet, twenty friends, and made a large gift to the monastery. Hans was still displeased that Martin had given up the law for monasticism and now the priesthood, and at the table when making the customary remarks he asked pointedly, "But have you not read in the Scriptures, 'Thou shalt honor thy father and thy mother'?" When in 1521 Luther wrote his *De votis monasticis,* dedicated to his father, he recalled that those words really moved him and raised doubts as to the rightness of his decision.

Luther was singled out among the seventy some brothers for theological study. His theological education was conditioned by scholasticism of the *via moderna* school, but the significance of that fact has still not been precisely spelled out and the implications are highly contested. He studied with Johannes Paltz and Johannes Nathin, who had been a student of Gabriel Biel (d. 1495), a nominalist theologian at Tübingen University, the most learned and the most creative of the late medieval nominalists. In preparing for his ordination Luther read Biel's *Exposition on the Canon of the Mass* and so received an early introduction to nominalist thought. Biel was completely deferential toward papal prerogatives and Luther seems not to have read William of Occam's (d. 1348) antipapal writings, indeed may not have studied Occam directly at all at Erfurt. It was, however, Occamist theology that influenced Luther and against which he gradually turned. Johannes von Staupitz, the Vicar-General of the Saxon Province of the Augustinians, recommended Luther to Elector Frederick for a position at the University of Wittenberg. This new university founded in Ernestine Saxony in 1502 was the Elector's pride and joy. In 1508 Luther left Erfurt for Wittenberg to teach moral philosophy on the basis of Aristotle's *Nicomachaean Ethics.* The next March he became a *Baccalaureus Biblicus,* which qualified him to lecture in theology as a *sentenarius,* commenting on Peter Lombard's *Sentences,* which had been drawn extensively from the writings of St. Augustine.

Luther now read St. Augustine with great gusto and began to travel that road away from Aristotelianism and scholasticism toward the new theology of the Wittenberg theologians based on the Bible, St. Augustine, and the old fathers. From 1509 to 1511 Luther returned to Erfurt to honor a teaching obligation there but was then returned to Wittenberg, where he was to remain for the rest of his life. Late in 1510 Luther was sent to Rome to accompany a senior member of the order who was to represent the case of seven Observantine Augustinian houses who were opposing amalgamation with the other Augustinian houses. The trip was arduous and when Luther first sighted the Holy City he fell to the ground and cried out, "Hail, holy Rome!" Pope Julius II was away from the city on a military campaign and Luther's mission was not resolved. He made the usual pilgrimages to the churches and climbed the stairs of Pilate's pretorium on his knees to earn indulgences for his grandfather. Luther seems not to have taken particular offense at the vices of the Eternal City and indeed the whole trip made no essential difference for him. When he returned Staupitz determined that Luther should prepare to assume his chair in biblical theology. On October 19, 1512, in a solemn ceremony in the Castle Church, Luther became a doctor of theology, assumed the *lectura in biblia,* and took an oath to defend and expound the Holy Scriptures. This was a decisive step in his life, for he took this calling so seriously that in the stormy years that lay ahead he often found comfort in the thought that he was being true to his calling and to the Word of God which he had sworn to declare. Moreover, the private monk now became a public figure required to teach and to preach in the congregations of the church. He was twenty-eight at the time, and for over three decades he entered the large auditorium twice a week and lectured on biblical theology, expounding the Scriptures as an exegete. His sermons were exegetical and his exegesis was often homiletical. Both were consistently biblical and theological rather than merely philological or philosophical. His lectures went on like a clock ticking away during a storm, even when the titanic events of the Reformation were crashing all about.

As a monk Luther had suffered through excruciating spiritual struggles, not carnal temptations in an ordinary sense but intense soul struggles or *Anfechtungen.* The fear-motivated piety of his youth was reinforced by the monastic demands for perfection. The words of Christ were: "Be ye therefore perfect even as your Father who is in heaven is perfect!" Overwhelmed by the thought of what it means as a sinner to stand in the presence of a righteous God *(coram deo),* he was driven to despair. Modernist theology which emphasized the power of the human will counseled him to do the best that was in him and God would not withhold His grace *(facere quod in se est deus non denegat gratiam)*. How could he be sure that he had done enough good works to satisfy God's demand for righteousness? How could he find a merciful God? From St. Augustine he learned something of the dichotomy of law and gospel, sin and grace, but he did not win relief from that father, whose anthropology was clouded by a Platonic overcast. The answer came to him gradually during the course of his biblical studies and then suddenly, or so it seemed to him, his evangelical breakthrough came to him as an unexpected insight, like the dawn after a long dark night of the soul.

Scholars have had a field day studying each phrase and inflection in his lecture notes on the Psalms, 1513–1515; and on the epistles of Paul to the Romans, 1515–1516; Galatians, 1516–1517; Hebrews, 1517–1518. One can find virtually all the basic elements of his theology in the *Dictata* or lectures on the Psalms, but they are not clearly stated and are intermingled with scholastic propositions, traditional phrases, Augustinian formulae, reflections of Lombard's *Sentences,* and retain the scholastic notion of the synderesis or moral structure and spark of basic good in man which enables him to choose to love God of his own free will. In the commentary on Romans he reveals clearly that he has learned from St. Paul the depth of sin and the magnitude of God's forgiving grace. He grew in certainty and in his appreciation of all the implications of the gospel and then returned to comment once again on the Psalms in the light of his new understanding. As an old man in 1545 he recalled his powerful "tower experience" *(Turmerlebnis),* the point at which he first discovered the key to his problem. Reading the huge Bible kept in the library in the tower room of the monastery, he puzzled over the meaning of the term "the righteousness of God" in Romans 1:17: "For therein is the righteousness of God revealed from faith to faith: as it is written, the just shall live by faith." He had previously understood the term "righteousness of God" *(justitia dei)* as an active, retributive, punishing, essential righteousness, the righteousness of the law which God demands of man. Now he saw that the Romans 1:17 passage must be understood in the light of Romans 3:24: "Being justified freely by his grace through the redemption that is in Christ Jesus." He now understood the "righteousness of God" as the passive imputed righteousness that God bestows upon man freely through Christ, whom one need merely trust for salvation. "I pondered night and day," he recalled, "until I understood the connection between the righteousness of God and the sentence 'The just shall live by faith.' Then I grasped that the justice of God is the righteousness by which through grace and pure mercy, God justifies us through faith. Immediately I felt that I had been reborn and that I had passed through wide-open doors into paradise!"

Luther recalls this dramatic episode as coming late, even after the indulgences controversy of 1517, a source of puzzlement to scholars, for in his lectures on Romans he seems already to have grasped the essentials of the doctrine of salvation by God's grace alone, received as a gift to the believer who accepts the benefits of Christ without depending upon his own merits. The resolution seems to be that after a long interior process of development and the shock of a public controversy Luther was reflecting upon Romans once again. Suddenly he came to realize the full implications of the idea that salvation depends entirely upon the divine initiative of God, who is love. Then he saw that the mercy of God is mercy which God bestows upon us, not that which He demands of us, the love of God is that which He shows toward us, not that which He asks of us, just as the righteousness of God is that which He gives us, not that which He requires of us. Luther saw clearly the distinction between law and gospel. His doctrine of justification by God's grace alone received only by faith in Christ's atoning work proved to be a powerful instrument for resolving his own religious struggle, for a critique of traditional theology and religious practice, and for the religious awakening of Europe.

Luther had achieved a certain prominence in the Augustinian order, becoming a subprior and regent of the monastery school in May, 1512, and district overseer of eleven monasteries in May, 1515. At Wittenberg the theological faculty developed a special emphasis upon St. Augustine and the Bible in contrast to the scholastic emphasis upon dialectic at the older universities. The most vociferous of the group, which included Nikolaus Amsdorf, Hieronymus Schurf, and Bartholomäus Bernhardi von Feldkirchen, was Andreas Karlstadt (1480–1541). He was a very assertive type who habitually plunged into things beyond his knowledge and abilities. Luther forged ahead in a more substantial way, spelling out the implications of his evangelical approach for theology. On September 25, 1516, he presided over a disputation in which Bernhardi, a student, defended quite radical theses on grace and free will. On September 4, 1517, he presided, as dean of the theological faculty, as another student,

Franz Günther, defended ninety-seven theses, which Luther had prepared as a "Disputation against Scholastic Theology." These theses represented a fundamental break with traditional theology, but the attack on the theory of a great institution aroused less attention than his attack on its practice was to do. Karlstadt swung over to Luther's side after reading Augustine and Günther's theses. Luther stirred up a minor storm among his Augustinian colleagues by denying the authenticity of the treatise *True and False Penitence* attributed to St. Augustine and cited in Lombard's *Sentences.* The question of penance and true repentance became the center of the indulgences controversy that triggered the Reformation.

About noon on October 31, 1517, Luther posted on the door of the Castle Church his *Ninety-five Theses or Disputation on the Power and Efficacy of Indulgences.* It was customary to nail such theses to the door, which served as a bulletin board for public events at the university, and many disputation theses had been posted there before. He wrote them in Latin with an academic preamble: "Out of love and zeal for truth and the desire to bring it to light, the following theses will be publicly discussed at Wittenberg under the chairmanship of the Reverend Father Martin Luther, Master of Arts and Sacred Theology and regularly appointed Lecturer on these subjects at that place. He requests that those who cannot be present to debate orally with us will do so by letter." No one came to dispute, but as an obedient son of the church, he sent copies to his ecclesiastical superiors in the secular hierarchy, Bishop Jerome of Brandenburg and Archbishop Albert of Brandenburg, asking their aid in opposing the flagrant sale of indulgences.

An indulgence or permission to commute the satisfaction to be made by a contrite sinner was attached to the sacrament of penance. Contrition of the heart for sins committed should be followed by oral confession and the performance of penitential acts, whereupon the sinner received absolution or pardon for his sins, on the condition that the penance or penitential acts were done sincerely and satisfactorily *(contritio cordis; confessio oris; satisfactio operis; absolutio).* As private penance administered by the clergy gradually replaced public penance, the sacrament became vulnerable to abuse, for the satisfactions required and eventually the money payments substituted for acts of satisfaction, such as pilgrimages or crusades, were used to increase the power and wealth of the church. Indulgences were granted for visits to the sacred shrines in Rome during jubilee years. Pope Boniface VIII granted a plenary indulgence, that is, a complete remission of all temporal punishments *(poena)* to be endured after absolution of the guilt *(culpa)*, to every penitent jubilee pilgrim. A separation developed between absolution, which removed guilt and eternal punishment, and the continuance of temporal punishment, that is, the good works and suffering to be endured as acts of satisfaction in this life and in purgatory beyond the grave. A scale of sins developed from less serious or venial sins requiring minor penalties to mortal sins, which merited eternal damnation. Thirteenth-century theologians such as Alexander of Hales (d. 1245) developed the idea of a treasury of merits earned by Christ and saints who had performed works of supererogation upon which the church could draw in granting indulgences. In 1457 Pope Calixtus III announced that indulgences could be applied for the relief of souls already in purgatory. In 1476 Pope Sixtus IV with the bull *Salvator noster* extended the remission of temporal punishment to include those still living as well as the dead. Although penitence was required and a distinction between guilt and temporal punishment was made, many purveyors of indulgences blurred the lines and countless common folk believed themselves to be buying the forgiveness of sins when they purchased an indulgence.

All this hit Luther close to home and jeopardized his pastoral care for his brothers and lay parishioners. Pope Julius II had in 1510 announced a jubilee indulgence with the proceeds to go to the construction of the new St. Peter's cathedral in Rome. Pope Leo X renewed this indulgence and made Archbishop Albert of Brandenburg the high commissioner of the sale in his archbishoprics of Magdeburg and Mainz. Albert owed the papacy an enormous sum for the pallium and for a dispensation for pluralism, because in 1513 Albert, age twenty-three, had been elected Archbishop of Magdeburg and administrator of Halberstadt and in 1514 had been elected Archbishop of Mainz, which office made him also one of the seven electors of the Holy Roman Empire. The Curia struck a deal with Albert that the sale of indulgences would last for eight years in northern Germany, with the exception that Albert's brother Elector Joachim of Brandenburg would open up his territories to the sale as well. Half of the receipts were to go to the papacy and half would go to Albert to enable him to repay the 29,000 gulden he had borrowed from the Fugger banking house to pay his ecclesiastical fees. Albert appointed as subcommissioner John Tetzel, a fat Dominican who had peddled indulgences as early as 1504. Elector Frederick the Wise had forbidden this sale of indulgences in electoral Saxony, for he had his own collection of relics, and he profited from the pilgrims who came to see them. His collection housed in the Castle Church had grown from 5,005 items in 1509 to 17,443 in 1518, including a piece of Moses' burning bush, parts of the holy cradle and swaddling clothes, 204 parts and an entire corpse of the Holy Innocents, 35 fragments of the True Cross, and milk from the Virgin Mary, and to these relics was attached an indulgence of 127,799 years and 116 days of remission of suffering in purgatory. When Tetzel approached the borders of Ernestine Saxony in April, 1517, and many Wittenbergers went to buy indulgences, the sale ceased to be a theoretical matter and became for Luther an urgent pastoral concern. He wrote to various bishops urging them to intervene and then prepared his *Ninety-five Theses* for academic debate and out of concern for the church. The first two theses set the tone: (1) "When our Lord and Master Jesus Christ said, 'Repent' [Matt. 4:17], he willed the entire life of believers to be one of repentance." (2) "This word cannot be understood as referring to the sacrament of penance, that is, confession and satisfaction, as administered by the clergy." Theses 8 to 29 dealt with the value of indulgences for souls in purgatory, theses 30 to 80 with their effectiveness for the living, and the remainder were made up of rhetorical thrusts and raised the standard of his reformation, the theology of the cross: (92) "Away then with all those prophets who say to the people of Christ, 'Peace, peace,' and there is no peace!" [Jer. 6:14]; (93) "Blessed be all those prophets who say to the people of Christ, 'Cross, cross,' and there is no cross!"; (94) "Christians should be exhorted to be diligent in following Christ, their head, through penalties, death, and hell"; (95) "And thus be confident of entering into heaven through many tribulations rather than through the false security of peace" [Acts 14:22].[2]

Luther did not intend to have the theses spread among the people. The first printing was made by Johann Grünenberg in Wittenberg on a folio sheet for posting on the church door and for a few friends. But in the early months of 1518 they were reprinted in many cities—Nuremberg, Leipzig, Basel—by humanist circles and printers, and created a tremendous stir. Luther had dutifully though naively sent a copy to Archbishop Albert of Brandenburg, with a letter asking his intervention to halt the harmful sale. Albert did not deign to reply but on December 1 asked the theologians at the University of Mainz for their opinion of the theses, and two weeks later he sent a copy of the theses to Rome, demanding action against this

2. *Luther's Works*, 31, *Career of the Reformer:* I, Harold J. Grimm, ed. (Philadelphia, 1957), pp. 17–33.

heretic. Tetzel, enraged at the impudence of this Augustinian who inter-
fered with sales, responded with a vehement blast. Dr. Johannes Eck,
professor at Ingolstadt University, leaped into the fray with denunciations.
On February 3, 1518, Leo X sent a brief to the prefect of the Augustinians,
Gabriel della Volta, or Venetus, ordering him to control Luther, who was
introducing novel doctrines to the people. At the beginning of March,
1518, Staupitz informed Luther of Rome's steps against him and that the
head of the Augustinian order had demanded that he recant in order to
head off a heresy trial. In a letter of March 31, 1518, Luther refused to
recant unless convinced on the basis of Scriptures and claimed his right
to dispute as a university professor. Elector Frederick volunteered protection for his subject, who was a star professor at his university.

On April 11, 1518, Luther set out for Heidelberg to defend his theology before the general chapter of the Augustinians of Germany, which
convened on April 25. He honored the request of Staupitz that he avoid
controversial subjects, such as indulgences, and prepared his Heidelberg
theses on sin, free will, and grace, returning to the central themes of his
theology in opposition to nominalism. Twenty-eight theses were on theology and twelve, prepared by his companion Leonhard Beier, were on
philosophy against Aristotle. These theological issues proved to be of even
deeper and more fundamental significance. The disputation took place on
April 26, Luther presiding and Beier defending the theses. It was a triumphant performance, for Luther not only maintained his position, but made
important converts such as the young Dominican Martin Bucer, thrilled
to have had lunch with Staupitz and Luther, who was to become the
reformer of Strasbourg, and Johannes Brenz, who became the leading
reformer of Württemberg.

Two developments were from the very beginning unfolding simultaneously, the theological controversy and the ecclesiastical legal process. In
May, 1518, Luther sent Leo X his *Resolutions,* or *Explanations of the Ninety-
five Theses,* published in August, which arrived while the Curia was preparing the case against Luther. This made no impression on the pope despite
the concessions to papal primacy and tradition. A Dominican Thomist,
Sylvester Prierias, master of the Sacred Palace, was commissioned to
provide a theological analysis of Luther's writings. In his *Dialogue Against
the Presumptuous Theses of Martin Luther Concerning the Power of the Pope,* he
declared Luther's theses to be erroneous, false, presumptuous, or heretical. He was supercilious and contemptuous and declared Luther to have

a brain of brass and a nose of iron. Luther was cited to appear in Rome within sixty days. The dialogue and the citation were dispatched to the general of the Dominican order, Thomas de Vio, better known as Cardinal Cajetan, and arrived in Wittenberg in August, 1518. An order of extradition was sent to Elector Frederick, and on August 25 the General of the Augustinian order commanded the provincial of Saxony, Gerhard Hecker, to seize Luther and send him to Rome. Luther now entered the months of his greatest peril. With the backing of Elector Frederick, Luther asked for a hearing before competent scholars on German soil. At this point an important political consideration came into play, for the pope wished to curry Elector Frederick's favor in view of the forthcoming election of a new emperor, which would follow upon the death of the aging Maximilian. He therefore agreed to a hearing for Luther before Cajetan, his legate to the Diet of Augsburg. Luther appeared before him October 12 to 14, gaunt and with deep-set eyes, Cajetan observed. The great Thomist, the author of a nine-volume commentary on the *Summa Theologica,* demanded that Luther repent, recant, promise never to repeat his errors, and refrain from mischief in the future. Luther was exasperated at Cajetan's refusal to take him seriously. At the end of their third meeting Cajetan dismissed him and told him never to come near him again unless he was ready to recant. As the days passed Luther's few friends panicked, and fearing for his safety, they spirited him away through the postern gate. They rode until they were forced to halt from sheer exhaustion. He had escaped just in time. Cajetan complained to Frederick of Luther's insolence and reported to the Holy See on Luther's damnable errors.

At Augsburg the Italian diplomat Urban de Serralonga touched on the very anxiety that must have been gnawing at Luther's heart. "Do you really believe that the Elector will go to war on your account?" he asked. "By no means," Luther replied. "Where will you go then?" asked Urban. "Sub Coelo" (under heaven), answered Luther. When Luther returned to Wittenberg he wrote Frederick a response to Cajetan, charging the papal legate with having broken his promise to the Elector in not allowing discussion and with condemning Luther in advance. Luther concluded by telling the Elector that he was willing to leave Saxony and go where God would have him go. Luther said his goodbyes and on December 1 gave a farewell meal to his friends during which two letters arrived, the first from Georg Spalatin, Luther's best advocate at the court, expressing surprise that Luther had not yet gone, and the second telling him to remain.

By December 18 the Elector had decided that Luther was to be safe-
guarded in Saxony until he had been convicted by due process. Luther
returned to the routine of university lecturing, for Wittenberg was pros-
pering, with a burgeoning enrollment. *Hamlet!*

On January 12, 1519, Emperor Maximilian died and political maneuvering was intensified. Instead of pursuing heresy with fire and gibbet, the
Curia turned to politics. The pope sent his chamberlain, Karl von Miltitz,
to flatter Elector Frederick with the gift of the Golden Rose, a coveted
decoration, and to temporize with Luther. In their meeting at Altenburg,
January, 1519, Miltitz suggested a more neutral arbitrator such as the
Archbishop of Salzburg or the Archbishop of Trier. Luther agreed to a
truce of silence, if his enemies also would cease attacking him. The silence
soon gave way to the din of renewed polemics as the relentless Dr. Eck
and the aggressive Karlstadt tangled once again. A debate was scheduled
to be held in Leipzig, June 27–July 15.[3] Luther superseded Karlstadt
during the course of the debate. He had been driven by Eck's arguments
in behalf of papal primacy and authority to the intense study of church
history and concluded that the extravagant claims of the papacy to supremacy of the last four hundred years were not representative of the first
eleven hundred years of Christian history. As he studied the forged De-
cretals upon which many of the papal claims to temporal power and
possessions were based, he developed an increasingly apocalyptic view of
the papacy and the first intimations of the pope as the Antichrist and Rome
the whore of Babylon glimmered in his consciousness. This picture of the
papacy hardened in his mind the following year when he read Ulrich von
Hutten's edition of Lorenzo Valla's exposure of the Donation of Constan-
tine, giving the keys of the city to Pope Sylvester. Eck accused Luther of
being a Hussite, a shrewd thrust, for the University of Leipzig had been
founded by German scholars who left Prague because of Hussitism. Luther acknowledged the correctness of some of John Hus's views, such as
his contention that there is one holy Christian church, and declared that
when the Council of Constance condemned some of his views the council
had erred. When Duke George of Saxony, Luther's fierce enemy, heard
that he exclaimed, "A plague on it!" Although Eck outpointed Luther in
the debate, Luther was not trapped into declaring that popes and councils

3. Kurt Victor Selge, "Der Weg zur Leipziger Disputation zwischen Luther und Eck im
Jahr 1519," in Bernd Moeller and Gerhard Ruhbach, eds., *Bleibendes im Wandel der Kirchengeschichte* (Tübingen, 1973), pp. 169–210.

had erred, but rather he boldly proclaimed it and brushed aside the timorous demurrers of his friends. "Farewell, unhappy, hopeless, blasphemous Rome!" Luther wrote. "The wrath of God come upon thee, as you deserve. We have cared for Babylon and she is not healed: let us then leave her, that she may be the habitation of dragons, specters and witches and true to her name of Babel, an everlasting confusion, a new pantheon of wickedness."[4]

During the years 1519–1521 Luther experienced a burst of enormous creativity as tracts and treatises, religious and devotional pieces, sermons, commentaries, and polemics poured from his mind and pen. He kept three printing presses busy and sent the first pages off to them while he was still writing the last pages. When a writer is at work, he once observed, the uninitiated believe that only three fingers are active, whereas in reality his whole being is involved, a much more difficult task than letting a leg dangle down each side of a horse as the knights do. He held, he explained, a sword with one hand and with the other built the wall; defend and teach. He preached a powerful sermon *On the Two Kinds of Righteousness* (1519) and published a treatise *On Good Works* (1520), showing that good works necessarily flow out of a living faith but are a result of and not the basis for man's justification, which depends entirely upon God's grace.

The three great treatises of 1520 proved his power as a publicist. His *Address to the Christian Nobility of the German Nation Concerning the Reform of the Christian Estate* followed his final conviction that Rome was incorrigible and his breach with the papacy irreparable. In a moving appeal to Christian laymen to take the initiative in reform because of the default of the hierarchy, he called on Emperor Charles V, who had succeeded Maximilian I as emperor in 1519, the princes and knights, and the imperial cities to act, but with spiritual weapons and not with arms. He attacked the three walls of the Romanists: their claim that the secular powers have no jurisdiction over them since the spiritual sword is superior to the temporal sword; their claim that only the pope has the authority to expound the Scriptures; and their claim that only the pope can summon a general council. Luther repeated the grievances of the German nation in a moving populist appeal. But the most radical thrust was a subtle theological one, the idea of the priesthood of all believers. All Christians belong to one estate *(stand),* that of redeemed sinners living under God's grace. The clergy, secular or regular, are in no way spiritually superior to the

4. *D. Martin Luthers Werke. Kritische Gesamtausgabe* (Weimar, 1883–), hereafter cited as *WA,* 6, 329, cited in Rupp, *Luther's Progress,* p. 82.

laity. Christians have different offices or service functions *(ampt),* but there is no qualitative distinction between them in religious terms. His *Babylonian Captivity of the Church,* done in Latin for scholars, attacked the sacramental-sacerdotal system which had subjected the children of the spiritual Israel to the tyranny of the Roman Babylon. Of the seven sacraments, only baptism, the Lord's Supper, and penance were dominical, instituted by Christ. The Lord's Supper had been subjected to three abuses: the withholding of the cup from the laity, the doctrine of transubstantiation, and the mass as a sacrifice. Ordination, marriage, confirmation, and extreme unction were not means of grace as were baptism and the Lord's Supper, which combined the scriptural promises of God's forgiveness of sins and a visible sign—the elements of water, bread, and wine. His *On the Liberty of the Christian Man* was accompanied by an open letter to Pope Leo X in which he decried the corruption in the court of Rome which had lasted for three hundred years, cited the example of St. Bernard's *De Consideratione,* in which Bernard chided the sins of the papacy, and wished Leo well personally. This beautiful treatise began with that paradoxical formulation of which Luther was so fond: "I shall set down the following two propositions concerning the freedom and the bondage of the spirit:

A Christian is a perfectly free lord of all, subject to none;
A Christian is a perfectly dutiful servant of all, subject to all.

These two theses seem to contradict each other. If, however, they should be found to fit together they would serve our purpose beautifully." The Christian who trusts in the saving work of Christ is completely justified in God's eyes, free of all sin, restored to his true manhood. Out of love he freely serves his fellow man, not to earn salvation which is already his, but out of a spontaneous desire to serve. In a way this third seemingly innocent treatise was more radical than the others, for it expressed the extreme Pauline theology of faith and ethics which undercut the dogmatic accretions or developments of the medieval church.

The affair now moved rapidly to a climax. Dr. Eck not only sent reports to Rome on Luther's heresies but went in person to poison the wells. He had a hand in preparing the papal bull of excommunication which Leo X published on June 15, 1520, citing forty-one heresies, calling for the burning of Luther's books, and giving him sixty days within which to recant. The bull, *Exsurge, domine,* began with the words: "Arise, Lord, and judge thy cause . . . for a wild boar has entered into thy vineyard." It condemned Luther's teaching as "poisonous, offensive, misleading for godly and simple minds, uncharitable, and counter to all reverence for the

Holy Roman Church, the mother of the faithful and the mistress of faith."
Luther's books were burned in the Piazza Navona and that fall Dr. Eck,
who brought the bull back to Germany, and the papal legate Girolamo
Aleander, staged a book burning. In retaliation the Wittenberg students
and faculty gathered outside the Elstergate on the morning of December
10, 1520, to burn copies of the canon law and scholastic writings. Luther,
trembling with emotion, quietly stepped out from the crowd and threw
upon the flames a copy of the bull of excommunication, with words such
as these: "Because you have destroyed God's truth, may the Lord destroy
you today in this fire." Nearly at the very end of his sixty-day period
Luther wrote a bitter tract *Against the Execrable Bull of the Antichrist.* On
January 3, 1521, Leo promulgated the bull of excommunication, *Decet
romanum pontificem:* "It seems fitting that the Roman pontiff should declare
Luther to be a heretic." That should have ended the matter, because
Luther, now an outlaw—for excommunication meant not only exclusion
from the church but brought with it the loss of all civil rights—should have
been turned over to the secular sword for execution. Emperor Charles,
however, even though he personally favored such action, could not do so
for political reasons. Aleander urged such direct action, but even he
sensed the powerful popular support for Luther, declaring that nine-tenths
of Germany was fanatically on Luther's side. In his election statement
Charles had promised that no one in Germany should be outlawed until
given a hearing. In February the Estates of the Empire refused to suppress
Luther's writings and insisted that Luther should appear before an imperial
diet. On the advice of his counselors Gattinara and Chièvres, who saw that
Charles would need the support of the Estates, Charles agreed to summon
Luther to the diet, which was to meet at Worms in April.

On March 6, 1521, Luther was summoned to appear before the emperor and the Diet of the Holy Roman Empire meeting in the city of
Worms, and the emperor issued him a safe-conduct. Luther was reminded
that a safe-conduct had not saved Hus at Constance, for it would be
considered invalid for an outlawed heretic. Elector Frederick clearly could
not protect him so far from home. Actually Luther had little choice but
to go, and he was determined to go "despite all the gates of hell" or, as
he put it later, "even though I should find there as many devils as there
are tiles on the roofs." His journey to Worms turned into a triumphal
procession, though it must have been disconcerting to see many hold up
pictures of Savonarola as he rode by.

About four o'clock on April 17, 1521, he was led, drawn and pale, before the diet. On a table in the center of the room were piled his books and he was asked two questions: Would he acknowledge the authorship of these books? and, Would he recant all or parts of them? He clearly was not to have a hearing but was being confronted with a demand to recant, or, as Luther put it, to rechant and sing a new song. Taken aback, he requested twenty-four hours for reflection. The next day at about six in the evening he was led into the crowded episcopal hall, which stood next to the great Romanesque cathedral, lighted by candles. There Luther made his stand before the emperor, the princes, the cardinals, and the powers of this world to declare his otherworldly faith. In a high clear voice he delivered in German a ten-minute speech which he later repeated in Latin. These words altered the shape of Christendom and changed the course of human history. When he concluded, the speaker for the emperor said he had not given a simple answer whether or not he would recant, whereupon Luther answered:

Since then your serene majesty and your lordships seek a simple answer, I will give it in this manner, neither horned nor toothed: Unless I am convinced by the testimony of the Scriptures or by clear reason (for I do not trust either in the pope or in councils alone, since it is well known that they have often erred and contradicted themselves), I am bound by the Scriptures I have quoted and my conscience is captive to the Word of God. I cannot and I will not retract anything, since it is neither safe nor right to go against conscience. I cannot do otherwise, here I stand, may God help me, amen.

Pandemonium broke loose in the hall. When Emperor Charles, angry and excited, rose to his feet and declared he had had enough of such talk, the meeting broke up. As Luther was leaving the auditorium the Spanish horsemen at the street gate shouted, "Into the fire!" Some spectators reported that as Luther left the hall, he held his clenched fist over his head like the victor in a tourney and cried out, "I am finished!" But what Luther believed to be the end was merely a beginning.

The emperor granted Luther three more days, April 22 to 24, for discussions with theologians, the Archbishop of Trier presiding, which proved to be unproductive. Luther wrote a letter to the emperor and the Estates thanking them for honoring the safe-conduct. "I have sought nothing beyond reforming the church in conformity with the Holy Scriptures," he wrote. "I would suffer death and infamy, give up life and reputation for his Imperial Majesty and the Empire. I wish to reserve nothing but the liberty to confess and bear witness to the word of God alone."[5] The next morning, April 26, the imperial herald Kaspar Sturm escorted Luther's carriage through the city gates for the journey home.

Aleander drew up the Edict of Worms, but Charles hesitated to sign it. On May 12, the troops of Franz von Sickingen were nearby, the Estates were showing resistance, the revolutionary sign of the *Bundschuh* had appeared on the walls overnight, the French had crossed the borders of Spain and the Habsburg Netherlands, and so the twenty-one-year-old emperor temporized. When the diet adjourned on May 25, Elector Frederick, Albert of Brandenburg, Philip of Hesse, and other princes had already departed. That same evening Charles V called together the remaining four electors, bishops, and princes and this rump session approved the Edict of Worms. On May 26, after attending a high mass in the cathedral, Emperor Charles signed it. Luther was under the great ban of the Empire, an outlaw who could be killed with impunity.

Meanwhile Luther's party, traveling back to Wittenberg, detoured to Moehre so that Luther could visit his grandmother and preach in the parish church. Toward evening of May 4 near Altenstein a company of horsemen attacked the party. Luther's companions fled into the woods, and when they returned Luther was gone. The horsemen, Elector Frederick's men, took Luther that night to the Wartburg Castle in the forest above Eisenach, where he was hidden away disguised as Knight George in "the Realm of the Birds," "the Region of the Air," or "the Isle of Patmos," the address he used on his letters. Word got out that Luther had been killed, to the anger and dismay of many. "O God," wrote Albrecht Dürer in his Netherlands notebook, "if Luther is dead, who from now on will proclaim to us the holy Gospel?"

2. LUTHER'S THEOLOGY

In the sixteenth century religious questions dominated intellectual life. Luther's reformation was theological, although the Reformation touched all aspects of life. He opposed his "theology of the cross and of suffering"

5. Cited in Ernest G. Schwiebert, *Luther and His Times* (St. Louis, 1950), p. 509. The whole legal process, ecclesiastical and secular, leading to Luther's condemnation is examined by Wilhelm Borth, *Die Luthersache (causa Lutheri) 1517–1524. Die Anfänge der Reformation als Frage von Politik und Recht* (Lübeck, 1970). A general account is that of Daniel Olivier, *Le Procès Luther 1517–1521* (Paris, 1971), English tr., *The Trial of Luther* (St. Louis, 1978).

to the traditional "theology of glory," which encouraged in man a false spiritual pride. Luther was professionally an exegete, not a systematician, a biblical theologian, not a philosopher. One can learn from him a way of thinking theologically rather than a theological system. His theology can best be understood by seeing all its parts arranged like rose petals around its center, the cross of Christ. Luther created his own seal by taking a rose from his family's coat of arms. He explained this seal to Lazarus Spengler, the city secretary of Nuremberg, as a symbol of his theology:

There is first to be a cross, black and placed in a heart, which should be of its natural color, so that I myself would be reminded that faith in the Crucified saves us. For if one believes from the heart he will be justified. Even though it is a black cross, which mortifies and which also should hurt us, yet it leaves the heart in its natural color and does not ruin nature; that is, the cross does not kill but keeps man alive. For the just man lives by faith, but by faith in the Crucified One. Such a heart is to be in the midst of a white rose, to symbolize that faith gives joy, comfort, and peace; in a word, it places the believer into a white joyful rose; for this faith does not give peace and joy as the world gives and, therefore, the rose is to be white and not red, for white is the color of the spirits and of all the angels. Such a rose is to be in a sky-blue field, symbolizing that such joy in the Spirit and in faith is a beginning of the future heavenly joy; it is already a part of faith, and is grasped through hope, even though not yet manifest. And around this field is a golden ring, symbolizing that in heaven such blessedness lasts forever and has no end, and in addition is precious beyond all joy and goods, just as gold is the most valuable and precious metal.[6]

Luther was able to explain his theology in simple catechetical language as well as to discuss it in the most sophisticated professional way.

The massive scholarship on every aspect of Luther's theology, literally thousands of volumes, has produced an interesting variety of approaches in the search for a single key or principle of organization. An older school emphasized Luther's "Copernican Revolution," which replaced the medieval anthropocentrism with a new theocentrism. Scandinavian motif research has pointed to certain themes believed to serve as the core of his theology, *agape* as God's undeserved love rather than *eros* as a love attracted by the lovableness of man as object, or *Christus victor* as the trium-

---

6. "To Lazarus Spengler, Coburg, July 8, 1530," ep. 221, *Luther's Works,* 49, *Letters II,* Gottfried Krodel, ed. (Philadelphia, 1972), pp. 356–359.

phant symbol of his Christocentrism. More recently scholars have stressed the breakthrough from formal systematic propositioned theology to a genuinely existential theology, contrasting Luther's existential thrust and Thomas Aquinas's sapiential balance. Some critics see in his work the outpouring of an uncontrollable inchoate flood of ideas which cannot be systematically stated. Others see the key to his thought in his biblical realism, a Hebrew approach to the big questions of life rather than the Hellenized metaphysics of medieval theology. He returned to the Bible, preeminently St. Paul, and preferred the early fathers, above all St. Augustine, to the scholastic doctors of the preceding three centuries. He did not merely repristinate Paul and Augustine, but aligned himself creatively with them. His was a theology of the Word, the Christ of the Scriptures. His personal encounter with God and demand for explicit faith in Christ undercut the medieval doctrine of a grace infused in man which enabled man to move beyond a merit achieved by doing the best one knows how (meritum de congruo) to a merit which is sufficient to permit one to stand in the presence of God (meritum de condigno). Luther's theology has been abstracted and absolutized in a very unhistorical manner, but a fruitful approach is to begin with an examination of the continuities and discontinuities of his theology with his medieval inheritance, then to examine the major facets of his thought, and finally to take measure of its unity and coherence. Clearly a theology with such impact on history had substance as well as surface appeal.

Luther owed a substantial debt to mysticism, scholasticism, and to Renaissance humanism, but he gradually came to differentiate his theology from that intellectual inheritance while retaining elements characteristic of each. Late medieval German piety was steeped in mysticism and Luther had absorbed a good deal during his youth. He may have encountered the voluntaristic mysticism of the Brethren of the Common Life in Magdeburg. The Rhenish mystic Wessel Gansfort had an important later influence. Luther in 1516 and again in 1518 edited the popular mystical German Theology by an anonymous author now believed to have been a member of the Order of the Teutonic Knights in Frankfurt. He agreed with the emphasis upon the "bitterness" of the true Christian life for proud and selfish human nature and for reason which seeks to avoid suffering and self-denial. Even though certain elements of its mystical anthropology and the quest for a deification and union in which man's will is dissolved entirely and replaced by God's will were not compatible with

Luther's views, he nevertheless praised this work as being superior to scholastic theology and in line with St. Augustine and the Bible.[7] He believed the little book to be "almost in the style of the illumined Doctor Tauler of the Dominican Order." Between early 1515 and mid-1516 Luther read and critically annotated John Tauler's (c. 1300–1360) sermons and though he rejected Tauler's basic ontological and anthropological presuppositions, he then and subsequently appreciated deeply Tauler's description of spiritual torments, soul struggle *(Anfechtung),* and resignation *(Gelassenheit),* for he taught "more of a genuine pure theology than all the scholastics of all the universities taken together." Luther retained from the mystics an emphasis upon the pervasive presence of God in all things, great and small, high and low, the indwelling of Christ in the heart of the believer, the personal involvement of the individual in faith and in producing the fruits of faith, the childbirth of social action. But Luther did his best to tear down the "heavenly ladders" set up by Dionysius the Areopagite for the mystical ascent into the presence of the naked majesty of God. Rather, God has come down to man in the incarnation in Christ. He rejected the mystical attempt to reduce all to the transcendental "I," the notion of the divine scintilla or spark of divinity in man which is reunited momentarily with God in the mystical union, and the steps in the mystical experience as described in the speculative mysticism of Meister Johannes Eckhart (1260–1327). The mystical ladder by which man ascends is but one more subtly disguised form of the "theology of glory" by which man asserts claims upon God rather than depends entirely upon the grace and mercy of God. Yet a quantum of experiential piety remained in Luther as a reminder of his consanguinity to mysticism.[8]

Luther's theological studies at Erfurt were based upon the *via moderna* or nominalist school of theology, as distinct from the *via antiqua* or Thomist school. Scholarly understanding of nominalism has made marked progress in recent years. The term nominalism was formerly used in a narrow sense for the philosophical position that denied to universals any extramental existence and substituted for a common nature or genus an atomistic world of particulars. It was used in a broader sense as a system of thought derived from this ontological and epistemological rejection of

---

7. Steven E. Ozment, *Mysticism and Dissent: Religious Ideology and Social Protest in the Sixteenth Century* (New Haven, 1973), pp. 17–25, 21–23.

8. Bengt R. Hoffman, *Luther and the Mystics: A Re-examination of Luther's Spiritual Experience and His Relationship to the Mystics* (Minneapolis, 1976), p. 218.

universals that destroyed metaphysics and made theological doctrines and ethical principles dependent entirely upon the arbitrary and omnipotent will of God. It was formerly also often charged that the nominalists interposed a wide chasm between reason and revelation, resorting to fideism to escape skepticism, and that because of their emphasis upon the power of man's will to choose the good, they were thoroughly Pelagian. Since William of Occam was the leading nominalist and the Occamists dominated most universities in the fourteenth and fifteenth centuries, scholasticism of this period has often been characterized as nominalist. Many revisions and refinements have lately been introduced which make possible a much more precise understanding of the theology that provided Luther's intellectual background.

There is now some agreement that Occam was, strictly speaking, epistemologically not a nominalist, but a realistic conceptualist. The term nominalist was applied to Occam's followers by their enemies and the term modernist would be more appropriate and less pejorative. Occam was moderate and orthodox, and among his most prominent followers Pierre d'Ailly, Gabriel Biel, and Gregory of Rimini followed a moderate path and only a few such as Nicholas of Autrecourt and John of Mirecourt took extremely radical positions on questions of epistemology, the possibility of knowledge, voluntarism, and the like. Some, such as Robert Holcot, once considered radical have been rehabilitated as safely orthodox by current scholarship. Modernism was as much a theology as a philosophy, for its special characteristic was less a different method of linguistic analysis than the dialectic of the two modes of God's power as expressed in nature and revelation. God's absolute power *(potentia absoluta)* is that unlimited power by which God is able to do that which He chooses to do, not merely abstractly the power by which He could do anything not self-contradictory that He wished to do, whereas God's ordered or regulated power *(potentia ordinata)* is that power in terms of which God chose to create an ordered world, to enter into a covenant with man, to reveal Himself in the Word, to atone for man's sin through Christ, to justify and to sanctify man through the Holy Spirit. This dialectic of the two powers was important not only for the tone and terminology of Luther's theology, but affected his thought in substance about the *deus nudus et absconditus* and the *deus revelatus,* God bare or abscondite and God revealed. New knowledge about Pierre d'Ailly's extensive dependence upon Gregory of Rimini (d. 1358), who gave St. Augustine a fourteenth-century voice, has led some scholars to assert that the *via Gregorii* in the fifteenth and sixteenth centuries was important especially for Erfurt and Wittenberg, but this is a highly dubious assumption. Nominalism and humanism were domesticated in Augustinianism, although both the nature of Luther's encounter with specific doctors and exactly which books in the Erfurt library he read are difficult to document. Gabriel Biel was the great recent authority for two of his most influential teachers at Erfurt, and it was immediately against Biel that the "new theology" of the Bible and Augustine at Wittenberg was directed.[9] Luther derived much insight from his father confessor Johannes von Staupitz, who was deeply read in St. Augustine, and directly from St. Augustine himself. The question as to the extent of his debt to the late medieval Augustinians is still open to discussion. In at least some of the passages in which Luther refers to Occam as "my dear master," he is speaking in irony, for scholastic theology contributed as significantly to Luther's development as an object against which he rebelled as it did in shaping his approach to theology. From Occam and the nominalists he gained an appreciation of experiential, and in a sense, of empirical knowledge. Luther objected to the scholastic assumption that man is able to keep God's law, that God will not withhold grace from those who do the best that is in them *(Facientibus quod in se est deus non denegat gratiam)*, that a certain moral structure or synderesis remains in man enabling him to prefer the things of God, that faith, according to St. Thomas, is formed by love *(fides caritate formata)* rather than love being induced by faith and accompanying the new spiritual life of the believer. Luther does not acknowledge that merit is rewarded with grace as an added gift *(donum superadditum)*. For him the difference between original and actual sin is not very consequential since the Scriptures do not distinguish those terms. In baptism or absolution the guilt is removed but man remains a sinner

9. On the current state of nominalism scholarship, see William J. Courtenay, "Nominalism and Late Medieval Thought: A Bibliographical Essay," *Theological Studies,* 33 (December, 1972), 716–734. Heiko Oberman, *The Harvest of Medieval Theology* (Cambridge, Mass., 1963), makes a major effort to establish the vigor and vitality of late scholasticism against the charges of decadence and confusion on the part of medievalists such as Étienne Gilson or Reformation scholars such as Joseph Lortz. See also Gordon Leff, *Gregory of Rimini: Tradition and Innovation in Fourteenth Century Thought* (Manchester, 1961), Leif Grane, *Contra Gabrielem, Luthers Auseinandersetzung mit Gabriel Biel in der Disputatio Contra Scholasticam Theologiam 1517* (Gyldendal, 1962), and *Modus loquendi theologicus. Luthers Kampf um die Erneuerung der Theologie (1515–1518)* (Leiden, 1975). Marilyn J. Harran, *Luther on Conversion. The Early Years* (Ithaca, 1983), is a careful, scholarly examination of a key concept in Luther's developing theology, 1509–1519, relating his theology to his own experience.

while here on earth. Luther continued in later life to use the method of dialectic when occasion demanded, to show that he could manage syllogism, but for demonstrating articles of faith he considered it a fools' game.

In the *Address to the Municipalities* (1524) Luther exclaimed:

How much I regret that we did not read more of the poets and the historians, and that nobody thought of teaching us these. Instead of such study I was compelled to read the devil's rubbish—the scholastic philosophers and sophists with such cost, labor, and detriment, from which I have had trouble enough to rid myself.

During the course of his early studies Luther did acquire a certain basic knowledge of the traditional classical Latin authors, Virgil, Plautus, Cicero, Livy, Terence, Horace, Quintilian, Ovid, and encountered Aristotle and Plato, and what he learned he retained. At Erfurt his contacts with Renaissance humanism were peripheral to his main course of study, and the circle of young humanists attached to Mutianus Rufus, a quite daring speculative poet-philosopher in nearby Gotha, coalesced only after 1505, when Luther was already in the monastery, although one member of that circle, Crotus Rubeanus, who later did the *Letters of Obscure Men* with Ulrich von Hutten, was a university friend of Luther's. Of the Italian humanists Luther's favorite poet was Baptista Mantuanus, the reforming general of the Carmelites. During the course of his theological studies he came to appreciate the value of the biblical languages and later observed that a florescence of literary studies had always been a sign that a spiritual summer was at hand. He was quick to adopt the latest philological and textual tools, turning to Erasmus's new edition of the New Testament in Greek halfway through his commentary on Romans.

For a few years there was a happy conjunction of the humanist program and Luther's reform efforts. From 1517 to 1521 the humanists in many cities were the chief propagandists and carriers of his cause. The radicality of his 1520 treatise *On the Babylonian Captivity* turned off some of the older, more conservative humanists, but attracted the young all the more. From 1517 to 1519 Luther adopted the signature Eleutherius, the liberator, and spoke of "our Erasmus," "our Reuchlin," and had in 1516 referred to Mutianus as the most erudite and humane of men. The humanists sincerely believed that their ideal was being realized openly: the rejection of Aristotle and scholasticism and their replacement by the Scriptures and early fathers. The philosophical Heidelberg Theses expressed a preference for Plato over Aristotle, praised Pythagoras, and referred to Parmenides and Anaxagoras. The fact that both the humanists and the reformers were concerned with hermeneutics made them partners in a serious scholarly conversation. In his first exposition of the Psalms Luther learned to understand the text historically. He also came to prefer rhetoric, which moves man, to dialectic, which merely instructs him. But also in matters of substance, not just the predilection for earlier sources and particular methods, Luther shared certain central positions with the humanists. In his little Galatians commentary of 1519 he sounded out characteristic humanist themes: true erudition is found with teaching, word and language; the gospel builds the new man with divine erudition; freedom is the indispensable premise for human self-realization, including ethical duty; the believer, though still a sinner, is on the way to full freedom; the justified man is the fully human being, cheerful, at peace, proving good to be victorious over evil; he despises hell, death, and the devil; he is the true ethical personality being gifted with the Holy Spirit. Culture, peace, freedom, and practical ethical conduct make the reform of church and society possible. In some passages in the *Explanation of the 95 Theses* he came close to the religious expressions of a Pico or Reuchlin. His assertion against Eck at the time of the Leipzig debate that "All men are equal in humanity, which is of all the highest and most admirable equality, from which men possess all dignity" was an early expression of his affinity with humanism. This assessment of rational man as the loftiest being in creation he affirmed throughout his life, as in the *Disputation on Man* (1536) and the last commentary he did, on Genesis. Under the influence of the younger Melanchthon from 1518 on, his interest in the *bonae litterae* was sustained throughout the years and even increased in some subjects such as history. His positive attitude toward the *studia humanitatis* proved to be of critical importance for the beginnings and the development of Protestantism, which, except for a very small number of radical cultural atavists, accepted and transmitted the educational and cultural values of Christian humanism.

Nevertheless, a theological gulf separated him from the optimistic anthropology of humanism and from the synergistic moralism of Christian humanism. Not only can natural man not keep the law of God perfectly, but he is alienated from God, curved in upon himself *(incurvatus in se),* and totally unable to believe in Christ as savior without the intervention of the

Holy Spirit. Moreover, humanist culture remained for him a relative and conditional good, for all culture is a human artifact, the achievement is time-bound and the rewards are temporal, no absolute validity can be ascribed to it. Theology is concerned with man's relation to God here in time and throughout all eternity, it is "infinite wisdom which can never be learned thoroughly."

"The cross tests all things," wrote Luther, "blessed is he who understands" *(crux probat omnia, beatus qui intelligit).* Luther was not only a forceful religious reformer, but also a professional theologian whose calling was to expound the Scriptures as an exegete. In his first theological writings, the annotations he prepared for his Erfurt lectures on the *Sentences* of Peter Lombard, 1509–1510, he expressed his opposition to the intrusions of the philosophers into theology, a point of view that was to ripen into an all-out assault upon scholastic philosophy for admitting Aristotle and other pagan philosophers as authorities in theology. His attitude even then was similar to that of Erasmus and the humanists and suggests an early break with his modernist teachers.[10] Theology for Luther was to be based upon concrete biblical revelation and was to be protected from extraneous metaphysical speculations. It was revealed theology rather than natural theology that concerned him. God is indeed Lord of nature and of history, but as such He can be known only indirectly, for nature is God's cocoon or mask *(larva, Mummenschanz),* and He is not immediately disclosed. God is active, absolute living will who keeps everything in the universe alive, for nothing is without God and His presence. In history God moves strangely as He acts not in a straight line but from opposing angles *(e contrario).* God is awesome and heroic, not bound by rules *(Genesis Commentary: Deus est heroicus sine regula).* This bare God *(deus nudus)* of nature and history is beyond the reach of man and human comprehension; He is God in His aseity. Man can find Him only where He lets Himself be found, as He has revealed Himself in Christ, the mirror of the heavenly heart. Only in Christ is the fullness of God's mercy and love for man disclosed. The Word reveals that it is the true nature of God to give what is good. Through the Word man learns of the promises of God and the benefits of Christ. Among unbelievers in the world He

10. Lawrence Murphy, S.J., "The Prologue of Martin Luther to the *Sentences* of Peter Lombard (1509): The Clash of Philosophy and Theology," *Archive for Reformation History,* 67 (1976), 54–75.

remains silent, but in Christ He reveals himself as love, as one who deplores sin and overcomes it, abhors death and triumphs over it, and transforms alienated, despairing people into men of faith and hope.

Christmas was for Luther a big day, for it celebrated the incarnation of God in Christ. In his commentary on the *Magnificat* he underlined the paradoxical nature of this revelation in Christ, that the king of glory should become this Nazarene, born of a virgin, Mary, of lowly origin, rejected, humiliated, persecuted, poor, and crucified as a criminal, suffering and dying vicariously for the sin of all mankind. Christ is both exemplar, showing how God deals with all mankind, delivering into death but resurrecting to life eternal, and example, providing a model for the sanctified Christian life of love and service. There is then a veiled and mysterious quality also to the nature of revelation.

Man needs God's grace, for the root condition of man is sinful. In his natural state man is dominated by concupiscence, turned in on himself, asserting self, and willingly acquiescing in his fallen condition. Luther heightened the conception of sin, for he followed St. Paul in describing it not merely as ethical fault or moral transgression against individual commandments, but rather as an unspiritual state. Sin consists not merely in not following the impulses of the body rather than those of the spirit; it is the condition of the whole man in the state of unbelief or alienation from God. Man is flesh when he lives life without trust in God; man is spirit insofar as he trusts in God and loves Him. Until the Holy Spirit calls man by the gospel, enlightens him with His gifts, man cannot of his own free will believe in Jesus Christ or come to Him. The man of faith has a *freed will* in the spiritual realm just as natural man has a *free will* in secular matters.

God speaks in a general way also in the Scriptures *(deus dicens),* but He speaks in a particular way when He addresses a single person *(deus loquens).* The word of God addresses man through the law saying: "Thou shalt or thou shalt not!" Luther emphasized the biblical concept of God's wrath, which had been revived by Augustine. But the wrath of God against sinful man is a strange and foreign work *(opus alienum),* whereas the showing of love and mercy reveals His real nature and is His proper work *(opus proprium).* God's grace does not suspend or undo standards of justice but includes justice within itself. The law is a schoolmaster for Christ and by His judgment He makes possible the actualization of His grace. Humility, repentance, brokenness must precede forgiveness and exaltation. The resolution of the conflict of sin and grace, law and gospel is seen concretely in the cross and resurrection. The gospel is the word of God in man, Christ dwelling in the believer's heart, promising forgiveness to all who accept the offer. The initiative is entirely God's and the thanks and glory belong to Him alone. As for man, Luther's motto was: We are acted upon rather than that we act ourselves *(Agimur potius quam agimus).* Grace is not a spiritual power extended to man *(habitus),* but a benignity, a specific act by which God forgives and reconciles to Himself a particular person at a particular point in time; salvation is His gift.

The Christian lives by faith alone, a faith which is trust in Christ *(fiducia)* not merely belief *(credulitas).* It must be the individual's personal faith *(fides explicita),* not a general agreement with the facts of the biblical account *(fides historica)* or acquiescence in the stand of the church *(fides implicita).* Faith is the life of the heart *(vita cordis)* which unsettles poise and insists upon man's transformation, growth in holiness of life. Luther hoped to be known as the doctor of good works *(doctor operum bonorum).* The man of faith produces good works; it is not the works that make man good, as Aristotle argues in the *Nicomachaean Ethics.* Man is at the same time righteous and sinner *(simul justus et peccator);* he is righteous in God's eyes when forgiven for Christ's sake, yet while on this earth he remains partially a sinner in his own eyes and in those of his neighbor. He is justified in hope, sinner in reality *(justus in spe, peccator in re).* Nevertheless, man can and should grow in holiness of life or sanctification. The most prominent emphases in Luther's ethics were responsibility, gratitude, and stewardship, as expressions of love of God and fellow man, the neighbor in need of love. In contrast to a heteronomous control of man's action by others from outside or an autonomous subjective control by the individual, Luther stressed theonomy, God acting within man but not without man, as he put it, for the reborn man lives in a dynamic relationship with God.

The Christian naturally seeks the company of his fellow believers in the church. The true church is invisible insofar as only the shepherd knows his sheep; only God knows who in his heart believes. Yet the association of Christians on earth constitutes the visible church which can be recognized by certain outward signs *(nota).* The marks of the true visible church are the preaching of the law and gospel, the administration of the dominical sacraments, baptism and the Lord's Supper, the

Office of the Keys, a faithful ministry and God-pleasing forms of worship. The Word and the sacraments are of central importance, whereas the organizational structure is secondary. Luther saw the confessing congregational form of church government as ideal, but was forced by circumstances to accept a form of state church in which the church was an independent spiritual authority but the state as secular sword or authority assumed responsibility for externals such as buildings and salaries. He viewed this function of the state, the kingdom of God's left hand, as an emergency situation and the princes and city councils as emergency bishops, until a better day would make the realization of a more ideal form of church government possible.

Luther understood the state to be not an institution in the modern abstract legal sense, but an authority (Obrigkeit) divinely established for a twofold purpose. On the one hand, he held with Augustine that the state exists by reason of sin (ratione peccati) and wields the sword against evildoers. On the other hand, the state is based upon the law of love (lex charitatis), which is fundamental to all moral and social laws, and to be legitimate must function as the servant of man and as an instrument of God's love for man. Christian social morality, he held, is one of equity, that is, of justice tempered with mercy. Christians must not participate in an unjust war such as a crusade or a war of conquest. He refused to condemn the state or abandon society to the realm of Satan, as some of the sectaries did.

The unity and coherence of Luther's theology was guaranteed by the centrality of Christ as the subject and object of his evangelical theology. He was the Copernicus of theology with a Son-centered universe. His method was characterized by dynamic concreteness, by his biblical realism, and by his acceptance of paradoxes that are essential to theology in which, unlike speculative metaphysics, the key to difficulties lies in the transcendent beyond. Luther's existential emphasis upon the concreteness and immediacy of religious experience lent a powerful personal thrust to his teaching. Its radical simplicity proved to be satisfactory to vast numbers of people who were longing for religious reassurance. The most important words in religion, he held, are the personal pronouns, I, thou, and he, my brother. In the powerful Invocavit sermons, which he preached on his return in 1522 to Wittenberg from his refuge on the Wartburg, he described life as a fortress under siege by death: "Everyone must fight his own battle with death himself, alone. We can shout into another's ears, but every one must himself be prepared for the time of death, for I will not be with you then, nor you with me. Therefore every one must himself know and be armed with the chief things which concern a Christian."[11] Luther was not interested in creating a grand theological structure but rather in reducing religious faith to the essential relationships. *Es gehört eine gewisse Bescheidenheit dazu,* he confessed; in theology a certain modesty is called for.

3. PUBLICATION, RESPONSE, AND REACTION

Luther was astonished at the rapid spread of his ideas through the literate public and the widespread popular response. In *Against Hanswurst,* 1541, he wrote: "So my theses against Tetzel's articles, which you can now see in print, were published. They went throughout the whole of Germany in a fortnight, for the whole world complained about indulgences, and particularly about Tetzel's articles."[12]

Years later Friedrich Myconius in his *Historia Reformationis* reported that the *Ninety-five Theses* had gone out into all parts of Germany "as if angels from heaven themselves had been their messengers." In Luther's *Resolutions,* which he dedicated to Pope Leo X on May 30, 1518, he wrote: "It is a mystery to me how my theses, more so than my other writings, or indeed, those of other professors, were spread to so many places. They were meant exclusively for our academic circle here."[13] Within a little more than a month they were said to have spread throughout nearly all Christendom. Moreover, they very shortly became the best-selling work in the Empire. The mystery had to do with the power of the press, for the Reformation was the first historical movement in the post-Gutenberg era and the printing press made it possible. There had been flurries of impact publication before, in the Savonarola incident, the Reuchlin affair, or even Karlstadt's controversy with the Thomists. But Luther's reform was the first fully to involve the power of publication as a historical force. In Wittenberg Johann Grünenberg printed the first edition of the theses, but the humanist sodalities in other cities quickly sponsored editions in German as well as in Latin, the *Sodalitas Staupitziana,* especially Christoph Scheurl and Kaspar Nützel, in Nuremberg with the printer Hölzel; in

11. *Luther's Works,* 51, *Sermons,* I (Philadelphia, 1959), 70. Luther's continued struggle for the integrity of the Reformation is described in Mark U. Edwards, *Luther's Last Battles* (Ithaca, 1983).

12. Kurt Aland, ed., *Martin Luther's 95 Theses with the Pertinent Documents from the History of the Reformation* (St. Louis, 1967), p. 35.

13. Hans Hillerbrand, ed., *The Reformation: A Narrative History Related by Contemporary Observers and Participants* (New York, 1964), pp. 47, 54.

Leipzig the printer Thauner; and in Basel the printer Petri, all by December 1517. The rapid publication of the theses was but an indication of the mighty deluge to come.

"I have only put God's Word in motion through preaching and writing," Luther wrote in 1522. "The Word has done everything and carried everything before it." But while he devoutly saw the spiritual force at work, he also quickly perceived the power of this new instrument, the press, which he called "God's highest and ultimate gift of grace by which He would have His Gospel carried forward." While he was in seclusion in the Wartburg, in eleven weeks he translated the New Testament from the second edition of Erasmus's New Testament (1516) into German, the first translation not based upon St. Jerome's Vulgate. This translation in the language of the people, known as the September Testament since it was published in September, 1522, embellished with woodcuts by Lucas Cranach, became a runaway best-seller. Some 5,000 copies were sold within two months, 50 printings in four years, over 200,000 over the course of the next twelve years, and it remains the standard German translation to this day. The September Testament along with Luther's translation of the complete German Bible (1534, rev. 1546) had a formative influence on the German language.

Luther was a skillful publicist in tune with the people. At Worms the emperor and his councillors could hardly believe that all the books piled upon the table before them were from one man's pen. Luther's thirty publications between 1517 and 1520 probably sold well over 300,000 copies. During the course of his lifetime he wrote some 450 treatises. There are 3,000 sermons and 2,580 letters extant, and the scholarly Weimar edition of his works runs to well over 100 folio volumes or 60,000 pages. "I deliver as soon as I conceive," he once commented and sent the first pages of his *Address to the Christian Nobility* off to the publisher while he was still writing the last. In 1519 Johannes Froben, the Basel publisher, wrote to Luther: "We have never had such glorious sales with any other book." Beatus Rhenanus, a young Erasmian, wrote to Zwingli on July 2, 1519, suggesting that a certain colporteur named Lucius should go from house to house offering exclusively Luther's writings for sale since that would "virtually force the people to buy them, which would not be the case if there were a wide selection."[14] In 1521 Aleander declared that "printers will not sell anything other than Lutheran writings." In 1524

14. *Ibid.,* pp. 124–125.

Erasmus observed that "in Germany hardly anything is salable except Lutheran and anti-Lutheran writings." Luther knew the value of the printed word. "Every great book is an action, just as every great action is a book," he commented in his *Table Talk.*

In the Koran Mohammed had already referred to the Christians as "people of the Book," like the Jews. Now Christians not only had the Bible in hand in vernacular translation, but they also had a tremendous reservoir of classical, patristic, medieval, and Renaissance works available. By 1520 all the major Latin authors had been published. Lorenzo Valla's *De Elegantiis Linguae Latinae* (1444) went through sixty editions between 1471 and 1536. Erasmus had taken up the torch of patristic scholars such as Ambrogio Traversari with his great editions of the church fathers and of the New Testament (1516).

The printer-scholars who published these works were educated laymen who rarely had formal university education, but who learned on the job. The first printeries were set up in commercial centers and after that in university towns. The printers were a competitive and alert breed, open to technical innovations and to new ideas as well. The use of paper instead of parchment had reduced the price of a book by 85 percent. The use of ink based on oil constituted a technical innovation similar to the introduction of oils in Renaissance painting. The bankruptcy rate was very high and few printers actually became rich, although some houses were large, such as Anton Koberger in Nuremberg, who had twenty-four presses and over a hundred workers. Some women, usually widows, such as Argula von Grumbach, managed publishing houses successfully. Printers sometimes published both evangelical and Catholic treatises or printed radical tracts anonymously. A very high percentage of the printers who did Protestant books and pamphlets became evangelical preachers, the ratio being ten to one compared with merchants, clothmakers, and masons, and four to one compared with the number of schoolmasters who became preachers.

If the printers did much to further the Reformation, the Reformation in turn did much for publishing. Within two generations after Gutenberg printing had spread to 250 towns. During the fifteenth century some 40,000 titles were published, so that if an edition averaged 250–300 copies, some 10,000,000 to 12,000,000 incunabula were produced. From 1500 to 1517 another 10,000,000 volumes were published. But under the impact of the Reformation, by 1550 around 150,000 titles or 60,000,000 had been published. "Thus we must continue to be disciples of those speechless masters which we call books," Luther admonished (Commentary on Psalm 101:1). In Germany the main centers of printing were Nuremberg, Wittenberg, Augsburg, Strasbourg, Magdeburg, Frankfurt, and Zurich, with some eighty printeries in forty other towns. Once the Reformation was under way the number of books, not including broadsides and leaflets, rose to 500 and then to 1,000 a year. In Wittenberg alone between 1518 and 1523, 600 different works appeared, religious and humanistic, whereas in the British Isles the sum total for those same years was under 300.[15] Luther's favorite printer, Hans Lufft, even became the mayor of Wittenberg.

The new social force unleashed by the pressures of the Reformation was the torrent of pamphlets, cartoons, and caricatures which carried to the masses the basic tenets of the Reformation, outcries against social and political grievances, polemical thrusts and broadsides, and radical revolutionary programs. Between 1517 and 1524, the "year of the flood," there was a tenfold increase in the number of tracts published. One of the largest collections was made by Gustav Freytag, 6,265 quite representative pamphlets. Three thousand of them are identified as to authorship, including 391 editions of Luther's works or 11.5 percent of the total. Three hundred ninety-one printers, 125 places of publication, and 894 authors are represented, including Melanchthon, Karlstadt, Urbanus Rhegius, Zwingli, Linck, Osiander, Flacius, Oecolampadius, Bugenhagen, Kettenbach, and Brenz.[16]

15. Harold Jantz, "German Renaissance Literature," *Modern Language Notes*, 81 (1966), 418. See also Maria Grossman, "Wittenberg Printing, Early Sixteenth Century," *Sixteenth Century Essays and Studies*, I (St. Louis, 1970), 54–74. A standard work is Rudolf Hirsch, *Printing, Selling and Reading, 1450–1550* (Wiesbaden, 1967). The brilliant articles by Elizabeth L. Eisenstein advance the thesis that the technological revolution of printing was a major force in sixteenth-century history: "The Advent of Printing and the Protestant Revolt: A New Approach to the Disruption of Western Christendom," *Annales, Économies, Sociétés, Civilisations*, 26, no. 6 (1971), 1355–1382; "Some Conjectures about the Impact of Printing on Western Society and Thought: A Preliminary Report," *Journal of Modern History*, 47 (March, 1968), 1–56. See also her book, *The Printing Press as an Agent of Change: Communication and Cultural Transformations in Early Modern Europe* (Cambridge and New York, 1979).

16. This analysis based on the Paul Hohenemser catalog (Frankfurt, 1945) is that of Richard G. Cole, an outstanding young Reformation scholar, who graciously lent me his manuscript on printing and the Reformation. See his articles, "The Dynamics of Printing in the Sixteenth Century," in Lawrence P. Buck and Jonathan W. Zophy, eds., *The Social History of the Reformation* (Columbus, Ohio, 1972), pp. 93–105; "Propaganda as a Source of Reformation History," *Lutheran Quarterly*, 22, 2 (1970), 166–171.

Perhaps the most famous and effective Lutheran pamphleteer was Johann Eberlin von Günzburg, a member of the Franciscan Observants, converted by Luther's writings of 1520. His fifteen pamphlets called the *Bundesgenossen,* or "Comrades," ran the whole gamut of religious issues and social ills, criticizing monasticism, social organization, the ineptness of Charles V, and offering a wide range of reform proposals. In his *Wolfaria* he sketched out a Lutheran utopia. In a satirical tract *I Wonder That There Is No Money In the Land (Mich wundert das kein Geld im Land ist),* 1524, he excoriated the printers themselves for publishing sensational profit-making books and pamphlets rather than serious history and decent literature. He considered printers to be "the schoolmasters of the people." One of his printers, Pamphilus Gengenbach, was a humanist dramatist in his own right.

Printing facilitated the publication of hymns and editions of the Psalms which served the newly forming groups of evangelicals. Since special type for musical notations was needed, the centers for this kind of pamphleteering were more limited: Wittenberg, Strasbourg, Zurich, with Nuremberg as the leader.[17] *A Book of Eight Hymns (Achtliederbuch)* was published in 1524. Luther's own hymns, such as "A mighty fortress is our God," were published for use in congregational singing, as was also his revised form of the liturgy. In the Erfurt *Enchiridion,* of twenty-six hymns eighteen were Luther's compositions. He wrote around twenty-seven hymns in all. Luther wrote an introduction to a *Small Song Book (Gesangbüchlein)* published by Johannes Walther with thirty-two hymns, embellished with woodcuts by Lucas Cranach. The poetry of Hans Sachs, the simple shoemaker and Meistersinger of Nuremberg, such as his description of Luther as the "Nightingale of Wittenberg," had a strong popular appeal. He replaced a hymn "O gentle Mary" with the famous hymn "O gentle Jesus." Lazarus Spengler composed the hymn "All mankind fell in Adam's fall." Paul Speratus composed doctrinal hymns which instructed the congregation as the people sang. Luther's *Small Catechism,* the *German* or *Large Catechism* (1529), and a book of family devotions *(Hauspostille)* became virtually omnipresent in evangelical schools and homes. His simple sermons *(Kirchenpostille)* for less well educated preachers were in most vestries or pulpits. A fairly broad reading public especially in urban centers now had access to new social ideas and religious alternatives via a mass medium

17. Rolf W. Brednich, *Die Liedpublizistik im Flugblatt des 15. bis 17. Jahrhunderts,* 2 vols. (Baden-Baden, 1974–1975).

using the vernacular. Luther's message was transmitted in a precise standardized form on the popular as well as on a highly technical theological level.

While printing was the novel means of communication, it would be a mistake to underestimate the power of the spoken word, the influence of preaching, for the pulpit carried with it great authority. While pamphlets could soften up a public for the reception of reform ideas, the pattern was that evangelical preachers would come or be called to a town, would rally the burghers, who with the guilds would put pressure on the reluctant city council in favor of reform. The monastic orders and especially the mendicants supplied thousands of evangelical preachers, many reeducated at the Lutheran universities, to man the pulpits. The reformers saw the great value of yet another form of oral communication, the religious drama in the tradition of the *Fastnachtsspiel* and the humanist plays. Drama combined poetry, rhetoric, and moral philosophy in presenting biblical and secular history as popular theater and as school dramas for the youth. The Swiss Niklaus Manuel, for example, wrote a play on the *Indulgences Hawkers (Ablasskrämer)* and on *The Pope and His Priesthood (vom Papst und seiner Priesterschaft)*. Burkard Waldi's *Parable of the Lost Son (Parabel vom vorlorn Sohn)* (1527) held up the pharisaism of the monks for criticism in the person of the prodigal son's self-righteous elder brother. The school dramas developed during the 1530s in Saxony and Switzerland spread to other evangelical areas and were taken up also by Catholics in the course of time. Finally, the oral witnessing and confession of faith spread the evangelical cause as merchants, journeymen, and other itinerants moved about Europe. "The church is a mouth-house," said Luther, "not a pen-house."

The popular response to the evangelical cause and to the promotional effort was overwhelmingly positive. The motives involved in this enthusiastic upsurge were mixed, of course, for some found in it an answer to their deep religious quest, others saw in Luther the liberator from intellectual bondage, some calculated that from the tumult would come amelioration of social or economic ills, still others were pleased to see authority flouted, church wealth shared, or the clergy humbled. In most cases the motives were doubtless mixed, as is usually true of human beings. To become a supporter of Luther required courage after 1520 and 1521, because he was now a declared heretic and outlaw, and one could not do so in many cases without grave danger to self, family, or property. The enrollment at the University of Wittenberg reflects that situation. The enrollment grew from 162 in 1516 to 552 in 1520, while Luther rode the crest of popularity. Then came the condemnation of Luther—and much tighter restrictions on students from Catholic areas such as Meissen, Bamberg, Würzburg, and Mainz—disturbances in Wittenberg, the knights' revolt and peasants' war, with the result that the enrollment dropped below one hundred in 1526 and then gradually rose to more than 750 in 1546 and over 800 in 1554. Between the years 1520 and 1560 approximately 16,000 students matriculated, coming from all parts of the Empire: 5,685 from northern Germany and 5,750 from southern Germany, an impressive number from Austria and Hungary.[18]

Much of the most intelligent leadership was drawn from among the many younger humanists who were attracted by Luther's radical evangelical theology and uncompromising assaults on abuses. *The Babylonian Captivity* of 1520 alienated many of the humanists over fifty but attracted a majority of the humanists under thirty. Johannes Bugenhagen (1485–1558) of Pomerania, for example, was enjoying a dinner at a priest's home in Treptow when someone handed him a copy. He hastily paged through it and exclaimed: "Since the days of Christ's passion many heretics have assailed the church, but none is so pernicious as the author of this book!" Later he studied it carefully, comprehended its full meaning, and is said to have exclaimed: "The entire world is blind—this man alone sees the truth!" Bugenhagen came to Wittenberg in 1522, became the city pastor there after 1523, helped reform Brunswick, Hamburg, Lübeck, Pomerania, Hildesheim, and Wolfenbüttel, introduced a new Lutheran church order in the duchies of Schleswig and Holstein, and in 1537 crowned the king and queen of Denmark and began the reorganization of the church in Denmark.[19] Wolfgang Capito (1478–1541) is another example of a young humanist won for the Reformation through Luther's influence. He was a professor and preacher at Basel, then served as chaplain and secretary to Archbishop Albert of Brandenburg, but became a professor of theology and one of the reformers of Strasbourg in 1523.[20]

Luther's strong character, firm faith, and charismatic leadership at-

18. Schwiebert, *Luther and His Times,* pp. 603–606.

19. Loui Novak, "An Historical Survey of the Liturgical Forms in the Church Orders of Johannes Bugenhagen (1485–1558)," (diss., Iliff School of Theology, Denver, 1974), p. 12.

20. James M. Kittelson, *Wolfgang Capito: From Humanist to Reformer* (Leiden, 1975), p. 243. In Capito the humanist movement influenced the Reformation in spite of how closely he appropriated Luther's evangelical religion.

tracted a body of very able and loyal supporters to his cause. Justus Jonas, a young humanist, in 1518 became professor at Erfurt; in 1521 he became provost of the Castle Church in Wittenberg and professor of theology; from 1541 to 1546 he reformed the church in Halle; and died in 1555. Nikolaus von Amsdorf had been a professor in Wittenberg from 1511 on; from 1542 to 1547 he served as evangelical bishop in Naumburg, from 1550 on in Eisenach, and died in 1565. Martin Bucer, a Dominican from Alsace, became Luther's admirer at the Heidelberg meeting of the Augustinians in 1518. In 1521 he became a secular priest, and from 1524 on he served as the chief pastor and reformer of Strasbourg. An influence on the reformation of many other cities in Germany, he favored strict church discipline and impressed John Calvin during his years as a refugee pastor in Strasbourg. He was involved in the controversy of the Lord's Supper, played a moderate role in seeking Protestant unity, and was the founder of the evangelical rite of confirmation. From 1549 to 1551 he worked in Cambridge to further the cause of the English Reformation.

Luther's most important co-worker was the brilliant young humanist Philipp Melanchthon (1497–1560). A grand-nephew of Johannes Reuchlin, Melanchthon studied at Heidelberg and Tübingen, where, not quite seventeen, he received his M.A. degree and lectured on Aristotle and other classical authors. Elector Frederick brought Melanchthon, a prodigy of twenty-one, to Wittenberg to become professor of Greek. In 1518 he gave his inaugural address *On Improving the Studies of Youth,* arguing for the humanistic curriculum. Filled with ideas of an Erasmian reform, he was quickly won over by Luther to the Augustinian and Pauline emphasis of the new evangelical theology. Although he continued as a classics professor, he became the outstanding theologian, writing the *Loci communes,* or "Theological Commonplaces," in 1521—revised and enlarged in 1543—in which he reduced Luther's prophetic and at times chaotic thoughts to a systematic statement. He became the principal author of the Augsburg Confession (1530) and the *Apology* or defense of the confession. He provided the key leadership in educational reform, drawing up the *School Plan for Electoral Saxony* (1528), directing the transformation of monasteries into schools, helping in organizing and inaugurating new *gymnasia* or secondary schools that combined a humanistic curriculum with evangelical instruction at Nuremberg, Magdeburg, and elsewhere. Johannes Sturm organized such a city-school at Strasbourg in 1535. Melanchthon enjoyed a special relation with Luther, the older, stronger leader, which lasted undisturbed until Luther's death. Luther, for example, conceded Melanchthon's superiority in Greek, and allowed him to lecture on Romans, while he himself took up the Hebrew Old Testament books for his own lectures. After Luther's death Melanchthon was called upon to assume the leadership of the movement, but his humanist moderation and pacific nature led him to compromises unacceptable to other Lutherans, with consequent strife.

The positive response to Luther's evangelical message was quite overwhelming, the extent to which Luther dominated the movement truly remarkable! The major role he played in directing the organization of evangelical city and territorial churches, especially during the final decade and a half of his life, is being given new historical attention. But there was predictably also a negative reaction of two kinds: from some of his followers who defected and from the Roman Catholic opponents. Signs of strain within the Protestant camp appeared early with the Wittenberg movement, while Luther was still in the Wartburg. In matters of church rites and external practices, Luther followed the sensible principle that whatever was good, useful, or beautiful in ceremony, art, and architecture should be preserved unless it was forbidden by the Scriptures. More radical spirits condemned anything and everything that was not specifically commanded by Scripture. The confrontation between the conservative and radical position was not long in coming.

The Wittenberg movement began on September 29, 1521, when Melanchthon and some of his students took the Lord's Supper in both kinds, bread and wine *(sub utraque)*, though the Catholic mass with only the host given to the laity continued to be celebrated. A few days later the Augustinian Gabriel Zwilling, who was being hailed by some as a prophet and a second "Martin," preached against the mass, and on October 31 the Augustinians ceased celebrating the mass altogether. In November fifteen of the forty Augustinians left the monastery, and by January there were only five or six left. In December students and citizens created tumults. At Christmas Karlstadt celebrated an evangelical communion with 2,000 partakers. The situation was further aggravated with the arrival on December 27 of the "Zwickau prophets," Nicholas Storch, a clothmaker, Thomas Irechsel, and Markus Stübner, a former Wittenberg student, associated with Thomas Münzer, who claimed revelations directly from the Holy Ghost. Luther lent the Wittenberg movement strong support and the leaders defended the reforms undertaken and codified in the Ordinance of the city of Wittenberg of January 24, 1522. Before he left the Wartburg Luther prepared an "Order of the Community Chest," the oldest Protestant poor law, and the city council resolved to pursue reform zealously. But then a specter arose, the beginnings of iconoclasm. Encouraged by Karlstadt, riotous mobs had begun to break statuary and to destroy stained-glass windows, taking literally the Old Testament injunction to "make no graven images of Him or likenesses." Luther had slipped into Wittenberg briefly in December to assess the situation, but now, on March 6, 1522, he returned, summoned by the Wittenbergers to restore order. On March 9–16 he preached the powerful *Invocavit* sermons to quiet the tumults, stressing that Christians must not offend the weak, should follow the law of love in evangelical freedom, and should establish no new laws. Luther charged that Karlstadt and Zwilling had given birth to a monstrosity and feared that violence and destructiveness would give a bad name to the evangelical renewal—they had proved to be false brethren.[21] Karlstadt was restricted in his university activities, became increasingly isolated, and from the fall of 1523 to 1524 worked as pastor in Orlamünde. In September of that year he was driven from Electoral Saxony, wandered about south Germany with his poor wife, daughter of a petty nobleman, and became involved in a further controversy with Luther over the real presence in the Lord's Supper. In December, 1524, Luther wrote a sharp polemic against the radicals, "On the Heavenly Prophets concerning Images and the Sacrament." "They have swallowed the Holy Ghost feathers and all," he quipped. Karlstadt sought refuge again in Electoral Saxony from 1525 to 1529, and for a time Luther kept his former foe in his own home. Karlstadt preached in Holstein and East Frisia and found asylum in Switzerland, where he worked as a preacher and professor in Basel until his death from the plague in 1541. Luther's opinion of these "false brethren" was much more bitter than his view of Catholic opponents because he believed that despite better knowledge they had betrayed the cause and undercut his own prophetic role.

In the great battle for men's minds the Catholic pamphleteers were at a distinct disadvantage. In sheer volume they were outnumbered about

21. Mark U. Edwards, *Luther and the False Brethren* (Stanford, 1975), pp. 6–7; "The Wittenberg Movement," pp. 6–33; "Carlstadt, The Republican Spirit," pp. 34–59. Ronald J. Sider, *Andreas Bodenstein von Karlstadt: The Development of His Thought, 1517–1525* (Leiden, 1974), offers a generally sympathetic treatment, but concludes that "Karlstadt knew what it means to begin with a petty intensely egocentric personality which badly needs God's regenerating grace."

twenty to one, and in propagandistic skill they were simply less effective, since they were forced onto the defensive and, having been schooled in cumbersome dialectic, they lacked the light touch and gift of brevity. Luther's opponents such as Johannes Cochlaeus, Hieronymus Emser, Johannes Eck, Hieronymus Dungersheim, and Augustinus Alveld unleashed a barrage of tracts against him, but the most effective polemicist at that level was the Franciscan poet laureate Thomas Murner (1475–1537), who adopted a style reminiscent of Sebastian Brant's *Ship of Fools* in such tracts as *The Big Lutheran Fool.* Luther responded in kind, referring to Cochlaeus as "Rotzleffel" (snot spoon), or as "Kochleffel" (cooking spoon); to Emser as "the goat of Leipzig"; to Eck as "Dr. Eck" or "Dreck" (dirt); and to Murner as the "pussycat."

Luther, confronted by a mighty host of opponents, chose carefully those whom he considered sufficiently weighty to merit a serious reply. The theologians of the older universities were in general very conservative. In October, 1522, the University of Cologne condemned eight articles of Luther's teachings. On November 9, 1519, the scholastic doctors of Louvain drew up articles of condemnation of fifteen of Luther's doctrinal statements. In April, 1521, on the same day that Luther entered Worms, the Sorbonne faculty of the University of Paris marched in solemn procession led by the zealous Syndicus Beda to mass at St. Marturinus. They then officially proclaimed 104 of Luther's articles to be heretical. Luther defended himself against the Louvainists and Paris doctors, but singled out one of the Louvain doctors, Jacobus Masson, known as Latomus, for a direct reply: *Against Latomus. Luther's Refutation of Latomus' Argument on Behalf of the Incendiary Sophists of the University of Louvain,* 1521, a representative polemical apology.[22] But the battle of the giants was the great debate between Luther and Erasmus on the question of man's contribution toward his own salvation or the freedom of the will in the religious context.

Luther had used Erasmus's *Novum Instrumentum* when doing his commentary on Romans, but he was doubtful about Erasmus's theological position and contrived to tell him so. On October 17, 1516 he wrote to Spalatin describing a deficiency in Erasmus's understanding of St. Paul and criticizing his predilection for St. Jerome, and asked that Spalatin pass this word along to Erasmus. On March 1, 1517, Luther wrote to Johannes Lang: "I

22. *Luther's Works,* 32, *Career of the Reformer,* II, George W. Forell, ed. (Philadelphia, 1958), pp. 133–260.

am reading our Erasmus but daily dislike him more and more. . . . I am afraid that he does not advance the cause of Christ and the grace of God sufficiently. . . . Human things weigh more with him than divine."[23] Between 1519 and 1524 Luther wrote in a friendly and even flattering way to Erasmus, referring to him as "our Erasmus," begging him to recognize him as a little brother (fraterculus), as Luther sought Erasmus's neutrality if he could not have him as an ally. Erasmus, more out of hostility toward the scholastics than out of love for Luther, on April 14, 1519, spoke to the Elector in Luther's favor, saying that he was in trouble for attacking the crown of the pope and the belly of the monks. Late in 1519 Erasmus wrote to Albert of Brandenburg arguing that it was not right that one should be dragged to punishment who at first merely proposed for discussion certain questions on which the schoolmen had always disputed and even doubted. But as Luther's position became more perilous, Erasmus increasingly disassociated himself from the cause, for, he held, Christendom has had many martyrs but few scholars. On July 5, 1521, he wrote to Richard Pace: "Not all have sufficient strength to face martyrdom. I fear I should act the part of Peter over again. I follow the Pope and the Emperor when they decide well because it is pious to do so, I bear their bad decisions because it is safe to do so."[24] But he was under increasing pressure to declare himself openly for or against Luther and he offered flimsy excuses for refusing to pass judgment himself, saying that he had not read Luther's writings and was too busy to do so, he was not qualified theologically, and he had no authority to intervene. Luther's increasing truculence, the radicality of On the Babylonian Captivity of the Church, and the growing turbulence of events alienated Erasmus further. In July, 1523, Ulrich von Hutten in his Expostulation attacked Erasmus for not committing himself to Luther's cause, and in September Erasmus published his Sponge to wipe out Hutten's charge. From the beginning of 1522 Luther's position had itself changed, for he no longer needed association with the humanist movement to establish his self-conscious position. Luther commented on May 28, 1522, that he would not provoke Erasmus, but if the great rhetorician attacked him, Erasmus would not find him a second Lefèvre d'Étaples, whom Erasmus claimed to have conquered.[25] In the spring of 1524 Luther wrote to Erasmus proposing a truce.

23. WA Br I, 90; Luther's Works, 48, Letters, I, pp.39–41.
24. P. S. Allen, ed., Opus Epistolarum Des. Erasmi Roterodami 4 (Oxford, 1922), lines 32–36.
25. H. Feld, "Der Humanisten-Streit um Hebraer 2, 7 (Psalm 8, 6)," Archive for Reformation History, 61 (1970), 5–35.

If Erasmus would not attack the Lutherans, Luther would see to it that they would keep quiet about him. That Erasmus was offended by this proposal is evident from his reply of May 8, but the die was cast and in September his attack on Luther, *On the Freedom of the Will (De libero arbitrio)*, was published.

In his diatribe Erasmus set forth the various views of grace and freedom held by the church fathers. Granting the authority of the Scriptures, he raised the question of how one can know whose interpretation is correct, discussed passages that seem to support free will and those that seem to oppose it, examined Luther's arguments in his *Assertio* of December, 1520, in which Luther had defended himself against Leo X's bull of condemnation, and then offered a mediating solution of his own: It is essential that man have freedom of choice or there would be no point to praise or blame, or to God's commandments which say, "Thou shalt." If men do not believe in free choice they will be irresponsible and lawless. If man acts out of necessity God cannot fairly reward or punish him. God's grace is necessary, but man must have the freedom to accept or reject it, for if men are damned for lack of grace they will at least have chosen damnation.

Luther considered Erasmus's argument for free choice "rubbish" from the point of view of biblical theology, and he had no intention of responding to it. But the diatribe received a wide circulation, and at last friends and his wife, Kathie, persuaded him to reply to the great Erasmus. His response *On the Bondage of the Will*, four times the length of the diatribe, attacked Erasmus's arguments point by point. He acknowledged the superiority of Erasmus's talent and congratulated him upon seizing the jugular, the question of man's salvation by God's grace alone or man's free choice, by which man can contribute to his own salvation. Man's salvation, he contended, has nothing to do with merit, for "all have sinned and come short of the glory of God." To make man's salvation dependent upon merit can only lead to legalism, to a vain effort to achieve salvation by good works, to self-righteousness and away from dependence upon the merits of Christ. God is not determined in what He does by what men do, but in His freedom God freely bestows forgiveness upon those whom He wills to redeem. God's freedom is the freedom of grace, the divine love in Christ which redeems sinners who do not merit salvation. Far from undermining the law, this proclamation of grace reveals the true meaning of God's law and commandments. God's demand for perfect love on the part of man shows man not what he should and can do but rather what he ought to do but cannot and in reality does not do unless he is completely transformed by the grace of God, by the Holy Spirit Himself. In response to Erasmus's confession that if it were not for the authority of the church he himself could be a skeptic, Luther responded with, "The Holy Spirit is no skeptic."[26] Luther's treatise ran through eight Latin editions and two editions of Justus Jonas's German translation within a year. Erasmus was deeply hurt and shaken and undertook to reply, *A Defense of the Diatribe (Hyperaspistes diatribae),* which was published in two parts, the first in June, 1526, and the second in September, 1527. But events had moved on and Luther never felt the need to answer. Ulrich Zwingli compared Luther to the heroic Ajax and Erasmus to the wily Odysseus. Eobanus Hessus, the poet, observed that Erasmus had pointed to the dead wood in the forest and Luther had seized the ax and chopped it down. There is some truth to these contemporary assessments. Luther commented once that Erasmus laughed at things that a Christian should rather weep over. Erasmus lived on another decade ignored or distrusted by both sides, a tragic denouement for a man who had once been the literary and intellectual arbiter of the age.

4. SOCIAL REVOLUTION

The religious Reformation was closely bound up with powerful social tensions and revolutionary impulses and served as a catalyst in the revolts of the 1520s. The new evidence underlines the importance of religious feeling and ideology for the revolutionary spirit of the time. Luther anticipated such disturbances, for they were a sign of the last times (Luke 21). To fearful Erasmus he said:

To wish to silence these tumults is nothing else than to wish to hinder the Word of God and to take it out of the way. For the Word of God, wherever it comes, comes to change and renew the world. . . . You do not see that these tumults and dangers increase through the world according to the counsel and the operations of God. And therefore you fear that the heavens may fall about our ears. But I by the grace of God see these things clearly, because I see the other tumults greater than these which will arise in ages to come, in compari-

---

26. "The Bondage of the Will," *Luther's Works,* 33, *Career of the Reformer,* III, Philip S. Watson, ed. (Philadelphia, 1972), Introduction, pp. 5–13, and text. A massive literature has been devoted to the famous controversy, but one of the more substantial recent studies is that of Harry J. McSorley, C.S.P., *Luther: Right or Wrong? An Ecumenical-Theological Study of Luther's Major Work, The Bondage of the Will* (New York and Minneapolis, 1969).

son with which these appear but as the whispering of a breath of air, and the murmuring of a gentle brook.[27]

The general economic trends of the century induced severe stress in a still quite feudal society: population pressure, inflation, inadequate adjustments in wages and rents. Moreover, the development of a more vigorous commercial life and urban growth as well as the consolidation of new power in the hands of the territorial princes worked to the disadvantage of the landed nobility and the peasants. Both of these social groups fought to restore or maintain their advantages by resorting to armed revolt.

The imperial knights *(Reichsritter)* constituted a large body of lesser nobility who were free lords of the Empire standing immediately below the emperor *(Reichsunmittelbarkeit)*, though they were not represented as an estate in the diet *(Reichstag)*. They were being ground between pressure from the territorial princes and the cities especially in southwestern Germany, where the Swabian League of cities and territories imposed order on them by force. These knights had suffered greatly from the agrarian crisis of the fourteenth century and they increasingly lost their utility as fighters with the development of armor-piercing guns and fortress-leveling artillery. They had castles and small landholdings and maintained themselves by hiring out as mercenaries to princes. Some of them preyed on the trade routes leading to Nuremberg, Augsburg, Trier, and other cities. The grandfathers of Ulrich von Hutten, for example, had formed a company of thirty-two knights who shared the loot equally from raids against merchant convoys. The leader of the Knights' Revolt of 1522 and 1523 was Franz von Sickingen, who had offered Luther sanctuary the year before. In August, 1522, he attacked the Archbishopric of Trier with a vague goal in mind of a political reform that would favor the nobility at the expense of the upper clergy, but four weeks later he had to abandon the attack and retreated to protect all the knights' castles, thus scattering his forces. The united princes bombarded the castle of Landstuhl, where he had taken refuge, and a timber hit by a shell tore a fatal wound in his side. The princes then moved from castle to castle in a ruthless mopping-up operation, reducing them to ruins. Even the strongest fortress, the Ebernburg under Ernst von Tautenberg, capitulated after a five-day bombardment.

27. *WA* 18, 626, 627.

Sickingen's ally Ulrich von Hutten, suffering a fatal case of syphilis, could not join the campaign. He fled to Switzerland seeking refuge with Erasmus in Basel, but the latter refused him shelter and persuaded the town council to expel him. Hutten then sought sanctuary with Huldrych Zwingli in Zurich. Erasmus even wrote to the Zurich city council urging them to refuse him shelter, but by then Hutten had died—on August 29, 1523—on the island of Ufenau on Lake Zurich, where he lies buried to this day. Luther, who believed violent revolution to be sinful, considered Sickingen's death a judgment of God on the knights' bloodshed. The revolt was a last hurrah for a class being ground down inexorably by socioeconomic forces.

The plight of the peasants plunged them into a war even more tragic and desperate. In the second half of the fourteenth and during the fifteenth century the peasants had gained concessions and improved their lot, due to the manpower shortage among other things. Now with the rural population on the increase and inflationary costs putting pressure on the landlords and princes both secular and ecclesiastical, the feudal overlords and the cities controlling the surrounding territories put the squeeze on the peasants, increasing dues and restricting privileges. It was more a case of battling not to lose ground than of gaining new advantages that drove the peasants to arms in a desperate and destructive rebellion.

Peasant revolts had been a frequent phenomenon in the late Middle Ages, and there were many local revolts in Germany before the major rebellion. In 1474, for example, Hans Böhm, the "Drummer of Niklashausen," proclaimed the forthcoming egalitarian millennium in which the lost rights of the peasants to the commons, woodlands, and streams would be restored. But the city walls of Würzburg were stormed and the insurgents suppressed. In the Swiss peasants' war of 1513–1515 the *Bundschuh,* or laced shoe and legging, served as a symbol for the peasants who declared for the old custom, law and justice against the new regulations. Württemberg experienced the "Poor Conrad" movement in 1514, analogous to the Jacques of French peasant revolts. In 1517 the *Bundschuh* was active on the upper Rhine under Joss Fritz, who in 1502 in Speyer and in 1513 in Breisgau had sought to change social conditions under the sign of the *Bundschuh* with the slogan "nothing but the righteousness of God" under a crucifix. Early in the summer of 1524 the Stühlingen peasants revolted against their lords when, in the middle of the harvest, the countess ordered them to gather snail shells in which she wanted to wind yarn, and that revolt became a signal for a more general insurrection.[28]

The Peasant is Becoming Sly, wrote Eberlin von Günzburg. In the early spring of 1525 three bands of peasants were roving about near Lake Constance. In March the Swabian peasants issued the "Twelve Articles" demanding their rights in matters of tithing, serfdom, fishing and game laws, foresting, feudal dues, rents, the commons, and the death tax. The first and twelfth articles reflected the influence of the religious Reformation in requesting that the entire community have the power and authority to call a pastor and offering to withdraw any article proven to be contrary to the Scriptures. In April the peasants took to arms and a ferocious slaughter ensued. Ironically the peasantry in the southwest was in a relatively good position with some property, with few compulsory services, with more personal freedoms than those in the east, and many possessed arms. The conflagration spread from the southwest eastward to Carinthia and Austria, northward to Thuringia and Saxony until a third of Germany was in an uproar. Only Bavaria, where the duke had restrained exploitation by lesser lords, escaped disturbances. In the southwest Georg Truchsess von Waldburg proved to be an efficient general for the Swabian League, and he suppressed the revolutionaries in short order. The peasants lacked both valor and leadership, and even Götz von Berlichingen, the "man with the iron hand," a robber knight and mercenary, proved ineffective in drawing the bands of peasants together into fighting unity. There was little coordination of battle plans; all too often the roving bands of peasants were victimized by some rabble-rouser, and in some cases they even consulted witches for counsel on strategy.

Some of the most violent revolts prior to this one had taken place in the lands of the ecclesiastical overlords, abbots and bishops, for the peasants were especially bitter over exploitation by prince-bishops, since secular

28. Hubert Kirchner, *Luther and the Peasants' War* (Philadelphia, 1972), p. 3. Robert N. Crossley, *Luther and the Peasants' War* (New York, 1974), provides a clear popular account. An older classic work is Günther Franz, ed., *Quellen zur Geschichte des Bauernkrieges* (Munich, 1963). Because of the interest of Friedrich Engels in the Peasants' War and Karl Marx's theory about the Reformation as an early bourgeois revolution, there is an enormous Marxist literature on this subject. A beautifully illustrated volume by Adolf Laube, Max Steinmetz, and Günter Vogler, *Illustrierte Geschichte der deutschen frühbürgerlichen Revolution* (Berlin, 1974), makes a distinct advance over earlier crude Marxist histories depicting the Peasants' Revolt as the real Reformation and Thomas Münzer as the true reformer. Laube's research on the mining industry and miners is of great value. See also Abraham Friesen, *Reformation and Utopia: The Marxist Interpretation of the Reformation and Its Antecedents* (Wiesbaden, 1974).

and church dues were so intermingled. The peasants for their part now could not separate social demands from religious beliefs. The fusion of social and economic demands with religious impulses entered a new phase when the revolution reached central Germany and fell under the spell of Thomas Münzer, a spiritual "enthusiast" who urged the peasants on with fanatical zeal. As a preacher in Zwickau, as early as 1520 he had showed enthusiastic *(Schwärmerische)* tendencies, declaring that the believer had to experience the pangs of hell, then the mystical state of resignation, to be followed by a supernatural enlightenment of the heart. He was given to visions and phantastic scriptural exegesis. In April, 1521, he was driven from Zwickau; he served as pastor in Allstedt from 1521 on, then in Mühlhausen in Thuringia, a man filled with bitter hatred of Catholics, Lutherans, and all worldly authorities. He preached revolution fanatically, was driven from Saxony, and fled to southwest Germany, where he published a harsh attack on Luther: "Against the spirit-less soft-living Flesh in Wittenberg." He became involved in the Peasants' War, preached to the peasants not to let the blood dry on their swords but to slaughter all godless rulers. The princes of Hesse, Brunswick, and Saxony joined forces against Münzer's peasant army in Thuringia. Before the final battle at Frankenhausen on May 15, 1525, Münzer is said to have promised to catch the enemy's bullets in his sleeves and the peasants went into battle singing "Come Holy Ghost, God and Lord." Münzer was captured that same day —found hiding in bed after the battle—and on May 27 he was beheaded.

Luther threw his energies into the cause of peace, urged the lords to recognize the justice of some of the peasants' claims, and admonished the peasants against a rebellion which meant taking the blood of the authorities in their own hands and unleashing the misery and injustice that makes anarchy less bearable than tyranny. In April, 1525, he published his *Admonition to Peace* on the Twelve Articles and the Memmingen Agreement adopted by the Swabian peasants. Early in May he published the Weingarten Treaty between the Swabian League and the Lake Constance Association *(Seehaufen),* with a preface and epilogue, as a positive model for agreements. In Thuringia he went out to the people and preached peace at Stolberg, Wallhausen, Nordhausen, Weimar, and Seeburg, though he was hissed and threatened and was in grave danger. Luther reprimanded the peasants for seeking economic gain in the name of the gospel and declared that they should leave the word Christian out of their demands. Now accounts of peasant atrocities poured in. On May

6, before Frankenhausen, he began writing his vehement tract *Against the Robbing and Murdering Hordes of Peasants,* urging the authorities or anyone else to smite, slay, and stab the rebels and to show no mercy until the rebels had been put down. It was published together with the *Admonition to Peace.* "If anyone thinks this too harsh," he concluded, "let him remember that rebellion is intolerable and that the destruction of the world must be expected every hour." This inexcusably harsh tract, detached and republished separately by some printers, appeared after the war had crested, and it alienated some popular support. After Frankenhausen he published *A Dreadful Story and a Judgment of God Concerning Thomas Münzer,* including a selection of letters found in Münzer's satchel with a commentary.[29] In July he wrote *An Open Letter on the Harsh Book Against the Peasants,* apologizing for his vehement language and urging equity and moderation on the lords and princes. It is sometimes said that Luther's stand in the Peasants' War brought to an end the Reformation as a spontaneous popular movement. The artisans and craftsmen in the towns had often made common cause with the peasants, and the lower echelons of society are thought to have been alienated by his opposition. In reality that does not seem to have been the case, for the advance of the Reformation into new areas actually gained momentum especially in the north and northeast, where the initiative in the cities came from below. Only with the continuous education of evangelical preachers did the manpower become available for the pulpits of country parishes. Luther's attitude toward princely tyranny and peasant violence was widely shared by many Catholics and other evangelical reformers such as Johannes Brenz, Andreas Osiander, Johann Lachmann, and Urbanus Rhegius, pastors in imperial cities. The popular pamphleteer Eberlin von Günzberg, at this time a pastor in Erfurt, opposed a lower-class uprising there in early 1525, and the next year as superintendent of the

29. The standard work in English is Eric W. Gritsch, *Thomas Müntzer: Reformer Without a Church* (Philadelphia, 1967). Walter Elliger, *Thomas Müntzer: Leben und Werk* (Göttingen: 1975), is the first all-encompassing biography of Münzer in German, depicting him as the propagator of a "renewed apostolic church." Other volumes of special interest are the historiographical account by the Marxist historian Max Steinmetz, *Das Müntzerbild von Martin Luther bis Friedrich Engels* (Berlin, 1971); Manfred Bensing, *Thomas Müntzer und der Thüringer Aufstand 1525* (Berlin, 1966); Paul Althaus, *Luthers Haltung im Bauernkrieg,* 2d ed. (Darmstadt, 1962). The text-critical edition of Münzer's works is by Günther Franz, 1968.

churches of Wertheim he published *A Warning to the Christians in the Burgau Mark to Guard against Revolt and False Preachers.* Most common folk seemed to understand this general conservative attitude.[30]

The mercenaries had a field day slaughtering the fleeing bands of insurrectionists. There were some cruel executions by way of example, but no mass hangings of the labor force. Arms were confiscated and punitive fines levied. Estimates as to the total cost in human life vary widely, the most extravagant being about one hundred thousand casualties. But the greatest casualty of all was clearly the peasantry itself, for it sank back into a state of resignation lasting for centuries. The power of the territorial princes increased through their victory, which led to a greater conservative reaction on the part of the Catholic princes and to still further influence of the evangelical princes over the church. The badly disorganized and decentralized peasants' revolt had never really had a chance to succeed, and it is quite unhistorical to play it up as though its failure were a lost opportunity to establish a proletarian society. It is equally idle to bemoan the role of the princes in Reformation history, for as the subsequent narrative shows, only the protection of faithful evangelical princes allowed the movement to survive the attacks of the powerful forces arrayed against it, and that barely.

5. EVANGELICAL MOVEMENT TO 1530

The social upheavals briefly slowed down but did not appreciably alter the continued spread of the evangelical movement. The high point of popular ferment had come in the years 1522–1524, with the focal centers in Wittenberg and south Germany. The first Protestant martyrs died in Brussels in 1523, Heinrich Voes and Johann Esch, two Augustinian monks from Antwerp. Several thousand heretics, most of them Anabaptists, were executed in the Netherlands, where the Habsburgs took a very hard line. Other Lutheran martyrs followed, preachers and Bible colporteurs, reenacting the history of early Christendom when, as Tertullian put it, the blood of the martyrs was the seed of the church. Luther, deeply moved, composed "A Hymn to the Martyrs"—their ashes will not rest, worldwide they spread through many nations! He bemoaned the fact that he himself

30. See the article by Robert Kolb, "The Theologians and the Peasants. Conservative Evangelical Reactions to the German Peasants Revolt," Archive for Reformation History, 69 (1978), 103–131. Editions of Luther's works published later in the century and thereafter were regularly bowdlerized, omitting his attacks on the princes.

was "not considered worthy of martyrdom." A Protestant mythology evolved which added an emotional ingredient reflected in such later martyrologies as Ludwig Rabus's *History of the Martyrs,* Jean Crespin's *Acts and Monuments,* and John Foxe's *Book of Martyrs.* A mere rehearsal of the spread of Lutheranism does not touch the human pathos involved—torn souls, divided families, exile, prison, torture, and death.

Defining the point at which a city or territory became Protestant is not a simple matter, for the criterion could be the suspension of the mass, the point at which evangelical doctrine was truly grasped by a majority, or a legal break and the introduction of a new church order. The process was usually gradual and taken in several steps, except where a ruler made the break and imposed reform from above, though even there much of the old order was frequently preserved. Proudly patrician Nuremberg, conditioned by a sodality of Staupitz's followers, welcomed the Lutherans before 1524. Albrecht Dürer was an early enthusiastic supporter. Lazarus Spengler, city secretary, was one of the first laymen to play a prominent role in promoting the Reformation. Andreas Osiander proved to be a powerful evangelical preacher. Augsburg humanists such as Conrad Peutinger had at the outset been interested in Luther's cause. The prior of the Carmelite monastery, Johann Frosch, played host to Luther during his hearings with Cajetan. The wealthy bankers and patricians resisted religious innovation and the city was divided in its loyalties. Ulm, Nördlingen, Esslingen, Colmar, and Constance in the south entered the evangelical camp. Constance was rather typical in the way in which the difficulties with the bishop, coupled with burgher unrest and bombardment with pamphlets, was followed by the installation of preachers, 1524–1527, who would expound the Holy Scriptures.[31] Strasbourg was a key city, for it became a leader of the movement in the southwest, a refuge for John Calvin, and the main center for the dissemination of Protestant propaganda in France during the first two decades of the Reformation. Matthew Zell was popular as preacher and his wife, Catherine, provided refuge for many evangelicals. The city moved toward the Reformation from 1524 and 1525 on, conclusively from 1528 on, led by Bucer and Capito. Two-thirds of the imperial cities joined the Reformation. In the south only Regensburg remained with the Catholic Church, overawed by the Wittelsbach dukes of Bavaria.

31. Hans-Christoph Rublack, *Die Einführung der Reformation in Konstanz von den Anfängen bis zum Abschluss 1531* (Gütersloh, 1971), an exemplary study.

Between the years 1528 and 1531 the leading cities in the north such as Bremen and Stralsund adopted the evangelical faith. Albert of Brandenburg, still money-minded, permitted Magdeburg and Halberstadt to adopt Lutheranism in return for a special tax levy in 1541. The Archbishop and Elector of Cologne, Hermann von Wied, invited Bucer and Melanchthon to introduce Protestantism in 1542 and planned to secularize his holdings, but he was overthrown before a fundamental change could be made. Franz von Waldeck, the bishop of Münster, Minden, and Osnabrück, emulated his example. The city of Hildesheim turned Lutheran, and large parts of the bishopric went along with the change. Luther wrote countless letters and sent trusted co-workers to guide these local reformations.

Whole territories were added to Lutheranism in those decades. In 1525 Albert of Brandenburg, Grand Master of the Order of the Teutonic Knights, ruling extensive territory in east Prussia, moved toward Lutheranism. He dissolved the Order, secularized its lands, and as the duke of Prussia became a vassal of the king of Poland. Landgrave Philipp of Hesse led his state into Lutheranism in 1526. The Margrave of Brandenburg-Ansbach followed suit in 1528, as did the dukes of Schleswig and Brunswick, and the count of Mansfeld. Motives were mixed, and in most cases genuine religious conviction coupled with hostility to the ecclesiastical hierarchy and the hope for gains from the appropriation of church properties many combined in the decision. Most of the secularized properties, perhaps as many as 80 percent, were subsequently devoted to educational and charitable purposes, so that a cynical reading of the rulers' motivation is not necessarily warranted, particularly considering at what perils they joined the cause, often risking the loss of everything they possessed.

During the 1520s Emperor Charles V was away from Germany engaged in war with France. Now the peculiar political structure of the Empire with its vagaries and complications came into play. Pope Adrian VI, the honorable reform-minded Dutchman and friend of Erasmus, sent as his nuncio Chieregati to the Nuremberg Diet of 1522, to demand the enforcement of the Edict of Worms. But the diet declared that it was impossible to enforce the edict and tabled the discussion of the Lutheran question until a church council could be held in Germany within a year. At the Nuremberg Diet of 1524 the papal legate Campeggio suffered the same frustration, for the cities flatly refused to enforce the edict, and the princes agreed to enforce it only "as much as possible." The Regency Council (*Reichsregiment*) dating from 1500 had become increasingly important and was now dissolved, so that only an imperial official stationed in Esslingen remained to implement the emperor's will. But the year 1524 witnessed a sinister development which presaged the formation of religio-political power blocs that might well lead to religious war. On Campeggio's urging, a number of Catholic estates, including Ferdinand of Austria, the Wittelsbachs of Bavaria, and the south German bishops, formed the Regensburg League in June, 1524, in order to enforce the Edict of Worms. The masterful hand of Frederick the Wise of Saxony, whose contribution to the Reformation has never been sufficiently appreciated by historians, was weakening. He died on May 5, 1525, but before his death, by receiving communion in both kinds and at the end rejecting extreme unction, he signaled his sympathy with the evangelical position. His successors, John the Constant (1525–1532) and John Frederick (1532–1547, d. 1554), were both close to Luther and loyal to the evangelical cause.

After the suppression of the peasants' revolt the princes were free to form new alliances for action on the religious question. In central and north Germany several Catholic princes—Luther's longtime enemies Duke George of Saxony, Joachim I of Brandenburg, Albert of Mainz, Erich and Heinrich of Brunswick—formed the League of Dessau in July, 1525, in order to root out heresy. Meanwhile the energetic young evangelical Landgrave Philipp of Hesse, very sharp and politically minded, joined with Elector John of Saxony in the League of Gotha—which was ratified in February, 1526, at Torgau, and was consequently known as the League of Torgau—joined shortly by other north German Protestant estates. Emperor Charles had in the meantime defeated the French in northern Italy in the key battle of Pavia, 1525. But at the first Diet of Speyer in the summer of 1526 he still had political difficulties and could not act decisively against the Protestants. The diet therefore resolved that the religious question should be referred to a church council to meet within a year and a half, and that until then every estate should act with respect to the Edict of Worms "as it hoped to be able to answer for before God and to the Imperial Majesty." Although the intent of the resolution was to preserve the status quo, the Protestant estates interpreted the resolution as legitimizing church reform in their own territories.

Charles V had gained relief from the French pressure, but the Medici Pope Clement VII, who was unwilling to accept a Spanish hegemony, kept him preoccupied with Italy. The emperor threatened the pope with an appeal for a general council and his mercenary troops moved down through Italy, got out of hand, and on May 6, 1527, sacked Rome. But no sooner had the pope been humiliated than the Turks renewed their pressure on the emperor. After their victory at Mohács in August, 1526, the Turks moved into Hungary and now were along the border of Habsburg lands. In 1529 they besieged Vienna itself and came close to taking it. The emperor needed the support of the Protestant princes. He resolved to return to Germany to seek a solution to the religious question and so came to the Diet of Augsburg in 1530.

The evangelicals had gained a decade in which to build up an independent church order. Luther's own home life and church activity served as a prototype of the evangelical parsonage. At the Wartburg he had written *On Monastic Vows,* dedicated to his father, in which he argued that celibacy and monastic asceticism were contrary to the Scriptures and were less a service to God than a useful life in society. When the Wittenberg Augustinians and colleagues began to marry, Luther exclaimed, "Good heavens! They won't give me a wife!" But nuns were leaving the cloister as well and though abducting a nun was a capital offense, Luther arranged for an old herring merchant of Torgau, Leonard Kopp, to help twelve nuns escape in his wagon from the nearby cloister of Marienthron on the Eve of the Resurrection, 1523. Eight of the nine who came to Wittenberg were provided with husbands. Luther refused to marry, for he expected death as a heretic at any time and now the Peasants' War was raging. The remaining nun, Katherine von Bora, let it be known that she was ready to marry either Amsdorf or Dr. Luther, who ruled it out of the question. On a visit with his parents, however, his father took the idea seriously and then, quite suddenly, Luther married. On June 13, 1525, he became publicly betrothed and on June 27 Luther and Katherine married at the portal of the city church, followed by a banquet at the Augustinian cloister and a dance at the city hall. The groom was forty-two and the bride twenty-six. He had married, he said, to please his father, to spite the pope and the devil, and to seal his witness before martyrdom. Archbishop Albert of Brandenburg, who was considering secularizing his lands, sent a present of twenty gold gulden. They had six children, two of whom died young, and Luther spent many happy hours in the family circle in the black Augustinian cloister which the Elector gave to them, playing the lute, singing to his children and telling them stories, such as Aesop's fables, which he also edited. Kathie managed well, for the house was always full of indigent students, friends, visitors, including royalty, from all parts of

Europe, where they regularly after dinner listened to Luther's famous *Table Talks*. [32] By his personal example Luther practiced what he had preached: that celibacy was a false ideal and not a way to win God's favor; for the Christian to do his duty in society is far more pleasing to God, a blow to one form of medieval religiosity.

On his return from the Wartburg Luther had been very reserved about changes in the forms of worship. Thomas Münzer introduced a very creative evangelical liturgy at Allstedt in 1523, and Johannes Lang composed a new liturgy for Erfurt. Luther wrote several orders of worship more compatible with evangelical theology, the *Formula missae et communionis*, 1523, and the *Deutsche Messe*, 1526, which gave the sermon a central position and included congregational singing of hymns. Wittenberg ended saints' days and at the end of 1524 eliminated all private masses *(Winkelmesse)* for the dead. In 1524 Luther wrote "To the Councilmen of the Cities in Germany" urging a progressive educational reform. With the introduction of the *Ordinance for a Common Chest at Leisnig* Luther contributed to poor-law legislation, which undercut the ethos of almsgiving to beggars as a charitable act rather than helping the poor to help themselves. In that *Ordinance* Luther expressed his ideal of congregational church government with the "establishment of a ministerial office with the calling, choosing, installation and deposing of the curators of souls" according to the divine Holy Scriptures. Where the mass and priesthood were abolished a new church order was needed.

Though congregations of confessing Christians might be an ideal—and it is not clear that Luther thought of a congregation as a collective of individuals rather than as a corporative form of representation—with the given circumstances such a system could not be realized. Luther was torn between the ideal of a confessional church and the need for a people's church which would serve all in a given community and instruct in good morals even those lacking in faith. In the end he had to settle for a great deal of influence and control over the external property and organization of the churches by city magistrates and territorial princes. He viewed them merely as Christian brothers in authority, emergency bishops *(Notbischöfe)* who should serve until times became better. They were to have no say in matters concerned with doctrine or the preaching of the gospel, for that would be a mixing of the secular sword into the affairs of the spiritual authority. Luther conceived

32. Roland H. Bainton, *Here I Stand: A Life of Martin Luther* (New York, 1950), pp. 286–304.

of spiritual and secular authorities *(Obrigkeiten)* rather than of church and state in a legal or modern institutional sense. Gradually during the years following 1526 the territorial church orders developed, in large part on the pattern established in electoral Saxony and Hesse.

The process began with a Visitation Program, first suggested by Nikolaus Hausmann, the Lutheran preacher in Zwickau. In January, 1526, a small trial visitation was made which immediately revealed the need. One visitation brought to light that only ten of some thirty-five ministers really had an adequate grasp of the gospel and one of the ten was a drunkard. As late as 1539 Justus Jonas reported that many preachers were still Catholic at heart and preached like evangelicals just for their salary. A shocking number of preachers were given to excessive drinking and other vices, and the morals of the laity had not improved over what they had been "under the papacy." Luther himself complained bitterly that even though the gospel was now clearly preached, the morals of the people did not improve, but everywhere rioting and drunkenness, vices of every kind, prevailed, signs of the ingratitude of the people to God. Innocence had not replaced ignorance and human nature remained unchanged. In that respect he judged the Reformation to be a failure. This sorry state of affairs in addition to the experiences of 1525, when local congregations were so easily led astray by radical enthusiasts, convinced Luther that more structure was needed for the church. Clearly firmer action was called for and an effort to reach the people with simple instruction. In 1527 he wrote a *Preface to the Instructions of the Visitors to the Preachers,* two electoral councillors and two theologians comprising the team of visitors. In 1528 Melanchthon in an *Instruction for the Visitors* specifically referred to the appointment of superintendents who would serve as surrogate bishops.

In Hesse the organization of the territorial church began with the Homburg Synod in October, 1526. A former Franciscan, Francis Lambert of Avignon, influenced this Homburg church order which rested upon a basic distinction between the confessing congregation of true believers and the great mass of the people who were merely nominal Christians. But Luther believed it to be too idealistic and impractical, and Hesse then followed the Saxon plan in 1527 with visitations and superintendents. In that year Philipp of Hesse on Lambert's advice founded the University of Marburg, the first university that was evangelical from the start.

Philipp also took the initiative in trying to get the Lutherans and the Swiss reformed Protestants to write in a common form. The sacramentarian controversy over the nature of Christ's presence in the Lord's Supper, involving Karlstadt, Zwingli, and the Lutherans, had split the Protestants into two camps. With imperial Catholic pressure increasing, Philipp believed Protestant unity essential for survival and arranged the Colloquy of Marburg in 1529, where Zwingli and Luther met to discuss fifteen articles of doctrine, but could not agree on a common interpretation of the Lord's Supper. As the political position of the Protestants grew worse, the Catholic princes applied renewed pressure.

At the Second Diet of Speyer, in the spring of 1529, the Catholic majority resolved to end the permissive final decree of 1526; the Edict of Worms should be enforced; territorial estates should refrain from further innovations or secularizations—they should tolerate Catholic worship and eradicate all Sacramentarians and Anabaptists. Against this resolution the evangelical minority could merely offer a Protest (hence "Protestants"). Six Lutheran princes and fourteen south German cities declared their right to answer to God alone for those matters which concerned "God's honor and the salvation . . . or the souls of each one of us." This impasse called for imperial intervention.

In 1530 Charles V returned to Germany in order personally to preside over the Diet of Augsburg summoned for that summer with the express purpose of settling the religious question. With the Turks threatening the Empire and the French in league with them, Charles V felt the need to negotiate. He wished to hear "the opinion, point of view, and belief of everyone." Melanchthon, assisted by Agricola, Jonas, and Spalatin, prepared the evangelical Augsburg Confession in German and Latin, using as a basis the Schwabach, Marburg, and Torgau articles. The confession emphasized the main doctrines that they held in common with the Catholic Church rather than such controversial matters as the power of the pope or transubstantiation of the elements in the sacrament. The first part discussed "Articles of Faith and Doctrine," such as God, sin, justification, the ministry, church, sacraments, civil government, freedom of the will, faith and good works, saints; the second part discussed "Articles about Matters in Dispute, in which an Account is Given of the Abuses which have been Corrected," such as the two kinds in the sacrament, marriage of priests, the mass, confession, foods, ceremonies, monastic vows, and the power of bishops. Their goal was to prove that they "have introduced nothing, either in doctrine or in ceremonies, that is contrary to Holy

Scripture or the universal Catholic church."[33] On June 25, 1530 the Saxon chancellor read this first Protestant confession before the emperor and estates of the Diet. It was signed by Elector John, Margrave George of Brandenburg, Duke Ernest of Lüneburg, Landgrave Philipp of Hesse, Duke John Frederick of Saxony, Duke Francis of Lüneburg, Prince Wolfgang of Anhalt, and the mayors and councils of Nuremberg and Reutlingen. In the Coburg Castle not far from Augsburg Luther paced nervously to and fro. On one wall he wrote, "Non moriar sed vivam et narrabo opera domini"—I shall not die but live and declare the works of God. He sent a stream of letters to Melanchthon and his colleagues urging them to stand fast, to yield nothing, to be strong.

The Roman party decided two days after the reading to write a refutation and assigned to the task a group of theologians headed by the legate and including Eck, Faber, and Cochlaeus. When this *Roman Confutation* had been read on August 3, the emperor demanded that the evangelicals should acknowledge that they had been refuted and should yield. Melanchthon prepared an *Apology of the Augsburg Confession,* ready for submission on September 22, but the emperor refused to receive it and the Lutherans had to leave the diet. Thereupon the Catholic majority, which remained behind, declared the Edict of Worms to be in effect and promised a church council within a year. "How absurd," Charles V once commented, "to try to make two men think alike on matters of religion, when I cannot make two timepieces agree."

6. POLITICS, WAR, AND THE PEACE OF AUGSBURG

From that moment in 1521 when Luther stood before him in Worms, Emperor Charles V never wavered in his hostility to the heretics and considered it his holy duty to win them over, to force them to conform, or to destroy them. To the widowed Queen Mary of Hungary, his sister, who was said to be somewhat favorably inclined toward Luther, he wrote: "I declare to you that if I had a father, mother, brother, sister, wife or child infected with Luther's heresy, I would consider them my greatest enemies." Not only was he thoroughly orthodox in his religious outlook, but he clung to the medieval ideal of two swords: a universal empire and a church universal. He was prevented from acting decisively by the pres-

---

33. Theodore G. Tappert, ed., *The Book of Concord: The Confessions of the Evangelical Lutheran Church* (Philadelphia, 1959), p. 95.

sures of duties in far-off Spain, where he had at the outset to struggle with the *comuneros* and a complicated governmental structure, by the wars with France, and by the advance of the Turks. But he never deviated from his original intention of suppressing Protestantism. He was "a lonely figure, not prone to laughter," as the chronicler and cosmographer Alonso de Santa Cruz portrayed him, and kept his own counsels.[34]

Charles's taciturn nature, added to a certain diplomatic guile, enabled him to deceive the evangelicals consistently. The wish was father of the thought in their case, and they wanted to believe that the emperor was not completely set against them. As late as June 30, 1530, Luther still wrote: "The Emperor to be sure has a pious heart, worthy of all honor and virtue, which so far as his person goes cannot be sufficiently honored; but, dear God, what can a mere human do against so many devils, if God does not help powerfully?" The evangelicals, especially Melanchthon, wanted to maintain Christian unity no less than did the Catholics. But Charles V badly misjudged them, for to the end he seemed to believe that the widespread support for Luther's doctrinal position was due to disaffection with ecclesiastical abuses and that as soon as these had been eliminated by a council that support would vanish. The emperor's support of Rome and the hierarchy did not prevent him from acting against the popes with their political chicanery, their catering to the French, the hostility of Clement VII, and the dubious attitude of Paul III. During the sack of Rome in 1527, when Charles's freebooters had Clement VII imprisoned in the castle of Sant' Angelo, Bartolomeo di Gattinara wrote to Charles: "We await the speedy instructions of your Majesty regarding the rule of Rome, whether, that is, any kind of of apostolic chair should remain in this city or not." Public opinion in Spain forced Charles to release Pope Clement, but this incident reveals what some advisers close to the emperor believed him capable of doing to the papacy. The Protestants genuinely believed from time to time that the emperor would call a council like that of Basel, on the example of the eastern emperors in the days of the great ecumenical councils, or that he would summon a national council for the German church. But in this they were to be disappointed, for although the popes feared a council under imperial auspices, the emperor used the idea more as a threat to them and as a pacifier for the Protestants. The emperor entertained the thought that a council would effect a moral reform which might turn back the tide of

34. Manuel Fernandez Alvarez, *Charles V: Elected Emperor and Hereditary Ruler* (London, 1975), pp. 49–50.

protest. Instead of that, the pope's council convened in 1545 and the emperor's road led to war in 1546, the year of Luther's death.

The evangelical states, growing increasingly apprehensive, formed a defensive military alliance, signed at Schmalkald on February 27, 1531, against the implementation of the Edict of Worms, provisionally for six years. The lawyers had to overcome the reluctance of the theologians to sanction armed resistance to the emperor with the theory that the authority of the territorial princedoms had been sanctioned by God and that the emperor's authority was derived from them through the electors. This Schmalkald League included Electoral Saxony, Hesse, Brunswick-Lüneburg, Brunswick-Grubenhagen, two counts of Mansfeld, the north German cities of Lübeck, Magdeburg, Hamburg, Bremen, and from December, 1531 on, Goslar, as well as several south German cities, above all Strasbourg under the leadership of Martin Bucer. Philipp of Hesse maneuvered against the Habsburgs by establishing diplomatic ties with France, England, Denmark, Hungary-Siebenbürgen, and even with the Catholic Bavarian dukes.[35] For a long time there had been increasing tension between the evangelical and Catholic princes. In 1528 the Pack affair had precipitated a severe crisis. A ducal Saxon official, Otto von Pack, told Landgrave Philipp of Hesse that he had discovered a secret treaty of the Catholic princes in which they pledged to exterminate the Lutherans. The letter intended to document the charge proved to be a forgery, but the legacy of fear and suspicion remained. Duke George and the Catholic princes now reacted to the formation of the Schmalkald League by organizing the Halle League in November, 1533, renewed as the "Christian Union" in the summer of 1538, with a constitution modeled after that of the Schmalkald League.

In the same year that the Schmalkald League was formed, religious war broke out in Switzerland. Bucer had not been able to persuade Zwingli to join forces with the Lutheran princes, so that Zurich, abandoned by Bern, was overrun and Zwingli killed at the battle of Kappel, October 11, 1531. In Germany itself the year passed without the outbreak of hostilities. The Turks increased their pressure when Suleiman prepared for

35. For background, details, and bibliography see Hermann Buck, *Die Anfänge der Konstanzer Reformationsprozesse, Österreich, Eidgenossenschaft und Schmalkaldischer Bund 1510/22–1531* (Tübingen, 1964); Ekkehart Fabian, *Die Entstehung des Schmalkaldischen Bundes und seiner Verfassung 1524/29–1531/35* (Tübingen, 1962); Gundmar Blume, *Goslar und der Schmalkaldische Bund 1527/31–1547* (Goslar, 1969).

another march on Vienna in April, 1532, and the emperor was forced to compromise. From the summer of 1532 on, for nearly a decade, Charles V was preoccupied by his wars with the Turks and the French, and so was forced to temporize, compromise, and negotiate with the Protestants, who pressed their advantage.

At the Diet of Nuremberg in the summer of 1532 a recess or temporary peace for the Protestants was agreed upon. They were to be tolerated within their present boundaries until the calling of a council within a year, and the cases against them pending before the Imperial Supreme Court were to be dropped. The years following the Nuremberg Recess were the best the Schmalkald League enjoyed. The evangelical movement won Württemberg and Pomerania in 1532 and ducal Saxony, following the death of Duke George, and Brandenburg in 1539, where Elector Joachim II (1535–1571) gave the Reformation a very conservative episcopal form. After the disaster of the Anabaptist kingdom of Münster in 1535 and the setback of the Zwinglians in the southwest, strict Lutheranism made greater advances and ministers were bound to the Augsburg Confession. Württemberg is an interesting case of the dynamics at work. Duke Ulrich returned in 1534 from his 1519 exile with the help of the French and Hessians. He called Ambrosius Blarer (a Zwingli-Bucer type) and Erhard Schnepf (a firm Lutheran). Johannes Brenz led in the reform of schools and churches. In 1538 Blarer was dismissed and a consistently Lutheran form of worship and doctrine was established.

In May, 1536, Bucer, Capito, and other south German theologians came to Luther's home and after earnest discussions came to a substantial agreement on the Sacrament of the Altar or Lord's Supper and other disputed matters. Melanchthon prepared a statement of their doctrinal agreement, known as the Wittenberg Concord, which brought harmony between the Lutherans of the north and the evangelicals of the south German cities, though it alienated the Zwinglians, since they insisted upon Zwingli's symbolical understanding of the sacrament. Luther remained on good terms with Heinrich Bullinger, Zwingli's successor in Zurich.

The situation polarized further in the second half of the decade. In accord with a tenuous agreement reached with King Ferdinand, states that accepted the Augsburg Confession were to be free to join the Schmalkald League. In April, 1536, at a meeting of the league in Frankfurt, Württemberg, Hanover, Pomerania, Anhalt, Frankfurt, Hamburg, and Kempten joined the league. When the league met in February, 1537, however, the imperial emissary, Vice-Chancellor Held, declared the addition of new members to be invalid. This blow was softened by the Frankfurt Interim of 1539, which extended a provisional and short-term permission to practice their religion. Moreover, in addition all Imperial Supreme Court cases on spiritual jurisdiction and church property were to be held in suspension. Both sides feared war.

With the Protestant and Catholic leagues staring eyeball to eyeball, the idea of a church council to resolve differences gained in appeal. Pope Paul III, more earnest about reform than his predecessors, wanted a general council under his leadership. Despite the renewal of war between the emperor and Francis I, Paul III summoned a council for May, 1537, to meet in Mantua. He sent his nuncio Peter van der Vorst to the meeting of the Schmalkald League in February, 1537, where some forty theologians and professors including Luther, Bugenhagen, and Melanchthon met. The latter held that one should not reject a council out of hand, but the others were convinced that the evangelical position would be condemned in advance, that Mantua was not a safe location, and that the evangelicals were truly catholic, not schismatic, needing no council for their own reform. Due to the Protestant opposition and continued war, the pope delayed the start of the council to November 1, 1537, then to May 1, 1538, now to be held in Vicenza, and finally postponed its opening indefinitely. But the reform committee appointed to prepare for the council continued its work, and in 1537 these largely Erasmian cardinals, such as Sadoleto, Contarini, and Giberti, published their brief, *De emendenda ecclesia,* listing the manifold abuses in the church in need of reform. Luther published an edition with his "I told you so" notes in the margin. The emperor in the next years followed a conciliatory policy by sponsoring religious colloquies. The first discussions in Hagenau, in June, 1540, produced no results, and a new colloquy was set up for Worms, from November, 1540, to January, 1541. Dr. Eck and Melanchthon debated on the question of how debilitating original sin was for man's ability to contribute to his own salvation. In April and May, 1541, the colloquies were renewed at Regensburg, where Melanchthon and Contarini arrived at a compromise formula on justification, promptly rejected by both the Curia and Luther. But a lively debate on the doctrine of transubstantiation ended the efforts at reunion through theological agreement.

The Protestants suffered a crippling blow due to the bigamy of Philipp of Hesse. In March, 1540, with the permission of his wife, Christina of

Saxony, he secretly took a lady of the court as his second wife. He had found continence impossible and on December 10, 1539, he won from Luther and Melanchthon as confessional counsel a dispensation to take secretly a second wife on the grounds that bigamy on the example of the patriarchs was less sinful than adultery. But rumors of his marriage spread and he was in great jeopardy under imperial law. The emperor took advantage of the situation to insist that Philipp desist from his opposition politics. Moreover, Duke Moritz of ducal Saxony (1541–1553), a Machiavellian type of politician without deep religious convictions, sided with the emperor and with Philipp of Hesse, his father-in-law, who had made a separate non-aggression treaty with the emperor on June 23, 1541. Elector Joachim II of Brandenburg stayed out of the Schmalkald League. The two Saxonies, electoral and ducal Saxony, were at odds with each other and fought in the bishopric of Meiszen. Philipp intervened to prevent an open war, but Moritz quit the League. Despite these difficulties, the evangelical movement made continued progress. In the south the Palatinate-Neuburg and Sulzbach, under the prince Ott-Heinrich, and the city of Regensburg turned evangelical. In the north the bishoprics of Naumburg, Merseburg, Meiszen, Brunswick-Wolfenbüttel, where Duke Heinrich was driven out by Saxony and Hesse, and somewhat later, the episcopal city of Hildesheim became Lutheran. In Mecklenburg the Reformation won out in 1547.

In the northwest the Elector and Archbishop of Cologne, Hermann von Wied, worked for reform from 1543 on and called Bucer and Melanchthon to advise him. His neighbor, Franz von Waldeck, the bishop of Münster, Minden, and Osnabrück, followed his example. Duke William of Cleves was feuding with Emperor Charles over the possession of Geldern. By the terms of Charles's and Philipp of Hesse's agreement, Duke William could not join the Schmalkald League. The Protestant princes failed to support Duke William, and Charles easily overthrew him and stopped church reform. Charles perceived the political myopia of the Protestants and calculated more strongly on it from that point on. A reaction in the northwest followed, and in 1546 Hermann von Wied was driven out of Cologne and died in 1552 as an evangelical. The advance of Protestantism in the northwest came to a halt.

Charles V managed to end his foreign war (1544–1545) and was ready now to take up his war with the heretics. At the same time he arrived at an agreement with the pope over the council. In November, 1544, Paul

III summoned a council for March 15, 1545, to meet at Trent, a town still within the Empire but heavily under Italian influence. At the Diet of Worms, March, 1545, the Protestant estates voted against sending delegates to Trent. Luther fired one parting shot *Against the Papacy in Rome founded by the Devil.* On February 18, 1546, he died of angina pectoris at Eisleben, the city of his birth, where he had gone to arbitrate in a legal quarrel of the two counts of Mansfeld. In January, 1545, Melanchthon had written the *Reformatio Wittenbergensis,* full of compromises and concessions. The quiet reformer seemed to sense the danger of the crisis which the evangelicals now faced. The emperor was ready to strike.

In the Schmalkald War, 1546–1547, the emperor totally defeated the Schmalkald League. With the help of the pope, King Ferdinand of Hungary, Duke William of Bavaria, and some evangelical princes whom he had won over through ecclesiastical concessions, the emperor overran the Protestants in the south in 1546 and in the north in 1546/47. In the battle of Mühlberg on April 24, 1547, he defeated the main army of the Schmalkald League and captured Elector John Frederick of Saxony. Landgrave Philipp of Hesse surrendered in June to the emperor, who imprisoned both princes. Emperor Charles stood at Luther's tomb in the Castle Church and when urged to have his body exhumed and burned, he replied, "I do not make war on dead men." In the Wittenberg Capitulation of May 19, 1547, the Albertines took away from the Ernestines the electoral privilege and the electoral district including Wittenberg.

The emperor now undertook the restoration of the Catholic Church and limited the freedom of the estates. The Diet of Augsburg accepted the Augsburg Interim in May, 1548. This Interim conceded the cup for the laity and marriage for priests, but only until the council met. For the rest it prescribed Catholic doctrine and usage. In the south the Protestants were forced to accept the Interim. In the north there was more resistance, particularly on the part of such cities as Magdeburg. Duke Moritz of Saxony had Melanchthon prepare a compromise formula, the Leipzig Interim of December, 1548. This formula provided an evangelical definition of justification and good works, set aside the mass, but under the rubric of adiaphora it retained Catholic rites and ceremonies, even including the *Corpus Christi.* Adiaphora were matters of belief and practice not clearly defined by scriptures and held not to be essential for salvation.

Just when the emperor seemed within reach of his lifetime goal, the wheel of fortune turned again. The people were embittered by the force and ruthlessness with which the Spanish ruler pressed his advantage. Moritz of Saxony, angered at the lengthy imprisonment of Philipp of Hesse and irked because the emperor had not given him Magdeburg and Halberstadt-Merseburg as promised, made a secret agreement with France securing support in exchange for Cambrai, Metz, Toul, and Verdun. Then in the spring of 1552 he took the emperor completely by surprise, overran his position at Innsbruck, and forced him to flee to Villach in Carinthia. The Council of Trent hurriedly adjourned. In the Treaty of Passau, August 2, 1552, the Protestants were given a truce until the next meeting of the diet. Philipp of Hesse was freed, John Frederick having been released earlier. At that juncture Moritz himself was struck down by fate. In 1553 he died of his wounds after a victorious combat at Sievershausen.

Emperor Charles V was weary of life and strife, while the evangelical states were chastened and anxious for peace. On September 25, 1555, at the Diet of Augsburg called by Charles and led by his brother King Ferdinand, the Religious Peace of Augsburg was ratified. The Peace of Augsburg has often been maligned as a provisional and makeshift document which merely reflected the particularist interests of the princes. But its provisions and subsequent political circumstances helped to preserve peace within the Empire for over half a century, while France and other nations were racked by religious wars, down to the outbreak of the Thirty Years' War in 1618. The Peace provided that the adherents of the Augsburg Confession were to be recognized by imperial law. Through the *Reservatum ecclesiasticum,* in the case of any future changes of religion the ecclesiastical properties were to be reserved to the Catholic Church. The Anabaptists, Zwinglians, Calvinists, and other groups were excluded from this new legal status. The Peace also set in concrete the confessional exclusiveness of each territorial state, a situation which lasted in Germany until the nineteenth century. The Peace did not proclaim religious freedom in a modern sense, for each ruler or council received the *ius reformandi* or right to reform. In actual fact, this was the principle of the *cuius regio, eius religio*—whose the rule, his the religion. The right to emigrate was generally acknowledged, a step forward toward liberty. There were many lesser provisions—for example, that the Imperial Supreme Court should henceforth have members from both confessions. The Catholic minorities in the imperial cities were to be tolerated. The Peace was at first considered provisional and the final treaty was to be achieved by peaceful

provisions of the Peace of Augsburg

means. But no clearer or more definitive treaty was concluded until the Treaty of Westphalia ended the long war in 1648.

The evangelical prince Duke Christoph of the Palatinate, riding along the Rhine reading the text of the Peace, was deeply moved by the small gains and great concessions even in matters of conscience that he thought the Protestants had made. He pondered whether it was Christian to agree to such things and answered: "If the evangelicals do not consider Christ and His Word with greater earnestness and zeal, they will not long go unpunished!"[36] The English ambassador to the Empire at one point summarized the feelings of the German princes toward the emperor with the words of Solomon: "The heaven for height, and the earth for depth, and the heart of kings is unsearchable" (Proverbs 25:3).

7. LUTHERANISM IN NORTH AND EAST EUROPE

The evangelical movement spread in two ways in north and east Europe. It was carried by German merchants, by letters and pamphlets, by students and traveling nobility, finding a foothold in the cities first of all and then among the landed magnates and peasants. In north Europe it was imposed by royal fiat from on top as a very conservative form of Lutheranism so far as ecclesiastical structure and cultus were concerned.

In the Baltic region, ruled by the Teutonic Knights before their subjection by Poland, the Catholic bishops had their sees in Riga, Pilten, Pernau, and Dorpat. The half-Christianized peasants inhabited primitive villages, and German merchants dominated trade in the small cities. The breakthrough came in Riga, where the first evangelical preaching took place in 1521. The following year Johann Lohmüller, a city councillor, wrote to Luther, who replied and dedicated an exposition of one of the Psalms to the "dear friends in Christ in Riga and Livonia." He urged them to support a pastor, instruct the children, and care for the poor. In 1527 Dr. Johann Briesemann came from Prussia to reform the order of worship. In 1539 an evangelical archbishop was elected. The church ordinance of Riga was adopted in Livonia, which comprised Latvia and Estonia. In 1535 a catechism in the Lettish language was printed in Wittenberg together with a low German text. In 1561 Gotthard Kettler, the master of the Livonian Brethren of the Sword in Courland became Lutheran and secula-

---

36. Viktor Ernest, *Briefwechsel des Herzogs Christoph von Wirtemberg III* (Stuttgart, 1900), no. 175, pp. 340ff. For a detailed general account of this period, see Johannes Bühler, *Deutsche Geschichte: Das Reformationszeitalter* (Berlin and Leipzig, 1938), pp. 425–472.

rized the land as a duchy, held in fief under the king of Poland. Sweden, Denmark, Poland, and Russia divided up the rest of the territory, in general tolerating Lutheranism.

In Scandinavia the Reformation was imposed upon the people by the throne. The Danish King Christian II (1513–1523) opposed the pope's candidate for the Archbishopric of Lund. Through his uncle, Elector Frederick the Wise, he arranged for the Wittenberg reformers to send Martin Reinhardt and Karlstadt to Copenhagen for a brief time, without lasting results. The opposition of the Danish clergy and nobility and of the Swedish aristocracy proved to be too strong. When the king attempted to break the resistance of the Swedes by killing the leaders in the "Stockholm Bloodbath," the reaction swept him away and he was forced by his own council to give up the throne and go into exile in 1523.

The Danish nobles elected as king Frederick I (1523–1533), who was favorably inclined toward the Reformation. He admired the success of his son-in-law, Albert of Brandenburg, who had turned Lutheran, and his own son Christian, duke of Schleswig-Holstein, who brought in evangelical preachers. In 1526 he appointed Hans Tausen, who had studied in Wittenberg, as court preacher. In that year at the Diet of Odense he proclaimed toleration for the Lutherans. Many burghers in the cities were growing favorable to the Reformation. Christian Peterson did a Danish translation of the New Testament. In 1530 Tausen, then pastor in Copenhagen, with other evangelical preachers debated "Forty-three Articles" with defenders of the Catholic Church at the Copenhagen Diet. Under Christian III (1533–1559) a full-scale reformation was achieved. Bugenhagen worked out a church order, substituting seven superintendents for the bishops, though the title bishop was later restored. Lacking consistories or synods, the bishops such as Peder Palladius of Sjelland, who had a master of arts and doctorate from Wittenberg, a literary figure, kept the church fairly independent of the state by their force of character.

Christian III forced Norway and Iceland, political dependencies of Denmark, to adopt the new Lutheran church order. The Catholic bishops were deposed and new superintendents were elected, church properties taken over, and the clergy made dependent on state support. The Danish liturgy, Bible, and hymnals were introduced. There was resistance on the popular level to the removal of images and relics, but it was repressed by officials. Two Catholic bishops in Iceland were deposed, one exiled and the other executed. From 1539 on the Lutheran form of worship was imposed. In 1540 an Icelandic New Testament was printed in Copenhagen, though it took decades to evangelize the island.

In Sweden ironically the introduction of Lutheranism was tied in with the drive for national independence from Denmark between the years 1521 and 1523. The Stockholm Bloodbath triggered a popular uprising among Sweden's independent peasants and the nobility against the hated Danish rule. Gustavus Vasa (1523–1560) emerged as the leader and was crowned by the Swedish Diet at Strengnäs on June 7, 1523. He was personally well disposed toward Lutheranism and believed that its introduction would strengthen both the monarchy and the independence movement. The church owned nearly half of the wealth of the country, with bishops such as Brask of Linköping exercising both spiritual and secular power. The new king was determined to make the church subordinate to the monarchy and assumed the power to appoint to church offices. At Westerôs in 1527 he forced the diet to approve of his transfer of ecclesiastical property to the king and to tolerate Lutheranism.

The king was aided by able reformers such as Olaf and Lars Petri, who had been educated in Wittenberg, and Lars Andersson. Olaf Petri's writings showed the influence of Luther's teaching on salvation by God's grace alone, the Scriptures, and the place of the vernacular, opposition to papal supremacy, the mass, monasticism, confession, and the invocation of saints. After his coronation, Gustavus Vasa made Laurentius Andreae, who had studied abroad and absorbed Lutheran ideas, his chancellor in Stockholm and installed Olaf Petri as pastor of the city church and secretary to the city council. Half the townsmen were Germans, and a Lutheran preacher served them. Olaf Petri produced a catechism and the New Testament in Swedish in 1526, a complete Bible by 1541. His *Mass in Swedish* and a *Swedish Hymn Book* of 1530 showed German influence. He also published a *Manual* in 1529, containing orders of worship and pastoral acts. Evangelical bishops such as Lars Petri replaced Catholics such as Bishop Brask, who fled the country. In 1531 the king married a German Protestant princess. The Diet at Westerôs in 1544 introduced a thoroughly Lutheran doctrinal and organizational program. Olaf opposed the emperor's Interim and the edicts of the Council of Trent. Under Gustavus Vasa, Sweden achieved national independence and a state religion.

As a territory of Sweden, Finland also moved into the Lutheran church. The key reformer was Michael Agricola (1508–1557), who had studied at Wittenberg from 1536 to 1539, and while there had begun a Finnish

New Testament and prayer book. These translations, plus the Psalms and various prophets, helped to develop Finnish as a literary language. Gustavus Vasa made Agricola bishop of Abo in 1554, but he died three years later when returning from a mission to Moscow.

In Poland the state authority was so decentralized that a reformation from above, such as the Scandinavians achieved, was not possible. In 1505 the Polish Diet decreed that new business could be considered by that body only with the consent of all three estates and that the king could not maintain a standing army. The landed magnates were virtually autonomous and that fact determined the pattern of the Reformation in that land. In 1525 Albert of Brandenburg, the head of the Order of the Teutonic Knights, acting on Luther's counsel and in agreement with Poland, secularized the Order's property in Prussia into a dukedom held as a fief under the feudal overlordship of Poland. He simultaneously introduced the religious Reformation into his lands. Lutheranism grew first in such German-speaking cities as Danzig (1523). From the 1540s on many Italian refugees of a Calvinist type came to Poland. A Pole, John à Lasco, spent time in the Protestant west and returned to Poland in 1556, where he worked as a reformer until his death in 1560. From 1548 on many Moravian Brethren, exiled after the death of the Protestants in the Schmalkald War, moved into Poland. King Sigismund II Augustus (1548–1572) was forced to make ever new concessions to the landed magnates, especially in "Little Poland," which was the southwestern territory of the Vistula valley. There were some 265 reformed congregations, most of them of a Calvinist persuasion, with some anti-Trinitarian groups splintering off. In western Prussia and "Large Poland" there were some 120 congregations, mostly Lutheran and Moravian Brethren.

Protestantism in Bohemia, Moravia, and Slovakia was related both to the Hussite tradition and almost by a popular association of Hus and Luther to the evangelical Reformation. In 1519 at the Leipzig debate Luther had himself become aware of the consanguinity of some of his ideas with those of Hus. In 1523 he dedicated a book to the Prague City Council, made up of Utraquists, and urged them to choose their own bishop regardless of Rome. Desiring a regular bishop, German settlers in Bohemia joined the Utraquists and established contacts with Wittenberg theologians who provided counsel and an ordinance through German superintendents. From about 1494 to 1528 the leader of the Bohemian Brethren, the more radical Hussites, was Luke of Prague. They favored

Lutheranism, but were restrained by the more conservative Utraquists, who had made their peace with the Catholic Church. The juncture of the Bohemian Brethren with Lutheranism was not completed until 1542, when they adopted Lutheran views of justification and the nature of Christ's real presence in the sacrament. But they retained their peculiar disciplinary system of public and private confession. Moravia remained their center, and thus later they received the name Moravian Brethren. Many migrated to Poland and there joined with the Calvinists from 1555 on. In Moravia the Lutherans were to be found chiefly in the cities such as Iglau. A small sect called the Amosites broke off from the Brethren of the Unity about 1500, attempting to live literally according to the precepts of the Sermon on the Mount. They were a kind of prototype of the radical Protestant sects that found refuge in Moravia. Bohemia was under the Habsburgs and after their victory in the Schmalkald War, King Ferdinand proceeded with some very repressive measures against the dissidents who had refused military service and support against the Protestants. The Prague Interim of 1549 was no more successful than the Augsburg Interim in the Empire, but the Utraquists and the Lutherans united in a demand for toleration. Ferdinand needed both the Utraquists and the Brethren and so did not—and, in fact, due to their strength, could not—completely suppress them. They eventually agreed not on the Augsburg Confession but on the *Confessio Bohemica,* which they presented at a diet. For some sixty years a truce between king and subjects was maintained in the interest of unity. By the end of the century the burghers and nobles of Bohemia and Moravia were for the most part evangelical.

In Slovakia Conrad Cordatus brought Lutheranism to the miners. From 1524 on he had often been in Luther's company and was the first to record his Table Talk. A Lutheran church persisted there during the following century.

In Hungary cities with a large German population turned Lutheran, as did a majority of the Magyar landed magnates such as the family of John Zapolya, king under the Turkish hegemony. Matthias Biro, who had studied in Wittenberg and was a friend of Melanchthon's, was the leading reformer. He returned from exile in Switzerland to lead the Reformation more along the lines of the Helvetic confession. Also in Turkish-occupied Hungary the evangelical movement spread. In Transylvania, in east Hungary, a region settled during the twelfth century by Saxons, Johann Honter (d. 1549), who labored in Kronstadt, led in the development of a "national" church of Lutheran persuasion. An evangelical church was organized also in Carniola among the Slovenes from 1561 on, the new Protestant literature forming the base for the Slovenian literary language.

In Austria, right under the domination of the Habsburgs, Lutheranism made astonishing progress. Like the Polish nobility, the Austrian landed nobility adopted Lutheranism to a surprising extent, sending sons to Wittenberg to study. The burghers of such cities as Steier, Graz, and Klagenfurt turned their cities into centers of Protestantism, and King Ferdinand was relatively tolerant in the interest of domestic tranquillity. But the Habsburgs, who staged some early Lutheran martyrdoms in 1524 and 1527, slowly tightened their grip and squeezed out Protestantism.[37]

The rapid advances of Protestantism into eastern Europe were facilitated by the diffusion of power and the mercantile ties that crisscrossed eastern Europe and provided avenues for evangelical missionary work.[38] By the same token, once stronger centralized powers took over in alliance with the revitalized Catholic Church, Protestantism had a difficult time maintaining itself in Habsburg lands or Poland, for example. In contrast, where Protestantism was established from on top by the central government over the opposition, in some cases, of the nobility and other groups, it maintained itself easily and remains well established to this day.

37. Conrad Bergendoff, *The Church of the Lutheran Reformation* (St. Louis, 1967), pp. 87–98; Grete Mecenseffy, *Geschichte des Protestantismus in Österreich* (Graz and Cologne, 1956), pp. 8–68. Eduard Boehl, *Beiträge zur Geschichte der Reformation in Österreich* (Jena, 1902), draws heavily on the Regensburg city archive. See also Konrad von Moltke, *Siegmund von Dietrichstein: Die Anfänge ständischer Institutionen und das Eindringen des Protestantismus in die Steiermark zur Zeit Maximilians I und Ferdinands I* (Göttingen, 1970).

38. For these economic ties see the volume of essays edited by Ingomar Bog, *Der Aussenhandel Ostmitteleuropas 1450–1650: Die ostmitteleuropäischen Volkswirtschaften in ihren Beziehungen zu Mitteleuropa* (Cologne and Vienna, 1971).

IMAGO MARTINI LVTHERI EO HABITV EXPRES-
SA, QVO REVERSVS EST EX PATHMO VVITTEN-
bergam. Anno Domini. 1 5 2 2.

Quæsitus toties, toties tibi Rhoma petitus,
En ego per Christum viuo Lutherus adhuc.
Vna mihi spes est, quo non fraudabor, Iesus,
Hunc mihi dum teneam, perfida Rhoma vale.

1.   This woodcut portrait of Luther, created by his friend Lucas Cranach the Elder in
1522 after the reformer's return to Wittenberg from the Wartburg, shows him in his
disguise at the castle as "Junker Jörg," rather
than in the habit of an Augustinian monk.
(*Bamberg, Staatsbibliothek*)

2.   This satirical woodcut portrait of Luther, when turned upside down, transforms
his visage into that of a fool. (*Worms, Museum
der Stadt Worms, Andreasstift*)

PESTIS ✳ ERAM ✳ VIVVS
MORIENS ✳ TVA ✳ MORS ✳ ERO ✳ PAPA

3. This early 16th-century engraved portrait of Luther by the Master W. S. (Wolfgang Stuber?) borrows Albrecht Dürer's famous composition of 1514 to emphasize the reformer's work as a scholar and translator. (*Coburg, Kunstsammlungen der Veste Coburg*)

HERCVLES GERMANICVS

4. This broadsheet casting Luther in the guise of "Hercules Germanicus" probably originated in the circle of Erasmus in Basel about 1522 and was illustrated by Hans Holbein the Younger. (*Zurich, Zentralbibliothek*)

5. Hans Holbein the Younger's exquisite, medallion-sized portrait of Melanchthon and its inside cover were probably painted about 1535 for an adherent of the Reformation in England. *(Hannover, Niedersächsisches Landesmuseum)*

QVI CERNIS TANTVM NON, VIVA MELANTHONIS ORA,

HOLBINVS RARA DEXTERITATE DEDIT.

6.   This fragment of a group portrait, painted by the Cranach workshop in the 1540s portrays Elector John Frederick with Luther, Melanchthon, and other reformers active in Saxony. (*Toledo, Ohio, Toledo Museum of Art*)

7. This woodcut portrait of Emperor Charles V appeared on the title-page of a treatise addressed to him by Huldrych Zwingli, published in 1530. (*Washington, D.C., The Folger Shakespeare Library*)

8. The printmaker Daniel Hopfer based his profile portrait of Francis 1 on classical precedents. (*New York, Metropolitan Museum of Art, The Elisha Whittelsey Collection*)

9. In Hans Holbein the Younger's theological allegory of about 1535, mankind is situated between the former Old Testament rule of mosaic law at the left and the New Testament gift of grace at the right. (*Edinburgh, National Galleries of Scotland*)

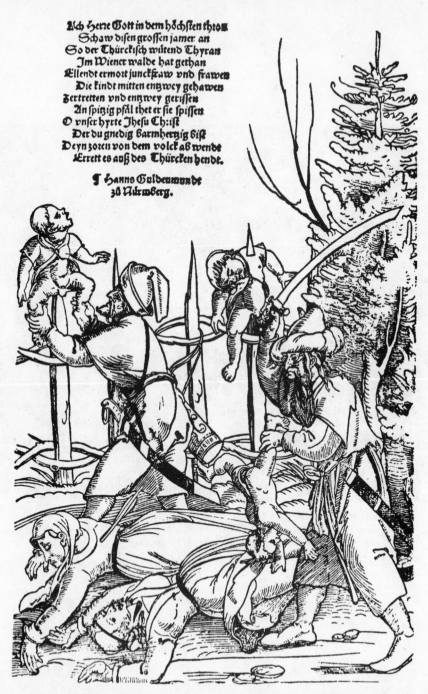

Ach Herre Gott in dem höchsten thron
Schaw disen grossen jamer an
So der Thürckisch wütend Thyran
Im Wiener walde hat gethan
Ellendt ermort junckfraw vnd frawen
Die kindt mitten entzwey gehawen
Zertretten vnd entzwey gerissen
An spitzig pfäl thet er sie spissen
O vnser hyrte Jhesu Christ
Der du gnedig barmhertzig bist
Deyn zoren von dem volck ab wende
Errett es auß des Thürcken hende.

❡ Hanns Guldenmundt
zu Nürmberg.

10. Erhard Schön's woodcut of 1530 records Turkish atrocities committed during the siege of Vienna: women and children were murdered, and some were impaled on fences. *(Vienna, Graphische Sammlung Albertina)*

11. This early 16th-century anonymous woodcut castigates the clergy's excessive indulgence in food and drink, gambling, and merrymaking. (*West Berlin, Staatliche Museen Preussischer Kulturbesitz, Kupferstichkabinet*)

12. This pen and ink drawing of 1521 by the Basel artist Urs Graf has been interpreted as a retrospective image illustrating the stunning defeat of the Swiss mercenaries at the battle of Marignano in 1515. (*Basel, Oeffentliche Kunstsammlung, Kupferstichkabinett*)

13. In this woodcut, designed about 1523-1524, Hans Holbein the Younger juxtaposed true repentance and forgiveness of sins at the left with the Catholic sale of forgiveness in the form of indulgences at the right. (*Basel, Oeffentliche Kunstsammlung, Kupferstichkabinett*)

14. The daily life and customs of peasants are reflected in these engravings by Hans Sebald Beham. (*Left: New York, Metropolitan Museum of Art, The Elisha Whittelsey Collection; Right: Metropolitan Museum of Art, Gift of J. Rockman*)

Der Bapst zwen Schlüssel hat gefürt/
Die Welt mit solchem schein bethört.
So nu der schein dauon verschwind/
So sihe man/das zwen schwengel sind/
Gemacht den Bapst zu hengen dran/
Mit Judas nemen gleichen lohn.

S. Petrus ad Christum.
HErr Jhesu Christ Richter gerecht/
Der ist/der dich sehr grewlich schmecht/
Dein Stathalter sich rhümet hoch/
Vnd ist des Teufels Diener doch.
Wil auch dazu mein Erbe sein/
Die Schlüssel haben gar allein.
Ein handel hat daraus gemacht/
Geitz/Stift/Raub damit tag vnd nacht.
Er bindet/Löset was er wil/
Auff das er geldes kriege viel/
Verkeufft/verteuscht/beid sind vnd recht/
Dein gantzen Menschlichem geschlecht.
Wohin die arme seele kom/
Da fragt sein Geitz vnd Stoltz nichts vmb.
Nichts denckt/denn wie er möchte sich/
Zum Gott erheben vber dich.
Die Schlüssel fürt er fur der welt/
Darunter nimpt des Judas gelt.
Las sehn man finds gewis also/
Vnder seinem Mantel aldo.

Gabriel ad Papam.
Wie paßt dir der Mantel so sehr/
Vnd ist der Zipffel dran so schwer.
Du wirst zu viel gestolen han/
Das hie/das sehn für jederman.

Papa ad Gabrielem.
Ah nicht mein lieber Gabriel/
Jch hab ein grosse beut vnd feil.
Da mir gros angelegen ist/
Das ja nicht seh der HErre Christ.

Gabriel ad Christum.
HErr Jhesu Christ Richter gerecht/
Die sach ist offenbar vnd schlecht.
Es ist Judas Beutel fürwar.
Das sehn wir albie offenwar.

Christus.
Lasse in mit Ketten binden an /
Vnd behalten neben Satan.
Bißsolang ich kom zum Gericht/
Da sol als denn der Böseticht/
Empfahen seinen rechten lohn/
Fur alles was er hat gethan.

Chorus XII. Apostolorum.
Nicht mehr sol er die Schlüssel füln/
Welch der Kirchen allein gebörn.
Des Judas Beutel sol er han /
Dinfort inn seinem Wapen stan.

Der Ebt vnd Bischoff hüt so viel/
Inn den Beutlin stecken on zil.
Annat vnd Pallia die sind/
Die er mit schalckheit fast geschwind.
Erticht/geraubt/gestolen hat/
Vnd noch nicht kan des werden sat.

Wil dazu mit der Könige Kron/
Sein Judas Beutel auch vol bon.
Damit er seine Cardinal/
Zu Herrn mache vberal.

M. Luther Antipapa curauit f.

15.   This parody of the papal coat of arms, published as a broadsheet in Wittenberg and consisting of a satirical text by Luther and a woodcut illustration by the Cranach workshop, draws an analogy between the pope and Judas. *(Coburg, Kunstsammlungen der Veste Coburg)*

16. This hand-colored broadsheet, illustrated about 1550 by the Monogrammist B.P. and issued in Magdeburg, satirizes the high living and corrupt morals of the members of the Augsburg Interim in a parody of the first psalm. (*Nurnberg, Germanisches Nationalmuseum*)

17.   Melchior Lorch's engraving of 1545 casts the pope in the guise of a wild man spewing forth monsters and vermin into the world. *(Wittenberg, Lutherhalle)*

Iudicabit iudices Iudex generalis
Hic nihil proderit dignitas Papalis
Siue fit Epifcopus fiue Cardinalis
Reus condemnabitur, nec dicetur qualis.

Hic nihil proderit quicquam allegare
Neque excipere, neque replicare
Nec ad apoftolicam fedem appellare,
Reus condemnabitur, nec dicetur quae.

Cogitate mifeti qui vel quales eftis,
Quid in hociudicio dicere poteftis:
Idem erit dominus, iudex, actor, teftis.

Hæc depinxit Iacobus Iſqueri de Ciuitate Taurini Pedemontio, anno Domini millefimo quatercentefimo primo.

18.   This Calvinist broadsheet satirizing the pope and the Catholic hierarchy was based on a mural dated 1401 in the Dominican convent in Geneva. (*Geneva, Bibliothèque publique et universitaire*)

Der Kirchen in Engelandt gelegenheit.

Ich bin Papst.

Die gefange Predickant in Engelande
Mit namen Cramerus. Hopperus.
Rydleius. Rogerus.

Stabsfoidns. Latimerus.

Vorrede.

Wirde ein Prophet vermessen sein
Vnd reden in den Namen mein/
Da ich im nichts gepoten han/
Oder rufft frembde Götter an.
Ein solch prophet verwercket hat
Sein leben/dis ist Gots gebot. Deu. 18.
A Der Teuffel Spricht Joan. 8.
Ihr trawte liebe Kinder mein/
Der ir euch artret nach mir sein/
Vnd reden in den Namen mein/
Von anfang ich ein Mörder bin/
B Das Lamb Spricht.
Was machte ir/ O wie nericke leut/
Das ir mich widerumb creutziget heut/
Mit einem Opffer in ewigkeit
Ich alle erwelte hab bereidt/
C Die Fürsten Spriech Luce. 19.
Wie gebe vns dieser Beerwolff an/
Wir wollen in nicht zum herscher han.

Die Bischoffe vn die Paffe Sprechē

Wir Schlucken dieses Lemlins Blut/
Vnd han do hay ein leichten mut.
E Der Beerwolff von Wintonien
Spriche.
Ein tuckischer/listiger fuchs gar klug
War ich vorzeiten vol betrug/
Nun aber/ da ich worden alt/
Brauch ich/gleich wie ein Wolff/gewalt/
Vorhin wurgte ich die Lemlin klein/
Gäns/enten/hüner/ingemein/
Jetz morde ich schaff/bock/vñ die wider/
Was ich antreff leg ich darnider.
F Das gemein pöbel in volck Spricht.
O heyliger vnd gelerter Man/
Allein vnstreflich lobinsan.
G Die gefangen Spriechen.
Vmb deinet willen wir viel tag
O Christe leiden vngemach/
Gleich wie vnschuldige lämmerlin
Zu wurgen vns sie al ir sinn.

Zum Leser.

Dis Bildnus lehrt dich frommer Christ/
Des Satans haß vnd arge list/
Wie er von anfang hat gethon/
Mit mörden vnd mit falscher lehr/
Der mörder vnd ertz liegener
Acht Jar leuchtet das Göttlich wort
In Engelande an allem ort/
Vndanckbarkeit die vrsach war/
Nun höret es den wider Christ/
Der zu Wintonien Bischoff ist.
Diß Gottsgericht/ O Teuscher Man
Solen allzeit vor augen han
Vnd Gott für sein wort danckbar seit
So wurdt er dirs auch lassen rein.
Darumb wer oren hat der hör/
Vonn lugen sich zur Warhait kere.

19. This German broadsheet commenting on the re-introduction of the Catholic faith in England during the years 1553-1554 was presumably issued contemporaneously by Protestants in Nuremberg. (*Zurich, Zentralbibliothek*)

Chapter Three

THE PROGRESS OF PROTESTANTISM

I. THE SWISS SETTING

A famous statue of Huldrych Zwingli behind the Wasserkirche in Zurich shows him standing with the Bible in one hand and a sword in the other. He lived by the book, but when he died on the battlefield of Kappel at age forty-six, he was there not only as a chaplain but as an armed and armored foot soldier fighting in defense of his city. Zwingli was the progenitor of reform in Switzerland, the creator of a theocratic form of church-state relations, and the most thorough and successful leader of the movement in the northern Swiss and southwest German city-states, where the Reformation took on a special urban character. Zurich provides a prime case study for the interaction of a strong clerical personality and powerful religious impulses with social and political forces in a relatively circumscribed environment.

The Swiss confederacy *(Eidgenossenschaft)* was a loose association of some thirteen very independent states whose only real tie was in the diet, which had to depend upon the individual states to carry out its resolutions, since there was no central government. The original core was made up of the forest cantons of Uri, Schwyz, and Unterwalden, with Lucerne and Zug close to them. When the confessional differences developed, these five formed the nucleus of the Catholic cantons, joined by Fribourg and Solothurn, despite pressure from Bern, which threatened them by westward expansions. Glarus was dependent upon Schwyz. Lausanne, at first dependent on Savoy for support against its bishop, on December 5, 1525, allied itself with Bern and Fribourg. Schaffhausen and Basel inclined toward Zurich and Bern, two city-states that enjoyed great independence thanks to their economic strength. The abbey of St. Gall was a dependency of Zurich, although the town of St. Gall sought to preserve its independence. The confederacy was completed with the admission of Appenzell on December 17, 1513. Geneva was officially protected by Bern against the duke of Savoy, but it remained technically outside the confederacy until 1815. Although the Swiss had renounced Maximilian as emperor in

1499, it was not until the Peace of Westphalia in 1648 that Swiss independence from imperial rule was given international recognition.

Switzerland was a poor little country with fewer than a million inhabitants. In western Switzerland about a fourth of the people lived in towns, whereas in the Zurich area only about 15 percent did so. The peasants were quite independent and conditions were tolerable despite the feudal dues paid to overlords, the church, and to the city oligarchies. During the Peasants' War of 1525 the peasants sympathized with those of Swabia and the Black Forest and, especially around Lake Constance, joined in the uprising. Overpopulation particularly in the forest cantons supplied manpower for the mercenary trade. The chronic economic imbalance caused by the importing of grain and salt was compensated for by the wages and booty brought home by mercenaries and by the pensions or retainers paid by foreign powers such as the king of France and the pope to city magistrates in return for their support in recruiting Swiss soldiery. In 1510 Pope Julius II made a treaty with the Swiss to supply him with 6,000 soldiers in exchange for an annual pension. The Swiss, who fought as pike-bearing foot soldiers in compact formations, had been hired out to the highest bidder, but in 1515 their defeat by the French at Marignano ended the myth of their invulnerability, and the next year the confederacy signed an agreement as part of the "Eternal Peace" that Swiss soldiers should thenceforth serve only under Francis I. In 1521 the French king, whose ambassador regularly paid pensions to friends of the king, renewed the agreement for a regular supply of mercenaries. The young Swiss, especially the peasants with their love of adventure, driven by poverty and greed, were ready volunteers, but all too many were killed or returned maimed and crippled for life. After the battle of Bicocca in 1522 Swiss soldiery no longer played a dominant role in the Italian wars, but the French and the pope continued to recruit them for their armies.

There was a great gap between the rich and the poor in the cities, with a middle range of people moderately well off. In Zurich 5 percent of the population, mostly patrician merchants, could be considered rich. The middle range consisted of merchants, landlords, masters of handworkers. The poorest class was made up of day laborers, widows, servants, artisans, and small shopkeepers. Masters and craftsmen were organized into guilds (*Zünfte*), which during this period were increasing their influence in city government. The moderately sized industries in Zurich, Basel, Constance,

Schaffhausen, Winterthur, St. Gall, and some in Bern began to recover during the sixteenth century from the depression of the fifteenth. The city-states of Switzerland experienced a growth in self-consciousness and self-confidence.

All signs also suggest a marked increase in piety during the late Middle Ages and early sixteenth century in Switzerland. Saint cults, relics, pilgrimages to local shrines, as well as to places as distant as Santiago de Compostela and Jerusalem, Mariolatry, veneration of St. Ann. in order to gain propitiation for sins and the grace of forgiveness, all provide evidence for such an increase in religiosity as well as superstition. The laity continued to pay rents, tithes, fees, oblations, and the traditional church dues. Just as in Germany, the sale of indulgences increased during these first decades of the century. In 1518 and 1519 the Italian Franciscan Bernhardi Samson attracted huge crowds in cities and in the countryside preaching and selling indulgences, promising to release souls from the fires of purgatory. He worked in Bern, Aargau, and in the Zurich area, until the Swiss Diet succeeded in getting Pope Leo X to call him away. As late as March 24, 1522, the mayor, council, and burghers of Bern counseled citizens to buy indulgences. The many new endowments of altars and churches reflected both an increased religiosity and the somewhat improved economic conditions.

New preacherships or "lectureships" were endowed in city churches, reflecting perhaps a new interest in biblical exposition. The number of clergy increased in order to man the additional altars and churches. In Zurich, for example, there were over two hundred clerics and monks in a city of 6,000 inhabitants. The cathedral alone had a staff of twenty-four canons, thirty chaplains, and a "common priest" *(Leutpriester)* with three assistants. On the other hand, there was a decline in the number of monks and friars and a detectable loss of morale and discipline. It is possible that the increased control of the laity over the city churches made them the preferred way of religious expression to the orders with their extraterritorial control and ascetic ideal.

The worldliness and misconduct of the bishops and higher clergy contributed here as elsewhere to the general demand for reform and to the aggressiveness of the city councils in assuming local control of the churches. The powerful Cardinal Matthew Schiner (1465–1522) played a fast political game, allied the papacy with Bern in its struggle with Savoy, brought Swiss mercenaries to Milan to fight for the pope, and bribed Swiss authorities freely, though he failed with Zwingli and Zurich. He even became a candidate for the papacy on the death of Leo X, but garnered only ten votes. The town-miter contest took place in nearly every city of Switzerland. There were constant quarrels over episcopal succession in Geneva, where the pressure of the dukes of Savoy, the French king, Fribourg, and Bern kept the bishops so politically involved they had no time for ecclesiastical reform. Bishop Aimon of Montfalcon (1491–1517) and his nephew Sebastian of Montfalcon (1517–1560) were in constant controversy with Lausanne. Basel was fortunate to have a pious and humanistically inclined bishop in Christoph of Utenheim, a doctor of laws, from Strasbourg. He summoned a diocesan synod, brought in the earnest Alsatian humanist Jakob Wimpheling for advice, and prescribed literacy and required readings for the recalcitrant priests. He was impressed with Luther's early writings, although he never became a Protestant; he died March 16, 1527. The bishopric of Constance was of critical importance to developments in Zurich. From 1496 to 1529 and again in 1531–1532 Hugo of Hohenlandenberg ruled as bishop, and the vicar general of Constance Johannes Faber played a key role from 1518 on. The struggle of the city councils with the bishops posed in those microcosms issues similar to the ones involved in the great medieval struggles of emperors and popes. Up to this point the spiritual headship of the pope and the spiritual authority of the bishops were not called into question. But increasingly on questions such as the control of properties, direction of monasteries, managing of prebends, clerical immunity from the jurisdiction of secular courts, and taxation the city councils challenged the authority of the bishops. Moreover, the councils were concerned with appointing preachers to the new preacherships which increased in number at the beginning of the sixteenth century. The parallel to the role played by the "Puritan lectureships" in the later English Reformation is striking, for the newly appointed preachers frequently inclined toward reform and some, such as Wolfgang Capito, preacher in Basel from 1515 to 1520, developed into full-fledged reformers.[1]

The powerful emanations of Renaissance humanism coming especially from Germany and from Italy, where Swiss involvement in the north

---

1. Rudolf Pfister, *Kirchengeschichte der Schweiz*, II, *Von der Reformation bis zum zweiten villmerger Krieg* (Zürich, 1974), pp. 3–11, provides an excellent discussion of religious and ecclesiastical conditions at the onset of the Reformation, including considerable detail on the bishoprics.

Italian wars stimulated interest in political and military aspects of Renaissance society, influenced Swiss culture most strongly in those very cities so crucial to Reformation history—Zurich, Bern, St. Gall, and, above all, Basel. Basel, situated on the Rhine, that great carrier of commerce and culture, was the most important center, with its schools, the only university in Switzerland, and its printing presses, paper mills, bookbinders, artists and illuminators, authors, and educated publishers. The presses of scholar-printers Johannes Amerbach (d. 1513) and his sons Bruno, Basil, and Boniface, of Johannes Froben, Adam and Hans Petri, Wolf Herwagen, and Andreas Cratander not only made texts available in the classical languages, but served as centers for humanist culture and attracted to Basel humanist scholars including the great Erasmus himself. His presence in turn provided a magnetic attraction for the *Sodalitas Basiliensis:* Glareanus (Heinrich Loritic), Capito, Louis Bär, Beatus Rhenanus (Beat Bild), the Roman legist Claudius Cantiuncula, and Oecolampadius (Johannes Hussgen), who arrived in 1515 and developed into the leader of reform. The printing industry attracted artists to Basel as well as advisers and illustrators: Lucas Cranach, Hans Holbein the Younger, Albrecht Dürer, who preferred etching to painting on the grounds of profit alone, Hans Leu, and Urs Graf (1485–1527), a pupil of Martin Schönauer of Colmar, best known for his woodcuts of the common people, mercenaries, peasants, and prostitutes. If the Swiss Reformation discouraged ecclesiastical art of the iconographical and decorative nature, it encouraged the development of new subjects and especially portraiture of individuals prominent in commerce, church, or state. Hans Asper (1499–1571) of Zurich did striking portraits of Zwingli, Bullinger, Oecolampadius, Pellikan, and Geralter. The Swiss cities of Basel, Zurich, St. Gall, Glarus, and Bern promoted scholarship and education.

In the area of historical writing the rich tradition of city chronicles provided a good background for the development of a humanist-Reformation historiography. Glareanus (1484–1563) wrote a *Helvetiae descriptio* which contained geographic and historical lore in such a way as to contribute to Swiss patriotism. Joachim von Watt, known as Vadianus, the humanist and reformer of St. Gall, wrote a *Chronicle of the Abbots of the Monastery of St. Gall,* an epic description of that ancient monastic establishment, the struggle of monastery and city, and the coming of the liberating Reformation. Giles Tschudi (1505–1572) modeled his Swiss chronicle after Caesar and Polybius. He showed a real grasp of the development of the Swiss

Confederacy, included the story of William Tell, and contributed to Swiss national consciousness. Two Swiss contributed to the natural sciences, Paracelsus in medicine and Conrad Gessner in botany and zoology. The printing presses of Basel had already during the early years of the century attracted authors such as Wessel Gansfort, Sebastian Brant, and Johannes Reuchlin, but greatest of all to be drawn to Basel was Erasmus of Rotterdam, prince of the humanists.[2]

Erasmus came to Basel for the first time in 1513 to work with Froben on his edition of the New Testament and the works of Jerome. Froben employed Oecolampadius and Nicholaus Gerbelius to assist in the production. The *Novum Instrumentum* was completed early in March, 1516, with the Greek text, Erasmus's Latin translation, a dedication to Leo X, address to the readers, and a concluding word by Oecolampadius. From 1521 to 1529 Erasmus lived regularly in Basel, then moved to Freiburg in Breisgau in a Habsburg domain to escape the Reformation. In 1536 he visited Froben once again and died in Basel on July 12.

The Erasmian circle in Switzerland included Glareanus, Oswald Myconius, Beatus Rhenanus, the Amerbachs, Vadian, reformer of St. Gall, and Oecolampadius, reformer of Basel. But his most eminent disciple was a common priest in Zurich, Huldrych Zwingli, destined to become the leading Swiss reformer, the "third man" of the Reformation. Shaped by the special sociopolitical circumstances of the confederacy and city-state, by the condition of the Swiss church and religious life, and by the new cultural surge of humanism, Zwingli emerged as the strong man of the Swiss Reformation.

2. ZWINGLI THE REFORMER

Zwingli had deep roots in the Swiss rock-ribbed soil. He was born on January 1, 1484, at Wildhaus in the Toggenburg, within the territory of the Abbot of St. Gall, as the third son of a fairly prosperous peasant and *Amman* or headman in the village. He had in all six brothers and two sisters, both nuns, none of whom became particularly distinguished people. The unusually gifted Huldrych was sent for fundamentals to study with an uncle Bartholomew, a priest in Wesen. At ten he traveled to Basel to study Latin with Gregory Büngli, a grammarian, and at thirteen he went to Bern for advanced instruction with a teacher named Heinrich Wölfflin,

2. G. R. Potter, "The Renaissance in Switzerland," *Journal of Medieval History,* 2 (1976), 365–382.

known as Lupulus. He also showed unusual musical talent, lute and voice, probably sang in the church and Dominican chapel, and the local Dominicans may have taken him in as a novice. But at fourteen his father sent him on to Vienna, a distinguished university known for its philosophical faculty. There was already a stirring of humanist interest there, with the presence of Johannes Cuspinian, the historian of the Habsburgs, among others. In October, 1497, Conrad Celtis, the German archhumanist, had arrived to promote classical learning and poetry. Huldrych was for some unknown reason expelled from the university, but reregistered two years later. In 1502 he was back in his homeland, where he earned an A.B. at the University of Basel in 1504 and an M.A. in 1506. His studies concentrated on the *via antiqua* scholastic philosophy—Thomas Aquinas, and above all, on the Aristotelian corpus of ethics, politics, metaphysics, and natural philosophy—Duns Scotus, and somewhat on humanist poetry and letters. Thomas Wittenbach, with whom he studied Peter Lombard's *Sentences,* an opponent of indulgences, directed him to Bible studies. He had just begun to attend lectures in the theology faculty when he was called to become the parish priest at Glarus, and the bishop of Constance ordained him in September, 1506. He celebrated his first mass at his own village church in Wildhaus on St. Michael's day. The fact that he had to pay off Heinrich Göldlin, a Zurich cleric then in the service of Pope Julius II, to whom the Glarus priesthood had been reserved, a sum that Zwingli later said came to one hundred gulden, must at least in retrospect have seemed to him to be a scandalous case of the evil of reservations.

Zwingli was an exemplary priest at Glarus, devoted to the office and dedicated to his studies. He read the Latin classics, taught himself Greek, and in addition to the Greek classics, he studied patristic writings east and west: Augustine, Athanasius, Cyprian, Chrysostom, and others. He was alert to new developments in literature and philosophy, encountered the writings of Pico della Mirandola and Jacques Lefèvre d'Étaples. But the deepest passion of this period was his love of his own Swiss soil and people. He was distressed that so many young Swiss in his parish were hiring out as mercenaries to foreign powers and were returning, if they came back at all, crippled, maimed, dissolute, and demoralized. He wrote an allegorical "Fable of the Ox," in which he portrayed the ox (Swiss) as a simple beast living peacefully in the meadow with its faithful dog Lycisca. But the leopard (French) comes with cats as counselors and persuades the ox that he owes it to the other animals to protect them from the predatory lion (Habsburg monarchy). The leopard takes advantage of the protection to rampage the territory of the fox (Venice), who asks protection from the shepherd (the pope) against the leopard and the lion. The shepherd, in turn, asks the ox to fight for him. There follows a general melée which leaves the ox without friends, and with innocence lost and pasture ravaged by goats. The mercenary trade was too enriching to be thwarted, and the Swiss combined to intervene in military campaigns in Italy and Burgundy. They won a victory at Pavia in 1512, and Zwingli himself accompanied the Glarus troops as chaplain in the battle of Novara the next summer, where the papal forces were defended and the French and Venetians defeated. Zwingli was also at the disastrous battle of Marignano, where the French artillery and troops slaughtered the Swiss, who left about nine thousand casualties on the field. He retreated with the survivors, about half the army, and made the long march back home. Zwingli began to doubt the wisdom of Cardinal Schiner's anti-French policy and Swiss sacrifices in behalf of a warring papacy. In *The Labyrinth* he called for peace and brotherhood. But he was identified in the minds of the people with a propapal policy, with its high cost in human life, and he was glad to move, on November 1, 1516, to Einsiedeln, a parish which attracted many pilgrims to see the miracle-working image of the Virgin Mary.

In Einsiedeln Zwingli found time for study and for an affair with a barber's promiscuous daughter. In April, 1515, Glareanus had introduced him to Erasmus and Zwingli now fell completely under that remarkable man's spell. Between 1515 and 1517 he adopted the great humanist's program for the renaissance of Christendom through good letters, the study of the Scriptures, and the Erasmian philosophy of Christ. He was in many ways a very conventional priest, corresponded with Glareanus about martyrs and relics, and in the critical year 1517 made a long pilgrimage to Aix-la-Chapelle. He gained a reputation as an effective preacher and on December 11, 1518, he was appointed common priest *(Leutpriester)* in the Great Minster of Zurich, the city that became the center of his Reformation movement. He was still enmeshed in the ecclesiastical pension system, receiving some fifty gulden annually. In 1518 the papal nuncio, Antonio Pucci, made him a papal acolyte chaplain for his services to the pope. All that was to change in Zurich.

On January 1, 1519, Zwingli, now thirty-five, announced that he would present a series of sermons on the New Testament, beginning with Matthew 1, ignoring the set Pericopes. He used the pulpit as the major platform from which to effect reform. In September he was struck down *plague* by the plague, which was ravaging Zurich, and was brought to death's door. His hymn on his recovery from the plague reveals a new Zwingli, more earnest and feeling totally dependent upon and grateful to God. His sickness unto death provided an experiential base for a high predestinarian theology, a position on sin and grace defined and reinforced by Pauline theology. He felt that he was among the elect. The more deeply he searched the Scriptures the more keenly he felt the contrast between the New Testament ideal primitive church and the ecclesiastical institution of his day. In 1520 he gave up his papal pension and criticized Cardinal Schiner for promoting the mercenary trade in behalf of papal armies.

Zwingli was not a sensational pulpit orator nor did he proceed rashly with radical reforms. He was a strong, measured man who spoke quietly but cogently from the pulpit. He showed restraint in action but prepared the people for change so that when it came, it seemed almost natural and necessary. He held out against extremists even while introducing major changes of his own. There was a puritanical streak in him which was foreign to Luther's nature. In church practice, for example, he sanctioned only those forms that he felt were authorized by the Scriptures, whereas Luther allowed everything decent, beautiful, and in order, whether it be stained glass windows or organs, so long as they were not expressly forbidden by the Scriptures. The question of Zwingli's relation to the Lutheran Reformation merits close examination, for despite the fact that Luther's public act opposing sales of indulgences took place in 1517 and Zwingli began his reformatory program in Zurich in 1519, Zwingli, especially from 1523 on, stoutly asserted his independence. The city of Zurich escaped the great ban by denying that it was Lutheran, nor was Zwingli excommunicated as a Lutheran. To answer the question with assurance requires a recapitulation of Zwingli's inner development.

At home Zwingli had acquired a passionate love of his fatherland—the soil, people, community, and church. His elementary schooling in the trivium was the usual, but in Basel and Bern he learned classical history. His contact with the Dominicans and his studies in Vienna and Basel, as well as possibly a semester in Tübingen or Paris, gave him a predisposition toward Thomism or the *via antiqua*. In Vienna he may have been awakened to Renaissance humanism. In the Glarus period he experienced a quickened sense of Swiss patriotism and encountered the great Erasmus with his individualistic cosmopolitan learned ideal and peace-mindedness.

He also developed a lively correspondence with a circle of young Swiss humanists with ideas about political and ecclesiastical reform. In Einsiedeln he studied Greek, began Hebrew, pondered over the New Testament, and read widely in Augustine. By the end of 1516 he developed an idea of the Scriptures as authority and of religion as an encounter with the living Christ. He began to feel responsibility for the reform of the church, a point that Zwingli was later to consider the beginning of his evangelical Reformation. But he was still very much in tune with the Erasmian *philosophia Christi*. In fact, he understood Luther's famous treatises of 1520 in a humanist reform sense. The plague experience and his studies of Paul's epistles in 1519 deepened his understanding of man's sinful condition and need for God's grace. He was much taken by Luther's stand in the Leipzig debate with Eck. By 1522 he was caught up by the Reformation emphasis on God's grace and the freedom of the Christian. His position was now defined and his theology was altered only in detail and emphasis by his study of the Christology of Hebrews, his encounter with the Anabaptists, and his dispute with Luther over the sacrament. Zwingli was, then, a reformer independent of Luther, but through the critical years much conditioned by Erasmus. He developed rapidly along Augustinian and Pauline lines, however, until his theology came very close to that of Luther. Certainly the evangelical movement in Germany began prior to that in Switzerland and had an enormous influence on the direction taken by the Swiss Reformation.[3]

Zwingli had introduced some minor liturgical changes and preached in an evangelical way in the Minster, but the first open challenge to ecclesiastical authority took place on Ash Wednesday, 1522, when the printer Christopher Froschauer, Leo Jud, the common priest at Einsiedeln, Zwingli, and a circle of co-workers and friends met in Froschauer's home and dared to eat sausage in defiance of church restrictions against eating meat during Lent. Zwingli did not eat any, in order not to offend some parish-

3. Gottfried Locher, *Huldrych Zwingli in neurer Sicht: Zehn Beiträge zur Theologie der Zürcher Reformation* (Zurich, 1969), pp. 184–186. For the changing interpretations of Zwingli see Locher's essay "Die Wandlung des Zwingli Bildes in der neuren Forschung," *ibid.*, pp. 137–171, and Ulrich Gäbler, *Huldrych Zwingli im 20. Jahrhundert: Forschungsbericht und annotierte Bibliographie, 1897–1972* (Zurich, 1975). Christoph Gestrich, *Zwingli als Theologe: Glaube und Geist beim Zürcher Reformator* (Zurich, 1967), pp. 108–109, comments on the lack of personal feeling and emotion in Zwingli's theological writings and attributes this fact, which concealed Zwingli's interior development somewhat, to a classical and medieval tradition of impersonal religious writing. He exaggerates Luther's influence on Zwingli, though he holds that Zwingli did not comprehend Luther's doctrine very accurately or fully.

ioners, but he was soon involved in the controversy. Froschauer appealed to the city government for support, but was met with an order to comply to the rules of fasting. Zwingli came to the fore with a sermon and a treatise *Concerning Choice and Freedom of Food,* published just before Easter, in which he argued on the basis of Acts 10: 10–16, that dietary restrictions ran counter to the freedom of the Christian as taught in the New Testament. The bishop of Constance, Hugo von Hohenlandenberg, and the vicar general, Johannes Fabri, reprimanded the dissidents, though they did not mention Zwingli by name, and the Diet of the Confederation, which met at Lucerne, scored disorderly and presumptuous preaching.

The second challenge was to the canonical rule of the celibacy of the clergy. The *de facto* common-law marriage of the clergy in Swiss towns and villages was widespread and actually favored by many of the laity. The bishops enjoyed a substantial income from fines levied for clerical wives and illegitimate children. Zwingli and his associates concluded, as had Luther in his 1521 treatise *On Monastic Vows,* that there was no scriptural basis for an enforced clerical celibacy and that it violated the freedom of the Christian. A growing number of the clergy now married and in 1522 Zwingli himself secretly married Anna Reinhart, a young widow with three children, an innkeeper's daughter of a good Zurich family. On April 2, 1524, they celebrated their marriage in a public church ceremony. Despite Zwingli's argument that celibacy was legalistically imposed during the papacy of Gregory VII in the eleventh century and that Paul had merely recommended and not commanded abstinence, the hierarchy remained firm against the marriage of the clergy. Zwingli published a defense of his evangelical position, *Apologeticus Archeteles* (The Beginning and the End), August, 1522, and received approval from the city council to stage a public debate in which he would clarify his stand on controverted issues.

This first public debate took place on January 29, 1523, before the city hall where over six hundred people were assembled to hear Zwingli present his reformed theology to the council. Bern and Schaffhausen were unofficially represented. The bishop of Constance sent Johannes Fabri and three other observers. Zwingli prepared the *Sixty-Seven Articles* for debate, a summary statement of his platform for reform. The first sixteen stated his positive positions on the meaning of the Gospel, the all-sufficiency of Christ's teaching, sacrificial life and death, and the true nature of the church as the communion of all believers in Christ. The remaining articles attacked papal power, the celebration of the mass as a sacrifice, rather than as a memorial, prayer for the intercession of Mary and the saints, compulsory fasting, pilgrimages as good works designed to earn forgiveness, clerical celibacy and monastic vows, the misuse of the Office of the Keys in excommunication and the great ban, rote prayers, the sale of indulgences, the doctrine of penance, the existence of purgatory, the role of the priesthood, the place of the state in religion, and other abuses. He argued that the medieval church had innovated and that he wished to restore the church to its original purity. Fabri intervened on some points, but Zwingli, armed with the Vulgate, his Greek New Testament and Hebrew Testament, outclassed all opponents and carried the day. The council was persuaded and declared that henceforth all teaching was to be based on the Bible alone, that all priests in the canton should support this position, and that the state would enforce this principle. The Zurich monasteries were dissolved and the council quietly took over their endowments as well as the control of the Great Minster. They turned the Dominican cloister into a hostel for the poor and the quarters of the Minster canons into a school. Thus in microcosm a reform was achieved that was to be repeated on a larger scale throughout Protestant Europe. Froschauer half a year later published Zwingli's *Interpretation and Substantiation of the Conclusions,* in which he contrasted church practices with the law of Christ and criticized traditional worship and liturgical music.

Attention now focused on the celebration of the mass and the veneration of images. Some Zwinglians cited the commandment against the making of graven images and a few incidents of iconoclasm occurred. In September Hans Hottinger, a shoemaker, overthrew a wayside crucifix at Stadelhofen, outside Zurich. Zwingli called for a second debate to discuss these issues. This second debate, in which Zwingli and Leo Jud were more ably opposed by a Catholic spokesman, Martin Steinli of Schaffhausen, began on October 26, 1523, and lasted three days. Some eight or nine hundred clergy and laity attended and Zwingli triumphed once again. Nevertheless, the council was cautious, voted to retain the mass and to tolerate the existence of images while permitting individuals to remove some of them, and appointed Zwingli and Jud to a commission to instruct the people in evangelical teachings. Zwingli penned a sharp attack on the veneration of and superstitious prayers before images, *A Brief Christian Introduction,* which reflected the influence of Ludwig Hätzer's *The Judgment of God Our Spouse as to How One Should Hold Oneself Toward All Idols and Images.* On December 28 a third disputation was held with the canons and clergy of Zurich, with the small and great councils present on the question of images and the mass. In April, 1524, the five forest cantons formed a Catholic alliance at Beckenried to oppose innovations. In a fourth disputation on January 19 and 20, 1524, Zwingli, Jud, and Engelhard thoroughly routed the opponents and convinced the council to adopt Zwingli's iconoclastic recommendations. On June 15, 1524, the council issued an order for the orderly removal of all images, pictures, and relics from the churches. Between June 20 and July 2 the "idols" were removed from the temples and the walls of the churches painted white. Zwingli's program of reform also called for the elimination of choir singing, organ music, congregational singing other than psalms, and anything not expressly authorized by Scriptures. A talented musician himself, Zwingli encouraged music and the fine arts in the home and in secular settings.[4] On April 12, 1525, the council with a narrow majority abrogated the celebration of the mass. During the Easter service the reformers celebrated communion in both kinds, bread and wine, from a table in the nave of the Minster, using wooden platters and tumblers. In the only truly systematic writing to come from his pen, his *Commentary on the True and False Religion,* dedicated to King Francis I, Zwingli had only a month earlier clearly stated his highly spiritual interpretation of the Lord's Supper, namely that Christ's presence in the sacrament could be received by faith alone in a communion that was intended to be commemorative and symbolic. The influence of the Erasmian philosophy of Christ and the emphasis on the spirit over the letter were evident in his exegesis, in his attitude toward material images, and in his sacramental doctrine. His personal theological views were skillfully parlayed into public positions and into concrete social realities. When the council suspended the mass, Zwingli's Reformation had triumphed in Zurich. The six years of life remaining to him he spent defending the reform in Zurich, attempting to extend it to other cantons, engaging in the sacramentarian controversy, struggling against the Anabaptist radicals, and in political and military maneuvering for the safety of Zurich against Catholic cantons, king, and emperor.[5]

4. Charles Garside, Jr., *Zwingli and the Arts* (New Haven, 1966), pp. 73–75.

5. These pages owe much to the insights of the authoritative biography of Zwingli, G. R. Potter, *Zwingli* (Cambridge, 1976), and a résumé, George Potter, *Ulrich Zwingli* (London, 1977). Walther Köhler, *Huldrych Zwingli* (Leipzig, 1943; 2d ed., Stuttgart, 1952), a

3. SACRAMENTARIAN CONTROVERSY

Zwingli's practical, rationalistic, and spiritualistic approach to the two dominical sacraments, baptism and the Sacrament of the Altar or Lord's Supper, led him into two major difficulties. In a striking way the Anabaptist movement in Zurich developed out of his own view of baptism as a sign and seal of regenerating grace rather than as a vehicle or means of grace in itself, through the power of the Word. The discussion of Anabaptism will be reserved for later pages, since the movement proliferated and belongs as much to the story of the Radical Reformation as to Zurich alone.

The other crisis related specifically to the Lord's Supper has come to be known as the sacramentarian controversy. Zwingli, in an Erasmian way, emphasized the commemorative, symbolic aspect of the celebration, the spiritual communion of the believer with Christ, and denied the corporeal presence of Christ's body and blood in the bread and wine. Like Luther, he opposed the medieval Catholic dogma of transubstantiation, that the essence or substance of the bread and wine are changed into Christ's body and blood by the sacerdotal act during the ceremony of the mass, a doctrine given official sanction by the Fourth Lateran Council in 1215. He also opposed the conception of the mass as a repeated though unbloody sacrifice of the original propitiatory death of Christ on the cross of Calvary. The eighteenth of the Sixty-seven Articles that Zwingli prepared for the First Zurich Disputation in 1523 reads:

> That Christ, having sacrificed Himself once, is to eternity a certain and valid sacrifice for the sins of all faithful, wherefrom it follows that the mass is not a sacrifice, but is a remembrance of the sacrifice and assurance of the salvation which God has given us.

theological liberal himself, saw Zwingli as torn between humanism and Reformation theology, strongly influenced by Luther. Oskar Farner, *Huldrych Zwingli,* 4 vols. (Zurich, 1943, 1946, 1954, 1960), for decades pastor in Zwingli's church and president of the cantonal church council, presented amazing detail on Zwingli in the local scene, but did not grasp his broader significance or wide influence. To be recommended also are the concise and perceptive studies of the Dominican scholar Jacques V. Pollet, *Huldrych Zwingli et la réforme en Suisse* (Paris, 1963) and "Zwinglianisme," *Dictionnaire de théologie catholique,* XV (Paris, 1950), cols. 3745–3928. The critical edition of Zwingli's works is at last nearing completion after more than seven decades: Emil Egli, Georg Finsler, *et. al.,* eds., *Huldreich Zwinglis Sämtliche Werke* (Berlin, Leipzig, Zurich, 1905–). Gäbler, *Huldrych Zwingli,* provides a review of Zwingli scholarship and an annotated bibliography of Zwingli literature 1897–1972, including 1,679 titles, updating Kurt Guggisberg, *Das Zwinglibild des Protestantismus im Wandel der Zeiten* (Leipzig, 1934).

While Zwingli agreed with Luther, then, on many major doctrinal aspects of the sacrament, they differed on the question of the real presence of Christ in the sacrament and on the nature of that presence. Zurich and Wittenberg were set on a collision course, although Luther and Zwingli did not attack each other's views openly until 1527. It is ironic that Luther's former Wittenberg colleague Andreas Karlstadt should have played an early role in the sacramentarian controversy which was to bring the magisterial reformers into direct conflict.

In 1524 Karlstadt wrote five tracts in which he developed a new conception of the Lord's Supper. He denied the real presence of Christ in the sacrament and offered the rather bizarre suggestion that when Christ on the night of the institution of the sacrament said, "This is my body," he pointed to his own body with his one hand at the same time as he gave bread to the disciples with the other. A dispute with Luther followed, and in the fall of 1524 Karlstadt was driven out of Saxony and fled to Strasbourg. Luther wrote an *Open Letter to the Christians in Strasbourg,* December, 1524, and a sharp treatise *Against the Heavenly Prophets concerning Images and the Sacrament,* January, 1525. The fact that it was one of his own false brethren who initiated the sacramentarian controversy, one who had also been involved in destruction of art and images in Wittenberg during his Wartburg days, led Luther to associate deviation on the sacrament with radical iconoclasm also in the case of Zurich.

In 1525 Zwingli made public his doctrine of the Lord's Supper, especially in the *Commentary on True and False Religion,* dedicated to Francis I. His formulation owed much to a Hague lawyer, Cornelis Henrixs Hoen, or Honius, who had written a letter about his ideas favoring a tropological interpretation of the words "This is my body"—that "is" really meant "signifies." He had developed this view under the influence of Wessel Gansfort's treatise *On the Sacrament the Eucharist* and combined a mystical with an Erasmian rationalistic spiritualist understanding of the text. Hoen had been imprisoned together with a Benedictine for being a "Lutheran" heretic. In 1524 Hinne Rode brought the elderly Hoen's letter to Zwingli, who was deeply impressed. Hinne Rode had earlier brought this same letter to Luther in Wittenberg, who replied that although he was by nature inclined to favor this symbolical interpretation, he found the scriptural statement too clear and too powerful to be tampered with. Although the Strasbourg reformers had rejected Karlstadt, Martin Bucer and others there inclined toward the symbolic interpretation. In Switzerland Oecolampadius sided with Zwingli. In Schwäbisch-Hall the Württemberg reformer Johannes Brenz came out in favor of Luther's position on the real presence. The lines were being drawn for the sacramentarian controversy that was to introduce the <u>first great schism into the evangelical camp</u>.

In 1525 Zwingli published Hoen's letter anonymously as *Certainly a Christian Epistle.* He wrote out his views in the form of a letter which he sent to friends and eventually published in March, 1525, as "A Letter to Matthew Alber concerning the Lord's Supper." He explained to the Lutheran reformer of Reutlingen that the Lord's Supper is a memorial, a joyous celebration for the redemption won by Christ's death. The words of institution are to be understood symbolically. Zwingli was attacked from the Catholic side by Joachim am Grütt of Zurich and decided that he would now present his position in German. He published *A Clear Instruction Concerning the Lord's Supper* on February 23, which evoked a strong response from his Catholic critic.

Meanwhile Luther was increasingly disturbed by the direction in which Zwingli was moving, for he perceived that this "reformed" way of conceiving of the nature of Christ's presence not only was far removed from the traditional understanding of the sacrament and interpretation of the words of institution, but that it involved some serious implications for Chalcedonian Christology. In 1526 he published against the Zwinglian teaching *A Sermon Concerning the Sacrament of the Body and Blood of Christ, Against the Fanatics.* Zwingli responded with *A Friendly Exegesis,* on February 28, 1527, in which part one was directed against Luther and part two offered an interpretation of the words of institution. In April Luther answered with a treatise *That These Words "This Is My Body" Still Stand, Against the Enthusiasts.* On June 20 Zwingli published *That These Words of Jesus Christ "This Is My Body Given for You" will eternally always have their Old Original Meaning. . . . Huldrych Zwingli's Christian Answer.* At the end of March, 1528, Luther published his *Great Confession Concerning the Lord's Supper* in which he developed the Wittenberg position and rejected Zwinglian "enthusiasm" or spiritualistic enthusiasm. His tone was condescending and Zwingli complained that he "did not like being treated like an ass." To Conrad Saum at Ulm he fumed, "That rash man Luther keeps killing human and divine wisdom in his books, though it would have been easy to restore this wisdom among the pious. But since the heretics, that is, his followers, together with the wicked, have become so deaf to all truth that they refuse to listen, I was for a long time doubtful about expending this enormous labor which I know would be vain. . . . May I die if he does not surpass Eck in impurity, Cochlaeus in audacity, and, in brief, all the vices of men!" Luther, in turn, wrote to Gregory Casel, "In a word, either they or we must be ministers of Satan. There is no room here for negotiation or mediation." The sacramental question remained in the center of attention, for the Catholic polemicists continued to defend the mass against innovators. At Baden in 1526 and at the disputation in Bern in January, 1528, an extensive discussion of the Lord's Supper took place. It seemed clear that the evangelicals would have to begin some form of colloquy in order to bridge the growing doctrinal division between them, but when the unity efforts were made, the motivation was highly political and the initiator was young Landgrave Philipp of Hesse.[6]

The immediate occasion for Philipp's determination to try for the political unification of the Protestants was the decision of the Diet of Speyer to enforce the Edict of Worms, which evoked the formal "protest" of the evangelical estates on April 19, 1529. Their situation was perilous, Philipp felt vulnerable, and soon after the diet adjourned he contacted Zwingli about religious discussions that would bring about the unity necessary for a common political program. On May 7 Zwingli responded with enthusiasm and asked when and where the meeting could take place. On July 1 Philipp sent Zwingli a formal invitation and shortly thereafter he also invited Luther, Melanchthon, Jakob Sturm of Strasbourg, Oecolampadius of Basel, Andreas Osiander of Nuremberg, and Johannes Brenz of Schwäbisch-Hall, the meeting to take place in Marburg on September 30. Zwingli traveled via Basel to pick up Oecolampadius, preached in Strasbourg, where Sturm, Caspar Hedio, and Martin Bucer joined his party, and arrived in Marburg on September 27. Luther and his group arrived on September 30; Osiander, Brenz, and Stephan Agricola of Augsburg came October 1. The colloquy lasted from the first to the third of October and made astonishing progress.

On the first day Luther met with Oecolampadius, and Melanchthon with Zwingli. The second day the main session began with the two leading Wittenbergers seated opposite the two Swiss. Luther wished to discuss a wide range of theological questions, and agreement was reached on fourteen of the fifteen points proposed for discussion. The Marburg Articles

6. René Hauswirth, *Landgraf Philipp von Hessen und Zwingli: Vorraussetzungen und Geschichte der politischen Beziehungen zwischen Hessen, Straszburg, Konstanz, Ulrich von Württemberg and reformierten Eidgenossen 1526–1531. Schriften zur Kirchen- und Rechtsgeschichte,* 35 (Tübingen and Basel, 1968), 100–166.

were a torso of the seventeen Schwabach articles devised earlier by the Lutherans, to which Ulm and Strasbourg would not subscribe. On the final question, the real corporeal presence of Christ in the sacrament, there was no possibility of agreement. Luther went so far as to refrain from describing the manner of Christ's real sacramental presence, but Zwingli remained adamant, insisting on the symbolic nature of the sacrament. To Bucer Luther spoke these words intended also for Zwingli: "You have a different spirit." Melanchthon, thinking perhaps of relations with the Catholics, opposed greater concessions to the Zwinglians. The fifteenth point of the Marburg Confession of October 4, then, was a carefully worded agreement to disagree on the question of the real presence of Christ in the sacrament, but expressed a common position denying the efficacy of the sacrifice of the mass for the living and the dead, affirming communion in both kinds, asserting that the sacrament was a divine gift of grace, and that it had to do with a "spiritual" benefit. All of the theologians present signed the Marburg Confession, but both sides were soon asserting that the other had yielded on the essential point in dispute.[7]

On January 21, 1530, Emperor Charles V issued his summons to the diet in Augsburg for April 8, including the Swiss. It was there that the Lutherans presented their basic Augsburg Confession. Four south German cities, Strasbourg, Constance, Memmingen, and Lindau, submitted their own *Confessio tetrapolitana,* or four-city confession. The Zwinglians were thus pushed aside, but Jakob Sturm asked Zwingli for a confession of faith, which he wrote as the *Fidei ratio* ("On account of the faith"), organized around the Apostle's Creed. He made no concessions on the sacramental question and it was quite evident that the division of Protestantism on the doctrinal level was final. Landgrave Philipp's plans for political unity in defense against the emperor and Catholic princes suffered a severe setback after Marburg. Philipp schemed, with Zwingli's approval, to set up an anti-Habsburg coalition of foreign powers—Denmark, Venice, and France. Luther opposed these efforts in part because of his inhibitions about opposing the constituted authority of the emperor and in part because of his doubts about the realism of such schemes. As the Catholic cantons in Switzerland allied more closely for resistance to the reformed city-states, Zwingli and Zurich were to pay a heavy price for their isolation from the Protestant estates of the Empire.

7. Walther Köhler, *Zwingli und Luther. Ihr Streit über das Abendmahl nach seinen politischen and religiösen Beziehungen, Quellen und Forschungen zur Reformationsgeschichte,* 7 (Gütersloh, 1953), 63–163.

4. CIVIL WAR IN SWITZERLAND

Zwingli's last years saw the further institutionalization of the Reformation in Zurich, diplomatic maneuvering on the part of the hostile camps, a fatal compromise with the world of politics, and finally the war that was to cost him his life. Much nonsense has been written about Zwingli's theocracy in Zurich, as though the Reformed Church and its leader dominated the city-state. Actually, Zwingli's ideal of the commonwealth envisioned a theocracy, but one in which both church and state under God, each in its sphere, served Christian ends and the good of all members of the religio-political congregation *(Gemeinde* or *Volck).* The institutionalization of the Reformation in Zurich marked the end of a long process by which the city magistracy's authority was extended over all aspects of the external affairs of the church, while the church with a new sense of purpose concentrated its efforts on the preaching of the gospel.[8]

Zwingli's ideal reflected the Gelasian principle of the relation of church and state prominent in the early Middle Ages before the attempts of the church to dominate the state or federal powers. The control of church external affairs by the city government was an urban case of the proprietary church arrangement characteristic especially of the later Middle Ages, which allowed the authorities not only control over the properties of the church within their legal jurisdiction, but also the decisive voice in the appointment of clergy to vacant ecclesiastical positions. In Zurich, an imperial city that joined the Swiss confederacy in 1351, there was a long tradition of republican freedom, with the franchise extended to the benefit of the artisan guilds at the expense of the landed gentry and merchant patricians. The city's Christian magistracy governed the whole body of the citizenry and there was little distinction between the people as members of the parish and the people as members of the commonwealth. It was not a novelty at all, then, for Zwingli to look to the city authorities for help in ordering the external affairs of the church. From Erasmus he had learned to be skeptical of the church's ability to reform itself and favored reducing its wealth and shifting control of its properties to the secular

8. Robert C. Walton, "The Institutionalization of the Reformation at Zurich," *Zwingliana,* XIII, no. 8 (1972), 497–575. Walton's important book, *Zwingli's Theocracy* (Toronto, 1967), p. 218, concludes that the desire to ensure the gospel its rightful place in the life of the community is the key to understanding Zwingli's attitude toward government. At every point, he says (p. 220), the development of Zwingli's political thought was conditioned by a corporate theory of society.

authorities so that the church could concentrate on its spiritual tasks, for the real church consisted of all those people who believed in Christ as the resurrected Savior and followed Him. He was acting consistently with his theory when in 1523 he requested the government to call an independent Reformation colloquy or disputation in order to settle disagreements over the preaching of the gospel which were disturbing public order, and when he petitioned for the second disputation to settle the issues of the mass and images which were causing civil strife. The magistracy, in turn, was acting in line with many pre-Reformation precedents when it intervened in this manner. In 1528 Zwingli proposed a plan for appointing clergy in the canton, which his successor, Heinrich Bullinger, put in final form and was accepted by the council on October 22, 1532. A committee of examiners was to interrogate candidates for vacant parish positions, and this committee was to include the members of the city Council of Fifty. The candidates were to swear obedience to the authority of Scriptures, to the doctrine of the Reformation, and to the magistracy.[9] The competence of the church synod was limited to matters of doctrine and to questions arising from the behavior of the clergy. All other "external" matters were to be referred to the council. Citizenship and churchmanship were inextricably interwoven. Zwingli was not merely being opportunistic, then, when he turned to the magistracy for help or when he involved himself in the cantonal relations and foreign affairs. The relation of church and state in Zurich was characteristic of many other city-states, and Zwingli's view of society was typical of the dominant political thought throughout most of sixteenth-century Europe.

As the Reformation spread from Zurich to the other Swiss cantons, their magistracies were also actively involved in developments. While the so-called forest cantons of Uri, Schwyz, and Unterwalden together with Zug, Lucerne, and Fribourg remained Catholic, Bern, Basel, St. Gall, Schaffhausen, Glarus, Appenzell, and lesser cities joined the Reformation. Joachim von Watt, or Vadian, who distinguished himself for his humanist learning at the University of Vienna, moved by his own study of the Scriptures to an evangelical reformed position between 1519 and 1523. He became the leader of the Reformation in St. Gall and was a stalwart

9. Robert C. Walton, "Institutionalization," p. 508. Hans Morf, "Obrigkeit und Kirche in Zürich bis zu Beginn der Reformation," *Zwingliana*, XIII, no. 3 (1970), 164–205, citing precedents, states that long before the Reformation the magistracy was responsible for ecclesiastical orders.

leader in that city, so long under the shadow of its famous monastery, until his death in 1551.[10] Zwingli's influence for a time was extended also to some south German cities. The spread of the Reformation came to a temporary standstill following the disputation at Baden in the Aargau in May, 1526. Baden, which had been moving in its own way toward reform, following Zurich's precedent, arranged a disputation. This time, however, the Catholic side was represented by able polemicists such as Johannes Eck, Johannes Faber, and Thomas Murner. The Protestant side was headed by Oecolampadius and Berchthold Haller, a former canon at Bern, who had read the Bible, but was no great scholar, and though considered to be a Lutheran was a supporter of Oecolampadius. Zwingli suffered loss of nerve and failed to attend the colloquy, apparently intimidated by the presence of Eck, a hostile Catholic audience, and the prospect of being seized and martyred. His absence marked the low point of his career and assured a Catholic triumph. The Zurich magistracy forbade him to go, fearing that it was a setup to declare him a heretic, but his failure to go seriously set back his cause.

The reformers, however, regained the initiative at the disputation in Bern held in January, 1528, where the evangelical cause was represented by Zwingli, Bucer, Capito, Haller, and others. In many ways this disputation was the climax of Zwingli's career. It was Zwinglian Bern that saved Geneva from Catholic domination and thus preserved it as an independent center for Calvin's activity. Doctrinal disputes were soon superseded by political and military alliances which led to war. Just as in the Empire Catholic and Protestant leagues of princes were forming, so in the microcosm of Switzerland the cantons allied in hostile groups and sought foreign support. First five Catholic cantons organized a defensive alliance. Thereupon Zurich joined with Constance in a "Christian Defense Alliance," which Bern, Basel, and lesser cities soon joined. The Catholic response was to form a firmer alliance of the five cantons with King Ferdinand, the Habsburg king of Austria-Hungary and brother of Emperor Charles V. For complex reasons Ferdinand decided against military support for the Catholic cantons and their dropping the Austrian alliance prevented a war and led to the First Peace of Kappel, 1529.

Zwingli's aggressive psychology asserted itself and clouded his good judgment. He developed a first-strike preventive war mentality and pro-

10. See the exemplary biography by Werner Näf, *Vadian und seine Stadt St. Gallen,* 2 vols. (St. Gallen, 1944, 1957).

posed economic sanctions against the Catholic cantons that would keep essentials like salt from reaching them. This move merely increased the desperation and hardened the resolve of the Catholic cantons to strike at Zurich, the main cause of their troubles. In 1531 the Five Cantons fielded an army against Zurich. The Zurichers, abandoned by Bern, hastily gathered a force which, only half-prepared and badly outnumbered, went out to meet the enemy. Zwingli, dressed in a green mantle under armor, fought as a common soldier in that battle at Kappel on October 11 and died on the field. An executioner had his body quartered and burned as a heretic's. The second Peace of Kappel, 1531, prohibited the further expansion of the Reformation in Switzerland. Ironically, with the coming of John Calvin to Geneva a very few years later, the French part of Switzerland became the center not only for a renewal of the reform movement in Switzerland but for the second surge of Protestantism in France and other parts of Europe.

The reformer of Basel, Oecolampadius, died just a few weeks after Zwingli and was succeeded there by Oswald Myconius.[11] Zwingli's son-in-law Heinrich Bullinger (1504–1575) became his successor in Zurich. By concentrating on theology and the spiritual mission of the church, Bullinger exercised an enormous influence on the development of Protestantism as far away as the Netherlands and England, under Edward VI, during succeeding decades. Within Switzerland the First Helvetic Confession (*Confessio Helvetica Prior*) of 1536 served as a common Zwinglian doctrinal statement for the Protestants. Bullinger and Calvin in 1549 negotiated the Zurich agreement (*Consensus Tigurinus*). Bullinger's private confession was published in 1566 by Elector Frederick of the Palatinate and it was accepted in Switzerland as the Second Helvetic Confession (*Posterior*), which characterized the Swiss Reformed Church down to present times.

5. ANABAPTISM

In a mighty spiritual movement such as the Reformation, all segments of the population were stirred up and swept along. In addition to the magisterial reformers and the main-line Protestant churches, the radical or left wing developed as well. If the Protestant church types were close to the Catholic in ecclesiastical structure and place in their societies, the

11. For a perceptive sketch of Johannes Oecolampadius, see Gordon Rupp, *Patterns of Reformation* (Philadelphia, 1969), pp. 1–46.

radicals deviated in two ways. Sects such as the Anabaptists moved as independent groups along a horizontal base line on a graph, but the individual spiritualist or mystical types and the evangelical rationalists or anti-Trinitarians, as they were once generally called, moved upward along the vertical line of the same graph. The Catholic and main-line Protestant churches, constituting over 95% of all Protestants, sought to hold a central position which embraced both social cohesion and concern as well as individual religions feeling and impulses. There has been an astonishing increase in contemporary scholarship devoted to the Radical Reformation in recent years, which can be attributed to the maturation of Mennonite scholarship, to a greater interest in church-state issues, and to the Marxist preoccupation with the Peasant Revolt, the Kingdom of Münster, and the communal aspect of the sectaries. There has also been an improved perspective on the origins of the radical sects. Ernst Troeltsch and older authorities saw the radicals basically as a spin-off from humanism and the Reformation. More recent studies point to the roots of many radical ideas in medieval heretical groups, in the long history of utopians pursuing the millennium, and in the laicizing and internalizing elements of the medieval ascetic tradition.[12] It is not merely by chance that the Reformation sectaries flourished as had the medieval heresies mainly in the Rhine valley and in the Netherlands.

Because the Anabaptist movement was so amorphous, scattered, and lacking in articulate and learned spokesmen, it is hazardous to offer a statement of its doctrines. The nearest thing to a formal dogmatic statement is the modest *Schleitheim Confession of Faith* in seven articles written mostly by the saintly Michael Sattler, who was burned to death in 1527 by the Austrian authorities as a seditious person and a heretic.[13] Yet most of these diverse groups given the common name Anabaptists by historians

12. Kenneth Ronald Davis, *Anabaptism and Asceticism: A Study in Intellectual Origins* (Scottdale, Pa., 1974), argues that Anabaptism derived its basic ideals and original impulse from the Christian ascetic tradition and was related more to this branch of the medieval Catholic church than to the tradition of medieval heresy and relates it more to Erasmian spiritualism than to the thought of the major reformers. While there is some truth in this thesis, it must be remembered that Zwingli, too, was Erasmian in basic ways. Moreover, what can be said of the initial leadership of Anabaptism does not preclude a spread of these groups still festering with medieval heretical notions.

13. John C. Wenger, "The Schleitheim Confession of Faith," *The Mennonite Quarterly Review*, XIX, No. 4 (Oct., 1945), 247–252. On Sattler's trial and execution, see Tilman J. van Braght's *Martyr's Mirror* (1660); George H. Williams, ed., *Spiritual and Anabaptist Writers*, The Library of Christian Classics, XXV (London, 1957), pp. 138–144.

shared certain emphases. Theologically they deemphasized the Holy Scriptures in favor of the mystical testimony of the inner Word or Light. They gave new prominence to the influence of the Holy Spirit, the third person of the Trinity. In anthropology they stressed sin as transgression rather than as a root condition of unbelief or unspirituality. They ascribed to man an important degree of free will, so that the Christian can truly imitate Christ and live according to the evangelical counsels of Christ's Sermon on the Mount. In ecclesiology they stressed adult or believer's baptism, after a person reaches the age of accountability, rebaptizing (hence the name Anabaptist) those baptized previously as infants. The Lord's Supper was given a strong symbolic or commemorative interpretation. Church discipline was rigorous as each local group considered itself to be a congregation of real saints on earth and any members deviating from pure doctrine and holy life were absolutely excluded from the community. Their church was to be coterminous with the kingdom of Christ here below. They were millenarian and awaited the eschaton or second coming of Christ at any moment, an expectation that cooled as the century moved on.

Certain Anabaptist tenets and practices seemed to the main-line reformers, the Catholic Church and the civil authorities, whether princes or city magistrates, to be subversive of faith and civil order. The magisterial reformers felt that the Anabaptists' appeal to an inner light for direct revelation from the Holy Spirit apart from Scriptures, undercut their stress on the Scriptures as the source and norm of doctrine. They thought that the Anabaptists' legalism and pretense to sainthood on earth subverted the proper relation of the sanctification of Christian life to justification by faith. The tendency to reject established churches in favor of a "gathered church" of saints and the hostility toward governments, even though on the level of passive resistance and endurance, aroused in society the fear of anarchy. Moreover, some groups practiced common possession of property and polygamy, and some were even said to share wives. The lunatic fringe contributed to their bad press, when, for example, a few extremists had intercourse on an altar less to show their contempt for the sacred than to demonstrate their ability to perform a sex act in all purity. The most extreme tenets and worst actions of the few tended to be ascribed to all, of course, so that the whole movement was held suspect by solid citizens and the authorities alike. It was not only the communism and fantastic apocalypticism of certain extremists like the Melchiorites that roused fear and anger, but such positions as refusal to take oaths at all, including swearing obedience to the civil authorities; denouncing all interest charges on loans, some refusing to engage in commerce at all; and favoring the abolition of all titles. The authorities, Protestant and Catholic alike, viewed them as subversives and treated them as such. A similar phenomenon of rebaptizers had arisen in the eastern Roman Empire in ancient times and the Roman law, now enjoying a revival, imposed the death penalty on them. Magistrates enforced the edict now and found beyond beheading and burning that drowning had an appropriate symbolic significance.

Zwingli's Reformation provided the soil from which Anabaptism grew. The first Anabaptists were Konrad Grebel, Felix Mantz, and the Waldshut pastor Balthasar Hübmaier. Grebel, of a patrician family, was born in 1498, studied in Basel, Vienna, and Paris, studied with Glareanus, and belonged to Zwingli's circle of friends. His sister married Vadian. Felix Mantz was a Zurich priest, born around 1500, and enjoyed some humanistic education. He studied Hebrew and sided with Zwingli in theology and reform. Zwingli's deliberate pace in effecting reform, however, was not sufficiently speedy for Grebel, Mantz, and their circle. On September 5, 1524, they wrote a letter to Thomas Münzer in Thuringia, under the influence of the spiritualistic Zwickau prophets, saying that the evangelical preachers (such as Zwingli) were not obedient to the Scriptures, for the church was a small minority of true believers and saints, not the whole community baptized as infants. Thereby the conflict about pedobaptism began. On January 17, 1525, Zwingli debated the issue with Grebel, and the members of the council who were present judged that Zwingli had made his case on the basis of Scripture for infant baptism and his view of the church. Grebel and Mantz were forbidden to speak further in public, while others of the group, including Ludwig Hätzer and Wilhelm Röubli, were banned from the city. On January 21, 1525, the circle assembled secretly, probably in the house of Felix Mantz's mother on the Neugasse near the Great Minster. There Grebel baptized Georg Blaurock, who, in turn, baptized all others present. The following day Grebel celebrated the Lord's Supper in the neighboring village of Zollikon, and the first adult baptism took place there. In less than a week thirty-five persons were baptized and formed the first Anabaptist congregation, the start of a new religious movement.

The persecution and exile of the Anabaptists in canton Zurich led to their dispersion to the Tyrolean Alps, Moravia, lower Rhine, and Friesia. Blaurock fled to the Tyrol, where he was executed in 1529, but was succeeded in the cause by Jacob Hutter. The Tyrolean Brethren attracted dissidents both from German and from North Italian areas. Hübmaier and Michael Sattler, chief author of that 1527 Schleitheim Confession, worked in the upper Danube area. Sattler was captured in Rottenburg on the Neckar River, was accused of civil disobedience and unwillingness to bear arms even against the Turk, and was tortured and burned to death in 1527. Hübmaier converted Hans Denck, whom Bucer called the pope of the Anabaptists. He was rector of the St. Sebaldus school in Nuremberg, but was driven out in 1529 for spiritualistic tenets, having rejected ceremonies, sacraments, and finally even the Scriptures in favor of direct inspiration by the Holy Spirit and the inner light. He died of the plague in Basel in 1527. Hübmaier went on into South Moravia, where he converted some landed nobility, who, in turn, made land available for the influx of thousands of Anabaptists, who organized dozens of communities. Hübmaier was executed by fire in Vienna in 1528, and his wife was drowned. Ludwig Hätzer, the former chaplain in Zurich, worked in Augsburg, Strasbourg, and the Palatinate, but was beheaded for adultery in Constance in 1529. Hans Hut, a real extremist, and a very popular preacher in Franconia, escaped from the battle at Frankenhausen, where Münzer was captured, but died in Augsburg in 1527 of a prison fire which the firebrand had started himself. Jacob Hutter from the Tyrol saved the movement by introducing communal farming and a very patriarchal form of community organization. By the time Hutter was executed in 1536 the Moravian Brethren or Hutterites were firmly established in Moravia, with even a few communities in Hungary.

The movement spread down the Rhine, as well as the Danube, though the cause was damaged by more fanatical leaders such as Melchior Hoffmann, a furrier from Schwäbisch-Hall, who preached the coming of the heavenly Jerusalem on earth. This fantasy-ridden man bothered Zwingli in 1523, visited Luther, wandered through Livland, Sweden, East Frisia, and the Rhineland preaching the apocalypse and the triumph of the 144,-000 virgins at the end of time. In 1529 he joined the Anabaptists in Strasbourg, a city with a tradition of relative tolerance, but he was driven out and wandered through the Netherlands prophecying the immanence of the Second Coming of Christ. He proclaimed himself to be the second Elijah preaching the day of wrath when all the unrighteous would perish.

He returned to Strasbourg just as the authorities had their fill of Anabaptists, was arrested, languished in prison for ten years, where he died in 1543. But his bitter harvest was not yet in.

The Melchiorites stirred up the common people in the Netherlands. Jan Matthys, a Haarlem baker, took up a theme already proposed by Münzer: the saints must wipe out the unrighteous and thus prepare the way for the coming of the Lord. But the Habsburg ruler and local authorities successfully controlled and repressed the extremists. Their big chance came in the city of Münster not far from the border in Westphalia. There the great Anabaptist catastrophe played itself out. By the early 1530s Lutherans controlled the council and town in opposition to the bishop, a kind of urban-feudal overlord hostility familiar in the history of such cities as Cologne from the twelfth century on. By 1533, due to the preaching of the chaplain Bernt Rothmann, himself close to the radical fringe, the Reformation won out. The mayor of the city, Bernt Knipperdolling, a textile merchant, had encountered Melchior Hoffmann in Sweden and inclined toward the enthusiasts. January, 1534, saw the influx of Melchiorites from Holland, who had heard of the triumph of radical reform in Münster. Both Rothmann and Knipperdolling joined forces with them in making Münster over into the new Jerusalem.[14] In February the Dutch Anabaptist prophet Jan Bockelson, an ex-tailor of Leiden, arrived and Jan Matthys, a baker from Haarlem, came shortly after to take over the control of the council and city. They forced all by law to be rebaptized and those Catholics and Lutherans who refused were driven by the mobs out of the city into the snow and onto the spears of the bishop's forces outside the walls. Matthys declared the state communist with the abolition of all private property. All books except the Bible were forbidden, confiscated, and burned. The bishop, Franz von Waldeck, put the city under siege. Matthys, proletarian dictator of the city, following a direct command from God, who promised him invulnerability, made a wild sortie outside the walls and was killed by the bishop's troops. Now Jan Bockelson of Leiden, a madman, crowned himself king over the Kingdom of Zion in Münster, ruled from a throne surrounded by courtiers, ruthlessly executed all oppo-

14. James M. Stayer, "Melchior Hoffmann and the Sword," *Mennonite Quarterly Review,* 45 (July, 1971), 265–277; "The Münsterite Rationalization of Bernhard Rothmann," *Journal of the History of Ideas,* 28 (April–June, 1967), 179–192. On Rothmann, see Jack W. Porter, "*Bernhard Rothmann,* 1495–1534: Royal Orator of the Münster Anabaptist Kingdom" (diss., University of Wisconsin, 1964).

nents, declared polygamy, created a new nobility and an armed guard, and began a reign of terror. From the early months of 1535 on the siege began taking its toll and famine stalked the streets. People ate rats and other vermin and in a weakened condition could not adequately man the walls. A few escapees betrayed the weak spots in the defenses to the forces of the bishop and of Margrave Philipp of Hesse, who had sent auxiliary troops. On June 25, 1535, they stormed the walls and captured the city, inflicting a fierce slaughter and penalties on the Anabaptists. They tortured King Jan and Knipperdolling to death and put the bodies of the leaders in an iron cage suspended from the church steeple as a warning to all. The city became once again officially Catholic. This fiasco of Münster gave to the entire Anabaptist cause a terrible reputation, and thousands died as martyrs in the persecution that followed.

After the way of force had proved to be such folly, the Anabaptists reverted to their earlier general pacific tradition.[15] In the Netherlands Menno Simons (1496–1561), a priest from Frisia who was converted to the cause in 1536, became the leader of the peaceful Anabaptists. They enforced rigid saintly discipline away from the world, typically rejecting infant baptism and the swearing of oaths, for Christ had said to swear not at all, but to let one's communication be merely yea, yea and nay, nay. For the rest their teachings did not vary greatly from the tenets of the Dutch reformed churches. They spread throughout east and west Frisia, along the lower Rhine, to Holstein and along the Baltic. After much persecution they finally were given toleration in 1572 in Holland and later in Switzerland and various north German cities such as Hamburg, Danzig, and Emden.

The Anabaptists were badly fragmented and only a part became Mennonites. Some followed the Delft glass painter David Joris, a radical follower of Melchior Hoffmann, who prophesied the imminent second coming of Christ. He withdrew, however, to Basel, where he lived incognito for twelve years, apparently as a good Zwinglian, until he died in 1556. Two years after his death the horrified council learned of his true identity, had his body exhumed, tied to a stake, and burned along with a box filled with his writings. Pilgram Marpeck was destined to become the major spokesman for Anabaptism in South Germany. Born in the small mining town of Rattenberg in the Tyrol around 1495, he became a town councillor and

15. On the problem of peacemindedness and power, see the well-researched volume by James M. Stayer, *Anabaptists and the Sword* (Lawrence, Kan., 1972).

municipal engineer. He was interested in Lutheranism, but moved on to Anabaptism. He abandoned his estate and in 1527 fled to Strasbourg. His views were socially oriented, he opposed injustices to the lower classes and usury, and, after Münster, he became the major spokesman for a responsible, pacifist, evangelical Anabaptism, orthodox in such dogmas as the Trinity, Christology, and eschatology. Bucer felt obligated to respond to his doctrinal statements in defense of the main-line Reformation. The council eventually imposed public silence on him and in 1532 he was obliged to leave Strasbourg. He wandered about to Ulm, Austerlitz, and various South German cities. He was involved in a great debate with the evangelical spiritualist Caspar Schwenckfeld, when he became disturbed over the defection of many moderate Anabaptists to the ways of inner light and lack of communal discipline. From 1544 on Marpeck lived in Augsburg and worked as an engineer in the city water works until his death in 1556, suffering only occasional warnings to cut his ties with the Anabaptists, which he ignored.[16]

Anabaptism appealed for the most part to the poor, the weak, the disaffected and resentful. It helped to cultivate in them a large measure of patience in suffering, peace-mindedness, gentleness, and basic piety, but this wholesome effect cannot conceal the fact that the in-group spirit often led to exclusiveness and intolerance toward the unwashed outsiders and unredeemed secular and ecclesiastical authorities. For example, Hans Hergot, beheaded in Leipzig in 1526, in a Joachimite way prophesied the coming of the third age of the world, the rule of the Holy Spirit which would eliminate all nobility, destroy the wealth of the monasteries, and inaugurate the age of the common man.[17] Münster, was, of course, a disastrous radical aberration from the norm, but an element of compensatory spiritual pride and contempt for those not numbered with the saints is also present elsewhere, revealing a proletarian *ressentiment.* They numbered less than one percent of the population and in many of the scattered villages where artisans and petty burghers adhered to the sect, there were frequently fewer than half a dozen members. They did not reshape political, economic, or social institutions or have any immediate major impact on the course of history. They clearly do not constitute a significant third

16. John C. Wenger, "The Life and Work of Pilgram Marpeck," *Mennonite Quarterly Review,* XII (1938), 137–166.

17. *Hans Hergot und die Flugschrift von der Wandlung eynes Christlichen Lebens. Faksimilewiedergabe mit Umschrift* (Leipzig, 1977).

force in the Reformation. Nevertheless, it would be a mistake to underestimate their long-term importance. Magistrates reacted with authoritarian and repressive measures. The established churches reemphasized the rite of confirmation and in the case of the Lutherans associated it with preparation for communion, to counteract late baptism. The sectarian aspect and puritanical pretensions of the Anabaptists, especially the Dutch Brethren, influenced the proliferation of sects in Elizabethan and Jacobean England. There was a very indirect influence on the modern constitutional provisions for the separation of church and state. But above all, the millenarian vision did not die with them. Until the eschaton, the end of time, however, it remains completely unrealistic to believe that society can be ruled by love rather than by government, law, and the sword.

6. SPIRITUALISTS AND EVANGELICAL HUMANISTS

The Radical Reformation as loosely related congeries of people bent on reform and restitution included in addition to the Anabaptist sectarian groups individuals with spiritualizing and humanistic tendencies. The spiritualists, whom the magisterial reformers regarded as "enthusiasts," were northern for the most part and were given to mystical speculative tendencies. The evangelical humanists, largely Italian in origin, inclined toward rationalism, and reflected Renaissance Neoplatonic and pantheistic influence. They were in the older historical literature characterized as anti-Trinitarian, but this deviation was related more to a rejection of Chalcydonian or Greek creedal terminology, while only a few went so far as to espouse genuine unitarianism, denying the deity of Christ.[18]

The spiritualists were religious subjectivists who wished to lead their lives guided directly by the Holy Spirit or an inner light without being bound by an objective authority such as the Scriptures or by external standards imposed by a religious community, whether the Catholic, Evangelical, Reformed, or Anabaptist church groups. They were related to the tradition of medieval religious mysticism, were in some cases touched by Renaissance Platonic nature mysticism, and were caught up by the accent of Pentecost and the gifts of the Holy Spirit recorded in

18. George Hunston Williams, *The Radical Reformation* (Philadelphia, 1962), xxiv, *et passim,* distinguished three types of radicals; the Anabaptists, spiritualists, and evangelical rationalists. The term evangelical humanists reflects more accurately the Renaissance influence on them and precludes any anachronistic suggestion of an anticipation of eighteenth-century rationalism.

the Acts of the Apostles. Since personally experienced revelation was the only source of certainty, they placed a great deal of emphasis upon psychological self-observation and frequently spun off into more or less fantastic speculation.

The lines between the three types of radicals were not clearly drawn, as can be seen from the case of Ludwig Hätzer, who associated with Anabaptist groups, but followed his own inner light. Hätzer, born around 1500, studied at Basel, came under humanistic influences, was ordained a priest, and became a supporter of Zwingli; but he was impatient with the slow pace of reform, became an iconoclast, and joined the Anabaptists. Exiled from Zurich in 1521, he was typical in his restlessness and instability, which, coupled with the hostility of magistrates, kept him on the move from Augsburg to Basel, Strasbourg, Worms, to Augsburg, again, then to Basel, where he was befriended by Oecolampadius, then to Strasbourg, where he encountered the spiritualist Hans Denck and became his follower. He and Denck went from there to Worms. In Constance he was arrested on the basis of a complaint from the city of Augsburg that he had created disturbances in many towns. On February 3, 1529, he was condemned to be beheaded. In the marketplace he admonished the crowds to keep the gospel in heart and life and said his last prayer at the very spot where John Hus had been burned at the stake more than a century earlier.

The archetypal figure of the spiritualists was Sebastian Franck of Donauworth (1499–1542), who ran the gamut from early humanist influence, to the priesthood in Augsburg, the Lutheran ministry in Nuremberg, from which he resigned in 1528, to life as a free spirit. In Nuremberg he supported himself as a printer and popular writer. He published his translation of a *Turkish Chronicle* written by a Transylvanian Saxon who had been a prisoner of the Turks for twenty-two years. In the preface he contrasted the simplicity of Turkish rites with the complicated liturgy and dogmas of Christendom. A new church of the spiritualists is now arising, he declared with approval, which will be an invisible spiritual church without exterior means and forms of worship. He disliked the legalistic Anabaptist groups as much as he did the main-line churches. In 1529 he moved to Strasbourg, where he was naturally attracted to Caspar Schwenkfeld, with his doctrine of the celestial flesh of Christ. "The Spirit and the Word of God" working within man was his only authority, not the "letters" of the Scriptures. He reinterpreted Christology and Trinitarian theology, and espoused a mythical ethic. His truly famous book, however, was the *Chronicle, Book of the Times, and History Bible (Chronica, Zeitbuch und Geschichtsbibel)*, 1531. This *Chronicle* gave an account of world history from creation to Christ in the first part, the history of the emperors from Augustus to Charles V in the second part, and a chronicle of the popes from Peter to Clement VII, the church councils, and the heretics down to the Anabaptists and Erasmus in the third part. Under pressure from Bucer, he left Strasbourg for Kehl, then Esslingen, where he became a soap maker. Then he moved to Ulm and published his geography *(Weltbuch)* in Tübingen, as a fourth part of his chronicle. In 1534 he published his *Paradoxa,* his basic theological work—much influenced by the mystical book the *German Theology (Theologia Deutsch)*—in which he pitted spirit against the world and literal Scripture. In 1539 he was exiled from Ulm with his printing presses and moved to Basel with wife and children. He continued to publish his own works in other cities, probably in order to evade the local censors, until his death in the fall of 1542. He maintained a basic hold on Luther's doctrine of justification by grace and faith alone, but his speculative mind and wide-ranging pen constantly got him into difficulty. He thought that there were good men among the pagans, Turks, and people of ancient times who were saved by the inner Word even though they knew nothing of the Word incarnate.[19]

One of the most interesting and influential of the spiritualists was the Silesian nobleman Caspar von Schwenkfeld, who was born in Ossig in 1489, and lived on the land, where he was hospitable to evangelicals and dissidents. He was for a while a follower of Luther, but they became estranged as Schwenkfeld drifted further and further away toward some rather strange spiritualist ideas about Christ's celestial body, the symbolic view of the sacraments, rejection of any literal interpretation of the Bible, a mystical ethic, and an exclusive stress on the church as the invisible indwelling of Christ in the believers. On the Lord's Supper he came close to Zwingli's position, and in 1527 Oecolampadius published his treatise *On the Course of the Word of God (De cursu verbi dei)*. Zwingli published his open letter on the Lord's Supper as well. In 1529 Schwenkfeld left Silesia for Strasbourg, where he stayed until 1533, and then moved on to Augsburg, Ulm, and Esslingen; he died in Ulm in 1561. A small sect of Schwenkfeldians continued in Swabia and back in Silesia, until they were

19. *Ibid.,* pp. 264–267, 457–465, 499–504, on his ongoing influence. See also Will-Erich Peuckert, *Sebastian Franck, ein deutscher Sucher* (Munich, 1943), not very critical in treatment, but appreciative and complete.

suppressed by the Jesuits in 1720 and fled to Freistatt, Pennsylvania, where they still persist to the present day.

The only other spiritualists really to form a sectarian group were the Familists, followers of Heinrich Niclaeas (c. 1501–c. 1570), a merchant who claimed direct inspiration from the Holy Spirit. He formed a sect with a unique hierarchical organization and many of the characteristically spiritualist tenets—late baptism, mystical-pantheistic piety, a love ethic—which some later developed into an antinomian libertarian way of life. Niclaeas traveled widely in northwest Germany, the Netherlands, and England, founding small groups of the Familists, a name derived from *familia charitatis,* or family of love. Their influence can be traced down to 1660 in England, and the Ranters in revolutionary times were heirs to this tradition.

While it is possible here to discuss only a few representative figures, there were many others at the time worthy of mention, such as Theobald Thamer, a student of Luther's who became a professor at Marburg, turned spiritualist, and eventually returned to the Catholic Church and died as a professor of Catholic theology at Freiburg in Breisgau. The tradition persisted into the century with such major figures as Valentin Weigel, Giordano Bruno, and Jacob Böhme. In a sense a nature enthusiast and religious spiritualist like Paracelsus (1493–1541) should be counted among them. Although he was a physician who was primarily concerned with establishing his own authority against that of Hippocrates, Galen, and Avicenna, he wrote very extensively on questions of theology and natural philosophy. At one point he was close to the Anabaptists, but then took a position against them, and really espoused opinions very close to those of Hans Denck or Sebastian Franck.[20]

The evangelical humanists emerged mostly in Italy and Spain, coming perhaps as an extreme reaction to conditions in the church and as a result of Renaissance culture in the Neoplatonic phase of humanist thought. They collectively have been called anti-Trinitarian and Arian, for they reworked the dogmas of the Trinity, Christology, and the sacraments, going behind the Hellenic terms embodied in the Nicene Creed to biblical terminology, and emphasizing Christ's humanity. To that group be-

20. Kurt Goldammer, ed., *Paracelsus, Theologische und religionsphilosophische Schriften, Sämmtliche Werke,* Bd. 4, 2. Abt. (Wiesbaden, 1955–1961); K. Goldammer, ed., *Paracelsus; sozialpolitische Schriften: Aus dem theologischreligionsphilosophischen Werke ausgewählt und eingeleitet und mit erklärenden Anmerkungen von Kurt Goldammer* (Tübingen, 1952).

longed Camillo Renato, Celio Secundo Curione, Matthias Gibaldo, George Blandrata, Valentin Gentilis, and Lelio Sozzini. Their movement fused with Swiss Anabaptism, but they remained a small group of intellectuals. In 1550 a convention held in Venice, more tolerant because of the city's antipapal tradition, attracted some sixty people. As inquisitional pressure on them increased in Italy, they emigrated to Switzerland.

Renato was the leader of this first generation of emigrants.[21] A Sicilian, he was a member of the Franciscan Order but left the Catholic Church before 1540 and was imprisoned. On November 9, 1542, he wrote to Bullinger from Chiavenna, where he had come with Curione, to present his creed, and by 1545, he was in conflict with Bullinger over his doctrines of the Trinity, sacraments, spiritual rebirth, and the immortality of the soul. He withdrew to Caspano where he lived into the 1570s. Francesco Calabrese and Girolamo Milanese left Italy for Switzerland in 1543, for they also harbored unorthodox views on infant baptism and soul sleep after death. Jacobus Acontius (d.c. 1567) fled Italy for Basel and Zurich —where he associated with Bernardino Ochino, another prominent dissident—and moved on to London in 1559 and became a member of the Dutch congregation of Austin Friars there. In his book *The Strategies of Satan (Stratagemata Satanae)* (Basel, 1565), he decried the divisions in Protestantism and insisted that only errors in doctrines essential to salvation should be considered heresies. Lelio Sozzini, born in 1525 in Siena, turned Anabaptist between 1540 and 1545. He lived in Padua and was in contact with a group of Anabaptists in Venice. In 1547 he left Italy for Chiavenna. He traveled to England, the Netherlands, and France and settled in Zurich, where he came into conflict with Bullinger over the doctrines of the sacraments, the deity of Christ, and the resurrection of the body. He died in Poland at the age of thirty-seven in the spring of 1562. Lelio's nephew, Fausto Sozzini (1539–1604), born in Siena, became the leader of the anti-Trinitarians in Poland. He founded the unitarian church of the Socinians, which centered in Rakow, with a catechism as a confession, and with both schools and churches. They were eventually suppressed, in 1658 were driven out of Poland by the Jesuits, and found refuge in Transylvania, the Netherlands, and other places.

The fusion of Italian evangelical humanism with Erasmianism is well illustrated in the thought of Celio Secundo Curione, who emigrated from

21. Delio Cantimori, *Eretici Italiani. del Cinquecento. Ricerche storiche* (Florence, 1967), pp. 73ff., 93ff., *et passim.*

Italy to Switzerland in 1542. He was active in Lausanne, where he lectured in the liberal arts. His first book was entitled *The Spider*, or *True Golden Book on the Providence of God*, published both in Venice and Basel, describing God's presence in all creatures in a nearly pantheistic way. In the fall of 1546 he moved to Basel and became a professor at the university. He was one of the most prolific of the émigrés, with a huge family and many books, textbooks, translations, commentaries, *The Institutes of the Christian Religion*, and a new history of the Turkish assault on Malta. His most important work was *Dialogues on the Amplitude of the Kingdom of God* (Poschiavo, 1554), dedicated to Sigismund II August of Poland. In the first book he cited all the Bible passages which seemed to suggest that only a small number of men would be saved. In the second he quoted all those that showed the all-embracing goodness of God, Who would save far more than were lost. Bullinger was critical of the book, which revealed how well Curione fit in with Erasmian humanism. When he died in 1569 he was buried in the transept of the Great Minster, not far from the prince of the humanists himself.

One of the most prominent Italian Catholic churchmen to turn Protestant was Pietro Paolo Vergerio the Younger (c. 1497/98–c. 1564/65), who served as papal secretary, chaplain, and legate. Born in Capodistria, he was educated in Padua, and served as a canonist in Verona, Padua, and Venice. Pope Clement VII sent him to the Diet of Augsburg in 1530. Pope Paul III dispatched him in 1535 to negotiate with the German princes about a proposed council in Mantua. He met Luther, whom he called a "beast" possibly possessed by a demon. In 1540 he attended the colloquy of Worms as a commissioner of Francis I, and in 1541 he was at the colloquy at Regensburg, discussing religious unity with Melanchthon and the Lutherans. For those occasions he studied the writings of Luther, was considered to have conceded too much to the Lutherans in negotiation, and was threatened. In 1545 he broke with the Catholic Church, was excommunicated in 1549, stayed in Switzerland until 1553, and devoted the remaining years of his life to the service of Duke Christoph of Württemberg. He was the author of many anti-Catholic books and pamphlets.[22]

The cause célèbre of anti-Trinitarians was the case of Michael Servetus, a Spaniard who was burned alive for heresy in Geneva on October 27,

22. Anne Jacobson Schutte, *Peter Paul Vergerio: The Making of an Italian Reformer* (Geneva, 1977).

1553. Servetus was born around 1509 in Villanova in Aragon. In 1530 he stayed with Oecolampadius in Basel, but because of his shocking ideas about the Trinity, he was driven out. He was expelled from fairly tolerant Strasbourg in 1531. In that same year he published in Hagenau his first major attack on the doctrine of the Trinity, *De Trinitatibus erroribus*. He took the thinly disguised pseudonym Villanovanus and worked as a corrector for a printer in Lyon. He then studied medicine in Paris and practiced in Charlieu and Vienne, where he wrote his main work on the *Restitution of Christianity (Christianismi Restitutio)*. He corresponded about this volume with Calvin in 1545–1546, but Calvin concluded that he was incorrigible and broke off the correspondence. In 1553 he was arrested by the Catholic inquisition in Vienne, escaped, though burned in effigy, but in Geneva on the way to Italy he was recognized and arrested. He rejected all the arguments and pleas of Calvin to renounce his "Arianism" and although the preachers urged a milder form of death for him, he was burned at the stake. Servetus was a brilliant though erratic man, who recognized the difference between the Christ of the Gospels and the Hellenic terms used in the early creeds to describe the two natures of Christ and the structure of the Trinity. His own theism was influenced by pantheistic Neoplatonism.

Sebastian Castellio (1515–1563), a Frenchman who had taught in Geneva, had had differences with Calvin and become a professor of Greek in Basel, was incensed at the death of Servetus. He excoriated Calvin and wrote an influential book *On Heretics, Whether They Ought to Be Persecuted*, in which he argued for love and understanding, stressing that no one had a monopoly on truth. The burning of Servetus was generally approved by the magisterial reformers such as Melanchthon and Bullinger, who feared that Servetus would lead many misguided souls to perdition. It shocked the Italian evangelical humanists, many of whom left Switzerland for Poland, Transylvania, Hungary, and other areas still hospitable toward radical reformers. The influence of the spiritualists and evangelical humanists cannot be measured in terms of numbers, for they were on the whole well educated and through their writings and disciples had an important impact during succeeding centuries.

7. URBAN REFORMATION

When Luther made his long journey to Worms in 1521, the city council of Wittenberg provided the transportation, for which he thanked them cordially. In 1525 he wrote to John Briessmann in Koenigsberg, a former Franciscan who had become the reformer of East Prussia and Livonia, "The imperial cities are now already consulting together to be able to remain on the side of the gospel in spite of the great threats made against them by the furious sovereigns."[23] Luther understood the importance of the cities to the Reformation and throughout his life corresponded with and sent messengers to the evangelical preachers and reformers active in the imperial and territorial cities, to lay readers in the movement, such as Lazarus Spengler of Nuremberg, and to the city councils and magistrates governing the cities. To the city council of Stellin in 1523 he gave the advice requested on exempting canons from taxation. To the city council of Leisnig he wrote the same year on organizing the office of the pastor and an order of worship. To the city council of Zerbst he wrote the following year suggesting flogging for adulterers rather than stoning or execution under imperial law. In 1524 he also wrote *To the Councilmen of All Cities in Germany That They Establish and Maintain Christian Schools.* In 1533 he gave his opinion on absolution and confession to the city council of Nuremberg. In 1530 he urged the pastors of Lübeck not to "change ritual first, which is dangerous" but to "deal first with the center of our teaching and fix in the people's minds what they must know about our justification." So prominent was the role of the cities in the progress of the Reformation and so freely did Luther, Zwingli, Bucer, and the other magisterial reformers acknowledge the fact, that it is strange to find historians only now engaged in detailed research on the "first" Reformation as an urban phenomenon.[24] They were possibly led astray by the promi-

23. *Luther's Works,* 49, *Letters,* II, Gottfried Krodel, ed. (Philadelphia, 1972), p. 124.

24. Alfred Schultze, *Stadtgemeinde und Reformation* (Tübingen, 1918), p. 7, observed that the legal historian Rudolph Sohm had in his outline of church history spoken of the Reformation as the first great movement in Germany in which the bourgeoisie played an independent decisive role. Two recent admirable volumes have undertaken to summarize scholarship on the Reformation in the cities, A. G. Dickens, *The German Nation and Martin Luther* (New York, 1974), and Steven E. Ozment, *The Reformation in the Cities: The Appeal of Protestantism to Sixteenth-Century Germany and Switzerland* (New Haven, 1975), which makes good use of the pamphlet literature to assess the appeal and of sociological analysis to appreciate the structure, process, and response to that appeal. Both owe much to the brilliant essay of Bernd Moeller, *Imperial Cities and the Reformation,* ed. and trans. by H.C. Erik Midelfort and Mark U. Edwards, Jr. (Philadelphia, 1972), pp. 41–115, originally, *Reichstadt und Reformation,* SVRG, no. 180 (Gütersloh, 1962). Hans-Christoph Rublack, author of *Die Einführung der Reformation in Konstanz von den Anfängen bis zum Abschlusz 1531* (Gutersloh, 1971), heads a Tübingen project for assembling on microfilm the relevant archival documents for the introduction of the Reformation to the cities of upper Germany and a definitive history must await the completion of many more monographs.

nence of Elector Frederick the Wise as Luther's protector, but Frederick was motivated by pride in this professor at his university, by the duty of protecting a subject, and by some appreciation of Luther's theology, although he remained basically a relic-gathering pious Catholic to his death in 1525. He saw Luther in person only once or twice and never spoke with him. For the first eight years most of the princes were indifferent or hostile to the Reformation and it was in the cities that the movement made sensational progress during the first two decades. The initiative and dynamic of the urban populace that carried it forward were propelled by the gospel preaching of evangelists and pamphleteers and by negative feelings such as anticlericalism, resentment against church dues, and anger at what were now perceived to be fraudulent indulgences. It remained a popular movement into the 1530s and longer.[25]

Young Margrave Philipp of Hesse became evangelical in 1526, under Melanchthon's tutelage, and Brunswick-Lüneburg followed shortly thereafter, but the "second" Reformation in which the princes figured in a more essential way belonged to the middle and later 1530s and in some cases the momentum of the urban Reformation in their territories carried them along. Württemberg, Pomerania, and Nassau turned evangelical in 1534, the Elector of Brandenburg in 1538, Albertine Saxony after the death of Duke George, in 1539, Mecklenburg-Schwerin and Brunswick-Calenburg in 1540. While at the Diet of Augsburg in 1530 the urban leaders were most prominent, by the time of the Schmalkald War, 1546–1547, the princes had moved to the fore and the cities continued their long decline. So important is the story of the urban reception of the Reformation that it merits a closer examination.

A map of Germany at the time would show the free imperial cities clustered heavily in upper Germany with a heavy concentration in the southwest. The territorial cities were more widely spread in the north and northeast than in the south, or in Franconia and central Germany. The structure typical of an imperial city consisted of a patrician group of wealthy merchants and landowners, a middle group of lesser merchants and landowners, a group of even lesser merchants and artisans, formed into guilds, which made up the great majority of the citizenry, and a smaller floating population not enjoying the rights of citizenship. The patricians ruled without remuneration, served on the city councils, repre-

25. Franz Lau, "Der Bauernkrieg und das angebliche Ende der lutherischen Reformation als spontaner Volksbewegung," *Luther Jahrbuch,* 26 (1959), 109–134.

sented the city at the diet or abroad, and were much concerned with the common good *(Gemeinwohl)*. There was a surprising amount of social mobility in cities such as Augsburg, where artisan families such as the Fuggers and the Höchstetters rose by their wealth to patrician status. With the decline of the cities the status of the patricians became less flexible and in the cities of the north the patrician class in these decades was much more rigid than in the south. The extent of patrician control of the cities varied substantially. In Nuremberg, Frankfurt, and northern cities such as Stralsund, Rostock, and Wismar, the patricians were in complete control of the councils. In Augsburg, Ulm, Strasbourg, Regensburg, Rothenburg ob der Tauber, and Schwäbisch-Hall the patricians shared their power with the guilds. In Schlettstadt and in Speyer the guilds controlled the councils. In cities in which the guilds played a role in the city government, as in Zurich, where the government, with its mayors, small and great councils, was formally based on the corporate division of the citizenry into a patriciate and twelve guilds, the Reformation made more rapid advances than in cities such as Lucerne and Bern, with more patrician governments. There were no social classes in the modern sense of the word, but rather estates or positions in society, and there was an impressive concern on the part of all, whatever their station in life, for the common good.[26]

That common good included in the general welfare a concern for Christian ethics, for salvation, and for the control of ecclesiastical appointments and properties. Each city considered itself a microcosm of the *corpus christianum*. The bishops and archbishops had long since been excluded from most cities, at Mainz, Worms, Speyer, Cologne, Strasbourg, Regensburg, and Magdeburg, for example. The Reformation was in part a defeudalization of the church in which the urban centers asserted their rights against the prince-bishops. The laity in the late medieval church had endowed preacherships in many cities, in nearly a third of the towns in Württemberg, though in only 16 percent of the Swiss towns, when they were dissatisfied with the quality of the priests. The city replaced the monastery as the center for literary culture; the city chronicles supplanted the monastic chronicles and annals. The humanists such as Rudolph Agricola and Jacob Wimpheling delivered many an exhortation to the clergy and urged a new social ethic. The reformers took up this theme:

26. Harold J. Grimm, "The Reformation and the Urban Social Classes in Germany," in *Luther, Erasmus and the Reformation*, John C. Olin, ed. (New York, 1969), pp. 75–86. See also Norman Birnbaum, *Social Structure and the German Reformation* (New York, 1980).

Luther concerned with the general principle of the Christian as servant of all and with specific proposals such as the common chest for the poor, Melanchthon habitually linking the good of the commonwealth with that of the church, Bucer urging in a tract of 1523 that *One Should Not Live for Oneself Alone but for Others, and How to Do It,* Zwingli, himself the choice of the elite of Zurich, leading the councils through comprehensive reforms. Religious reform necessarily involved social reform, for with the emphasis on the priesthood of all believers the medieval distinction of clergy and laity disappeared. Assaults on the privileges and tax exemptions of the canons and clergy, criticism of the confraternities, attacks on monasticism and closing of monasteries, freeing endowments for schools and hospitals, all such steps had social as well as religious implications. Laymen, in turn, became evangelical missionaries, such as the eight Hanse merchants whom Sir Thomas More had arrested in the Steel yard in London and incarcerated for having in their possession pestiferous Lutheran books. The late medieval religiosity generated in laymen a sense of uncertainty about salvation, just as it had in Luther, and the evangelicals now shared with the laymen the certainty of the gospel. A Lutheran pamphleteer, Eberlin von Günzburg, even described a Protestant Utopia, *Wolfaria,* in which religious and social reform renewed urban institutions and provided for the welfare of all.[27]

The process by which the Reformation became established in the cities was nearly everywhere the same. In no case did the patricians initiate the reform. There were, to be sure, individual patricians in nearly every German city who embraced Lutheranism or Zwinglianism quite early, and did so against their own economic and social best interests. The pressure for reform came from the populace down below. Evangelical preachers and pamphleteers, either local converts or itinerant missionaries, arrived and began preaching, for despite the impact of printing, the spoken word was powerful in a still very illiterate age and pamphlets were often designed to be shown and read to the masses. The artisans were generally receptive to the evangelical teachings of the reformers and responded readily to the criticisms of clerical privileges and abuses. Although in Nuremberg they for the most part owned some property—a small family house, perhaps, and a garden plot—in some cities, like Augsburg, nearly

27. See Susan Groag Bell, "Johann Eberlin von Günzburg's *Wolfaria*—The First Protestant Utopia," *Church History,* 36 (1967), 122–139.

half of them owned no property and another 40 percent paid only a minimal property tax, so little did they possess. The most volatile element in the population, the members of the small guilds such as the gardeners, vintners, and small farmers, some of whom lived in the city, others in adjoining villages, joined the movement first, followed by the major artisan guilds and small merchants. As the number of evangelicals increased, pressure on the magistrates to adopt the Reformation grew.

There was a natural rapport between the evangelical Lutheran preachers who spearheaded reform in the cities and the middle and lower strata of society so receptive to their message. Many evangelical preachers were drawn from the ranks of the secular clergy, and like the late medieval clergy on the parish level, they came for the most part from an artisan or craftsman background. They were drawn also in part from positions that required a basic literacy such as printers, teachers, sextons, and clerks.[28] The Augustianians provided a sizable number of recruits, not only because Luther was a member of their order and the Dominicans a common foe, but because of the Pauline nature of one dimension of St. Augustine's theology of sin and grace. The Franciscans, too, provided a considerable number of first generation Protestant ministers, who made good itinerant preachers in the mendicant tradition. It is interesting to note that three decades later a very high percentage of the evangelical preachers were sons of pastors—nearly two-thirds of them in some states—of bourgeois parents, children of artisans, peasants, and teachers, with very few drawn from the nobility or wealthy merchant or provostial levels of society.[29]

A few case studies will illustrate the general pattern in the cities. In Nuremberg, with more sympathetic councilmen, a humanist circle, and the *Sodalitas Staupitziana* or followers of Luther's confessor, Johannes von Staupitz, the magistracy accepted the Reformation early and with unusual enthusiasm.[30] In Augsburg, on the other hand, the bankers like the Wels-

28. Bernhard Klaus, "Soziale Herkunft und theologische Bildung lutherischer Pfarrer der reformatorischen Frühzeit," *Zeitschrift für Kirchengeschichte,* 80 (1969), 22–49; Martin Brecht, "Herkunft und Ausbildung der protestantischen Geistlichen des Herzogtums Württemberg im 16. Jahrhundert," *ibid.,* 163–173; H. Meylan, "Le recrutement et la formation des pasteurs dans les Églises réformées du XVIᵉ siècle," *Miscellanea Historiae Ecclesiasticae,* III (Louvain, 1970), 127–150.

29. Bernard Vogler, *Le Clergé Protestant Rhénan au siècle de la Réforme (1555–1619)* (Paris, 1976), pp. 17–78: "Recrutement et Formation du clergé," especially p. 18.

30. Cf. Gottfried Seebass, "The Reformation in Nürnberg," pp. 17–40, and Jackson Spielvogel, "Patricians in Dissension: A Case Study from Sixteenth Century Nürnberg," pp.

ers and Fuggers were so tied to the Habsburgs by political loans and mining concessions that they had good reason to oppose the Reformation, and when the city joined the Reformation many patricians dissociated themselves from the scene.[31] The city of Ulm, in a vulnerable position, was unable to complete its reformation until the years 1531–1532 and impose it upon the countryside under its jurisdiction, a total of 60,000 people. In 1520 the Catholic Church in Strasbourg seemed solidly established, but a small and determined minority took a mere five years to impose its view upon a fragmented and uncertain opposition.[32] The guilds and lower orders were lively and independent, the humanists were very active, and were followed by reformers such as the preacher Mattheus Zell, in the tradition of Geiler von Kaisersberg, Martin Bucer, Wolfgang Capito—one of the highest-placed clergy to defect—and Caspar Hedio, court preacher in Mainz, who became a preacher in Strasbourg in 1523 and the first Protestant church historian. In Luther's own city of Erfurt the situation was complicated by social disturbances, the presence of the university with thousands of students, strong churches and cloisters, and the fear of the Elector. The final solution was to embody in law the coexistence of both religions, the only city in which such mutual sufferance was guaranteed by a treaty of state prior to the Peace of Augsburg in 1555.[33]. It would be interesting to multiply instances, but these examples must suffice to illustrate that despite local variations, the basic pattern by which the Reformation was established in south and central German cities, was the same: preachers and pamphleteers, positive response from the lesser merchants and artisan guilds, pressure on the patrician-dominated councils, and eventual capitulation by the magistracy.

The pattern of reformation in the north and northeast was much the

---

73–92, both in Lawrence P. Buck and Jonathan W. Zophy, eds., *The Social History of the Reformation* (Columbus, Ohio, 1972).

31. See Rolf Kiessling, *Bürgerliche Gesellschaft und Kirche in Augsburg im Spätmittelalter: Ein Beitrag zur Strukturanalyse der oberdeutschen Reichstadt* (Augsburg, 1971), for a sociological analysis of Augsburg's special situation. Eberhard Naujoks, *Obrigkeitsgedanke, Zunftverfassung und Reformation* (Stuttgart, 1958), develops a picture of city constitutions as representative of a guild-dominated city-state.

32. This story is well told by Miriam Chrisman, *Strasbourg and the Reform* (New Haven and London, 1967). A superb book on the background to the Reformation in Strasbourg, the anticlericalism and other factors, is F. Rapp, *Réformes at Réformation à Strasbourg: Église et Société dans le Diocèse de Strasbourg (1450–1525)* (Paris, 1974).

33. R.W. Scribner, "Civic Unity and the Reformation in Erfurt," *Past and Present,* 66 (Feb., 1975), 29–60.

same. The overall difference lay in the fact that in the Hanse cities and the towns of Westphalia, Brandenburg, Mecklenburg, Pomerania, and East Prussia, the patrician estate was much more closed and static. Those oligarchies were entrenched in seeking their own interests and resistant to change. But the burghers, the lesser merchants and more prosperous artisans, of the cities along the North Sea, the Baltic Sea, and in the *Hinterland* were not slow in joining the Reformation. They bore the brunt of taxation, for those above—especially the clergy—enjoyed various forms of tax exemptions, and those below—about one-fifth of the population in Hamburg and up to one-half in some other cities—were propertyless artisans. Due to shifting economic patterns and trade routes, most of those cities were experiencing financial difficulties and social strain. The coming of the Reformation exacerbated the social conflicts within the cities and deepened the rifts. Luther's criticism of the Roman Catholic Church and his simple intense evangelical message won the support of the restless middle and disaffected lower strata of society. The first audiences, in such cities as Stralsund, Rostock, and Wismar, who listened intently to sermons sometimes lasting three and four hours, were made up of lesser merchants, master craftsmen, artisans, and harbor workers.[34] They organized citizens' committees in many cities to represent the wishes of the people alongside the patrician councils and imposed their reformatory will upon them.

While the overall pattern of urban reformation in the north was similar, there were some noteworthy variations. In the old Hanse towns of Bremen, Hamburg, and Lübeck the Reformation developed quite rapidly and comprehensively. Bremen enjoyed quite a liberal constitution which allowed for admission of newly rich families to the council. As was true in the south, this openness facilitated the early acceptance of reform, the major threat coming from the Archbishop of Bremen, who awaited an opportunity to regain the power his predecessors had gradually surrendered to the lay council. A former Augustinian and a student of Luther's, Heinrich von Zütphen, served as an evangelical preacher at St. Ansgar's chapel in 1523 and 1524. But in the fall of 1524 he dared enter the Ditmarschen in western Holstein in order to convert the free peasants there; he was kidnapped by drunken peasants urged on by the local

34. Johannes Schildhauer, *Soziale, Politische und Religiöse Auseinandersetzungen in den Hansestädten Stralsund, Rostock und Wismar im ersten Drittel des XVI. Jahrhunderts* (Wismar, 1959), a work in which a formal Marxism does not obfuscate the results of careful research.

Dominican prior, lynched, and burned on December 10. Luther wrote a very moving memorial on *The Burning of Brother Henry*.[35]. Any abstract discussions of statistics and social stratification fail to do justice to the real human, heroic, and often tragic substance of history.

The story of the Reformation in Hamburg is beautifully documented and conforms to the classic pattern. This old Hanse city with 13,000 to 15,000 inhabitants was slightly smaller than Lübeck at that time. The city was heavily churched with a strong cathedral chapter and several monasteries. The tax-paying citizens were resentful of the ecclesiastical exactions and the tax exemptions given the canons and orders when the council raised taxes to strengthen the municipal fortifications and build a canal. There were sixteen to twenty-three canons, a hundred priests at the four parish churches, plus two hundred clerics saying masses and other services. The leading intellectual on the eve of the Reformation was Dr. Albert Krantz, noted historian, who read Luther's Ninety-five Theses with approval just before his death on December 7, 1517. A mandate from the city council in 1521 warned against the errors of Luther. But soon evangelical preachers were active in the city. Students went to study at Wittenberg and Rostock, famous for their humanist curricula. On the Leipzig and Zurich pattern, disputations were held which led to some Protestant gains. In St. Catherine's church Stephan Kempe, a Franciscan, emerged as a Bible-preaching reformer. Johann Widenbrügge, a Premonstratensian, came to the city from a nearby monastery to instruct the people in the Scriptures. Soon demonstrations involving 500 to 2,000 people protesting the Protestants developed, but the movement gained new converts. In 1524 St. Nicholas church called Johannes Bugenhagen, city pastor in Wittenberg, but the city council would not approve the call. Not until 1528 did the council, with new members, yield to the pressure and allow Bugenhagen to come to Hamburg. He preached, lectured, colloquized, counseled, persuaded, and organized. Before he left he prepared a church order that was accepted by the council and the citizens and celebrated in a service of thanksgiving on May 23, 1529. Bugenhagen's church order was put into effect by Dr. Johannes Hoeck, called Aepinus (d. 1553), Hamburg's first superintendent over the course of the next two decades. His work was embodied in a second great church order, the Aepinian Order of 1556. The Reformation had triumphed thoroughly against the determined opposition of canons, nuns, monks, papal emissaries, and a

35. *Luther's Works*, 32, *Career of the Reformer*, II, George W. Forell, ed. (Philadelphia, 1958), pp. 261–286.

conservative patrician council. Hamburg followed the classic social pattern, but the Reformation was in a very real way the work of heroic and dedicated individual men.[36].

In Lübeck, that red-brick museum of the Hanse's better days, the laity had asserted itself in rivalry to the ecclesiastical powers in earlier centuries, building the huge church of St. Mary on a grander scale than the episcopal church. Now Lübeck was in deep economic difficulty as its trading operations declined. Taxation was heavy for the reduced city income, and discontent was rife. The middle strata of society set up a citizens' committee in order to pressure the council to impose heavier taxes on the secular clergy, canons, and monasteries. They demanded "good preachers" and welcomed the Lutheran missionaries who arrived to serve. By 1530 they had won the day for the Reformation. Luther sent Bugenhagen, back in Wittenberg, to the north to supervise the abolition of the mass, the dissolution of the monasteries, and the organization of an evangelical church. Unfortunately for Lübeck, the leader of the citizens' committee, Jörgen Wullenwever, elected mayor in 1533, involved the city in an enervating Danish War. In the summer of 1534 the Lübeck forces captured Copenhagen, but a new king, Christian III, rallied the Danes and forced a truce on Lübeck. Wullenwever was taken by the Archbishop of Bremen as he crossed the Archbishop's territory and turned over to the duke of Brunswick, who tortured and executed him in 1537. Although the old patrician council then regained its power, Lutheranism was so well established that it could no longer be eradicated.[37]

In the Prussian provinces to the east Lutheran preachers were very active, and the critical turning point came with the conversion of the Grand Master of the Order of the Teutonic Knights, Albert of Brandenburg, by Osiander of Nuremberg, with Luther's encouragement. He secularized the Order, adopted the title of duke, and undertook a sweeping reformation. The support of the progressive element in the cities—largely German, including Danzig—made it possible for Albert to move so fast against the determined opposition of the bishop of Ermeland, Moritz Ferber (1523–1537), a Danzig patrician in family background. So the urban reformation was an important factor in the success of one of the first "princely" reformations in the north.

36. See Heinrich Reincke, *Hamburg am Vorabend der Reformation* (Hamburg, 1966), and George Daur, *Von Predigern und Bürgern. Eine hamburgische Kirchengeschichte von der Reformation bis zur Gegenwart* (Hamburg, 1970), pp. 13–80: "Die Reformation setzt sich durch."
37. Dickens, *The German Nation*, pp. 163–165.

In the northwest the cities and towns of Westphalia played an equally crucial role. Once again there were negative feelings, anticlericalism, resentment against church dues and clerical tax exemptions. The Reformation won the support of the master craftsmen and artisans. The Augustinians lent support to Luther's cause. But perhaps because of its greater distance from Wittenberg and Zurich, the progress of reform was slow and inconsistent, as compared with progress in the north and northeast as well as the southwest.[38]

The initial Reformation in the Empire and in Switzerland was an urban reformation. The extension of the evangelical movement into the country, to the peasants in the villages, began seriously only during the three decades following the Peasant Revolt in 1525. Seventy-five to 85 percent of the population lived in the country, nearly all in villages, although there were some districts with separate rural households. It took many years until a sufficient number of pastors could be educated or retrained in evangelical theology to care for the country parishes. Preaching was necessary, since few peasants could read and Luther's stress on the spoken word of the gospel reinforced the place of the pulpit. During the early years the sects made gains in the countryside through the work of the unauthorized "hedgerow" preachers; but with the advent of a better-educated clergy, paid miserably but very dedicated, the situation stabilized. The Protestant cities as well as the princes at a later stage, through the consistories and following visitations, introduced and supervised the introduction of the Reformation to the countryside. Religious feeling was strong in the villages as can be seen by the many village churches enlarged in the late Middle Ages by adding in front a Gothic structure to a frequently Romanesque nave. It is naive to think that the visitation reports represent a true picture of the religious life of the people, since in accord with the instructions to the visitors from 1527 through the century, the visitors for the most part reported on the evil life, ignorance, and doctrinal deviations needing correction, not on the positive aspect of religious life or evangelical impact on the villages, where catechetical instruction proved an effective means and level of teaching.[39]

38. H. Stratenwerth, *Die Reformation in der Stadt Osnabrück* (Wiesbaden, 1971).

39. Johannes Hermann, "Reformation auf dem platten Lande," in Franz Lau, ed., *Das Hochstift Meissen: Aufsätze zur sächsischen Kirchengeschichte* (Berlin, 1973), pp. 207–221, 208–209. On the miserable pay of Lutheran preachers in at least one territory, see Suzanne K. Boles, "The Economic Position of Lutheran Pastors in Ernestine Thuringia 1521–1555," *Archive for Reformation History*, 63 (1972), 94–125, a tribute to their spiritual motivation or lack of better alternatives.

As the urban reformation developed, many of the cities in the southwest which were initially in line with the Zwinglian or Swiss reformed church turned Lutheran. Even after Zwingli's death the Swiss reform movement continued its spread into southwest Germany until only Reutlingen among the imperial cities stood firmly for Lutheranism. The Zurich model seems to have been an important factor. Moreover, the reformed city councils undertook mission work in other cities. The momentum was gradually lost, however, as two formidable forces came into play, the power of the territorial princes and the Catholic counterattack. By the late 1530s the princely overlords had opted for Lutheranism. Luther had stressed the importance of the authorities or government to check evil, to serve the people as instruments of God's left hand, and the corresponding necessity for obedience to authority. As areas such as Württemberg, under the leadership of Johannes Brenz, turned Lutheran, the influence on the cities became crucial. As the Catholic and Protestant forces firmed up opposing alignments, the cities of the southwest within the Empire were pressured in a Lutheran direction. After the victory of Emperor Charles V at Mühlenberg in the Schmalkald War, some thirty cities between the years 1548 and 1552 were forced back into the Catholic fold. The Jesuits and the Calvinists whittled away at the Swiss reformed areas as well. Martin Bucer left Strasbourg for England, an act symbolic of the general despair in the city-states of Germany. The Peace of Passau in 1552 and the Peace of Augsburg in 1555 excluded all religious groups from legal recognition except the Catholic Church and all who subscribed to the Lutheran Augsburg Confession of 1530. The cities were being eclipsed politically as the territorial princedoms and the emperor applied military pressure. They resumed that economic and social decline which humanism and the Reformation emphasis on civic duty and the common good had only temporarily arrested. The urban reformation had to be a magistrates' reformation if it was to endure. Now more powerful magistrates, princes and kings, were to assert their authority embodied in the principle "whose the rule, his the religion." But cities such as Erfurt, Frankfurt, and Augsburg had made a lasting contribution to the idea of toleration, for in permitting Catholic and Lutheran churches to coexist within their walls, they showed that religious uniformity was not essential to peaceful civic life.

Chapter Four

THE SECOND SURGE

1. PROTESTANT PENETRATION IN FRANCE

JOACHIM DU BELLAY, a member of The Pleiades, in 1559 praised France as the "mother of the arts, of arms, and of laws" (*Les Regrets,* IX). Compared with the fragmented Empire, France in that year did seem to be in a relatively fortunate position, but she was about to enter the disastrous period of the wars of religion. When the dust settled and the blood dried after those wars and the St. Bartholomew's Massacre in 1572, France, the eldest daughter of the Church, remained Catholic and the number of Protestants fell to less than 10 percent of the population. The reasons why France alone among the lands of northern Europe, besides Ireland, which was virtually untouched, was not won over to the Reformation and withstood the challenge even of militant Calvinism lay in part in its history and in part in its political and social structure.

While all France was not "crying for Reformation," there is ample evidence of general ecclesiastical uneasiness, of popular discontent with conditions in the church, anger at the abuses common in French church life as well as in the rest of Christendom, and desire for renewal. Among the humanists, Rabelais was not alone in mocking monastic abuses, nor Erasmus exceptional in decrying scholastic education in Paris and turning to the Scriptures and early church fathers for guidance. But popular or intellectual criticism seemed less acrimonious than in the Empire and had a less overtly antipapal tone. One basic reason was that the political and financial privileges of the Roman Catholic Church were much more restricted than they were in the Empire. The Gallican church had gained many special privileges by the Pragmatic Sanction of Bourges, subscribed to by King Charles VII in 1438, such as the right to forbid judicial appeals to Rome, the restriction of papal control over benefices, and the freedom to substitute voluntary contributions for official dues. In 1516 King Francis I concluded the Concordat of Bologna with Pope Leo X, which secured to the French king the right to nominate persons to vacant bishoprics and abbacies in France, while it granted the pope the authority to collect the annates from those offices. The great liberties of the Gallican church and the control exercised by the king lessened any resentment against the Renaissance popes and Roman exploitation.

It is ironic that the victory of the medieval popes in the investiture controversy and the undermining of the power of the emperor in the sixteenth century prevented a strong Catholic emperor such as Charles V from containing the Reformation. Conversely, the emergence of the new French monarchy with a centralized bureaucracy, fairly effective agents in the provinces, a productive taxation system, and a royal army during the decades that followed the chaotic Hundred Years' War, enabled Francis I, Henry II, and his widow Queen Catherine de' Medici to cope more successfully with the forces of Protestantism. Perhaps geography played a role with Paris as the focal point of the royal domains with the network of rivers and roads extending outward. It seems more than a coincidence that the heretical Cathari and Waldensians survived in the south and that after the Catholic resurgence, Calvinism retained its adherents best in the south and west, in areas such as Languedoc, farthest from Paris. The argument that the aristocratic social structure worked in favor of the conservative alliance of throne and altar is not tenable, for Protestantism made converts on all levels of society, not just or even predominantly the bourgeoisie, and Calvinism won over very powerful noble families, which made the contest for control of the monarchy during the wars of religion more than just a struggle for survival by a desperate minority.

The full story of the spread of Protestantism has never been told. The single source theory explains the spread as the transfer of ideas from Luther and the rapid expansion or radiation of Lutheranism in all directions. The parallel source theory emphasizes the indigenous nature of the Reformation in various countries, a general northern European zeitgeist, similar discontents, and parallel revolutionary ecclesiastical movements. The origin of the Reformation in France poses intriguing problems, for not only has Protestantism in France often been mistakenly equated with the emanation of Genevan Calvinism into France, but a strong argument has been made for the indigenous nature of the French Reformation. The Genevan source is patently mistaken, for it overlooks the fact that Calvin himself was converted only in the early 1530s, that he did not take up permanent residence in Geneva until 1541, and that he directed major attention to the world beyond Geneva only from 1555 on. Only from then on did the Company of Pastors systematically provide a missionary ministry for France, and the Genevan academy for the education of missionaries was not founded until 1559, which leaves two to three decades of evangelical expansion in France unaccounted for. By 1559 there were already some two thousand Protestant congregations in France. In that year, after nearly forty years of persecutions, Cardinal Charles of Lorraine declared that more than two-thirds of the inhabitants of France had already turned Lutheran. This was a wild exaggeration, of course, but does indicate the growing strength of the Protestants.

The argument for the indigenous source of the French Reformation poses genuine difficulties of definition.[1] Bishop Guillaume Briçonnet of Meaux sought to enliven spiritual life in his diocese and ordered Lefèvre d'Étaples's French translation of the New Testament to be distributed free to the poor. That dissemination of the Gospels gave a special intensity to the piety of the fullers, wool carders, and clothmakers on whose industry the prosperity of the region depended. He had assembled a circle of reform-minded, religiously concerned humanists at his court. When this group was suppressed in 1525, Marguerite d'Angoulême, the sister of Francis I, the wife of Duke Charles of Alençon and later of Henry d'Albret, King of Navarre, took them under her protection. This remarkable woman had learned enough Italian from her mother, Louise of Savoy, to read Dante and Petrarch's sonnets, and she could read Latin and perhaps some Greek as well. Influenced by Boccaccio's *Decameron,* she wrote a *Heptameron* of short stories, some with obvious moral messages, some risqué and bloody with a very dubious ethical point, reflecting the society of her times. She was inwardly an intensely spiritual person and she expressed her deeply religious nature in many poems and treatises, the most notable being her *Mirror of a Sinful Soul,* reflecting her deep mystical piety. Marguerite intervened repeatedly in defense of reforming Christian humanists and mystics. When the Sorbonne condemned the poet Clément Marot, the translator of the French Psalter, Marguerite interceded for him with Francis I and gained for him royal clemency. She intervened similarly for Bishop Briçonnet, with whom she corresponded, and in 1531 gave the most famous member of the group, Lefèvre d'Étaples, also known as Faber Stapulensis, refuge at her court.

Lefèvre d'Étaples (1455–1530) was religiously the most profound of the French humanist reformers. He received his doctorate in Paris, studied at Florence, where he encountered Neoplatonism, and at Padua,

1. The classic statement of the problem and argument for a Reformation antedating Luther's influence is Lucien Febvre, "Une question mal posée: Les origines de la Réforme française et le problème des causes de la Réforme," republished in *Au Coeur religieux du XVIe Siècle* (Paris, 1957), pp. 3–70

where he studied Aristotle with Ernolao Barbaro. He read deeply in the medieval mystical tradition, the writings of Meister Eckhart, Johannes Tauler, and Raymond Lull. He published in 1514 an edition of the works of Nicholas Cusanus (d. 1564), the great German Neoplatonist whose philosophical ideas of the learned ignorance, the coincidence of opposites, and panentheism were so rich and challenging, but raised the specter of relativity. But Lefèvre was influenced most strongly by Jean Gerson, whose emphasis on the spiritual meaning of the biblical text as the quintessential literal meaning which could be grasped only with the aid of the Holy Spirit proved to be of great significance to Lefèvre and through him for Luther. His extensive reading of the Greek and Latin church fathers added a further dimension to his synthetic theology. But it was his preoccupation with the text of the Scriptures that came to have the greatest historical impact. In an edition of John of Damascus which he published in 1505, he declared that the Scriptures must be the sole source and authority for man's statements about God. In the *Quintuplex Psalter,* 1509, he published five Latin versions of the Psalms in parallel columns to illustrate the variant readings and thus to show the need for precise philological and textual criticism. In his *Commentary on the Epistles of Paul* he presented the Vulgate texts, his own translation based on the Greek texts, and a commentary. In his Romans commentary he developed a high predestinarian doctrine and stressed, following St. Paul, salvation by the grace of God alone, received as a gift by faith alone without any merit or contribution of good works on man's part. He spiritualized the sacraments and denied that they worked *ex opere operato.* Both the Psalms and the Pauline epistles editions were of importance to Luther in his commentaries on the Psalms and Romans. Lefèvre also did a *Commentary on the Four Gospels,* 1522, and a French translation of the New Testament and the Psalms, based mainly on the Vulgate. Bishop Briçonnet appointed him his vicar general to reform the clergy and to inspire them with his mystical spiritual teachings. Hostility to his efforts was so great that in 1525 he was charged with pro-Lutheran sympathies and had to seek temporary refuge in Strasbourg. He was recalled and became tutor in the royal family and royal librarian in Blois. From 1531 on he lived under the protection of Marguerite in Nérac, where Calvin is said to have visited him in 1533. The reformers Gérard Roussel and Guillaume Farel also knew him personally and were influenced by his thought.

Calvin's associate and successor in Geneva, Theodore Beza, observed that in France one commonly speaks of "the Lutherans of Meaux." The

Meaux group certainly made an important contribution to both Luther and Calvin, but they can hardly be considered reformers in the same sense as the Protestant leaders. In fact, in 1523 the Bishop of Meaux warned against Luther's influence: "The whole world is filled with books. The common people, enamored of novelty and license and seduced by the vivacity of [Luther's] style, seem to be giving themselves over to his imaginary and fallacious liberty." Their mystical piety and Christian humanism could easily be accommodated within the bounds of tradition and they remained good Catholics to the end. They were religious renovators rather than theological revolutionaries in the Protestant sense or revisionists in the Counter-Reformation sense.[2] Lefèvre was cautious in his attitude toward the institutional church and respectful toward traditional authorities. Luther's evangelical movement had a powerful impact in France between the years 1520 and 1550, and while figures are imprecise, it could be argued that the Protestant tide reached its height in mid-century, ran into difficulties when Genevan clericalism and presbyterianism imposed itself upon the congregationalism of the earlier less well organized evangelicalism, and then receded under Catholic pressure during and after the wars of religion.

There is abundant evidence of an early and widespread distribution of Luther's books in France. In February, 1519, Johannes Froben, the Basel printer, wrote Luther that his writings had reached France, Spain, Italy, England, and Brabant. Wolfgang Capito at the same time wrote to Luther, "Your writings have been made public throughout Italy, France, Spain, and England." Lefèvre in April asked Beatus Rhenanus to greet several men whom he "cherished in Christ," and included Luther among

2. See the lucid discussion of the problem by Hans J. Hillerbrand, "The Spread of the Protestant Reformation of the Sixteenth Century. A Historical Case Study in the Transfer of Ideas," *The South Atlantic Quarterly,* LXVII, No. 2 (Spring, 1968), 265–286.

The main source of the identification of French Protestantism with Calvinism was very likely Theodore Beza's *Ecclesiastical History,* which minimizes the importance of Protestantism in France before 1550 as being small in number, disorganized, without a regular ministry, and tainted with heresy, and glorifies the period of Genevan hegemony within French Protestantism. The myth of an indigenous French Reformation was created some eighty years ago by a Protestant preacher, O. Douen, in an article entitled "Is the French Reform the Child of the German Reformation?" He saw Lefèvre as a French Protestant nationalist reformer. René-Jacques Lovy, *Les Origines de la réforme française. Meaux, 1518–1546* (Paris, 1959), stresses the evangelical nature of the Meaux group and affinity to the Lutheran evangelicals. The most complete, precise, and satisfactory work on the influence of Luther on early French Protestantism remains that of Will Moore, especially his *La Réforme allemande et la littérature française: recherches sur la notoriété de Luther en France* (Strasbourg, 1930).

them.[3] In November, 1520, the Swiss humanist Heinrich Glareanus wrote to Zwingli from Paris, "No books are more eagerly brought up than those of Luther ... One bookshop has sold 1400 copies. ... Everywhere people speak highly of Luther. But the chain of the monks is long." In April, 1521, the Sorbonne condemned Luther's doctrines and in June the Parlement in Paris imposed rigorous censorship on his books. In the fall of 1521 Luther's books were burned in front of Notre Dame in Paris, a *publica combustio!* In August, 1523, the first Protestant was burned in Paris. By 1525 the Parlement was taking measures which suggest that Luther's evangelical teachings were infiltrating all the dioceses within its jurisdiction. Robert Estienne and Pierre Robert, called Olivétan, published a vernacular translation of the Bible. In his *Acts and Monuments,* Jean Crespin refers to the early martyrs as "Lutherans," and refers to the small books passed from hand to hand as "silent ministers for those deprived of sermons." The small octavo book containing between five and ten sheets fitted easily into a peddler's pack. In this form, difficult to spot and confiscate, an avalanche of evangelical literature reached widely different classes of society: translations of Luther's sermons and treatises, polemical tracts, and prayerbooks. Printers and schoolmasters, as is evident from the court actions against them, were particularly receptive to Protestant propaganda.[4]

octavo book

The spoken word was still very important in that age, and the itinerant preachers without portfolio wandered from town to town spreading the Word. They were even more effective on the scaffold and at the stake than in their improvised pulpits. Crespin tells of a certain Anne Audubert, burned at Orléans in 1550, who "when bound with a rope in the usual way exclaimed: 'Lord God! What a fine belt my betrothed has given me,' and when she saw the tumbrel she cheerfully asked: 'Is this what I am to get into?' "[5] Florimond de Raemond, a Bordeaux magistrate and a friend of Montaigne's who had turned Protestant and then reverted to Catholicism, in his *History of the Birth, Progress and Decadence of Heresy in This Century,* 1605, marveled at the way the martyrs of the early Reformation

3. For Froben, *WA Br.* I, 331; for Capito, *WA Br.,* I, 332; cited in Hillerbrand, "Spread of the Protestant Reformation," p. 276, a contemporary source observed that Luther "wrote several books which were printed and distributed through Germany and France." V.L. Bourilly, ed., *Journal d'un Bourgeois* (Paris, 1910), p. 80, cited in Hillerbrand, p. 277, n. 42.

4. Henri Hauser, *Études sur la Réforme française* (Paris, 1909), pp. 225 ff. "Petits Livres du XVIe Siècle."

5. Jean Crespin, *Actiones et Monumenta Martyrum* (Geneva, 1560).

faced death. His graphic descriptions tell the story more forcefully than abstract analytic paragraphs could:

Meanwhile, fires were being kindled everywhere. . . . the stubborn resolution of those who were carried off to the gallows, where they were seen, for the most part, to be deprived of life rather than courage, stupefied several people. Because when they saw innocent, weak women submit to torture so as to bear witness to their faith, facing death calling out only to Christ, the Savior, and chanting various psalms; young virgins heading more joyfully for the gallows than they would have gone to the bridal bed; men exulting upon seeing the dreadful and frightful preparations for and implements of death which were readied for them, and half charred and roasted, they looked down from the stakes with invincible courage at the blows incurred from the hot pincers, bearing a brave mien; and sustaining themselves joyfully between the bayonets of the hangmen, they were like rocks standing against waves of sorrow, in short they died while smiling.[6]

Heresy crept very near to the very Parlement of Paris commissioned to deal with it. Florimond de Raemond recorded the death of a certain counselor to the Parlement and its effect on young onlookers:

When Anne de Bourg, a counselor to the Parlement in France was executed, all of Paris was astonished at the constancy of that man. We burst into tears in our colleges upon returning from that torture and pleaded his cause after his demise, damning those unjust judges who unjustifiably condemned him. His sermon on the gallows and at the stake caused more harm than one hundred ministers could have done.[7]

Not all the evangelical witnessing was of such a dramatic kind. German merchants certainly played a role, although there is less concrete evidence for this than in the case of England. It is possible that German students at French universities served as carriers of Lutheran ideas. At the University of Orléans, for example, where John Calvin studied for a year and a half, there was a lively *Natio Germanorum*, which suggests the possibility of such infiltration.[8]

6. Florimond de Raemond, *Histoire de la Naissance Progrèz et Décadence de l'Hérésie de ce Siècle* (Rouen: Chez David Ferrand, 1648), p. 864. Translation by Solomon Langermann.

7. Ibid., p. 866.

8. Detlef Illmer, Hilde de Ridder-Symoens, and Cornelia M. Ridderikhoff, *Die Matrikel der deutschen Nation an der Alten Universität Orléans,* Vol. I: Premier Livre des procurateurs de la nation germanique de l'ancienne Université d' Orléans, 1444–1546; Part 2: Biographies des étudiants; Vol. II: Biographies, 1516–1546; Vol. III: Tables, Illustrations (Leiden, 1971).

There were many avenues of access to France for Lutheran evangelicals, but the city of Strasbourg played a key role not only because of its strategic geographical location, but also because it adopted the Reformation early, was relatively tolerant of a range of Protestant opinion, and was hospitable toward refugees from abroad, playing host, for example, to a congregation of French refugees which Calvin came to serve as pastor from 1538 to 1541 when he was exiled from Geneva. Strasbourg more than Geneva was the mother to French Protestantism up to mid-century. One of the charges against the fourteen martyrs of Meaux in 1546 was that they had celebrated the Lord's Supper as they do in Strasbourg. Once again Florimond de Raemond grasped part of the picture allowed to fade away by many later, more scientific historians:

It was in your Strasbourg, which they called the New Jerusalem, the city which prided itself on being a neighbor to France, where the hydra-headed heresy set up its arsenal and gathered part of its strength to attack her. It was the refuge and meeting place of Lutherans and Zwinglians, led by Martin Bucer, a great enemy of the Catholic faith. It became the receptacle for those banished from France and the host city to the one who gave his name to Calvinism. It was there that the Talmud of the new heresy that he constructed, the principal instrument of our downfall, was built and shaped. In brief, it was there that the first French church, as they call it, was established to serve as a model and patron for the others which we have observed everywhere established in France.[9]

The aggressive Lutheran leader Philipp of Hesse, converted by Melanchthon, kept close ties to Strasbourg, corresponded with Marguerite d'Angoulême, and had the church ordinance for Hesse prepared by Francis Lambert of Avignon, a Franciscan convert, who favored the congregational system of church government.

The pejorative name of Lutheran was applied to nearly any and all Protestants in those first decades and it covered a multitude of religious dissidents. It is more difficult to assess Luther's personal influence abroad than in Germany itself, for his powerful German treatises were of little use abroad and his published Latin writings were limited in number during the early years, ten in 1518, thirteen in both 1519 and 1520, nine in 1521. His Latin writings were naturally accessible first of all only to the educated, which meant a certain trickle-down process was needed to reach the

9. Florimond de Raemond, *Histoire de la Naissance Progrèz et Décadence de l'Hérésie de ce Siècle* (Rouen: Imprimerie de Pierre Maille, 1647), p. 838. Translated by Dr. Barbara Tinsley.

masses. There were some translations of popular writings into Latin and French, however, and the printing press worked its magic. Eight collections of his treatises were printed by 1520 and perhaps as many as one million copies of his tracts and treatises were in circulation by 1524, an indeterminate number reaching foreign lands. Since Luther's technical exegetical commentaries on the Psalms, Romans, and other biblical books were not published, it was not the theological system as such that was transmitted, but rather some general religious ideas derived from his impact writings, criticism of abuses, repudiation of the papal hierarchy, rejection of human traditions and superstitious accretions, assertion of the Scriptures as authority, the Christological emphasis, Christ rather than the cult of saints, salvation by faith in the Savior rather than through works and the medieval sacramental-sacerdotal penitential system. Congregations developed in many cities and towns mostly under lay auspices and sometimes under the protection of the nobility. It is easy to see why John Calvin would feel the compunction to get French Protestantism organized, systematized in theology, and structured under proper clerical guidance, not to say control. That effort introduced stress within French Protestantism between congregationalism and lay prominence on the one hand and presbyterianism and clericalism on the other. Whether a more highly organized and militant form of Protestantism enabled the movement to survive at all during the Catholic resurgence of the second half of the century or whether it alarmed the authorities and brought on the repression is a question well worth pondering.

The Valois kings were not very consistent or effective persecutors of Protestants. Francis I (1515–1547) was preoccupied with his wars with the Habsburgs. With Renaissance artistic interests, he was at the outset reasonably tolerant. He even protected the raucous Louis de Berquin, but returned one time to find him burned for printing the writings of Erasmus and Luther. But the Affair of the Placards, October 17–18, 1534, angered and alarmed him. There appeared mysteriously overnight Protestant flyers, one attached to the door of the king's own bedchamber in Amboise and one in a bowl where he kept his kerchief. These scurrilous pamphlets, now thought to have been printed by Pierre de Vingle in Neuchâtel, mocked the mass, referred to a "God of dough," and spoke of "a man of twenty or thirty concealed in a morsel of dough" which might be eaten by worms or mice. This affront alarmed Francis into taking a stronger stand against the heretics. Francis, the "father of letters," now tried to suppress printing presses altogether, although we do not have the text of that edict. But he must have thought better of it, for the government began publishing pamphlets as "white papers" in defense of public policy as well as a constant flow of official edicts to suppress religious dissension. In 1537 Robert Estienne, for example, published *The Texts of Letters by Which Francis, the Most Christian King of France, Is Defended Against the Slanders of His Enemies.* Two years later he became the official printer to the king. In 1542 the Paris Parlement issued an ordinance condemning the *Institutes* of Alcuin (Calvin). King Henry II (1547–1559) unleashed sporadic persecutions. His queen, Catherine de' Medici, a niece of Pope Clement VII, despised the Protestants, although she was anything but a deeply religious Catholic herself. In 1548 Henry set up the *chambre ardent* as a special court in the Parlement of Paris to deal with heretics. In 1551 the Edict of Châteaubriand codified laws for handling heretics, set up lower courts to expedite their trials, and set up special sessions of the courts to deal with judges who were themselves suspect. The edict forbade all emigration from France and the importation of any books from Geneva. The Edict of Compiègne, 1551, commanded judges to show no leniency to the Protestants. It was not until after the conclusion of the Treaty of Cateau-Cambrésis with Philip II of Spain in 1559, however, that both monarchs were able to devote full attention to the problem of heretics within their lands. Henry was killed in a freak accident in a tournament a few months later and could not himself follow through on his plans for repression.

It is important to understand in what years Genevan influence began to determine the direction Protestantism was to take in France. Calvin had an early influence upon important people in ruling circles. He dedicated his *Institutes* in 1536 to Francis I. He corresponded with Marguerite through the years. Her daughter, Jeanne d'Albret, mother of the future King Henry IV, became a convinced Calvinist. Jeanne's husband, Duke Antoine d'Condé and king of Navarre, was claimed by the Protestants, although he died a leader, with Guise and Montmorency, of the Catholic armies in the first war of religion. The Prince of Condé, his brother, turned Protestant. Later the nephew of the powerful High Constable Ann de Montmorency, Gaspard de Coligny (1519–1572), admiral of France and commander of the French infantry, became a Calvinist. The Calvinist orientation of these high personages has contributed to the association of

French Protestantism with Calvinism. But it was not until 1552 that the French Protestants came generally to be known as Huguenots, suggesting the Swiss connection. The first French Calvinist church with a consistory of elders and a Genevan form of worship and celebration of the sacraments was established in Paris in 1555. Geneva had an earlier direct influence in the south through Lyon and eventually helped to sustain Calvinism in the south when it was in retreat in the north. Calvin's major effort to create a "rightly constituted church" in France on the Genevan model with local, district, and national synods to replace the casually organized and doctrinally imprecise or indifferent "Nicodemites" developed from 1555 on, after Calvin was securely established himself in Geneva and had triumphed over his opposition.[10] In 1555 the first formal mission was dispatched from Geneva to France when Jacques l'Anglois was sent to the Poitiers church, which long remained a mother congregation of the French reformed church. The Registers of the Company of Pastors reveal that some 105 pastors were sent to France, two to colonies, from Geneva between 1555 and 1562. Sources supplementing the Registers show 1561 as the peak year with more than 100 men sent out. Only seven years passed between the beginning of the Geneva Company's concentrated missionary effort and the start of the religious wars in France. The use of the printing press in Geneva for religious books accelerated at the very same pace. There was a steady rise in the total number of titles, reaching a peak in the years 1557–1562, with an all-time high of forty-eight titles in 1561, and then a slow decline after 1563. Geneva's oral and written influence on France clearly came late and corresponded to the years of Calvin's dominance in the city.

The first provincial synods and the national synods of Paris in 1559, Poitiers in 1561, and Orleans in 1562 saw congregationalism and lay leadership embattled and they eventually succumbed to the Calvinist consistory system with its clerical prominence. The National Synod of Paris adopted the "Confession de foi" *(Confessio Gallicana)* and the "Discipline ecclésiastique" which Calvin prepared. They reflected the theology and church polity of Calvin's *Institutes.*

Some of the nobility and a few intellectuals held out against the Genevan pattern. Jean Morely argued against the consistories and for greater democ-

10. Robert M. Kingdon, *Geneva and the Coming of the Wars of Religion in France, 1555–1563* (Geneva, 1956), pp. 2, 99.

racy within the reformed church; Charles du Moulin, the distinguished jurisconsult, served as an articulate spokesman and litigious opponent of the Calvinist ecclesiastical system; and Peter Ramus preferred the Zurich to the Genevan pattern. The Massacres of St. Bartholomew's day, August 24, 1572, put an end to the quarrel over the appropriate structure of the reformed church because of the general paralysis induced in French Protestantism from which it has not entirely recovered down to the present day.[11]

The demography of French Protestantism is rather imprecise. It is estimated that around mid-century about one-fourth of the population was Protestant. By order of the king a census of Protestants was taken in 1598, which showed 274,000 Protestant families, or about 1,250,000 people. This tally indicates that after the religious wars the number of Protestants had fallen to about 10 percent of the population. One-tenth of them were nobility. By 1670 that number had dropped to a mere sixteenth of the population. Moreover, after 1550 the Protestants were increasingly concentrated in the south, and by 1670 three-fourths of all Protestants were in the south.

The prosopography of French Protestantism reveals an equally interesting and revisionist picture. Contrary to an old view which saw Calvinism and the bourgeoisie as natural partners, newer studies indicate that French Protestantism was not exclusively a middle-class phenomenon, but embraced all social classes. The social composition of the movement was in constant flux, and the predominant group varied from region to region. In Languedoc the artisans made up over 60 percent of the Protestants, the professions such as law and medicine provided another 30 percent, the nobility constituted 3 percent, and the peasants merely 5 percent. The French peasantry seemed to be impervious to Protestant ideas, possibly because of the literacy problem, general conservatism, and the fact that no territorial province enforced a change in religion, as in the Empire. Though numerically small, the nobility provided most of the leadership during the sixteenth century, but yielded to the bourgeoisie during the next century.

11. Robert M. Kingdon, *Geneva and the Consolidation of the French Protestant Movement 1564–1572: A Contribution to the History of Congregationalism, Presbyterianism, and Calvinist Resistance Theory* (Madison, 1967), pp. 46–62, 96–111, 138–148, 200–202. On the effect of the Massacre throughout Europe, see the essays in Part I: St. Bartholomew and Europe, in Alfred Soman, ed., *The Massacre of St. Bartholomew: Reappraisals and Documents* (The Hague, 1974), pp. 15–96.

2. GENEVA

A contemporary of John Calvin noted the strategic location of Geneva: where "Germany, France, and Italy meet." The city at the headwaters of the Rhône had lively commercial ties to Lyon and lay on major trade routes, especially north and south. Its fairs made it an important mercantile capital.[12] It was the episcopal center of a large diocese of 443 parishes in 1447. In some ways it fit the pattern of late medieval cities, casting off the feudal overlord and the bishop's yoke in order to establish its communal independence, but it was unique in that it won and kept its independence during the Reformation period. In 1537 Geneva had a population of 10,300, which was swelled in the 1550s and early 1560s by religious refugees—a large number from France, a substantial number from Italy, and a few from Spain. The city's economic prosperity increased very slowly from the low levels of the 1530s which followed upon the protracted struggle for independence from Savoy and the bishops, most of whom belonged to the house of Savoy. "The Reformation at Geneva was more political than religious. It was less a conversion than a revolution," the historian C. L. de Haller asserted, not without some justification.[13]

The break with the Catholic Church and confiscation of its properties, a bold step which the city magistrates took with much hesitation in 1535, can be seen as the final stage in a war for urban independence. The city council justified this step in the name of "reformation," the restoration of the pure gospel and of primitive Christianity, the ecclesiastical counterpart to the city's "ancient liberties."[14] Calvin and the religious Reformation which he created had to make their way through tumultuous decades within the free city until his final years. Geneva did indeed help to shape the character of the Calvinist Reformation, just as Calvin reformed Ge-

12. See the Braudel-inspired work by Jean-François Bergier, *Genève et l'économie européenne de la Renaissance*, I (Paris, 1963), on commerce and communications, for fairs and markets, especially part 2: "Les Foires de Genève et la conjoncture commerciale jusqu'au milieu de XV e siècle," pp. 217–356, and part 3, "La Crise des foires de Genève, 1450–1480," pp. 357–436.

13. Ch.-L. de Haller, *Histoire de la révolution religieuse ou de la Réforme protestante dans la Suisse occidentale*, p. 169, cited in Henri Naef, *Les Origines de la Réforme à Genève*, II (Geneva, 1968), p. 1. See Robert M. Kingdon, "Was the Protestant Reformation a Revolution? The Case of Geneva," *Transition and Revolution: Problems and Issues of European Renaissance and Reformation History* (Minneapolis, 1974), pp. 53–107.

14. E. William Monter, *Calvin's Geneva* (New York, 1967), p. 59.

neva and made it the center from which radiated outward the second surge
of Protestantism. By the time Calvin arrived in Geneva the political revolution was already over and it had succeeded only after a protracted
struggle and several dangerous crises.

The feudal overlord of Geneva was its bishop, usually chosen from the
House of Savoy. Duke Charles III of Savoy was determined to take over
Geneva completely. The party within the city that favored Savoy was
known as the "mamalukes" and the party opposed to Savoy was called the
"Eidguenots." Fribourg and Bern supported the Eidguenots, and when
the Savoy troops besieged Geneva in September, 1530, the confederates
invaded the Savoyan district of Vaud and forced on the duke the Peace
of St. Julien. According to the Peace, if Savoy again disturbed Geneva the
allies were to have the right to reoccupy the Vaud.

Within Geneva a humanist circle led by Heinrich Cornelius Agrippa,
influenced by Lefèvre and Erasmus, inclined toward the Reformation.
They had learned of the Lutheran Reformation from the Tuchers, Nuremberg merchants who did business in Geneva. In 1527 the bishop withdrew
from Geneva. The notary, Robert Vandel, secretary to the bishop and later
of the city and chatelain of Bonivard, favored the Reformation. So around
1530 there was a small but influential group of citizens who favored a
reformation in the Protestant sense. When in that year the Bern garrison
arrived to occupy Geneva, their chaplain Kaspar Groszmann preached in
the cathedral of St. Pierre. The following year the council appointed
Claude Bigottier, a Lyon priest who was secretly evangelical, as school
superintendent. In 1532 the first public disturbances began. Pope Clement
VII had issued a jubilee and special indulgences, but when the people
arrived at the church door on Sunday, June 8, they found placards posted
with telling sentences from the Gospel. Now Pierre Olivétan (Olivier), an
evangelical cousin of Calvin from Noyon, replaced Bigottier as teacher and
Guillaume Farel came to Geneva and gathered the evangelicals around
him. On October 3 he was summoned before the bishop's council and
ordered to leave town immediately. He fled across the lake the next morning and a French stocking weaver, Guerin Muète, held the group of evangelicals together. Another evangelical, Antoine Froment from the Dau-
phiné, arrived on November 3 and began teaching reading, writing, and
religion. His following grew, but when he attempted to preach in public the
councilmen present prevented him from continuing.

A Sorbonne doctor, Guy Furbity, came to the city to oppose the heretics. On December 10 a Bern herald arrived with Farel, Froment, and Guillaume du Moulin. Bern demanded a trial for Furbity, who was eventually jailed. Farel and a young evangelical, Pierre Viret, now assumed the leadership over the evangelicals. Farel began preaching evangelical sermons in the Franciscan church, and a religious colloquy was held in the Franciscan monastery. When Bishop Pierre de la Baume left the city, July 14, 1533, he plotted with Duke Charles III of Savoy for a renewed war with Geneva. On August 22 he placed Geneva under an interdict. The city declared a state of siege and the Council of Two Hundred razed all the buildings outside the walls of the city to remove shelter and approaches for a siege force. Political and religious revolt were fused in this moment of crisis.

As at Wittenberg and Zurich, the excitement of the moment triggered an iconoclastic streak, so that a group of wreckers invaded the convent of the Sisters of St. Clare on October 24, 1534, and destroyed the images of the saints. Then came the crucial political turning point, the election of new syndics favorable to the Reformation. On April 2, 1535, the council installed Farel and Viret as the preachers in the church of the monastery of Rive. On April 4 some four hundred people celebrated the Lord's Supper in both kinds at the Rive monastery. The council sponsored a disputation which began May 30 and dragged into January between the evangelicals and the Catholics and obliged all clerics to take part. It followed the classic Swiss pattern of disputation, with Farel and Viret backing up Jacques Bernard, guardian of the Rive, the principal spokesman for the evangelicals; but the Catholics were poorly represented only by Jean Gacy, the spiritual of the convent of the Sisters of St. Clare, and a Dominican, Jean Chappery. The debate centered on such articles as the fullness of the gospel, church, customs, purgatory, images, the mass, and Christ as the sole sacrifice and mediator. Farel meanwhile preached in the church of the Madeleine and on August 8, with a large crowd, moved to the cathedral of St. Pierre. Iconoclasts destroyed the statuary there and in the Augustinian church. The Council of Two Hundred on August 10 heard Farel, Viret, and Bernard declare their teachings to be in accord with Scriptures. The council decided that the disputation had been decided in favor of the evangelicals and forbade the mass, which triggered a general exodus of Catholics from Geneva. All priests who would not participate in an evangelical service were ordered by the council to leave the city. The

1535. Council edicts in favor of Reformation

council ended the secular rule of the bishop, sequestered church properties, using the proceeds to liquidate debts to Bern and to set up a hospital in the Sisters of St. Clare convent. It began to coin its own money. It officially opened up the cathedral and the church of St. Gervais for evangelical preaching. The Reformation had reached a point of no return! The restoration of the gospel and reclamation of the city's "ancient liberties" were linked together in the minds of the councilmen, who, as "conservative revolutionaries," introduced radical change.

War with Savoy came as expected. Between October, 1535, and March 2, 1536, Bern and Savoy, with some French interference, vied for control over Geneva, yet by an adroit balancing act Geneva emerged from the struggle as a republic and maintained itself for 250 years as a state very different from the prince-bishopric it had been back in 1519. On December 27, 1535, the Bern Council declared its support of Geneva. On January 16, 1536, Duke Charles III of Savoy received the Bern declaration of war. The Bernese army of 6,000 men and 1,000 auxiliaries from Alpine villages and neighboring cities marched out on January 22, occupied the Vaud, and arrived in Geneva on February 2. By the end of March the key Savoy fortresses had surrendered, the upper part of Lake Geneva was secured, and on March 31 the Bernese entered Lausanne. The power of Savoy over Geneva was broken forever.

The Council of Two Hundred in Geneva moved to complete the Reformation. In April it ordered all priests in the countryside to submit to the Reformation and forbade the celebration of the mass in its territories. The Small Council asked the Council of Two Hundred to summon the general assembly of citizens in order to demand that "each one live according to the new reformation of the faith as it is preached." On May 21 all citizens assembled at St. Pierre summoned by the ringing of the great bell and with a fanfare of trumpets. With upraised hands all swore that they would henceforth "live according to the holy evangelical law and the Word of God." They swore to reject all Catholic ceremonies and resolved to appoint a headmaster for a school which all children must attend. On November 10, 1536, Farel presented to the Council of Two Hundred a plan for providing leadership to the reformed church. It seemed providential to many that at that point there had already arrived in Geneva a brilliant and zealous young French reformer named Jean Calvin.[15]

15. Rudolf Pfister, *Kirchengeschichte der Schweiz*, II, *Von der Reformation bis zum zweiten Villmerger Krieg* (Zürich, 1974), pp. 154–159.

In 1536 Calvin emerged as the new leader of Protestantism. In March the Basel publishers Balthasar Lasius and Thomas Platter published his systematic presentation of evangelical theology, the *Christianae religionis Institutio*, with a conciliatory preface addressed to Francis I. He may have written this catechetical handbook during his stay at Angoulême, after his flight from Paris, although a strong argument has been made for its speedy composition in Basel just before publication. Immediately after its publication he journeyed with his university friend Louis de Tillet to the court of Ferrara, where the Duchess Renée d'Este, daughter of Louis XII and a cousin of Marguerite d'Angoulême, was said to be inclined toward evangelical religion. She was pretty much hemmed in, however, by the duke and the pro-Roman clergy, so after a few weeks Calvin and his friend returned to Basel. Du Tillet went to Geneva and Calvin to Paris to set his affairs in order, sold his land in Noyon, and prepared to emigrate to Strasbourg. However, a state of war existed and in order to evade the marauding bands he traveled by way of Lyon and Geneva, accompanied by his sister and brother. Du Tillet alerted Farel to Calvin's presence, and Farel went to see him at the Hotel De'Ours in order to persuade him to stay and help with the work of reform in Geneva. Calvin wished to withdraw and live in studious seclusion, but as he put it later, "God thrust me into the game." Farel laid it on young Calvin, twenty years his junior. "If you refuse to devote yourself with us," he thundered, " . . . God will condemn you." Calvin recalled in his Psalms exegesis published in 1557 that at that moment he felt as though God had from on high laid His mighty hand on him. Calvin stayed in Geneva. His religious development up to that fateful moment is itself a fascinating story of a young Frenchman's road to Reformation.

3. CALVIN'S ROAD TO REFORMATION

Calvin was born on July 10, 1509, in Noyon in Picardy as the fourth son of Gérard Calvin, who served as secretary to the bishop and notary for the local cathedral chapter. He was pointed toward a career in the church and was educated in the household of the Hangest family, a noble family that had produced many bishops of Noyon, and in that environment Calvin perhaps acquired something of his poise and aristocratic reserve. In May, 1521, he received the first of several benefices in order to finance his education, was probably tonsured, and two years later he went off to Paris to study at the Collège de la Marche. There he learned an excellent Latin from Mathurin Cordier. He transferred to the Collège de Montaigu, where Noel Beda had inaugurated a severe scholastic regimen. Erasmus and Rabelais had studied there, unhappy with the discipline, and Ignatius Loyola was to come later. But Calvin made friends there who were to play an important role in his life, Nicholas and Michel Cop, his own relative Olivétan, who translated the Bible into French, and the great French humanist and distinguished Hellenist Guillaume Budé.[16] He took the M.A. degree, but then under pressure from his father, who had quarreled with the canons in Noyon and felt alienated from the church, he took up the study of law.

In March, 1528, he transferred to Orléans, where he attended the lectures of the jurist Pierre de l'Estoile, and in the fall of 1529 he went to Bourges to study with Andrea Alciato, an authority on Roman law, who demonstrated that historical and literary evidence could be applied to the understanding of legal texts.[17] Calvin studied Greek there with Michael Wolmar, who had definite Lutheran sympathies. In May, 1531, Calvin's father died and he returned to Paris, where he studied Greek and began the study of Hebrew with royal lecturers. In April, 1532, Calvin proved his humanist interests by publishing a Latin commentary on Seneca's *De Clementia*. Even though Calvin was at that time living at the home of Étienne de la Forge, an aristocratic Protestant who was later executed for his beliefs, there is no hint of Lutheranism in the Seneca commentary. He then returned to Orléans and completed his doctoral degree in law.

Calvin was drawn ever closer to associates of evangelical persuasion. In October, 1533, back in Paris, he was involved in an incident fraught with danger. His friend Nicholas Cop, as the newly elected rector of the

16. On Budé, see Josef Bohatec, *Budé und Calvin. Studien zur Gedankenwelt des französischen Frühhumanismus* (Graz, 1950), and David O. McNeil, *Guillaume Budé and Humanism in the Reign of Francis I* (Geneva, 1975). Bohatec argues for the essential humanism of Calvin on the grounds of his preoccupation with the three great ideas of God, freedom, and immortality. Quirinus Breen, *John Calvin: A Study in French Humanism,* 2d ed. (Hamden, Conn. 1960; 1st ed., Grand Rapids, 1931), pp. 113–124, says that "none of Calvin's contemporaries exceeds Budé in influence upon the young French humanists." On Calvin's early training, see particularly Alexandre Ganoczy, *Le jeune Calvin* (Wiesbaden, 1966).

17. Myron P. Gilmore, *Humanists and Jurists. Six Studies in the Renaissance* (Cambridge, Mass., 1963), p. 32.

university, delivered an inaugural address in which he presented the views of spiritual reformers such as Lefèvre and dared to use citations from a sermon of Luther. Although he praised all the sciences for their utility, he pronounced them relatively unimportant when compared with the time-honored philosophy "that God's grace alone redeems from sins." The reaction against the "Lutherans" was immediate and Calvin fled from Paris with Cop. His room was searched but he returned for his belongings before taking refuge early in 1534 in Angoulême, where he lived with his friend Louis du Tillet. He made a journey to Nérac for a brief visit with Lefèvre, who was spending the evening hours of his life under the protection of Marguerite d'Angoulême. In his *Life of Calvin* Theodore Beza reconstructed the conversation between the old Christian humanist and the young emerging reformer. Lefèvre urged him to moderation so as not to tear down the house of God he wished to purify. Calvin responded that the structure was too rotten to be renovated, but needed to be torn down and a new one built. Whereupon Lefèvre declared that Calvin would be chosen to be a mighty instrument of the Lord through whom God would erect His kingdom in France!

Calvin was always so reserved when speaking of his own life and inner self that dating his conversion experience has eluded even his most diligent biographers, some placing the event as early as 1528 and others as late as the spring of 1534. In the preface to his *Commentary on the Psalms,* Calvin years later recounted his experience:

God by a sudden conversion subdued and brought my mind to a teachable frame, which was more hardened in such matters than might have been expected from one of my early period of life. Having thus received some taste and knowledge of true godliness, I was immediately inflamed with so intense a desire to make progress therein that, although I did not altogether leave off other studies, I yet pursued them with less ardor.

His conversion had a very intellectual character and his teaching vibrated with a real religious experience. In Calvin's case these two characteristics cannot be dissociated from each other. Calvin had known of evangelical reform at least from the time of his first arrival in Paris at the very time that Jean Vallière was burned as a Lutheran. He knew of the Sorbonne's condemnation of Luther's teachings. At Paris and Orléans, possibly already at Noyon, he came under Olivétan's influence, a man more Lefèvrean than Lutheran, but a biblical reform type. His circle of friends included people of Protestant persuasion as well as those of Lefèvre's intellectual group such as Gérard Roussel and François Daniel. The year 1534, however, was decisive for Calvin's public declaration of his Protestant persuasion. In May he traveled to Noyon to resign his ecclesiastical benefices. He was briefly imprisoned twice, went to Paris, Orléans, and Poitiers, where he is said to have celebrated the Lord's Supper according to the reformed rite for the first time in a grotto near the city using a slab of rock as a communion table, although this report is not well substantiated. In 1534 he also wrote his first theological tract, the *Psychopannychia*, in which he argued against the notion held by some Anabaptists of soul sleep between death and resurrection. His 1534 preface to Olivétan's French translation of the Bible reveals his evangelical convictions. Although of a timid disposition, Calvin was, because of his conviction, brilliance, and eloquence, pressed toward a position of leadership in the Reformation. Then came the Affair of the Placards, October 18, 1534, and the royal reaction. Francis I dramatized his horror and anger at the Placards' denunciation of the papal mass by accompanying a solemn religious procession to the Cathedral of Notre Dame with lighted tapers to purify the city of Paris from the abomination. He imprisoned hundreds of Protestants, burned thirty-five of them, executed one of Calvin's own brothers. The following year, in order to please Pope Paul III, he issued a general decree suppressing heresy.

Life became increasingly precarious for Calvin and he retreated first to the security of Angoulême, but then was forced into exile, journeying with Louis du Tillet to Basel, where he assumed the pseudonym Martianus Lucanius. In Basel Calvin withdrew to study and to write and saw very little of anyone, but he enjoyed the support of such stalwart reformers as Pierre Viret, Oswald Myconius, and Heinrich Bullinger. It was there that he published his *Institutes of the Christian Religion* with its dedicating letter addressed to Francis, calling him to account for his persecution of the saints. Since Francis had referred to all evangelicals as Anabaptists in order to justify the severity of his persecution in the eyes of other rulers, Calvin spelled out the true evangelical doctrines in his catechetical handbook. There followed that sequence of circumstantial events that led him to Geneva.

4. CALVIN IN GENEVA

The magisterial reformers were men of the Book. Like Luther, the *doctor in Biblia,* and Zwingli, who preached his way into the Zurich reform, Calvin's first office in Geneva was as *lecteur en la sainte Écriture.* As a relatively unknown Frenchman he began a series of sermons expounding St. Paul's epistles in the cathedral of St. Pierre. A year later the magistrate with the consent of the people elected him as preacher. This timid gentleman soon proved that he could be bold in behalf of the Gospel. In a debate with Catholic apologists in Lausanne in October, 1536, during which he displayed an impressive knowledge of the church fathers, and in a disputation with the Anabaptists in March, 1537, he brilliantly defined his doctrinal position between the papists and the radicals. He so totally routed his opponents in the latter encounter that the Council of Two Hundred stopped the debate and expelled the Anabaptists. Up to this point Geneva had adopted Protestantism only in terms of the decision of May, 1536, to live according to God's law and God's word and to abandon idolatry. The way was now cleared for the construction of a reformed church order in Geneva.

Farel and Calvin had already in 1536 begun work on a church order for Geneva. On January 16, 1537, they presented to the Small Council their *Articles Concerning the Organization of the Church and of Worship at Geneva.* It was designed to provide a constitution for the reformed church which would assure it of existence apart from the actions of the government. Calvin, very likely the principal author, at the very beginning emphasizes that the Lord's Supper should be celebrated and attended often and church discipline exercised. Excommunication was necessary so that the sacrament would not be profaned by those partaking unworthily. Calvin wished the Lord's Supper celebrated every Sunday, but in practice he had to settle for once every three months. To enforce discipline the *Articles* requested that "certain persons of good life and repute among all the faithful" be appointed in every quarter of the city to observe the moral conduct of the citizens and to report open and manifest sins to one of the ministers. The steps of admonition outlined in Matthew 18 were then to be followed and if the brother remained impenitent, he was to be excluded from the church. Especially those people such as recalcitrant papists, "wholly contrary to us in religion," were to be excluded. Certain magistrates and the ministers were to test the doctrinal soundness of the people. Calvin urged the singing of Psalms to "lift up our hearts" and counseled that a catechism should be prepared for the instruction of the people. The *Articles* included stricter marriage laws as well.[18]

The Small Council approved the *Articles* but the magistrates were not eager to enforce them. The council had for centuries through sumptuary laws and other restrictions controlled much social behavior, but the new feature of the *Articles* was the tie-in of personal behavior with church discipline designed to prevent the unworthy from participating in the Lord's Supper. The church officials, not the state, should decide upon each communicant's fitness, with the magistrates merely enforcing a decree of excommunication. The magistrates were reluctant to give up their control over the social behavior of the citizens and a certain tension developed.

Calvin prepared a short *Instruction in Faith*, published early in 1537, in which he summarized the central doctrines of the *Institutes*. In November, 1536, he delivered to the magistrates a *Confession of Faith which all the citizens and inhabitants of Geneva and the subjects of the country must promise to keep and hold*. It begins with the affirmation that "we desire to follow Scripture alone as rule of faith and religion," runs through the teachings on sin, law and gospel, justification, faith, prayer, the sacraments, the church, excommunication, and ministers of the Word. It concludes with a declaration that the supremacy and dominion of kings, princes, and other magistrates and officers are a holy thing and a good ordinance of God. In his doctrine of the church and of the ministry Calvin was still in a living and vital contact with the Catholic tradition. He did not wish to break but to reestablish continuity with the true church of Christ and His apostles. He opposed adversaries in the name of that rediscovered continuity. He believed that for all its limitations and imperfections the local church in Geneva was the true church and that the universal church should be reformed on that pattern.[19]

Calvin's thrust was clearly in the direction of decency and order. Enforcing the demand for a common confession of faith by the citizens precipitated a predictable reaction. Farel, still the dominant figure, and Calvin, with the agreement of the council, had the confession printed and dis-

18. John T. McNeil, *The History and Character of Calvinism* (New York, 1954), pp. 138–140.

19. Alexandre Ganoczy, *Calvin Théologien de l'Église et du Ministère* (Paris, 1964), II: "La Doctrine Calvinienne du Ministère," pp. 141–402; "Conclusion Générale," pp. 403–434.

tributed on April 27, 1537, to every household by the head of each *dizaine* or subdivision. After a few weeks these "block wardens" were to lead the citizens of their division of their city quarter to St. Pierre, where they were to swear on oath to the confession. Only those who subscribed to the reformed confession could remain members of the church and thus also part of the civic community. This process was to be completed by September, 1537, but many were still remiss and so the confession was repeated on November 11. On November 15 the council resolved to banish all those who had not subscribed. Opposition in the council was strong and punishment was threatened but not carried out. However, on November 25 the council decided on punishments for those who were recalcitrant. A furor resulted with most of the hostility directed against Farel and Calvin.

Opposition developed both outside and within Geneva. The chief pastor at Lausanne, Pierre Caroli, charged that Calvin's *Instruction in Faith* (1537) and *Confession of Faith* (1536) were wrongly usurping the place of the ecumenical creeds of the ancient church and that Calvin was guilty of Sabellianism and Arianism. Caroli, however, a brilliant scholar but a highly unstable character, was brought before a synod in Lausanne, May 15, 1537, with the Bernese present and discharged from office for saying prayers for the early resurrection of the dead. At a later synod in Bern (May 31, 1537) Caroli was accused of leading an immoral life and was forbidden to preach. Calvin proved to be a tower of strength and easily vindicated his position on the basis of the Scriptures and his knowledge of the ancient church. The city of Bern also criticized the new confession and ordinances and demanded that Geneva adopt the Bernese church order prevailing in the Vaud. Within Geneva the chief opposition was led by Jean Philippe and was directed mainly against withholding the Lord's Supper from the unworthy.

On February 4, 1538, new elections brought the opposition into control. The new leadership was not so much antireform, but rather favored the Bernese pattern of reform with less extensive liturgical changes, for the Bernese were Geneva's best protection against Savoy. The Bernese order allowed the use of baptismal fonts, unleavened bread in the Lord's Supper, the observance of certain traditional feast days, and the like. While these were adiaphora to Calvin, he insisted that the ministers and not the magistrates should have the authority to make such decisions. The blind evangelical preacher Elie Corault was forbidden by the council to preach, and when he defied the magistrates he was imprisoned. When Calvin and Farel protested, they were forbidden to preach. But on Easter day, April 21, the reformers defied the order, Calvin preached at St. Pierre and Farel at St. Gervais. The Small Council, the Council of Two Hundred, and the General Assembly agreed that the preachers must go and they were sent into exile on April 23.

Farel and Calvin went to Bern to tell the council there about developments in Geneva. The Bern Council urged the Geneva magistrates to exact a less harsh punishment, but their admonition went unheeded. The two reformers moved on to Zurich, where they reported to a conference of evangelicals which met there April 29 to May 4. Then Farel returned to Neuchâtel, where he was to live out his days as preacher, and Calvin went first to Basel and then to Strasbourg, where he was befriended by the evangelical reformers and a tolerant city council.

Calvin's three years in Strasbourg were happy and highly productive, important for his own development. Martin Bucer, eighteen years his senior, influenced him by his example in his generosity in caring for refugees, his concern for forms of worship, and his churchmanship. Wolfgang Capito arranged for Calvin to give public lectures. Johannes Sturm appointed him a lecturer in the Holy Scriptures at his gymnasium. He became the pastor of the French refugee congregation which numbered some five hundred souls. He was very pastoral in his personal relations with the members, counseled with concern, preached daily, introduced the singing of psalms and liturgical change, and was beloved by the congregation.

In August, 1540, Calvin married a member of his congregation, Idelette de Bure, the widow of Jean Stordeur, artisan from Liège, whom Calvin had converted from Anabaptism. Calvin had written to Farel that should he marry he would seek a wife who would be modest, obliging, not fastidious, thrifty, patient, and apt to care for his health. In Idelette he found such an "excellent companion" and "precious help." She had a teenage son and a daughter, but the only child she had by Calvin, Jacques, who was born on July 28, 1542, died within a few days, a "severe wound" to Calvin. Idelette was herself very frail and died in 1549. Calvin was always dignified and reticent to speak of his personal life, but it is clear from his expressions of grief that his marriage was a very good one. He resolved to live out his years in solitude.

During the Strasbourg period Calvin's literary production was impressive. He did a new edition of the *Institutes* in 1539 and his own French translation in 1541, which became a classic of the French language. His *Commentary on Romans* was based on lectures which he had begun in Geneva. He tried for an even treatment in order not to concentrate in overmuch detail on difficult passages. He was also involved in congregational worship, music and liturgy. He compiled a book of music in 1539. He provided the text for *Some Psalms and Canticles with Notes,* although he was not satisfied with his own rendition of the Psalms and later substituted Clement Marot's translation. His liturgical effort, *The Form of Prayers and Manner of Ministering the Sacrament According to the Ancient Church,* printed in 1540, owed much to the influence of Martin Bucer's liturgy. His *Little Treatise on the Holy Supper of Our Lord* was a layman's guide to the doctrine of the communion, offering in some sixty short chapters Calvin's views of the centrality of the sacrament. Melanchthon's son-in-law, Christoph Pezel, recounted that Luther picked up a copy in a bookshop and praised it with the words: "I might have entrusted the whole affair of this [sacramentarian] controversy to him from the beginning. If my opponents had done the like, we should soon have been reconciled."[20]

Calvin's interest in church unity led him to attend the series of meetings aimed at the reconciliation of evangelicals and Catholics within the Empire. He participated in the conference on Christian reunion sponsored by Charles V at Frankfurt in March, 1539. There he had a long conversation with Melanchthon and was disturbed by his readiness to compromise. He was one of Strasbourg's representatives at the conference at Hagenau, 1540, and attended the disputation at Worms, 1540–1541. At Regensburg in 1541, where Contarini and Melanchthon arrived at a compromise statement on the doctrine of justification, Calvin was displeased with the willingness of Melanchthon and Bucer to cover differences with "ambiguous formulae." In June, 1541, he left Regensburg escorted by an official herald from Geneva. He journeyed to Strasbourg to arrange his affairs and then left the city, shedding tears of sorrow, for Geneva. He was most apprehensive about returning to Geneva, for as he had written to Viret half a year earlier, "There is no place under heaven that I am more afraid of." But duty called and when he entered Geneva on September 13, 1541, he was given a great public welcome.

During Calvin's absence city politics had hardly been tranquil as the

20. McNeil, *History and Character,* p. 153.

populace polarized with one party, the *Articulans,* nicknamed the *Artichauds,* favoring Bern and its organization of reform, and the other party named the *Guillermins,* after Guillaume Farel, favoring the Genevan pattern of reform and considering themselves the true patriots. The new preachers, Antoine Marcourt of Neuchâtel and Jean Maraud from Cully, were less impressive personalities than Farel and Calvin and could not provide effective leadership. In March, 1539, Calvin's influence in Geneva was inadvertently given an effective boost by Cardinal Jacopo Sadoleto, bishop of Carpentras, who addressed an irenic epistle to the citizens of Geneva urging them in the name of Christian love and the unity of the church to return to the faith of their fathers. The Genevans could find no one able to respond and sent an official to Strasbourg to ask Calvin to write a reply. In mid-August Calvin in six days wrote his brilliant *Responsio ad Sadoletum,* in which he opposed the ancient church and the Word of God to the Catholic concept of the enduring unerring papal church.[21] The reply was printed in Strasbourg by Wendelin Rihel and in Geneva in 1540 in Latin and in French, strengthening Calvin's image in the city.

The tide began to turn in favor of the pro-Calvin cause. The new elections in February, 1539, had already brought in magistrates less hostile to Calvin. On October 19 and 20, 1540, the councils and assembly decided to ask Calvin to return to the city; the General Assembly on May 1, 1541, formally removed all obstacles to his return. The new preachers (after Marcourt and Moraud had left), the councils of Basel and Zurich, Heinrich Bullinger and Farel all wrote to Calvin to persuade him to come back to Geneva. And so it was that Calvin in fear and trembling returned to the city from which he had been driven. He had, he said, sacrificed his heart to God.

The Sunday after his return he preached in St. Pierre, basing his sermon on the Scripture passage he had been expounding when he was forced to leave the city. He now determined to establish a reformed church order which had matured in his mind during his Strasbourg experience. Within two weeks he had written the *Ecclesiastical Ordinances,* which went through various revisions until they received their definitive form in 1561. They became important for reformed presbyterian church polity on the continent, in Britain, and America. The *Ordinances* established four orders of

21. John C. Olin, ed., *John Calvin and Jacopo Sadoleto: A Reformation Debate. Sadoleto's Letter to the Genevans and Calvin's Reply* (New York, 1966), p. 20.

office, pastors, teachers, elders, and deacons, and a ruling body called the consistory made up of pastors and elders to guide church affairs. The pastors preached the Word and administered the sacraments and with the elders cared for the Christian life of the congregation. The teachers or doctors included those who instructed in the Christian faith on all levels from elementary teachers to professors of theology. The elders were chosen from various sections of the city so that they could watch over the Christian lives of the congregation members and exercise church discipline. Some deacons called procurers were in charge of alms for the poor and others entitled hospitalers cared for the sick and the hospitals. The Company of Pastors met regularly on Friday to study the Scriptures. The consistory met on Thursday to act on church discipline and discuss moral behavior. At this point the city council still retained the power to enforce exclusion from the sacrament or excommunication, but Calvin was determined to make this a matter for church discipline, despite the civic implications of excommunication, a point of contention during the years ahead. The *Ordinances* included instructions for baptisms to be held during the services, frequent communion, liturgical advice, and hymnody. The call for frequent communion was amended before adoption by the government to read four times a year. The system of municipal government by the city councils remained unchanged, but the interrelations between the councils gradually shifted and the interaction with the influential consistory altered the church and state relationship. It took fourteen years of intense effort and the support of a large influx of French Protestant refugees before the new discipline could be firmly established.

Many of the old families opposed the new discipline and some of Calvin's staunchest supporters moved to the opposition. Ami Perrin, a staunch partisan of Calvin and an influential syndic, was alienated when his father-in-law, François Favre, was excluded from participation in the sacrament on charges of an unethical life. His own wife was cited to appear before the consistory for allowing forbidden dances at a wedding. The morals check infuriated those Genevans, whom Calvin called libertines, who had been accustomed to the traditionally lax enforcement of the morality or sumptuary law code. Pierre Ameaux, who designed playing cards and was a member of both the Small Council and the Council of Two Hundred, said privately among friends that Calvin was a worthless Picard who preached false doctrine. On Calvin's insistence the council made him walk bareheaded through the streets carrying a torch and wearing a penitent's shirt. When on June 27, 1547, a defamatory sheet was found on the pulpit of St. Pierre calling Calvin a hypocrite who wanted to be worshiped as a pope, an unlucky fellow named Jacques Gruet was condemned as the author by the city and executed.

Calvin looked beyond Geneva toward doctrinal unity with the other reformed Swiss. The main problem lay in the differences over the Lord's Supper, for Calvin held to a real presence of Christ in the sacrament, with Christ's body and blood given by the Holy Spirit to the believers. He sought middle ground between Luther and Zwingli, for Luther held to the ubiquity of Christ and the sacrament as a means of grace whereas Zwingli had stressed the symbolic or commemorative aspect, since Christ is away in heaven. In 1545 Heinrich Bullinger published a treatise directed against Luther in defense of the Zwinglian position, *A True Confession of the Servants of the Church.* In 1546 he published two further treatises and sent them to Calvin, who then became involved in correspondence, the exchange of treatises, and visits to Zurich in an effort to negotiate agreement on the sacrament. On May 20, 1549, Calvin left Geneva for Zurich and picked up Farel in Neuchâtel on the way. The conference in Zurich within two hours came to an understanding on the spiritual presence of Christ in the sacrament, and the Zwinglians joined with Calvin in subscribing to the *Consensus Tigurinus,* or Zurich agreement. Other theologians such as Martin Bucer, now in England, and John à Lasco, the Polish reformer, concurred. Melanchthon was favorably inclined toward the *Consensus.* A staunch Lutheran, however, Joachim Westphal, wrote against the *Consensus,* eliciting an apology from Calvin in 1554, and the hope that the Lutherans would subscribe was in vain.

Theological controversies arose within Geneva which had the end effect of strengthening Calvin's position as he triumphed over each successive opponent. There was an early brush with Sebastian Castellio, whom Calvin had previously befriended. Born in Nantua, Savoy, in 1515, Castellio fled to Strasbourg because of his reformed ideas, and in 1540 Calvin took him into his house. He followed Calvin to Geneva, where Calvin made him head of the Latin school, the Collège de Rive. Castellio wrote a text which greatly pleased Calvin, *Religious Dialogues in Latin and French, for the Linguistic and Ethical Instruction of the Young,* 1543. Tension developed over the Old Testament book the Song of Solomon, Calvin holding to the traditional view that it represented the love of a believing soul for Christ, but Castellio asserting that it was a secular love song that should be excluded from the canon. Castellio was denied ordination. They differed also on the question of Christ's descent into hell, Calvin maintaining that I Peter 3:19 and the phrase in the Apostle's Creed referred to Christ's pangs of conscience when he took upon himself the sins of the world, but Castellio insisting upon a literal interpretation. When Calvin was critical of Castellio's French biblical translation tension mounted to the point that Castellio left for Lausanne, where Viret provided a teaching position for him at Calvin's suggestion, but then moved on to Basel.

Calvin's position on election and double predestination hardened into firm doctrine under the attacks of Albert Pighius and Jerome Bolsec, a former Carmelite monk of Paris who had become a Protestant and served as a personal physician to a Protestant nobleman at Veigny around 1550. He frequently came to the meetings of the Company of Pastors for theological discussions. He charged that Calvin's doctrine of election necessarily meant that God was the author of sin and evil. Calvin's bad temper clothed in righteous wrath led him to accuse Bolsec of being a tool of Satan, and the magistrates jailed him. The Small Council was to try him, consulted the clergy of Bern, Basel, and Zurich, but received no clear-cut responses. In December, 1551, they banished Bolsec, who returned to France, rejoined the Catholic Church, and wrote a slanderous life of Calvin, 1577, not unlike Cochlaeus' *On the Life and Acts of Luther*. Bolsec died in 1584 totally alienated from Protestantism.

The case of Michael Servetus had a similar effect in hardening Calvin's dogmatic position and adding to his prestige as the ideological leader of Geneva. Since February, 1553, Calvin's opponents were in the majority on the council, and his most passionate enemies took Servetus's side in the notorious anti-Trinitarian case. Calvin was embattled at that critical juncture not only in defense of the Nicene Trinitarian formula, but for his own position of leadership as well. The deliberations of the Company of Pastors on the Servetus case relate the dialogue between Servetus and the ministers, but the first signature on the protocol is that of John Calvin.[22] Servetus persisted in his error and though Calvin argued in vain for beheading, he was burned alive on October 27, 1553, on order of the civil magistrates. Heresy of such magnitude was thought to be dangerous to the state, risking the wrath of God. Anti-Trinitarianism was not to be tolerated, as the trial and imprisonment of the Italian Valentine Gentilis in 1558 reconfirmed.

---

22. Robert M. Kingdon and Jean-François Bergier, eds., *Registres de la Compagnie des Pasteurs de Genève au Temps de Calvin*, II, *1553–1564* (Geneva, 1962), pp. 3–41.

The election of February 3, 1555, brought to office four syndics completely supportive of Calvin. On February 24 the council agreed that excommunication was a matter for the consistory, not the councils, to decide. Calvin's archfoe Ami Perrin led an abortive uprising of the Libertines on the evening of May 16, 1555, in an effort to regain power. Four Genevans including François-Daniel Berthelier were condemned to death and Ami Perrin fled the city. From April 16 to May 9 sixty French refugees were given citizenship in Geneva, and subsequently the number increased, all loyal to Calvin.

From 1555 to his death in 1564 Calvin's prestige and influence in Geneva were very great. But his power was only indirect and depended upon persuasion rather than upon political office or personal tyranny, so that it is a mistake to refer to this period as one of theocratic rule.[23] He continued his pastoral work as before, preached daily, and based his homilies on his exegetical studies. The total number of over two thousand sermons, most taken down by official stenographers, provide his commentary on every book of the Bible except for the Song of Solomon and the Apocalypse, a book which Calvin confessed he could not fathom.

He worked continuously on the *Institutes* and published the final Latin text in 1559 and the final French edition in 1560. The second edition of 1539 was twice the size of the first edition and this final eighth edition was twice the size of its immediate predecessor. It was based upon a masterful knowledge of the Scriptures and the church fathers. Instead of the twenty-four chapters of the edition of 1550, this final edition had eighty chapters, divided into four books: "On the Knowledge of God the Creator," "On the Knowledge of God the Redeemer in Christ," "On the Manner of Receiving the Grace of Christ," "On the Outward Means by Which God Invites Us into the Fellowship of Christ and Maintains Us in It."

The proudest achievement reflecting Calvin's Christian humanism was his reform of the educational system and the founding of the Genevan academy which developed into the University of Geneva. The elementary schools were reorganized, one for each of the three parishes at first, with a fourth parish and school added following the influx of French refugees.

23. The idea that Calvin enjoyed almost dictatorial power and influence was popular in the older literature such as Eugène Choisy, *La Théocratie à Genève au temps de Calvin* (Geneva, 1897), pp. 187 ff., "Le régime théocratique victorieux." For a detailed study of the Genevan institution which administered charity and engaged in support of the mission enterprise, see Jeannine Fahsl Olson, "The *Bourse française*: Deacons and Social Welfare in Calvin's Geneva," (diss., Stanford, 1980).

The ministers directed the schools. The students with greater ability moved up through the central system, learned Latin, and were prepared for the institution of higher learning which Calvin established on the model of the Strasbourg academy. In October, 1557, Calvin visited Strasbourg and was given a moving reception at Johannes Sturm's academy. When he returned to Geneva he persuaded the council to establish a similar academy in a new substantial building to be constructed on elevated land with a view of the lake. The secretary of the council observed: "The enthusiasm of the magistrates and the people rose above their poverty."[24] The academy, endowed with gifts and through wills, came into being and the building was completed by 1563. The faculty was recruited at the outset from the company of ministers in Lausanne, including as rector Theodore Beza (1519–1605), destined to become Calvin's successor as leader of the movement, Pierre Viret, and others. On June 5, 1559, the inaugural service was held at St. Pierre's with an address by Beza and a few comments by Calvin, stressing the liberal arts and especially the language emphasis of the curriculum. Calvin served in effect as the leading professor of theology. The Genevan academy became a citadel of Calvinist theology and classical studies, as well as a mighty instrument for the training and reeducation of dozens and eventually hundreds of Calvinist pastors and missionaries to other parts of Europe, especially to France.

Those final years were not without anxiety and danger from outside. In April, 1559, France and Spain agreed upon the peace treaty of Cateau-Cambrésis which freed the French king to concentrate upon the repression of Protestantism. The duke of Savoy undertook the recovery of the hereditary lands so that Geneva was threatened anew.

Calvin himself, never a robust man, paid the price for his increasing labors, many a day, he said, when he did not see the blessed sun and many a night when he paid no offering to sleep. On February 6, 1564, he wrote to the medical faculty at Montpellier asking for advice on how to treat his various illnesses—gout, asthma, intermittent fever, intestinal ulcer, and renal disorder. On Wednesday, February 2, 1564, he delivered his last lecture at the academy and the following Sunday he preached his last sermon. On Thursday, February 27, the members of the Small Council called on him to say farewell. The next day the Company of Pastors came to take final leave of their leader. Calvin reviewed his life, confessed to

24. McNeil, *History and Character*, p. 193.

mistakes, recommended Theodore Beza as his successor, and urged them to make no changes in the structure of the church or style of worship. Farel, now seventy-five, came from Neuchâtel to say adieu. Calvin died in Beza's arms at sunset, on May 27, 1564, with the words of the Psalmist, "How long, O Lord?" He was buried the following day according to his wish in an unmarked grave in the common cemetery of Plain-palais. The city secretary wrote in the protocol of the Council, "God gave him a character of great grandeur."[25]

5. CALVIN'S THEOLOGY

Born a generation after Luther, Calvin was greatly indebted for the substance of his theology to the Wittenberg reformer, as well as to Melanchthon, Bucer, and somewhat to Zwingli, though the structure of his theology and ecclesiology was characteristically his own. If Luther's theology was formed against the background of late medieval Catholic theology, Calvin's took form under the pressure of official oppression and a resurgent militant Catholicism. If his personal religious conversion lacked the dimension of personal struggle and liberating faith such as Luther experienced, his religious conviction was cast in the mold of his iron will and expressed with the force and clarity of his strong mind. The man of faith, Calvin firmly believed, has been predestined or chosen by God for salvation from all eternity without any merit or contribution on his part. The elect can never fall away, but will be preserved in faith to the end.

The most convenient summary of Calvin's theology can be derived from the four books of the final edition of the *Institutes,* a masterpiece of luminous argument. Calvin was the great dogmatician and his *Institutes* were the most complete systematic theology produced by a major reformer. Book I, "On the Knowledge of God the Creator," draws upon Cicero's *On the Nature of the Gods* to establish a natural theology context for theology proper, spelling out the interrelatedness of the knowledge of God and man. The knowledge of God in creation and conscience puts man under obligation for religious belief and ethical behavior. But because man's reason is clouded over by sin God revealed Himself in the Scriptures through the prophets, evangelists, and apostles. Through the Word of God man's mind can be enlightened through the "internal testimony of the Holy Spirit." There follows an orthodox exposition of the

25. Pfister, *Kirchengeschichte*, p. 225.

doctrine of the Trinity, creation, and Providence true to the Chalcedonian formula and the Nicene and Athanasian creeds.

Book II, "On the Knowledge of God the Redeemer in Christ," depicts man in his sinful estate, since the fall of Adam alienated from God and in need of salvation. The law of God convicts man of his sin and disobedience. The Gospel brings to man the good news of his salvation through the atoning work of Christ, who suffered and died vicariously for the sins of the whole world. The elect who trust in Christ the Savior receive the benefit of his sacrifice. The law also serves as a rule and guide to a sanctified and holy life on the part of the believers who are justified by grace.

Book III, "On the Manner of Receiving the Grace of Christ," deals with the work of the Holy Spirit, the third person of the Trinity. The Holy Spirit through the Word works faith in Christ as Redeemer in the believer's heart and provides faithful assurance that he is a child of God. The Spirit leads the regenerate man to live a sanctified life, to battle the lusts of the flesh, and to grow in love and righteousness. God from all eternity freely chose those persons who would be saved for eternal life and condemned the others to eternal damnation.

Book IV, "On the Outward Means or Help by Which God Invites Us into the Fellowship of Christ," describes the role of church and sacraments. The church is in one sense invisible, for it is made up of the elect from the beginning of the world and only the Lord "Knoweth them that are His." But the church is also visible in the present world wherever men publicly confess Christ and worship the one true God. The marks of the true visible church are the preaching of God's Word in its truth and purity and the correct administration of the sacraments of baptism and the Lord's Supper. This book spells out the structure of the church and the role of the pastors, doctors, elders, and deacons. The concluding chapter discusses the state, and Calvin makes clear his preference for a mixed constitution, a representative government serving a literate populace, but with an aristocratic element to serve as a check on the volatile nature of the common people. The state has historically taken many forms and the powers that be are ordained by God. A truly legitimate government must protect true religion and a tyrant who opposes the gospel should be resisted by those lesser magistrates with authority, just as the ephors in ancient Sparta were appointed to oppose tyrants.

Certain emphases stand out as being particularly characteristic of Calvin.

The most obvious of these is his stress upon the importance of predestination. This doctrine of election, derived from the Old Testament account of Israel as the chosen people (Deut. 7:7–8), from St. Paul, and from Augustine, looms larger in Calvin than in Luther. He did not make it an adjunct to the doctrine of God as a special application of divine Providence, but like Luther he develops the doctrine in order to emphasize that salvation is by God's grace alone without any merit or worthiness on man's part. Whereas Luther emphasized that the Lord is not willing that any should perish and that man is himself to blame if he remains unbelieving and reprobate, Calvin was not satisfied with an agnostic answer to the question why some are saved and not others. He boldly stated that God made that choice in all eternity and cannot be questioned any more than a clay pot can challenge the potter. He did not even shrink from saying that God willed the fall of Adam. Calvin was deeply concerned to honor and glorify God as the all-powerful sovereign.

A second unique characteristic was the quality of Calvinistic piety. The Calvinist, convinced of his election and assured of his preservation in faith, developed a heroic activism in the world. The Calvinist was noted for self-discipline, rigid morality, an inclination toward legalism, and a strong sense of vocation not only to the religious life but to his secular occupation as well. The Calvinists developed a certain moral earnestness and a militancy not known among the evangelical Lutherans. Strong will and the example of Calvin's own self-control, as well as an emphasis upon the Old Testament law and prophets, an identification of the spiritual Israel with the people of the old covenant, were elements that contributed to the peculiar form of Calvinist piety.

In the question of the Lord's Supper Calvin sought to find a middle ground between Luther and Zwingli on the question of Christ's real presence in the sacrament or the symbolic and behavioral aspect of the sacrament. Together with them he rejected the doctrine of the transubstantiation of the elements into the body and blood of Christ as formulated by the Fourth Lateran Council and reaffirmed by the Council of Trent. He also with them opposed the idea of the mass as a renewed sacrifice and wrote "Antidotes" to the decrees of the Council of Trent. On the question of Christ's presence in the sacrament he developed a formula which emphasized Christ's real but spiritual presence, for he visualized Christ as bodily in heaven. The difference between Calvin and Luther on this point was basically one of Christology and not merely a quibble as to whether *est* in "this *is* my body" was the equivalent of *significat*. Luther stressed the communication of attributes between the divine and human natures of Christ, the ubiquity of Christ whose glorified body was not limited by the time and space continuum experienced in this present world. Zwingli limited Christ's local presence to heaven, where he sits at the right hand of God, a phrase Luther viewed as allegory or poetic imagery, and he understood the communion to be a memorial service with symbolic value, not as a means of grace employed by God for man's conversion and renewal. Calvin was close to Luther in emphasizing Christ's real though spiritual presence, the regenerative power of the Holy Spirit working through the Word of promise given in the sacrament, and the importance of the sacrament in congregational worship. Calvin's Christology and sacramental teaching were closer to the Antiochan patristic type, Luther's more like the Cyrillic, that is to say, a trend toward a disjunction of the two natures of Christ on the one hand and an emphasis upon the full unity and deity of both natures in the person of Christ on the other.

Calvin's order of worship and liturgical innovations marked a distinct change from the pattern set by Luther. Luther had basically kept the formula of the mass purified of nonevangelical elements, had emphasized the centrality of the sermon, and had insisted upon the celebration of the sacrament as an integral part of every main worship service. Calvin simplified the liturgy further, was unable to make participation in the sacrament obligatory more than four times a year, and, despite his wishes to the contrary, had to accommodate to a separation of preaching and communion services. Due to his passionate antipapism and the influence of Zwingli, directly and indirectly through his Strasbourg experience, Calvin was more radical than Luther in reforming the church calendar by reducing the festival days to Christmas, Easter, and Pentecost and in renovating the churches by removing images, crosses, side altars, candles, and organs, anything that could serve as an intermediary object between the worshiper and God. The singing of Psalms was to be preferred to the sensuous tones of an organ. All worship was designed to favor and glorify the sovereign God. It is easy to see how Sabbatarianism and blue laws could in later years develop in accord with this stark ideal of worship. Calvin did indeed state formally in the *Institutes* in a sermon on Christian liberty that wine and other such gifts were given by God for our benefit. Calvin himself had an unusually good wine cellar. God does not forbid us to laugh, he said, and was himself very adept at punning. But he seems controlled and austere compared with the spontaneity and raucous good humor of the older reformer. In his ecclesiology Calvin was very close to Luther in his doctrine of the invisible church, and the essential nature of the kingdom of God, but he differed in his views of external church organization. Luther preferred a congregational order but was able to accept and live with the consistory and episcopal system that developed in the territorial and urban churches, since the external form of organization and support seemed to him not to be of the essence of ecclesiology. Calvin, however, believed that the form of the church that developed in New Testament times with the four prescribed offices was mandatory for the true church in all times. Despite the common picture of a Genevan theocracy, Calvin was deeply concerned to separate the church with its spiritual functions from state control, as was evident from his struggle to take the power of excommunication out of the hands of the magistrates and to place it under the control of the consistory. This insistence upon an independent church structure and organization was to prove to be of immense historical importance during the decades ahead, for it enabled militant Calvinism to survive and to make headway in countries in which Protestantism was a minority and the government hostile.

6. THE INTERNATIONAL APPEAL

Calvinism was well adapted to expansion and survival in a hostile environment. Luther had his preferred congregational form of church organization, but he did not consider organizational structure to be crucially important and was able to accept various adaptations of the episcopal system and management by consistories. Calvin's self-contained system of ecclesiastical polity was designed to assure the independence of the church from the state. The rise of Calvinism corresponded to the time of the Council of Trent and the beginning of the Counter-Reformation, which put Calvinism into a militant situation from the outset. The *Institutes,* the Genevan Psalter, the *Geneva Catechism* (1541, 1545), and other doctrinal statements in Latin and in French served as convenient handbooks for the propagation of the faith. Finally, Calvin's theology was clear and precise compared with the dialectic and paradoxes of Luther's theology of the cross, a logical reduction, as in the case of double predestination or the real presence of Christ in the sacrament. These elements of Calvin's ecclesiology and theology proved to be advantageous in Calvinism's spread and struggle for survival. The expansion of Calvinism lies for the most part beyond the scope of this volume, but well before Calvin's death the mission drive of Calvinism developed momentum.

In Switzerland itself the *Consensus Tigurinus,* 1549, had arrived at a statement on the Lord's Supper acceptable to Zwinglians and Calvinists alike. Nevertheless, the following decade witnessed further tensions between Zurich and Geneva. In the Vaud Pierre Viret as the leader of the church spread Calvinism among the clergy to the displeasure of Bern, which felt its Zwinglianism threatened. Conflicts about polity and predestination finally led to the banning of Viret in 1559 and the emigration of a large number of Calvinist preachers. In Lausanne the college or academy became an influential center for Calvinist teachings. In November, 1548, Theodore Beza came to teach and in 1552 he became the director, active until called to Geneva. The famous jurisconsult François Hotman, who was to develop theories of resistance to tyranny, taught there from 1550 to 1556. In Neuchâtel the church order of 1542 combined Bernese and Calvinist elements. There, despite his frequent absences on mission journeys, Farel was the determining influence until his death a year after Calvin's. In Fribourg despite early humanist support for Luther and Zwingli, a determined reaction set in, and from 1524 on the council sought to protect Catholicism from Protestant inroads. In 1556 François Hotman wrote to Calvin that in Geneva was engendered that spirit which raised up a new race of "Martyrs in Gaul, whose blood is the testimony of thy doctrine and thy church." Calvin's heart was with his fellow Frenchmen and he sincerely hoped that all of France would one day be reformed. He carried on an enormous correspondence with true believers and with princes, nobles, burghers sympathetic to reform whom he hoped to win over to the evangelical cause. His correspondence included letters to powerful men such as King Francis I, King Antoine of Navarre, Admiral Coligny, and Prince Louis of Condé, but also myriad letters to his young missionaries, imprisoned Protestants, and martyrs. His letters of spiritual counsel were jewels of pastoral concern, but he also concerned himself with practical affairs, jobs for the unemployed, support for the needy, tutors for the children of gentlemen, recommendations for students, and encouragement for evangelists. As noted earlier, although the parlements trying heretics continued to refer to "Lutherans," by the decade of the 1550s French Protestantism was taking on a Calvinist cast as French exiles returned from Geneva and as Calvinist literature reached increasingly large numbers of people. From 1559 on alumni of the Geneva academy became effective missionaries, often called by congregations of Calvinists who met in the estates of nobles, in private houses, in open fields, groves, or caves in order to escape the soldiery and judges of Francis I and Henry II. The French secular rulers had won extensive control over the Catholic Church and could not tolerate the independence of the "Lutherans" or Calvinists any more than their heretical teachings.

It is ironic that the Swiss, in accordance with their treaty with Francis I, continued to supply mercenary troops to the French for three years beyond his death, and maintained their contract of 1506 with the Papal states to provide Swiss guards down to the present time. On June 7, 1549, eleven cantons and some smaller cities, but without Zwingli's Zurich and Bern, contracted with Henry II to supply mercenaries, some of whom were used in later years to combat the Huguenots. The Swiss continued sending mercenaries to France later in the century for the armies of Charles IX and Zurich sometimes balked, but there was no stopping the prolific Catholic cantons. How little the Swiss remembered of Zwingli's sermons against this trade in young men!

The missionary drive of the Calvinists in France is well illustrated by the efforts of Calvin's own senior colleague Guillaume Farel. From Neuchâtel he worked for the introduction of reform in the priest-bishopric of Basel. He preached in the country of Montbéliard in 1525. Under the protection of Count George and Duke Ulrich, Farel's student Pierre Toussain introduced the Reformation to Württemberg, between 1538 and 1542. Farel was also personally active in Metz in Lorraine. In 1542 the evangelicals demanded a preacher and Farel went to serve. He preached in Montigny and in Gorze. In 1543 some two hundred citizens went from Metz to celebrate communion according to the reformed rite in Gorze. Government troops attacked them and in the general melée Farel escaped to the castle. When the garrison fell, he was lucky to get away alive and returned to Neuchâtel in 1544. He died there in 1565 at the age of seventy-six. The fiery pioneer who had won Calvin for reform in Geneva served as an inspiration for the young Calvinist missionaries who were to risk their lives for the cause.

It was during the period of the reign of Henry II (1547–1559) that several powerful noble families joined the Huguenots. The most eminent were Louis of Condé, Admiral Caspar of Coligny of the house of Châtillon, and Jeanne d'Albret, daughter of Marguerite d'Angoulême, the wife of Antoine d'Condé and mother of the future king Henry IV.[26] The Catholic party coalesced around the Guise family, Lorraine nobility claiming descent from Charlemagne, which had never been subservient to the king. The Catholic party was led by Duke Francis, his brother Charles, Archbishop of Reims, and their ally Constable d'Montmorency. Through the marriage of their niece Maria Stuart of Scotland to the dauphin Francis in 1558, the Guises established a relationship to the French royal family. Constant tension and skirmishing between the contending politico-religious parties led to the bloodbath at Vassy by Duke Francis of Guise on March 1, 1562, precipitating the horrendous French wars of religion.

In the Netherlands Charles V had been able to keep the Lutheran and Anabaptist movements in check by force. Pope Adrian VI supplied two experienced inquisitors. Genevan Protestantism made more notable headway, first of all in the southern French-speaking provinces. Calvin's own wife was a Walloon and he was interested in that land. French Calvinist refugees crossed the border into the southern provinces. Guy de Brès, who had been educated in Geneva, prepared a Calvinist confession that was adopted by a synod at Antwerp in 1566. The movement in the northern provinces was reinforced by the later arrival of English Protestant refugees, so that over the decades Calvinism became more firmly established in the north than in the south as the Dutch Reformed Church.

The abdication of Charles V in 1555 had unfortunate consequences for the Protestants in the Netherlands. Because of his early years in the Netherlands Charles had been reasonably well liked by the people, but his son Philip II, a Spaniard, was distrusted. He not only laid on heavy and arbitrary taxation, but adopted a repressive ecclesiastical policy and kept Spanish troops in the provinces as enforcers. He declared that he would rather die a hundred deaths than be king over heretics. He reorganized the hierarchy in the Netherlands, raised Cambrai, Mechlin, and Utrecht into archbishoprics, and increased the number of bishops with the intention of using them for the suppression of heretics. This move ran directly counter to the general European trend of city councils assuming greater prerogatives over the church at the expense of the bishops. The burghers of Antwerp resented having a bishop imposed on them. The nobility and the abbots of wealthy monasteries were angered by the taxation and the confiscation of property to support the new episcopal sees. Philip's per-

---

26. See the excellent biography by Nancy L. Roelker, *Queen of Navarre: Jeanne d'Albret, 1528–1572* (Cambridge, Mass., 1968).

sonal rule in the Netherlands was disturbed by the war with France and
a war with Pope Paul IV, but the Treaty of Cateau-Cambrésis, 1559,
established peace with France; Philip II would have had a free hand to
suppress Protestantism had not developments in Spain required his presence, and he left the Netherlands in August.

Margaret of Parma remained behind as Philip's regent, who was to rule
with the aid of a Council of State. But the council soon divided on the
question of the loss of Dutch liberties through the suppression of heretics.
Lamoral, Count of Egmont, a military hero, and William, Prince of Orange, who had served as a counselor to Charles V, opposed the repressive
policies pushed by Antoine de Granvelle, Archbishop of Mechlin, primate
of the Netherlands, and by the other two members of the council. Early
in 1559 William of Orange had learned of the resolution of Henry II of
France and Philip II to crush all heretics and he saw this plan as a threat
to justice and traditional liberties. He secretly resolved one day to "drive
the Spanish vermin from the land." When this secret resolution later
became known, he was called William the Silent, though he was in no way
taciturn. Egmont and William evolved as leaders of an opposition party
and the stage was set for the bitter struggle for the liberation of the
Netherlands.

Calvinism entered the Netherlands at the right time to become an ally
in the rising Dutch nationalist or independence movement. There had
been earlier influences from Strasbourg, refugees from France, the teaching of the Polish reformer John à Lasco, preacher in Emden, in East Frisia.
In 1545 Calvin had dedicated his Latin catechism "to the faithful ministers
of Christ throughout East Friesland." The Dutch were a trading people,
and traveling merchants as well as colporteurs brought in Calvinist literature. Despite the death penalty imposed on printers and owners of heretical books by Charles V, Protestant publications increased in number. The
coalescing of the patriotic and religious causes is best symbolized by
William the Silent himself. At the time of his famous resolution he was still
Catholic, though in reality a *politique.* In 1561 he married a Saxon Lutheran princess, and in 1573 he followed many of his countrymen in becoming a Calvinist.

Calvinism made little headway in the Holy Roman Empire itself until
the year following Calvin's death. Calvin was well known, of course, to
the Wittenberg reformers. His Strasbourg period and attendance at the
religious colloquies established further contacts and his publications cir-

culated, especially in the Rhineland. Strasbourg itself, however, joined the Schmalkald League and after the Interim turned staunchly Lutheran. The Calvinist pastor of Calvin's own congregation was expelled in 1555 and Jerome Zanchi, a Calvinist professor of theology, was forced to resign. The area most congenial for Calvinists was the Rhenish Palatinate, where the elector Ott-Heinrich was a tolerant prince. At Heidelberg University an angry quarrel arose between the Calvinists and the orthodox Lutheran theologian Tilemann Hesshus, who attacked Melanchthonians, Calvinists, and Crypto-Calvinists. Ott-Heinrich and his successor, Elector Frederick III (1559–1576), were offended. Frederick III actively promoted Calvinism, and Heidelberg became a center for Calvinist theology.

In eastern Europe Calvinism made its greatest gains in Poland and Hungary in the second half of the century. The pattern was similar in the two cases, with the landed magnates favoring Calvinism and eventually the monarchs under the influence of Jesuits repressing it. With the accession of King Sigismund II August (1548–1572) in Poland, Calvinism made its first inroads. Sigismund had corresponded with Calvin and was impressed with the *Institutes*. In 1554 Calvin proposed to him a plan for the reform of the Polish church under an evangelical archbishop and with Calvinist bishops, an odd kind of adaptation on Calvin's part, except for the fact that local church life was still to be organized on the familiar presbyterian pattern. This pattern appealed to the middle and lesser Polish nobility, for it provided for lay membership at the consistories and lay participation at the provincial and national synodical levels, analogous to their political interests. As a militant form of Protestantism, Calvinism was set against the Roman Catholic hierarchy and absolute monarchy. Moreover, Lutheranism was associated too closely with competing German provinces, as in the case of Duke Albert of Prussia. King Sigismund II was a loser, having permitted the hereditary union of East Prussia with Brandenburg under Elector Joachim, having lost his war with Ivan IV of Muscovy, and proving incapable of checking the landed magnates. The diet of nobles through a law called "Execution" took over most government functions, passed legislation that further weakened the cities, and in the Union of Lublin, 1569, brought Poland and Lithuania into a closer union, with one king and one diet. In Lithuania the powerful landed magnate Nicholas Radziwill, Sigismund's chancellor, became a Calvinist with all of his feudal estates and dependencies.

The leading religious figure in Little Poland was John à Lasco. He had become a Lutheran and helped reorganize the church in ducal Prussia. He veered toward Calvinism, however, and served refugee congregations in Frankfort, Emden, and in London, for three years during the reign of Edward VI. In 1557 he returned to Poland where he promoted Calvinist theology and polity.

Until mid-century Lutheranism dominated the Protestant movement in Hungary, as in Austria, but then the appeal of Calvinism to the landed magnates made itself felt. Matthias Biró (Dévay) established the Genevan pattern in the city of Debrecen. In Transylvania the Lutherans or "Transylvania Saxons" were increasingly challenged by Calvinism. John Zapolya had stood off both the Habsburgs and the Turks, who tolerated his rule, and the relative independence of Transylvania was favorable to the local rule of the church favored by the Calvinists. Villages and towns were given authorization to choose preachers congenial to them. Calvinism maintained itself more successfully in Hungary than in Poland, but both areas suffered from a lack of creativity and energy comparable to Calvinism in Switzerland, France, and the Netherlands. Resurgent Catholicism was soon to win the upper hand also in Hungary, where the Habsburgs put the reformed church under heavy pressure.

Protestantism made few serious inroads into Italy and Spain. The fact that Italy was the homeland of the papacy was considered an asset. The financial exactions by the Catholic Church were less burdensome than those imposed in Germany. The reawakened Catholic piety stimulated some spiritualists and evangelical humanists to follow their individualist lights, but no real Protestant church movement developed. There were small circles of evangelicals in Venice, Modena, Ferrara, Lucca, and Naples. In Venice at one point there were said to be only eight hundred "Lutherans." In Ferrara Duchess Renée, whom Calvin had gone to visit, protected a group of evangelicals, but she was isolated at the court by her husband Duke Ercole II, and eventually her own son, Alfonso, drove her out and back to France. There the remarkable woman Olympia Morata held a spiritualized faith not unlike Marguerite d'Angoulême's. The largest reformed community in Italy was probably Lucca, led by Peter Martyr Vermigli, an Augustinian canon, until the 1542 crackdown. A high percentage of the Italian emigrants to Geneva were Lucchese.

In Naples the Spaniard Juan de Valdés (c. 1500–1541), twin brother of Alphonso, the reform-minded counselor in the chancellory of Charles V, developed a circle of religious humanists. Valdés, Erasmian and mystical, moved from Naples to Rome in 1531 to serve as an attendant to Pope Clement VII. He returned permanently to Naples in the fall of 1533. He did poetry and prose politico-religious writings such as his *Diálogo de Mercurio y Caron* and philological treatises such as his *Diálogo de la Lengua,* 1533. Valdés was most deeply involved, however, in biblical studies and devotional writing. His coterie included such reform-minded religious spirits as Peter Martyr Vermigli, Marcantonio Flaminio, Vittoria Colonna, Margravine of Pescara, a celebrated religious poet, and her sister-in-law Giulia Gonzaga, Bernardino Ochino, and Pier Paolo Vergerio the younger. Pietro Carnesecchi (1508–1567) attributed his acceptance of the doctrine of justification by faith to the influence of Valdés. The most famous writing to come out of this circle was the *Il Beneficio de Cristo* commonly attributed to the Augustinian monk Benedetto de Mantova, although it may have been the work of Flaminio or of multiple authorship. It drew heavily upon the ideas on sin and grace of Valdés, Luther, and especially Calvin.[27]

The spiritual revival affected some Catholic churchmen who remained within the church such as Gasparo Contarini, who negotiated at the religious colloquies with the Lutherans, Cardinal Giovanni Morone, who played a significant role at the Council of Trent, and Cardinal Reginald Pole, who was alternately accused of Protestantism and Papism.[28] But the fate of the movement was decided by repression. With the passing of Valdés in 1541, the spirit of the movement also ebbed away. In 1542 Paul III decided on the renewal of the Inquisition, which shattered these evangelical circles and scattered their adherents. A stream of refugees such as Vermigli, Ochino, Vergerio, fled to the north, to Calvin's Geneva and beyond, Vermigli to Oxford, Ochino to London.

In Spain the evangelical movement was even more isolated. The Spanish Inquisition repressed Erasmians and Lutherans alike. As early as 1521 severe penalties were established for possessing heretical books. Nor did Calvinism make any headway in Spain. The Inquisition acted against the small circles of evangelicals in Seville and Valladolid in 1557 and 1558 and the autos-da-fé of 1559 and 1560 destroyed the movement completely.

The career of Bartolomé Carranza (1503–1576) illustrates well the

27. The new edition of *Il Beneficio di Cristo,* Salvatore Caponetto, ed., in the *Corpus Reformation Italicorum* (Florence and Chicago, 1972), includes sixteenth-century editions in English, French, Croatian, and supplementary documents.

28. See Paolo Simoncelli, *Il Caso Reginald Pole Eresia e Santita' nelle Polemiche Religiose del Cinquecento* (*Uomini e Dottrini,* 23), *Edizioni di Storia e Letteratura* (Rome, 1977).

tight control exercised over theologians and ecclesiastical administrators. He studied at the Alcala, became one of the most learned men in Spain, but was denounced by the Inquisition for Erasmianism and favoring limitations on papal power. Exonerated of these charges, he represented his order in Rome, where he encountered Valdés and gained the confidence of Paul III. He returned to Spain where he became a censor of books for the Inquisition. Charles V sent him as emissary to the Council of Trent. In 1557 Philip II had him made Archbishop of Toledo. He was at the deathbed of Charles V and gave him extreme unction. But even this establishment man was accused by the Inquisition of Lutheran sympathies. Philip II had him arrested and imprisoned for almost eight years. He appealed to Rome, where he was taken in 1566, and held in the Castello San Angelo for ten years. He was found innocent of heresy but was kept in the Dominican cloister of Santa Maria sopra Minerva. He finally abjured sixteen errors of which he was accused and died seven days later. Calvin had considered him a Nicodemite who failed to confess his faith openly.

Calvinism's clearest triumph came in the far north with the Reformation of Scotland, a story best told together with that of the English Reformation.

Chapter Five

THE ENGLISH REFORMATION

1. THE POPULAR GROUNDSWELL

JOHN DRYDEN perhaps spoke more wisely than he knew when he penned the lines

> But 'tis the talent of our English nation,
> still to be plotting some new reformation.

In the case of the English Reformation, the entire nation was involved to a greater extent than historians formerly realized. The English Reformation was not merely a matter of state and statute, an official governmental change initiated and directed from above, but was anticipated and made viable by the changes in popular religious feeling below.[1] Those changes were not simply the immediate product of social and economic forces. Despite the fact that England was subject to the same general pressures evident on a European scale such as population increase and price rises, the country differed sufficiently from the Protestant lands on the continent that an easy parallel to the continental Reformation can not be drawn. Nevertheless, the social structure and economic activities of various classes of people did incline them toward dissidence and brought them more readily into contact with Protestant ideas. The spread of Protestant ideas, anticlericalism, anti-Romanism, evangelical religion, and biblical theology played a very important role in facilitating the break with the Roman Catholic Church and the launching of the Reformation in England. Moreover, Christian humanism contributed to a public philosophy among politicians, statesmen, royal officials, and members of Parliament favorable to reform in the commonwealth. A climate of public opinion and passion developed that made possible the schism from Rome under Henry VIII.

Conventional religion on the eve of the Reformation conformed to the

---

1. A classic example of the traditional "the King's Great Question" and Parliament historiography is Sir Maurice Powicke, *The Reformation in England* (London, 1941), which begins (p. 1) with the statement: "The one definite thing which can be said about the Reformation in England is that it was an act of state."

general European patterns of late medieval piety. Erasmus in a famous colloquy mocked the superstitious saints' cults and the pilgrimages to Mary of Walsingham, with the crass commercialization of the shrine and ignorance of the canons. But Henry VIII made his pilgrimage there as well as the least of his subjects. Fear of demons was rife and cults of the saints flourished. Since Christ was viewed as the stern judge of the Last Day, people sought the intercessions of Mother Mary and the saints. Fear of eternal torments in hell for the damned was accompanied by dread of intense suffering in purgatory immediately after death in order to purify the soul for entrance into heaven. Time spent in purgatory could be reduced by the purchase of indulgences and intercessory masses provided for in advance, in one's will, or by one's survivors. Henry VII ordered 10,000 masses for his soul at sixpence each, and in his will Henry VIII provided for many masses to be said for his soul. In the *Supplication of Souls* Thomas More depicts souls of the dead begging for prayers and intercessory masses. Popular books such as the *Lay Folke's Mass Book* circulated widely containing the offices of Our Lady and of the dead, the litany of the saints, and collections of prayers for the dead. Despite the limited circulation of religious books, the common people acquired a catechetical knowledge of church teachings. Although sermons were infrequent in village churches, the oral tradition was strong and some sound teaching by pious and good priests was transmitted along with the superstitions.

In limited circles mysticism and the new devotion of the Brethren of the Common Life added a deeper dimension of spirituality to church life. The works of fourteenth-century mystics still circulated in the sixteenth century. Richard Rolle (c. 1300–1349), the "hermit of Hampole," led a contemplative life and opposed papal supremacy. His works included *The Mending of Life, The Form of Perfect Living,* and *The Fire of Love.* Walter Hilton (c. 1330–c. 1395), an Augustinian canon of Thurgarton Priory, Nottinghamshire, was the author of the *Ladder of Perfection. The Cloud of Unknowing* by an anonymous author was especially influential. Among the regular clergy in England, none had the perfect record of the Carthusians, two of whom, John Norton and Robert Methley, wrote mystical treatises. Thomas More lived for some years with the London Carthusians and wore a hair shirt throughout his life to chasten his sinful flesh. The more practical or voluntaristic mysticism of the Brethren of the Common Life entered English religious life along with other influences that accompanied commercial contacts with the Netherlands. Thomas à Kempis's *The Imitation of Christ* circulated during those decades. But there were two weaknesses in these otherwise promising signs of religious vitality. First, mysticism is almost by definition personal and internalized, providing no program for social reform or community life. Second, the Bible in English was a very rare book. In 1408 any translation not sanctioned by the bishops was prohibited, in contrast to the twenty complete translations which appeared between 1466 and 1522 in Germany. The Bible as a forbidden book circulated underground through the counterculture of Lollardy.

[margin note: New Bible in English]

Lollardy was still a vital force during the first three decades of the sixteenth century. The evidence comes largely from the trial records of the "secret multitude of true professors," the name John Foxe gave to the Lollards in his *Book of Martyrs*. According to the records, many more abjured than became martyrs, but the statistics of those accused of Lollardy are impressive. In the diocese of London in 1510 Bishop Fitzjames brought fifty Lollards to trial and in 1518 nearly as many. His successors Tunstall and Stokesley forced at least 218 heretics to abjure, and other dioceses show smaller but significant numbers. Even when Lutheran doctrines surfaced in the trials the predominant element remained Lollard.[2] The term "Lollard," of uncertain origin, designated a fourteenth-century sect in the Netherlands related to the Beghards and Beguines. The Irish Cistercian Henry Crump applied the term, which suggested a "mumbler" of prayers, to the followers of the heretical John Wycliffe (1320–1384), antipapalist and critic of the doctrine of transubstantiation. This underground heretical movement had no precise confessional statement, but certain positions were common to most groups. The author of *The Wycket*, mistakenly attributed to Wycliffe, criticized transubstantiation. A group of Lollard supporters in the House of Commons in 1395 drew up "Twelve Conclusions" which condemned transubstantiation, clerical celibacy, prayer for the dead, pilgrimages, images, useless liturgical trappings, and the subordination of the English church to the papacy. In his *Acts and Monuments*, John Foxe wrote of the Lollards: "In four principal points they stood against the church of Rome: in pilgrimage, in adoration of saints, in reading of Scripture Books in English and in the carnal presence of Christ's body in the Sacrament." The Lollards were unanimous in stressing

[margin note: Lollards]

2. A. G. Dickens, *Lollards and Protestants in the Diocese of York 1509–1558* (London, 1959), pp. 8, 9. A. G. Dickens, *The English Reformation* (London, 1964), is the most excellent comprehensive history of the period synthesizing modern scholarship. See also John A. F. Thomson, *The Later Lollards 1414–1520* (New York, 1965).

the need for gospel preaching and the study of the Bible in English. Whatever historical legitimacy may be claimed for the concatenation of influence from Wycliffe to Hus to Luther, it is clear from Lollard teachings that there was a preestablished harmony between them and the tenets of Lutheranism. In 1523 the London bishop Cuthbert Tunstall complained that Lutheranism was adding "new arms" to Lollardy.

Although there is little evidence connecting the Lollards with Robert Barnes and other early Lutherans, there were some ties, such as the use by some Lollards of William Tyndale's English New Testament. Tyndale, in turn, published two old Lollard tracts to show that Lutheranism was not a novelty. The White Horse Inn group of Cambridge intellectuals owed nothing to Lollards as to doctrine, but their associates, the "Christian Brethren," who financed the selling of Lutheran books, included men with Lollard associations.[3] One of the Cambridge group, Thomas Bilney, preached to Lollard communities in East Anglia. During the 1530s the Lollard and Protestant movements tended to fuse, though identifiable groups holding characteristic Lollard tenets persisted through the reign of Henry VIII and beyond. There is some slight evidence of association between Lollardy and Anabaptism of Dutch mediation, at least in the minds of conservative Protestants such as Hugh Latimer. Most Lollards were common people, simple unlearned laborers and craftsmen rather than husbandmen. Those elements of the middle and lower classes that had greater mobility and continental contacts became the first carriers of Protestant ideas and in certain ranges of society there was a distinguishable overlap with communities of Lollards. The merchant classes who traveled to the continent or had contact with continental merchants in English ports and marts were prominent in the circulation of Protestant books and ideas. Weavers and other clothmakers had contacts with foreign immigrant workers and were themselves mobile among the textile centers. Lawyers and judges in the common law tradition had for two centuries sought to bring ecclesiastical jurisdiction within the limits of the statutes of *Praemunire*. Their resentment against special privileges and exemptions of the clergy grew into a generalized anticlericalism. The many country gentry and others who studied law at the Inns of Court imbibed an atmosphere critical of the hierarchy.

Anticlericalism contributed much to the climate favoring change. At

3. Dickens, *Lollards and Protestants*, p. 10.

the very top of the English hierarchy, Cardinal Thomas Wolsey (1471–1530) served as the prime example of clerical arrogance, political ambition, and material aggrandizement. The son of a cheating butcher in Suffolk, Wolsey rose through the church and Oxford, where he became bursar of Magdalen College, and caught the attention of Henry VIII, who appointed him chancellor in 1515. Pope Leo X in 1518 named Cardinal Wolsey his *legatus a latere* in the provinces of both York and Canterbury. As legate and chancellor, Wolsey held the reins of both church and state in his hands. But if ever he were to lose church backing he would have no counterpoise to the will of his headstrong young monarch. Wolsey enjoyed power and used it to aggrandize his personal honor and fortune. He held multiple benefices as Archbishop of York, bishop of Durham and Winchester, deputy for nonresident alien bishops at Worcester, Salisbury, and Llandaff, and abbot of St. Albans. He made his illegitimate son dean of Wells and archdeacon of York and Richmond, with two rectories, six prebends, and one appointment as chancellor. He dissolved twenty-eight smaller religious houses in order to divert their endowments to found his own college at Oxford, later known as Christ Church College, and to a new preparatory school at Ipswich. He loved ostentatious display, built palaces such as Hampton Court Manor, and played a grand role on state occasions.[4] Wolsey had strong points as well, occasionally protecting the poor against the powerful. In the interests of the peasants being forced off the land, he worked to slow down enclosures of common lands. Moreover, he had a corner of his mind open for education and new ideas. No one was burned for heresy when Wolsey was at the height of his power. Nevertheless, because of his visibility he stood in the popular mind as the prime example of the worldliness and corruption of the higher clergy.

With such concrete examples before their very eyes, the people were easily stirred up by anticlerical writings of publicists such as Christopher St. Germain, a common lawyer and eminent theorist, and Simon Fish, a scurrilous pamphleteer, who attacked abuses harshly in the years 1529–31. Simon Fish, an Oxford student who entered Gray's Inn about 1525, belonged to a circle of young men in London who were critical of Wolsey and the clergy. In his vicious pamphlet *A Supplication for the Beggars, Written About the Year 1529,* he complained to the king that the poor

4. Charles W. Ferguson, *Naked to Mine Enemies: The Life of Cardinal Wolsey* (Boston, 1958), pp. 121–232.

beadsmen were being devoured by ravenous wolves in sheep's clothing —the bishops, abbots, priors, deacons, archdeacons, suffragens, priests, monks, canons, friars, pardoners, and summoners—strong, puissant, and counterfeit holy and idle beggars and vagabonds. Following a quarrel with Wolsey, Fish was forced into exile and was subsequently instrumental in distributing copies of Tyndale's English New Testament. In his *Acts and Monuments* John Foxe relates that Anne Boleyn gave a copy of the *Supplication* to Henry VIII, who asked to meet the author, who was hiding nearby. The king embraced him, took him as a hunting partner, and gave him the royal signet to protect him from Chancellor Thomas More, foe of heretics. Fish was to die instead of the plague in 1531. His widow married a Protestant whom More had whipped in his garden.

Several scandalous instances of clerical tyranny roused the public against clerical privileges, immunities, and special courts. The Convocation of the Clergy had the power to make ecclesiastical laws and fix penalties for clergy, even though these acts affected laymen. Ecclesiastical courts had jurisdiction over probating wills, often charging exorbitant fees. The most notorious incident occurred in 1514 when Richard Hunne, a London tailor, was found hanged from a beam in his prison cell in the Lollard's Tower at St. Paul's. The rector had sued Hunne for the burial cloth used for his dead child. Hunne's house was ransacked, allegedly Lollard tracts were found, and he was tried for heresy. His death in prison was said to be a suicide, but at the coroner's inquest the investigating jury charged Bishop Richard Fitzjames's chancellor with murder. The bishop petitioned Wolsey to remand the case to a special board of inquiry, for he believed that if his chancellor were to be tried by "any twelve men in London, they be so maliciously set in favor of heretical depravity that they will cast and condemn my clerk, though he were innocent as Abel." The special board found the chancellor innocent and Thomas More, who attended the inquiry, believed Hunne to have been a heretic who died in despair by his own hand. The incident and the way it was handled roused lay sentiment against the clergy.

Popular anticlericalism surfaced as a very real threat to clerical privileges in the debates and bills of the House of Commons. In 1515 Wolsey dissolved the Parliament due to anticlerical feeling. It met again in 1523, to provide subsidies to pay for the war and royal expenditures. In 1529 Bishop Fisher complained to the upper House: "My Lords, you see clearly what bills come hither from the Common House, and all is to the destruction of the church. For God's sake, see what a realm the kingdom of Bohemia was, and when the church went down, then fell the glory of the kingdom. Now with the Commons is nothing but down with the church." Unconsciously the good bishop was identifying the church directly with clerical interests, a very dangerous development. The attitudes of the people were reflected in Parliament, and anticlericalism added fuel to the fire once the "official Reformation" was under way.

If medieval heresy and mounting anticlericalism fused in the popular mind, Christian humanism and early Protestant influences combined to create a mindset among the educated favorable to religious change and a public philosophy inclined to reform. It is a mistake to categorize individuals as though they were representatives of an abstract idea or exclusively moved by humanism, Protestantism, or desire for commonwealth reform. The cross-play of beliefs weighed differently in different people. An amalgam of ideas and personal motivations in a general reformist yearning characterized most individuals involved in the early years.[5] Classical humanism penetrated England during the fifteenth century through various agencies. Italians came as churchmen, merchants, and artists, patronized by English bishops, by noblemen such as Duke Humphrey of Gloucester, Henry V's brother, and by Henry VII and Henry VIII themselves. English clergymen such as William Grey, bishop of Ely, and John Shirwood, bishop of Durham, studied with Italian humanists or served in Rome. At the end of the century serious study of the classics began at Oxford with Thomas Linacre (c. 1460–1524), William Grocyn (c. 1466–1519), and William Latimer (c. 1460–1543), who had studied in Florence

---

5. G. R. Elton, *Reform and Renewal: Thomas Cromwell and the Common Weal* (Cambridge, 1973), p. 1. In a review of recent literature, pp. 2–5, Elton points to the pioneering achievement of W. Gordon Zeeveld, *Foundations of Tudor Policy* (Cambridge, Mass., 1948), and the contributions of Fritz Caspari, *Humanism and the Social Order in Tudor England* (Chicago, 1954), Stanford Lehmberg, *Sir Thomas Elyot, Tudor Humanist* (Austin, Tex., 1960), Arthur B. Ferguson, *The Articulate Citizen and the English Renaissance* (Durham, N.C., 1965). Despite his excessive zeal in attributing to Erasmianism nearly every social, religious, or political reform proposal from the mid-twenties to the mid-fifties, James McConica, *English Humanists and Reformation Politics under Henry VIII and Edward VI* (Oxford, 1965), offers much insight into the reform-mindedness of literate people and their influence on political figures and policymakers from the days of Wolsey through Cromwell to Catherine Parr to Somerset and the Commonwealth men. W. R. D. Jones, *The Tudor Commonwealth, 1529–1559* (London, 1970), is less inclined to find patterns of thought than a reaction on the part of the reform-minded to socioeconomic developments. Elton's own approach is to begin with Thomas Cromwell as "both the organizer and the agent of the intellectuals."

and had even acquired a limited knowledge of Greek.[6] Grocyn in turn was the teacher of the so-called Oxford reformers, Thomas More, John Colet, and even Erasmus.[7] These three humanists marked the transition from pre-Reformation to Reformation England.

An earnest man, John Colet (c. 1467–1519) was moved by the Neoplatonic religious philosophy of Marsiglio Ficino and by his study of the Scriptures to a desire for the reform of the clergy, the church, and theology. The son of a London merchant, he took his degrees at Cambridge and studied with Grocyn and Linacre at Oxford. With some knowledge of Greek, he went to Italy in 1493, made contact with Ficino, and fell under the influence of the philosophy of Dionysius the Areopagite and Augustinianism. In 1496 he began a series of lectures at Oxford on St. Paul's Epistle to the Romans. In contrast to Ficino's commentary, Colet stressed that sin is an essential part of human nature and that man is a "stench in the nostril of God." Through the Scriptures man's mind is divinely inspired and by God's grace he is imbued with trust in Christ the Redeemer. Colet moved away from the traditional fourfold interpretation of the Scriptures toward an exegetical method which emphasized the spiritual content of the text which he held to be the literal meaning intended by the author in writing by the inspiration of the Holy Spirit. Colet can be described as a Paulinist because of his stress upon sin and grace. He believed that scholastic philosophy clouded over the pure doctrine of Christ. In a famous sermon to the Convocation of the Clergy on the appointment of Archbishop Warham in 1512, he cited the evils in the church and exhorted the ambitious and greedy clergy to reform. He instructed Wolsey on the duties of a cardinal and courageously criticized England's continental military adventures. Colet took his doctorate in 1505 and became the dean of St. Paul's Cathedral. In 1508 he received his inheritance and with it founded St. Paul's School for boys, with a curriculum modeled in part on the humanist schools of Italy but with a strong emphasis upon morality and religion. He chose William Lilly, who

6. See Lewis Einstein, *The Italian Renaissance in England* (New York, 1902), and Roberto Weiss, *Humanism in England During the Fifteenth Century,* 2d ed. (New York, 1957).

7. Frederic Seebohm, *The Oxford Reformers* (London, 1896), fixed the name "Oxford reformers" to Colet, More, and Erasmus, however inappropriately, for Colet was a Cambridge man and more theologically than classically oriented. Erasmus, too, is more properly identified with Cambridge and More with London. On Colet, see Ernest Hunt, *Dean Colet and His Theology* (London, 1956).

taught Latin and Greek, as headmaster. The governance of the school was vested in the London Company of Mercers, lay rather than clerical trustees. His contribution to education and his association with More and Erasmus were the main reasons for his reputation as a humanist.

Thomas More (1478–1535) is one of the least understood men of the English Reformation. He has been turned into a soporific saint, idealized after the biography of his son-in-law Roper as a man for all seasons, but no assessment to date has brought out his true dimensions. He was a man of principle, wit, strong will, and outsized proportions, but he was a firm, hard, and consequential man who could whip and persecute heretics, deal out death as, indeed, he could take it. He was a distinguished humanist, man of letters, author of the *Utopia,* but he also wore all the while a hair shirt and smarted under a conscience sensitized during his years in the London Charterhouse of the Carthusians, where he beat himself each Friday in remembrance of Christ's scourging by the Roman soldiers and slept on the floor with a wooden block for a pillow to humiliate his flesh. He kept a religious perspective on worldly success and a concept of the right that enabled him to cope with the king's great question even unto death. He was, that is to say, not the plaster-cast image depicted in the books and plays, but a man of greater dimensions, good and bad.

On his reentry into secular life his career went well. He became under-sheriff of the city of London in 1502, married Jane Colt of good family in 1505, learned to know Erasmus well, and earned with his *Utopia,* 1516, a reputation as a humanist. He became treasurer of the exchequer in 1521, speaker of the Commons in 1523, Lord Chancellor in 1529, succeeding Wolsey, a position from which he resigned on May 16, 1532, because he could not in good conscience accept the king's renunciation of papal supremacy. When the Act of Supremacy in 1534 made the English monarch the "supreme head" of the English church, More was unable to acquiesce and was executed for treason on July 7, 1534. His head was exposed on London Bridge as a warning to all who put pope above king. More was basically a political figure and an orthodox stalwart, who fought Luther, Tyndale, Lollards, and Protestants with pen, thong, and sword.[8] His *Utopia* was a critique of the England and Europe he knew in the light of his idealized image of what a commonwealth could be, if it followed

8. John M. Headley, ed., *Responsio ad Lutherum,* V, *The Complete Works of St. Thomas More* (New Haven, 1969), p. 305. More denounces Luther as a "sophistical fellow" who holds that "he alone must be believed on all matters."

the precepts of religion and natural reason, to say nothing of Christianity. The institutions of that fortunate island were designed to inhibit man's basic impulses toward sloth, greed, and pride.[9] It was not to be the conservative Catholic More, however, who was to lead England into its era of reform, but younger men imbued with humanist and Protestant sentiments.

Christian humanism or, to personalize the metaphor, Erasmianism, had an ongoing effect on subsequent religious life in England. Erasmian humanism may have moderated the orthodoxy of the conservative Catholic episcopal party, the thought and action of men such as Tunstall, Warham, Foxe, Longland, Pole, Gardiner, John Fisher, and even the scourge of heretics, Thomas More. It may also have prevented the establishment of a dogmatic Protestantism while contributing to the mediating mentality of young Protestant statesmen such as Richard Morison and Thomas Starkey, shapers of Tudor policy. One might even argue that Erasmian humanism supported the *via media* which emerged in the early years of Edward VI's reign and eventually led to the Elizabethan settlement. Then again, it is more likely that the peculiar political circumstances of the English realm had more to do with the development of the Reformation than did gentle Erasmianism, for it was a harsh century. England's first Protestants were made of stern stuff and their metal was tempered with blows and tried in the fire.

2. ENGLAND'S EARLIEST PROTESTANTS

The first wave of Lutheran ideas washed ashore surprisingly soon after the 1517 indulgences affair. Lutheran books and pamphlets were carried by travelers and merchants aboard ships from Germany and the Netherlands. The merchants were the least traditional social group in England. They resented ecclesiastical restrictions and taxation and were open to new religious ideas. Protestantism spread and all through the century flourished in the southeast, while the north and west remained a refuge for Catholicism although the seaports even in Cornwall and Devon showed signs of Protestant infiltration. While behind the continent in the development of printing, the English press so reduced the cost of publication that by 1520 it was possible to buy works of Erasmus and Luther at Oxford for about fourpence or sixpence.[10] As early as 1519 Lutheran

9. J. H. Hexter, *More's Utopia: The Biography of an Idea* (Princeton, 1952), makes this point well.

10. C. S. L. Davies, *Peace, Print and Protestantism 1450–1558* (St. Albans, 1977), p. 133.

pamphlets were circulating in the universities. In March, 1521, Archbishop Warham, the chancellor of Oxford, complained to Cardinal Wolsey of Protestant influence in the university. "I am informed," he wrote, "that divers of the university be infected with the heresies of Luther and others of that sort, having a great number of books of the said perverse doctrine." Wolsey's response was to order the burning of Lutheran books on Market Hill in Cambridge and at St. Paul's Church in London. There Wolsey with an assembly of bishops and abbots graced a platform built for the occasion to view the burning of Luther's books. Protestants observed that he was robed in purple like a "bloody Antichrist." Wolsey ordered the bishops to have announcements proclaimed from all pulpits that anyone having Lutheran books must surrender them to the ordinaries or their officials. But by 1518 the flood of Lutheran tracts was so great that Bishop Tunstall granted Thomas More a license to read Lutheran books in order to write refutations in English, an assignment he worked at fulfilling for the next five years. Bishop John Fisher fought back against Luther with an *Assertionis Lutheranae confutatio* (1523) and two years later defended the king against Luther.

King Henry VIII himself entered the lists against Luther. As a boy and while his older brother Arthur lived, Henry had been intended for the church, and he was a man of considerable theological learning. Furious at Luther's treatise *On the Babylonian Captivity of the Church,* Henry published his response in defense of the seven sacraments, *Assertio septem sacramentorum,* dedicated to Pope Leo X. From the very moment of its publication the authorship of the *Assertio* has been a disputed question, some ascribing it to Richard Pace, John Fisher, Wolsey, or Erasmus. Luther thought that Edward Lee was probably the real author, but he responded to it as though it were Henry's, for, he declared, either a fool wrote it or a fool let it go out under his own name. For his efforts on behalf of orthodoxy, the pope bestowed upon the king the title *fidei defensor* on October 11, 1524.

During the 1520s a group of Cambridge dons met to discuss the new Protestant ideas at the White Horse Inn, which came to be known as "Little Germany." This coterie provided the key leaders of the movement in England: Robert Barnes, John Frith, Hugh Latimer, Thomas Bilney, Nicholas Ridley, John Bale, John Foxe, and possibly William Tyndale. Some of them were martyred or exiled by Henry VIII and some fell victim to "bloody Mary." Thomas Becon paid them tribute in the preface to *The Flower of Godly Prayers:*

God, once again having pity on this realm of England, raised up His prophets, namely William Tyndale, Thomas Bilney, John Frith, Doctor [Robert] Barnes, Jerome [Barlowe], [Thomas] Garret, with divers others, which both with their writings and sermons earnestly labored to call us unto repentance that by this means the fierce wrath of God might be turned away from us. But how were they entreated? How were their painful labors regarded? They themselves were condemned and burnt as heretics, and their books condemned and burnt as heretical. O most unworthy act![11]

The person-to-person spread of the evangelical movement was chronicled by John Foxe in his *Book of Martyrs.* He reported that it was through Tyndale that Frith "received into his heart the seed of the Gospel and sincere godliness." In 1524 Latimer presented a bachelor of divinity thesis directed against Melanchthon, but Bilney persuaded him of the rightness of the Lutheran position. In order to build the faculty of his new college at Oxford, in 1526 Cardinal Wolsey brought scholars from Cambridge, but six of the eight appointees were from among the reform-minded group.

Tyndale was the most effective propagandist for Protestantism in England. Thomas More considered him his most dangerous opponent. Born about 1495 in Gloucestershire, he took an M.A. at Oxford and continued his study at Cambridge. He felt the need for a good translation of the Bible and after attempting without success to persuade Bishop Tunstall to permit him to render the New Testament into English, he traveled in 1524 to Wittenberg. Influenced by Luther's German version, he published in Worms the first printed English translation of the New Testament. During the next years he collaborated with Miles Coverdale in translating large parts of the Old Testament. The Bible and his tracts were smuggled into England. In his later years Tyndale lived in the English house of the Merchant Adventurers of Antwerp, where he was immune from arrest by the Habsburg imperial officials. Thomas More plotted for his death. In May, 1535, Tyndale was tricked into leaving the house by an Englishman who posed as a convert. He was arrested and imprisoned in a castle near Brussels. Sixteen months later he was tried for heresy and on October 6, 1536, he was

11. Marcus Loane, *Pioneers of the Reformation in England* (London, 1964), p. vi. William Clebsch, *England's Earliest Protestants 1520–1535* (New Haven, 1964), describes the careers, theological ideas, and Reformation programs of Barnes, Frith, Tyndale, George Joye, William Roy, Jerome Barlowe, Simon Fish, and other early pioneer Protestants.

strangled at the stake and his body burned to ashes. His last words are said to have been: "Lord, open the king of England's eyes."

The fiery-tempered prior Robert Barnes provided another personal link with Wittenberg. On Christmas Eve, 1525, he delivered an impassioned sermon in which he leveled twenty-five criticisms at the church and made heretical statements. Wolsey had his Cambridge rooms searched for Lutheran books which Barnes foresightedly had hidden elsewhere. On the advice of Bishops Gardiner and Foxe he abjured his preaching "against the worldliness of the church" and did penance by kneeling during Bishop John Fisher's sermon at St. Paul's Cathedral on February 11, 1526. In addition, he was forced to carry a faggot in procession around the church. Under house arrest in 1528, he dressed in lay clothes and fled via Antwerp to Wittenberg. There he became a guest and close friend of Luther. In 1531 the Wittenberg theologians sent him as their representative to Henry VIII, but Chancellor Thomas More attempted to have him arrested as a heretic and apostate monk. He escaped by disguising himself as a merchant. During the last conservative years of Henry's reign, his luck ran out and, condemned to death for opposing Bishop Gardiner and the king, he was burned at Smithfield on July 30, 1540. In his final confession he declared: "I trust in no good works that ever I did, but only in the death of Christ. I do not doubt but through him to inherit the kingdom of heaven." Thus did "St. Robert" die, as Luther affectionately called him.

The authorities became increasingly alarmed as Lutheran and Zwinglian reformed ideas spread. The Archbishop of Canterbury, William Warham, feared that various parts of the realm were "infected with Lutheranism." At first penalties were light and recantations came rather easily, but gradually the authorities toughened. Death sentences became common and Protestant confessors steeled themselves for martyrdom. In 1526 some German merchants were tried for introducing Lutheranism into the Steelyard, the Hansa's London headquarters. The Cambridge group was decimated. Shy and gentle "little Thomas Bilney" was burned at the stake in 1531. When Henry VIII broke with Rome he used the Protestants as a ploy to threaten the pope with a possible defection to Lutheranism, but quickly changed his tactics to one of severe persecution in order to demonstrate that despite his break with the papacy he was still an orthodox Catholic. In May, 1530, the king issued a royal proclamation against all Lutheran literature. Bilney's two most famous converts to "the gospel" were Barnes and Hugh Latimer. It was the aged Latimer who during the reign of Queen Mary cheered his fellow martyr at the stake with the immortal words: "We shall this day light such a candle by God's grace in England as I trust shall never be put out." Some of England's earliest Protestants, then, provided leadership decades after their university years.

3. THE OFFICIAL REFORMATION

Thomas More once said of King Henry VIII, "If the lion knew his strength, hard were it for any man to rule him." In 1515 Henry declared: "We are the King of England and the King of England in times past never had any superior but God. . . . You interpret your decrees at your pleasure; but as for me, I will never consent to your desire any more than my progenitors have done." The proud monarch was harking back to the days when medieval church and state were locked in combat, Pope Alexander III against King Henry II in the twelfth century or Innocent III against John Lackland in the thirteenth century. He saw his own struggle for the independence of the realm from all foreign ecclesiastical control in the light of history, although the occasion for it was both immediate and urgent. The king's great question concerned an annulment of his marriage and his remarriage to obtain a male heir to the throne. A prince could provide greater security to the kingdom. England had emerged from the ruinous civil War of the Roses only a few years before, thanks to the strong arm of Henry VII. At his father's death on April 22, 1509, Henry succeeded to the throne. He was "a man of unbounded selfishness," Bishop William Stubbs has written, "a man of whom we may say . . . that he was the king, the whole king, and nothing but the king; that he wished to be, with regard to the church of England, the pope, the whole pope, and something more than the pope."[12] Erasmus admired his brilliance when he saw Henry in court as an eight-year-old boy. But he remained an unpredictable and willful *enfant terrible* who loved popularity and power. His conscience and profit had a way of coinciding. H. A. L. Fisher has said of him that when "he made a voyage of exploration across that strange ocean, his conscience, he generally returned with an argosy."[13] When the papacy under pressure from Emperor Charles V refused to sanction his so-called divorce, this "defender of the faith" examined his conscience

12. William Stubbs, *Seventeen Lectures on the Study of Medieval and Modern History*, 3d ed. (London, 1900), pp. 300–301.
13. Cited in T. M. Parker, *The English Reformation to 1558*, 2d ed. (London, 1966), p. 14.

and took the whole kingdom out of the Roman Catholic Church. The stage for that dramatic move was set during the administration of Cardinal Thomas Wolsey, who dominated English affairs from 1515 to 1529.

During the first two years of Henry's reign Archbishop Warham of Canterbury and mild Richard Foxe managed the realm. Very soon the ruthless Cardinal Wolsey rose to prominence, took advantage of Henry's dislike of routine matters to make himself an indispensable administrator, and drew into his own hands the reins of both church and state in England. Within six months after Henry's accession Wolsey was Royal Almoner, and within two years he was a close confidant and spokesman of the king. In 1512 he directed the French war and by 1515 he was Lord Chancellor of England and Cardinal Archbishop of York. In 1518 Pope Leo X wished to send Cardinal Campeggio to England to recruit aid for a crusade against the Turks. The pope was informed that the law of the land forbade the reception of such legates, but that Campeggio would be received if Wolsey were made a papal legate *a latere* in equal terms. Thus Wolsey became the pope's plenipotentiary in England and now held in his hands the power of both church and state. He could treat the English church as a unitary institution rather than as a mere province of Rome. The lesson that ecclesiastical and secular power could be combined was not lost either on the king or on one of Wolsey's officials, Thomas Cromwell. Superficially it may have seemed that the church through Wolsey had gained great power in England. Wolsey, moreover, paid relatively little attention to England's domestic affairs and seemed to view the country as a source of revenue for a foreign policy and military intervention on the continent. Both policies were devoted largely to furthering the interests of the papacy, for Wolsey was ambitious to become pope himself. But he was and remained essentially the king's creature subject entirely to his caprice. When he lost royal favor over what Henry considered the mishandling of his marriage case, he was quickly ruined and, as Shakespeare put it, left naked to his enemies.

Henry's desire for glory and Wolsey's adventurism coincided in foreign policy and war. In 1511 Henry joined Spain—ruled by his father-in-law Ferdinand—the papacy of Julius II, and Naples in their Holy League designed to force France, England's traditional enemy, out of Italy and to divert its forces away from Navarre, which Ferdinand was invading. Early reverses drove Henry to lead his troops himself, and in 1513 he crossed the channel, won the "Battle of the Spurs," and directed the successful

sieges of Thérouanne and Tournay. Wolsey managed the campaign effi-
ciently and negotiated a truce with France in August, 1514. Henry married his sister Mary to King Louis XII of France. While Henry's allies
negotiated for a separate peace, Wolsey and Henry outfoxed them, or so
it seemed. King James IV of Scotland took advantage of England's involvement on the continent to invade from the north, but he lost his life
in the battle of Flodden.

Upon the death of Ferdinand of Spain in 1516 and of Emperor Maximilian of Austria in 1519, their grandson Charles V became the heir to all
the Habsburg lands. The young French king Francis I, who ascended the
throne in 1515, was Charles's major rival for power on the continent.
Wolsey promoted Henry as the arbiter between the Habsburgs and the
Valois. On his way to his coronation in Aachen, Charles journeyed to Kent
to court Henry's favor. At the fabled meeting on the Field of the Cloth
of Gold in 1521 Francis sought Henry's support. At a conference in Calais
in 1521 Henry played the role of arbiter for all of Europe, but he shortly
afterward on Wolsey's advice tilted against Francis and in 1522 and 1523
directed a futile military expedition against him. The balance of power
shifted in favor of Charles V, who captured Francis at the battle of Pavia,
1525. Spain's power reached new heights, including influence over and
even control of the papacy, just as Henry's marriage to Catherine of
Aragon, his dead brother's widow and Charles V's aunt, was beginning
to cloy. Henry viewed Wolsey's foreign policy with increasing skepticism
and resentment. Wolsey forged an alliance with France in 1526 with the
Treaty of Cognac and in the end clung desperately to it, but he could not
regain credibility. His alliance failed to protect the pope, for in 1527 a
mutinous imperial army sacked Rome and imprisoned Pope Clement VII.
Because of Henry's divorce problem, Wolsey needed the support of the
pope and emperor, but he lost both. When the king became wrathful,
Wolsey fell from power.

These foreign adventures compounded the crown's financial difficulties,
and the domestic economy was not faring well. Despite a slight increase
in textile production and export, England was still very dependent upon
the sale of raw wool, especially to the Lowlands. But the demand was
down and the price of commodities was up, an ironclad law of war and
the price index. Wolsey had had to summon Parliament in 1523 to ask for
subsidies. Thomas More was then speaker of the House of Commons, and
Parliament refused to grant the money. Wolsey was reduced to making

forced loans and by 1526 he was obliged to undertake recoinage and to debase the currency to ease the money situation.

When Wolsey fell from royal favor and power, it was basically because he failed to win a papal annulment of the king's marriage to Catherine so that Henry could marry dark-eyed Anne Boleyn, the sister of his favorite mistress and a lady-in-waiting to the queen. Of five children Catherine had borne to the king, the only one living was Mary. Except for the disputed reign of Queen Matilda centries before, there had been no regnant queen of England. Henry was concerned about the succession and the stability of the land. Anne Boleyn's ambitious mother reacted to Henry's desires as have mothers throughout history by insisting upon an honorable marriage and the elevation of their house.

Henry had dedicated his *Assertio* against Luther to the pope as "a sign of his faith and friendship" and stated absolutely that "the whole church not only is subject to Christ, but, for Christ's sake, to Christ's only vicar, the pope of Rome." To deny obedience to the highest priest on earth is a blasphemy like idolatry, he held. His position subsequently remained the same in theory, although he asserted royal prerogatives in church matters with increasing insistence, as did many secular princes of the day. It was the "king's great question" of his marriage that changed his mind with respect to papal authority. Catherine had been married to Arthur, who died at the age of fifteen without the marriage's having been consummated. Wolsey's task was to secure from Clement VII an annulment of Henry's marriage on grounds of consanguinity. Pope Julius II had exempted the royal couple from those laws to make the marriage legitimate in terms of church law, for according to Leviticus 18:6–18 a man should not contract a marriage within five or even six degrees of relationship, a defense against incest and inbreeding in ancient Israel. The key injunction is Leviticus 20:21: "If a man takes his brother's wife, it is impurity; he has uncovered his brother's nakedness; they shall be childless." Henry contended that the dispensation of 1503 had been obtained under false pretenses and was therefore not valid, although he had lived almost eighteen years married to his brother's wife. That Deuteronomy 25:5 sanctioned marriage to a brother's widow in order to conceive children in his name or that marrying Anne after living with her sister in a "common-law marriage" presented an analogous problem did not move him. He searched his conscience and found that he had to stay with his plan for divorce. The king had a powerful though confusing and illogical conscience.

Wolsey now undertook to do the king's bidding. In 1527 the primate of Canterbury summoned the king before his ecclesiastical tribunal for violating the code of Leviticus. Bishop John Fisher of Rochester declared that such a decision had to be made in Rome. Thereupon Wolsey's secretary was dispatched to Rome to present Henry's case. He asked the pope to annul the marriage with Catherine and provide a dispensation so that Henry could marry Anne Boleyn. The Medici Pope Clement VII equivocated due both to his personal indecisiveness and to political circumstances, since the pope was at war with the emperor. On the king's insistence Clement VII sent Cardinal Campeggio to England, but the bull he brought was burned immediately. In 1529 the ecclesiastical court under Campeggio and Wolsey opened proceedings. Queen Catherine refused to recognize its validity and appealed directly to Pope Clement, who had in the meantime made peace with Charles V. Charles insisted that the pope suspend the authority of the legates and remand the trial to Rome. Despairing of persuading Pope Clement to grant an annulment, in the summer of 1529 Henry shifted from blandishment to threat. There was precedent for declaring England's independence from papal dominion in the statute of Provisors of 1351 and in the statute of *Praemunire* of 1353, which outlawed any appeal to Rome not sanctioned by the king. Henry recognized the potential use of Parliament to blackmail the pope. Henry's envoy in Rome let it be known that unfavorable papal action could lead to the destruction of the church and the loss of England, whereupon Clement replied that it would be better for England to be lost because of righteousness than through unrighteousness. Since Wolsey had failed to deliver the annulment and dispensation, he was removed from power. He was arrested, ironically, under a writ of *praemunire,* which accused him as a papal legate of acting as a foreign agent. He died traveling to his trial, a broken man.

To popular acclaim the great seal was transferred to the new Lord Chancellor, Sir Thomas More, on October 25, 1529. More was a firm but reserved opponent of the divorce. Henry's design was to put pressure on the pope through Parliament. From the outset the king and his chancellor were on a collision course. Thomas Cranmer, the former chaplain of the Boleyn family, suggested that he secure the support of the universities for his cause. This move to solicit the *opinio communis doctorum* proved to be only partially successful. The universities of Naples and Spain predictably came out in support of the legitimacy of his marriage with Catherine, and Paris declared for an annulment only under pressure from Francis I and over the protest of forty-three doctors. Luther and the Wittenberg theologians volunteered the opinion that the marriage to Catherine was perfectly valid. At this juncture Henry came under the influence of the brilliant Thomas Cromwell, who had served in Wolsey's administration. He advised Henry to follow the example of the German princes and free himself from Rome. Henry at the end of 1530 accused the clergy of having violated the statute of *Praemunire* in appealing to the pope and the Convocation of the Clergy agreed to pay the sum of £100,000 rather than risk the loss of all church properties. The convocation adopted a motion of old Archbishop Warham of Canterbury declaring: "Of the church and clergy of England, whose especial Protector, single and supreme Lord, and, as far as the law of Christ allows [a phrase added by Bishop Fisher], even Supreme Head, we acknowledge his Majesty to be." The House of Commons passed a series of bills controlling church practices, fees payable for probate, burials, and other charges for clerical services.

After the death of Warham the king made Thomas Cranmer the primate of England. Unwilling to serve as the king's tool, Thomas More resigned as Lord Chancellor, succeeded by the king's man Audley. In response to the resolution of the Convocation of the Clergy the pope issued a sharp warning, to which Parliament responded by blocking the payment of annates. The new strong man to emerge as Henry's key adviser, the manipulator of Parliament, and the scourge of the clergy was Cromwell, a man of extraordinary ability, strong will, boundless ambition, and flexible political ethics. There is still some debate as to whether Henry or Cromwell primarily directed the course of events, but there is a growing appreciation of Cromwell's contribution to the reorganization of the government in rationalizing administration, streamlining laws, and increasing efficiency in taxation. Cromwell's aim was to deliver centralized control to the king and Parliament, but not to make the monarchy absolute. Schooled in the common law, Cromwell worked through the House of Commons, which meant that the legislation of the Reformation Parliament (1529–1536) was decisive.[14]

Cromwell's personal background prepared him well for the rough and tumble of Tudor politics. He was born in Putney about 1485, a man, as

14. G.R. Elton, *The Tudor Revolution in Government: A Study of Administrative Changes in the Reign of Henry VIII* (Cambridge, 1953), made the strongest case for Cromwell's contribution, and two decades later Elton continued to see Cromwell as the organizer of the Reformation and the agent of the humanist-reforming intellectuals in *Reform and Renewal*, pp. 9ff. A. G. Dickens, *Thomas Cromwell and the English Reformation* (London, 1959), provides a balanced view.

the phrase goes, of humble origins. In his teens he became a soldier of fortune as a French mercenary and then served for two years as a clerk for the Frescobaldi bankers in northern Italy. With this financial experience he became an economic adviser to English merchants in the Lowlands, watching closely and shrewdly developments in the growing market of Antwerp. Along the way he acquired a knowledge of Latin and Italian literature. He was still relatively innocent politically and did not, as Cardinal Reginald Pole later accused, learn the art of politics from Machiavelli's *Prince,* though he read the work. His real schooling came as a member of Wolsey's household. Wolsey used him, for example, to carry out his liquidation of the smaller monasteries. George Cavendish, who was Wolsey's servant and biographer, described Cromwell immediately after the fall of his master Wolsey:

It chanced me upon All-hallow day to come there into the *Great Chamber* at Asher, in the morning, to give mine attendance, where I found Master Cromwell leaning in the great window, with a Primer in his hand, saying of our Lady matins, which had been since a very strange sight. He prayed not more earnestly than the tears distilled from his eyes.

Cromwell then confessed to Cavendish that he was weeping not over Wolsey's misfortune, but over his own, and told of his plans to abandon the sinking ship.[15] Before long Cromwell rode off to London to ingratiate himself with the king. After holding minor offices he was made a member of the king's council by January, 1531. He applied his banking expertise to the king's finances, became his principal secretary in 1534, and gradually made himself the indispensable manager of all the king's business.

Cromwell was concerned not only with excluding the power of the pope from the realm, but with reducing the church in England to subservience to the crown. The Supplication of the Commons Against the Ordinances limited severely the authority of the Convocation of the Clergy to make ecclesiastical laws independently of the Commons and attacked the capricious and unfair actions often taken against laymen by the church courts. At the king's request the Convocation on May 15, 1532, in the Submission of the Clergy, appealed to the king to protect their prerogatives against the Commons and offered to him the control over their legislative functions in exchange for his protection of their ecclesiastical courts. The Submission reads:

15. Parker, *English Reformation,* p. 15.

We your most humble subjects, daily orators and beadsmen of your clergy in England, having our special trust and confidence in your most excellent wisdom, your princely goodness and fervent zeal to the promotion of God's honor and Christian religion, and also in your learning, far exceeding in our judgment, the learning of all other kings and princes that we have read of, and doubting nothing but that the same shall continue and daily increase in your majesty—First, do offer and promise, *in verbo sacerdotii,* here unto your highness, submitting ourselves most humbly to the same, that we will never from henceforth exact, put in use, promulge, or execute, any new canons or constitutions provincial, or any other new ordinance, provincial or synodal, in our Convocation or synod in time coming, which Convocation is, always has been, and must be, assembled only by your highness' commandment or writ, unless your highness by your royal assent shall license us to assemble our Convocation, and to make, promulge, and execute such constitutions and ordinances as shall be made in the same, and thereunto give your royal assent and authority.[16]

The most decisive legislation of all was the Act in Restraint of Appeals which Cromwell put through Parliament in March, 1533. The statute of *Praemunire* of 1353 had forbidden appeals to Rome except with the king's consent, but the Act in Restraint of Appeals forbade such appeals unconditionally. The Act was repeated in the legislation of 1534. The flavor of the Act can be savored from the well-known preamble:

Whereas by divers sundry old authentic histories and chronicles, it is manifestly declared and expressed, that this realm of England is an empire and so hath been accepted in the world, governed by one supreme head and king, having the dignity and royal estate of the imperial crown of the same, unto whom a body politic, compact of all sorts and degrees of people divided in terms and by names of spirituality and temporally, be bounden and ought to bear, next to God, a natural obedience. . . . In consideration whereof the king's highness, his nobles and Commons . . . establish, and ordain, that all causes testamentary, etc. . . . shall be from henceforth heard, examined, discussed, clearly, finally, and definitively adjudged and determined within the king's jurisdiction and authority, and not elsewhere. . . .[17]

According to this statute all matters having to do with the king's business were to be handled in the Upper House of Convocation, which under the

---

16. S.P., Henry VIII, v. No. 1023; in Henry Bettenson, *Documents of the Christian Church* (New York and London, 1947), pp. 308–309.
17. 24 Henry VIII, cap. 12: *Statutes of the Realm,* iii, 427, in Bettenson, *Documents,* pp. 309–315.

king had final jurisdiction without any recourse to appeals outside the realm, which meant essentially to the papacy in Rome.

The king's marriage became an increasingly urgent matter. Henry and Catherine had been separated and six months after his secret divorce from her, he secretly married Anne Boleyn, January, 1533. There was some apprehension that the legality of the divorce would not be upheld, but Anne was expecting a child, as became increasingly obvious, and the legitimacy of the heir had to be established in order to make succession secure. The Act in Restraint of Appeals allowed Archbishop Cranmer to pronounce the marriage with Catherine annulled and the marriage to Anne valid without fear of his being countermanded by the pope. Anne was crowned queen in June. When in a matter of days the new Pope Paul III excommunicated Henry, the king declared that he did not care a straw if the pope promulgated ten thousand excommunications. In actual fact when Pope Paul III on August 30, 1535, issued a bull, *Eius qui immobilis*, condemning Henry and declaring that the king "had incurred the penalty of the deprivation of his kingdom" and had "been sundered forever from all faithful Christians and their goods,' he was unable to promulgate the bull, for he could find no prince prepared to carry it into effect. The country was no longer concerned with papal pronouncements. In September, 1533, Anne gave birth to Princess Elizabeth. Parliament came through with the First Succession Act, which made it treason not to accept the validity of Henry's marriage to Anne.[18]

Two major pieces of parliamentary legislation completed the English Reformation by statutes. In November, 1534, Parliament passed the Act of Supremacy, which in ponderous phrases declared the king and his successors to be the only earthly head of the English church who alone had the power to suppress and root out errors, heresies, abuses, and offenses. Papal spiritual powers, in other words, were now in the hands of the king as head of the Church of England:

Albeit the king's majesty justly and rightfully is and ought to be the supreme head of the Church of England, and so is recognized by the clergy of this realm in the convocations, yet nevertheless for corroboration and confirmation thereof, and for increase of virtue in Christ's religion within this realm of England, and to repress and extirp all errors, heresies, and other enormities and abuses heretofore used in the same; be it enacted by authority of this

18. H. Gee and W. J. Hardy, *Documents Illustrative of English Church History* (London, 1896), pp. 232–243.

present Parliament, that the king our sovereign lord, his heirs and successors, kings of this realm, shall be taken, accepted, and reputed the only supreme head on earth of the Church of England, called *Anglicana Ecclesia;* and shall have and enjoy, annexed and united to the imperial crown of this realm, as well the title and style thereof, as all honors, dignities, pre-eminences, jurisdictions, privileges, authorities, immunities, profits, and commodities to the said dignity of supreme head of the same Church belonging and appertaining; and that our said sovereign lord, his heirs and successors, kings of this realm, shall have full power and authority from time to time to visit, repress, redress, reform, order, correct, restrain, and amend all such errors, heresies, abuses, offenses, contempts, and enormities, whatsoever they be, which by any manner spiritual authority or jurisdiction ought or may lawfully be reformed, repressed, ordered, redressed, corrected, restrained, or amended, most to the pleasure of Almighty God, the increase of virtue in Christ's religion and for the conservation of the peace, unity, and tranquillity of this realm; any usage, custom, foreign law, foreign authority, prescription, or any other thing or things to the contrary hereof notwithstanding.[19]

The Convocation of 1531 had recognized the king as supreme head of the Church of England, but now the saving clause "as far as the Law of Christ allows" was eliminated. In anticipation of opposition, the Treason Act of November, 1534, protected the Tudor monarch and his heirs from subversion and rebellion. Erastianism, the dominance of state over church, had triumphed. Stephen Gardiner (c. 1470–1555) in 1535 wrote *De Vera Obedientia* in support of royal supremacy, but in that same year Thomas More repudiated it. Gardiner, however, due to his opposition to Reformation doctrine was to be imprisoned under Edward VI, and made Lord Chancellor under Mary until his death in 1555. More went to martyrdom under Henry. The spirits were dividing.

There was surprisingly little resistance to this governmental revolution leading to schism from the Roman Catholic Church. Pope, Curia, and clergy had long been unpopular with the people. Many of the bishops had been chosen from among the king's most subservient followers. There was some opposition among the regular clergy, especially among the Carthusians, who refused the oath and were jailed. The prior of the London Charterhouse was martyred. Some starved in prison, eighteen of them were executed, as well as an Augustinian, a member of the order of St. Bridget, and several strict Franciscans and secular priests.

Two distinguished martyrs, Bishop John Fisher and Sir Thomas More, were sacrificed to drive home with terror the price of resistance to the king. Fisher had been imprisoned on a charge of collusion with the ecstatic Nun of Kent, who prophesied Henry's damnation for his second marriage. Fisher was now taken to the Tower of London, where he and More were held for more than a year prior to trial. Pope Paul III sealed Fisher's doom by making him a cardinal while he was being held in the Tower. Henry is said to have responded, "Well, let the pope send him a hat when he will, but I will provide that whensoever it cometh, he shall wear it on his shoulders, for his head he shall have none to set it on." Fisher lost his head to the swordsman on June 22, 1535.

Sir Thomas More was to become Saint Thomas More by following his conscience, much better informed and much better defined than that of his monarch, even unto death. His wife reminded him during the long year in the Tower of all the wealth and preferments he could enjoy by the simple expediency of acknowledging the royal supremacy over the church. His favorite daughter tested him severely with, oddly enough, the same question that had plagued Luther, "Are you alone wise?" Who was he to pit his opinion against that of many churchmen who denied papal supremacy and acknowledged the king as supreme head in the realm while he turned against his own monarch? This argument proved to be difficult, but he responded, "Daughter, I never intend to pin my soul on another man's back!" In making his final speech after the verdict had gone against him, More expressed those convictions which led him to embrace martyrdom. The text comes from Nicholas Harpsfield, who wrote More's first formal biography under the reign of Queen Mary, and is based in part upon the account of William Roper, More's son-in-law.

"Seeing that I see ye are determined to condemn me (God knoweth how)," he said, "I will now in discharge of my conscience speak my mind plainly and freely, touching my indictment and your statute withall. And forasmuch as this indictment is grounded upon an Act of Parliament directly repugnant to the laws of God and his holy Church, the supreme government of which, or any part whereof, may no temporal prince presume by any law to take upon him, as rightfully belonging to the see of Rome, a spiritual pre-eminence by the mouth of our Savior himself, personally present upon earth, only to St. Peter and his successors, bishops of the same see, by special prerogative granted; it is therefore in law amongst Christian men, insufficient to charge any Christian man."[20]

20. "Thomas More Discharges His Conscience," in A. G. Dickens and Dorothy Carr, eds., *Documents of Modern History: The Reformation in England to the Accession of Elizabeth I* (New York, 1968), pp. 70–72.

Having stated the issue clearly, More went on to argue his case by analogy and history. For the Church of England to be ruled by laws at variance with that of the church universal is as unacceptable as the poor city of London making a law against an act of Parliament to bind the whole nation. More's great fear in the Tower had been that he might under the treason laws be disemboweled rather than beheaded. Under such stress he wrote beautiful religious treatises such as a *Dialogue of Comfort Against Tribulation*. Roper related that when mounting the scaffold he indulged in a bit of gallows humor, saying to the jailer, "I pray you, Master Lieutenant, see me safe up, and for my coming down let me shift for myself." He asked the axman to spare his beard, for it had committed no treason. His head was exposed on London Bridge as a warning to all who thought of opposing the supremacy of the king.

Cromwell took advantage of the anti-Roman and anticlerical mood of king and country to despoil the monasteries and ease the problems of the royal treasury. England's defenses had to be strengthened against the Spanish threat, the Irish were stirring up new trouble, the French no longer paid a pension to their ally, and the king found economy difficult. Cromwell, however, found new taxation problematical. He saw in the monastic holdings a vulnerable target and planned the suppression of the monasteries. The monasteries were in much better shape in terms of morality and learning than Tudor propaganda and the reports of Cromwell's inspectors suggest.[21] There were some ten thousand monasteries and lesser religious foundations with an income estimated at one-fifth of the national income.

In February, 1536, Cromwell's visitors reported to Parliament on the "enormities" and immoralities of the monasteries. The first Act of Dissolution closed some 295 smaller houses with incomes of less than £200. Another act set up the Court of Augmentations to transfer their wealth to the crown. In 1539 the larger monasteries suffered the same fate. They were charged with maintaining useless ceremonies, suggesting that the value of prayer for the dead was being questioned. The monks were driven out and commanded to marry. The possessions were partly bestowed upon friends of the king and partly sold outright, to local gentry or merchants with ready cash wishing to have landed property. The new

21. The definitive study is that of Dom David Knowles, *The Religious Orders in England,* 3 vols. (Cambridge, 1948–1959).

owners understandably became the strongest supporters of the new order. In 1539 the abbots of Glastonbury, Reading, and Colchester were executed by hanging, although if the truth be told they were more the victims of politics than the heroic martyrs for the faith. The last monastery to submit was Waltham Abbey in Essex, which yielded on March 23, 1540. The king's despotism and the ruthlessness of Cromwell, whom Henry had made his vicar general in church affairs, reached a grotesque high point in the trial against Thomas à Becket, an English prelate who had opposed his monarch, dead nearly four hundred years. His body was taken from its grave, his name removed from the calendar, and the treasures adorning his tomb were taken to London, all on the order of the king. Other shrines were despoiled, such as that of Our Lady of Walsingham, a pilgrimage site for centuries. The benefits of pilgrimages and prayers to the saints were questioned and the wealth of the shrines coveted.

By the 1540s the spoils from the dissolution increased the annual income of the crown by more than £100,000, which was about the amount of the whole crown revenue when Cromwell came to office, but it did not, of course, meet Henry's needs. With the dissolution of the monasteries the regulars were gone. One of the great creations of the medieval church was destroyed forever and there could be no return. Not only nobility but also the gentry benefited by the dissolution, contributing to the rise of that class and to its involvement in national government. On a lower level the enriched squires dominated local government more than before. The gentry class, anything but in decline, was impressive in its adaptability and flexibility. They educated their scions at the universities and Inns of Court and regularly joined their wealth with that of urban families, just as old merchants conversely moved onto the land. The revenue from the sale of monastic holdings was used not only to fill the king's purse but to endow six new sees, to pension some former nuns and monks, to support many new and enlarged grammar and cathedral schools, to complete Christ Church at Oxford, and to establish Trinity College at Cambridge. Five Regius professorships were established at both universities.

The country was in economic difficulty. The rising inflation that afflicted Europe in general was felt acutely in England in these decades and throughout the rest of the century. Production of food and goods remained fairly static while the population continued to grow. This meant that from 1500 on there had been a rapid decline of wage earners' living standards, as determined, for example, by a comparison of the money wages of a builder's laborer with the cost of a "composite unit of consumables." Wage earners constituted only a small part of the labor force, it is true, but their income serves as a useful index of how common folk were faring at the time. The increase of enclosures to meet the continued demand for wool further dislocated the peasantry and depopulated the countryside. The higher farm prices increased competition among tenant farmers and led landlords to extort ever higher rents (rack-renting). Moreover, between 1526 and 1551 the royal treasury debased the currency to pay government obligations, a devaluation that added to price inflation.[22]

A series of rebellions occurred during the latter part of 1536, known collectively as the Pilgrimage of Grace. These uprisings reflected both a traditionalist disaffection with Cromwell's policies, especially the dissolution of the monasteries, which were more generous landlords than secular or absentee ones, and the general economic distress of the lower classes, peasants and artisans in villages and towns. Revolts took place in Lincolnshire, in Lancashire, the northeastern counties, and in Yorkshire, where there were two separate rebellions between October, 1536, and January, 1537, the main pilgrimage being led by Robert Aske. Anti-Reformation sentiment was mixed with economic distress in the minds of the rebels. The revolts were easily suppressed, for the king promised relief to the rebels, whereupon the largest contingent dispersed. The royal troops then moved in for a mopping up operation and executed Aske and over two hundred other insurgents. The net result was that the king asserted even more direct control over the north.

4. THE EMERGENCE OF ANGLICANISM

The final decade of King Henry's reign saw a polarization of those who wished to make England more Protestant, and here the influence of Zwin-

22. Of the extensive literature devoted to these complex economic questions, attention may be drawn especially to the pioneering work of J. E. Thorold Rogers, *History of Agriculture and Prices in England,* 7 vols. (Oxford, 1866–1900); Peter Ramsey, *Tudor Economic Problems* (London, 1963), a short introduction; Peter Ramsey, *The Price Revolution in Sixteenth Century England* (London, 1971); R. B. Outhwaite, *Inflation in Tudor and Early Stuart England* (London, 1970); Joan Thirsk, ed., *The Agrarian History of England and Wales, 1500–1640* (Cambridge, 1967); and the article by E. H. Phelps Brown and Sheila V. Hopkins, "Seven Centuries of Building Wages," *Economica,* n.s., 22 (1955), 195–206. Page 204: "The most salient feature of all is the extent of the rise for the craftsman, from 3d a day under Henry III to 445d for 10 hours' work under Elizabeth II—multiplication by nearly 150." During the period from 1532 to 1660 the average annually compounded rate of rise was 0.86 percent. During the Tudor inflation (1532–1580) it was 1.46 percent.

gli and Swiss reformed theology was important, and those who wanted the church to remain Catholic in doctrine even without papal supremacy. The king remained theologically conservative and from 1532 to 1540 he was under pressure from both the progressive group under Cromwell and Cranmer inclined toward Lutheranism—men such as Hugh Latimer, bishop of Worcester, Nicholas Shaxton, bishop of Salisbury, and Edward Foxe, bishop of Hereford—and the conservative group represented by the duke of Norfolk and Stephen Gardiner, bishop of Winchester, who supported the royal supremacy but was doctrinally very Catholic. Henry tried to keep the two factions in tow, but in effect, until Cromwell's fall in 1540, the progressives enjoyed great success. Thereafter it was the turn of the conservatives, whose views coincided more closely with those of the aging Henry.

It is customary to describe Anglicanism as a *via media,* for it was comprehensive territorially, including all but a few diehard Catholics in hiding and some radical sectaries underground, and doctrinally, for it sought compromises on confessional statements and liturgical formulations that would accommodate the largest spectrum of belief possible. Thomas Babington Macaulay described the Church of England as "the fruit of the union" between the government and the Protestants, the result of compromise by both parties to its conception. The accommodation between the parties was fraught with tension and vacillation so that the center shifted to and fro, anything but a stable "middle way." The *via media* followed a zigzag course reflecting the pressures of the moment. Among the makers of Tudor policy were such young counselors as Richard Morison, whose private papers reveal him to have been genuinely evangelical in religious faith and influenced strongly by Luther, and Thomas Starkey, an Erasmian humanist and for a time a member of the Padua circle of Reginald Pole, who had chosen exile to a martyr's death. In *An Exhortation to Unity and Obedience* Starkey argued that all good citizens were bound by God's law and by all good civility to follow the middle way between superstition on the one hand and division, controversy, and sedition on the other. He followed Melanchthon's doctrine that *adiaphora* should not be made binding upon conscience or considered necessary for orthodoxy. This concept of "indifferent things" bore within it the seed of toleration, though some said it was rather the source of indifference.

The conservatives such as Stephen Gardiner shared the concept of the divine right of kings. In his treatise *De Vera Obedientia* (1535) he devel-

oped a theory reminiscent of Marsiglio of Padua's emphasis on the obedience that all true Christians owe to their anointed monarch, God's representative on earth, a father to his children and a master to his servants.
Since the king and Parliament had separated the English people from
Rome, all should obey this authoritative decree. When Queen Mary ascended the throne Gardiner excused his book on the grounds that he
wrote it in fear of suffering the fate of Fisher and More in view of his
Catholic beliefs. Others showed an uncanny ability to survive the turmoil
of the times. William Barlow, for example, as a Catholic wrote a book on
continental Protestantism, *A dyaloge descrybyng the orygynall ground of these
Lutheran faccyons and many of theyr abusys* (London, 1531), in which he
described the Lutheran, Zwinglian, and Anabaptist factions, giving a jaun-
diced picture especially of the radicals and providing much ammunition
for Thomas More and other apologists. But Barlow very shortly joined the
reformers and he rose to become bishop of St. Asaph's (1535), St. David's
(1536), Bath and Wells (1548). He survived the Marian period to become bishop of Chichester in 1559, consecrated Matthew Parker as
Queen Elizabeth's archbishop, and became involved in the controversy
over the validity of Anglican ordination.

The king was interested in peace and unity in the realm with loyalty to
royal supremacy as the touchstone. In 1545 he gave a famous speech in
Parliament which made the point well:

> What love and charity is there among you when one calleth another heretic
> and anabaptist, and he calleth him again papist, hypocrite, and Pharisee?
> . . . I hear daily that you of the clergy preach one against another, without
> charity or discretion. . . . Yet the temporality be not clear and unspotted of
> malice and envy. For you rail on bishops, speak slanderously of priests, and
> rebuke and taunt preachers, both contrary to good order and Christian frater-
> nity. . . . Be not judges of yourselves of your fantastical opinions and vain
> expositions. . . . Be in charity with one another like brother and brother.[23]

As a theological dilettante Henry took a keen personal interest in the
theological constructions, articles, and injunctions which went into the
building of a national church. To say that Henry remained an orthodox
Catholic and that the conservative Six Articles reflect his true personal
convictions and final view is too simplistic, for he held deviant opinions
on the sacraments, orders, headship, authority of the Scriptures, and other

23. David H. Pill, *The English Reformation 1529–58* (Totowa, N.J., 1973), p. 101.

points to the end of his days and appointed men of Protestant leanings to tutor and guide his heir. The role of Thomas Cranmer (1489–1556) was crucial, for Henry trusted him, protected him from Norfolk and Gardiner, and on his deathbed pressed Cranmer's hand to signal his faith in Christ as his Savior. Cranmer was a kind, flexible, persuasive man, though not creative or a forceful leader. As a fellow at Jesus College he took priestly orders and became a doctor of divinity. He served the king on several missions to the Lutherans, on one of which he met and married the niece of the Nuremberg reformer Osiander, and to the emperor in Vienna and to northern Italy. In 1533 Henry made him the Archbishop of Canterbury, a position that enabled him to do the king's bidding in the matter of the divorce and to coax the English church along a reformed path.

The first independent doctrinal statement of the Church of England was the Ten Articles of 1536. Without denying the other four sacraments, the Articles declared the necessity of baptism, penance, and the eucharist, in line with Luther's earlier opinion. The saints were to be honored but not adored like God. Prayers for the dead were to be retained, but the word purgatory which was fundamental to the Catholic doctrine of the expiation of sin and guilt for the departed soul was eliminated. The real presence of Christ in the sacrament of the altar was asserted but without spelling out the mode, so that Catholic and Protestant interpretations could be accommodated. Justification by faith was confessed, but the necessity of good works for salvation was also asserted. The Articles were a masterpiece of compromise phraseology, but by not being explicitly Catholic in such matters as transubstantiation, for example, they left the side door open for further Protestantization. A few weeks after the publication of the Ten Articles, state injunctions were issued to the secular clergy ordering them to explain the Articles to the people, to denounce the pope and superstitious practices, to catechize the laity, teaching them the Lord's Prayer, the Apostles' Creed, and the Ten Commandments in English, and to lead exemplary lives themselves. In 1537 the Convocation of the Clergy issued the *Institutions of a Christian Man,* more generally known as the *Bishops' Book,* designed for study by the clergy. It stressed the duty to teach, the call to preach the Word, and made no mention of celebrating the mass as a sacrifice. While these and other Protestant emphases may not have pleased the king, he allowed them to pass, and must have been gratified to read that the universal church was composed of free and equal national churches.

Cranmer, with the enthusiastic support of Cromwell, promoted the publication of the English Bible and the introduction of an English liturgy. The English Bible of 1537 was based upon Tyndale's translation, but Tyndale's unorthodox conception of the church and other offensive phrases were altered. First published as the Matthew's Bible in 1535, Matthew being the editor John Rogers' pseudonym, it was revised by Miles Coverdale and published as the Great Bible. Injunctions of 1538 ordered that a copy be placed in every church for the parishioners to read. Moreover, the Injunctions ordered the clergy to keep exact parish records of baptisms, weddings, and burials for the better regulation of the parish. A few years later Archbishop Cranmer prepared an English litany which became a part of the *Book of Common Prayer* with its splendid Coverdale Psalter and beautiful cadences.

Cranmer shifted gradually from a nearly Lutheran position on the sacrament of the eucharist toward a more Zwinglian spiritualistic understanding. But just when it seemed that the progressive Protestant group was in the ascendancy, Cromwell fell from grace over the marriage he had negotiated for Henry with Anne of Cleves, the woman Henry called the "Flemish mare." Henry was unlucky in his matrimonial affairs due to his personal instability, disease, and the exigencies of international politics. Vivacious Anne Boleyn, like Catherine, produced no male heir but only a daughter, Elizabeth. Convicted of committing adultery with a young courtier, Anne was beheaded in 1536, the same year that Catherine died. Partly to please the Protestant party Henry then married colorless Jane Seymour, who produced a male heir at last, sickly Prince Edward, and then died in 1537. At that point Henry was negotiating with the Schmalkald League of German Lutheran princes as a counterpoise to Charles V. A delegation of Lutheran theologians came to England and agreement was reached on thirteen articles of faith. Charles V and Francis I met in the summer of 1538 and in January, 1539, and pledged not to ally themselves with Henry except by mutual consent, and the English monarch feared isolation. But at the Imperial Diet at Frankfurt the Lutheran princes arrived at an accommodation with Charles V. The theological discussions were suspended, but Cromwell continued the marriage negotiations regarding Anne with the duke of Cleves, who, though not Lutheran himself, had Lutheran ties. Thus was Henry ensnared in the marriage with Anne of Cleves, a plain woman who proved to be physically repugnant to

Henry, and one can imagine the feeling to have been mutual. Cromwell's enemies, Norfolk and Gardiner, seized the moment to turn Henry against his chancellor by using slanders of heresy and treason. The king divorced Anne and beheaded Cromwell on July 28, 1540.

The conservative party arranged his next marriage with Norfolk's niece, Catherine Howard. The king had Norfolk present to Parliament six articles of doctrine which emerged over Cranmer's objection as the Six Articles Act. It was truly Henry's own, for he revised the initial draft himself and sat in on the debate in the House of Lords. The Six Articles reverted to (1) a Catholic definition of transubstantiation in the sacrament; (2) celibacy of the clergy as a divine order; (3) the binding character of the oaths of regular clergy; (4) communion under one kind; (5) the appropriateness and necessity of private masses; and (6) private confession. The penalties were so savage, death by burning, for example, and the confiscation of all property, if one denied transubstantiation, that the Articles were called a "whip with six bloody strings." Cranmer sensed the dangers and sent his wife to safety with relatives in Germany. Two pro-Protestant bishops, Shaxton of Salisbury and Latimer of Worcester, gave up their bishoprics. Over five hundred Protestants were arrested in London alone. The Act claimed some Protestant martyrs, but the conservatives failed to dislodge Cranmer, who kept the king's confidence despite charges of heresy against him. Henry laughingly even put Cranmer in charge of his own investigation. In 1542 Henry had Catherine Howard beheaded for adultery and in his last years he found comfort in the company of motherly Catherine Parr, who survived her royal spouse. He died on January 27, 1547, ministered to by his faithful Cranmer. Characteristically, Henry on the one hand nominated for his son a Council of Regency that was dominated by the Protestant element, but on the other hand provided in his will for the saying of many masses for his soul.

5. TRIUMPH OF PROTESTANTISM

It is ironic that after all of Henry's efforts to produce a male heir, his son Edward VI should have been king so briefly and never have ruled England. Edward VI was a mere boy of nine when he came to the throne. Although Holbein's portrait of him at age two shows Edward to be a healthy child, he was always frail and sickly so that his death at sixteen came as no surprise. His childhood was plagued by tutors such as Roger Ascham, who taught him the classical languages and French. At the age of thirteen he was able to read Aristotle's *Nicomachaean Ethics* in Greek, to translate Cicero's *De Philosophia* into Greek, and, like his father, could carry on complicated conversations about theology. The real rulers during his reign were not the Council appointed by Henry but two strong men who assumed power. The first three years the power behind the throne was the handsome, affable, ambitious, and greedy Protestant Edward Seymour, brother of Jane Seymour, earl of Hertford, duke of Somerset. During the last years of Edward's life the role passed to the unscrupulous and ruthless John Dudley, earl of Warwick, who became duke of Northumberland. During Edward's reign religious, social, and economic problems were predominant rather than questions of foreign policy.

Within a few hours after Edward was proclaimed king, the Council voted Somerset protector, and within a few weeks he was given a patent which enabled him to assert direct personal power. Cranmer enjoyed continued influence and Somerset promoted Protestantism along with his own interests. He was undone mainly by being too favorable to the poor and powerless and conversely by offending the rich and mighty. In one session of Parliament the new government indulged in a "self-denying orgy" by repealing the Six Articles with the severe penalties, rescinding Henry's punitive additions to traditional heresy and treason laws, allowing the unrestricted printing, sale, and exposition of the authorized version of the Scriptures, and annulling the act that gave royal proclamation the force of law. The stability of the regime, however, required fiscal solvency and Somerset followed the example of King Henry.

In 1545 Henry's Parliament had passed an act vesting chantry property in the crown. The act was intended only for the lifetime of the king, but a new act transferred to the crown all chantries, which were essentially endowments for the saying of private masses for the souls of the dead, presumably in purgatory. The act included the endowments also of all free chapels, colleges, prayer fraternities, and religious guilds. The moneys once devoted to the papist errors could now be used for "the erecting of grammar schools to the education of youth in virtue and godliness, the further augmenting of the universities, and better provisions for the poor and needy." It has been estimated that there were some 2,374 chantries, 90 colleges, and 110 hospitals, most of which disappeared at the dissolution, with the exception of some chapels in remote areas far from a parish church. Some chantry schools were transformed into Edward VI grammar schools and the confiscated chantry holdings were applied to increase their endowments a third. Some of the chantry wealth was used to support military garrisons and fortifications and some to enrich Somerset's family fortune. Some episcopal lands were secularized as well, one device being to appoint bishops on salary who in turn gave episcopal manors and lands to secular rulers. Somerset himself acquired the site of his palatial Somerset House by tearing down three bishops' town houses and a church and gaining building material for it by demolishing the cloister of St. Paul's Cathedral and part of the Priory Church of St. John of Jerusalem.

Somerset had many Lutheran convictions, was in contact with Calvin, and favored further reform of the church. Already in the summer of 1547 royal commissioners traveled through the diocese on visitations similar to those in Lutheran lands two decades before. They issued injunctions ordering all parishes to acquire Erasmus's *Paraphrases* as a clear and critical interpretation of biblical passages, Cranmer's sermon collection known as the *Book of Homilies,* and insisted that the English Bible was to be available in every church. Bishops Gardiner of Winchester and Bonner of London resisted and were imprisoned.

During this period a stream of refugees and immigrants came from the continent to England, reflecting the successes of the Habsburgs and Valois in repressing heresy. Some refugees journeyed to England from Italy via Geneva. Most of those who came were inclined toward Zwinglianism or Calvinism. When Emperor Charles V imposed the Interim as many as four hundred Lutheran ministers were forced from their pulpits. The most prominent among them was Martin Bucer of Strasbourg, who came to England at the invitation of Cranmer, who thought he would be a mediating influence. Bucer accepted a Regius professorship at Cambridge, completed there his book *On the Kingdom of Christ,* and helped compose the Edwardian prayerbook. He died in February, 1551. Among the former Strasbourg reformers who came to England were Peter Martyr Vermigli, who accepted a Regius professorship at Oxford, Paul Fagius, who became a reader in Greek at Cambridge, where he was succeeded by John Immanuel Tunellius, whom Cardinal Reginald Pole had converted from Judaism to Christianity. The Polish reformer John à Lasco, who had been the Calvinist superintendent of the reformed church in Friesland, served a congregation of over five thousand religious refugees in the church of the Austin Friars, a fitting gesture since some of the Augustinians were among

the first to respond to Luther. There was a congregation of French refugees in London. The Calvinist Valérand Poullain served a group of
Flemish weavers, whom the Protector had set up in the ruins of the former
Glastonbury Abbey. Bernardino Ochino, like Peter Martyr, was an Italian
Protestant who came to England from Strasbourg and was made a canon
of Canterbury Cathedral. Originally from Spain came the pro-Lutheran
nobleman Francisco de Encinas, known by the pseudonym Dryander. And
from Scotland came the rambunctious pro-Genevan John Knox, poised for
further action in the north. Anabaptists and other radicals were considered
subversive to the civil order and were as unwelcome in England as elsewhere.

Lutheranism became less influential at the universities, and Swiss reformed notions, such as the prohibition of images in churches, increased
in influence in the Council, which issued a decree leading to the destruction of roods and side altars and even the whitewashing of church walls.
The Edwardian bishops who shouldered the main burden of Anglican
reform represented a theological spectrum ranging from the conservatives
who still upheld transubstantiation, such as Bonner of London, Tunstall
of Durham, Day of Chichester, and Heath of Worcester, to the Puritan-
like John Hooper, Goodrich of Ely, Holbeach of Lincoln, and Nicholas
Ridley of Rochester, who held positions varying from nearly Catholic to
almost Zwinglian on the real presence of Christ in the sacrament. The
question of celibacy or marriage for the clergy still stirred controversy. A
statute of February, 1549, allowed clerical marriage, which was usually
accepted by the parishioners, although the wives were sometimes maligned. The great liturgical creation was the *First Prayer Book,* which
trimmed down parts thought to be superstitious leftovers, added English
prayers in preparation for the eucharist, the general confession, absolution, comforting words from Scripture, the Prayer of Humble Access, and
the blessing. Its beautiful cadences reflect Cranmer's Lutheran beliefs and
mastery of the English language. It was a splendid piece of studied ambi-
guity, sufficiently traditional to satisfy the conservatives and yet so
phrased, especially as to the eucharist, to permit the more advanced reformed to use it in good conscience. Soon services were conducted entirely in English at St. Paul's Cathedral and other Lincoln churches. In
1549 Parliament passed an Act of Uniformity to bring order out of the
variety of services.

These religious changes together with economic and social pressures led to a series of rebellions in 1549. Although the penalty for not using the new service was six months in jail and the loss of a year's salary, some priests refused to follow it. Such resistance coupled with resentment at new taxes on sheep and cloth and other grievances led to trouble in Devonshire, the Western Rebellion in Cornwall, skirmishes in Exeter, and smaller revolts in Yorkshire, Buckinghamshire, and Oxfordshire. In Norfolk a more serious revolt developed, known as Kett's Rebellion. Robert Kett, a tanner and landholder, led peasants and townsmen against the Norfolk gentry whom they held responsible for the continuous spread of enclosures, which were blamed for nearly all the economic ills of the area. The Commonwealth Party, which opposed enclosures, won Protector Somerset to their position. He in response created the impression that he would help the oppressed against the landlords. These East Anglia rebels produced a long list of grievances and demands, including free fishing rights in the rivers. The rebels captured Norwich, and the government decided to take strong measures. An army of German mercenaries and recruits from neighboring counties attacked the disorganized rebels and routed them. Over three thousand died in the battle and forty-nine rebels, including Kett, were executed.

Protector Somerset was in a vulnerable position. He was still known to the poor and oppressed as the "Good Duke," but many sensed that his government was weak and unstable. The military commander in the west, Russell, refused to come to the Protector's aid. His sinister foe John Dudley, earl of Warwick, was in command of the army that defeated Kett. Warwick skillfully won support in the Council, ingratiated himself with the young king, whom he invited to Council meetings and managed to turn against Somerset. With the king on his side Warwick made his move, and on October 14, 1549, Protector Somerset was sent to the Tower. Warwick released Somerset and made him Earl Marshal, but fearing a new surge of popularity for his opponent, Warwick had him executed in 1552, the price paid for failure in Tudor England. Indeed, even a fraternal relationship offered no protection against Warwick, who had his own brother beheaded for treason. In 1551 Warwick took the title duke of Northumberland and is generally known as such. Having tricked the Catholic faction into supporting him against Somerset, he proceeded as victor to promote the Reformation more radically than Somerset had ever done and enriched himself with the grossest kind of spoils.

The Church of England had been purified of all that the English reformers and the influential continental immigrants considered to be medieval superstitions. The mass as a sacrifice of the body and blood of Christ had been replaced by a communion service which was a memorial of the Last Supper. The sermon had become the center of the service. These changes were reflected in the *Second Book of Common Prayer* in 1552. Now a commission of thirty-two members was appointed, half clerics and half laymen, to develop a new church law to replace the old canon law. The new code for the Church of England was the *Reformation of Ecclesiastical Laws,* which reaffirmed the independent jurisdiction of the church and its courts over both clergy and laity, a matter of dispute for common law jurists. This code was a statement of faith composed largely by Cranmer and drawing heavily on the Lutheran Augsburg Confession of 1530 and other doctrinal statements. The articles condemned papal teachings about purgatory, indulgences, images and relic adoration, prayers to the saints, and the mass. They taught justification by faith, election to salvation, and other doctrines reflecting Lutheran and Calvinist teachings. The statement on the nature of Christ's presence in the eucharist, article 24, has been called "the perfect summary of the Zwinglian belief of the Real Absence" of Christ from the sacrament and from the world according to his human nature. Christ is removed from this temporal reality and sits at the right hand of God the Father. The English church had indeed moved fast and far from the Six Articles of 1539 to Cranmer's Forty-two Articles of 1553.

In 1552 Edward VI's health began to fail noticeably and by May, 1553, it was obvious to all that he was not long for this world. Northumberland maneuvered to perpetuate himself in power. He married his son to Lady Jane Grey, the sixteen-year-old Protestant grandniece of Henry VIII, and then he persuaded Edward to name Lady Jane as his successor rather than his older sister Mary, a Catholic. Northumberland foolishly failed to put Mary in a secure prison. Edward died on July 6, and innocent Lady Jane reigned for only a few days. Mary had slipped away to East Anglia and the people came to her support as the rightful heiress to the throne. Lady Jane and her young spouse were imprisoned and Northumberland was sent to the Tower. Until the very day of his execution he tried to save himself by exhorting all to abjure heresy and to embrace Catholicism. Mary had him and the unlucky young pretender beheaded.

6. THE CATHOLIC QUEEN AND THE ELIZABETHAN SETTLEMENT

Toward evening on July 18, 1553, the great bells of St. Paul's Cathedral began to peal followed by the ringing of all the church bells in London to announce the accession of Queen Mary. A *Te Deum* rose heavenward toward the cathedral's high dome. The people lit bonfires in the streets to celebrate her new reign. On October 1 Mary was crowned queen. As an omen of things to come, Queen Mary's first gesture was to hang up a forbidden crucifix in the chapel of her castle at Framingham. Her whole life had been marred by tragedy and her brief reign of less than six years was full of disappointment and sorrow. While a mere infant she was used in the marital chess games of Francis I and Charles V. Henry had forced his own daughter to acknowledge herself as illegitimate, but then in the Act of Succession he made her next in line after Edward and before Elizabeth. Her mother, Queen Catherine, with whom she lived years at a time away from court, brought her up as an ardent Spanish Catholic. She thought of herself as Spanish and the Venetian ambassador at her court reported that she despised being English and was proud of her Spanish descent. She alienated her countrymen by marrying King Philip II of Spain. She was relatively simple and direct and could show mercy despite her fanaticism. But she also undeniably had a prominent trait of her father, stubborn self-will. History's name tag "Bloody Mary" is too harsh a judgment on a woman so sincere and well-intentioned. She was narrow-minded but not cruel.

Her first move was to rid the government of Edward's Protestant officials. Some former Council members who had turned against Northumberland in time were reappointed and some new members were among those who had been supportive while Mary had been in peril. But the key bishops and ministers were replaced with her men. She made Stephen Gardiner Lord Chancellor. Bishops Bonner, Tunstall, Heath, Day, and other conservatives were returned to office and restored the Latin mass and liturgy. Cranmer, Latimer, and Ridley were imprisoned, and many of the reformers fled to the continent. Among those Marian exiles who became refugees in Strasbourg, Frankfurt, Zurich, Emden, Wesel, even Copenhagen, were Peter Martyr, John à Lasco, who left with his congregation, Poullain with his Glastonbury weavers, Richard Cox, dean of Christ Church in Oxford, John Cheke, Thomas Lever, and Edward Sandys of

Cambridge, as well as several dozen students, merchants, gentry, and laborers. Abroad these exiles maintained their independent congregations and used the Prayer Book of 1552.

The first Parliament, which met from October to December, 1553, declared Henry's divorce illegal and Mary the legitimate heiress to the throne. It repealed all the laws relating to religion passed during Edward's reign, the two Acts of Uniformity, acts concerning the election of bishops, marriage of the clergy, iconoclasm, and church festivals. Church services were to be in accordance with the practice during Henry's last year. The second Parliament in session in April and May, 1554, showed signs of foot dragging. It consented to the marriage of Mary and Philip of Spain, but rejected Gardiner's move to allow Mary to disinherit Elizabeth and bequeath the crown by will. The English were not ready to accept a Spanish monarch. Parliament also rejected the restoration of the harsh laws against Lollards, the reinstatement of the Six Articles, and the reestablishment of the monasteries. Gardiner wished also to eliminate the title of Supreme Head of the Church for the queen. The Parliament revoked all statutes against papal authority enacted since 1529. The Convocation of Clergy condemned Cranmer, Ridley, and Latimer as heretics. Following an injunction against married clergy in March, 1554, two thousand or more, one-fourth of the total, were deprived of their livings.

When Mary announced that she intended to marry Philip of Spain, English national feeling ran high. The Commons sent a commission to ask her not to marry a foreigner. The most serious of a number of rebellions was led by young Sir Thomas Wyatt, who roused the county of Kent against the Spanish king and marched with some four thousand men to the very gates of London before being driven back. The frightening success of this revolt led Mary to have Lady Jane Grey beheaded, because she reluctantly concluded that as long as a Protestant pretender remained alive there would be rebels ready to take up arms in her cause. Mary's marriage with Philip proved to be a failure. They were unable to produce an heir, and Philip sailed off to look after his own interests on the continent. After she had watched her husband in his white-silk gold-brocaded suit disappear toward the horizon, an embittered Mary turned to the task of seriously persecuting Protestants.

On November 24, 1554, Cardinal Reginald Pole arrived from Italy as the papal legate with a papal brief to absolve the kingdom for its disobedience to the Holy See. For a renowned Christian humanist he turned out to be a determined leader of the Marian reaction. On January 29, 1555, the persecution of Protestants began in deadly earnest when Cardinal Legate Pole commissioned bishops Gardiner, Tunstall, Capon, Thirlby, and Aldridge to begin trying heretics. Through an underground network the exiles kept in touch with the dissidents inside the kingdom. In response to the London Bishop Edmund Bonner's articles against marriage of the clergy, the English Prayer Book, and in favor of the mass, the exiled Protestant bishop of Ossory, bilious John Bale, wrote: "This limb of the devil and working tool of Satan, bloody Bonner, seeketh to deprive you of faith, true doctrine and God's religion." "What is this idolatrous mass and lousy Latin service," he asked, "but sow's belly swillbowl, and the very draught of Antichrist and dregs of the devil?"[24] Protestant divines who had stayed in England had more limited freedom of expression although they may have shared Bale's sentiments. John Rogers, editor of the Matthew's Bible, Hugh Latimer, Nicholas Ridley, John Hooper, Miles Coverdale, and other prominent Protestants were imprisoned. Rogers was burned at the stake on February 4, 1555. The famous preacher Hugh Latimer was taken along with Ridley to the great ditch opposite Balliol College, Oxford, and burned at the stake. Latimer, a humble man, cheered Master Ridley and then, as John Foxe related in his *Book of Martyrs*, he "received the flame as it were embracing it. After he had stroked his face with his hands, and, as it were, bathed them a little in the fire, he soon died, as it appeared, with very little pain or none." A recent list numbers the victims of this persecution at 282. Not all were heroic, for some of the rich bought themselves free. A recent study of the psychology of English martyrdom has suggested that some masochistically sought suffering and death. A good many of those burned for heresy were simple artisans. Some were merely jailed or flogged. When a critic chided Bishop Bonner for whipping an old man in a "pelting chafe" he replied: "If thou hadst been in his case, thou wouldst have thought it a good commutation of penance to have thy bum beaten to save thy body from burning."

Thomas Cranmer's hour, too, had come. He had been permitted to say King Edward's funeral service from the *Book of Common Prayer,* but he was marked for judgment and the death sentence. The Spanish king and English queen wished to have his case remanded to Rome and he was ordered to appear there within eighty days. But the secular sword, in a

24. *Ibid.,* p. 185.

medieval fashion, was now wielded in the interest of the spiritual sword. Cranmer's trial was held in England in the Oxford University church of St. Mary the Virgin. Bishop Brooks as the representative of Pope Paul IV graced a platform ten feet high before the altar while the royal prosecutors below him accused Cranmer of incontinence, blasphemy, and heresy. He was, of course, found guilty on all charges, stripped of his insignia of office in a humiliating ceremony, and condemned to die at the stake. Cranmer feared the fire and after his degradation he signed seven submissions and recantations. It was all to no avail. As the formulator of so much of Henrican and Edwardian Protestantism, he had to die. On March 21, 1556, his enemies placed him on a stage in St. Mary's where he stood the "very image and shape of perfect sorrow" with tears streaming down his cheeks. He exhorted all men to have obedience toward rulers and love for all men. Then he surprised all by recanting all his recantations, declaring that should he be brought to the fire the hand that had signed them should burn first. He denounced the pope and confessed that his own book on the eucharist represented his real convictions. Torn from the stage, he was dragged to the ditch where Ridley and Latimer had died at the stake. The *Book of Martyrs* recounts that "When the wood was kindled and the fire began to burn near him, stretching out his arm, he put his right hand into the flame which he held so steadfast and immovable (saving that once with the same hand he wiped his face) that all men might see his hand burned before his body was touched. . . . Using often the words of Stephen, Lord Jesus receive my spirit; in the greatness of the flame he gave up the ghost."

Mary's Catholic restoration had a retrospective, medieval, and monastic cast to it and did not take into account that England had experienced fundamental changes and that the Catholic Church was also in motion. While the conservative north and west supported her quite strongly, the east and southeast, especially London, were more divided and ambivalent toward her. Mary's Archbishop of Canterbury Reginald Pole failed to take advantage of the new forces at work in Catholicism, rejecting Ignatius Loyola's offer to train seminarians for service in England. Foreign affairs added to miserable Mary's grief since she was put in the position of seeing her own kingdom in a "state of war with the Pope himself." One of the reasons why Philip had married Mary was to bring England into a Habsburg alliance against France and the Papal States. As a Neapolitan, Pope Paul IV was resolved to free Naples from Spanish domination. Philip struck first against Rome, but King Henry II of France initiated hostilities on behalf of the pope. Perceiving England to be an ally of Spain, crafty Pope Paul summoned Cardinal Pole to Rome for an investigation of heresy. Henry II now attacked the remaining English foothold on the continent and captured Calais, a severe blow to English pride and a humiliation that was widely blamed on Mary. Nature struck further blows as pestilence and disease decimated her largely older clergy while the Marian exiles waited on the continent to fill the vacancies. Mary lost her will to live and in the early morning hours of November 17, 1558, she died at St. James's. Some twelve hours later Cardinal Reginald Pole died in his sleep.

The accession of Queen Elizabeth, a young woman of twenty-five, was greeted with tremendous enthusiasm by the people, who rallied to her at Hatfield even as her half-sister Mary lay dying. Her forty-five-year reign saw England turn thoroughly and irrevocably Protestant and emerge as the leader of the Protestant states. With its strategic location on the Atlantic and fine harbors, England under Elizabeth built up a world empire abroad and enjoyed a cultural flowering at home which constituted the country's real renaissance. While historians formerly exaggerated Elizabeth's personal contribution to England's development, it remains true that she was a shrewd, calculating, and worldly ruler who used Parliament to advantage and served as a symbol for the will, hope, and aspirations of her energetic people.

The people fully expected Queen Elizabeth to marry, but she preferred to keep the reins of government in her own hands. A strong, fairly tall woman with pinkish red hair, an olive complexion, graceful hands given to regal gestures, expressive eyes, and a dignified bearing, she was a daughter worthy of her imperious father. She could play on her femininity or turn ice cold in making quick and firm decisions or coolly delaying until she could act to attain the maximum advantage. Tutored by Roger Ascham, she had a fine taste for literature and spoke Latin, French, and Italian. Philip II of Spain offered her marriage, but marriage with her sister's former husband would have provided an interesting replay of her father's problems with consanguinity laws. After Mary's unhappy experience with Philip, clever Elizabeth knew well to reject that alliance at any price. Robert Dudley, earl of Leicester, her passionate lover, was at least an Englishman, but he was mercurial, spoiled, and suspected by some of having arranged a fatal fall for his wife. Although attracted to him, Elizabeth put the welfare of the kingdom above her own personal feelings. She remained the virgin queen whose longest-lasting love affair was with the English people.

As in the case of Henry, it is difficult to say absolutely to what extent Elizabeth planned to follow the *via media* and to what extent she simply steered her way by necessity between extremes or was pressured by equal forces. In any case, most of her rule demonstrated moderation and a striving for compromise and consensus. Her choice of advisers and ministers reflected her policy. She chose William Cecil, who became Lord Burghley, as her closest adviser. A moderate Protestant, Cecil had served under both Protector Somerset and Northumberland, and briefly under Mary. He held office during almost all of her reign, as secretary of state and as lord treasurer. Elizabeth had an exclusively Protestant council, men theologically more Protestant than she and some even favorable to Puritanism. She believed strongly that England needed peace at home and abroad for its prosperity. She therefore favored an Anglican settlement in matters of polity and doctrine and kept Catholics and radicals under close surveillance and control. The Scots reformer John Knox complained that Elizabeth was "neither good Protestant nor yet resolute Papist." She named Matthew Parker, her mother's chaplain and her own tutor, as Archbishop of Canterbury. Theologically a moderate and a disciple of the mediating Martin Bucer of Strasbourg, he had many friends among the Marian exiles. He and Elizabeth filled many strategic bishoprics with returned exiles who were more favorably inclined toward Calvinism than was the queen.

Like Henry, Queen Elizabeth worked very effectively through Parliament, which evolved in a significant way during the course of the century from a basically legislative and taxing body which met only intermittently into a powerful force of government, especially the House of Commons. Henry had increased the political power of the Commons because it agreed with his political aims. Elizabeth controlled the Commons, heavily representing the gentry, by manipulation and by their common national feeling. On January 25, 1559, Parliament met and speedily enacted reform legislation. Within two weeks the Commons was working on a bill to "restore the supremacy of the Church of England to the crown of one realm." The Convocation of the Clergy held to the Catholic doctrines of transubstantiation and the sacrifice of the mass, since most of the bishops had been appointed by Mary. So Parliament took the initiative, with the

Protestant council working along with the House of Commons. In April Parliament passed the Act of Supremacy, which ended papal jurisdiction in England. A later supremacy bill acknowledged the queen to be the supreme head of the Church of England. This third Act of Supremacy eliminated the Marian heresy laws and revived certain Henrican statutes such as annates and appeals. The Act of Uniformity, 1559, restored the ecclesiastical statutes of Henry and reintroduced the *Second Prayer Book* of Edward with some more traditional passages added from the 1549 edition. The Tudor queen and Protestantism were once again solidly established. To deny the supremacy of the crown over the church or to refuse to take an oath of loyalty resulted in immediate deprivation of office. To acknowledge the authority of any foreign prince or prelate was defined as high treason and made punishable by death. Clergy who refused to conform were gradually replaced with Elizabeth's appointees. While there were pockets of resistance to the settlement and recusants maintained significant numbers, the country as a whole seemed to welcome the establishment of peace and order in the realm.[25] It is not without cause that the English sometimes think of the age of Elizabeth as the greatest in their history.

7. THE REFORMATION IN SCOTLAND AND IRELAND

The direction that the Reformation took in both Scotland and Ireland was of an importance for England and America far out of proportion to the size of those two countries. A Catholic Scotland would have meant a continuation of the alliance with France and encirclement for England. A Protestant Ireland might have meant eventual absorption into Britain along with Cornwall, Wales, and Scotland. The Reformation came to Scotland late and the triumph of Protestantism was not assured until 1560. Scotland was less developed economically than was the south of England and its politics were dominated locally by the clans. There was virtually no bourgeois middle class inclined toward the Protestant work ethic or reinforced by it. The reform pattern was more one of protest against ignorance and criticism of the immorality of the priests. The canons regular were a constructive force, although the monks played a relatively minor role either as causes of complaint or as leaders of reform. Anticlericalism was directed primarily against the priests and the hierarchy. Despite

25. An admirable study of how a single county away from the orbit of the capital and the universities stood out against change is Christopher Haigh, *Reformation and Renaissance in Tudor Lancashire* (Cambridge, 1975).

an act of Parliament of 1525 forbidding the importation of Lutheran books into Scotland, merchants and travelers brought them in through the port towns. In 1528 Patrick Hamilton was burned at the stake for evangelical preaching, an incident followed by a number of other executions and iconoclastic demonstrations. Cardinal Beaton emerged as the villain in the scenario, and when he burned the gospel preacher George Wishart at St. Andrews in 1546, there was great popular outrage. Beaton was waylaid and assassinated three months afterward in his castle at St. Andrews. As in England, hostility toward the clergy played a major role in the Reformation.

One man stamped his imprint on the Reformation in Scotland in a special way. He was John Knox (1505–1572), the "thundering Scot." He was a priest of peasant lineage and remained an earthy man of the people. He was Wishart's supporter and on his death, Knox fought with a Protestant garrison which defended the St. Andrews castle against French troops sent to protect the power and Catholic religion of Mary of Guise, the widow of James V and regent for their daughter Mary. The French triumphed in August, 1547, and took Knox and the garrison captive. For nineteen months Knox was forced to labor as a galley slave, chained to the rowing bench. In April, 1549, he made his getaway to England. When Mary acceded to the throne, Knox became an exile in Calvin's Geneva. In 1556 he wrote to a certain Mrs. Locke about Geneva, "whair I nether feir nor schame to say is the nearest perfyt school of Chryst that ever was in the erth since the dayis of the Apostillis." In 1559 the Scottish Protestants called Knox back to his homeland. Knox denounced Mary of Guise as an "unruly cow saddled by mistake." In 1558 he had published his notorious *First Blast Against the Monstrous Regiment of Women* aimed at the three Marys, in which he declared that to "promote a woman to have rule above any realm is repugnant to nature, contumely to God, a thing most contrarious to His revealed will and approved ordinance, and finally it is subversive of good order, of all equity and justice." These were words he was to regret in the presence of Elizabeth. The English sent an army to help Knox and his Protestants drive out the French. Mary of Guise died during the war. The Treaty of Edinburgh, July 6, 1560, marked the victory of Protestantism, and on August 24 the Parliament outlawed Catholicism. From his pulpit in St. Giles Knox sent shudders through his audience and tremors throughout Scotland. He now embarked on reorganizing the country with a Calvinist presbyterian polity. The *Confession of Faith,* the *Book of Common Order,* and the *First Book of Discipline* became the key documents of the Reformed Church. Moreover, with his *History of the Reformation in Scotland* Knox left to posterity a moving account of what had transpired.

On the death of her husband Francis II in 1561, Mary Queen of Scots, a girl of eighteen, returned from France. After a mild beginning she swung over to a hard line against the Protestants and was driven out in 1567 to find refuge in England. The success of Knox and the triumph of Protestantism was remarkable both for its rapidity and its thoroughness.

The standard view of the Reformation in Ireland is that the Reformation was a foreign implant, that its supporters were colonists, English government officials, or local opportunists, that from the outset the common people were hostile to a reformation, and that the Irish parliamentarians who appeared to support it did so more because of English pressure than out of genuine conviction.[26] In reality, as in England there was a deep vein of discontent due to abuses and scandalous irregularities. Anticlerical sentiments were accompanied by the penetration of Protestant ideas early in the reign of Henry VIII. The Irish chiefs were as ready as the English gentry to benefit from Henry's suppression of the monasteries.[27] During the reign of Edward VI Sir Anthony St. Leger and then Sir Edward Bellingham imposed the royal will in Ireland. Bellingham brought the O'Mores and the O'Connors under control so that chiefs and nobles were forced to respect the English monarch, although the O'Mores continued to give trouble to the English until the end of Elizabeth's reign. Anglicanism as such was viewed by most Irish as a foreign import. The royal order officially establishing Protestantism in Ireland was withheld until 1551. When Edward Staples preached in Dublin against the mass and the invocation of saints, he met with animosity on all sides. He challenged George Dowdall, Archbishop of Armaugh, to a debate, which naturally proved indecisive. When Dowdall fled, Cranmer sought a Protestant for St. Patrick's chair. John Bale became bishop of Ossory, but his crudeness and lack of tact worked against his success in the Protestant cause. Edward's agents turned to conquest and extermination. Queen Mary removed Staples,

---

26. The classic statement of this view is that of R.D. Edwards, *Church and State in Tudor Ireland: A History of the Penal Laws Against Irish Catholics 1534–1603* (Dublin and London, 1935).

27. Brendan Bradshaw, *The Dissolution of the Religious Orders in Ireland under Henry VIII* (Cambridge, 1974), gives a good account of the period 1533–1556, but mistakenly assumes that Protestantism was at that point blocked and made no further progress.

deprived other Protestant bishops of their sees, and reappointed men like Dowdall. She failed to restore the monastic lands and followed her English interests with a policy of expropriation and the establishment of military colonies.

Upon Queen Elizabeth's accession Sir Henry Sidney was sworn in as lord-justice with a full Catholic ritual, but when his successor, Thomas Radclyffe, earl of Sussex, became lord-lieutenant, the litany was chanted in English, the walls of the cathedral were painted and biblical texts substituted for "pictures and popish fancies." In 1560 the Irish parliament restored the ecclesiastical laws of Henry VIII and Edward VI. The *congés d'élire* of the church were abolished and heretics were to be remanded directly to royal commissioners or to parliament rather than to the Convocation of the Clergy or to synods. Some Irish bishops took the oath to royal supremacy, although some were deprived of their sees. However, Elizabeth was a realist and except in the Pale and in larger towns she did not attempt to enforce uniformity. A long delay in undertaking a mission drive and educational effort meant that throughout most of Ireland the Reformation struck only shallow roots. This does not mean that the Counter-Reformation was sure to flourish, except for progress in some towns. The evidence suggests that neither the Reformation nor the Counter-Reformation was the final victor in Ireland in early modern times, but that the majority of the native population clung tenaciously to pre-Tridentine religious practice.[28] Elizabeth's plans for Protestantization and colonization in Ireland came to grief, and despite her efforts at "pacification" the Emerald Isle remained a sullen, unreliable part of her realm, ready to erupt at the first opportunity.

28. This is the revisionist argument of Nicholas Canny, "Why the Reformation Failed in Ireland: Une Question Mal Posée," *The Journal of Ecclesiastical History,* 30, no. 4 (Oct., 1979), 423–450. See also for the later period John Bossy, "The Counter-Reformation and the People of Catholic Ireland, 1596–1641," *Historical Studies,* 8 (Dublin, 1971), 155–171.

Chapter Six

CATHOLIC RENEWAL AND RESPONSE

I. SPIRITUAL RENEWAL

AN ecclesiastical parole that well describes the history of the Roman Catholic Church reads *ecclesia reformata reformanda,* for all through its history the church and its orders have suffered decline and experienced renewal. The history of the church in the Reformation era falls within this old historical pattern although the Protestant Reformation with its radical doctrine and schism was the most serious crisis the church had faced since the Arian heresy. Though driven by Protestant pressure to reform, the church also drew upon deep wells of spiritual strength and a long medieval tradition of self-renewal.

During the fourteenth and fifteenth centuries the church had experienced a decline in spirituality and institutional crises that weakened its structure and inner resources. Many of the very churchmen who should have served as models of good behavior and sources of inspiration were openly worldly and cynical. Álvarez Pelayos, a strong ultramontane, stormed: "Those who rule in the church are wolves: they feed themselves with blood, every soul is burdened with blood." The reign of the Renaissance popes, for all intents and purposes Italian princes with typical parochial and familial interests, followed upon a time of troubles: the "Babylonian Captivity of the Church," or seventy years of exile from Rome in Avignon under domination by the French monarchs; the Great Schism, which saw two and then three rival popes; the conciliar movement which challenged the monarchical episcopate of the bishop of Rome and was not brought to the point of a moratorium until 1449, when the papacy brought the Council of Basel to its close; and 1460, when Pius II issued his *Execrabilis,* declaring it an execrable thing and a heresy to appeal to a council over the head of the pope. Conciliarism was not then dead, but at most dormant until humanists like Ulrich von Hutten and reformers like Luther called for *concilium.* The Hussite revolt was contained but not mastered, for the Utraquists remained the established church of Bohemia

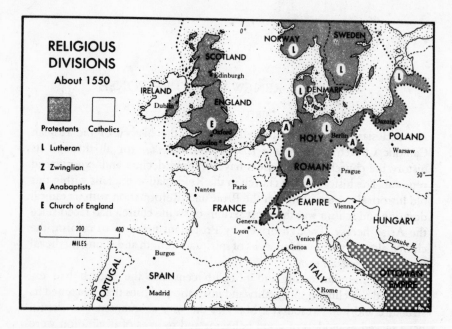

RELIGIOUS
DIVISIONS
About 1550

Protestants   Catholics

L Lutheran

Z Zwinglian

A Anabaptists

E Church of England

0   200   400
MILES

until after the Battle of the White Mountain in 1620, and some groups such as the Bohemian Brethren have persisted in the Czech and Moravian areas until the present time.

The crisis within the "interior castle" was reflected in various spiritual and intellectual developments. Mysticism, a "perennial philosophy" in the West, though less so than in the East, flourished in the late Middle Ages. It has been described as a reaction to scholastic rationalism, though the interaction between mysticism and scholasticism was extensive. The flourishing of mysticism has also been viewed as a withdrawal from an oppressive and corrupt society and church to the inner self. A highly personal way of apprehending spiritual reality through immediate experience, insight, or intuition, mysticism is not readily communicable and therefore not an effective platform for direct social change. Its symbolic value is significant, reflecting malaise vis-à-vis society and a deeper individual spiritual feeling. Moreover, insofar as individuals change history, its historical impact is important. One need merely at this point recall the place of the *Theologia Germania* and the *Devotio Moderna* in Luther's formation.

Mysticism in varying dimensions remained an operative force for most Catholic religious reformers and emerged in strength especially in Spain in the latter half of the sixteenth century in such figures as Teresa of Avila and John of the Cross.

The scholarly teapot still gives off steam over the question of the vitality and creativity of late scholasticism. The humanists and reformers were quite uniformly of the opinion that this rationalistic approach to theology based upon classical dialectic and ancient pagan sources had not only outlived its usefulness but was harmful to theology. Whatever claims may be made for scholastic theology as represented in the thought of Marsiglio of Inghem or Gabriel Biel in the fifteenth century, originality and constructive contribution cannot be among them. Yet a scholastic approach to theology not only persisted into the time of Catholic reformation, but underwent a notable revival. Thomas de Vio (1469–1534), for example, later to become Cardinal Cajetan and Luther's opponent, wrote a famous exposition of Aquinas's *De Ente et Essentia* and did voluminous commentaries on his *Summa Theologica* between 1507 and 1522. Although Cajetan's Thomism was brittle and formal compared with Thomas, this neo-Thomism remained as a vital force in the theological definitions of the Council of Trent in the mid-century and in the thought of Dominican apologists and philosophers such as Francisco de Suarez (1548–1617) as the Catholic Reformation gained momentum.[1] Overall late scholasticism was not so decadent as its contemporary and subsequent critics held. Nominalism was not so skeptical or corrosive of theology. Epigoni and pedants abounded in the universities, but many humanists could match them in midget mentality and pusillanimous polemic. But the alternatives that Christian humanists and reformers offered to scholasticism had more appeal to their contemporaries, so that the cultural momentum was with them.

The decline of intellectual vigor in evidence was of less importance than the religious chasm that was developing between the growth in religious intensity on the popular level during the century and a half preceding the Reformation and the inability of the institutional church to satisfy those powerful religious impulses stirring throughout society. Both complaints

1. A perceptive monograph on this problem is that of Gerhard Hennig, *Cajetan und Luther: Ein historischer Beitrag zur Begegnung von Thomismus und Reformation* (Stuttgart, 1966). A masterful overview is provided by Steven Ozment, *The Age of Reform 1250-1550: An Intellectual and Religious History of Late Medieval and Reformation Europe* (New Haven, 1980), of the scholastic traditions, pp. 22-72, and the spiritual traditions, pp. 73-134.

such as the *gravamina* of the German diets, formalized in complete lists from 1510 on, and the disappointment with the failure of the church of the Renaissance popes to respond created a revolutionary situation. This disjunction was operative also between Catholic reformers and un-reformed ecclesiastics. Political pressures generated by national monarchs such as Louis XII and Francis I, Charles V and Henry VIII against the papacy created tremendous stress for churchmen also in countries that remained within the Roman Catholic jurisdiction. As events unfolded, it became evident that the papacy at times had more to fear from its friends than from its enemies, when, for example, the renegade forces of Charles V sacked Rome in 1527 and when Spain took control of the Italian peninsula as far north as Milan as well as south of Rome. The popes of the Reformation enjoyed some very limited power as Italian princes and somewhat more as the spiritual heads of Catholic Christendom, but their European reach was a far cry from what it had been in the days of Innocent III, *verus imperator.*

If Protestant reformers had predecessors in the likes of Wycliffe, Hus, and Marsiglio of Padua, Catholic reformers had forerunners in men such as Ximenes, Savonarola, Baptista Mantuanus, and others. Cardinal Ximenes (Jimenez de Cisneros, 1436–1517) was the Franciscan who became the confessor to Isabella of Spain, high chancellor of Castile, founder of the Alcalá, sponsor of the Complutensian Polyglot, and moral administrator of the Spanish church. Savonarola stood as the great prophetic figure in Flo-rence on the eve of the Reformation. A charismatic preacher, he called for repentance and summoned the imminent judgment of God upon a sinful world.[2] Baptista Mantuanus (1448–1516) as prior general of the Carmelite Order wrote religious poetry ornamented with classical figures of speech and invigorated the Carmelites morally and spiritually so that they entered the crisis period in better condition than did most orders.

Gian Matteo Giberti, bishop of Verona from 1524 to 1543, set an example in the reform of the parishes in his diocese. In 1528 he left the Curia and stayed in his diocese until his death. He founded a Confraternity of the Blessed Sacrament, set a personal example in dedication and frugal-ity. Many of his reforms were incorporated both in the prescriptions of a papal commission in 1537 and in the list of necessary reforms agreed on at Trent. Giberti's good example was reinforced by many new editions of

---

2. Savonarola's representative sermon *On the Renovation of the Church,* 1495, is to be found in John C. Olin, ed., *The Catholic Reformation: Savonarola to Ignatius Loyola. Reform in the Church 1495–1540* (New York, 1969), pp. 4–30.

ancient and medieval treatises on the ideal bishop and by such works as Contarini's *De officio episcopi,* which stressed the need for a bishop to lead an exemplary life, carry out pastoral visits to parish churches, improve the education of priests, and provide devotional and catechetical materials for priests and laymen. The printing press in the fifteenth and early sixteenth centuries especially in Catholic lands poured out a great number of medieval inspirational and devotional tracts, lives of the saints, catechisms, and hymnbooks, books such as the *Legenda Aurea* or Ludolph's *Life of Christ.* It is difficult to place certain figures such as Erasmus and the Erasmians. In a sense they represented a liberal wing of Catholic reform, since to their personal discomfiture they lived on into the Reformation decades, but in spirit and intellectual posture they belong rather to a less passionate time. When they sought to find a prescription for reform, Luther commented that they were still trying to sweep the Augean stables with fox tails. He was the Hercules who diverted through those stables the rivers Alpheus and Peneus, which reached flood heights. It is truly difficult to conceive of Cardinal Jacopo Sadoleto, with his Petrarchan yearning for the *vita studiosa* or *contemplativa,* fighting the battles that the French humanist John Calvin fought.[3] Also Catholic reformers for the most part were made of sterner stuff than the Erasmians. Humanist educational ideals informed individual Catholic reformers and especially the Jesuits.

A line of continuity can be traced from the late medieval and Renaissance period to Catholic reform with respect to mysticism, humanism, and education, and in theology in terms of a strong Augustinian tradition and resurgence. As an Augustinian, Luther may be seen as part of a strong Augustinian revival during the fifteenth and sixteenth centuries. From Petrarch Augustinianism influenced one important segment of humanist thought while Stoicism influenced another.[4] Beyond the broader stream

3. See the admirable sketch drawn by Richard M. Douglas, *Jacopo Sadoleto, 1477–1547: Humanist and Reformer* (Cambridge, 1959).

4. William J. Bouwsma, "The Two Faces of Humanism, Stoicism and Augustinianism in Renaissance Thought," in Heiko A. Oberman, Thomas A. Brady, eds., *Itinerarium Italicum. The Profile of the Italian Renaissance in the Mirror of its European Transformations* (Leiden, 1975), pp. 3–60. See also William Bouwsma, "Renaissance and Reformation: An Essay in Their Affinities and Connections," in Heiko A. Oberman, ed., *Luther and the Dawn of the Modern Era* (Leiden, 1974), where he argues that the deepest assumptions of earlier humanist culture found theological expression in the Protestant Reformation and that the Protestant Reformation was even "the theological fulfillment of the Renaissance" p. 129. Ozment, *The Age of Reform 1250–1550,* p. 315, believes that as with the humanist and Protestant concepts of man, the similarity between humanist and Protestant interest in rhetoric "may be more structural than material."

of Augustinian influences specifically within the scholastic tradition Augustinianism remained a vital force. It has been argued that Luther was decisively influenced by Augustinian thinkers such as Archbishop Thomas Bradwardine, the famous general of the Augustinian order in the fourteenth century, Gregory of Rimini and his *via Gregorii,* Jacobus Perez of Valencia (d. 1490), and Agostino Favaroni, the fifteenth-century general of Luther's order. Luther may possibly have encountered their books in the Erfurt library and been introduced to the main outlines of their thought by Karlstadt or Staupitz, although specific evidence is lacking.[5] His thought was formulated in its essential structure before his reading of Johannes Wesel, Pupper von Goch, or Wessel Gansfort, Augustinian mystics. Indisputably for Luther the decisive factors were his study of St. Augustine and St. Paul. For Catholic reformers the line of Augustinian theological descent is demonstrable in the case of the most important sixteenth-century representative of this tradition, Girolamo Seripando, whom Luther may have met in Rome at the convent of Porta del Popolo, where he stayed in 1510–11. Three decades later Seripando was accused of having Lutheran tendencies, because of his Augustinian views of man's sinfulness and salvation by grace alone. Seripando was, nevertheless, made a cardinal and at the Council of Trent he represented an Augustinian position distinct from dominant Thomism.[6]

A "Catholic evangelism" movement emerged in Italy during the 1530s and 1540s which shared some common emphases with Protestantism, such as the all-sufficiency of Christ's sacrificial life and death, the Scriptures as carrier of the gospel, faith as trust, and the value of the spoken Word. Some converts to this movement eventually became Protestant, such as Bernardino Ochino, vicar general of the Capuchins, Peter Paul Vergerio the Younger,[7] bishop of Capo d' Istria from 1536 to 1549 and several times a

5. Adolar Zumkeller, "Die Augustinerschule des Mittelalters: Vertreter und philosophisch-theologische Lehre," *Analecta Augustiniana,* 27 (1964), 167–262; Heiko A. Oberman, "Headwaters of the Reformation. *Initia Lutheri—Initia Reformationis,*" *Luther and the Dawn of the Modern Era,* Heiko A. Oberman, ed., pp. 40–88; David C. Steinmetz, "Luther and the Late Medieval Augustinians: Another Look," *Concordia Theological Monthly,* 44 (1973), 245–260. In his latest work, *Luther and Staupitz: An Essay in the Intellectual Origins of the Protestant Reformation* (Durham, N.C., 1980) Steinmetz again refers to the nature and importance of Augustinianism, pp. 13–16, 25–26, et passim.

6. Hubert Jedin, *Papal Legate at the Council of Trent: Cardinal Seripando* (St. Louis and London, 1947).

7. Anne Jacobson Schutte, *Pier Paolo Vergerio: The Making of an Italian Reformer* (Geneva, 1977), "The Convert to Evangelism (1536–1540)," pp. 105–138.

papal legate to Germany, and Peter Martyr Vermigli, former prior of the Augustinians in Naples and then in Lucca.[8] Vermigli fled the Inquisition, became a professor at Oxford, and defended the Calvinist doctrine at the Colloquy of Poissy. The Venetian pamphlet *De beneficio Christi* (1543) incorporated large sections from the writings of Calvin stressing the centrality of Christ and justification by faith alone. This Catholic evangelism flourished largely in northern cities where Protestant pamphlets and witnesses were most influential. But the most important figure was Juan de Valdés in Naples, whose circle, known as the Blessed Fellowship, included such noblewomen as Giulia Gonzaga and Vittoria Colonna. One of the Valdesiani, Pietro Carnesecchi, had been apostolic protonotary at the court of Clement VII. He was tried for heresy in 1545 and released, but when he was summoned to appear by the Inquisition in 1559 he fled to Geneva. Cosimo d' Medici brought him back to Florence by guaranteeing his personal safety, but he was eventually condemned to death for heresy. The bishop of Bergamo, likewise a member of Valdes's Blessed Fellowship, was imprisoned for two years and in 1558 dismissed from office.

So much attention has been directed toward the reformed or newly organized orders that outstanding individuals who were brave and dedicated defenders of the faith have not been given their due. There were the apologists such as Eck, Erasmus, Cochlaeus, Murner, Reuchlin, Clichtove, Pole, More, Fisher. There were some who defected to Lutheranism and then returned to the mother church, such as Georg Witzel. And there were those who remained within the old church but went as far as was institutionally and dogmatically possible to reach an accommodation with the Lutherans, such as Gasparo Contarini. Johannes Eck, Luther's early and most relentless enemy, was no mean opponent. A man of considerable humanist learning, he had before Luther's emergence on the scene gained international attention with his critique of traditional strictures against usury, favoring, as Luther was to do, a charge of 5 percent interest. His books *On the Primacy of Peter*, 1521, and the *Enchiridion*, 1525, against Luther's theology went through ninety-one editions by 1600 and were translated into several languages. In 1537 he published a German Bible for Catholics.[9] Eck was an all-purpose apologist who took on Zwingli and the Anabaptists as well.

8. Philip McNair, *Peter Martyr in Italy* (Oxford, 1967), documents the influence of the reformers' writing on Vermigili.

9. A. G. Dickens, *The Counter Reformation* (New York, 1979), pp. 56–58, a sprightly brief account.

Although Erasmus was pressured against his will into attacking Luther, his *On the Freedom of the Will* was a worthy polemic which grappled with a central issue of theology. His vituperative *Hyperaspistes,* responding to Luther's *On the Bondage of the Will,* however, was a bitter attack revealing the smarting of a wounded ego. Another humanist apologist was Josse van Clichtove, a member of Lefèvre d' Étaples's circle and later a professor at Paris. Besides an *Anti-Lutherus,* 1524, he wrote many volumes of sermons and biblical exegesis and was widely read in the Catholic world. Reuchlin rewarded Luther's early support in his own controversy with the Cologne scholastics over Hebrew books by siding with Eck and the theologians at Ingolstadt, where he went to teach, against Luther and Melanchthon. Reuchlin had used the Jewish Cabala as a source to prove the truth of Christianity and was not pro-Jewish, just as his opponent Pfefferkorn was not the anti-Jewish villain the humanists Ulrich von Hutten and Crotus Rubeanus made him out to be in the *Letters of Obscure Men.* But Reuchlin was aging and was not long involved in the Reformation struggle.

Some Catholic apologists were more publicists and pamphleteers, such as Johannes Cochlaeus and Thomas Murner. Cochlaeus participated in the Regensburg Conference in 1546 to achieve agreement on the eve of the Schmalkald War. His sharpest thrust against Luther was his commentary on Luther's life and works published three years after Luther's death. It was a mine of calumnies used by polemicists and even serious Catholic historians for centuries. Cardinal Aleander warned against its publication, fearing that the reaction would make it counterproductive. There were men of greater substance with an irenic bent, such as Johannes Gropper (1502–1559) and Julius Pflug (1497–1564). Gropper studied law and theology at Cologne and wrote his *Enchiridion Christianae institutiones,* regarded by some Catholic theologians as a suitable basis for reconciliation with the Lutherans. He participated in the doctrinal colloquies with the Protestants in 1540–41 and was active at the Council of Trent in 1551–52. Pflug was a well-educated man of humanist learning who was elected bishop of Naumburg-Zeitz in 1541 and took part in the Regensburg Conference with the Lutherans in that year. He helped to draft the Augsburg and the Leipzig Interim. The theologian Georg Witzel (1501–1573) was a priest who turned Lutheran in 1524, married, but in 1527 wrote two works critical of Lutheran theology. He resigned his charge in 1531 and the next year wrote a work *In Defense of Good Works,* followed by an *Apologia.* He worked as a Catholic for church reunion but spent his life fleeing from one city to the next as Protestantism spread, moving from Dresden to Bohemia, Berlin, Fulda, and Mainz, pouring out nearly a hundred books and treatises in defense of the church. In England the saintly Fisher, Reginald Pole, and preeminently Thomas More wrote works in defense of the faith against the Lutherans, Zwinglians, and Anabaptists. To consider Christian humanism as a "third force" or "second Reformation" is to overestimate its cohesiveness and independent theological structure. Humanists as classical scholars, rhetoricians, historians, poets, and educators used their talents for the Reformation or the Catholic cause, as their religious convictions required. Nor were apologists of humanist background consistently more moderate, reasonable, civil, or controlled than men of more modest learning. Catholic polemicists gradually learned from Protestant success that rhetoric and good style in Latin or the vernacular made for more effective impact writing than did scholastic treatises.

2. THE RELIGIOUS ORDERS

The religious vitality of the Catholic Church, particularly in Italy and Spain, was further evidenced by the renewal within the older orders of monks and friars and by the establishing of new oratories and orders during the first decades of the Reformation. Withdrawal, mystical contemplation, and the religious life of the regulars retained their appeal for the very devout. The whole history of monasticism and of the mendicants had been characterized by the gradual erosion of the founders' ideals of poverty, chastity, and humble obedience and the intrusion of worldliness with an increase in wealth, followed in turn by reform and renewal. The evolution of the monastic ideal had seen a steady progression from the original hermetic isolation to complete involvement in the world. From individual hermits the move was toward cenobitic groups, then to communal living by groups as in Benedictine monasticism, behind walls away from the world, often in remote valleys or on high crags and hills. The monks served the world in the scriptorium, schools, fields, and vineyards. The mendicant friars retained the ideal of poverty but entered the world and trod the dusty crowded streets with or without sandals. The Jesuits and Theatines now in the sixteenth century entered the world with a vengeance. Even while retaining intramundane an ascetic ideal, they served as counselors to the high and the mighty in courts and princely houses and as scholars in the secondary schools and universities. In Europe, Asia, and the New World they engaged Protestants and pagans in a contest for men's souls. On the eve of the Reformation the condition of the various older orders presents a mixed picture, not so bad in general as secular priests, anticlerical laymen, humanist critics, and earnest reformers claimed, but not so good and inspiring as had been true at times in centuries gone by.

The Franciscan order experienced a double regeneration. First of all, certain friars and houses joined the Observance movement for strict adherence to the Franciscan rule, whereas the Conventuals accommodated themselves to wealth and the amenities it offers. This movement spread to other orders of friars such as the Augustinians. Secondly, a reform movement among the Franciscans led to the founding of an independent group known as the Capuchins, for their four-pointed hoods. The leader was Matteo de Bascio (1495–1552), of Italian peasant stock, who became an itinerant evangelist. The pope recognized them in 1528. Through their work with the common people throughout Italy they helped hold them for the Catholic Church. They survived the defection of their vicar general Bernardino Ochino to Protestantism in 1542 and by the end of the century had nearly fifteen hundred houses. Various offshoots from the spiritual wing of the Franciscans sprang up. St. Peter of Alcantara (d. 1502), an austere Spanish mystic, led the Order of the Discalced or sandal-less Franciscans from 1556 on. He influenced St. Teresa of Avila, who in turn founded the female Discalced Carmelites. In Naples the Capuchins were founded by Maria Laurentia Longo (d. 1542), who followed the strict rule of Santa Clara, the associate of St. Francis himself. The Dominicans produced a notable reformer in Battista da Crema and influential preachers including Savonarola. The Carthusian Order had held quite faithfully to its ideal of solitary meditation and separation from the world. Its influence was more through individuals who were inspired by their precepts and examples. The Camaldolese, an old reformed order of Benedictines, were revitalized and founded a huge number of new enclosed houses. Like the Carthusians, their influence was spiritual and indirect. The reformed Augustinian canons in the Netherlands were closely allied with the Brethren of the Common Life in their practical mysticism, educational ideals, and care for poor students. The importance of the Brethren for northern Christian humanism has been generally recognized, and the Lutheran reformers were very charitably inclined toward the Brethren. They were absorbed and ebbed away as the century progressed.

New orders in tune with the needs of the time arose. Close to the heart of Pope Leo X's court a reformatory movement stirred. Devout laymen and select clerics met regularly at the Church of Saints Sylvester and Dorothea for prayer and meditation. Under the leadership of Gaetano da Thiene (St. Cajetan) and Gianpietro Caraffa, this group organized as the Oratory of Divine Love and boasted such distinguished members as Giberti, Sadoleto, and Contarini. Out of the Oratory of Divine Love grew the new order of Theatines founded by Gaetano da Thiene, Caraffa, Bonifacio da Colle, and Paolo Consiglieri. Named for the city of Chieti (Theate) in southern Italy where Caraffa was bishop, the chief aim of the order was to recall the clergy to a godly life and to inspire the laity to virtue. On September 14, 1524, they made their solemn profession before the altar of St. Peter's Cathedral in Rome. Many pious aristocrats were included in their congregations. They not only founded oratories and hospitals but were very mission minded, evangelizing at home and sending missionaries to the Near East and the East Indies. In 1575 one of the leaders of the Catholic Reformation, St. Philip Neri, founded a community of secular priests patterned after the Oratory. These men were bound by a strict rule of obedience, although they followed active lives in the world.

The Theatine concept of secular clergy and laymen living under orders or rules caught on. The Barnabites or Clerks Regular of St. Paul in Milan were founded in 1533 by St. Antonio Maria Zaccaria. They evangelized in public meetings and later assisted St. Carlo Borromeo, the bishop of Milan, in reforming his diocese in conformity with the Tridentine decrees. The Somations or Somaschi were founded in 1528 by a Venetian nobleman, Girolamo Aemiliani, and chartered by Pope Paul III in 1540. They concentrated their efforts on poor relief, orphanages, and hospitals mostly in northern Italy and eventually in France.[10]

The most remarkable new order for women was that of the Ursulines, founded by Angela Merici in 1535. She had cared for the sick and needy for years in Brescia and neighboring towns. She developed a family of

10. For documents in English on the Oratory, the Theatine Rule of 1526, Giberti's Constitutions, and the Capuchin Constitutions, see Olin, *Catholic Reformation*, pp. 16–26, 128–132, 133–148, 149–181. On the Barnabites and other Catholic reformatory movements, see Émile G. Léonard, *A History of Protestantism, I, The Reformation* (Indianapolis, 1968), pp. 270–271. Léonard describes these Catholic foundations as "flimsy screens in the path of the great Lutheran conflagration, and some of them were soon to be caught up in its flames."

devoted helpers and gradually conceived the notion of an order that would care for the Christian nurture of girls. From this beginning grew their role as the leading teaching order for women, although their first school was not founded until 1595 in Parma. These decades saw the founding of religious brotherhoods and prayer fellowships in which prayers could be said *en masse* and their spiritual benefits shared by all members. The School of St. George, for example, and the School of St. Rochas in Venice were supported by wealthy merchants and enriched by their bequests. St. Rochas supported the painter Tintoretto for life in exchange for three wall and ceiling paintings a year for their *scuola,* which remains an artistic treasure house to this day. The stream of popular religion flowed on in Italy for centuries thereafter, little disturbed by cultural or political upheavals.

It is in the context of the new orders out in the world that the story of the Jesuits properly belongs. But Loyola and the Jesuits were so effective as a counterpoise to Protestantism that their origin and role will be reserved for the discussion of the Counter-Reformation. While Italy proved to be the most fertile matrix for the revitalization of older religious orders and the source of new ones, the Jesuits owe their origins to Spain and the spirit of the Spanish church.

3. POPES AND PRELATES

For decades the papacy and Roman Curia proved to be strangely impervious to pressures for reform. Following more than half a century of Renaissance popes, the "papacy of princes"—Nicholas V, elected 1447, Calixtus III, Pius II, Paul II, Sixtus IV, Innocent VIII, Alexander VI, and Julius II—the popes who had to cope with the Protestant revolt had first gradually to become masters of themselves and of their own household. The two Medici popes, Leo X (1513–1521) and Clement VII (1523–1534), came from a worldly background that rendered them singularly unprincipled, vacillating, and uninspired, inept at dealing with the less sophisticated but sincere reformers. The brief interregnum of the aged Dutchman Adrian VI (1522–1523) did nothing consequential to restore a pious regime. Paul III (1534–1549) of the Farnese family, Julius III (1550–1555), a del Monte, and Marcellus II (1555), a Cervini, represented a transition to the reforming mentality. Paul IV (1555–1559), Caraffa, finally breathed the fire of a true Counter-Reformation pope. He was succeeded by the Medici Pius IV (1559–1565) and the very effective Pius V, Ghisleri, who carried on Paul IV's work of reform and reconstruction in Rome.

Despite warnings that to delay reform or not to take Luther seriously would be hazardous, Leo X chose rather to busy himself with his splendid Renaissance court, with frivolous entertainments and the beautiful artistic creations of Michelangelo, Raphael, and Bramante. A generous patron and lavish spender, his debts already ran to more than 125,000 ducats in 1513. His pontificate was known as the Leonine Age. The serenity of his rule was disturbed not only by the Protestant revolt, but by the Turkish threat which led him to organize the Brotherhood of the Holy Crusade in 1513, an impotent effort. Not a warrior like Julius II, he was rather a wily diplomat who skillfully managed the Fifth Lateran Council (1512–1517), constituted almost exclusively of reliable Italian bishops, so that the series of proposals for reforming abuses such as absenteeism or nonresidence of bishops in their dioceses, simony, and nepotism, came to naught. The bulls he issued to follow up on the council's resolutions remained ineffectual. Leo X died on December 1, 1521, near the close of the very year during which Luther had emerged at the Diet of Worms as a world figure.

The cardinals by this time recognized the seriousness of the situation. On January 9, 1522, they elected as pope an earnest Dutch theologian, Adrian of Utrecht, to inaugurate the reform of the church. Adrian VI had studied with the Brethren of the Common Life at Zwolle, had been close to Erasmus, had tutored Charles V, and been at Louvain as a student and professor for thirty years. He was named a cardinal in 1517. He understood the Spanish scene, for he had been bishop of Tortosa, papal legate in Castile and Aragon, and regent of Spain in the absence of Charles. But to break up the sequence of Italian and Spanish popes with a northerner proved to be a poor move, since his zeal could not overcome the resistance of the Italian churchmen to this earnest outsider, the last non-Italian pope elected until John Paul II, four and a half centuries later. Adrian arrived in Rome in August and died in September of the following year. The importance of his career lay not in his achievements but in his aims. In his personal Instruction to Chieregati, papal nuncio to the Diet of Nuremberg, 1522, he outlined seven charges against the Lutherans and then continued:

You will also say that we frankly confess that God permits this persecution to afflict His Church because of the sins of men, especially of the priests and prelates of the Church. . . . We know that for many years many abominable things have occurred in this Holy See, abuses in spiritual matters, transgressions of the commandments, and finally in everything a change for the worse. No wonder that the illness has spread from the head to the members, from the Supreme Pontiffs to the prelates below them. All of us (that is, prelates and clergy), each one of us, have strayed from our paths; nor for a long time has anyone done good; no, not even one.[11]

At least by intention he may rightly be called the first pope of the Counter-Reformation.[12] Adrian's epitaph serves as a fitting commentary on his short reign: "Alas! How the power even of a most righteous man depends upon the times in which he happens to live!" With the election of Giulio de' Medici, a cousin of Leo X, as Clement VII reform again became a secondary concern. Family interests, Italian politics, the French-Spanish struggle for the peninsula, patronage of the arts, took priority over reform for this witty, easygoing, vacillating Medici, who was the son of Lorenzo de' Medici's brother Giuliano, murdered in the *duomo* by the Pazzi. Pope Clement sent Cardinal Campeggio, a moderate and learned man, as his nuncio to the Diet of Nuremberg in 1524. He was authorized to make concessions such as allowing the marriage of the clergy and giving sacramental wine to the laity. But polarization was increasing and pressure for a council growing. Clement adopted Fabian tactics, fearing that a council would delimit papal prerogatives and that a German national council would be controlled by Charles V and the princes. But he finally realized that a council offered the only remaining hope of overcoming the schism and saving the church. In early May, 1532, he agreed to a council, but on September 25, 1534, he died without yet having convoked one.

Paul III was more resolute about reform and more favorable toward a council. He summoned a council to meet in Mantua on May 23, 1537. He appointed a blue ribbon panel of nine cardinals to prepare a preliminary examination of the condition of the church. The commission included several reform-minded Christian humanists such as Caraffa, Pole, Sadoleto, Aleander, Giberti, and Contarini, who served as chairman. The

11. Olin, *Catholic Reformation*, p. 125.
12. Cardinal van Roey et al., *Adrien VI, le premier pape de la Contre-Réforme (Bibliotheca Ephemeridum Theologicarum Loraniensium)*, 14 (Gembloux, 1959).

commission met regularly from early in November, 1536, to mid-February, 1537, and on March 9 Contarini presented to Paul III the *Consilium de Emendenda Ecclesia,* which scored such abuses as nepotism, simony, pluralism, absenteeism, immorality, easy dispensations, and venality. The *Consilium* did not get into the deeper theological issues raised by the reformers, merely recommending, for example, that indulgences should not be granted more often than once a year in the larger cities but without discussing their religious value or doctrinal basis. The authors concluded with these words:

You have assumed the name of Paul; therefore we hope that you will imitate him and manifest the love for the church which he did. St. Paul was chosen as a good instrument for preaching the name and merit of Christ among the heathen [Acts 9:15]. Now we hope that you are chosen to raise up again the name of Christ, obscured both by the heathen and by us clerics, and to restore it, and to heal the sickness in our hearts and works, to bring the little sheep of Christ into one single fold, and also to turn away from us the well-deserved wrath and vengeance of God, which we can see is ready to fall down upon our heads.

The text of this *Counsel 11. Concerning the Reform of the Church* was published prematurely through an indiscretion and as in the case of Pope Adrian's Instruction was used by the Protestants to substantiate the truth of their charges against the church. Luther himself published a Genevan edition with his ironic marginal comments.[13]

Gasparo Contarini (1483–1542) did take doctrine seriously and played a key role in the final efforts to attain a theological agreement with the Lutherans. He was of a noble Venetian family, was a member of the Great Council in Venice, had served as a Venetian ambassador to the court of Charles V, and was a celebrant at Charles V's coronation in Bologna in 1530. Paul III made him a cardinal and appointed him to head the commission of cardinals. He now used him to try to heal the schism in the Empire, a task for which he was eminently qualified, since he knew the gravity of the situation in the Empire at first hand, was diplomatically talented, had an easy disposition, and was learned theologically. As a mediating theologian who understood Augustine well, Contarini played

13. "Counsel of a Committee of Several Cardinals with Luther's Preface," tr. by Robert R. Heitner, *Luther's Works,* 34, *Career of the Reformer IV,* Lewis W. Spitz, ed. (Philadelphia, 1960), pp. 231–267. The English text of the *Consilium* is also to be found in Olin, *Catholic Reformation,* pp. 186–197.

an important role in the final Catholic efforts to negotiate with the Lutherans toward church unity.

In 1535 Vergerio visited Wittenberg and discovered that the reformers were still open to theological discussions with the Catholics. Charles V was keenly interested in religious unity in the Empire, under pressure as he was from the French and the Turks. Paul III overcame his fears that Charles V might emulate the example of Henry VIII and create a national church. Paul therefore sent a delegation to the colloquies for religious conversations summoned by Charles V. In 1540–41 religious colloquies were held at Hagenau and Worms. In April, 1541, the colloquy was moved to Regensburg where the Imperial Diet was in session. The colloquy in Hagenau, 1540, included as Catholic participants King Ferdinand I, the younger brother of Charles V; Cardinal Giovanni Morone, bishop of Modena and papal nuncio to Germany; Johannes Faber, a humanist friend of Erasmus nicknamed *Malleus Haereticorum* or "Hammer of Heretics" after one of his works; Johannes Eck; and Johannes Cochlaeus. The evangelicals were represented by Johannes Brenz, Martin Bucer, Wolfgang Capito, Casper Cruciger, Friedrich Myconius, Andreas Osiander, Urbanus Rhegius, and the young John Calvin. With such a formidable lineup on each side, doctrinal differences were emphasized and little ecumenical progress achieved, but they resolved to try again. The next colloquy was held November, 1540, to January, 1541, in Worms. There were eleven Catholic representatives, including Granvella as Charles V's delegate and Campeggio as papal legate. Melanchthon was the chief Lutheran spokesman. While a detailed discussion with Johannes Eck was under way, the colloquy was adjourned to Regensburg.

The leading discussants at Regensburg on the Catholic side were Johann Gropper, Julius Pflug, and Johannes Eck and on the evangelical side Melanchthon, Bucer, and Johannes Pistorius, who had participated in the earlier colloquies as well. The papal legates were Contarini and Morone. The discussions were based upon the Regensburg book of twenty-three articles developed in secret discussions between Gropper and Gerhard Veltwick, a counselor of Charles V, on the one side, and Bucer and Capito on the other, and read by Luther, Philipp of Hesse, and various other Protestant princes. Agreement was reached on the first four articles dealing with man before the fall, free will, the cause of sin, and original sin. No agreement was reached on the matters of doctrinal authority, ecclesiastical hierarchy, church discipline, and the sacraments. A compromise agreement was reached on the central doctrine of justification by faith, an accommodation formulated covering a "double justification," which was worked out by Contarini and Melanchthon. Simply put, the formula stated that justification was dependent wholly on the basis of the merits of Christ and was bestowed upon the sinner by God's grace alone and received by faith alone, but that justifying faith must prove itself to be alive and efficacious through good works of love and charity. Contarini spelled out his views in an *Epistola de Justificatione;* he pushed his Augustinian views of sin and salvation by grace alone as far as he possibly could. But when Melanchthon returned to Wittenberg he found Luther unwilling to accept the verbal formulation, which Luther believed merely obfuscated a real difference. When Contarini returned to Rome he was accused of heresy, but mercifully died a year later. Charles V exerted strong pressure to induce the Protestants to accept the disputed articles, but by mutual agreement the remaining differences were referred for settlement to a future general council. In early 1546 another conference was held in Regensburg, and the failure of that meeting was soon followed by the outbreak of the Schmalkald War between the Catholic emperor and the Protestant princes and cities.

Despite his misgivings Paul III sincerely intended to summon a general council to deal with the schism, but political circumstances forced repeated postponements and precious time was lost. Mantua proved in 1537 to be an unacceptable location for a council, thanks to the duke's opposition. Next Vicenza, in Venetian territory, was chosen for a council convoked for May 1, 1538, but due to continued warfare the delegates did not appear. In 1543 the reopening of the war between Francis I and Charles V made it impossible for all but a few prelates to come to a council called for Trent. Watching this tragicomedy of errors from Wittenberg, Luther laughingly compared the pope's repeated failures to convene a council to the story of the medieval scoundrel Markolf whose final request was that he be allowed to choose the limb from which he would be hanged and spent years leading his judges from tree to tree. At last the Council of Trent, which was convoked for March 25, finally convened on December 13, 1545, for the first session.

Paul III died of his infirmities in 1549 and was succeeded by Cardinal del Monte, a genial Tuscan who adopted the name Julius III. He was persuaded to reconvene the Council of Trent in 1551 but adjourned that second session the following year. He was followed upon his death in

1555 by Marcellus II, who died soon afterward. With the election of Caraffa as Pope Paul IV the Counter-Reformation began in earnest.

4. COUNTER-REFORMATION

The failure of the religious colloquies not only had portentous consequences in the Empire, but it marked the transition from a conciliatory and ineffective approach on the part of the Catholic Church toward Protestantism to a new hard and repressive line. The shift to a policy of rigid reform and repression in 1541–1542 coincided with the rise of Caraffa to prominence and a turn to the Spanish model of Counter-Reformation. The Erasmian spirit in Spain crested in the years 1527 to 1532, followed by a conservative reaction led by the Franciscans and Dominicans. Erasmians were tagged as Lutherans and were imprisoned or exiled along with the *conversos* and the *Allumbrados* whose mystical illuminations were suspect. The Spanish orthodox crusading spirit, a carry-over from the centuries-long drive against the Moslems, the taking of Granada in 1492, and the expulsion of the Jews, translated forcefully into hatred for heretics. Gianpietro Caraffa as papal nuncio in Madrid in 1536 saw the Spanish Inquisition move ruthlessly against the Erasmians and root out their influence in a matter of months, or so it seemed on the surface. In 1531 Clement VII had subjected the clergy of Spain to the Inquisition and had forbidden any appeals from its judgments. To be sure, Caraffa had himself been a member of the Oratory of Divine Love along with worthy Erasmian intellectuals, but his personal convictions were less liberal and permissive than theirs. With his election to the papacy in 1555 his hour had come; an individual met the social and political needs of an institution. What was operative was not the hand of unseen forces, but a highly personal bent of mind. Caraffa was certain that only a hard line against the Protestants would be effective, and history has proven him to have been right, within the terms of his definition of success. Spain was known as "the hammer of heretics" and the "sword of Rome." Caraffa was impressed.

In Italy popular resistance restrained the Inquisition. In the Spanish domains and in Sicily the Inquisition did not function until 1518 and was then directed primarily against the Jews. Caraffa was convinced that the papacy had to support the Inquisition and he pressured the pope to set up a new congregation in Rome which would revitalize the old Dominican tribunal for handling heretics. Paul III hesitated at first but, shocked by the growth of heresy as close as nearby Lucca, he yielded to Caraffa's importuning. Two Spaniards in Rome at that time supported this repressive approach, Juan Alvarez of Toledo, Archbishop of Burgos with its Gothic cathedral, and none other than Ignatius Loyola. On July 21, 1542, Paul III formally established the Roman Inquisition with the bull *Licet ab Initio*. Caraffa, given broad powers to act, purchased a large residence in which he set up interrogation chambers, instruments of intimidation, and prison cells until an official tribunal could be organized. "If our own father were a heretic," he fervently declared, "we would carry the faggots to burn him!" His Roman tribunal was granted jurisdiction over all Italy with the same powers as the Spanish Inquisition. "No man is to lower himself by showing toleration toward any sort of heretic," Caraffa thundered, "least of all a Calvinist!" Caraffa struck at the high and mighty in society as well as lowly heretics. As the arbiters of theological orthodoxy, the Dominicans acted as judges under the supervision of six cardinals appointed by the pope to serve as inquisitors general. Caraffa was one of the inquisitors general.

The cooperation of the revitalized orders and of the civil authorities helped to make the Inquisition an effective instrument for suppressing nonconformity and dissent. It has been said that the Inquisition effectively ended Renaissance humanist culture in Italy, but it can be argued with equal plausibility that the prior denouement of the Renaissance of culture paved the way for the Counter-Reformation repression of ideas. The inquisitors claimed a depressing number of victims such as the Spanish nonconformist Juan de Enzinas, who was burned in Rome in March, 1547. A stream of Protestants were now driven into exile. Among them was Pietro Paulo Vergerio, who was summoned from the safety of Venetian territory to Rome. Excommunicated on July 3, 1549, he went into exile in Grisons. The pattern varied from state to state in Italy. Lucca resisted but finally yielded to the Inquisition in 1551. In Tuscany, on the other hand, Cosimo I, narrow-minded grand duke of Florence, welcomed the Inquisition as one more instrument of social control. In Ferrara the Inquisition pressured Duke Hercules d'Este to move against the evangelicals whom the Duchess Renée was protecting. When Renée, on whom Calvin had pinned his hopes for the reformation of Ferrara, was driven out by her fanatical son and returned to France, Ferrara remained safely within the Catholic fold. Caraffa was made the Archbishop of Naples in 1549, and with the cooperation of the Spanish authorities he repressed what remained of the Valdés circle. The Dominican Michele Ghislieu, the commissary general of the Holy Office, took a hard line on heretics. He was to become Pius V, who outdid Caraffa himself as a severe and uncompromising pope of the Counter-Reformation.

The authority of the Roman Inquisition extended as far as the church itself and was effective where the secular ruler proved cooperative. In France, for example, the introduction of the Inquisition coincided with the decision of Francis I to suppress the Huguenots by force. The Inquisition imprisoned and took the lives of Protestants in Toulouse, Rouen, Grenoble, and Bordeaux. In Meaux, once the home of an indigenous reform movement, on October 4, 1546, sixty-one Protestants were arrested by the authorities, tried by the Inquisition, and fourteen of them burned for heresy. The civil authorities cooperated with the Inquisition in suppressing Protestants. In 1547 a special tribunal of the Parlement of Paris was given exclusive authority in matters of heresy and burned so many that it came to be called the *chambre ardente*. But heresy invaded the Parlement itself, which created a difficult situation in Paris. King Henry II (1547–1559) proved to be a fanatical foe of Protestantism and he promoted restrictive legislation on publication, professorships, and communication with Geneva, Strasbourg, and other Protestant cities. In 1549 a special royal edict spelled out the legal powers of the civil and ecclesiastical authorities in matters of heresy. Throne and altar worked together in a time-honored historical alliance.

The burning of books and bulls was a part of the battle from the very beginning of the Reformation. From 1521 on the theological faculties at Paris, Louvain, Cologne, and other universities had compiled and circulated lists of dangerous and prohibited books. The first complete list valid for the entire church was the *Index librorum prohibitorum* which Paul IV had published in 1559. The *Index* included not only titles by heretical Protestants, but many of the early works of Catholic theologians such as Erasmus and Contarini and humanist literary works such as Boccaccio's *Decameron* written in a less austere day but now thought to be harmful to faith and morals. This list contained titles that seemed innocuous to some and the *Index* of Trent, 1564, removed them. It was now a common practice to publish bowdlerized versions of Renaissance classics in order to evade the *Index*, just as the nudes in the murals of the Borgian apartments of the Vatican were modestly clothed.

When Paul IV died the resentment that had been building up in Rome against his authoritarian ways spilled over into rioting. The offices of the

Inquisition were pillaged and heretics in prison set free. The cardinals chose as his successor a Medici who was a canon lawyer and a diplomat, Pius IV (1559–1565), who proved to be more lenient than Paul IV and who worked together with the final session of the Council of Trent. Paul IV had set its tone, however, as a hard line without concessions to heresy or sacrifices for conciliation. The very art of the Counter-Reformation stressed the dogmatic themes that had been challenged by Protestantism.

The most characteristic creation of the Catholic Reformation was the Society of Jesus, generated by Spanish spirituality and in the heart and mind of a religious genius, Iñigo or Ignatius Loyola. So effective was the Jesuit order in polemics, education, and politics that it has been regarded too exclusively as a force to combat Protestantism rather than as an order first designed for mission work, much in the medieval tradition and in tune with other new orders. In addition to the traditional threefold monastic vows, the Jesuits took a fourth vow, that of absolute obedience directly to the pope, which gave them a unique role to play in the reestablishing of papal authority.

Ignatius Loyola is one of history's most dramatic characters, a soldier who became a peaceful warrior for the church militant. Born in 1491 of a noble Basque family in the province of Guipuzcoa in Castile, he served as a page at the court of King Ferdinand where he was schooled in courtly manners and military tactics. He served with the troops of his feudal overlord, the duke of Najera, and when the army of Francis I invaded Navarre he was gravely wounded. Defending a breach in the wall of Pamplona on May 21, 1521, he was struck by a French cannonball which smashed his right leg and wounded his left one. A French doctor tried to set his leg but it had to be broken and reset twice with the result that he was lamed for life. During his long convalescence at the family castle he read the German Carthusian Ludolph of Saxony's *Life of Christ,* and Jacopo de Voragine's *Legenda Aurea,* or golden legend of the lives of the saints. Caught up in a mystical religious experience, he underwent a conversion to a new vision of God. Transferring his chivalric ideals to the realm of religion, he conceived of his life as devoted service to Our Lady and to the salvation of souls. He set out as a pilgrim and penitent to the shrine of Our Lady at Montserrat where he hung up his dagger in the church and dedicated it to Mary. Like Francis of Assisi, he gave away his rich garment to the poor and donned a cloak of sackcloth which reached to his feet. He withdrew to the small town of Manresa, near Barcelona, for the better part of a year where he wrestled intensely with spiritual questions such as whether man with the aid of grace is able to control his will in such a way as to conform to the will of God and achieve salvation. Like Luther before him, he also struggled with the spiritual temptation of scruples. There he encountered Thomas à Kempis's *Imitation of Christ.* He worked out a preliminary outline of his powerful *Spiritual Exercises,* though he did not give them their final form until 1541.

Early in 1523 Ignatius made a pilgrimage to Jerusalem and returned to acquire the education he needed to serve as an apostle of Christ. He studied at the Alcalá, at Salamanca, and from 1528 to 1535 at the University of Paris, first at the Collège de Montaigu and then at the Collège de Sainte Barbe. He received the licentiate in theology in 1534 and an M.A. degree in 1535. Ironically at the Alcalá where he had gathered a group of followers, the Inquisition had briefly imprisoned him on suspicion of heresy and now in Paris he was denounced by the Inquisition but escaped persecution. His zeal attracted like-minded disciples and on August 15, 1534, Ignatius and six companions in a small chapel in Montmartre joined in taking the vows of poverty and charity and resolved to go to Jerusalem to devote themselves to the conversion of the Turks, and if that were not possible to put themselves at the service of the pope. Ignatius, Pierre Favre, Francis Xavier, Diego Laynez, Alfonso Salmerón, Nicholas Bobadilla, and Simon Rodriguez met in Venice along with three new members, Claude Le Jay, Paschase Broet, Jean Codure, in order to begin their missionary journey to the Near East. Prevented by war from traveling, they went instead to Rome to carry out their alternate plan. In the summer of 1539, with the help of Cardinal Contarini, they submitted their plans of organization to Paul III and on September 27, 1540, the pope issued the bull *Regimini militantis ecclesiae* establishing the order. By then Francis Xavier had already left Rome—in March, 1540—for his great mission to the Indies, which was eventually to take him as far as Japan.

The Jesuits were an elitist corps and accepted into membership only the most intelligent, dedicated, physically strong and attractive men of sound character. After a two-year novitiate they took the traditional threefold monastic vow. There followed another year of general studies and three years of philosophy, at which point they taught grammar or philosophy to the younger members. After four more years of theological study they were ordained as priests. A year devoted to the study of practical theology, preaching, and the following of spiritual exercises was succeeded by a second year of proving themselves. Only then were they permitted to take the fourth vow of obedience to the pope and incorporated into the Society of Jesus. Ignatius spent his last years at his desk in the Casa Professa in Rome handling the order's vast correspondence with members throughout the world. Although the founding bull had limited membership to sixty, by the time of Ignatius's death the membership had reached over a thousand. Most of the early growth was naturally in Italy and Spain, but twelve years after their founding they had 318 Portugese members. Loyola still lived to see the establishment of around a hundred colleges and seminaries. The election of Caraffa as pope filled him with fear and apprehension lest the new pope dismember his organization or damage his cause. Loyola died peacefully and almost alone in July 1556, while saying his prayers.[14]

The spirit of the Jesuits is best expressed by reading or following the *Spiritual Exercises*. The "first principle and foundation" expresses Ignatius's sense of devotion to God:

Man is created to praise, reverence, and serve God our Lord, and by this means to save his soul. The other things on the face of the earth are created for man to help him in attaining the end for which he is created. Hence, man is to make use of them in as far as they help him in the attainment of his end, and he must rid himself of them in as far as they prove a hindrance to him. Therefore, we must make ourselves indifferent to all created things, as far as we are allowed free choice and are not under any prohibition. Consequently as far as we are concerned, we should not prefer health to sickness, riches to poverty, honor to dishonor, a long life to a short life. The same holds for all other things. Our one desire and choice should be what is more conducive to the end for which we are created.[15]

The *Spiritual Exercises* are divided into four "weeks" of meditations. The first corresponds roughly to the purgative way in the spiritual life, purifying the soul and putting one's life in order. In the second and third weeks the meditations are for the most part taken from the public life and passion

14. The best introduction to Loyola and the Jesuits is afforded by the books of James Broderick, S.J., *The Origin of the Jesuits* (New York, 1940), *The Progress of the Jesuits (1556–1579)* (New York, 1947), *Saint Ignatius Loyola, The Pilgrim Years, 1491–1538* (New York, 1956), and others. H.O. Evenett, *The Spirit of the Counter-Reformation,* John Bossy, ed. (Cambridge, 1968), places Loyola and the Society of Jesus within the general setting of the Catholic Reformation. Hugo Rahner, S.J., *The Spirituality of St. Ignatius Loyola* (Westminster, Md., 1953) assesses the mystical and theological dimensions of his thought and inner being.

15. Louis J. Puhl, S.J., ed., *The Spiritual Exercises of St. Ignatius* (Westminster, Md., 1957), p. 12.

of Christ. The fourth week is drawn from Christ's postresurrection life and is intended to engender unselfish love, joy in Christ's glory, and an unchanging trust in Christ the Consoler. Crowning the whole work is the "Contemplation to Attain Divine Love," which draws together the progression of the four weeks so that one lives one's life for God alone in joyous service to Him and one's fellow man.[16]

Attached to the *Spiritual Exercises* is an appendix called the "Rules for Thinking with the Church," composed by Ignatius during his stay in Paris. It embodies his view of the church, the kingdom of Christ on earth, and the need to conform one's thinking to the teaching of the church. Most articles are moderate, make positive statements in behalf of scholasticism and defend regulations, feast days, veneration of the saints, and other points controverted by the Protestants. But Rule 13 came under sharp criticism from Protestants for its supposed abdication of personal judgment and conscientious accountability: "If we wish to proceed securely in all things, we must hold fast to the following principle: What seems to me white, I will believe black if the hierarchical Church so defines. For I must be convinced that in Christ our Lord, the bridegroom, and in His spouse the Church, only one Spirit holds sway which governs and rules for the salvation of souls. For it is by the same Spirit and Lord who gave the Ten Commandments that our holy Mother Church is ruled and governed."[17] In practice the Jesuits evidenced special concern for the conscience of each member.

The technique of spiritual growth applied in the *Exercises* was adaptable. They could be used in a full-scale retreat under a director or for an hour or two a day while engaged in one's occupation. They together with the "Rules" engendered a sense of discipline and sacrifice that kept the order and its lay supporters mobilized for a tremendous educational, missionary, and political effort that turned back the tide of Protestantism and made the Catholic Church a major force in the modern world. The order reflected Ignatius's military spirit and organizational talent, which kept open the lines of communication between the general of the order and the lowest echelon.

Jesuit attention to homiletics paid huge dividends. In the 1540s Laynez preached in Parma, Padua, Venice, and Florence; Salmerón in Verona,

16. Robert W. Gleason, S.J., Introduction, *The Spiritual Exercises of St. Ignatius,* Anthony Mottola, tr. (Garden City, N.Y., 1964), pp. 14–15.

17. Olin, *Catholic Reformation,* p. 210.

Modena, and Belluno; Brouet in Faenza; and Le Jay in Ferrara. The *ratio studiorum* of their excellent schools incorporated much humanist educational philosophy although they stressed dialectic over history for apologetic reasons. In Italy, with the support of princes, high churchmen, and aristocrats, they founded colleges in Bologna, Messina, and Palermo. Loyola himself founded the Collegium Romanum in 1550. The Jesuits won back many important ruling houses to the faith through the strategy of supplying learned tutors for young princes such as Ferdinand of Styria and Sigismund of Poland. In the Holy Roman Empire the Dutchman Peter Canisius led in the re-Catholicization of Protestant lands largely through his catechism and by founding excellent secondary schools and colleges such as the Jesuit Academy in Vienna. Duke Albert V of Bavaria assisted the Jesuits in founding a college at Ingolstadt in 1555 and a second one in Munich in 1559 which helped to keep Bavaria a bastion of the Counter-Reformation in the Germanies. Other Jesuits such as Pierre Favre, Claude Le Jay, and Nicholas Bobadillo worked in the Empire. The German College in Rome, later headed by Cardinal Bellarmine, was an important center for training German priests. William Allen founded a seminary at Douay across the channel from England and directed the infiltration of missionary priests into Protestant England. It was there that the Catholic Douay English Bible was translated. This college, as well as the English College in Rome, was modeled on those of the Jesuits, whom Allen much admired. The volatile Jesuit Simon Rodriguez gained a powerful influence over King John III of Portugal. The transition from being the tutors of princes to confessors and confidants of rulers was a natural one. In later decades the Jesuits became so involved in politics that they were expelled by the rulers, and from 1773 to 1814 the Society was suppressed everywhere except in Russia, where it was favored by Catherine the Great.

The Society of Jesus never lost sight of its original goal of world missions. Since its phenomenal growth corresponded to the first great period of European expansion, its opportunities for carrying out Christ's commission to "go into all the world and preach the gospel" were greater than the church had enjoyed since the fourteenth century when the Franciscans had undertaken their Asian missions. The motives of the European explorers and conquistadors were mixed, mostly materialistic and political, but in part religious. In the Christianization of Europe the growth of the church had usually proceeded within the lines of the Holy Roman Empire through the expansion of parishes and dioceses, whereas beyond the lines the conversion of the pagans was largely the work of the missionary monks and friars. In this period of worldwide expansion beyond Christian Europe it was once again the regular clergy who served as the reconnaissance troops and manned the overseas missions. Although the Franciscans, Dominicans, and Augustinians were the most involved in Mexico and Peru, the Jesuits, thanks to their early influence on King John of Portugal, played the leading role in Brazil, under the direction of Father José de Anchieta, and in Paraguay. It was possible in Latin America to effect with persuasion and arms the conversion of entire Indian populations. The task was much more difficult in Asia, where there were more complex ancient cultures with established higher religions having their own holy books and developed religious philosophies.

The greatest Jesuit missionary was Francis Xavier, one of Loyola's first companions, the "apostle of the Indies and Japan." Xavier was born in 1506 in his family castle at the foot of the Pyrenees. He met Loyola, who was impressed by this bright, handsome, and personable young noble, at the Collège de Sainte Barbe in Paris. Xavier was with Loyola in Venice, where he worked in a hospital for incurables, accompanied him to Rome, and returned to Venice, where he was ordained into the priesthood. In response to a request by King John III of Portugal for six Jesuit missionaries to journey to the East Indies, Loyola named Xavier and a companion as ready to be sent. From Lisbon Xavier sailed to southern India, arriving in May, 1542, where he preached for three years in the Portuguese colonies at Goa, Cochin, San Thomé, and along the coast of Travancore, serving European sailors and merchants more than Asians. He then journeyed on to the Portuguese colonies in Malacca, Malaya, the Moluccas and Ceylon, evangelizing for two and a half years. He reached Japan in 1549 and his labors there until 1551 enjoyed astonishing success. Unhampered by the bad reputation of European sailors and merchants or by the opposition of Moslems or Jews, he succeeded in gaining converts at Kagoshima, Yamagutsi, and other cities. He established native Christian communities that still survive despite the cruel persecutions of 1596–1598, the exclusion of Europeans in 1640, and the atom bombs dropped in 1945 on two cities with many Christian inhabitants. Xavier died in a cold and miserable hut on St. John's Island of a fever at the age of forty-six while preparing to begin a mission to China. The China mission was continued by Father Matthew Ricci (1551–1610), who was well received by the emperor in

Peking and honored for his learning and piety. The reports of the Jesuit missionaries which are known as the Jesuit relations brought volumes of fairly reliable information to the Europeans about Asia, Africa, and the Americas.

5. THE CONCILIAR SOLUTION

Not since the fourth and fifth centuries after Christ, days of heresy and schism, had the church faced a crisis of the magnitude it now confronted. Then the ecumenical councils—Nicaea, Constantinople, Ephesus, and the subsequent assemblies—had arrived at confessions agreed upon by the orthodox. In the late Middle Ages at the close of the Christian era well-meaning conciliarists had once again proposed councils as a solution to the ills of the church. But the conciliarists of Constance (1414–1418) and Basel-Ferrara-Florence (1431–1443) had posed a threat to the monarchical episcopate, and the papacy had fought back vigorously and successfully. Pope Pius II celebrated the triumph of the papacy over the conciliar movement with his bull *Execrabilis,* 1460, in which he pronounced it "useless, illegal, and wholly detestable" to appeal over the head of the pope to a council, and declared anyone who did so automatically excommunicated. Nevertheless, appeals for a council to resolve the problems of the church persisted, with humanists and reformers calling for a council and monarchs threatening to call national councils. That *Execrabilis* was widely disregarded is evident from the fact that the Fifth Lateran Council meeting under Leo X was obliged to reassert its injunction. Ulrich von Hutten, a German humanist partisan of Luther, published a daring tract with the cry "Consilium! Consilium! Consilium!" The papal legate to Germany Girolamo Aleander wrote from Worms in 1520, "All the world cries out 'Council, Council!'"

Luther's own attitude toward a council was ambivalent. On the one hand he urged a true ecumenical conference for the reform of church doctrine and practice, but as a realist he feared little good would come of one and that the papacy would use such a council to suppress the evangelical movement. On November 28, 1518, he called earnestly for a council, but during the Leipzig debate in 1519 he argued for the authority of the Word of God over popes and councils. His ideal of a council was the meeting of the apostles in Jerusalem described in Acts 15. If council members are chosen from the people of God in whose hearts the Holy

Spirit dwells, there would be a true council ruled by the Spirit.[18] In his *Address to the Christian Nobility*, 1520, he cited the ills of the church with which a council would have to deal. In his treatise *On the Councils and the Church*, 1539, he expressed his ambivalence: "We cry out and appeal for a council and beseech all of Christendom for its advice and help!" but "You say that there is no hope for such a council any longer. I suppose I agree with you."

The popes' fear of a council controlled by secular rulers was very real, and they were determined to hold a council in a location free of hostile control. The French kings Louis XI, Charles VIII, and Louis XII had repeatedly threatened to call a national council. In September, 1511 Louis XII even had several cardinals convoke a council in Pisa which Pope Julius II circumvented by calling the Fifth Lateran Council in Rome in April, 1512. In 1517 the University of Paris urged the calling of a general council as a protest to the Pragmatic Sanction of Bourges. In the Empire Frederick III and Maximilian I had threatened to call a council to consider the *gravamina* of the Imperial Diet against the church. Charles V, under pressure from the Lutheran princes, insisted upon a council, and after his victory at Pavia, 1525, and the sack of Rome, 1527, it seemed that the pope would have to yield to his demand. Clement VII, however, delayed, despite the emperor's threat to summon a national council with the Lutherans as participants. After the failure to convene councils at Mantua and Vicenza, Paul III summoned a council to meet at Trent which was technically on German soil but actually in northern Italy. After the Peace of Crépy with France, September 18, 1544, Charles V was ready to accept Paul III's proposal. The *Bull of Convocation of the Holy Ecumenical Council of Trent* acknowledged the "evils that have long afflicted and well-nigh overwhelmed the Christian commonwealth." All who opposed the summons to the council would "incur the indignation of Almighty God and of His blessed apostles Peter and Paul." At long last the opening session of the council was held on December 13, 1545. Thus began the nineteenth ecumenical council, by official enumeration, which proved to be the most important council since that of Nicea in 325.

The Council of Trent sought to deal with the confessional schism, to achieve self-definition, and to begin self-renewal. Would history have been very different if the council had been held a quarter of a century

---

18. WA 50, 643–644. Luther favored a "true free Christian council," *WA* 54, 206–207, 212–213.

earlier, in 1520 rather than in 1545? Or did the church have to suffer the traumatic experience of a full-scale revolt before it was ready to reform itself? Some insight into these questions can be gained by a retrospective glance at the Fifth Lateran Council which met from 1512 to 1517, on the very eve of the Reformation.

The Fifth Lateran has been called "the last attempt at a papal reform of the church before the break-up of Christian unity."[19] Julius II had called the council in July, 1511. At that time the warrior pope, disdained by Erasmus in his *Julius Exclusus,* was at war with Louis XII of France and wished to circumvent Louis's council at Pisa. The bull of convocation and the opening address of Egidio da Viterbo (1469–1532), the general of the Augustinian Order, indicate that there was a longing for reform. Egidio's role at the council has been overestimated, but his address remains indicative of at least his own conservative reform intentions. "Men must be changed by religion, not religion by men."[20] He was a classicist, Hebraist, and Platonist. As general of the Augustinians, he had set into motion changes within the order that had brought the young Augustinian Luther to Rome in 1510–1511, a visit that had great impact upon the young monk. Egidio had proven himself to be a reformer. His reform programs consisted in a reaffirmation of authentic values and institutions received from the past and a return to what was ancient and more genuine. He urged the pope to give up weapons for the "arms of light," to work for peace among the princes, who should direct their forces against Mohammed. The council "is the one and only remedy for all evils, the sole port for the ship in distress, the single means of strengthening the commonweal." The council, however, failed to respond concretely to demands for reform. The council called for a crusade against the Turks and called for higher financial assessments on the secular state, even permitting the taxation of the clergy in some states. The response of the secular rulers was, however, cynical. The Venetians believed that the money would simply be used by Leo X to finance his war against Urbino in order to gain territory for his Medici family. In the final session the council reaffirmed Boniface VIII's claims in the bull *Unam sanctam* (1302) to a fullness of spiritual power and real, though indirect, authority over all rulers. The council composed largely of Italian prelates met over the course of five

19. Hubert Jedin, *A History of the Council of Trent,* I (St. Louis, 1957), p. 128.

20. John W. O'Malley, S.J., *Giles of Viterbo on Church and Reform, A Study in Renaissance Thought* (Leiden, 1968), pp. 139ff., reform in concept and practice; p. 191, conclusion.

years and in the end produced few concrete results. It adjourned in that fateful year 1517. Now twenty-eight years later another council faced reform with half of Christendom lost to heresy and schism.

Throughout the summer of 1545 the prelates came struggling into Trent. When the first session opened it included only four archbishops, twenty-one bishops, five generals of monastic orders, and fifty canon lawyers and theologians. Cardinals del Monte, Cervini, and Reginald Pole were appointed as papal legates to preside over the council. In his opening address Cardinal del Monte cited the growth of heresy and the need to reform abuses as the two main reasons for the council. He blamed both on the negligence of the bishops, whom he admonished to confess and to beg God's forgiveness. All knelt and prayed for God's pardon, though some resented the fact that the Roman Curia had been omitted from censure. After the reading of the collect and gospel for the day, the choir sang *"Veni, Creator Spiritus"* and the *"Te Deum,"* whereupon the council was declared to be in session. Three crucial procedural decisions were made; first, to recognize papal supremacy; second, to limit voting rights to bishops, heads of religious orders, and representatives of monastic congregations rather than to have voting by nations as was done at the councils of Constance and Basel; and third, not to allow absent bishops to vote by proxy, which put churchmen from distant lands at a distinct disadvantage. The council also decided to debate the issues of dogma and reform simultaneously.

In the matter of the reform of abuses, the council had guidance from the Erasmian cardinals' *De Emendenda Ecclesia* (1537) and Giberti's *Constitutions* (1527). They attacked the problems of plurality of offices, plurality of benefices, incompetence in cathedral churches, ignorance and illiteracy of clergy, neglect of visitations, and fiscal mismanagement. In the matter of dogma the question of Holy Writ or Holy Church and the question of sin and justification were central concerns. On questions of dogma the council basically followed the order of the articles of the Augsburg Confession of 1530, opposing to them their own orthodox definitions and condemning them with anathemas. The fourth session dealt with the question of the canonical Scriptures and the role of tradition. Some of the bishops as a gesture toward the Protestant stress upon *sola Scriptura* wished to state that the Scriptures contain all that is necessary to salvation. Cardinal Pole, however, argued that many beliefs and practices depend upon tradition. The final statement concluded simply that the Scriptures and tradition were to be considered equally valid. But the statement did not spell out precisely whether truth is to be found partly in the Scriptures and partly in tradition or whether the whole essential truth is to be found in each, with the Scriptures the norm that authenticates later tradition. In the decree *De canonicis scripturis* the council declared Jerome's Vulgate Latin translation to be authoritative for the church.

The central issues of sin and justification were taken up in the fifth and sixth sessions. The varying doctrinal emphases now came into sharp conflict. To the right Jacopo Seripando with his Augustinian grounding on questions of sin and grace worked for a solution that would not further alienate the evangelicals. Contarini had developed the "double justification" theory, which distinguished an "inherent justification" of man before God as a result of right action and an "imputed justification" acquired when God bestows upon man vicariously the merits of Christ, which are appropriated by man through faith or trust in Christ the Savior. The righteousness that man thus receives constitutes the supreme end of faith. The desire of the moderates like Contarini, who clung to a mediating position, was to subordinate works to faith without denying the necessity of good works. A third approach was that of the Jesuits, who emerged as a new force in ecclesiastical decisions. Laynez and Salmerón, Jesuit theological spokesmen, had at Loyola's request stayed very much in the background until that point in the discussions, but they now entered the debate vigorously. In line with the emphasis of their order, they insisted absolutely on the necessity of good works for justification and salvation. They refused to accept any formula that would subordinate doing good works to faith. Argument on this critical issue was long and heated, and in the end the council in its decree on justification adopted a definition in agreement with the position of St. Thomas Aquinas. Chapter seven explained in good scholastic fashion the final, efficient, meritorious, instrumental, and formal causes of justification. The final cause, said the fathers, is the glory of God and of Christ and life everlasting. The efficient cause is the merciful God Who washes and sanctifies gratuitously, signing and anointing with the Holy Spirit of promise, Who is the pledge of our inheritance. The meritorious cause is His most beloved only begotten, the Lord Jesus Christ Who merited justification for man by His most holy passion on the wood of the cross and made satisfaction for us to God the Father. The instrumental cause is the sacrament of baptism. Finally, the single formal cause is the justice of God, not that by which He Himself is just, but that by which He makes us just, that, namely, with which we being endowed by Him, are renewed in the spirit of our mind, and not only are we reputed but we are truly called and are just, receiving justice within us, each according to his own measure, which the Holy Ghost distributes to everyone as He wills, and according to each one's disposition and cooperation.[21] Leaving nothing open to misinterpretation, the council then added thirty-three canons on justification which condemned every conceivable Protestant position on the subject. Whereas many points of dogma had throughout the medieval period been left without detailed definition, Catholic doctrine was now defined with a verbal precision that left little room for deviation or elbow room for liberal maneuvering. On the positive side, the church now had a doctrinal platform on which all who repaired to her banner could take their stand. Moreover, there was really no doctrinal novelty for, as Bossuet reminded Leibniz, who had urged the suspension of the canons and decrees of Trent in the interest of Christian unity, every assertion of the council was to be found authorized in earlier papal and conciliar documents.

The Council of Trent was proceeding beautifully when political and military realities raised their ugly heads. Charles V had been at war with the Lutheran Schmalkald League, had during the first year overrun southern Germany, and after his triumph in the battle at Mühlberg on April 24, 1547, seemed to be in a position of unrivaled strength. He issued his Interim, May 15, 1548, with its concessions to the Lutherans. A plague hit Trent and the pope transferred the council to Bologna, where the Italian prelates gathered for the eighth session. The Spanish delegates began asserting themselves with new confidence. Charles forbade the German delegates to move to Bologna, feeling that the Lutherans would not accept decrees of a council meeting held within the papal states. Cardinal Cervini, the future Pope Marcellus II, feared that Charles V might arrive in person to force his will on the council. The pope began to organize the Holy League to keep Charles V in check. In November the Imperial Diet at Augsburg refused to acknowledge the legality of the council's decrees. Paul III recessed the council on February 15, 1548, and he died late in 1549 without reconvening it. Thus at the very moment that the close cooperation of the pope and emperor might have succeeded in restoring the old order, fear and suspicion between the two intervened to prevent it.

Cardinal del Monte was elected pope on February 7, 1550. As Julius

21. H.J. Schroeder, O.P., ed., *Canons and Decrees of the Council of Trent* (St. Louis, 1960), p. 33. See also the master work on Trent, Hubert Jedin, *A History of the Council of Trent,* II (St. Louis, 1961), pp. 307–309.

III he was willing to oblige the emperor and reconvened the council in Trent on April 29, 1551. The second meeting of the Council of Trent was destined to last only a year, and its accomplishments were much more limited than the first. Charles V was not feeling very secure about his control of the situation in the Empire, where the Lutheran cities and princes were negotiating secretly for support with Henry II of France. The Lutherans had declared in advance that the decrees of the council would not be binding on them because they were not represented and their position was not given a fair hearing. At this second meeting of the council the Italian and Spanish delegates were in the majority, but there was much rivalry between them. The trend of the council away from doctrinal accommodation to the Protestants was perhaps best symbolized by the fact that Julius III chose two Jesuits, Laynez and Salmerón, as his spokesmen. The council reviewed the questions of reform and dogma and reconsidered at length the question of the mass or Lord's Supper. They reasserted a Thomistic definition of the sacrament, reaffirming transubstantiation, adoration of the host, and the utility of private masses. They reaffirmed the necessity of oral confession, penance as a sacrament, and the sacrament of extreme unction.

These sessions at Trent were sparsely attended, but they were augmented surprisingly from January to March, 1552, by representatives of the German Lutherans. In October of 1551 the council had yielded to the demands of Charles V and had issued safe conducts to Lutheran delegates from Saxony, Württemberg, and the southwest German evangelical cities. These representatives were angered that the council had already decided most of the controverted issues and allowed discussion only of the questions of marriage of the clergy and communion in both kinds, which the emperor had already conceded to them in the Interim. The German prelates present urged that communion in both kinds be permitted, but even that was denied by the council. Laynez and Salmerón urged the council to confirm traditional positions on penance, the sacrament, and extreme unction. The decision to uphold all the decrees of the first assembly coupled with this action effectively closed off the dialogue with the evangelicals.

Once again political events upset the course of the council. Moritz of Saxony had turned against the emperor, nearly captured him at Innsbruck, and rumor had it that he was preparing to march on Trent. On April 28, 1552, Julius III in a panic adjourned the council for two years, but it was not to meet again until 1562. During that intervening decade momentous changes took place. The Peace of Augsburg, 1555, recognized the legal right of the Lutherans to coexistence with the Catholics in the Empire. Pope Paul IV reigned for four years as the harsh Counter-Reformation pope. Cardinal Morone, who had been active at Trent, was imprisoned for being soft on Protestants, and even Reginald Pole was summoned to Rome on the charge that he had been too conciliatory toward the Protestants, though Queen Mary refused to let him go. On the international scene Charles V abdicated in 1555 and the Treaty of Cateau-Cambrésis, 1559, achieved a new, far-reaching settlement.

Pius IV reconvoked the council for April 8, 1561, and deliberations were renewed in January, 1562. It had been called in part to avoid a French national settlement, and so for the first time the council had a significant French representation led by the Cardinal of Lorraine. Emperor Ferdinand, Charles V's brother, hoped to minimize conflict in the Empire, and he urged acceptance of marriage of the clergy and communion in both kinds. There were few German prelates present, however, and with the Italians in a majority, backed by the Spaniards, who were opposed to any doctrinal change, no genuine concessions were made to the Protestants. It became increasingly evident that as the sessions went on the papacy had emerged from the struggle of these decades with new prestige and authority. The Jesuits were active agents and proponents of papal power. One Jesuit even advocated including a statement on papal infallibility. Papal representatives initiated proposals to the council, and the council referred important questions to the pope for arbitration and decision. Cardinal Morone closed the council on December 4, 1563 with an appropriate ceremony. Of the 255 churchmen who attached their formal signatures to the canons and decrees, 189 were Italian. On January 26, 1564, Pius IV gave his approval and on June 30, 1564, the bull *Benedictus Deus* added papal authority to the work of the Council of Trent. The papacy was triumphant within the church.[22] Before the century was over the cupola was set in place atop the dome of St. Peter's Cathedral in Rome, a symbol of the fact that the church had risen again and could hold her head aloft with good conscience and justifiable pride.

22. The story of post-Tridentine reform is continued in Marvin R. O'Connell, *The Counter-Reformation 1559–1610* (New York, 1974), "Chapter III: Reform of Head and Members." See also the stellar collection of articles, "Catholic Reformation," *The Sixteenth Century Journal,* XI, no. 2 (Summer, 1980).

Chapter Seven

EUROPE: EAST AND WEST

1. THE CENTER—STRUGGLE FOR MASTERY

ARNOLD J. TOYNBEE was fond of toying with the idea of small states at the center of a continent and civilization engaged in internecine warfare while peripheral states grew as giants eventually to dominate the heartland. Thus the small Italian city-states bled each other for centuries while the transalpine national monarchies grew to the point where Italy was dwarfed and dominated alternately by the French, Spaniards, or Germans. Similarly the European nation states built their proud towers and fought over specks of land such as Alsace-Lorraine while Russia and the United States grew to giant size. The Reformation era witnessed a phase between the Renaissance microcosm and the shrinking of Europe. At the center the Habsburgs of the Empire and Spain fought for decades with the Valois of France without a decisive resolution. All the while Latin Christian Europe was retracting in the East before the onslaught of the Ottoman Turks, though Russia and with it the Russian Orthodox Church was moving eastward across Asia to the north of the Turks. And in the West the Atlantic seaboard states were embarked on an overseas expansion that was to give to Portugal, Spain, the Netherlands, and England worldwide empires.

The survival of the Protestant Reformation depended at critical junctures not merely upon the mutual imperial and papal suspicion and rivalry but also upon the fact that the emperor was caught between the French to the west and the Ottoman Turks advancing from the east.[1] Repeatedly Emperor Charles was almost in a position to crush the Protestants when he was distracted by renewed warfare to the west or east. Charles inherited from his Habsburg ancestors Austria, the Netherlands, Luxembourg, Burgundy, Alsace, Castile, Aragon, Naples, Sicily, and the Spanish dominions

---

1. Stephen A. Fischer-Galati, *Ottoman Imperialism and German Protestantism 1521–1555* (Cambridge, Mass., 1959), develops this theme, although he overstates the case when he writes, p. 117: "The consolidation, expansion, and legitimizing of Lutheranism in Germany by 1555 should be attributed to Ottoman imperialism more than to any other single factor."

The Habsburg Empire under Charles V, 1557

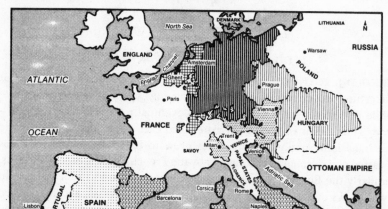

DOMINIONS OF CHARLES V

From Maximilian of Austria	From Ferdinand of Aragon	The Holy Roman Empire
From Mary of Burgundy	From Isabella of Castile	Acquisitions of Ferdinand, Charles V's brother

in the New World, as well as a high probability of election as the Holy Roman Emperor, a throne to which the Habsburgs had established a nearly perpetual claim. His realm was double the size of France and encircled that kingdom on three sides. Charles exhausted himself administering, defending, and expanding his holdings, but despite the limitations of his achievements, he made an original contribution thanks to his vision of a universal empire embracing many well-treated component parts, an idea perpetuated in the Austro-Hungarian Empire and in certain ideals of world federation and even possibly of the United Nations. He conceived of his kingship as a divine regency to be carried out with a sense of dignity and calling.

Charles V was born on February 24, 1500, in Ghent, the heir to a proud tradition.[2] His father was Philip the Fair, son of Emperor Maximilian I and Mary of Burgundy, and his mother, Joanna, later given the sobriquet "The Mad," was the daughter of Ferdinand and Isabella of Spain. While Charles was still an infant his parents moved to Spain and left him to the care of Margaret of York, who was the widow of Charles the Bold of Burgundy. He imbibed the spirit of Flemish piety and of Burgundian chivalry, which remained two of his most prominent personality traits. His policy upon succeeding to the throne was directed toward the recovery of Burgundy from the French, but upon his election as emperor of the Holy Roman Empire in 1519, he was involved in Italian affairs and reasserted the medieval imperial claims to Milan, Naples, and Tuscany. He made Spain his real power base from 1521 on, and operating from there and secondarily from the Empire, he sought to exclude the French from the Italian peninsula and to control the papacy, for its own good, of course. For nearly four decades he was involved in diplomatic intrigue, marriage schemes, and constant warfare to achieve his goal of a universal dynastic empire. Though he was not a powerful man physically, he was agile and athletic, with the long and narrow melancholy Habsburg face, alert eyes, and slim body. Well-armored and riding a white horse, he fought alongside his troops on the battlefield. He took a personal interest in the administration of his vast empire, as thousands of letters in his own handwriting attest, and was personally interested in the religious questions raised by the reformers, although he was more pious than learned about theology.

Strategically Charles V's French opponents had the advantage of centrality and interior lines, whereas Charles had to work around them, sending troops from Genoa northward to the Spanish Netherlands and the Holy Roman Empire or by sea, through the rough waters of the Channel, running the gauntlet between the French and the English. His eastern domains along the Danube lay directly in the path of the Ottoman armies. A national solution in the Empire would have unified the Germanies, but when Charles moved his real base of power away from Germany and Burgundy to Spain, both Germany and Italy were left to their fates,

2. Manuel Fernández Alvarez, *Charles V, Elected Emperor and Hereditary Ruler* (London, 1975), provides an excellent picture of Charles as a person and ruler, dealing with the intricate political questions and economic foundations in an adequate way. The classic study is Karl Brandi, *Kaiser Karl V. Werden und Schicksal einer Persönlichkeit und eines Weltreiches*, 2 vols., 7th ed. (Munich, 1964), English tr. *The Emperor Charles V* (London, 1939).

not achieving national unity until the nineteenth century, and then with overkill.

The jockeying for the imperial election began well before the death of Emperor Maximilian, which came on January 12, 1519. One ambitious candidate was Francis I, king of France since January 1, 1515. That year his victory over the Swiss mercenaries at Marignano inflated his reputation and his ego. The Treaty of Brussels, 1516, provided that France was to have Milan and Spain Naples and southern Italy. From 1517 on Francis maneuvered for his own election as emperor, fearing that if Charles were elected his interests in Italy would be endangered. Of the seven electors, Archbishop Richard of Trier supported Francis; Frederick the Wise of Saxony, himself thought by some to be a possible candidate, kept his own counsel; and the other five electors took bribes from both Charles and Francis. Just before the election Frederick of Saxony declared for Charles. On June 2, 1519, the electors chose Charles and on October 22, 1520, he rode into Aachen for his coronation in the cathedral where Charlemagne lies buried.

Typically Habsburg, Charles skillfully enlarged the dynastic holdings by convenient marriages. He achieved a temporary unity of Spain and Portugal through his own marriage with Isabella of Portugal. He followed through on his grandfather Maximilian I's design for uniting Habsburg Austria with Bohemia and Hungary by joining the Habsburg and Jagiellon lines. He married his brother Ferdinand to Anne, who was the sister of King Louis II of Hungary and Bohemia and married his sister Mary to King Louis himself. He gave the Spanish base priority and made Ferdinand regent of Austria, Tyrol, Vorarlberg, and Württemberg. He had him rule over Alsace, Pfirt, and Hagenau on the condition that these possessions would revert on his death to the Burgundian inheritance. The shift of Charles' own interest to Spain had fateful consequences for central Europe. By tying the Netherlands with Spain he prepared the way for the Dutch wars of liberation and cut them off from their natural place in the Empire, from which they were cut loose formally in 1648. By suppressing the Hanseatic cities and opposing Christian II of Denmark, his own sister Isabella's spouse, he prevented the development of a strong state in the north. By frustrating France's ambitions in Italy, he diverted France toward Lorraine and weaker targets in the Empire with faithful consequences for later history. Through his relative neglect of the Holy Roman Empire he allowed the particularist interests of the territorial princes,

Catholic as well as Protestant, to develop. Shortly after the Diet of Worms in 1521, Charles went to the Netherlands and then to Spain and was not to return to the Empire for eight years, during which time the Lutherans made great gains.

Francis I was twenty-one when he became the king of France and Charles V nineteen when he became emperor. Practically coevals, they were fierce rivals their whole lives. The stakes were high, far beyond their immediate territories. The winner would control the Mediterranean, the Atlantic, and the wealth and lands of the New World. The small principalities of Italy were merely pawns in this power struggle and quickly lost their independence.

The first years Charles outmaneuvered Francis diplomatically and defeated him decisively in battle. At Calais, June 7, 1520, Francis hoped to win over Henry VIII to his side with a lavish display and tourney in what is known as the Field of the Cloth of Gold. But that maneuver came to naught. Instead Henry VIII signed the Treaty of Windsor, 1522, with Charles V, promising an invasion of France. Charles promised to help Henry with the return of the old Angevin claims, while Charles himself would take everything in eastern and southern France that had once belonged to the Empire, plus the part of Navarre that lay north of the Pyrenees. Leo X sided with Charles in order to help him control the Protestants. Francis, in turn, tried to attack the kingdom of Navarre from Spain, assisted rebels in Castile, and allowed a mercenary adventurer Robert von der Mark to attack the Empire in the west. Charles felt gratified that Francis started hostilities. His mercenary troops under Georg von Frundsberg and an imperial army under the count of Nassau invaded France, but made only limited progress, for the main action took place in Italy. Charles' troops took Milan on November 19, 1521. The imperial general Pescara, reinforced by twelve fresh contingents of troops led by Frundsberg, captured Genoa on May 20, 1522. Constable Charles of Bourbon, a French landed magnate hostile to Francis's royal ambitions, invaded southern France in July 1524, and besieged Marseilles. Francis I now staged a major campaign to retake Milan. With more daring than prudence he moved out of a protected position in the park of Mirabello near Pavia and rashly gambled all on one desperate battle on February 24, 1525. French losses were reported to have been over ten thousand men and Francis I himself was taken captive.

The capture of King Francis and his imprisonment in Madrid had a devastating effect on France. French soldiers drifted around the country aimlessly, shouting for Bourbon or Burgundy. The armored nobility had suffered heavy losses and the cities took the occasion to assert greater independence from feudal control. The people in general blamed the Queen Mother Louise and Chancellor Duprat more than the young king himself. Charles V was not prepared for this total success. Henry VIII urged Charles to put Francis out of commission for good, but Charles feared that such an act would create a fierce reaction in France that would not be forgotten. Charles decided to release Francis on certain conditions. The Treaty of Madrid, January 14, 1526, made several demands on France. The king was to renounce his claims on Burgundy, the Netherlands, and Italian territories, Charles of Bourbon was to have his lands returned, Francis was to marry Charles's sister Eleanor, and Francis's two oldest sons were to be sent as hostages to Madrid as a guarantee that Francis would keep the terms of the treaty. His wife, Francis never allowed Eleanor, who remained childless, to influence his policy. In true Machiavellian fashion, once released he refused to honor the treaty on the predictable grounds that he had signed it under duress. The pope agreed that the Treaty of Madrid was invalid because it had been extracted from Francis under duress, although actually the pope was concerned with the complete domination of the continent and Italy by Emperor Charles and Spain. Before the year was out Pope Clement VII, France, Venice, Florence, and Duke Sforza of Milan joined in the League of Cognac to oppose imperial ambitions.

Charles was deeply concerned, for in that very year, 1526, at the battle of Mohács, the army of Suleiman the Magnificent had destroyed the Hungarian forces under King Louis of Hungary, who lost his life in the battle. When the first Diet of Speyer was held in 1526, the emperor, besieged on all sides, had to make concessions to the Lutherans. Moreover, Charles was furious at the duplicity of Clement VII in turning against him. He asked him how the vicar of Christ could shed one drop of blood for worldly possessions. The pope, he charged, was damaging Christendom, for as emperor he could now neither fend off the Turks nor suppress the heretics. If the pope went on acting as a factional leader rather than as a father, as a robber rather than a shepherd, he would appeal to a council! Within a year Charles' troops sacked Rome and Clement retreated to the fortress of Sant' Angelo.

The *sacco di Roma* still lingers on in Roman folklore as a catastrophe analogous to the fall of Rome. Some see it as an outward act symbolizing the end of the Renaissance. In November, 1526, Georg von Frundsberg, the tough old mercenary, crossed the Alps with an army of some fifteen thousand soldiers. In February, 1527, Charles of Bourbon joined his forces with some five thousand poorly disciplined French and Spanish soldiers. Frundsberg died of a stroke after confronting the rebellious troops demanding their pay. The army rolled on toward Rome like an undisciplined mob. Living off the land, looting and robbing, they assaulted the walls of Rome on May 6. Charles of Bourbon was shot while mounting a scaling ladder. By midnight the invaders were inside the city and began a rampage of pillaging and murder that lasted several days. Charles V regretted the damage to Rome and allowed Clement VII to retain his secular power in the Papal States, asking that he work for peace and call an ecumenical council.

Francis I meanwhile was preparing for a second war with Charles. He built a defensive system of fortresses with the latest Italian methods of constructing earthworks and stone structures angled to deflect artillery shots. He also recruited soldiers into provincial militias. Then he maneuvered diplomatically for security, making a peace treaty with Henry VIII in August, 1527. He was now prepared for another Italian campaign. He recaptured Genoa and besieged Naples by land while Andrea Doria with a Genoese fleet blockaded the city by sea. At that juncture the French were decimated by a plague, Andrea Doria went over to the emperor in anger over French treatment of Genoa, and an imperial army occupied Lombardy and lifted the siege of Naples. In the battle of Landriano, 1529, Charles won a decisive victory, his last on Italian soil, and Francis by now was ready for peace. In the Peace of Barcelona, June 29, 1529, Clement VII confirmed the imperial claim to Naples and promised to allow the unhindered passage of imperial troops across the Papal States in return for the emperor's promise to suppress the Lutherans. The Treaty of Cambrai officially ended the war on August 5, 1529. This treaty, sometimes called the "Ladies' Peace" because the Queen Mother Louise and Margaret of Austria, Charles's aunt, initiated the negotiations, followed the same basic lines as the Treaty of Madrid. It recognized the supremacy of Charles in Italy. The Sforzas were restored in Milan but under Spanish control. The emperor acknowledged the French claims to Burgundy in return for Francis's renunciation of his overlordship of Flanders and Artois and his promise never again to invade Italy or the empire. Francis's sons were freed in return for a high ransom in a single gold payment. On February 25, 1530, Clement crowned Charles emperor in Bologna in an elaborate ceremony, the last time in history that a pope was to crown an emperor.

Once again perfidious and desperate Francis declared the peace treaty invalid because he had signed it under duress. In 1533 he married his second son to the pope's niece, Catherine de' Medici, thus strengthening his ties with Clement. The most Christian king of France next moved to form an alliance with the Turks against the emperor. While a prisoner in Madrid Francis had managed to make contact with Suleiman I and very likely encouraged his attack on Hungary. In 1535 Francis sent an ambassador, Jean de la Forêt, to the sultan, who received him in May while returning from Iraq to Azerbaijan. He proposed joint action against the Habsburgs. On February 18, 1536, they made a trade agreement, subsequently called the Capitulations, and followed it with a formal alliance. The next month Francis attacked Savoy and moved into Italy while the Turks attacked the Habsburg lands along the Danube toward Vienna and the Venetians at sea. The French invaded the Netherlands while Charles's troops attacked Piedmont and Provence. Hard pressed by the Turks, the emperor had to negotiate concessions with the Lutherans at Nuremberg in exchange for military support. Charles gathered an army of some 80,-000 men. Suleiman withdrew from Hungary, which he left to his puppet John Zapolya to rule for the time being. In the Mediterranean the corsair Khair ad-Din Barbarossa with a Turkish fleet was destroying Spanish commerce. Charles struck back by seizing Tunis and destroying the Turkish fleet. The French helped Barbarossa, who had escaped, rebuild his fleet and resume the pirating. Barbarossa and the sultan planned a major expeditionary force in 1537 of 300,000 men who were to march from Istanbul to Albania and then be transported by Barbarossa's fleet across the Adriatic for a direct assault on Italy while the French invaded northern Italy. But the French retired from northern Italy and Suleiman directed his forces against some lesser Venetian bases along the coasts of Dalmatia and Albania in September, 1537. Out of fear of the Turks, Pope Paul III was relieved to negotiate a peace between Charles and Francis on June 18, 1538. The kingdom of France was to retain most of Piedmont and drop its alliance with the Turks, and Charles was to keep control over Milan. Charles and Francis met at Aigues Mortes and planned a joint effort against the Turks, Protestants, and Henry VIII. But Francis still intended to break the Habsburg grip once and for all.

Francis's fourth and final effort to defeat the Habsburgs came close to ending in disaster for France. In the summer of 1542 his ally Suleiman I coordinated a renewed attack on Hungary with a French attack on Spain and Luxembourg. A combined French and Turkish fleet raided the cities along the coast of the western Mediterranean, except, of course, for those in France. Charles in turn made an alliance with Henry VIII, sent an army down the Rhine to crush the Protestant Prince William of Cleves, an ally of Francis, and then began a direct attack on France itself. In June, 1544, an imperial army of some 35,000 men invaded France and came within fifty miles of Paris. Charles felt uneasy, however, about the Protestant princes and the Turks and so negotiated a relatively generous peace settlement with Francis. He promised that if the French king's third son married his daughter he would give her either Milan or the Netherlands as her dowry. Charles then turned on the Lutherans and emerged as victor in the Schmalkald War. Francis died on March 31, 1547, and was succeeded by Henry II. Charles abdicated his imperial throne in 1555 in favor of his brother Ferdinand. Working out a more permanent peace was left to their successors. Forty years after Charles had been elected emperor and a year after his death the Treaty of Cateau-Cambrésis was signed, April 1–3, 1559, formalizing the relationship among France, Spain, and the Empire for decades thereafter. France agreed to give up her claims to Italy and yielded Savoy and Piedmont. As so often in history, Italy was the real loser, for the country was divided a new way: Siena went to the Medici, western Lombardy to Savoy, the south and the east to the Farneses and Gonzagas. France kept the income from the bishoprics of Metz, Toul, and Verdun, an omen of her future moves on Lorraine. The stability of the peace owed less to the goodwill of the treaty's signators than to the fact that France was weakened by internal religious dissension and civil war and to the Spanish preponderance in the second half of the century.[3] France and the Empire at the center of the continent, the old Carolingian domain, had effectively come to a standstill while the initiative and momentum lay with powers in the east and west.

3. An account sympathetic to Francis I is to be found in Roland Mousnier, *Les XVIe et XVIIe Siècles* (Paris, 1956); Henri Hauser and Augustin Renaudet, *Les Débuts de l'Âge moderne* (Paris, 1946), remains a classical account of the period and of his reign. Given the political and military pressure on Francis I, his patronage of Renaissance culture is all the more remarkable. See Anne Denieul-Cormier, *A Time of Glory: The Renaissance in France, 1488–1559* (Garden City, N.Y., 1968).

2. THE EAST—APOGEE OF THE OTTOMAN EMPIRE

The peak of Ottoman grandeur coincided with the reign of Suleiman the Magnificent, 1520–1566.[4] The only son of Sultan Selim I, he ascended the golden throne in the same year in which Charles V was crowned emperor and, like Francis, became his lifelong opponent. In Europe he was called the "Grand Turk," but his own people named him *Kanuni,* the "Lawgiver." Although while still in the shadow of the powerful Selim he was thought to be shy and retiring, scholarly and introspective, once in power he became a ruler without equal. He emerged as an energetic warrior, a lawgiver, diplomat, administrator, builder, patron of letters, and a man of justice and surprising tolerance. He inherited from Selim the Janissary corps of elite troops and enjoyed an enviable strategic position both in the east and west, thanks to the conquests of Bayezid II and Selim I. Suleiman himself proved to be the greatest Ottoman military leader. He accompanied his armies on thirteen major campaigns and spent ten years in the field, even wintering on the front to avoid the long trip back and forth from Istanbul. Suleiman managed to deal alternately with his foes in the east and west, thus avoiding a two-front war. All the while he worked at internal reforms, building a system of justice with an enlarged number of courts that would minimize arbitrariness and discrimination, adjusting taxation to the ability to pay and eliminating confiscatory punitive assessments, reorganizing the administration with a merit system for appointment and promotion with safeguards against arbitrary dismissal, and providing for the general and advanced education of scholars and jurists to work on adequate legal codes.

His reign was not, of course, free of internal problems. Although during the early part of his reign, Suleiman was to continue building a world empire by expansion in Europe, he was beset with difficulties at home and in the east. The former Mamluks in Syria led by Canberdi al-Gazza, the governor of Damascus, hoped to take Egypt and use it as a base for rebuilding the Mamluk empire, which the Ottomans had destroyed. Suleiman's governor of Aleppo suppressed the revolt, and the whole Mamluk administrative structure was replaced by the Ottoman system of feudal dependence. Suleiman had to destroy heavy fortifications on the island of

4. The standard biography remains A. D. Merriman, *Suleiman the Magnificent, 1520–1566* (Cambridge, Mass., 1944).

Rhodes, the last Christian redoubt in the eastern Mediterranean, since the island was used as a base for naval action and piratical assaults on Ottoman shipping. After a siege lasting half a year, Rhodes fell on December 20, 1522. Shortly after that triumph, however, the Mamluks in Egypt revolted under Arnavut Ahmet Paşa in January, 1524. Ahmet Paşa declared himself to be sultan, but he was assassinated the next year. Suleiman replaced him with Grand Vizier Ibrahim Paşa, who rebuilt the government in conformity with Suleiman's enlightened standards. Ibrahim represented a new type of Ottoman official who rose by his own ability. He was a member of the *devşirme* class which now gradually pushed aside the hereditary aristocracy. This class was ambitious and self-seeking and was soon divided into political factions. The rivalries of the harem groups further complicated the domestic political scene.

One of the *devşirme* men in Suleiman's court, Lüfi Paşa (d. 1562), a legal scholar and superb administrator, directed as second vizier the codification of provincial administrations into laws *(kanuns)*. A new general code of laws *(kanunname)* was developed dealing with justice and finance. This code established regulations for the timar holders. Timars were subdivisions of the *sancak* border districts which were administered by beys.[5] It also established new port regulations, rationalization of custom duties, and tightened controls on freeing of foreign slaves for bribes. Suleiman was very tolerant in allowing the religious practices of all faiths provided only that they remain nonpolitical. During Suleiman's reign the population of the empire nearly doubled from twelve to twenty-two million. Economic pressures led to illegal taxation and to the restoration of forced labor to increase food production. During his last years Suleiman was preoccupied unwillingly with two campaigns in the east while at home a political disintegration set in which presaged the growing decline of Ottoman vitality and military success.

Suleiman's mosque in Istanbul symbolizes the grandeur of the sultan's imperial ambitions. His military objectives in the west during these decades were to clear up the Christian enclaves and defenses along the Danube, to take Belgrade, which was the key to the rich Hungarian plains to the north, to control Hungary at first indirectly and then through occupation, and to drive back the Habsburgs from the Austro-Hungarian-Bohemian region. Despite the excellence of his Janissary assault troops

5. On the timar, Nicoară Beldiceanu, *Le Timar dans l' État Ottoman (début XIVe—début XVIe siècle)* (Wiesbaden, 1980).

and officers, and the experience and fighting spirit of his troops, Suleiman had two major military disadvantages. The one was the length of his communications and supply lines from Istanbul to the Adriatic and middle Danube front. The second was the fact that many soldiers and officers in the vast armies he amassed came from the feudal militia recruited in the landed provinces. These men had to return after the summer campaigns to look after the management of their estates. The campaign season therefore lasted, at the most, from April to the end of October.

Suleiman took advantage of the declaration of war by Francis I against the Habsburgs in April, 1521, to move against them from the east. He transported an immense army of Janissaries, regular troops, and siege guns out of Istanbul and up the Danube, led by himself and his personal troops. His cavalry overran the countryside around Belgrade and cut off the city to the west and north so that reinforcements could not reach it. Ottoman gunboats controlled the river. A heavy bombardment followed by a direct assault forced the defenders to retreat to the citadel. The Serbian and Hungarian soldiers quarreled over tactics and on August 29 the fortress surrendered.

The Persians provided a temporary diversion, but in April, 1526, Suleiman's army moved out again. After Pavia Francis I negotiated an alliance, it will be recalled, with Suleiman for a coordinated attack on the Habsburgs. King Louis II of Hungary led a relatively small army of brave Magyars such as the Esterházys against the Turkish army and engaged them on the plain of Mohács, on the right bank of the Danube south of Buda, on August 29, 1526. To the east flowed the Danube, to the west and south there was a barrier of wooded hills which screened the Turkish forces from view. The Magyars' armored cavalry charged the center of the Turkish line and drove it back. But then the Turkish troops came out of the woods to the west and struck the Hungarian right flank while Ottoman artillery shells killed masses of men. The armored nobles, including King Louis II, not killed by the Turks drowned while fleeing through the marshes along the Danube. Buda and Pest fell ten days later.

While the noble Magyars died at Mohács, John Zapolya, prince of Transylvania and leader of a national movement of lesser nobles, stood aside with a large army. Now he received his reward, for Suleiman accepted Zapolya's offer to acknowledge Turkish suzerainty and make Hungary a tributary in exchange for the kingship. His claim was naturally disputed by Archduke Ferdinand I, Charles V's brother, who had married

Louis II's sister Anna and claimed the Hungarian throne. The Ottomans kept a few garrisons in Hungary but the largest part of the army withdrew with the sultan.

Suleiman was preoccupied from 1526 to 1527 with revolts in Anatolia. The Turkomans resented the efforts of the governor, Ferhad Paşa, to end their autonomy and to bring them underneath a central administration. Moreover, many of the old aristocracy, resentful of the rise of the devşirme types in government, joined the Celali movement to maintain their traditional rights and privileges. The most serious revolt was led by Kalender Çelebi. It was not until June 23, 1527, that the Ottomans were able to destroy Kalender and scatter his army. From 1527 to 1529 Suleiman was free to launch his second Hungarian expedition.

While Zapolya was busy in Transylvania, Ferdinand, having set his house in order in Austria and Bohemia, invaded Hungary at the call of the Hungarian nobles. He called on Sigismund I of Poland for help, but under pressure from some of his landed magnates Sigismund temporized and did not enter the fray. At Tokay Ferdinand defeated Zapolya on September 26, 1527, and occupied nearly the whole country. He had himself proclaimed king at Bratislava/Pressburg, the Hungarian capital. Zapolya appealed to Suleiman, who began his second invasion of Hungary. His army left Istanbul on May 10, 1529, and he took Buda on September 3. He then proceeded up the Danube in order to besiege Vienna.

Turkish troops appeared before Vienna on September 21 and began a siege of the city which lasted until October 15. Ferdinand and his court fled from Vienna. The battle for the city was fierce and desperate. The Turkish army plundered the countryside and surrounded Vienna, which had some 20,000 defenders. The suburbs were destroyed and the Turks tunneled under the walls and mined them. On October 9 they blew up a sizable section of the wall between the Carinthian gate and the fortress and began to storm through the gap. But the largely German troops filled in the breech with a wall of cannons lowered to aim at ground level and backed by guns and lances. They inflicted enormous casualties with their withering gunfire. Two days later the Turks blew up another section of the wall but were driven back by German and Spanish troops in ferocious hand-to-hand combat. After three new attacks on October 12 yet another section of the wall was blown up and the Turks made a final assault. Once again their attack led them into the very mouths of the enemies' cannons and they suffered great losses. The Janissary corps had become restless during the siege and Turkish raiding parties attacked Regensburg in Bavaria and Bremen in Bohemia, striking terror throughout the Empire. Meanwhile Charles V had been able to negotiate the peace of Cambrai with Francis I on August 3, 1529, which had freed some of his army to reinforce Vienna. Count Frederick of the Palatinate, field marshal of the Empire, gathered a relief force in Linz while Ferdinand gathered troops in Moravia. The Swabian League also bestirred itself to cooperate in the defense of the Empire. The nights were getting colder and longer, and Vienna still had not fallen. Suleiman weighed the difficulties and broke off the siege on October 15. He retreated through the snow back to Belgrade and made the long trek back to Istanbul. From Suleiman's point of view the thrust at Vienna did keep much of Hungary under his control through Zapolya. It also so gutted Austria and northern Hungary that Ferdinand could not counterattack, and by keeping Hungary as a buffer state he was not in direct contact with the Habsburg lands. The failure of the siege, however, convinced many that the logistics of supply had carried the Ottomans as far west as they could go while operating out of Istanbul.[6]

During the campaign season of 1532 Suleiman made another try for Vienna. The first attack had been almost an afterthought and not by design, but this time the city was his prime target. After the first assault Christendom was alarmed and there was talk of a crusade against the Turks. Even Francis vowed to join Charles V in an offensive, but, of course, that was all rhetoric and neither the pope nor the French could be counted on, since the French with their own motives and self-interest had repeatedly allied themselves with Asian powers against Europe. Ferdinand I therefore wisely remained cool to the idea of a crusade, and he and Charles concentrated on strengthening their defenses against the Turks. Suleiman needed time to develop his internal reforms, especially the juridical system, so that this basically wise Turk also had reasons for holding off. As Luther commented about rulers, "A smart Turk makes a better ruler than a dumb Christian." But by 1532 when Suleiman made his move, Ferdinand, too, was better prepared than in 1529. Suleiman moved through Hungary during July and August with what seemed like an invincible army of 300,000 men. His scouting companies could not

6. Stanford Shaw, *History of the Ottoman Empire and Modern Turkey*, I: *Empire of the Gazis: The Rise and Decline of the Ottoman Empire, 1280–1808*, I (Cambridge, 1976), p. 93, pp. 87–111, an excellent account used extensively here.

make contact with the main Austrian army and after some devastating raids across Austria he withdrew into Hungary and returned home. Suleiman concluded that the territory to be gained was hardly worth the risks and cost. This campaign obliged Charles, however, to curry further support from the Lutheran princes. Ferdinand also recognized Suleiman as "father and suzerain," gave up his claim to rule in Hungary except for the territories he had been holding, and paid an annual tribute to the sultan.[7] The peace of 1533 signaled a stalemate, with each side fortifying its side of the line between them.

Suleiman now turned his attention to Mesopotamia and Iran, where the Shia heresy was spreading and the Sunni shrines were being destroyed. As the leader of the orthodox Sunni Moslems, Suleiman moved against the Shi'ites, sending the Grand Vizier Ibrahim Paşa with a contingent of soldiers. He himself followed with the main army. Wintering in Bagdad, Suleiman restored Sunni rites, though the Shi'ites dominate Iran to this day.

Suleiman also rebuilt the Ottoman fleet to oppose the Portuguese in the Indian Ocean and the Spanish in the western Mediterranean. The Mediterranean fleet under Khair ad-Din Barbarossa worked havoc on Spanish and Venetian shipping and raided coastal cities in the western Mediterranean, sparing France. The struggle at sea was as desperate as the battles on land. Andrea Doria in 1532 scored a triumph over the Ottoman fleet. In 1535 the imperial fleet took the city of Tunis and destroyed it. Charles planned to take Algiers from the Turks and free all of Tunisia in the summer of 1536. He even hoped to move out of Naples and assault Istanbul, but was advised against such a rash action. It was not until 1541 that the imperial fleet attacked Algiers, but his landing force had just hit the beach when a storm destroyed a large number of his ships and made withdrawal necessary. In 1543 Barbarossa attacked the coast of Italy and Spain. He caused panic in Naples and Rome, and tried to take Nice with a siege from August 20–September 8. The Ottoman fleet wintered safely in the French harbor of Toulon. Thirty years later in the battle of Lepanto, 1571, Don Juan of Austria, Charles V's illegitimate son, defeated the Turkish fleet, but the Turks conquered Tunis in 1574 and kept a base of operations in the western Mediterranean.

In the eastern seas the Ottomans took up the war with the Portuguese

7. *Ibid.*, p. 94.

that the Egyptian Mamluks had waged ever since the Portuguese naviga-
tors had rounded the Cape of Good Hope in 1488. In 1502 the Portuguese fleet blockaded the Persian Gulf and Red Sea to establish a
monopoly on the Europe-India trade. The ports of Suez and Alexandria
suffered economically and the Mamluks were unable to build up their fleet
to oppose the Portuguese. The Ottomans reactivated the shipyard at Suez
and by the 1530s built a second fleet at Basra in Iraq. When a Moslem
ruler in western India appealed to Suleiman for help against the Portuguese he sent a fleet from Suez on June 13, 1538, under the command
of Hadrin Suleiman Paşa, governor of Egypt. They took control of the
coast of Yemen but upon reaching India were rejected by the son of the
Moslem leader who had succeeded his father and had to return to Suez.

The contest with the Habsburgs continued in the Danube basin for half
a dozen years. In February, 1538, Zapolya willed Hungary to Ferdinand.
Sigismund I of Poland subsequently married his daughter Isabella to
Zapolya. Isabella then gave birth to a son whom Zapolya now wanted to
have succeed him. When Zapolya died on August 22, 1540, Ferdinand
tried to assert his claim to Hungary. Suleiman in response occupied Hungary and annexed it outright to the Ottoman Empire. Ferdinand launched
a crusade in 1542 to free Hungary but failed to capture Buda. In 1543
Suleiman sent another army to take Habsburg strongholds in Hungary.
Suleiman and Ferdinand finally agreed to a truce, November 10, 1545,
which essentially recognized the status quo. After Francis I's death the
truce was made a permanent peace on June 13, 1547.[8] Hostilities were
renewed in 1549 following Habsburg intervention in Transylvania and
the sea war was resumed from 1551 to 1562, with the fleets of Algiers and
Tripoli continuing piratical raids on shipping with few restraints. After the
Treaty of Cateau-Cambrésis, April 3, 1559, the French lost incentive for
drawing in the Turks against the Empire. Moreover, Suleiman was aging
and was beset with internal difficulties. On June 1, 1562, the Ottomans
and Habsburgs signed another peace treaty which basically renewed the
provisions of the peace of 1547. The old warrior still had some fight left
in him, however, enough for an attack on Malta, which had been fortified
by the knights from Rhodes, and for another Hungarian expedition,
which he led in person in 1566. He died on September 7 and was succeeded by Selim II.

8. *Ibid.,* p. 103.

The cultural legacy of the Ottoman Empire remained important for eastern Europe for centuries thereafter. A large Moslem population comprised mostly of converted Christians and a minority of Turkish colonists left a heritage of language, place-names, folklore, ethnic ways, and epic literature that has enriched Balkan life down to the present time.[9] The Eastern Orthodox Church did not flourish under Turkish rule, for although the Turks were generally tolerant of the Christian cult, they confiscated much of the wealth of the church and laid such a crushing burden of taxation on Christian subjects that there was little revenue left to support the clergy or to keep the churches in repair; many of them, especially in Asia Minor, decayed and were abandoned. Many learned men had fled to the west. Some prelates such as the metropolitan of Pisidia were really titular bishops with no constituency. Some Greek merchants and shipbuilders created family fortunes and supported the church. The sultans, like the Byzantine emperors before them, controlled the election of the Patriarch of Constantinople and normally sold the see to the Patriarch, whom the sultans removed again at will. The Ottomans encouraged strong central control by the Patriarch over the metropolitan bishops and gave them important juridical functions over the Greeks. The Turks took at least one church in each town they captured and converted it into a mosque, as they had done to the Hagia Sophia and eight other Byzantine churches in Constantinople. The Turks rarely destroyed churches, except for some lost in taking towns. The monasteries at Athos were not disturbed and the monastery of St. Catherine's at Mount Sinai, as well as the shrines in Jerusalem, were preserved, although the monks were heavily taxed. Pilgrimages persisted and on the popular level local Christian customs were adopted by the Moslem inhabitants and vice versa.

The Orthodox Church carried on negotiations with Melanchthon and other Lutherans in the interest of unity or union. In 1559 a Lutheran translated the Augsburg Confession into Greek and a chaplain, Stephen Gerlach, offered it to Jeremiah II, Patriarch of Constantinople, in order to promote doctrinal agreement. But political considerations frustrated the good intentions of the Orthodox churchmen and the Lutherans. During the sixteenth-century some young Orthodox theology students were even permitted to study in Italian universities with the result that western theological questions, such as the mode of Christ's real presence in the

9. Wayne S. Vucinich, *The Ottoman Empire: Its Record and Legacy* (Princeton, 1965), pp. 116–123.

sacrament, were introduced into the Greek Orthodox milieu. The persistence of Greek Orthodoxy in eastern Europe was a tribute to its closeness to the people on the village level as well as to the fairly tolerant attitude of the Ottomans, despite some massacres and desecrations.[10]

3. THE EAST—CONSOLIDATION OF RUSSIA

Sixteenth-century Russia continued the dual achievements of the princes of Moscow, absorbing the few principalities that remained independent of their control and increasing their monarchical control over Muscovy. The Grand Prince Ivan III (1462–1505) had been successful in his policy of the "gathering of the Russian lands" because his reign was comparatively free of internal disturbances. He destroyed the liberties of the rich city of Novgorod and annexed her colonies. He took possession of Tver because it had allied itself with Lithuania. He controlled his own brothers effectively, not allowing what they considered to be their ancient rights of sharing in ruling. As "Sovereign of all Russia" and the "Tsar [Caesar] and Autocrat" of Russia he drew more and more power into his own hands. He controlled the boyars or hereditary aristocracy of Muscovy, who traditionally served as advisers and shared control of policy. Encouraged by the church, he moved toward autocracy, but in 1480 he was confronted with a revolt by his own brothers Andrey and Boris, which he handled effectively, as well as a later palace intrigue. The centralization of government brought new men in as a "service class." These officials were rewarded by the granting of *pomestya* or lands on the basis of life tenure. As land came into short supply, over eight hundred boyars and merchants were moved from the black lands of Novgorod to eastern Muscovy to make room for the *pomestya* grants to "service men." The Orthodox Church had to fend off secularization of its lands, especially the monastic lands. Ivan III needed the support of the hierarchy for his crusade against the infidel Latins of Lithuania. Against dissidents such as Nil Sorsky, who believed that monks should live in poverty and labor with their hands, Joseph of Volokolamsk argued that unless monasteries had lands to support them they could not attract and sustain pious monks. His followers, who were known as Josephians or "possessors," won the contest, but secularization of church lands remained a tempting target for the tsars.

10. Owen Chadwick, *The Reformation* (Baltimore, 1964), pp. 348–360.

When Ivan III died on October 27, 1505, he left to his eldest son Basil, or Vasily, two-thirds of his estates and divided the remaining third among Basil's four brothers. Just as Ivan III had taken the land of his deceased brother, the escheats of any younger brother were to revert to the grand prince. The cadets lost many other rights, such as minting their own coins and pursuing independent relations with foreign powers. Basil annexed the two remaining territories in Great Russia, taking Pskov, much in the way in which Ivan III had taken Novgorod and Ryazan. Basil took additional land away from Lithuania and became involved in a war with Sigismund I, king of Poland and of the grand principality of Lithuania. When Mikhail Glinsky, the largest landowner in Lithuania, deserted to Moscow with his private army, the Lithuanians had to sign a treaty in 1508 acknowledging nearly all of Ivan III's conquests as now belonging to Moscow. In 1512 Basil invaded Lithuania again and in July, 1514, took the city of Smolensk. But Basil had serious problems to the south and east. The Crimean Tatars in 1521, encouraged by the Ottoman Turks and the Lithuanians, attacked from the south while an army of Kazan Tatars led by Sahib struck at Moscow from the east. Moscow survived the siege only because the Astrakhan Tatars attacked the Crimea, forcing a retreat by the Crimean Tatars. Basil's wife, the Grand Princess Elena, did not produce a son until 1530, and in 1533 Basil died leaving his principality to a child, Ivan IV, who was to earn the sobriquet Ivan the Terrible (1533–1584).[11]

During Ivan's minority his mother and rival princely families, the Shuiski, the Bêlski and the Gemski, governed the land. At age thirteen, Ivan, as a tool of one of the rival factions, had palace servants murder Prince Andrey Shuiski. At the age of seventeen Ivan IV had himself crowned by the metropolitan as the tsar of all Russia. He married Anastasia, who belonged to the old Moscow family of Zakharin. During the late 1540s and early 1550s he undertook internal reforms under the direction of a "Chosen Council," which was influenced by Adashev, a court favorite, and Sylvester, a priest. His aim was to achieve greater centralization and efficiency of government. In particular, local governments and the taxation system were rationalized, with elective officials replacing the arbitrary traditional officials, the *kormlenshchiki*. They resettled those service men or officials working for the central government

11. See the lucid account of this period by J.L.I. Fennell, "Russia, 1462–1583," *The New Cambridge Modern History,* II, *The Reformation,* G. R. Elton, ed. (Cambridge, 1958), pp. 534–561, used extensively here.

close to Moscow in *pomestya* commensurate in size to the importance of the official service rendered. Thus the public administration and the military command developed greater centralization and the duties of the various ministries were more clearly defined. But in 1560 the Chosen Council fell into disfavor with Ivan, who dismissed Adashev and Sylvester, and exiled or murdered their supporters.

In 1564 Ivan suffered a series of setbacks which seem to have upset his equilibrium. These adversities consisted of a defeat in Lithuania, the desertion of Prince Kurbsky, his close adviser and general, and the threat of a two-front invasion. Ivan left Moscow for Alexandroskaya Sloboda, halfway to Rostov, from where he wrote back to Moscow denouncing the treachery of the clergy and saying he had no grievance against the merchants and people of Moscow. They sent a delegation to ask Ivan to return to the city. Ivan's paranoia increased as some of the great nobles, fearing they might be expropriated and executed as had many boyars, fled and gave their support to the prince of Lithuania. Ivan set up his own council of boyars, special courts, and what amounted to an elite private army of some six thousand shock troops called the *Oprichniki,* completely loyal to him. Then began a twenty-four-year reign of terror which won him the name of "the Terrible." He devastated whole districts seemingly for no other reason than that of setting an example to intimidate the country. In Novgorod he massacred thousands of citizens, including women and children, in order to break their independent municipal loyalty. Ivan IV succeeded in establishing a totally autocratic rule.

In foreign relations the Moscow state made important advances eastward. The Golden Horde of the Mongols had broken up into a number of independent khanates, the largest of which were Kazan, Astrakhan, and the Crimea. These khanates, constantly jealous and frequently at war with each other, were also weakening internally. Ivan IV annexed Kazan and Astrakhan in 1552–1554 and the Bashkirs in 1556. The Tatars of the Crimea managed to maintain their independence for some two centuries due to the support of the Ottoman sultans. Although a Tatar force pillaged Moscow as late as 1571, the Mongols were no longer a cohesive force or real threat to the Russians. Settlers moved eastward to develop agricultural villages and gradually dispossessed the nomadic Asiatics. Since these settlers were frequently attacked by the Tatar herdsmen, they organized their own militia defense. The seminomadic so-called Cossacks were frontier fighters, horsemen who became legendary fighters in the wild east.

The Muscovites had territorial ambitions in the west as well. Both Lithuania and Poland had vast stretches of thinly populated and very rich land, and were politically weak, more conglomerates than unified states. Toward the end of the fourteenth century they had been united under one ruler, but there remained great internal tensions, for the majority of the inhabitants of Lithuania were Russian and Orthodox in religion, whereas in Poland nearly all were Polish and Roman Catholic. Although the country was a hereditary monarchy in name, the landed magnates had reduced the monarchy to the point where the kingship became elective and the landed nobles independent to the point that virtual anarchy reigned. Ivan III had taken some nineteen municipalities away from Lithuania. Basil had attempted to win the election as grand prince of Lithuania, but Sigismund of Poland had been elected instead. Now Ivan the Terrible reached farther than the mere annexation of Lithuanian lands, wishing to drive all the way to the Baltic, so that he could develop commercial and cultural ties with the west by sea. He was frustrated in this grand design not only by Poland-Lithuania, but by the opposition of the Teutonic Knights, the Livonian Order, the Swedes, and the Danes, who feared the advance of the Muscovite barbarians toward their borders.

Ivan IV tried to import German artisans from Saxony to develop his arsenal, but this move was blocked by the Livonian Order. He did, however, establish free trade relations with the English via the White Sea and North Cape during the reign of Queen Mary. But that route was distant and closed off during the long winters, so he again took up his drive toward the Baltic. During the final decades of his reign he was engaged in a series of wars with the Baltic powers. He forced the Grand Master of the Livonian Order to put himself under his protection, a move that led to a war with Poland lasting from 1563 to 1570. When that war came to an inconclusive end, he became involved in a war with Sweden from 1572 to 1583 and fought again with Poland from 1579 to 1581. When he died in 1584 he still hoped for an alliance with England, which would enable him to gain the window to the west he wished Moscow to have. He should perhaps have been labeled Ivan the Tenacious by historians.

The Orthodox Church expanded northward and eastward along with the Muscovite state. Ivan III had married Sophia, who was the niece of the last Roman emperor of Constantinople. He saw himself as the heir to the Roman Empire and Moscow as the third Rome. Philotheos, a monk, wrote to Basil: "Two Romes have now fallen, and the third one, our

Moscow, yet standeth; and a fourth one there shall never be. . . . In all the world thou alone art the Christian Tsar." As the Muscovite state expanded, the Orthodox Church established parishes in the new settlements. Throughout the sixteenth century monasteries continued to colonize and tame the wilderness. In 1589 the patriarchate was created when Jeremiah II of Constantinople consecrated the tsar's candidate as the first patriarch of Moscow, taking rank after Jerusalem.[12] It was the only Orthodox patriarchate not under Moslem rule. Thus the church reflected in its way the two major trends of Russian political life during the Reformation century, greater centralization and autocratic control, and continuous territorial expansion and consolidation.

4. THE WEST—INTO ALL THE WORLD

During the fifteenth century the Portuguese and Spaniards, with the help of Italian navigational expertise, had launched an age of exploration and discovery. In the sixteenth century the Portuguese and Spaniards led the way in trade, conquest, and colonization. During the seventeenth century England, the Netherlands, and France built worldwide colonial empires. The "shift" away from the Empire and Italy in the center, then, transpired over a two-century period, but the time span from 1517 to 1559 was significant as a phase in the Portuguese and Spanish advances in the New World and in south and southeast Asia.[13]

The building of a Spanish colonial empire is one of the grand sagas of western history. The romantic tales of conquistadors braving the ocean in small wooden vessels, plunging later by foot into jungles and across deserts never seen by European eyes, engaging in battle native tribes that vastly outnumbered them, winning treasures and organizing lands that dwarfed in size their homelands, all this is calculated to excite the imagination of any student of history. The Catholic kings and their captains thought of their travels as missionary journeys to save souls and to extend the kingdom of Christ as well as a search for earthly treasures and a kingdom of this world. Where they went, the Augustinians, Franciscans, Dominicans, Jesuits, and lesser missionary orders went also. The Spanish adventure during these decades focuses on the conquests and explorations of Hernán Cortés, Francisco Pizarro, Ferdinand Magellan, and Sebastián

12. Chadwick, *The Reformation*, p. 361.
13. J. H. Parry, "The New World, 1521–1580," *The New Cambridge Modern History*, II, *The Reformation*, pp. 568–569 and pp. 562–590.

del Cano. The story of the Spanish colonial empire at this stage is one of bold advance by the conquistadors and initial organization followed by the efforts of the government at home to centralize control and regularize or bureaucratize the administration of these new lands.

Hernán Cortés (1485–1547) was a natural-born leader. He could make difficult decisions and stick by them. After his 1519 conquest of Mexico he decided to rebuild the Aztec city of Tenochtitlán-Mexico as the capital of New Spain. Despite the fact that it was a marshy island without its own food or fresh water supply and was attached to the mainland by causeways, vulnerable to siege, Cortés believed that it was of crucial importance to suggest the continuity of rule from the Aztecs to the Spaniards by keeping the key city. With thousands of Indian laborers, many of whom died of exhaustion, accidents, and smallpox, Cortés rebuilt Mexico City in 1522 and 1523. The Spaniards inherited from the Aztecs a system of tributary labor and an agricultural supply system which sustained the corporate towns they built for social, administrative and, somewhat less, for military purposes. Each conquistador ensured that his own followers were put in charge of the municipal administration. The soldiers of Cortés, for example, became legally enrolled householders or *vecinos,* and from them Cortés appointed the city council of twelve members. These councillors or *regidores* in turn chose two magistrates acceptable to Cortés to rule for one year.

The system of settlement and administration that the Spaniards introduced was known as the *encomienda.* Under this system a village or several villages with the land around them were commended to the care and control of a Spaniard and his household. He did not own the land nor did he possess jurisdiction over it in his own right, but he was made responsible for the education, religious instruction and services, and the protection of the native population, in return for Indian labor in building chapels and household structures, in agriculture, in road construction, and in whatever else needed to be done. Except for the land arrangement, the analogy to the feudal system in Spain is striking. The *encomienda* system allowed the Spanish soldiers to build up vast estates which in some cases contained thousands of Indians within their domains. The Indians were more docile than the Moors had been in Spain, and in a way the Spaniards merely replaced the ruling Aztecs at the top of the heap. The system was open to abuse and efforts were made to substitute for it a system of *repartimiento* under which the Indians were still obliged to work for the Spaniards but under contract, on a temporary basis, and for wages. But the original *encomienda* system lasted into the eighteenth century and for a long time the two systems existed simultaneously. Cortés did win royal approval of his plans, but the king and his councillors had their misgivings about the *encomienda* system, since the potential for feudalization ran counter to the drive toward centralization that characterized the national monarchy.

The church could not abdicate its responsibilities for missionary work, parish worship, and educational undertakings. Cortés asked the emperor to send Franciscan missionaries, the first of whom were the twelve who came in 1524 under the leadership of Fray Martín de Valencia. The first Dominicans under Fray Domingo de Betanzos arrived in Mexico in 1525. Fray Juan de Zumárraga became the first bishop of Mexico in 1527. These mendicant missionaries emphasized catechization and biblical teaching along with baptism so that the conversion to Christianity would be more than a mere formality. They encouraged the Indians to cluster in towns or villages around a church or convent and thus affected the social pattern of the Indians who formerly had lived thinly scattered over the land. Impressive churches, strongly built as fortifications just as in the early Middle Ages, and complicated ceremonies appealed to the Indians and replaced the void left in their lives by the initial destruction of their temples and the banning of pagan ceremonies.

Cortés continued exploring the coast looking for the fabled passageway to India. At this juncture, however, he ran into a number of difficulties. In going down the coast toward the south he encountered Pedro Arias de Avila and his company, who were moving up toward the north from Darien. A conflict between the two Spanish conquerors seemed imminent. One of his underlings named Olid rebelled and Cortés marched across Honduras to suppress the rebellion, though someone murdered Olid before he arrived. Alvarado conquered the Mayans in Guatemala and became the governor. In 1526 Cortés returned to Mexico and found things in disarray. It was not until 1529 that Cortés visited Spain to plead his own interests at court. He ran afoul of Nuño de Guzmán, who was the president of the court of appeals established in 1527. A personal enemy of Cortés and a partisan of the governor of Cuba, Velásquez, Nuño used the inquiry into the charges against Cortés to harass him interminably. Nuño himself was given control over New Spain, but Bishop Zumárraga, enraged at Nuño's ruthless conquests, enslavement, and harsh treatment of the Indians, denounced him to the crown. Nuño was arrested in 1536, returned to Spain, and died in prison a few years later. The crown made Cortés a captain-general, but left the *audiencia* or advisory council, composed of civilian lawyers, in charge of the civil administration of New Spain. Then out of fear of the fragmentation of the colonial area, the crown appointed in 1535 a viceroy, Antonio de Mendoza, to rule New Spain. Cortés was given an *encomienda* in Oaxaca but in 1539 he retired to Spain, where he died in 1547.

The second major Spanish triumph of arms in the New World was the conquest of Peru. Ever since the Spaniards had settled in Darien they had heard rumors of the fabulously rich highland kingdom to the south. High in the Andes the Incas and the dynasty of the Quechua people had maintained for some four centuries an empire that now extended nearly two thousand miles. Its capital city of Cuzco served as the center of an intricate system of roads and bridges binding the empire together. The llama served as the beast of burden.

Two adventurers, Francisco Pizarro and Diego de Almagro, and a priest named Luque, had settled on *encomiendas* in Darien, on the coast of Central America. After some years of coastal exploration Pizarro returned to Spain and received a commission as governor of the region he would conquer. He then returned to Panama where he organized his expedition to conquer Peru. He set out in 1530 with only about 180 men and twenty-seven horses. Fortunately for him the Incas were less warlike than the Aztecs. Pizarro made a surprise attack on Cajamarca, which the Inca ruler Atahualpa had established as his capital after he had usurped the reign from his half-brother in Cuzco. Pizarro captured Atahualpa and held him for a large gold ransom. He then led his men along with reinforcements from Panama against Cuzco, which he sacked in November, 1533, and seized a fabulous amount of gold. Two years later he established a new Spanish capital at Lima, the city of the kings. He reasoned that he could receive supplies and reinforcements from Spanish ships, but by setting up an entirely new capital he broke the continuity of rule and sharpened the division of Spaniards and Indians. His execution of Atahualpa caused further embitterment.

The crown commissioned Almagro to conquer and rule the area south of Pizarro's Peruvian region, and he claimed Cuzco as part of his domain. After spending some two years exploring as far south as Bolivia and Chile, Almagro returned to Cuzco, defeating a rebel named Manco. A war between the two Spanish leaders developed. Hernando Pizarro, brother of Francisco, defeated Almagro in 1538, captured him, and had him strangled. In 1541, in turn, the illiterate and headstrong Francisco Pizarro was murdered by men who had belonged to Almagro's faction. A number of captains who had served under Pizarro took over the rule of various regions, but the government and the work of the church were less effective than they had been in New Spain.

Bishop Bartolomé de Las Casas (1474–1566) was a great champion of humane treatment for the Indians. His father had accompanied Columbus on his second voyage and Bartolomé had an early and lasting interest in the New World. The Indians were not well suited for heavy labor in the heat and were easily subject to the white men's diseases. Las Casas was incensed at their exploitation and abuse, but his own remedy was problematical. The remedy that Las Casas proposed with characteristic fervor was the importation of Negroes, who could stand the heat of the Antilles and the lowlands. As early as 1505 Negroes were sent to work in the mines in the Antilles. There had been slavery in Africa, blacks "owning" blacks, and the Aztec and Inca Indian societies had both been based on servitude and a system of enforced labor and tribute. Las Casas himself took seven Negroes to Venezuela as his personal slaves. He had argued that the Indians should be placed under the protection of the church, and he was given the northeastern coast of South America that is now Venezuela as an area for experiment. The experiment failed. After establishing a post at Cumaná, he left to give an account of his stewardship. The Indians then attacked and killed the Europeans and sacked the warehouse in which Las Casas had stored supplies for their care and education. Too late he realized what many an idealist has had to learn the hard way, that in his zeal to help the Indians he had done a grave disservice to the blacks. Moreover, he was so disillusioned with his efforts on behalf of the Indians that he opposed all colonization of the New World. He joined the Dominicans and spent the rest of his life fighting for the rights of the Indians. Many Spaniards shared his concern and the crown was sympathetic, but it was a labor-short society and harsh economic realities overruled human sympathies and humane considerations. Las Casas retired to a Dominican monastery on the island of Santo Domingo and wrote his *Historia de las Indias,* in which he gave a gruesome account of the Spanish colonization, exaggerating the number of Indians on the island at the time of discovery and magnifying every injustice into an act of revolting cruelty. Las Casas had a marked influence on the crown and helped encourage a reorganization of the colonies, with more centralized control and greater concern for the Indians.

The Spaniards' colonial administration developed into an impressive organizational structure. Their colonies were administered by viceroys in Mexico and Peru. Men of means frequently served for honorific reasons. An advisory council or *audiencia* was appointed in the main city of each of the larger provinces to serve as implementors of the viceroy's policies. Occasionally the viceroy sent inspectors to check up on the local administrations. The *residencias* reviewed the viceroy's record after his term expired. In Spain the Council of the Indies, calling on the experience of the viceroys and the local administrators, directed the overseas empire. Given the long lines of communication, the rapidly changing conditions, and the size of the geographic areas involved, it was difficult for the viceroys to direct their operations effectively. The crown received the "king's fifth" of all the spoil taken from the Indians and the profits of private entrepeneurs. The Spanish premercantilist policy was designed at obtaining bullion and raw materials for the homeland. Colonists were not to compete with such Spanish industries as the production of wine and olive oil. The full effects of the inflationary spiral contributed to, although it was not simply caused by, the importation of gold and silver from the New World. It was felt first in Andalusia, then in the rest of Spain, the Spanish Netherlands, and the rest of Europe. By the end of the century prices in Spain were three or four times as high as when the sixteenth century began.

The Spanish convoy system for escorting fleets of ships for New World treasure and produce worked very well and was used to the end of the eighteenth century. Hurricanes and tropical storms took the heaviest toll of Spanish ships. Despite the English legend of Elizabethan seadogs and Dutch raiders decimating Spanish shipping from 1562 on, there were few totally successful raids on Spanish convoys by their Protestant enemies.

One of the greatest Spanish achievements in these decades was Ferdinand Magellan's and Sebastian del Cano's circumnavigation of the globe. Magellan left Seville for the Indies in 1519 on a voyage that was to cost his life. The expedition experienced a shipwreck and mutiny off the coast of Patagonia, found its way through the treacherous straits that now bear Magellan's name, then headed across the Pacific and ran out of food. The men were reduced to eating rats and leather. They encountered hostile natives in the Ladrones and the Philippines, and witnessed the death of Magellan and forty other men in a local war. Magellan's successor as leader of the expedition was Sebastian del Cano, who sailed the two remaining ships past Borneo and reached the Moluccas, where the Portuguese were already trading, in November, 1521. The sultan of Ti'dore gave del Cano a friendly reception and he traded their goods for supplies. One of the two remaining ships was captured by the Portuguese, but del Cano sailed the *Victoria* back across the Indian Ocean and around the Cape of Good Hope, arriving home three years after first setting sail.

Charles V sent out two further expeditions to the Moluccas, one under Frey Garcia de Loaisa direct from Spain and another from the west coast of Mexico under Alvaro de Soavedra, but both proved to be disasters. In the Treaty of Zaragoza of 1529, Charles V signed away his claims to the Moluccas or Spice Islands to Portugal for 350,000 ducats but retained his claim to the Philippines. The Spaniards then concentrated on their colonial empire in the Americas and did not get involved in the Far East until they settled in force in the Philippines in the 1560s. The Portuguese developed the Far Eastern trade and fought off the competition in those decades.

In May, 1493, the Spanish pope Alexander VI had drawn the line of demarcation between the Portuguese and the Spanish colonial possessions. To the Spaniards he gave everything lying one hundred leagues or nautical miles west of the Cape Verde Islands and the Azores. The Portuguese were not pleased and negotiated directly with Spain. In the Treaty of Tordesillas, 1494, the line was moved 340 miles west of the Cape Verde Islands. Both Spanish and Portuguese were not so much thinking of dividing up the newly discovered territories as they were seeking to define and to limit the two ways of reaching India, south and east for the Portuguese and west for the Spaniards. This division effectively gave Brazil, which extends eastward, to Portugal and the rest of the New World to Spain. Little Portugal with a population of only two million was able, because of its seafaring ability, to rule over an empire several hundred times its size. Thanks to Henry the Navigator's explorations down the African coast and then around the Cape of Good Hope to India and to Cabral's discovery of Brazil in 1500, Portugal became a global colonial power. The Portuguese did not have the population on which to draw for the colonization or local administration of large areas. By 1503 they had learned that garrisons of a few thousand soldiers stationed at the mouths of rivers or other strategical coastal spots could dominate a large and populous hinterland. Lisbon became the center of the spice trade and of a lively new commercial empire. Francisco Almeida worked out a comprehensive plan based on sea power for maintaining trade factories and outposts without trying for political domination. The viceroy of Albuquerque envisioned an empire fanning out from power centers such as Goa, Cochin, Calcutta, and Molucca. The years 1512 to 1516 saw the greatest expansion in the Far East, largely under the king's authority. The king of Portugal automatically reserved a fourth of all trade profits for the crown. After 1520 the king's authority weakened and private trade flourished. The Portuguese, however, contented themselves with overseas trading and did not get involved in selling their goods directly in the European markets, thus missing an opportunity for further enrichment. The Portuguese were stretched out too thinly and were overextended. During the second half of the sixteenth century attrition began to take its toll. Colonial administration became more rigid and by 1580 when Spain took over Portugal itself, the Portuguese government in Asia was quite weak. The Dutch arrived in the East in 1595. Control of the sea remained the key to empire for centuries to come.[14]

The wars for dominion overseas certainly did not follow confessional lines, Spanish against Portuguese, later English against Dutch. The expansion of Europe into the rest of the world had important consequences for the European self-consciousness. The full realization of what had happened was slow in coming. Luther, for example, referred to the New World only three times or so. He was nine when Columbus discovered America and was at Worms in the year in which Magellan's ship returned to Spain. But as a citizen of the Empire at the center he was preoccupied with church, state, and Turks in Europe. Artists continued doing portraits of the societal elite with little attention to the new worlds and peoples to be portrayed. Indians were often presented, even later in Dresden china, like Negroes, wearing feathers. Economically, too, the full effects of the American bullion and the wealth of the Indies were not felt until the second half of the sixteenth century. Silver from the mines of Potosí in Peru became a really important factor from 1545 on to the end of the century. From 1520 on prices went up in Spain and doubled between 1500 and 1550. But these social and economic changes took place gradually and the sensational achievement of these decades had a less immediate, dramatic, and revolutionary effect than has often been supposed.

14. I. A. Macgregor, "Europe and the East," *ibid.,* pp. 591–614.

Chapter Eight

SOCIETY AND CULTURE

EUROPEAN history from the world of humanism to the Counter-Reformation was notable for its dramatic beginnings, the titanic struggle for the hearts and minds of people, and for the ongoing nature of its most striking features. From the mass of data on population, economics, climate, social relations, and politics presented at the beginning of this volume the narrative moved on to consider single individuals and to explore the recesses of their hearts and minds. It is one of the great paradoxes of history, as Veronica Wedgwood has reminded us, that even though individuals are like grains of sand, waves in the sea, leaves in the forest, real people make history. If Luther had died in his cradle, there would still have been a "reformation," but it would certainly not have been the same historical event that it was, thanks to his presence. Historians know so little, though they know so much more than do those who are ignorant of history. Still, Lord Acton was quite right when he wrote: "Better one great man than a dozen immaculate historians." It should be clear from the history of this conjuncture in European history that events have resulted from the interaction of societal forces and individual drives and decisions. The present volume has undertaken the historical study of a great religious movement within society as a whole. It should be useful in summary to point up some of the outstanding social and cultural developments of the era and to suggest the directions in which they led, directions spelled out more fully in the later volumes in this series. The age of the Protestant Reformation had an enduring impact upon later European, American, and world history.

I. RELIGIOUS CHANGE

One of history's perennial problems is that of continuity and change and clearly the Reformation changed radically the religious and ecclesiastical framework and structure of the past. In that respect it was revolutionary.

Nevertheless, the Reformation also reasserted Christian tenets long forgotten or half-forgotten in the church. With their single-minded reemphasis on basic Christian teachings, the reformers gave Christendom a new lease on life. In a way the Reformation can be seen as a part of those missionary and reformatory efforts of the late medieval period which sought at last to Christianize a culture which still retained much that was pagan and superstitious.

The successes and limitations of the Reformation as a religious movement can be assessed in various ways, but the most obvious is in terms of the goals that the reformers set for themselves, not their highest hopes or wildest expectations, but their realistic aims. Such a judgment cannot be made merely with respect to the correction of the abuses, which medieval reformers had already criticized, or on the basis merely of the ethical and cultural improvement of society. The disappointments and disclaimers of the reformers and the harsh criticisms of the visitation reports in Protestant parishes emphasize the failings in these respects. These reports were critical and corrective in interest and cannot be relied upon exclusively for a full picture of the local scene. The Reformation was not in the first instance directed against abuses or toward moral reform. In his *Lectures on Galatians* in 1531 Luther made his intention clear, for, he declared, if the church of Rome had practiced its cult with the purity and rigor of the hermits, and of Jerome, Augustine, Gregory, Bernard, Francis, and Dominic, the Reformation would still have been necessary for the correction of Rome's false doctrine.[1] The real aim of the reformers transcended earthly goals and pointed to the eternal welfare of man in this life and in the world to come. Luther's question was not, Did the Reformation succeed? but, Have I preached the gospel clearly, faithfully, and fearlessly? The results he left to God.

The central teachings of the magisterial reformers, salvation by God's grace alone, by trust in Christ alone, guidance by the Scriptures alone, provided a positive evangelical message and a doctrinal structure. They had a coherent religious platform and a standard to which millions could repair. On the one hand, in this respect they had a great advantage over late medieval reformers who excoriated abuses but offered no alternative system of belief. On the other hand, once the pope and councils had been

1. "Lectures on Galatians" (1535), *Luther's Works* 26, 459.

pushed aside and no longer had the final word in dogmatic definitions, the problem of authority in religious formulations and belief came to be of crucial importance for the reformers. It became the Achilles heel of Protestantism. The mystery is that the half of Christendom that defected from the authority of the bishop of Rome did not totally fragmentize. In actual fact, however, nearly 90 percent of all Protestants adhered to one of the major confessions—Lutheran, Reformed, Calvinist, or Anglican. The reasons for this coherence in the face of potential group disintegration are very likely that there was a clerical infrastructure in the various cities and territories involved, that it was in the interest of the political powers to maintain a basic uniformity in religious profession within their jurisdiction, and that the Protestants from the time of the Augsburg Confession in 1530 to the Formula of Concord (1577) and the Reformed decrees of the Synod of Dort (1618–1619) developed confessions that served as expressions of a common cause and rallying points for the various Protestant constituencies. What the reformers basically achieved was not an ethical reform, but a reassertion of basic evangelical teachings which gave to Christianity renewed vitality—one more, and perhaps the final, lease on life. This thrust even redirected the mother church once more toward its religious mission, when she had been so misled by false pastors to material concerns of wealth and power. That is how to judge the success or failure of the Reformation in the reformers' terms.

Luther's central affirmation that man is justified in God's eyes by His grace alone for the sake of Christ, whose propitiatory life, death, and resurrection saved man from his sin and brought him the gift of eternal life, became the keystone of Protestant theology and was reflected in the confessions of all communions from the radicals to the Anglicans, whatever variations developed in formulation, sacramental teaching, or in practice. A reading of the sermons, catechisms, hymns, liturgies, and tract literature makes clear the astonishing fact that this highly spiritual theological insight was widely and correctly understood by a broad spectrum of clergy and laity on all levels of society. As a dogmatic formula, however, his deep insight proved to be unstable and was challenged in a series of doctrinal controversies about human nature, reason and will, predestination, the place of good works, and related issues. Luther's essential insight and biblical theology were subject to objective misunderstanding and oversimplification into a dogmatic formula. Certain emphases had a direct social impact such as the new sense of vocation or calling, a new work ethic, a new cultus or worship service and, especially in Calvinism, a strong conviction of the divine covenant of God with man.[2]

Luther, Zwingli, Calvin, the radicals, on one level devastated the old order. They challenged the traditional authorities, popes, councils, ecclesiastical customs, the role of the clergy as a special state above the laity, its hierarchy, the validity of canon law, dogmas about purgatory, the sacrifice of the mass and all the related practices, such as private masses, the saying of masses for the dead, for souls in purgatory, prebends for the saying of masses, and other medieval practices. They questioned the sacramental system and the Catholic teaching of transubstantiation. They challenged the whole system of man's contribution by good works to his salvation. The centrality of Christ's all-sufficient vicarious sacrifice for the sin of all mankind in Protestant teaching undercut nearly the whole medieval superstructure of religious practices such as the invocation of saints, cult of images, reliquaries, holy water, amulets, pilgrimages, processions, monastic asceticism, the "religious" or regular clergy as separate and superior to "secular" clergy and lay Christians, religious sanctions for begging and for almsgiving and the like. The abandonment of the allegorical method and the whole fourfold interpretation of the Scriptures revolutionized exegesis and led to a new historical-spiritual interpretation of the Bible. The Word of God, Christ, became the central focus in the theological interpretation of the Bible with the new emphasis on the promises of God and the benefits of Christ.

For all that, Protestantism was less radical than might appear on the surface. In fact, it even reemphasized truths long since forgotten or neglected by the Catholic Church. It left the whole supernatural or religious world view intact. Angels, devils, demons, witches, signs and wonders, astrology, strange portents and forebodings filled the air. Hopefulness for life on earth and the usefulness of education were partially countermanded by a basic pessimism about human nature and the possibility of real social progress. Predestination of the chosen few for salvation, the church as the sole ark of the saved, eschatological fervor, and the anticipation of Christ's imminent second coming for judgment, insofar as this was taken seriously, inhibited social optimism or even meliorism. The rejection of overt reli-

2. The idea of the covenant, with Judaic roots, so important for the Reformed Protestant tradition has been most recently discussed in relation to Zwingli's successor, Bullinger, in an excellent work by J. Wayne Baker, *Heinrich Bullinger and the Covenant: The Other Reformed Tradition* (Athens, Ohio, 1980).

gious asceticism in a works-righteousness context led to a form of in-tramundane asceticism which produced a new kind of layman. If marriage was sanctified anew, sexual pleasure as such continued to be viewed with suspicion, and reproduction and suppression of lust continued to be viewed as the main functions of sex in marriage. In balance, the Reforma-tion did effect radical change, but still within the well-marked boundaries of Christendom. Compared with the dogmatic struggles of the first to the fifth century, the Protestant Reformation was an intramural scrimmage. Clearly merely looking at a religious map of Europe divided between a Protestant north and a Catholic south does not tell us much about the shadings, similarities, and differences.

Popular religion in both Protestant and Catholic areas continued to help people cope with their personal anxiety and with social disorder. Ecclesias-tical and social rites reflected in part a behavioral response to perennial problems of survival in a still predominantly agricultural society. People continued to understand their daily life on the familial and social level, even as urban dwellers who belonged to the guilds, in the context of a supernatural and sacramental world view. Calvin, after all, like Luther, stressed the need for frequent communion. The Lutheran and Anglican liturgies, and with modifications the Reformed cultus, retained the tradi-tional ritual cycle of the church year, related as it was to the annual calendrical cycle. Ecclesiastical feasts were reduced in number in Protes-tant areas with the elimination of saints' days and the change in their significance, for saints were now models of Christian life and no longer intercessors before God. Feast days continued to be connected with solar and lunar cycles. Seed time and harvest, summer and winter, day and night continued as before. The religious and cultural inheritance remained pow-erful, if modified, until the industrial revolution brought about fundamen-tal change and a truly large-scale urban culture evolved.[3]

2. POPULAR CULTURE AND SOCIAL CHANGE

The Spanish humanist Juan Luis Vives in his treatise *De Tradentis Disci-plinis* declared: "We scholars must transfer our solicitude [from princes]

3. Valuable insights are to be gleaned from the work of social anthropologists such as Clifford Geertz, *The Interpretation of Cultures* (New York, 1973). For example, Natalie Zemon Davis, *Society and Culture in Early Modern France* (Stanford, 1975), offers brilliant essays applying social science approaches and anthropological insights to sixteenth-century religious and social history.

to the people." Historians today have heeded this admonition so that social history is very much in vogue. Attention has shifted from castles and mansions to houses and huts, from kings and parliaments to subjects and citizens. There is a new interest in the permanent qualities of everyday life.

Anyone who has read the local history and social histories of the nineteenth century will be unable to join the chorus of adulation of the "new history" or "urban reformation," when most of what appears today with often obstructive abstract social scientific terminology was well-known to historians long ago. Nevertheless, the material bedrock of daily living merits close examination. People are not the sum of geographic, geological, technological, or physical forces, be it in the Mediterranean or in the rocky highlands of Scotland. Climate, fickle weather, harvests or famines, birthrates, food, furniture, nose-blowing habits, the cookery, cash boxes, horse power, discount rates, hygiene, toilet facilities, or the availability of luxuries, such as aperitifs, sugar, pepper, or forks, all grace or disgrace life.[4] It was not until 1596 that a crazy Englishman invented the water closet, and so until then, in the absence of the *cabinet d'aisances,* people used chamber pots, windowsills over the moat, outside latrines, gutters, or bushes. There was little privacy and the extended family shared the limited and open space of the household, be it a palace or a peasant hut. The churches served as an extension of indoor communal space. Much living was done outdoors—in courtyards, the streets, town squares, and even cemeteries.[5]

The bulk of the people—the peasants, artisans, and small traders—lived close to subsistence level, and life was extremely precarious, subject to economic disasters, market fluctuations, war, famine, epidemics. Their condition showed no marked improvement during the first half of the sixteenth century. Despite all the instability, during these decades towns grew. There was an increase in social mobility as "new people" rose. About a fifth of the landed income in England fell into new hands, and the secularization of

4. The greatest assemblage of lore about daily living in the preindustrial world between 1400 and 1800 is Fernand Braudel, *The Structures of Everyday Life* (New York, 1982).

5. Peter Clark, ed., *The Early Modern Town* (New York, 1976), contains such interesting chapters as Braudel on premodern towns, Charles Pythian-Adams on ceremony and the citizen in Coventry, 1450–1550, and J. F. Pound on the social and trade structure of Norwich. Philippe Ariès, *Essais sur l'histoire de la mort en Occident du moyen-âge à nos jours* (Paris, 1975), tr. *Western Attitudes Toward Death: From the Middle Ages to the Present* (Baltimore, 1974), discusses changing attitudes toward death, the development of funeral customs and the role of the graveyard in village and city life.

land in Germany and Scandinavia had a similar effect. In England the tenant farmer, known as a copyholder, was elevated by the profits derived from escalating wool prices to the level of a substantial farmer.

Despite the gradual growth of an urban society, the a priori assumption that the rising bourgeoisie now pressed for and in large part succeeded in obtaining control of society has had to yield before the fact of the resiliency, adaptability, educability, assertiveness, and even economic control by the nobility. The notion of the Reformation as an "early bourgeois revolution," which Marxist historians have substituted for the questionable and even to them no longer tenable thesis that frenetic Thomas Münzer was the true hero of the Reformation, has gained some acceptance among lesser western historians. What remains after the historiographical "storm over the gentry" is the picture of the English gentry powerfully asserting itself against the powers above and the commoners below them. In France the nobility of office (*de la robe*) grew in influence and power, while in Spain the nobility drew close to the monarchy in order to dominate all other elements in the population. As the sixteenth century advanced the territorial princes in Germany and their noble underlings asserted their power as the bourgeois elements in the cities lost initiative and confidence. The "late Reformation" in the cities progressed into the second half of the sixteenth century, but from the time of the inception of the Schmalkald League, the princes, Protestant and Catholic, were clearly the dominant force.[6] Similarly in Italy the Spanish domination introduced feudal aristocratic forces and mores that had become foreign to the culture of the earlier Italian Renaissance. Moreover, the domination in eastern Europe by the great landholders and upper nobility led to the suppression of the lesser nobility, the decline of the market towns, and the reduction to serfdom of the peasants who had emigrated to the east in order to enjoy the privilege of new land and greater personal freedom. Across Europe, then, except in northern Burgundy and in Holland and Zeeland, where the bourgeois element gained in strength, the nobility showed not only surprising staying power, but a new vitality. Sixteenth-century society was and remained hierarchical, with its pyramidal social structure basically intact.[7]

6. See the admirable monograph by Kaspar von Greyerz, *The Late City Reformation in Germany: The Case of Colmar 1522–1628* (Wiesbaden, 1980), for a case study of the "late Reformation."

7. A commendable study is Norman Birnbaum, *Social Structure and the German Reformation* (New York, 1980).

Urban development and the growth of capitalism added to the numbers and to the importance of the bourgeoisie. One cannot speak of classes in a modern postindustrial sense, but those burghers, many of them represented in guilds, who were below the nobility in the social hierarchy and above the artisans and peasants, grew in numbers and financial power during the sixteenth century. At mid-sixteenth century people lived their daily lives much as they had at the start of the sixteenth century. The "extended family" rather than the nuclear family remained the norm. Luther did, on biblical precept, stress the importance of parents and children, but he, or rather his well-organized wife, Kathie, presided over an extended household of forty or more relatives, indigent students, colleagues, and friends. Dietary and personal habits in 1559 were the same as in 1517, with interesting innovations such as snuff taking, tobacco smoking, and coffee drinking originating only later on, with imports from the New World and from Turkey. It cannot be said with any show of authenticity that the first half of the sixteenth century marked a change of life-style in terms of daily living for the vast majority of Europeans.

So traditional, viewing Europe overall, were these decades that the role of women was closely connected with their social position and was "class oriented" rather than sex oriented, and thus might operate to a woman's benefit or detriment, depending on her social standing.[8] Family ties, occupations, inheritances of businesses by widows, who ran them successfully in many cases, patronage or clientage and corporate membership were more important for women's personal identification than was their sex.[9] On the one hand, the upheaval of the Reformation left intact women's traditional roles as housekeepers, mothers, spinners, weavers, midwives, doctors, helpers to their peasant, artisan, or tradesman husband. On the other hand, the general disturbances during the first half of the century introduced a certain fluidity resulting in an enlarged role for women which carried some beyond the household or estate. Women all too often in history have been condemned to be the silent partners in the unfolding of events, but they played an important role in the Reformation movement. Women such as Katherine Zell, wife of Matthias, in Strasbourg

8. Sherrin Marshall Wyntjes, "Women in the Reformation Era," in Renate Bridenthal and Claudia Koonz, eds., *Becoming Visible: Women in European History* (Boston, 1977), p. 167. This chapter, pp. 167–191, provides a brief, excellent overview for western Europe, especially valuable for the Calvinist areas.

9. Wyntjes, "Women," p. 167. Susan V. Lenkey, "Printers Women in the Time of Humanism," *Gutenberg Jahrbuch* (1975), pp. 331–357.

played an important part in the introduction of the Reformation.[10] Some radical groups established virtual equality for women within their sects.

In denying the meritorious value of celibacy Luther correspondingly elevated marriage as a reflection of God's natural order of creation. His own wife, Kathie, had fled with other nuns from a convent, and he learned to love and to appreciate her deeply through the years, recommending the married estate to others. The fact that literally thousands of monks and priests married alleviated the disparity in the numbers of men and women available for marriage. The founding of the Protestant parsonage was important for the time, for underpaid as they were, the ministers and their wives not only cared for their own children but provided shelter for ex-nuns and monks, for religious refugees, and for poor relatives. The parsonage produced an outsized number of famous men of science and letters in subsequent centuries, as biographical dictionaries such as the *Deutsche Nationale Biographie* and the *Dictionary of National Biography* suggest. In the former, of the approximately 1,600 Germans included, 861 were sons of pastors. The convent had become a depository for expendable women just as the monastery and the priesthood had been used for younger sons for whom there was no land or inheritance. Some of those now forced out had trouble readjusting, but most found a place in a household, though, of course, not an independent career.

The reform effort against concubinage, prostitution, illegitimacy, fornication, and adultery served to increase respect for women. The Genevan ordinances and the acts of the Genevan consistory controlling morals in the city were well-known instances of such reform, but increased moral vigor was evident throughout Protestantism. The polygamy of the Anabaptists in Münster was a notorious exception to the rule. The fact that Luther made marriage a civil act having to do with this world and not a sacrament, which is a means of grace, had important implications for a woman's position in subsequent centuries. In the Middle Ages the church allowed divorce or annulment only for consanguinity or adultery. After the Reformation the woman's right to divorce because of the husband's

10. Roland Bainton, *Women of the Reformation,* 3 vols. (Minneapolis, 1971–1977), provides biographical vignettes of women in the Reformation, but without providing a broader historical analysis. There is a long tradition of books of this sort. Over a century ago, for example, James Anderson, a Scottish minister, published *Ladies of the Reformation: Memoirs of the Distinguished Female Characters Belonging to the period of the Reformation in the Sixteenth Century . . . England, Scotland and the Netherlands.* (London, Edinburgh, Glasgow, and New York, 1855).

faults, including impotence, became more widely recognized. Civil laws were more readily subject to change than were church laws. The idea that by eliminating the cult of Mary and of female saints the reformers damaged the position of women is fairly absurd, for they reemphasized the place of Mary and other holy women as models of the godly life, even while denying the need for them as intermediaries between sinners and a gracious God.[11]

The regard of the reformers for women of high estate is evident from the letters of Luther to a patroness of students, Argula von Grumbach, and of Calvin to Jeanne d'Albret, daughter of Marguerite of Navarre. Prominent noblewomen such as Charlotte de Bourbon-Montpensier and Louise de Coligny were leading Calvinists and became the third and fourth wives respectively of William of Orange in the Netherlands. The threads of religious and political allegiance were closely interwoven for women as for men. Women were spared military action, though some were executed for subversive roles in aiding and abetting rebels during the time of the French religious wars and the Dutch revolt against Spain. Women of the so-called middle class became publicly increasingly prominent, just as noble and aristocratic women had been during the Renaissance. Toward the end of the century and during the century following there was a steady loss of status for women until the efforts for equality of the sexes in modern times.[12]

God's chosen, long-suffering, and sometimes forgotten people, the Jews, constituted a religio-social minority group of priceless value to European culture. An island, or rather, a large cluster of islands in a Catholic sea during the Middle Ages, the fortune of the Jews reached low tide in the last centuries of the Middle Ages. How the Reformation affected their situation is a question of great interest. Suddenly the formal unity of the *Corpus Christianorum* was fragmented and sects of all kinds arose and in due course won legal recognition. There was some expectation that the situation of the Jews, too, would improve, but it took the long-range

11. Wyntjes, "Women," p. 179.

12. Natalie Zemon Davis, "City Women and Religious Change in Sixteenth Century France," in Dorothy Gies McGuigan, ed., *A Sampler of Women's Studies* (Ann Arbor, 1973), pp. 17–46, discusses the vigorous part played by women in the economic life of cities on the eve of the Reformation, discusses the changes and long-range effects of Protestantism on the relation between the sexes, and concludes that the Protestant solution still left women unequal, for the world of the sixteenth century remained a man's world in terms of economics and political power.

historical development of religious pluralism and enlightenment before that hope was realized. In the short run, due to the intra-Christian battles, the Jews realized a temporary reprieve from immediate pressure, but they enjoyed no real change of attitude on the part of most Christians of either Catholic or Protestant persuasion.

The expulsion of the Jews from Spain in 1492 marked the climax of Spanish crusading fervor and fanaticism. Aragonese intolerance extended also to Sicily and Naples and brought to an end the Jewish settlement in southern Italy. The existence of many small states both in Italy and Germany prevented uniform legal repressive measures, so that Jewish congregations could seek out less hostile states in which to live. Despite the fact that the very word "ghetto" derives from the Jewish quarter of Venice founded in 1516 near the old *geto* or foundry, the Jews fared better in Italy than in most countries of Europe during the Renaissance period. Ironically they were best situated in Rome and the Papal States, where their utility as financiers and bankers was much appreciated. The inhibitions about usury had made moneylending and pawnbrokerage suspect activities, suitable only for non-Christians, so the Jews had access to high places in Rome, the center of Italian banking. There was agitation in the fifteenth century to establish charitable public pawnbroking to replace the Jews, but for the most part the tolerance and religious indifference characteristic of certain levels of Renaissance society worked to the advantage of the Jews.

The Jews made a distinctive contribution to higher culture during this period. In Spain they had developed cabalism, Jewish mysticism, and an exquisite poetry. Italy, France, and Germany were notable for their concentration on Talmudic studies. In Italy the Jews entered the mainstream of philosophy and vernacular literature. Leon Ebreo (d. 1535), as a member of the Florentine Neoplatonic circle, wrote love poems such as the *Dialoghi d'amore.* Elijah del Medigo of Crete introduced Pico della Mirandola to Aristotle and to the Platonic mysteries of the cabala. Egidio da Viterbo, the general of the Augustinian order, who addressed the opening session of the Fifth Lateran Council (1512–1517), was the patron of the leading Hebrew grammarian of the time, Elias Levita (1469–1549), who had the Zohar translated into Latin. Azariah de' Rossi of Ferrara (1514–1578) introduced a more systematic method to Jewish studies and drew renewed attention to Philo and the Apocrypha. Sixteenth-century Jewish chroniclers such as Gedaliah ibn Jahia of Imola and Joseph haCohen of Genoa added much new knowledge about the history of their people. By

1475 two presses in Italy were publishing Hebrew books and during the decades following the number of presses doing Hebrew proliferated in northern Italy, usually manned by German immigrants. Venice became the center of Hebrew publishing in the sixteenth century. The most prominent printer was a gentile, Daniel Bomberg, who dominated the Jewish book trade for many years.[13]

In Rome the Medici popes Leo X and Clement VII proved to be the most tolerant. Leo X even patronized the publication of the Talmud. Clement VII protected a Jewish adventurer, David Reubeni, who claimed to be a brother of Joseph, king of the tribe of Reuben, sent to gain the support of the European rulers in a war against the Moslems. But toleration fell victim to the Catholic Counter-Reformation. In 1553 all copies of the Talmud found in Rome were burned in public. Pope Paul IV (1555–1559) ordered measures to be taken against the Jews, and twenty-four men and one woman were burned at the stake. On July 12, 1555, he issued a bull that renewed all the oppressive medieval legislation against the Jews, excluding them from professions, limiting their financial and commercial activities, forbidding them to own real estate, and humiliating them by obliging them to wear yellow hats. The ghetto system spread throughout the Catholic half of Europe.[14]

The Reformation seemed at first to offer a respite and new hope for the Jews. The trauma of the late Middle Ages for the Jews had meant expulsion from more than ninety cities in Germany, from Strasbourg in 1388 to Regensburg and Rothenburg ob der Tauber in 1519. It was a mark of distinction and a cause for imperial privilege for states such as Württemberg to be free of Jews (*Jüdenfrei*). Such expulsions diminished during the sixteenth century, in part because attention was directed elsewhere, to the fragmentation of Christendom and the struggle for survival by Christian heretical minorities. But not infrequently did the Jews serve as scapegoats for the troubles of the "last times."

Much attention has been focused upon Luther's attitude toward the Jews, although they were quite peripheral to his reformatory concern, as a comparison of the very few pages on the Jews with the total output in the 110 folio volumes of his collected works suggest. Luther was, nevertheless, the

13. See the collection of text and commentary by Walther Bienert, *Martin Luther und die Juden. Ein Quellenbuch mit zeitgenössischen Illustrationem mit Einführungen und Erläuterungen* (Frankfurt am Main, 1982).

14. *Ibid.*, pp. 241–243; 246–248.

major figure of the time and had a wide and long lasting influence.[15] At the outset of his career, Luther seems to have had little hope of converting the Jews. Then for a brief time he believed that most Jews would be converted. His optimism was grounded in the naive assumption that their conversion would occur once papal scandals were ended and the loving gospel of Christ was preached clearly. It was also based on the eschatological expectation that God's chosen people would be converted just before the second coming of Christ. Between his treatise *That Jesus Christ Was Born a Jew* (1523) and *On the Jews and Their Lies* (1543) he vacillated between a messianic hope for their conversion and a traditional hatred for these people who considered the savior of the world to have been the illegitimate child of Mary. The Jews watched the battle between Luther and the popes with fascination, although the outcome proved to be of little solace to them at the time. They naturally were even held by some to be responsible for the schism within Christianity. Luther's theological precept that not the Jews but the sin of all men brought about the death of Christ was lost sight of in the very time that religious enlightenment introduced a general tolerance of different traditions.[16] Although Johannes Eck, Luther's dedicated opponent, and others wrote vitriolic attacks on the Jews, some of Luther's colleagues, such as his dear friend Justus Jonas, present at Luther's deathbed, and Andreas Osiander, reformer in Nuremberg, were very understanding of the position of the Jews. A more tolerant attitude toward the Jews was not a gift of Christian humanism as such but in some cases of a true understanding of the gospel of love. Erasmus was harshly anti-Judaic, not anti-Semitic, a modern racist term, and Reuchlin was not the hero who fought for all Jewish literature.[17]

15. The pioneer scholarly work, remarkable for its calm impartiality, is that of Rabbi Reinhold Levin, *Luthers Stellung zu den Juden, Neue Studien zur Geschichte der Theologie und Kirche*, 10 (Berlin, 1911). Carl Cohen, "Die Juden und Luther," *Archiv für Reformationsgeschichte*, 54, no. 1 (1963), 38–51, offers an excellent brief summation of the issues. See also M. Stohr, "Luther und die Juden," *Evangelische Theologie*, 20 (April, 1960), 157ff. An exemplary historiographical survey is Johannes Brosseder, *Luthers Stellung zu den Juden im Spiegel seiner Interpreten: Interpretation und Rezeption von Luthers Schriften und Äusserungen zum Judentum im 19. und 20. Jahrhundert vor allem im deutschsprachigen Raum* (Munich, 1972).

16. Heiko A. Oberman, *Wurzeln des Antisemitismus: Christenangst und Judenplage im Zeitalter von Humanismus und Reformation* (Berlin, 1981), p. 165, in a highly personal book, makes this observation. It was secularism, difficult for both Jews and Christians, the new paganism, and modern racism that unleashed the holocaust in "modern" times, much more than a religious situation within which dialogue is still under way.

17. On Reuchlin and the revisionism regarding the Cologne school, see James H. Overfield, "A New Look at the Reuchlin Affair," *Studies in Medieval and Renaissance History*, 8 (1971), 165–207.

One of the most interesting Jewish leaders of this period was Josel or Joselman of Rosheim near Strasbourg (1480–1554), who observed the battle of Clement VII and Charles V with the mere monk Martin Luther and sided with the emperor.[18] In 1507 Josel prevented the expulsion of the Jews from Oberehnheim in Alsace. In 1510 he became the civil spokesman for the Jews in lower Alsace and later for Jewish communities in the whole Empire. After the crowning of Charles V in Aachen in 1520, Josel managed to have the privileges of the Jews in the Empire confirmed. Neither rich nor learned, he had a political sense for the trends of the time and the needs of his coreligionists. In 1530 he triumphed in a disputation with a former Jew who had been baptized a Christian, Antonius Margarita, and also persuaded the Strasbourg city council to prevent the publication of Luther's tract *On the Jews and Their Lies,* which understandably led him to hate Luther. He appeared in the background at the courts of Maximilian and Charles V and was present at the imperial diets. He even obtained a decree that gave a regulated legal basis to Jewish business transactions in the Empire. He deserves credit for much of the improvement in the condition of Jewry in the Empire during the sixteenth century, with expulsions and violence reduced and the protection of public law extended, even though the diet of 1551 once again restricted the privileges of Jews.

Overall the impact of the Reformation throughout Europe on popular culture and social change was not very obvious during the four decades under examination. But the long-range radical effect of the Reformation would prove to be enormous. If Rome was not built in a day, neither could it be leveled in a few decades. The Reformation was a mere chapter, though a critical one, in the chronicle of old Europe.

3. ECONOMIC AND POLITICAL CHANGE

Following the Diet of Worms Luther wrote to Melanchthon on May 26, 1521: "If the pope will take steps against all who think as I do, then Germany will not be without uproar . . . God is arousing the spirits of many, especially the hearts of the common people. It does not seem to me likely that this affair can be checked with force; if the pope begins to put it down, it will become ten times bigger. Germany has very many Karst-

18. Selma Stern, *Josel von Rosheim: Befehlshaber der Judenschaft im Heiligen Römischen Reich Deutscher Nation* (Stuttgart, 1959); (Eng. tr., Philadelphia, 1965).

hansen [peasant followers of Luther]."[19] Luther understood very well the symbiotic relation of religion and socioeconomic and political forces. It remains for the historian with the wisdom of hindsight to venture some conjectures on their interrelation at that time.

The demographic pressures of the sixteenth century clearly contributed greatly to social instability and change. With more limited food supplies, due in part to the cool humid summers from 1500 to 1550, coupled with the cold winters about 1540, and a rapidly growing population, inflation created a difficult situation for all. The effect of the supposed climatic change in 1540 was not immediately reflected in either demographic or economic indices, be it said. Given an increase in population and an inelastic agricultural supply and demand, food prices rose sharply. Although with more labor available industrial output rose, the residual income left to wage earners after providing themselves with food was limited, and thus the demand for industrial output was weak. Food prices rose more rapidly than those of industrial goods and the difficulty thus created for the common folk in this situation is obvious.[20] The population growth also made peasants more expendable, while increasing the cost of goods they had to buy. Fearing the loss of privileges gained during the preceding century and a half of labor shortage, they were ready to fight for their rights. They were increasingly reluctant to share their diminished wealth with lazy monks and ignorant clergy, with silk-clad cardinals and the papacy at Rome. Luther touched a responsive chord when in his *Address to the Christian Nobility of the German Nation*, 1520, he wrote:

How is it that we Germans must put up with such robbery and extortion of our goods at the hands of the pope? If the Kingdom of France has prevented it, why do we Germans let them make such fools and apes of us. . . . And we still go on wondering why princes and nobles, cities and endowments, land and people grow poor. We ought to marvel that we have anything left to eat![21]

There was clearly economic pressure, but also a German national feeling operative. Nevertheless, Luther's cause was religious and the response to his message reflected the deep religiosity of the time.

One might speculate about the continued economic pressures in Eng-

19. *D. Martin Luthers Werke. Briefwechsel* (Weimar, 1930–), II, 347–349; *Luther's Works*, Gottfried Krodel, ed. (Philadelphia, 1972), Letters, I, pp. 48, 233.

20. Anna J. Schwartz, "Secular Price Change in Historical Perspective," *Journal of Money, Credit and Banking*, 5, no. 1, part 2 (Feb., 1973), 243–269; 251.

21. *Luther's Works*, James Atkinson, ed., 44 (Philadelphia, 1966), pp. 142–143.

land correlating with the continuous Protestantization throughout the century, but it would be difficult to demonstrate the connection there or elsewhere in Europe. After all, Spain and Italy, too, experienced economic ills without turning Protestant, and France is possibly the most complex case of all. The middle class was expanding and urban centers enlarging, but the Reformation was not an early bourgeois revolution. It occurred within the bosom of the church, began in an area relatively unaffected by urban culture, even though through mining as well as agriculture the region was involved in economic change. Calvinism was born in France, though berthed in Geneva, and involved a wide range of social estates. It found a second home in Scotland with no middle class to speak of. There is then no one-on-one correlation to be made between economic change and the religious solution of a particular state. Rather, one can assert without fear of contradiction that the economic stress particularly on the common people served to create the social tensions that generated an environment open to religious change throughout half of Europe. The opening of the globe in the age of discoveries was to have enormous economic and political implications for Europe, but the full impact was realized only after the decades under consideration. The question of the relation of Protestantism to capitalism in terms of the Tawney-Weber hypothesis regarding Puritanism, vocation, the work ethic, and the like properly belongs to a later period. During the later 16th and 17th centuries materialistic factors such as the commercial and industrial needs of the western countries, especially of England and Holland, which were Protestant, worked together with religious emphases to produce a new capitalist society.

Politically during the course of these four decades tendencies long under way developed further and more rapidly. If economic activity shifted to the Atlantic seaboard, political trends of the future were also more obviously in evidence in the west. While absolute monarchy in early modern Europe is a creation of the historians, nevertheless in England and France, and by the end of the century also in Spain, the move was clearly in evidence toward greater centralization of power in the hands of the monarch, increased governmental concentration, and the development of a central bureaucracy. The power of the monarchy was also furthered by military success in controlling the nobility and various centers of power and by dominating the church within the particular state. In the Holy Roman Empire Charles V struggled in vain to stem the tide of polycentralism so that the Empire continued as the many Germanies. Except for the Habsburg personal domains, the farther east and north one went, the weaker the royal control became, as in Lithuania and Poland, for example. The tendency toward the consolidation of territorial states militated against the strength of loose conglomerations of lands under some monarch dependent on traditional or inherited legal authority. This overall pattern, described in the initial chapter of this book, was merely accentuated during the decades of the Reformation.

It remains to offer some judgments on the impact of the Reformation on church and state issues. The Protestant Reformation changed certain political realities and forced people to reconsider the traditional concepts of church and state. This rethinking was not a mere prolongation of the medieval struggle between the spiritual and temporal powers, long since resolved to the advantage of the state. The reformers recast theory to accommodate new beliefs and changing circumstances.

In their varying ways the reformers from Luther to the radicals sought to restore the New Testament conception of the church as the communion of saints and a community based upon love rather than upon power and coercion. In that aim they, of course, by and large failed, but there is virtue in their having tried. They sought to turn the church to its spiritual tasks and to destroy the claims of the hierarchy to temporal power.

The reformers altered the concept of the church, shifting the focus from the one visible institution directed by the hierarchy to the church as the communion of saints, all those true believers in Christ, the sole head of the church. The members of that church are known only to God, though the church is not a "Platonic city," but is made up of individual human beings. The marks of the true visible church on earth, Luther held, must necessarily be the preaching of the Word of God and the celebration of the sacraments according to Christ's institution, for the gospel and the sacraments are the means of grace. Zwingli added discipline and Calvin ceremonies as aids in identifying the true evangelical church. Some Anabaptist and other sects held the church to be made up of saints in their groups living holy lives here and now. In matters of church polity, Luther left many questions open, suspended between his ideal of Christian congregations and the reality of community churches (*Volkskirche*), so that the Lutheran church structures ran the gamut from congregationalism to high episcopal.[22] In the Empire the territorial churches managed by consisto-

22. George H. Williams, " 'Congregationalist' Luther and the Free Churches," *Lutheran Quarterly*, 19, no. 3 (August, 1967), 283–295.

ries, usually composed of some laymen, governmental officials, and clergy, became the dominant type. City councils sometimes managed the church in the urban setting. Given his Swiss city-state background, Zwingli made many concessions to state-churchism. Calvin sought the independence of the church from the state. Although in Geneva the church was intertwined with city government, in the context of larger states such as France within which the Calvinists formed a minority group, the presbyterian form of church government made an independent organization possible. The Anabaptists were the most consistent in holding the visible church to be a sanctified body separated from the state, civil society, and civic duties. The nature of England's Reformation led to a different solution, and Anglicans thought of their church as the universal church in England under royal headship. Scandinavian Lutheranism was to develop a pattern not unlike that of England.

The reformers asserted the absolute distinction between the spiritual and the secular authorities, citing the words of Christ: "Render unto Caesar the things that are Caesar's and unto God the things that are God's," historically one of the most influential texts in the New Testament, Leopold von Ranke asserted. The secular authorities were to care for the external needs of the church but were not to interfere with doctrine, worship, and sacraments. In reality all too often the one who paid the piper called the tune, but the seed of the idea of the separation of church and state was planted.

The Protestant emphasis upon Christian vocation helped to transcend the medieval dualism of sacred and secular callings. Now the secular order was given authenticity on the basis of natural law *(lex charitatis)* and was not on a lower plane than the spiritual authority, not dependent for its authority upon ecclesiastical sanction. Unlike Jacob Burckhardt, Lord Acton, and other modern theorists who saw power as necessarily evil, for the reformers power was not in itself evil and the state was an instrument of justice and social good, not merely there for the repression of evil. It was, as Luther put it, the "Kingdom of God's left hand" and positive law was to reflect natural law or the law of love. None of the reformers, however, had any notion of a secular state in the modern western democratic or totalitarian sense, divorced from religious or ethical ties. Luther, Calvin, Zwingli, Knox, and some Anglicans sought to sharpen the consciences of rulers. They enlarged the state's area of responsibility in charities and education, for example, in tune with the overall tendency in evidence already in late medieval cities and states. Like Erasmus and the

Christian humanists, the reformers thought it desirable for rulers to be and to act as Christians, but their authority did not depend on their church connection but upon natural law.

The problem of resistance to tyrannical governments came into sharp focus for the Protestant minorities subjected to violence and coercion by Catholic rulers, *et contra*. Luther went through a personal development on this point, for he moved from a position that essentially required obedience to "the powers that be that are ordained of God" and at the most allowed for passive resistance or martyrdom, to a position that permitted resistance to the emperor on the part of the estates, princes, or electors, if the emperor defied the laws of the empire over him. Moreover, by emphasizing "obedience to God rather than man," Luther substituted a quickened personal conscience for traditional rules, a view reflected in the *Apology to the Augsburg Confession,* which called for obedience "not only because of punishment but on account of conscience." When Charles V's armies had overrun Saxony and other Lutheran lands in the late 1540s, the doctrine of the right of lesser magistrates under the law to resist superiors received a clear formulation in the *Confession and Apology of Magdeburg.*

Calvin never went quite so far as Luther in his resistance theory, but in the context of repression in France the Calvinists such as Pierre Viret, the Monarchomachs, Philippe Mornay, and others went much farther. The *Vindiciae Contra Tyrannos* used the Roman law principle of co-tutorship to legitimize the right of higher magistrates to restrain the monarch. The covenant idea in Calvinism, derived from Calvin's own preoccupation with the history of Israel, contributed to social-contract thinking, a precondition of constitutionalism. This idea, taken up by Heinrich Bullinger in Zurich and others, joined with natural law concepts, the idea of the universal priesthood of all believers, and the fact that religious uniformity had been broken, all contributed to the growth of representative government. On the Catholic side the Sorbonnists of the early sixteenth century such as Maur and Almain and the Spanish neo-Thomists of the last half of the century such as Vitoria and Suarez provided a scholastic basis for constitutionalism, contract theory, and absolutism.[23] In political theory our four decades experienced a gap between Machiavelli and Bodin which the writings of Budé, Cujacius, Ponet, Starkey, and others could not fill.

23. On Reformation political theory, see the most intelligent recent statement by Quentin Skinner, *The Foundations of Modern Political Thought,* II, *Age of the Reformation* (Cambridge, 1978).

Perhaps the greatest political contribution of the reformers to political thought may have been an element of stability derived from their theocentric orientation. They had a way of putting earthly potentates into perspective. In the final edition of Calvin's *Institutes* he wrote these concluding words:

And that our hearts may not fail us, Paul stimulates us with another consideration—that Christ has redeemed us at the immense price which our redemption cost him, that we may not be submissive to the corrupt desires of men, much less be slaves to their impiety.

In his *Commentary on Psalm 2* Luther wrote:

Our job . . . is to have a large open eye so that we can with one glance take in all the kings with all their wisdom and power and take them for a burning straw which He who established heaven, earth and all things can extinguish with one breath.[24]

For the wars of religion, for independence and the age of the great revolutions to come, the type of inner-directed citizen rather than mere subject constituted the solid core of modern political progress. "On their feet before God, on their knees before men; on their knees before God, on their feet before men" is an old saying not without relevance in early modern times.

4. CULTURAL CHANGE

Ironically the Renaissance in Italy lasted into the first decades of the Reformation. It is a moot point whether the Catholic Reformation ended the Renaissance or whether the end of the Renaissance made possible the frigidity and repressiveness of the Counter-Reformation. The Savonarola incident in Florence suggests that below the surface glitter of Renaissance culture a deep sea of traditional attitudes, loyalties, superstitions, resentments, and anti-intellectualism existed. The Medici popes Leo X and Clement VII, as well as Paul III, who has been called the last of the Renaissance popes, presided over high Renaissance culture even as they tried to cope with the religious revolution in the North.

Leonardo da Vinci died in 1519 and Raphael in 1520, but Michelangelo Buonarroti (1475–1564) was fated to live on into a century far different in spirit from that which they had known. Apprenticed to Domenico Ghirlandaio, he worked as a tyro for Lorenzo de' Medici. In the Medici

24. *Luther's Works,* Jaroslav Pelikan, ed., 12 (St. Louis, 1955), p. 12.

circle he encountered the spirit of grandeur and high style that had such a profound influence on his work. There he heard discourses on Neoplatonic philosophy that conditioned his highly personal poetry and his theory of art. Given to melancholy and brooding, he worked with restless fury on papal commissions, the Sistine ceiling, Julius II's tomb, the Medici chapel tombs. The two Medici popes, Leo X and Clement VII, became his patrons though he was not devoted to them. During the brief restoration of the Florentine Republic (1527–1530) he was made responsible for the city's fortifications but with the return of the Medici he reluctantly reentered their service and did the four giant figures in marble of *Day, Night, Dawn* and *Twilight* for the Medici chapel. Paul III had him do *The Last Judgment* for the front wall of the Sistine Chapel, commissioned him to design the Farnese Palace in Rome and a number of buildings to crown the Capitoline Hill, and appointed him chief architect of St. Peter's Cathedral in 1547. He reworked the designs of his predecessors on a grander scale, supervised the construction of the supports and lower sections of the giant dome. How ironic that indulgences sold to help pay for its construction triggered the Protestant revolt. After sixty he took up less strenuous labors, wrote passionate sonnets to a young Roman aristocrat, Tommaso dei Cavalieri, and suffered intensely when Vittoria Colonna, a young widow of great mind and piety died, ending a devoted friendship of twelve years.

A very different character was Benvenuto Cellini (1500–1571), whom Michelangelo once called "the greatest goldsmith of whom the world has ever heard." A supreme egotist and brawler, he was often in flight from the law. He fled from Rome, where he had been accused of stealing jewels from the papal tiara, and entered the service of Francis I of France. His most famous masterpiece was the gold and enamel saltcellar made for the king, with reclining figures of Neptune and a sea nymph in a setting of waves, dolphins, and other sea creatures. He returned to Florence where he lies buried in the Church of the Annunziata.

Venice, as a city, had a flair for artistic rites and public ceremonies. The queen of the Adriatic developed a distinctive school of art notable for its use of oil as binder for pigment and for the use of canvas rather than plaster-covered walls or wooden panels. The tradition of Gentile and Giovanni Bellini was carried forward by such leading Venetian artists as Giorgione and the long-lived Titian (c. 1477 1576), known for his voluptuous Venuses and beautiful landscapes. In 1516 he became the official state painter and received commissions to do paintings such as *The Assumption of the Virgin* and *The Martyrdom of St. Lawrence* for the city's churches. He did numerous portraits of famous men, among them Charles V, Paul III, Cardinal Alessandro, and Duke Ottavio Farnese. Tintoretto (1518–1594) and Veronese (1528–1588) continued deep into the sixteenth century the Venetian tradition of rich colors, gorgeous landscapes, fleshy human bodies, classical mythology, and secular themes. The architect Andrea Palladio (1518–1580), who designed his Villa Rotundo with a classical dome and pilasters, carried on the classical motifs.

Michelangelo, Titian, and Tintoretto, while they carried forward the best Renaissance traditions of classical measure and balance in art, in their individual ways lost the decorum of their more confident period and yielded to less controlled emotion. The next generation of artists gave way to sometimes violent and openly expressed emotions. Their style has been referred to as mannerism, a mere transition between the Renaissance and the baroque. Giorgio Vasari, the author of the most famous history of art, *Lives of the Most Eminent Painters, Sculptors, and Architects* (1550), commended eclecticism and seemed to suggest that the *belle manière* meant a variety of things. Modern art historians seem to be rehabilitating mannerism despite the extravagance and emotionalism of the artists of this period. Parmigianino, Il Rosso Fiorentino, and Bronzino, for example, are more highly appreciated for their personal vision of their work.

By the end of the fifteenth century Italian artists had absorbed the technical skills of Flemish artists such as Jan and Hubert van Eyck and Roger van der Weyden, with their mastery of minute detail. At the turn of the sixteenth century northern artists were coming to Italy to learn and Italian artists were invading the north, serving the courts, secular and episcopal. Among the northerners who studied in Italy were Quentin Metsys (1466–1530), Lucas van Leyden (1494–1533), Bernaert van Orley (1493–1541), and the best artist of them all, Albrecht Dürer (1471–1528).

Dürer of Nuremberg was a master of woodcuts, copper etching, silverpoint, charcoal, watercolors, and oil painting. He journeyed both to Venice (1505–1507) and to the Netherlands seeking to perfect his technique. In Venice he learned to know Giovanni Bellini and absorbed the Renaissance spirit of inquiry about flora and fauna, anatomy, the proportions of the human body, and perspective, and he later wrote treatises on *The Doctrine of Proportion* and on *The Art of Measurement*. Dürer became an ardent follower of Luther, whose evangelical teaching, he said, helped him out of great anxieties. His conversion was reflected in both his subject matter and style. As a Catholic he had transmitted to the north the Renaissance spirit of classical antiquity, alongside medieval themes. As a Lutheran he practically abandoned secular subjects, except for scientific illustrations, traveler's records, and portraits. He abandoned the "decorative style" almost entirely and centered his attention on religious subjects such as the apostles, evangelists, and the passion of Christ, all done with a strangely impassioned austerity.[25]

The Reformation made both a negative and a positive impression upon the fine arts. Initially the Protestant areas suffered a decline in artistic quality and creativity. There was no worthy successor to Dürer in the north until Rembrandt. The moral rigor of the Counter-Reformation at first inhibited the free classical expression of Renaissance art and the individualism and emotionalism of mannerism, but the Catholic Reformation gave birth to the baroque style, which gave expression to the renewed religious ardor of the church.

Luther strongly favored religious art and admired the skill of artists and craftsmen. His religious principle was that the beautiful should be kept so long as there was nothing in the Scriptures forbidding it. Thus ecclesiastical art should enhance worship and adorn the house of God, but should not be put to idolatrous use. When the Zwickau prophets and Wittenberg radicals began an iconoclastic destruction of religious statues and stained-glass windows, he came down from the Wartburg and stopped the mayhem. He spoke out again against the wanton destruction of church and monastic art in 1525 during the violence of the Peasants' War. The iconoclasm inherent in the "Puritan" element of Protestantism, which like Islam took literally the Old Testament commandment "Thou shalt make no graven images," persisted from Karlstadt and Zwingli to Cromwell. Zwingli thought that any artistic representation of Christ and the saints in a church was inherently idolatrous. He prepared the way for the "cleansing of the temple" when the reformed laity stripped the Great Minster in Zurich of its artwork and whitewashed the walls, like those of a Moslem mosque. Anabaptists and spiritualists had no need for religious art. Sculpture fell into a precipitous decline. Calvin was closer to Luther's positive position, although he favored simplicity in church art and architecture, a

25. Erwin Panofsky, *The Life and Art of Albrecht Dürer* (Princeton, 1955), p. 199.

table, for example, for communion rather than a high altar, which suggested renewed sacrifice.

The Reformation overall was important for art and architecture in four ways.[26] First, the attitude of the major reformers toward art in general and toward ecclesiastical art in particular was important for their fate in the centuries following. The tension, for example, between the constructive attitude of Luther and Calvin and that of the literalistic Zwingli and the destructive radicals persisted into the conflict of Anglicans and Puritans in the seventeenth century both in old England and in New England.

Second, the Reformation teachings were given expression by Reformation artists. The altar pieces, pulpit decorations, and other religious paintings of Lucas Cranach and others emphasized Christ crucified, the Word, law and gospel, the Lord's Supper as a communion of reformed believers, baptism as a congregational event, and the like. The Lutherans had no immediate need to develop a distinctive architecture, for they inherited many more churches and chapels in the overchurched cities than they needed, and they even, as in Augsburg, shared church structures with the Catholics. The Reformed Protestants, on the other hand, when able to move from private dwellings to public houses of worship inclined toward a meetinghouse structure rather than the traditional basilica or Gothic church emphasizing the altar. It is sometimes said that the doctrine of the priesthood of believers gave impetus to the portraiture of laymen, but the shift to the portrayal of individual patrons and to secular themes outside of ecclesiastical art took place also in Catholic countries.

Third, the reformers' emphasis upon the Book and the printed word directed artists to book and pamphlet illustrations, not only of religious but also of scientific works. Cranach, for example, did many illustrations for Luther's books and pamphlets. The stress on the printed word, however, may have been subversive to the visual arts in directing attention away from image to word, from pictures to verbally expressed ideas.

Fourth, social upheavals attendant on the Reformation affected adversely the lives and prosperity of the artists themselves. Til Riemenschneider, the exquisite wood carver, had his fingers smashed in punishment for his role in the Peasants' War. The wars of religion made the lives of the artists insecure. The economic decline of the Empire and lack of

26. Carl C. Christensen, *Art and the Reformation in Germany* (Athens, Ohio, and Detroit, 1979), is the most recent examination of the subject. See also his article "The Reformation and the Decline of German Art," *Central European History,* VI, no. 3 (Sept., 1973), 207–232.

wealthy patrons forced an artist like Hans Holbein the Younger, famous for his portraits of Erasmus, to leave for England, where he painted English royalty and aristocracy, and died in London in 1543. Hans Baldung Grien died in 1545, Lucas Cranach in 1553, leaving no worthy successors. Nevertheless, the next great period of European art developed in the Netherlands, where Dutch Reformed religion and capitalist prosperity combined to make life for artists viable. The portraiture, self-portraits, civic consciousness, household scenes, and the tempestuous spirit of the time were reflected in the paintings of that period, culminating in the work of Rembrandt. Jacob Burckhardt himself took religious differences into account when contrasting Rembrandt and Rubens.

Catholic art suffered during the first half of the sixteenth century from the military catastrophes and the political degradation of Italy. From the invasion of Charles VIII of France in 1494 to Spanish domination directly in southern Italy and indirectly through puppets such as Duke Lorenzo I de' Medici in Florence, Italy was subjected to foreign domination and exploitation. The immediate consequence of the prudery and moralistic rigor of the Counter-Reformation was to produce a reaction against the pagan elements and nude figures in Renaissance art. "Breeches painters" were assigned to clothe the nudes in the Borgian apartments of the Vatican and even some of the figures in Michelangelo's *Last Judgment* in the Sistine Chapel. In Florence Ammanti apologized publicly for having done the nudes on the fountain of Neptune. Artists were directed to stress those very doctrines under attack by the Protestants such as Mary as *Semper Virgo* and Queen of Heaven, the assumption of Mary into heaven, the apotheosis of saints, Corpus Christi processions, and triumphant pontiffs holding in their hands the keys of St. Peter.[27] Sculpturing was protected in Catholic areas such as Italy, Austria, and Bavaria, which made possible the creative genius of a Giovanni Bernini and his masterpiece *The Ecstasy of St. Teresa.*

Rome itself gave birth to the baroque as the most characteristic style of the Catholic revival. It may be argued that all the elements of the baroque are to be found in the works of Michelangelo, especially the tendency toward heroic proportions. Baroque artists and architects built churches, palaces, and piazzas as large as finances made possible. The main church of the Jesuits, the Il Gesú, became the prototype of baroque churches

---

27. See the classic work of Charles Dejob, *De l'influence du Concile de Trente sur la littérature et les beaux-arts chez peuples catholiques* (Paris, 1884), and Erwin Iserloh et al., *Reformation and Counter-Reformation* (New York, 1980), pp. 565–566.

throughout Europe. It is possible that its architects derived ideas from Michelangelo, who had offered to design it. Giacomo Vignola (1507–1573) directed its construction, with a broad tunnel vaulted nave, a modest-sized dome over the crossing, and a small series of side chapels along each side in place of side aisles. The high ceilings and domes of baroque edifices were used for enormous paintings depicting the apotheosis of saints, the ascension of Christ, or the assumption of Mary.

If the effect of the Reformation on the visual arts was ambivalent, its positive contribution to music is clear. The sixteenth century has been called the golden age of music. Luther considered music the noblest of the arts; like theology, it could calm the soul and drive away evil spirits. One panel of the porcelain stove in his living room depicted Frau Musica as queen of the arts. He wrote a famous letter in 1530 from the Feste Coburg to the Catholic Swiss musician Ludwig Senfl (c. 1492–1555), the Wittelsbach court musician in Munich, expressing admiration for his work and asking him to compose a polyphonic arrangement of an antiphon he had loved since his youth. He loved the compositions of Josquin des Prez (d. 1521) and declared that his music preached the gospel of grace. Each meal in the Black Cloister ended with all singing a song. He was talented with the lute and composed some eight original hymns such as "A mighty fortress is our God" and the Christmas hymn "From heaven above to earth I come." He composed the first part of the German mass and adapted German popular tunes to religious stanzas. Congregational singing of chorales and other hymns became a standard part of every worship service. Music was no longer the province of a chanting priest or choir, for all participated in the service, and the first Lutheran hymnal was published as early as 1524. The Lutheran musical tradition is familiar to all who know the compositions of Heinrich Schütz, Paul Gerhardt, or Johann Sebastian Bach.

Zwingli had a magnificent baritone voice, loved music, and encouraged it outside the church. Within the church he applied his principle that nothing other than those things expressly commanded by the Scripture should be used in worship, and so he had the organs removed from the churches in Zurich, believing that their sensuous tones distracted the mind from pure worship.[28] After his death, however, Zurich enjoyed the restoration of the organ to the Minister and the reintroduction of congrega-

28. See Charles Garside, *Zwingli and the Arts* (New Haven, 1966).

tional singing. Calvin favored congregational singing of the Psalms and he approved the first edition of the French Psalter in 1562. His own teacher, the French poet Clement Marot, composed most of the 150 or so versified renditions of the Psalms, and Calvin's colleague Theodore Beza finished the edition. As in the case of Luther's use of folk tunes, this popular songbook adapted French *chansons* to the versified Psalms. One of the best Calvinist composers, Claude Goudimel (1505–1572), published several editions of musical settings for the Psalms. Music, too, served the cause of religion. Through Methodism Lutheran music was to influence evangelical church music in England and America.[29]

The late fifteenth-century masters of the Flemish school, such as Jean d'Okegem (d. 1495) and Jacob Obrecht (d. 1505), were the great innovators in music by developing polyphony and introducing a new technique of imitation with voices beginning one after another rather than simultaneously. Adrian Willaert (c. 1480–1562), a Flemish musician, served as choir director of St. Mark's in Venice. Italy made its contribution in the sixteenth century, especially in Rome and Venice, though not in theory. The most renowned composer of the century was Giovanni da Palestrina (c. 1525–1594) who built on the Flemish composers and developed their contrapuntal technique. He was the authentic musical voice of the Catholic Reformation, serving as the composer for the papal choir and as music director of churches in Rome for over forty years. He was declared by the Council of Trent to be the official model for all musical composers serving the church. In music as in art, the contribution of Venice came later in the century, as did the greatest musical invention of the century, opera, which interpreted in music the visual scenes of drama on the stage.

One area of obvious continuity between the Renaissance and Reformation was in education. The humanists had reemphasized the importance of the classics, following especially Quintillian and Cicero, and new methods of instruction. The humanist curriculum played down dialectic, dear to the scholastics, in favor of rhetoric, grammar, poetry, history, moral philosophy, and classical languages. Their schools were elitist and served the higher circles of society. The reformers emphasized three main points in their educational philosophy: (1) universal compulsory education; (2) teaching as a divine vocation; (3) the importance of the humanistic curriculum.

29. H. G. Haile, *Luther: An Experiment in Biography* (New York, 1980), pp. 49–54, especially p. 54.

Luther and his followers stressed the importance of universal, popular, compulsory education for boys and girls and special education for those with greater ability. The motivation was basically religious in order to eliminate illiteracy and to make catechetical instruction and Bible reading for each Christian possible. In his *Address to the Municipalities, Sermon on Keeping Children in School* and many other pedagogical writings, Luther hammered away at this theme. A great effort was made, of course, to improve the education of the clergy, for the clergy were the cultural leaders in all communities.[30] Education for girls was to help them be better wives, household managers, culture bearers as well as child bearers. While this well-circumscribed aim may be displeasing to some who rightly hope for more for womankind, in the context of the time—not to say in the perspective of other cultures throughout the world—this insistence on education for girls was very important. In later centuries many went on to higher education, and a few did then.

Like Luther, Melanchthon, who has gone down in history as "the preceptor of Germany," declared that education was essential not only for the church but for the state. As Melanchthon expressed it: "the ultimate end which confronts us is not private virtue alone but the interest of the public weal." In the *Ordinances* of 1541 Calvin wrote: "Since it is necessary to prepare for the coming generations in order not to leave the church a desert for our children, it is imperative that we establish a college to instruct the children and to prepare them for both the ministry and civil government." As early as 1536 the Geneva citizens in a public assembly on Calvin's urging swore that they would "maintain a school to which all would be obliged to send their children." Scotland and several Protestant states in Germany were the first in the world to eliminate illiteracy in the nineteenth century, a fact attributable to the early emphasis on schooling in the sixteenth century based upon the religious idea of the universal priesthood of all believers and the Bible open to all readers. In Scotland John Knox and his coreligionists drew up *The First Book of Discipline,* which

30. Gerald Strauss, *Luther's House of Learning: Indoctrination of the Young in the German Reformation* (Baltimore and London, 1978), largely on the basis of the parish visitation reports and reflecting the reformers' own disappointment with the success of the Reformation, points up the limitations of the Protestant achievement in elevating the clergy and educating the people in literacy and morality. The visitation reports were, of course, intended primarily to nose out abuses and weaknesses, not to celebrate successes. One can do much in a few decades, but, as G. R. Elton once observed, the reformers could not change human nature.

provided for a national system of education with parish schools, Latin schools in larger places, and education for all.

What does not happen locally does not happen at all. A look at a single diocese such as York reveals a much broader spread of education than was once held. While many parish priests were not well educated, lived like yeomen, and knew barely enough Latin to say mass, others were eager students of patristic and medieval authors. Besides the chantry schools and endowed grammar schools, many clergy gave the youth of their parishes some elementary education. There were more grammar schools than once was thought, about forty-six of them during the first half of the sixteenth century, and no fewer than eighty new schools were added between 1545 and 1603 to serve a population of some 20,000 boys. The Protestant clergy included a far higher proportion of literate and even learned men than any other social group, and the number of cultured laymen, including the gentry, increased during the Tudor period.[31] While the picture of the initial impact of the Reformation on a regional society in mid-Tudor England cannot be applied everywhere, it is quite evident that with wide variations Protestantism did promote education and that Protestant Europe as the centuries wore on outstripped Catholic Europe in that respect.

The belief that teaching is a divine vocation, as Luther put it, "next to the ministry the most useful, greatest and the best," created an ethos for the teacher in church and public schools which has survived to the present time. The reformers also developed secondary schools for boys capable of further education and advancing toward the university. In the medieval period mere children in their mid-teens went from school to the university, but the founding of the gymnasium in Germany and the lycée in France altered the educational structure. The Jesuit academies followed the new pattern. Melanchthon provided the inspiration and guidance in the founding of Protestant gymnasia in Nuremberg, Strasbourg, and many other cities. The evangelical gymnasium in Strasbourg founded by Johannes Sturm with its objective of "wise and eloquent piety" became a model for such secondary schools in northern Europe. Sturm and Roger Ascham, tutor to Elizabeth I and great Tudor educator, were close friends and educational confrères. Claude Baduel, who studied with Melanchthon, observed Sturm, and knew Calvin in Geneva, became the reformer and refounder of the academy in Nîmes. So the network of schools spread.

31. A. G. Dickens, *Lollards and Protestants in the Diocese of York 1509–1558* (London, 1959), pp. 5–6.

The impact of the Reformation on the universities was of critical importance. Luther had declared the universities to be disaster areas badly in need of reform and along with several Augustinians he began with the reformation of the University of Wittenberg. Students who came to the theological faculty preconditioned by years of scholastic training in dialectic could not grasp the new evangelical approach to biblical texts. Luther favored rhetoric, classical languages, history, poetry, in fact, the whole humanist curriculum on the arts level. Largely through Melanchthon, the Wittenberg reformers became a loose model for the reform of older universities in lands that became Protestant and for the newly founded Protestant universities beginning with Marburg, founded by Philipp of Hesse, Rostock, Jena, Altdorf, and several others.[32] During the sixteenth century the universities once again assumed an importance for cultural leadership which they had enjoyed in the thirteenth and fourteenth centuries and were not to regain thereafter until the nineteenth and twentieth centuries.

The other great magisterial reformer, John Calvin, was a humanist and a university man. When he founded the Geneva academy, which became the University of Geneva, he provided for a "humanist" curriculum with a special emphasis on the classical languages and basic humanist subjects. His address at the opening of the academy and that of Theodore Beza served as a platform for the Calvinist universities, combining humanism and evangelical religion into a powerful and long-lived amalgam. The Calvinists, too, founded new universities in Montauban, Nîmes, Saumur, Sedan, Edinburgh, Leiden, Amsterdam, Groningen, Utrecht, and Franeker in the decades that followed. In some Calvinist areas they reformed universities such as Heidelberg and founded Emanuel College in Cambridge. The reformers viewed higher education as serious business, a *negotium cum deo,* an activity carried on together with God.

Within the Catholic Church the Brethren of the Common Life had cultivated a classical tradition, teaching and preaching the safe and moral classics. Their movement died out during the sixteenth century, as many members moved over to the evangelical cause. But the Jesuits now took over the humanist curriculum in their schools. The students read such literary and moral philosophical works as Cicero's *Tusculan Disputations* and letters, plays of Terence, Virgil's *Eclogues,* Ovid's *Tristia,* the histories of Sallust, and Horace's *Ars poetica.* Humanistic subjects took on an in-

32. See Chapter 1, "The Impact of the Reformation on the Universities," Leif Grane, ed., *University and Reformation* (Leiden, 1981), pp. 9–31.

creasingly school-like character as the century wore on in both Protestant and Catholic schools, compared with the verve which once characterized the enthusiasm for the classics in the Italian and northern Renaissance.

The impact of the Reformation on letters is less obvious than that on art. During the four initial decades of the Reformation a few humanist writers lingered on and the full flower of literary achievement in Montaigne's France, the Spain of Cervantes, Elizabethan England, or the Germanies of Schiller and Goethe had not as yet been realized. The leading minds of the time were devoted to religious subjects. Luther's literary and poetic productions were prodigious, and his marvelous translation of the Bible helped shape the German language and has remained a literary influence down to the present time. Calvin through his many French writings and relentless logic became a formative influence upon the French language and mind. In England Cranmer's liturgy revealed a remarkable poetic talent and the whole *Book of Common Prayer* is itself a moving literary achievement. The Protestant publicists contributed to the strength and flexibility of that linguistic glacial moraine, the English language.

Following on the Renaissance humanist assertion that Latin is the truly legitimate language for literature, the reformers brought the European vernacular languages to adulthood. Yet, ironically, the reformers' insistence upon the normative value of the classical languages meant that much literature of the Reformation period, prose as well as poetry, continued to be produced in Latin rather than in the vernacular.[33] Of course, Hans Sachs, the shoemaker, wrote poetry in the vernacular, calling Luther the "nightingale of Wittenberg" and inspiring the opera on the "Mastersingers of Nuremberg" (Wagner). And another Lutheran artisan, Jacob Boehme, seemed to be a simple man, but offered poetic visions of the world and universe that were to inspire one whole scientific approach to the understanding of nature. Silesia was to become a vital center of humanistic, evangelical, and scientific progress in the decades following. A price was paid for the theological preoccupation of the best minds of the time, for the religious struggle directed the intellectual energies of the most able people away from letters to immediately serious and pressing subjects.

33. A point that seems to escape the brilliant British historian G. R. Elton, "Introduction: The Age of the Reformation," *The New Cambridge Modern History,* II, *The Reformation,* pp. 17–18. On this subject see the chapter on "The Course of German Humanism" in Heiko A. Oberman, ed., *Itinerarium Italicum* (Leiden, 1975), pp. 371–436.

Devotional literature, polemical treatises, sermon books, catechisms, hymnals, and religious poetry all constituted an important part of Protestant literature and the printed works of the time.

The writing of history took a great step forward during the Reformation. In preparation for the Leipzig debate with Dr. Eck in 1519, Luther was obliged to study the positions on doctrinal issues not only of the Scriptures but of the fathers of the church and of church councils. He called history the "mother of truth." He prepared a chronological chart on which he tried to harmonize the dates of biblical and secular history. He wrote the forewords for a number of histories such as that of Cuspinian, historian to Charles V, and Galeatus Capella, historian of the Sforzas. He lamented the fact that as a student he had been forced to spend years on a sterile dialectic and was not given the opportunity to study history and poetry. Melanchthon wrote a preface to Carion's *Chronicle,* enlarged it, and rewrote most of it. Sebastian Franck wrote a notable history of the world which in its independence, originality, and scope was superior to the traditional chronicles. The two most outstanding historians of the time were Johannes Aventinus (d. 1534), who wrote his *Bavarian Chronicle* by going back to the sources, and Johannes Philippson, called Sleidanus, author of an excellent work, *Commentaries on the State of Religion and on the Reign of Charles V.*

History was to become a weapon for controversy in the hands of Matthias Flacius Illyricus (1520–1575), who had studied in Venice, Basel, and Tübingen before coming to Wittenberg, where he became professor of Hebrew in 1540. In his *Magdeburg Centuries,* organizing the history of the church by centuries, he sought to prove that the papacy rested on false foundations. His work became the center of a long-lasting polemic, attacked by Catholic apologists such as Cardinal Baronius, Cardinal Bellarmine, Florimond de Raemond, and many others. This type of polemical history persisted into the next century, with Veit Ludwig von Seckendorf embroiled in historical controversy with the Jesuit Louis Maimbourg. Protestant historians in general accepted humanist historical assumptions, the stress on going back to the sources, the idea that history has pragmatic utility, the prejudice against the Middle Ages as the dark ages, a "thousand years without a bath," and the assumption that the Renaissance and Reformation marked the beginning of the modern age. Given their religious fervor, they also stressed a providential interpretation of history and saw the hand of God in history, rewarding and punishing.

French literature came alive during the reign of Francis I. Étienne Dolet (1508–1546) in his *Commentaries on the Latin Tongue* celebrated the progress of literature in his day. He trusted in the power of secular scholarship to reveal the truth and assumed that if people knew what was right, they would do it. He was burned in Paris as a freethinker, the "martyr of the Renaissance." His friend François Rabelais (c. 1495–1553), a witty satirist, was a Benedictine monk and a physician. His works *Gargantua* and *Pantagruel* became world literary classics. They are full of digressions and serve as a catchall for the intellectual currents of French humanist society. His work is in the tradition of Christian humanism, a kind of Erasmian *Praise of Folly*. But the humorless Sorbonne censured his works and the Parlement forbade their sale. During the period of repression toward the end of Francis I's reign, Rabelais thought it the better part of valor to move to Metz, an imperial city, to practice medicine.

The most learned man of the time was Guillaume Budé (1468–1540), a classical scholar, master of Greek, commentator on Roman law, student of numismatics and the ancient monetary system. Erasmus called him the "marvel of France." Francis I thought him to be an ornament of his court. Along with Jean du Bellay, bishop of Narbonne, he persuaded Francis to form the Collegium Trilingue in 1530, which evolved into the Collège de France. Budé also used his influence on the king to get him to found a library at Fontainebleau, which developed into the Bibliothèque Nationale. He was suspected of being a crypto-Calvinist and after his death his widow moved to Geneva, where his son was active in serving the Bourse Française, Calvin's charitable organization, also used as a front for Protestant subversive activities in France.

In spite of the religious wars and the fact that Henry II and later kings were not the generous patrons Francis I had been, some of the members of the Pléiade, a circle of poets and literary figures, such as Joachim du Bellay, author of the *Defense and Illustration of the French Language,* wrote in this period. But the story of Ronsard, Peter Ramus, and Montaigne belongs to the half century following.

Spain suffered a definite loss in literary culture because of the Inquisition's persecution. The *Alumbrados,* a mystical movement centering in the Benedictine monastery up a craggy cliff at Montserrat, were viewed as heretics despite their strongly Christocentric piety. In 1555, Pope Paul IV condemned the *Espiritualistos* of Spain. The inquisitors could not distinguish between Erasmians and Lutherans and fiercely suppressed them all. Small groups of "Lutherans" met secretly in Valladolid and Seville, but they were discovered and tortured, and eventually fled. Many of them in exile joined the Calvinists. In this dangerous environment such leading intellectuals as the Erasmian Juan de Valdés (1500–1541) and his brother Alfonso chose to leave Spain. Juan, the author of *The Dialogue of Mercury and Caron,* dreading the Inquisition, moved to Naples in 1530, and Alfonso entered the service of Charles V in the Empire. Juan de Valdés moved from Naples to Rome, where he served Pope Clement VII as an attendant, and then in 1533 returned to Naples. He wrote brief commentaries on Paul's epistles to the Romans and Corinthians and influenced Peter Carnesecchi (1508–1567) to accept the doctrine of justification by faith. He also influenced Bernardino Ochino, Peter Martyr Vermigli, Giuls Gonzaga, and Vittoria Colonna toward an evangelical understanding of Christianity. Juan Luis Vives (1492–1540), an Erasmian vitally interested in education, spent his life outside Spain, in France, England, and the Netherlands. The foremost humanist Antonio de Nebrijo (1441–1522), a splendid Latinist and Castilian grammarian, taught a whole generation of students at Salamanca, a university with a gorgeous Renaissance facade gracing its main entrance. But facade it remained, and Spanish letters had to await Miguel de Cervantes (1547–1616) and his *Don Quixote* for a first-rate man of letters.

It is quite wrong to view England in the sixteenth century as so wracked by religious turmoil or suppressed by Tudor tyranny as to have suffered a cultural decline. The period between the first mature phase of English humanism, with Colet, More, and Erasmus, and the Elizabethan Renaissance, with Francis Bacon, Sir Philip Sidney, Edmund Spenser, and Shakespeare, saw the spread of humanistic culture beyond the elite circles at court and the academy to a broader range of the upper and middle classes. New and improved schools brought classical culture and higher learning to a growing number of Englishmen. In his *The Boke Named the Gouvenor* in 1531 Sir Thomas Elyot combined the educational ideals of Erasmus and Vives with Castiglione's concept of the "gentleman." His goal was to apply the wisdom of the ancients for the good of society through the education of the upper-class leaders. Roger Ascham (1515–1568), the greatest English educator of the time, embraced the same humanistic ideals. He wrote *The Schoolmaster,* 1570, an outstanding work on education. The spread of those ideals from court circles to a larger part of the population prepared the way for the cultural surge during the reign of Elizabeth I.

The rise of modern science during the seventeenth century and the development of an industrial society in the eighteenth and nineteenth centuries mark the advent of the modern world as we know it today. The state of science and the relation of the Reformation to science in our four decades merits at least a few comments. The relation of Protestantism to the rise of modern science has generated a storm among the savants nearly as violent as that over the relation of Protestantism and capitalism. Like this latter problem, it comes into play more with the seventeenth-century Puritan ethic and the key date 1640. Michelet once burbled that the early modern period covers "from Columbus to Galileo, from the discovery of the earth to that of the heavens." One problem that surfaced during the early decades of the Reformation was that of the Copernican theory, for Copernicus was, as Melanchthon put it, that Sarmatian astronomer who "made the sun stand still and made the earth move."

Luther has often been referred to as the Copernicus of theology, with a Son-centered religion, and Copernicus as the Luther of astronomy, who broke with the geocentric view of the universe. Luther taught that the scholastics and the humanists did not appreciate nature fully and he held that the doctrines of creation and the incarnation called for a high regard of the external material world of nature. Luther's biblical naturalism, not dissimilar to the "Gothic" naturalism of St. Francis, offered a positive approach to natural science. The reformers reemphasized those very elements in Jewish and Christian theology that had prepared the West for its interest in natural science, namely the idea that creation was *ex nihilo,* not an extension of God's being, which de-divinized nature; the divine commission to Adam to name and subdue all creatures; the thought that the God who created human reason also legislated the natural laws governing the world outside; and the assumption, derived from Roman law, canon law, exegetical and hermeneutical rules, that nature, too, operates according to the rule of law. The combination of this rational interpretation with experimentation and the language of mathematics, a gift from the Greeks, made modern science possible. The theological interpretation of miracles was that such extraordinary events involved the introduction of a higher law of nature, not the cancellation or arbitrary suspension of natural laws.

Necessity is the mother of invention, to be sure, and the commercial demands especially in the western Protestant lands required advances in astronomical and nautical techniques. But the mind set, *mentalité,* if the reader will pardon the expression, was essential to scientific progress. The reformers included natural science in the term "philosophy." They held the world of nature to be open to the exploration of human reason and its capacity for inquiry. They believed in multiple discourse, two levels of knowledge, the divine for things beyond our experience, like the world hereafter, the natural for the examination of the world about us.

The Germanies of Luther's day were hospitable to scientific and technical advances. With a history of invention, gunpowder and artillery, the printing press and books, mechanical clocks and deadlines, the Germans enjoyed a reputation for scientific progress. Georg Agricola with his *De re metallica* produced a precisely illustrated book on mining technology. Gerard Kremer of Flanders drew up his great map of the world (1539), a "Mercator" projection. Sebastian Münster, who was both a mathematician and a geographer, in 1544 published his *Cosmographie.*

Luther spoke twice of the discovery of the "New World" and declared that if the Germans were not grateful for the gospel the *translatio evangelii* would carry it to new peoples farther west. Luther attacked the superstitions of the astrologers but admired some conclusions of the astronomers as, for example, that the moon was the smallest and lowest of the stars. He commented that when the Scriptures referred to the sun and moon as "great lights," they were accommodating themselves to human perception. This accommodation theory applied to Copernicus's theory might have circumvented a controversy over the geocentric and heliocentric theories that was to last for a century even in intellectual circles.

The implications of Copernicus's heliocentric theory spelled out in his *Commentariolus* and his *De Revolutionibus Orbium Caelestium* (1543) were uncongenial to both the humanist and the reformed view of man on this earth. In one of his rambling *Table Talks* Luther made a snide comment about some "new astrologer" who was trying to prove that the earth moves and not the sun and moon. It was, the astronomer argued, like a man in a moving boat who believed that he was standing still while the land and the trees were moving. Nowadays, Luther observed, everyone has to produce a theory of his own, if he wants to be clever, but he himself would stay with the Scriptures, which report that Joshua commanded the sun to stand still. In 1539 Melanchthon had sent a colleague, Georg Rheticus, to consult with Copernicus himself, then canon at Frauenburg in Ermland, Poland. He was convinced by Copernicus of the correctness of the heliocentric theory and returned to publish the *Commentariolus* in Nuremberg. Calvin apparently did not know of the theory, for the one prejudicial comment ascribed to him is spurious. The Lutheran theologian Osiander of Nuremberg wrote a favorable though equivocating preface to Copernicus's major work, published in the year of his death (1543), in which Osiander suggested that the theory was merely a hypothesis that simplified the mathematics of astronomical calculations.[34]

The year in which Copernicus's work was published saw a second scientific book of monumental importance, for in that year the Flemish anatomist Andreas Vesalius published his *De Fabrica,* on *The Structure of the Human Body.* By doing actual dissections on human bodies, not on simian apes, he pointed out the mistakes of the Greek anatomist Galen, whose findings were used in medical training from the second century A.D. on.[35]

A physician of another sort was a Swiss doctor, Paracelsus, Theophrastus Bombastus von Hohenheim (1493–1541), known to be bombastic, who attacked the ancient authorities in medicine and burned the book of Galen in the courtyard of the University of Basel. He operated on the victims of mine disasters and experimented with new drugs for diseases, contributing to the science of iatro-chemistry. His medical theories were interwoven with theological and theosophical ideas of great interest. Servetus, a medical doctor, speculated on the circulation of the blood. A Swiss biologist, Conrad Gesner (1515–1565), developed a new system for cataloging flora and fauna. A German botanist named Leonard Fuchs (1501–1566) produced a glossary of botanical terms with woodcuts of plants.

34. On the reformers and the Copernican theory, see John Dillenberger, *Protestant Thought and Natural Science* (New York, 1960), who believes that for the first fifty years after Copernicus common sense observations favored the geocentric theory, the next fifty years the evidence was debatable, but that after Galileo and the telescope only the retrograde mind could oppose the Copernican theory. See also Robert Westman, "The Wittenberg Interpretation of the Copernican Theory," in O. Gingerich, ed., *The Nature of Scientific Discovery* (Washington, D.C., 1975); "The Melanchthon Circle, Rheticus and the Wittenberg Interpretation of the Copernican Theory," *Isis* (June, 1975); and "The Diffusion of the Copernican Theory, 1540–1560: Philosophical and Historiographical Issues," *History of Science* 13 (1975), ; and B. A. Gerrish, "The Reformation and the Rise of Modern Science: Luther, Calvin, and Copernicus," in *The Old Protestantism and The New. Essays on The Reformation Heritage* (Chicago, 1982), pp. 163–178.

35. See the excellent biography by Donald O'Malley, *Andreas Vesalius* (Berkeley, 1964).

Italy, too, during the first half of the sixteenth century contributed significantly to scientific progress. In mathematics, the language of science, Niccolo Tartaglia (1500–1537) was the first to solve the cubic equation and to develop the use of coefficients. Girolamo Cardano (1501–1576) developed a new theory of numbers and worked out an algebraic synthesis. Centers of scientific interest in physics and astronomy such as Padua and Pavia carried on a scientific tradition without which a Galileo in the next century would not have been possible. In this half century there was clearly no difference in scientific contributions between Catholic and Protestant Europe.

As a theologian, Luther, as the other reformers, was primarily concerned with man in his relation to God and man's eternal destiny; but within its proper sphere, this life within this present world of nature, science had a God-pleasing task to perform.[36] One of Luther's sons became a theologian; the other became a medical doctor. To set up a "warfare of science and theology" in this period is an exercise in futility and a reflection of a nineteenth century materialism now happily transcended.

5. CONTINUITY AND CHANGE

The great historian of Tudor England, G. M. Trevelyan, once said of Lord Thomas Babington Macaulay that reading his histories was like "looking through a small magic window into the past." This volume has unfortunately been demystified and cannot compare with Whiggish Macaulay's wondrous pronouncements upon the fantastic progress of the Protestant, liberal, educated, and democratic north compared with the Catholic, reactionary, ignorant, and tyrannous south.[37] In the late twentieth century historians have a genuine appreciation of the socioeconomic as well as the political and idealistic and ideological factors involved in historical movements. Economic pressures such as climate and food supply, population increase and inflation, political factors such as dynastic power struggles, national consciousness and linguistic barriers, religious feeling such as increased intensity of piety opposed to a bureaucratized

36. John Warwick Montgomery, *In Defense of Martin Luther* (Milwaukee, 1970), pp. 87–113, argues that Luther was not an opponent of Copernicus but rather one who encouraged scientific research.

37. See Thomas Babington Macaulay, *The History of England from the Accession of James the Second,* 7th ed. (London, 1850), Vol. 1, pp. 47–48.

church and a mechanical scheme for salvation, all are involved in the complex multilateral causation of history.

These four decades in the history of that highly volatile subcontinent Europe saw tremendous changes, the transition from medieval to early modern times, for the Reformation was far more radical than the Renaissance as a social and intellectual solvent. Change is far more readily discernible over the continent in the areas of religion, culture, economics, and politics, far less in social relations and the daily life of the common person. This overview has revealed yet another historical fact, that change was far greater in central and even more so in western Europe than in eastern Europe. Change in Russia, Poland-Lithuania, and the domains of the Ottoman Turks is far more difficult to perceive and describe for these decades than it is for western Europe. Clearly this dynamism of the western lands made for the rise of modern Europe during the centuries that followed so that Europe imposed its ways upon the rest of the world, for better or for worse, down to the present time. Why did the empire westward wend its way and why did the surge eastward which characterized the late medieval period end? Just why this was to be defies explanation by a mere historian. Perhaps Jacob Burckhardt was right when he wrote in his *Civilization of the Renaissance in Italy* that "mighty events like the Reformation elude, as respects their details, their outbreak and their development, the deductions of the philosophers, however clearly the necessity of them as a whole may be demonstrated." The Protestant Reformation does indeed defy final explanation, for it was a movement of the human spirit, broad in its historical dimensions, and of monumental importance for modern Europe, America, and all the world.

BIBLIOGRAPHY

"La bibliographie est le vestibule de la science!"
The volume of literature and the vitality of current research on the Reformation are so tremendous that only a highly selective bibliographical essay on major topics, emphasizing books and a strictly limited number of articles, is feasible. At the risk of seeming to make arbitrary choices, the author offers here a bibliographical survey of those volumes deemed most immediately useful to the serious student of the period. The bibliography is arranged to correspond to the sequence of chapters and sections of the narrative. In historical criticism, Marc Bloch, the great medievalist, wrote (*Annales*, V, 5, 8–9), the important thing is *Non numerantur, sed ponderantur*, "Les témoignages se pèsent, et ne se comptent pas."

REFORMATION EUROPE

Without recapitulating the general bibliographical aids available to students of European history, attention may be drawn to special resources for the study of the early sixteenth century. They include Karl Schottenloher, *Bibliographie zur deutschen Geschichte im Zeitalter der Glaubensspaltung 1517–1585* (7 vols., Leipzig, 1933–1966); *Sixteenth Century Bibliography*, a series of publications by the Center for Reformation Research, St. Louis, on a wide variety of subjects, including James Hinz, "Toward the Control of Bibliography for the Study of the Sixteenth Century," *Bulletin*, 6 (1971), giving hints on the use of bibliography aids and bibliography of bibliographies; *Luther Jahrbuch; Literature Review (Literaturbericht)* of the *Archiv für Reformationsgeschichte*, I (1972) on; Comité internationale des sciences historiques, *Bibliographie de la Réforme 1450–1648: Ouvrages Parus de 1940 à 1955* (6 vols. to date, Leiden, 1958–1982); The Historical Association Leaflet no. 66, *The History of the Church: A Select Bibliography* (2nd ed., prepared by Owen Chadwick, London, 1966); Alfred A. Strand, "Renaissance-Humanismus, Reform und Reformation Literaturbericht," *Römische Historische Mitteilungen*, 21 (1979), 187–231; A. G. Dickens, "Recent Books on Reformation and Counter-Reformation," *Journal of Ecclesiastical History*, 19, no. 2 (1968), 219–226; Shirley Jackson Case, *A Bibliographical Guide to the History of Christianity* (Chicago, 1931); *The Bibliography of the Reform 1450–1648 Relating to the United Kingdom and Ireland for the Years 1955–1970* (Oxford, 1975); Conyers Read, *Bibliography of British History, Tudor Period: 1485–1603* (London, 1959); *Répertoire bibliographique de l'histoire de la France* (Paris, 1921–); *Jahresberichte für deutsche Geschichte* (Berlin, 1878–); Friedrich Dahlmann and Georg Waitz, eds., *Quellenkunde der deutschen Geschichte* (Leipzig, 1932; 10th ed., 1969ff.); D. Shapiro, ed., *A Select Bibliography of Works in English on Russian History* (Oxford,

1962); Herbert M. Adams, ed., *Catalogue of Books Printed on the Continent of Europe 1501–1600 in Cambridge Libraries* (2 vols., London and Cambridge, 1967); Theodore Besterman, *Early Printed Books to the End of the Sixteenth Century: A Bibliography of Bibliographies* (4th ed., 5 vols., Geneva, 1965); Steven Ozment, ed., *Reformation Europe: A Guide to Research* (St. Louis: Center for Reformation Research, 1982); Roland H. Bainton and Eric W. Gritsch, eds., *Bibliography of the Continental Reformation: Materials Available in English* (2nd ed., Hamden, Conn., 1972). Also of special value is the *Historical Abstracts* published by ABC—Clio Information Services, Santa Barbara, California, and Oxford, in which, for example, vol. 35, Part A, no. 1 (1984), one can find brief descriptions of the contents of books and the periodical literature for Modern History, 1450–1914.

A few titles broad in scope on the historiography of the Reformation may be of special value: Abraham Friesen, *Reformation and Utopia: The Marxist Interpretation of the Reformation and Its Antecedents* (Wiesbaden, 1974); Ulrich Kremer, *Die Reformation als Problem der Amerikanischen Historiographie* (Wiesbaden, 1978); Harold Grimm, *The Reformation in Historical Thought* (New York, 1946). There is as yet no equivalent for the Reformation of Wallace K. Ferguson's *The Renaissance in Historical Thought* (Boston, 1948), although A. G. Dickens and John Tonkin are preparing such a volume. Bernd Moeller, ed., *Luther in der Neuzeit: Wissenschaftliches Symposion des Vereins für Reformationsgeschichte* (Gütersloh, 1983), includes essays focusing on the German Reformation but dealing with the scholarship in various lands—England, Denmark, America, and others. Philippe Joutard, ed., *Historiographie de la Réforme* (Paris, 1977), emphasizes French titles. Lewis W. Spitz., ed., *The Reformation: Basic Interpretations* (Lexington, Mass., 1972), offers the sometimes conflicting views of leading historians.

Among the many general histories of the Reformation period one may refer with confidence to *The New Cambridge Modern History*, 2, *The Reformation*, G. R. Elton, ed. (Cambridge, 1958); Roland Bainton, *The Reformation of the Sixteenth Century* (Boston, 1952), a popular account; Owen Chadwick, *The Reformation* (Baltimore, 1964), third volume of the Pelican History of the Church, a lively account leaning heavily on the English church for illustrative incidents; H. G. Koenigsberger and George L. Mosse, *Europe in the Sixteenth Century* (New York, 1968); Hans J. Hillerbrand, *The World of the Reformation* (New York, 1973); Jean Delumeau, *Naissance et Affirmation de la Réforme* (Paris, 1968; 2nd ed., 1973), with a discussion of historiographical debates; A. G. Dickens, *Reformation and Society in Sixteenth Century Europe* (New York, 1966), popular, well-written and beautifully illustrated, as is also Dickens' *The Age of Humanism and Reformation: Europe in the Fourteenth, Fifteenth, and Sixteenth Centuries* (Englewood Cliffs, N.J., 1972); Geoffrey R. Elton, *Reformation Europe, 1517–1559* (Cleveland, 1963), offers a brief survey; Harold J. Grimm, *The Reformation Era, 1500–1650* (2nd ed., New York, 1965), strongest on Germany and Lutheranism; Erich Hassinger, *Das Werden des neuzeitlichen Europa, 1300–1600* (Braunschweig, 1959), a useful handbook stressing aspects pointing toward modern developments; Hans J. Hillerbrand, *The Protestant Reformation* (London, 1968); Erwin Iserloh, Joseph Glazik, and Hubert Jedin, *Reformation and Counter-Reformation,* V, *History of the Church,* ed. by Hubert Jedin and John Dolan (New York, 1980), a Catholic church history mainly the work of Jedin, the distinguished historian of the Council of Trent; Émile G. Léonard, *Histoire Générale du Protestantisme* (3 vols., Paris, 1961–64); English tr., 2 vols., London, 1966–67), a general history by a leading Protestant authority on French church history, dealing with the Reformation in the first volume. Charles Nauert, *The Age of Renaissance and Reformation* (Hinsdale, Ill., 1977), a useful text; Eugene Rice Jr., *The Foundations of Early Modern Europe, 1460–1559* (New York, 1970), a nicely illustrated brief account; Gerhard Ritter, *Die Neugestaltung Europas im XVI. Jahrhundert* (Berlin, 1950) and *Die Weltwirkung der Reformation* (2nd ed., Munich, 1959), the first of these an adaptation of the *Propyläen Weltgeschichte* volume and the second containing famous essays on the sixteenth century as a historical epoch, the spiritual roots of the Reformation and the like; Henri Daniel-Rops, *L'Église de la Renaissance et de la Réforme* (vol. 2, Paris, 1955; Eng. tr., London, 1961), by a French Catholic writer, somewhat tendentious; Preserved Smith, *The Age of the Reformation* (New York, 1920), still of some value; Lewis W. Spitz, *The Renaissance and Reformation Movements* (2 vols., 2nd ed., St. Louis, 1980); Hermann Tüchle, *Geschichte der Kirche,* III (*Reformation und Gegenreformation* (Einsiedeln, Zurich, Cologne, 1965), an admirably done Catholic general church history.

A few of the better general works stressing the intellectual, theological, or cultural aspects of the period are Steven Ozment, *The Age of Reform 1250–1550: An Intellectual and Religious History of Late Medieval and Reformation Europe* (New Haven, 1980); Enno van Gelder, *The Two Reformations of the Sixteenth Century: A Study of the Religious Aspects and Consequences of the Renaissance and Humanism* (The Hague, 1961), clearly preferring the Erasmian solution; Pierre Chaunu, *Église, culture et société: Essais sur Réforme et Contre-Réforme 1517–1620* (Paris, 1981), stressing France but including all of Europe except the Eastern Orthodox world; Carl Andresen, *Handbuch der Dogmen-und Theologiegeschichte,* 2, *Die Lehrentwicklung im Rahmen der Konfessionalität* (Göttingen, 1980); Olivier Fatio and Pierre Fraenkel, eds., *Histoire de l'Exégèse au XVIᵉ Siècle* (Geneva, 1978), presents the papers on major Catholic and Protestant figures given at a colloquium in 1976. Richard Stauffer, *Interprètes de la Bible: Études sur les Réformateurs du XVIᵉ Siècle* (Paris, 1980), offers twelve studies from 1512 to 1561, including Lefèvre, Luther, Calvin, Zwingli, and some radical reformers. George Tavard, *Holy Writ or Holy Church: The Crisis of the Protestant Reformation* (New York, 1959), deals with the problem of Scripture and tradition. Hans J. Hillerbrand, *The Reformation: A Narrative History Related by Contemporary Observers and Participants* (New York, 1964), is especially useful for his translation of left-wing sources and political documents.

Economic History: E. E. Rich and C. H. Wilson, eds., *The Cambridge Economic History of Europe*, IV, *The Economy of Expanding Europe in the Sixteenth and Seventeenth Centuries* (Cambridge, 1967), is a reliable reference work. Carlo M. Cipolla has a number of basic studies: *Before the Industrial Revolution: European Society and Economy, 1000–1700* (New York, 1976); *The Economic History of World Population* (Baltimore, 1962); ed., *Fontana Economic History of Europe*, II, *The Sixteenth and Seventeenth Centuries* (Totowa, N.J., 1974; reprint, 1977). See also Douglass C. North and Robert Paul Thomas, *The Rise of the Western World: A New Economic History* (Cambridge, 1973), part 3, 1500–1700, describing France and Spain as the "also-rans" and the Netherlands as the success story of economic growth; Frédéric Mauro, *Le XVIᵉ Siècle Européen: aspects économiques* (Paris, 1966); and Harry A. Miskimin, *The Economy of Later Renaissance Europe 1460–1600* (London and New York, 1977), an exemplary study by a distinguished Yale historian. Immanuel Wallerstein, *The Modern World System: Capitalist Agriculture and the Origins of the European World Economy in the Sixteenth Century* (New York, 1974), offers an idiosyncratic theory to explain the advance of Europe to the forefront among world economies, preferable to Marxist or deterministic dogmas, but to be taken with reservations. Ingomar Bog, ed., *Der Auszenhandel Ostmitteleuropas 1450–1650* (Cologne and Vienna, 1971), has essays on land to market patterns and trade routes in east-central Europe. Of special interest is Peter Burke, ed., *Economy and Society in Early Modern Europe: Essays from Annales* (New York, 1972). Fernand Braudel, the author of *The Mediterranean and the Mediterranean World in the Age of Philip II* (New York, 1973), has two books done into English on the economy of this period, *Capitalism and Material Life, 1400–1800* (New York, 1973) and *Afterthoughts on Material Civilization and Capitalism* (Baltimore, 1977). Works specifically on agriculture include N. S. B. Gras, *A History of Agriculture* (New York, 1925; 2nd ed., New York, 1940); R. H. Tawney, *The Agrarian Problem in the Sixteenth Century* (London, 1912); Harriett Bradley, *Enclosures in England* (New York, 1918); Emmanuel Le Roy Ladurie, "A Long Agrarian Cycle: Languedoc, 1500–1700," in Peter Earle, ed., *Essays in European Economic History, 1500–1800* (Oxford, 1974), edited for the Economic History Society. One cannot write about economic history in this period without reference to the classical works of Henri Hauser, *Les débuts du capitalisme* (Paris, 1927) and *Les ouvriers du temps passé, XVᵉ –XVIᵉ siècles* (Paris, 1899). The rise of Antwerp, superseding the older centers of medieval trade such as Bruges and the Hanse cities, has received careful attention: Hermann van der Wee, *The Growth of the Antwerp Market and the European Economy* (3 vols., The Hague, 1963); S. T. Bindoff, "The Greatness of Antwerp," in G. R. Elton, ed., *The New Cambridge Modern History* (II, Cambridge, 1958), pp. 50–69; and John J. Murray, *Antwerp in the Age of Plantin and Brueghel* (Norman, Oklahoma, 1970), depicting the city as the wealthiest and most renowned city of the century.

Demography: The population growth following the disasters of the black death in 1348–1350 had a critical impact upon the first half of the sixteenth century. More recent studies include Karl F. Helleiner, "The Population of Europe from the Black Death to the Eve of the Vital Revolution," in E. E. Rich and C. H. Wilson, eds., *The Cambridge Economic History of Europe,* IV, *The Economy of Expanding Europe in the Sixteenth and Seventeenth Centuries* (Cambridge, 1967), pp. 1–95; Roger Mols, *Introduction à la démographie historique des villes d'Europe du XVe au XVIIIe siècle* (Louvain, 1954), which is difficult for those not skilled in statistics; Marcel R. Reinhard and André Armengaud, *Historie Générale de la Population Mondiale* (Paris, 1961); Edward A. Wrigley, ed., *An Introduction to English Historical Demography* (London, 1966), a brief manual; Edward A. Wrigley, *Population and History* (London, 1969); Ernst Wolfgang Buchholz, *Vom Mittelalter zur Neuzeit,* III, *Raum und Bevölkerung in der Weltgeschichte. Bevölkerungs-Ploetz* (4 vols., Würzburg, 1966); William H. McNeill, *Plagues and Peoples* (Garden City, N.Y., 1977), especially chapter 5 on transoceanic exchanges, 1500–1700; William F. Langer, "Europe's Initial Population Explosion," *American Historical Review,* 69 (1963), 1–17, on the humble potato and the "vital revolution"; and the historiographical article by Eugene F. Rice, "Recent Studies on the Population of Europe, 1348–1620," *Renaissance News,* 18 (1965), 180–87.

Price Revolution: The great pioneering work in this field was Georg Wiebe, *Zur Geschichte der Preisrevolution des XVI. und XVII. Jahrhunderts* (Leipzig, 1895). Other writings that have attained near classical status are Earl J. Hamilton, *American Treasure and the Price Revolution in Spain, 1501–1650* (Cambridge, Mass., 1934), and E. J. Hamilton, *Money, Prices and Wages in Valencia, Aragon and Navarre, 1351–1500* (Cambridge, Mass., 1936), emphasizing the importance of the new world's bullion for the price rise. John H. Elliott, *The Old World and the New* (Cambridge, 1970), describes the present state of the case of the impact of American silver on the European economy. Studies concerned with the impact of New World bullion and trade include P. and H. Chaunu, "Économie atlantique, Économie mondiale," *Cahiers d'histoire mondiale,* I (1953), 91–104; P. and H. Chaunu, *Seville et l'Atlantique* (11 vols., Paris, 1955–1959), a monumental achievement based on a close study of the export-import documents for the major part of the period; and Fernand P. Braudel and F. Spooner, "Prices in Europe from 1450–1750," *The Cambridge Economic History of Europe,* IV, *The Economy of Expanding Europe in the Sixteenth and Seventeenth Centuries* (Cambridge, 1967), pp. 378–486, with ample charts and graphs. Adolf Laube, *Studien über den erzgebirgischen Silberbergbau von 1470 bis 1546* (Berlin, 1974), brings out the fact of the bullion increase due to new mining techniques and operations in central Europe itself. Inclined more to the "realistic" solution in explaining the price rise and resulting social pressures for Europe and especially England are E. H. Phelps Brown and Sheila V. Hopkins, "Wage-rates and Prices: Evidence for

Population Pressure in the Sixteenth Century," *Economica*, 24 (1957), 289–306; E. H. Phelps Brown and Sheila V. Hopkins, "Seven Centuries of the Prices of Consumables, Compared with Builders' Wage-Rates," *Economica*, 23 (November 1956), 296–314; Alexandre R. E. Chabert, "More About the Sixteenth-Century Price Revolution," in Peter Burke, ed., *Economy and Society in Early Modern Europe: Essays from Annales* (New York, 1972); Peter H. Ramsey, ed., *The Price Revolution in Sixteenth Century England* (London, 1971); J. D. Gould, *The Great Debasement: Currency and the Economy in Mid-Tudor England* (Oxford, 1970); R. B. Outhwaite, *Inflation in Tudor and Early Stuart England* (London, 1969). Of at least tangential relevance are the following studies: John U. Nef, "Industrial Europe on the Eve of the Reformation," *Journal of Political Economy*, 49 (1941), 1–40, 183–224, and his book by that title; James B. Wadsworth, *Lyons, 1473–1503: The Beginnings of Cosmopolitanism* (Cambridge, Mass., 1962); J. R. Partington, *A History of Greek Fire and Gunpowder* (Cambridge, 1960), an account of the changes in military technology that put pressure on sixteenth-century political and financial institutions.

Climate: Two samples of the recent historiographical emphasis on climate are Robert I. Rotberg and Theodore K. Rabb, eds., *Climate and History* (Princeton, 1981), made up of seventeen papers originally published in the *Journal of Interdisciplinary History*, 10 (1980), which offer a valuable sampling of recent research on the effects of climate on historical change, and Emmanuel Le Roy Ladurie, "History and Climate," in Burke, ed., *Economy and Society*, pp. 135–63. See also Ladurie, *Histoire du climate depuis l'an mil* (Paris, 1967).

Social Relations and the Common People: A potpourri of the many new volumes on the social history of the period should include Gareth Jones, *History of the Law of Charity* (New York, 1969), which shows the harshness of life for most people; Brian Pullan, *Rich and Poor in Renaissance Venice* (Oxford, 1970); Frederick George Emmison, *Elizabethan Life: Disorder* (Chelmsford, 1970), playing up the contrast of rich and poor; Hermann Rebel, *Peasant Classes: The Bureaucratization of Property and Family Relations Under Early Habsburg Absolutism, 1511–1636* (Princeton, 1982), which discusses the economic and occupational characteristics of the Upper Austrian peasantry and shows how the developing Habsburg monarchy made the peasant household an organ of the state; Teodor Shanin, *Peasants and Peasant Societies* (Harmondsworth, Middlesex, England, 1971); W. N. Parker and E. L. Jones, eds., *European Peasants and Their Markets* (Princeton, 1975); J. M. Potter, M. U. Diaz, and G. M. Foster, eds., *Peasant Society: A Reader* (Boston, 1967); Winfried Schulze, *Bäuerlicher Widerstand und feudale Herrschaft in der frühen Neuzeit* (Stuttgart, 1980), with a thorough bibliography; Paul Böckmann, "Der gemeine Mann in den Flugschriften der Reformation," *Deutsche Vierteljahrsschrift für Literaturwissenschaft und Geistesgeschichte*, 22 (1944), 186–230; R. Lutz, *Wer war der gemeine Mann?: Der dritte Stand in der Krise des Spätmittelalters* (Munich, 1978);

Wolfgang J. Mommsen, et al., eds., *Stadtbürgertum und Adel in der Reformation: Studien zur Sozialgeschichte der Reformation in England und Deutschland* (*Veröffentlichungen des Deutschen Historischen Instituts London*, 5) (Stuttgart, 1979), which includes articles by Dickens, Scribner, Press, Moeller, Ozment, Brady and others; Henri Mendors, *Sociétés paysannes* (Paris, 1976); Jean Louis Flandrin, *Familles: parenté, maison, sexualité dans l'ancienne société* (Paris, c. 1976; Cambridge, England, 1979); Jean Louis Flandrin, *Les Amours Paysannes* (*XVIᵉ-XIXᵉ siècle*) (Paris, 1975); Jack Goody, *The Development of the Family and Marriage in Europe* (Cambridge, 1983); Peter Laslett, *Family Life and Illicit Love in Earlier Generations: Essays in Historical Sociology* (Cambridge/New York, 1977).

Political Thought: Arthur S. McGrade, *The Political Thought of William of Ockham: Personal and Institutional Principles* (Cambridge, 1974), significant because of the importance of Ockham for Luther's understanding of the two-kingdoms theory, according to the argument of Helmar Junghans, *Ockham im Lichte der neueren Forschung* (Berlin, 1968). Paul E. Sigmund, *Nicholas of Cusa and Medieval Political Thought* (Cambridge, Mass., 1963), is significant because of Cusanus' yielding on conciliar theory to the monarchical episcopate of Rome. A similar pre-Reformation subject of relevance is to be found in Nicolai Rubenstein, "Marsilius of Padua and Italian Political Thought of his Time," in *Europe in the Late Middle Ages,* John Hale, et al., eds. (London, 1970), pp. 44–75, seeing the *Defensor pacis* as an attempt to apply the Paduan solution to church-state conflicts in Europe as a whole. See also William F. Church, *Constitutional Thought in Sixteenth-Century France* (Cambridge, Mass., 1941).

Political Institutions: G. Benecke, *Society and Politics in Germany 1500–1750* (London, 1974), drawing on the example of Lippe rehabilitates the Holy Roman Empire as an example of viable federalism; Eduard Fueter, *Geschichte des europäischen Staatensystems von 1492 bis 1559* (Munich, 1919; repr. Osnabrück, 1972), the old classic by the noted Swiss scholar on the international relations; Arthur J. Slavin, ed., *The New Monarchies and Representative Assemblies: Medieval Constitutionalism or Modern Absolutism?* (Lexington, Mass., 1964), a problems book by a noted scholar of Tudor England; Henry J. Cohn, *Government in Reformation Europe 1520–1560* (London, 1971); H. G. Koenigsberger, "The French Renaissance Monarchy as Seen Through the Estates General," *Studies in the Renaissance,* 9 (1962), 113–25; H. G. Koenigsberger, *Estates and Revolutions: Essays in Early Modern European History* (Ithaca, 1971), including the parliaments of Piedmont and Sicily; J. N. Stephens, *The Fall of the Florentine Republic, 1512–1530* (Oxford, 1983); G. R. Elton, *The Tudor Revolution in Government: Administrative Changes in the Reign of Henry VIII* (Cambridge, 1953); Perez Zagorin, *Rebels and Rulers 1500–1660* (2 vols., Cambridge, 1982).

Institutional Church: An excellent work on the church on the eve of the Reformation is Francis Oakley, *The Western Church in the Later Middle Ages* (Ithaca, N.Y.,

1979). Several volumes of collected essays merit special mention, such as Charles Trinkaus and Heiko A. Oberman, eds., *The Pursuit of Holiness in Late Medieval and Renaissance Religion* (Leiden, 1974); F. Forrester Church and Timothy George, eds., *Continuity and Discontinuity in Church History: Essays Presented to George Huntston Williams* (Leiden, 1979), with a section on the radical reformation; Heiko A. Oberman, ed., *Luther and the Dawn of the Modern Era* (Leiden, 1974); and Peter Newman Brooks, *Reformation Principle and Practice: Essays in Honour of Arthur Geoffrey Dickens* (London, 1980). See also Heiko A. Oberman, *Forerunners of the Reformation: The Shape of Late Medieval Thought* (New York, 1966). Thomas N. Tentler, *Sin and Confession on the Eve of the Reformation* (Princeton, 1977), sheds light on the penitential system related to indulgences, a key Reformation issue. Erwin Iserloh, *Gnade und Eucharistie in der philosophischen Theologie des Wilhelm von Ockham: Ihre Bedeutung für die Ursachen der Reformation* (Wiesbaden, 1956), labels Ockham's theology as one of possibilities that belittle the teaching of Scripture and tradition. E. Jane Dempsey-Douglass, *Justification in Late Medieval Preaching: A Study in John Geiler von Keisersberg* (Leiden, 1966), offers a good insight into the message of one of several late medieval preachers preparatory to the religious Reformation. Ludwig von Pastor, *The History of the Popes from the Close of the Middle Ages* (vols. 1–8, St. Louis and London, 1938–1950), remains a classical resource for church history in the period.

Popular Religion: Natalie Zemon Davis, "Some Tasks and Themes in the Study of Popular Religion," in Trinkaus and Oberman, eds., *Pursuit of Holiness,* pp. 307–36, discusses challenges of this aspect of history from the bottom up. See also her *Society and Culture in Early Modern France: Eight Essays* (Stanford, 1975). General studies of popular religion include Imogen Luxton, "The Reformation and Popular Culture," in Felicity Heal and Rosemary O'Day, eds., *Church and Society in England: Henry VIII to James I* (London, 1977), on Lollard demands for vernacular Bibles for the laity and pastoral attention to duties; James Obelkevich, ed., *Religion and the People, 800–1700* (Chapel Hill, N.C., 1979), a collection of studies on the history of popular religion; Keith Thomas, *Religion and the Decline of Magic* (London, 1971), which argues for a growing individualist piety opposed to or indifferent to the rituals of official church practice; and Lionel Rothkrug, *Religious Practices and Collective Perceptions: Hidden Homologies in the Renaissance and Reformation, Reflexions Historiques* 7, no. 1 (Spring 1980). Studies of popular religion in various countries and local areas of special value include Bernd Moeller, "Piety in Germany Around 1500," in *The Reformation in Medieval Perspective,* Steven E. Ozment, ed. (Chicago, 1970), pp. 50–75; Gerald Strauss, ed., *Manifestations of Discontent in Germany on the Eve of the Reformation* (Bloomington, Ind., 1971); Jacques Toussaert, *Le sentiment religieux en Flandre à la fin du Moyen-Âge* (Paris, 1963), a classic in the field; William A. Christian, Jr., *Local Religion in Sixteenth-Century Spain* (Princeton, 1981); A. N. Galpern, *The Religion of the People in*

Sixteenth-Century Champagne (Cambridge, 1976); Mary O'Neil, "Discerning Superstition: Popular Errors and Orthodox Response in Late Sixteenth Century Italy" (diss., Stanford, 1981), part one based on Inquisition trials in Modena; and Carlo Ginzburg, *The Cheese and the Worms: The Cosmos of a Sixteenth-Century Miller* (Baltimore, 1980), a fascinating case study making use of inquisitorial records, as did Emmanuel Le Roy Ladurie, *The Peasants of Languedoc* (Urbana, 1974; Paris, 1969).

Humanism and Reform: The great work on the thought of the Italian Renaissance humanists is that of Charles Trinkaus, *"In Our Image and Likeness": Humanity and Divinity in Italian Humanist Thought* (2 vols., Chicago, 1970). The essay by E. F. Jacobs, "Christian Humanism," in *Europe in the Late Middle Ages*, John Hale et al., eds. (London, 1965), merits a reflective reading. Roberto Weiss, *The Spread of Italian Humanism* (London, 1964) addresses the diffusion problem. On the Brethren of the Common Life, see Albert Hyma, *The Christian Renaissance: A History of the Devotio Moderna* (New York, 1925; Hamden, Conn., 1965); Albert Hyma, *The Brethren of the Common Life* (Grand Rapids, Mich., 1950); and R. R. Post, *The Modern Devotion: Confrontation with Reformation and Humanism* (Leiden, 1968), revising downward the importance of the Brethren as educators. Rudolf Arbesmann, *Der Augustiner-Eremitenorden und der Beginn der humanistischen Bewegung* (Würzburg, 1965), explores an avenue pointed to by Paul Oskar Kristeller decades ago, the importance of the regular clergy for humanism. Two books by beloved professors of Reformation history merit special mention, Quirinus Breen, *Christianity and Humanism: Studies in the History of Ideas* (Grand Rapids, Mich., 1967), and E. Harris Harbison, *The Christian Scholar in the Age of the Reformation* (New York, 1956). Jerry H. Bentley, *Humanists and Holy Writ: New Testament Scholarship in the Renaissance* (Princeton, 1983), deals with Valla, the Complutensian Polyglot, and Erasmus as editor of the New Testament.

For German humanism a recent collection of sources in English is useful. Reinhard P. Becker, ed., *German Humanism and Reformation* (New York, 1982). Lewis W. Spitz, *The Religious Renaissance of the German Humanists* (Cambridge, Mass., 1963), deals with the religious thought of the major figures. Maria Grossmann, *Humanism in Wittenberg 1485–1517* (Nieuwkoop, 1975), takes humanism into the incubus of the Reformation itself. The following are a few of the biographies of German humanists worth special notice: Charles Nauert, *Agrippa and the Crisis of Renaissance Thought* (Urbana, 1965); Hajo Holborn, *Ulrich von Hutten and the German Reformation* (New Haven, 1937); Heinrich Lutz, *Conrad Peutinger: Beiträge zu einer politischen Biographie* (Augsburg, 1958); Lewis W. Spitz, *Conrad Celtis the German Arch-Humanist* (Cambridge, Mass., 1957); Gerald Strauss, *Historian in an Age of Crisis: Johannes Aventinus 1477–1534* (Cambridge, Mass., 1963); H. Ankwitz van Kleehoven, *Johannes Cuspinian* (Graz, 1969); P. E. Willehad and C. von Imhof, *Willibald Pirckheimer, Dürers Freund* (Vienna, 1971); Niklas Holzberg,

Willibald Pirckheimer: Griechischer Humanismus in Deutschland (Munich, 1981); James M. Kittelson, *Wolfgang Capito: From Humanist to Reformer* (Leiden, 1975); and Noel Brann, *The Abbot Trithemius (1462–1516): The Renaissance of Monastic Humanism* (Leiden, 1981). Two articles have been particularly influential in the reassessment of the relation of humanism and scholasticism, Charles Nauert, "The Clash of Humanists and Scholastics: An Approach to Pre-Reformation Controversies," *The Sixteenth Century Journal,* 4 (1973), 1–18, and James Overfield, "Scholastic Opposition to Humanism in Pre-Reformation Germany," *Viator,* 7 (1976), 391–420. It is obviously impossible to recapitulate here a list of all the older works still of basic importance, such as Willy Andreas, *Deutschland vor der Reformation: Eine Zeitenwende* (5th ed., Stuttgart, 1948), or the works of Paul Joachimsen, Michael Seidlmayer, and Richard Newald. Among newer works that of Frank L. Borchardt is outstanding, *German Antiquity in Renaissance Myth* (Baltimore and London, 1971). A colloquy held at Tour produced an unusually rich collection of essays on German humanism, *XVIIIe Colloque International de Tours: L'Humanisme Allemand (1480–1540)* (Munich and Paris, 1979).

More extensive bibliography on French and English humanism will be included later in this survey, but here attention may be drawn to a few titles. Augustin Renaudet, *Préréforme et Humanisme à Paris* (2nd ed., Paris, 1953), remains a standard work. Werner Gundersheimer has edited a useful volume, *French Humanism, 1470–1600* (New York, 1969). Michael Screech has two studies on Rabelais updating the position of Lucien Febvre on the religion of Rabelais, *L'Évangélisme de Rabelais* (Geneva, 1959) and *Rabelais* (Ithaca, N.Y., 1979). Douglas Bush, *The Renaissance and English Humanism* (Toronto, 1939), continues to sparkle. The *Festschrift* dedicated to Paul Oskar Kristeller and edited by Heiko A. Oberman and Thomas A. Brady, Jr., *Itinerarium Italicum: The Profile of the Italian Renaissance in the Mirror of its European Transformations* (Leiden, 1975), contains chapters dealing with the reception of the Italian Renaissance in France by Sem Dresden, in the Low Countries by Josef Ijsewijn, in England by Denys Hay, in the Germanies by Lewis W. Spitz.

Erasmus: The prince of the humanists has proved to be a phoenix in the late twentieth century. Unlike the magisterial reformers, he has no official church body to serve as a natural interest group, but in this age has attracted a great following of his own. In addition to P. S. Allen, *Opus Epistolarum Erasmi* (12 vols., Oxford, 1906–1958), the eighteenth-century Leiden edition of his works is being superseded by the new Amsterdam *Opera Omnia* under the direction of Cornelis Reedijk and made available in English by the University of Toronto Press edition, James McConica, ed., which has already published six volumes of correspondence, two volumes of literary and educational writings, and the *Adages.* One of several bibliographical surveys is Jean-Claude Margolin, *Douze Années de Bibliographie Érasmienne* (Paris, 1963).

Among the biographies are Roland H. Bainton, *Erasmus of Christendom* (New York, 1969), much more favorable to him than Jan Huizinga's *Erasmus of Rotterdam* (New York, 1924; Harper Torchbook, New York, 1957), a critical assessment of his self-serving psychology; Albert Hyma, *The Youth of Erasmus* (Ann Arbor, 1931; 2nd ed., New York, 1968); Margaret Mann Phillips, *Erasmus and the Northern Renaissance* (London, 1949; Woodridge, 1981), the new edition containing bibliographical additions; Preserved Smith, *Erasmus: A Study of His Life, Ideals and Place in History* (New York, 1923); Louis Bouyer, *Erasmus and His Times* (Westminster, Md., 1959), a Catholic assessment; and György Faludy, *Erasmus of Rotterdam* (New York, 1970).

Works on various aspects of his thought include James D. Tracy, *Erasmus: The Growth of a Mind* (Geneva, 1972), correlating his intellectual and personality characteristics, and *The Politics of Erasmus: A Pacifist Intellectual and his Political Milieu* (Toronto, 1978); Georges Chantraine, S.J., *Mysterium et Sacramentum dans le 'Ratio Verae Theologiae' d'Érasme* (Namur, 1972); John B. Payne, *Erasmus: His Theology of the Sacraments* (Richmond, Va., 1970); Ernst W. Kohls, *Die Theologie des Erasmus* (Basel, 1966); Albert Rabil, Jr., *Erasmus and the New Testament: The Mind of a Christian Humanist* (San Antonio, Tex., 1972); W. H. Woodward, *Erasmus Concerning the Nature and Aims of Education* (Cambridge, 1904). The skilled translator and editor of the *Colloquies,* Craig R. Thompson, edited the key piece, *Inquisitio de Fide: A Colloquy by D. Erasmus of Rotterdam 1524* (New Haven, 1950; 2nd ed., Hamden, 1975).

Lawrence V. Ryan, "Art and Artifice in Erasmus' 'Convivium Profanum,'" *Renaissance Quarterly* 31 (1978), 1–16, analyzes Erasmus' criticism of required fasting and the reactions it provoked. See also Bruce E. Mansfield, *Phoenix of His Age: Interpretations of Erasmus c. 1550/1* (Toronto, 1979), and Myron P. Gilmore, "Italian Reactions to Erasmian Humanism," in Oberman and Brady, eds., *Itinerarium Italicum,* pp. 61–115, describing Erasmus' position as one of resigned acceptance of Rome and repudiation of Luther. One cannot omit a reminder of Marcel Battaillon's classic account of Erasmus' broad influence especially as a teacher of piety in the Spain of 1515–1530, *Érasme et l'Espagne* (Paris, 1937), or of Augustin Renaudet's *Études érasmiennes (1521–1529)* (Paris, 1939). Also worthy of special attention are Richard DeMolen, ed., *Essays on the Works of Erasmus* (New Haven, 1978), and the books of Marjorie O'Rourke Boyle, *Erasmus on Language and Method in Theology* (Toronto, 1977); *Christening Pagan Mysteries. Erasmus in Pursuit of Wisdom* (Toronto, 1981); and *Rhetoric and Reform. Erasmus' Civil Dispute with Luther* (Cambridge, Mass., 1983), an idiosyncratic and questionable emphasis on their differences in style and method rather than on the incompatibility of basic theological substance.

Erasmus and the Reformation has received much scholarly attention. Philip S. Watson and B. Drewery have translated and edited *Luther and Erasmus: Free Will and Salvation* (Philadelphia, 1969), their treatises on the free or enslaved will. In *The Library of Christian Classics,* Matthew Spinka edited *Advocates of Reform from Wyclif to Erasmus* (Philadelphia, 1953). To be recommended is Karl Heinz Oelrich, *Der späte Erasmus und die Reformation* (Münster, 1961).

THE LUTHERAN REFORMATION

German scholars, like their French and English counterparts, tend to write on the Reformation in their own country, and the result has been a formidable array of general histories on Luther and the German Reformation requiring severe selectivity. Heinrich Lutz, *Das Ringen um deutsche Einheit und Kirchliche Erneuerung von Maximilian I. bis zum Westfälischen Frieden 1490 bis 1648,* IV, *Propyläen Geschichte Deutschlands* (Berlin, 1983), with a thorough bibliography, supersedes older works such as Johannes Bühler, *Deutsche Geschichte: Das Reformationszeitalter* (Berlin and Leipzig, 1938). Hajo Holborn, *The Reformation* (London and New York, 1959), is the first volume of his *A History of Modern Germany,* stressing political history. A. G. Dickens, *The German Nation and Martin Luther* (London, 1974), has brief chapters not only on nationalism, humanism, printers, and the cities, but also on the changing historiography of the Reformation. A. G. Dickens, *Martin Luther and the Reformation* (London, 1967), is useful for beginning students. Hans J. Hillerbrand, *Men and Ideas in the Sixteenth Century* (Chicago, 1971) outlines major events 1517–1598. Franz Lau and Ernst Bizer, *A History of the Reformation in Germany to 1555* (London, 1969), also presents a good summary of events. Leopold von Ranke's *History of the Reformation in Germany* was edited in a new edition by Robert A. Johnson (New York, 1966). Philip Schaff, *The German Reformation,* vol. 7, 2nd rev. ed. of his *History of the Christian Church* (New York, 1910), is still of value for its moderate judgments. Three heavy basic German tomes are: Karl Brandi, *Deutsche Geschichte im Zeitalter der Reformation und Gegenreformation* (3rd ed., Leipzig, 1941), Fritz Hartung, *Deutsche Geschichte im Zeitalter der Reformation, Gegenreformation und des Dreissigjährigen Krieges* (2nd ed., Berlin, 1963), and Paul Joachimsen, *Die Reformation als Epoche der deutschen Geschichte* (Munich, 1951). Peter Blickle, *Die Reformation im Reich* (Stuttgart, 1982) is a recent brief entry. A splendid book with strong essays on various nonreligious aspects of the Reformation is Heinz Angermeyer and Reinhard Seyboth, eds., *Säkuläre Aspekte der Reformationszeit* (Munich and Vienna, 1983), especially Erich Methuen on humanism.

The pioneer of an ecumenical Catholic approach was Joseph Lortz, whose *Die Reformation in Deutschland* (2 vols., 4th ed., Freiburg, 1962), has been translated infelicitously into English, *The Reformation in Germany* (2 vols., New York, 1969), depicting Luther as a *homo religiosus,* more sincere than Erasmus, but too subjective and unable to submit himself to ecclesiastical authority. Two other of Lortz's works have been done into English, *How the Reformation Came* (New York, 1964) and *The Reformation. A Problem for Today* (Westminster, Md., 1964). Peter Manns and

Harding Meyer, eds., *Luther's Ecumenical Significance: An Interconfessional Consultation* (Philadelphia, 1983), features an exchange between Manns, Lortz's successor as director of the church history section of the Institute for European History in Mainz, and Otto Pesch, learned scholar of Luther and Thomas Aquinas' theology, on the nature of Lortz's contribution and new direction in the ecumenical assessment of Luther. John Dolan, *History of the Reformation: A Conciliatory Assessment of Opposite Views* (New York, 1965), is less a history of the Reformation than it is a collection of studies of historiographical controversies and the failings of the medieval church. The old polemical work of Johannes Janssen is still a mine of interesting information, *History of the German People at the Close of the Middle Ages* (17 vols., London and St. Louis, 1896–1925).

Luther the Reformer: The great scholarly edition of Luther's works, now over 110 folio volumes, is *D. Martin Luthers Werke* (Weimar, 1883–) in four parts, Works, Correspondence, Table Talks, and the German Bible. A new edition of his Bible has been edited by Hans Volz and Heinz Blanke, *D. Martin Luther: Die gantze Heilige Schrifft Deutsch Wittenberg 1545* (2 vols., Munich, 1972). The new English translation of his writings is *Luther's Works: American Edition,* Jaroslav Pelikan and Helmut T. Lehmann, eds. (55 vols., St. Louis, 1955– , Philadelphia, 1957–), with a companion volume by Pelikan, *Luther the Expositor* (St. Louis, 1959). Two aids for the use of these works are Kurt Aland, *Hilfsbuch zum Lutherstudium* (3rd ed., Witten, 1970), and Heinrich J. Vogel, *Vogel's Cross Reference and Index to the Contents of Luther's Works* (Milwaukee, 1983). Josef Benzing, *Lutherbibliographie; Verzeichnis der gedruckten Schriften Martin Luthers bis zu dessen Tod, Bibliotheca Bibliographica Aureliana,* X, XVI, XIX (Baden-Baden, 1965–1966).

Luther has been blessed with hundreds of biographers so that it is not possible to cite even the most distinguished of them from Julius Köstlin (1883) on, but merely more recent and readily available volumes. Two source books are of special value, Otto Scheel, *Dokumente zu Luthers Entwicklung (bis 1519)* (2nd ed., Tübingen, 1929), and Reiner Grosz, et al., *Martin Luther 1483–1546: Dokumente seines Lebens und Wirkens* (Weimar, 1983), documents from the state archives of the G.D.R. The most popular biography in English remains Roland H. Bainton, *Here I Stand: A Life of Martin Luther* (Nashville, Tenn., 1950). The most replete with information is E. G. Schwiebert, *Luther and His Times: The Reformation from a New Perspective* (St. Louis, 1950), stressing the university setting. Helmar Junghans, *Wittenberg als Lutherstadt* (Göttingen, 1979), reveals an amazing familiarity with every nook and cranny of Luther's town. Other biographical works, whose titles must speak for themselves, are Heinrich Boehmer, *Martin Luther: Road to Reformation* (Cleveland, 1967); E. Gordon Rupp, *Luther's Progress to the Diet of Worms* (New York, 1964); Ian Siggins, *Luther and His Mother* (Philadelphia, 1981); R. H. Fife, *The Revolt of Martin Luther* (New York, 1957); James Atkinson, *Martin Luther and the Birth of Protestantism* (London, 1968); Gerhard Ritter, *Luther: His*

Life and Work (New York, 1963); John Todd, an English Catholic, *Luther: A Life* (New York, 1982); Eric W. Gritsch, *Martin—God's Court Jester: Luther in Retrospect* (Philadelphia, 1983); H. G. Haile, *Luther: An Experiment in Biography* (New York, 1980), on the years 1534–1546; Heiko A. Oberman, *Luther: Mensch zwischen Gott und Teufel* (Berlin, 1981); Oskar Thulin, *Illustrated History of the Reformation* (St. Louis, 1967); and Peter Manns and Helmuth Loose, *Luther: An Illustrated Biography* (New York, 1982).

Several excellent monographs address particular biographical problems: Daniel Olivier, *The Trial of Luther* (St. Louis, 1978; Paris, 1971): Erwin Iserloh, *The Theses Were Not Posted: Luther Between Reform and Reformation* (Boston, 1968); Kurt Aland, *Martin Luther's 95 Theses* (St. Louis, 1967); Heinz Bluhm, *Martin Luther, Creative Translator* (St. Louis, 1965); Mark U. Edwards, *Luther and the False Brethren* (Stanford, 1975); Mark U. Edwards, *Luther's Last Battles: Politics and Polemics 1531–46* (Ithaca, N.Y., 1983); Mark U. Edwards and George Tavard, *Luther: A Reformer for the Churches* (Philadelphia and New York, 1983); Martin Ebon, *The Last Days of Luther* (New York, 1970).

The approach and arrival of the quincentennial year (1983) of Luther's birth inspired many of the leading German Reformation scholars to do biographies of Luther, among them the following: Martin Brecht, *Martin Luther: Sein Weg zur Reformation 1483–1521* (Stuttgart, 1981), an excellent, thoroughly reliable account based on new research on the young Luther; Walther von Loewenich, *Martin Luther: The Man and His Work* (Minneapolis, 1983; Munich, 1982), a last tribute from the great Erlangen Luther scholar; Heinrich Bornkamm, *Luther in Mid-Career* (Philadelphia, 1983; Göttingen, 1979); Hans Mayer, *Martin Luther: Leben und Glauben* (Gütersloh, 1982), an original but popular effort lacking citations; Michael Meisner, *Martin Luther: Heiliger oder Rebell* (Lübeck, 1981; 2nd ed., 1983); Helmar Junghans, ed., *Leben und Werk Martin Luthers von 1526 bis 1546: Festgabe zu seinem 500. Geburtstag* (2 vols., Berlin, 1983); Bernhard Lohse, *Martin Luther: Eine Einführung in sein Leben und sein Werk* (Munich, 1981), offering a masterful overview of important problems of Luther research; Joachim Rogge, *Martin Luther: Sein Leben. Seine Zeit* (Berlin, 1983), a beautifully written and illustrated work.

Luther's Theology: Three works helpful by way of understanding the development of Luther interpretation are Bernd Moeller, ed., *Luther in der Neuzeit* (*S.V.f.R.,* 192) (Gütersloh, 1983); Jaroslav Pelikan, ed., *Interpreters of Luther: Essays in Honor of Wilhelm Pauck* (Philadelphia, 1968), interpreters from Luther himself to Harnack, Troeltsch, and Tillich; and Pfarrer Wilfried Beck, *Jesus Christus—Unsere Erlösung* (2 vols., Giessen, 1983), a critical assessment of philosophizing and politicizing tendencies in German Luther literature. Among the many more recent presentations of Luther's theology as a whole, the following are worthy of special notice: Walther von Loewenich, *Luther's Theology of the Cross* (Minneapolis, 1976; 5th ed., Witten, 1967); Gerhard Ebeling, *Luther: An Introduc-*

tion to His Thought (Philadelphia, 1970; Tübingen, 1964), with an existential emphasis; Heinrich Bornkamm, *Luther's World of Thought* (St. Louis, 1958); Paul Althaus, *The Theology of Martin Luther* (Philadelphia, 1966), by the Erlangen Lutheran theologian; Werner Elert, *The Structure of Lutheranism* (St. Louis, 1962; reprint, 2 vols., Munich, 1958). Two superb introductions by Catholic scholars are Otto Hermann Pesch, *Hinführung zu Luther* (Mainz, 1982), and Daniel Olivier, *Luther's Faith: The Cause of the Gospel in the Church* (St. Louis, 1983; Paris, 1978).

On Luther's own "tower experience," see Uuras Saarnivaara, *Luther Discovers the Gospel* (St. Louis, 1951), for a late dating. Marilyn J. Harran, *Luther on Conversion: The Early Years* (Ithaca, N.Y., 1983), analyzes Luther's developing thought on conversion from about 1509 to 1519, with a final word on his own "conversion" to an evangelical position. On Luther's christology and his understanding of sin, grace, faith, and reason the following works are to be highly recommended: Marc Lienhard, *Luther, Witness to Jesus Christ: Stages and Themes of the Reformer's Christology* (Minneapolis, 1982; Paris, 1973); Gordon Rupp, *The Righteousness of God: Luther Studies* (London, 1953); P. S. Watson, *Let God Be God!* (London, 1947); Brian Gerrish, *Grace and Reason: A Study in the Theology of Martin Luther* (Oxford, 1962); Reinhard Schwarz, *Fides, Spes und Caritas beim jungen Luther* (Berlin, 1962); Jared Wicks, S.J., *Man Yearning for Grace: Luther's Early Spiritual Teaching* (Washington, D.C., 1968), and *Luther and His Spiritual Legacy* (Wilmington, Del., 1983). Gerhard Ebeling, *Lutherstudien* I (Tübingen, 1971), *Lutherstudien* II in two parts, *Disputatio de Homine* (Tübingen, 1977, 1982), is a profound treatment of Luther's anthropology based on his disputation of 1536.

Several additional monographs should be cited as well: Michael G. Baylor, *Action and Person: Conscience in Late Scholasticism and the Young Luther* (Leiden, 1977); Heinrich Bornkamm, *Luther and the Old Testament* (Philadelphia, 1969); Bengt R. Hoffman, *Luther and the Mystics* (Minneapolis, 1976); David Steinmetz, *Luther and Staupitz* (Durham, N.C., 1980); Scott Hendrix, *Luther and the Papacy: Stages in a Reformation Conflict* (Philadelphia, 1981); Steven Ozment, *Mysticism and Dissent: Religious Ideology and Social Protest in the Sixteenth Century* (New Haven, 1973); J. S. Preus, *From Shadow to Promise: Old Testament Interpretation from Augustine to the Young Luther* (Cambridge, Mass., 1969); Steven Ozment, *Homo Spiritualis: A Comparative Study of the Anthropology of Tauler, Gerson, and Martin Luther (1509–1516)* (Leiden, 1968); Leif Grane, *Contra Gabrielem: Luthers Auseinandersetzung mit Gabriel Biel in der Disputatio contra Scholasticam Theologiam 1517* (Gyldendal, 1962), a brilliant analysis of Luther's rejection of scholastic philosophy; Leif Grane, *Modus Loquendi Theologicus* (Leiden, 1975); and Heiko Augustinus Oberman, *The Harvest of Medieval Theology* (Cambridge, Mass., 1963). Otto Pesch, *Theologie der Rechtfertigung bei Martin Luther und Thomas von Aquin* (Mainz, 1967), offers a masterful analysis of Luther and the *via antiqua* embodied in Thomas. Peter Newman Brooks, ed., *Seven-Headed Luther: Essays in Commemoration of a Quincentenary 1483–*

1983 (Oxford, 1983), may serve as a final entry marking the surge of publications on Luther up to this present year.

   Printing and the Reformation: From Luther the publicist, who thought the press to be God's last great gift to man for spreading the gospel, to the present, the linkage of printing and Reformation has been well appreciated. But scholarship on the subject has reached a fever pitch the past twenty years. Only a partial selection of important titles can be offered here. For a survey see C. S. L. Davies, *Peace, Print and Protestantism, 1450–1558* (London, 1976). Henry S. Bennett, *English Books and Readers, 1475 to 1640* (3 vols., Cambridge, 1952–1970), of which the first volume covers 1475–1557, states that half of Caxton's output was "religious." Elisabeth Eisenstein, *The Printing Press as an Agent of Change* (2 vols., Cambridge, 1978) emphasizes printing's role in intellectual change. Lucien Febvre and Henri-Jean Martin's earlier French work has now appeared as *The Coming of the Book: The Impact of Printing 1450–1800* (London, 1976). Rudolf Hirsch's highly regarded journal articles have appeared in a reprint edition, *The Printed Word: Its Impact and Diffusion, Primarily in the Fifteenth to Sixteenth Centuries* (London, 1978). See also Rudolf Hirsch, *Printing, Selling and Reading 1450–1550* (Wiesbaden, 1967). Two important studies in German focus on our period, Josef Benzing, *Die Buchdrucker des 16. und 17. Jahrhunderts im deutschen Sprachgebiet* (Wiesbaden, 1963), and Hans Joachim Bremme, *Buchdrucker und Buchhändler zur Zeit der Glaubenskämpfe* (Geneva, 1969). Maria Grossmann writes of printing in Wittenberg, which at one point was producing more publications than all of England: "Wittenberg Printing, Early Sixteenth Century," *Sixteenth Century Essays and Studies,* I (St. Louis, 1970), 54–74. A superb study centering on a key city is Miriam Chrisman, *Lay Culture, Learned Culture: Books and Social Change in Strasbourg* (New Haven, 1982).

   The impact of printed books but especially also of pamphlets has received attention as an instrument of religious and social change. Representative studies include Robert W. Scribner, *For the Sake of Simple Folk: Popular Propaganda for the German Reformation* (Cambridge, 1981); Richard G. Cole, "Dynamics of Printing in the Sixteenth Century," *The Social History of the Reformation,* Lawrence P. Buck and Jonathan W. Zophy, eds. (Columbus, Ohio, 1972), pp. 93–95; Hans-Joachim Köhler, *Flugschriften als Massenmedium der Reformationszeit* (Stuttgart, 1981); Rolf W. Brednich, *Die Liedpublizistik im Flugblatt des 15. bis 17. Jahrhunderts* (2 vols., Baden-Baden, 1974–1975); W. Wettges, *Reformation und Propaganda* (Stuttgart, 1978); Michael A. Pegg, *A Catalogue of German Reformation Pamphlets (1516–1546) in the Libraries of Great Britain and Ireland (Bibliographica Aureliana* 45) (Baden-Baden, 1973). Scholars of the older generation, such as Otto Clemen and Karl Schottenloher, appreciated the popular influence of pamphleteers such as Eberlin von Günzburg, Pamphilus Gegenbach, Sebastian Lotzer, Thomas Murner, Daniel von Soest, and even the shoemaker-poet Hans Sachs and did editions and lists of their pamphlets. Recently many works have appeared on the pamphlet and the knights' revolt, the peasants' revolt, the urban reformation, and social protest, not just the religious pamphlets of the reformers. See Steven Ozment, "Pamphlet Literature of the German Reformation," in his *Reformation Europe: A Guide to Research,* pp. 85–105. Pamphlet literature and the importance of printing for the French Reformation will be included later under the bibliography for chapter 4.

Melanchthon, Bucer, and Brenz: Luther's "lieutenant" Philip Melanchthon, who organized and systematized Luther's thought, was the principal author of the first Protestant confession, the Augsburg Confession, and led the movement after his death. His works are in the *Corpus Reformatorum* and in the various supplements. A few of the many works on him must be included in this survey: Clyde L. Manschrek, *Melanchthon: The Quiet Reformer* (New York, 1958); Lowell C. Green, ed., *Melanchthon in English: New Translations into English with a Registry of Previous Translations* (*Sixteenth Century Bibliography,* 22) (St. Louis, 1982); Peter Fraenkel, *Testimonia Patrum: The Function of the Patristic Argument in the Theology of Melanchthon* (Geneva, 1961); Carl Maxcey, *Bona Opera: A Study in the Development of the Doctrine in Philip Melanchthon* (Nieuwkoop, 1980). The best work on the younger Melanchthon is that of Wilhelm Maurer of Erlangen, *Der junge Melanchthon* (2 vols., Göttingen, 1967, 1969). Martin Greschat points to Luther and Melanchthon's close cooperation against the argument that the younger man went his own way in *Melanchthon neben Luther: Studien zur Gestalt der Rechtfertigungslehre zwischen 1528 und 1537* (Witten, 1965). For further Melanchthon studies see Peter Fraenkel and Martin Greschat, *Zwanzig Jahre Melanchthonstudium* (Geneva, 1967). Two standard Bucer biographies are Hastings Eels, *Martin Bucer* (New Haven, 1931), and Constantin Hopf, *Martin Bucer and the English Reformation* (Oxford, 1946). Various studies by Martin Brecht are of special value for Johannes Brenz and in English: James M. Estes, *Christian Magistrate and State Church: The Reformation Career of Johannes Brenz* (Toronto, 1982).

Karlstadt: J. S. Preus, *Carlstadt's Ordinaciones and Luther's Liberty: A Study of the Wittenberg Movement 1521–1522* (Cambridge, Mass., 1974); Calvin A. Pater, *Karlstadt as the Father of the Baptist Movements* (Toronto, 1983); Gordon Rupp, *Patterns of Reformation* (Philadelphia, 1969), Part II: Andrew Karlstadt; Ronald J. Sider, *Andreas Bodenstein von Karlstadt: The Development of His Thought, 1517–1525* (Leiden, 1974); R. J. Sider, eds., *Karlstadt's Battle with Luther: Documents in a Liberal-Radical Debate* (Philadelphia, 1978); L. B. Volkmar, *Luther's Response to Violence* (New York, 1974).

Luther's Catholic Opponents: John P. Dolan, "The Catholic Literary Opponents of Luther," *Journal of Ecumenical Studies,* II (1974), 447–66, is one of the more recent bibliographical studies. Remigius Bäumer, ed., *Von Konstanz nach Trient: Festgabe für August Franzen* (Munich, 1972), contains excellent articles such as P. Fraenkel on Eck and More. Ford Louis Battles has translated John Eck, *Enchiridion* of Commonplaces Against Luther and Other Enemies of the Church (Grand Rapids, Mich., 1979). On Cajetan, see Marvin O'Connell, "Cardinal Cajetan: Intellectual and Activist," The New Scholasticism, 50, 3 (1976), 310–22; Jared Wicks, Cajetan Responds: A Reader in Reformation Controversy (Baltimore, 1978); Gerhard Hennig, Cajetan und Luther: Ein historischer Beitrag zur Begegnung von Thomismus und Reformation (Stuttgart, 1966). John C. Olin et al., eds., Luther, Erasmus and the Reformation: A Catholic-Protestant Reappraisal (New York, 1969), offers articles by Catholic and Protestant authors such as Wilhelm Pauck, Harold Grimm, and a bibliography of recent studies of Luther and the Reformation. Luther and Erasmus in their famous exchange on freedom or bondage of the will have received an inordinate amount of attention, the texts translated and edited in the Library of Christian Classics, 17, by E. Gordon Rupp and A. N. Marlow et al., Luther and Erasmus: Free Will and Salvation (London and Philadelphia, 1969). Harry J. McSorley, C.S.P., Luther, Right or Wrong?: An Ecumenical-Theological Study of Luther's Major Work, The Bondage of the Will (New York and Minneapolis, 1969), offers a close examination of the issues. Setting the debate into the general context of Luther's theology is Ernst-Wilhelm Kohls, Luther oder Erasmus: Luthers Theologie in der Auseinandersetzung mit Erasmus (Basel, 1972). A recent work is R. D. Jones, Erasmus and Luther (Oxford, 1968).

Peasants' War: Studies historiographical and bibliographical in nature are Tom Scott, "The Peasants' War: A Historiographical Review: Parts I and II," Historical Journal, 22 (1979), 693–720, 953–74; U. Thomas, Bibliographie zum deutschen Bauernkrieg und seiner Zeit (Stuttgart, 1976–77), since 1974; R. W. Scribner and Gerhard Benecke, The German Peasants' War 1525: New Viewpoints (London, 1979); H. C. Erik Midelfort, "The Revolution of 1525? Recent Studies of the Peasants' War," Central European History, 11, no. 2 (June, 1978), 189–206, a review article including other literature reviews. Franz Günther, Der deutsche Bauernkrieg (Munich, 1933; 11th ed., Darmstadt, 1977), the standard work on the peasants' revolt. See also his edited volume Bauernschaft und Bauernstand 1500–1970 (Limburg/Lahn, 1975). Robert N. Crossley, Luther and the Peasants' War (New York, 1974), is a popular account. Excellent is Peter Blickle, The Revolution of 1525, trans. by Erik Midelfort and Thomas A. Brady, Jr. (Baltimore, 1982; 1st ed., Munich, 1975, 2nd ed., 1983). Also important are the symposium edited by Blickle, Revolte und Revolution in Europa: Referate und Protokolle des Internationalen Symposiums zur Erinnerung an den Bauernkrieg 1525 (Memmingen, 24.–27. März 1975), Historische Zeitschrift, Beiheft 4 (Munich, 1975); Janos Bak, ed., The German Peasant War of 1525 (Library of Peasant Studies, 3) (London, 1976); Hans Ulrich Wehler, ed., Der deutsche Bauernkrieg 1524–1526 (Göttingen, 1975); Rainer Wohlfeil, Der Bauernkrieg 1524–1526 (Munich, 1975); R. Wohlfeil, ed., Reformation oder frühbürgerliche Revolution (Munich, 1972); Bernd Moeller, ed., Bauernkrieg-Studien (Gütersloh, 1975); David Sabean, Landbesitz und Gesellschaft am Vorabend des

Bauernkriegs (Stuttgart, 1972). Two books make clear that the German peasantry did not after 1525 lapse into nonviolent and apolitical apathy, Winfried Schulze, *Bäuerlicher Widerstand und feudale Herrschaft in der frühen Neuzeit (Neuzeit im Aufbau 6)* (Stuttgart, 1980), and Peter Blickle et al., *Aufruhr und Empörung?: Studien zum bäuerlichen Widerstand im Alten Reich* (Munich, 1980). For the Habsburg realms, see Hermann Rebel, *Peasant Classes: The Bureaucratization of Property and Family Relations Under Early Habsburg Absolutism, 1511–1636* (Princeton, 1983), and a monograph on the Tyrol, Aldo Stella, *La Rivoluzione Contadina del 1525 e L'Utopia di Michael Gaismayr* (Padua, 1975).

The old party line of the Marxists was set down by Friedrich Engels, *The German Revolutions: The Peasant War in Germany* and *Germany: Revolution and Counter-Revolution,* ed. Leonard Krieger (Chicago, 1967), originally written 1850. This view held Luther to be the reactionary and the peasants' war with Thomas Müntzer as a key figure to represent the true reformation or revolution. Marxist historiography has shifted emphasis to Luther's reformation as the early bourgois revolution, a trend evident in the following newer books: Gerhard Brendler and Adolf Laube, eds., *Der deutsche Bauernkrieg 1524/25: Geschichte, Traditionen, Lehren* (Berlin, 1977); Adolf Laube, Max Steinmetz, and Günter Vogler, *Illustrierte Geschichte der deutschen frühbürgerlichen Revolution* (Berlin, 1974); M. Bensing and S. Hoyer, *Der deutsche Bauernkrieg* (Berlin, 1965); A. Laube and H. W. Seifert, eds., *Flugschriften der Bauernkriegszeit* (Berlin, 1975); Max Steinmetz, *Das Müntzerbild von Martin Luther bis Friedrich Engels* (Berlin, 1971); Günter Vogler, *Nürnberg 1524/25: Studien zur Geschichte der reformatorischen und sozialen Bewegung in der Reichsstadt* (Berlin, 1982).

Thomas Münzer: The text-critical edition of his works is by Günther Franz and Paul Kirn, *Schriften und Briefe von Thomas Müntzer; Kritische Gesamtausgabe,* 33, *Quellen und Forschungen zur Reformationsgeschichte* (Gütersloh, 1968). Hans J. Hillerbrand, *Thomas Müntzer: A Bibliography (Sixteenth Century Bibliography,* 4) (St. Louis, 1976), and Hans Joachim Berbig, "Thomas Müntzer in neuer Sicht," *Archiv für Kulturgeschichte,* 59 (1977), 489–95, on the literature 1973–76, provide bibliography. Eric W. Gritsch, *Reformer Without a Church: The Life and Thought of Thomas Müntzer, 1488?–1525* (Philadelphia, 1967), and Walter Elliger, *Thomas Müntzer: Leben und Werk* (Göttingen, 1975), the first all-encompassing biography in German, are the two best biographies. Hans-Jürgen Goertz, *Innere und Äussere Ordnung in der Theologie Thomas Müntzers* (Leiden, 1967), is one of the works stressing Münzer's religious and spiritualist side. From a Marxist perspective, see Max Steinmetz and Siegfried Hoyer, eds., *Der deutsche Bauernkrieg und Thomas Müntzer* (Leipzig, 1976), and Manfred Bensing, *Thomas Müntzer und der Thüringer Aufstand, 1525* (Berlin, 1966).

The Progress of the Lutheran Reformation: Johannes Bühler, *Deutsche Geschichte,* 3, *Das Reformationszeitalter* (Berlin and Leipzig, 1938), has a detailed general account of this period. On the political side, the Schmalkald League is examined in the following works: Hermann Buck, *Die Anfänge der Konstanzer Reformationsprozesse, Österreich, Eidgenossenschaft und Schmalkaldischer Bund, 1510/22–1531* (Tübingen, 1964); Ekkehart Fabian, *Die Entstehung des Schmalkaldischen Bundes und seiner Verfassung 1524/29–1531/35* (Tübingen, 1962); Gundmar Blume, *Goslar und der Schmalkaldische Bund 1527/31–1547* (Goslar, 1969). The Augsburg Confession and other confessional writings are represented by Joseph Burgess, ed., *The Role of the Augsburg Confession: Catholic and Lutheran Views* (Philadelphia, 1980); Bernhard Lohse and Otto Hermann Pesch, eds., *Das 'Augsburger Bekenntnis' von 1530: Damals und heute* (Munich, 1980); *La Confession d'Augsbourg. 450e anniversaire: Autour d'un Colloque oecumenique international* (*Le Point Theol.*, 37) (Paris, 1980); Erwin Iserloh, ed., *Confessio Augustana und Confutatio: Der Augsburger Reichstag und die Einheit der Kirche* (Münster, 1980); Edmund Schlink, *Theology of the Lutheran Confessions* (Philadelphia, 1961); Werner Elert, *The Structure of Lutheranism* (St. Louis, 1962; Munich, 2 vols., 1931, rev. ed., 1958); Conrad Bergendoff, *The Church of the Lutheran Reformation* (St. Louis, 1967). On the clergy, see B. Vogler, *Le clergé protestant rhénan au siècle de la Réforme (1555–1619)* (Paris, 1976); Suzanne Karant-Nunn Boles, "The Economic Position of Lutheran Pastors in Ernestine Thuringia 1521–1555," *Archiv für Reformationsgeschichte*, 63 (1972), 94–125, and *Luther's Pastors: The Reformation in the Ernestine Countryside* (*Transactions of the American Philosophical Society*, 69, 8) (Philadelphia, 1979).

Lutheranism in Northern and Eastern Europe: E. H. Dunkley, *The Reformation in Denmark* (London, 1948); K. E. Christopherson, "Hallelujahs, Damnations, or Norway's Reformation as a Lengthy Process," *Church History*, 48 (1979), 279–99, a historiographical essay; Conrad Bergendoff, *Olavus Petri and the Ecclesiastical Transformation of Sweden, 1521–1552* (New York, 1928); Paul Fox, *The Reformation in Poland* (Baltimore, 1924); Grete Mecenseffy, *Geschichte des Protestantismus in Österreich* (Graz, 1956); Konrad von Moltke, *Siegmund von Dietrichstein: Die Anfänge ständischer Institutionen und das Eindringen des Protestantismus in die Steiermark zur Zeit Maximilians I und Ferdinands I* (Göttingen, 1970); Karl Reinerth, *Die Gründung der Evangelischen Kirchen in Siebenbürgen* (Vienna, 1979); J. S. Szabo, *Der Protestantismus in Ungarn* (Berlin, 1927); Mihály Bucsay, *Der Protestantismus in Ungarn, 1521–1978* (2 vols., Vienna, 1977–); Imre Révész, *History of the Hungarian Reformed Church* (Washington, 1956); David P. Daniel, *The Historiography of the Reformation in Slovakia* (*Sixteenth Century Bibliography* 10) (St. Louis., 1977), and "Highlights of the Lutheran Reformation in Slovakia," *Concordia Theological Quarterly*, 42 (1978), 21–34.

THE PROGRESS OF PROTESTANTISM

Swiss Background: Rudolf Pfister, *Kirchengeschichte der Schweiz*, II, *Von der Reformation bis zum zweiten Villmerger Krieg* (Zurich, 1974), pp. 3–11, provides an adequate discussion of the ecclesiastical and general religious conditions at the beginning of the Reformation in Switzerland. Since the city council played such a crucial part in the Zurich reform, of special interest is Hans Morf, "Obrigkeit und Kirche in Zürich bis zu Beginn der Reformation," *Zwingliana,* 13 (1970), 164–205; George R. Potter, "The Renaissance in Switzerland," *Journal of Medieval History,* 2 (1976), 365–82.

Zwingli: H. Wayne Pipkin, *A Zwingli Bibliography* (Pittsburgh, 1972), for basic titles. G. R. Potter, *Zwingli* (Cambridge, 1976), and his work for scholars, *Ulrich Zwingli* (London, 1977), are based on good archival work in Zurich. Biographical and immediate historical works on Zwingli include Walther E. Köhler, *Huldrych Zwingli* (Leipzig, 1943; 2nd ed., Stuttgart, 1952); Wilhelm H. Neuser, *Die reformatorische Wende bei Zwingli* (Neukirchen-Vluyn, 1977); Arthur Rich, *Die Anfänge der Theologie Huldrych Zwinglis* (Zurich, 1949), a definitive study; Jean Horace Rilliet, *Zwingli: Third Man of the Reformation* (Philadelphia, 1964); Jacques Pollet, *Huldrych Zwingli et la Réforme en Suisse* (Paris, 1963); Jaques Courvoisier, *Zwingli: A Reformed Theologian* (Richmond, Va., 1963); Fritz Büsser, *Huldrych Zwingli: Reformation als prophetischer Auftrag* (Zurich, 1973), very positive; Martin Haas, *Huldrych Zwingli und seine Zeit* (2nd ed., Zurich, 1976), the best biography according to some authorities, but not so strong on theology as Büsser; Oskar Farner, *Huldrych Zwingli* (4 vols., Zurich, 1943–1960) and *Zwingli the Reformer,* trans. by D. G. Sear (New York, 1952); the old English-language classic, Samuel Macauley Jackson, *Huldreich Zwingli: The Reformer of German Switzerland 1484–1531* (New York, 1901). On Zwingli and the Zurich government: Robert Clifford Walton, *Zwingli's Theocracy* (Toronto, 1967). On Zwingli, visual arts and music: Charles Garside, *Zwingli and the Arts* (New Haven, 1966). Zwingli and theology: S. Rother, *Die religiösen und geistigen Grundlagen der Politik H. Zwinglis* (Erlangen, 1956); Walther Köhler, *Das Marburger Religionsgespräch 1529* (Leipzig, 1929); Walther Köhler, *Zwingli und Luther: Ihr Streit über das Abendmahl nach seinen politischen und religiösen Beziehungen,* 2 vols., *Quellen und Forschungen zur Reformationsgeschichte,* 6–7, 63–163 (Leipzig, 1924–53); Ernst Bizer, *Studien zur Geschichte des Abendmahlstreits im 16. Jahrhundert* (Gütersloh, 1940, repr., Darmstadt, 1952); Hermann Sasse, *This Is My Body: Luther's Contention for the Real Presence* (Minneapolis, 1959).

Zwingli and Bullinger: G. W. Bromiley, *Zwingli and Bullinger (Library of Christian Classics,* 24) (Philadelphia, 1953); André Bouvier, *Henri Bullinger: Réformateur et conseilleur oecuménique* (Zurich, 1940); J. Wayne Baker, *Heinrich Bullinger and the Covenant: The Other Reformed Tradition* (Athens, Ohio, 1980).

Vadian: C. Bonorad, *Vadians Weg vom Humanismus zur Reformation* (St. Gallen, 1962); Werner Näf, *Vadian und seine Stadt St. Gallen* (2 vols., St. Gallen, 1944, 1957).

Anabaptism: On the sectarian mentality in general, Norman Cohn, *The Pursuit of the Millennium* (3rd ed., London, 1970), has become a classic of sorts. The massive study is George H. Williams, *The Radical Reformation* (Philadelphia, 1962), who also edited *Spiritual and Anabaptist Writers: Documents Illustrative of the Radical Reformation* (Philadelphia, 1957). Some bibliographical aids are Hans J. Hillerbrand, ed., *A Bibliography of Anabaptism* (Elkhart, 1962), and *A Bibliography of Anabaptism, 1520–1630: A Sequel, 1962–1974* (*Sixteenth Century Bibliography*, 1) (St. Louis, 1975); George H. Williams, "Studies in the Radical Reformation (1517–1618): A Bibliographical Survey of Research Since 1939," *Church History,* 27 (1958), 46–69, 124–160; André Sequenny, ed., *Bibliotheca Dissidentium: Répertoire des non-conformistes religieux des seizième et dix-septième siècles,* vol. 1 (*Bibliographica Aureliana,* 79) (Baden-Baden, 1980); Hans J. Hillerbrand, *A Bibliography of Menno Simons (c. 1520–1630)* (Elkhart, Ind., 1962). General studies of the movement and of the spectrum of Anabaptist religious thought include Claus-Peter Clasen, *Anabaptism, a Social History, 1525–1618: Switzerland, Austria, Moravia, South and Central Germany* (Ithaca, N.Y., 1972); Kenneth R. Davis, *Anabaptism and Asceticism: A Study in Intellectual Origins* (Scottdale, Pa., 1974); Hans-Jürgen Goertz, *Die Täufer: Geschichte und Deutung* (Munich, 1980), the first comprehensive interpretation to transcend idealizing of their theology; Franklin H. Littell, *The Origins of Sectarian Protestantism: A Study of the Anabaptist View of the Church* (New York, 1964); Michael Mullett, *Radical Religious Movements in Early Modern Europe* (London, 1980); Steven Ozment, *Mysticism and Dissent: Religious Ideology and Social Protest in the Sixteenth Century* (New Haven and London, 1973); Werner Packull, *Mysticism and the Early South German-Austrian Anabaptist Movement* (Scottdale, Pa., 1977); Paul Peachey, *Die soziale Herkunft der Schweizer Täufer in der Reformationszeit, 1525–1540* (Karlsruhe, 1954); Cornelius Krahn, *Dutch Anabaptism: Origin, Spread, Life, and Thought, 1450–1600* (The Hague, 1968); James Stayer, *Anabaptists and the Sword* (Lawrence, Kan., 1972); James Stayer and Werner Packull, eds., *The Anabaptists and Thomas Müntzer* (Dubuque, Iowa, 1980), a historiographical anthology with a critical introduction; Robert Friedmann, *The Theology of Anabaptism* (Scottdale, Pa., 1973); Leonard Gross, *The Golden Years of the Hutterites* (Scottdale, Pa., 1980); Peter J. Klassen, *The Economics of Anabaptism, 1525–1560* (The Hague, 1964); Walter Klaassen, *Anabaptism: Neither Catholic nor Protestant* (Waterloo, 1973); Walter Klaassen, ed., *Anabaptism in Outline: Selected Primary Sources* (Scottdale, Pa., 1981); Guy E. Hershberger, ed., *The Recovery of the Anabaptist Vision: A Sixtieth Anniversary Tribute to Harold S. Bender* (Scottdale, Pa., 1957); Harold Bender, *The Anabaptists and Religious Liberty in the Sixteenth Century* (Philadelphia, 1970); K. N. Kirchhoff, *Die Täufer in Münster 1534/5: Untersuchungen zum Umfang und zur Sozialstruktur der Bewegung* (Münster, 1973); R. Po-chia Hsia, *Society and Religion in Münster, 1535–1618* (New Haven, 1984); Jarold Zeman, *The Anabaptists and the Czech Brethren in Moravia, 1526–1628: A Study of Origins and Contacts* (The Hague, 1969); Lowell P. Zuck, *Christianity and Revolution: Radical Christian Testimonies, 1520–1650* (Philadelphia, 1975).

Biographical Studies Worth Special Mention: Harold S. Bender, *The Life and Letters of Conrad Grebel* (Goshen, Ind., 1950–), 1, entitled *Conrad Grebel ca. 1498–1526: The Founder of the Swiss Brethren, Sometimes Called the Anabaptists;* Roland H. Bainton, *David Joris* (Leipzig, 1937); Torsten Bergsten, *Balthasar Hubmaier: Seine Stellung zu Reformation und Täufertum* (Kassel, 1961); John L. Ruth, *Conrad Grebel: Son of Zurich* (Scottdale, Pa., 1975), admiring and a bit uncritical; Klaus Deppermann, *Melchior Hoffman: Soziale Unruhen und Apokalyptischen Visionen im Zeitalter der Reformation* (Göttingen, 1979); E. Geldbach, "Toward a More Ample Biography of the Hessian Anabaptist Leader Melchior Rinck," *Mennonite Quarterly Review,* 48 (1974) 371–84; James M. Stayer, The Münsterite Rationalization of Bernhard Rothmann," *Journal of the History of Ideas,* 28 (April–June, 1967), 179–92; Walter Klaassen, *Michael Gaismair: Revolutionary and Reformer (Studies in Medieval and Reformation Thought,* 23) (Leiden, 1978); Hans-Jürgen Goertz, *Profiles of Radical Reformers: Biographical Sketches from Thomas Müntzer to Paracelsus* (Scottdale, Pa., 1982; Munich, 1978).

Two works by Marxist scholars are Gerhard Brendler, *Das Täuferreich zu Münster 1534/35* (Berlin, 1966), and Gerhard Zchäbitz, *Zur Mitteldeutschen Wiedertäuferbewegung nach dem grossen Bauernkrieg* (Berlin, 1958). Two books on the Anabaptists and magisterial reformers: Heinold Fast, *Heinrich Bullinger und die Täufer* (Weierhof, 1959), and John S. Oyer, *Lutheran Reformers Against Anabaptists: Luther, Melanchthon and Menius, and the Anabaptists of Central Germany* (The Hague, 1964).

Spiritualists and Evangelical Humanists: Delio Cantimori, *Eretici italiani del Cinquecento: Ricerche storiche* (Florence, 1967; 1st ed., 1939); Domenico Caccamo, *Eretici italiani in Moravia, Polonia Transilvania (1558–1611)* (Florence, 1970); E. M. Wilbur, *A History of Unitarianism, Socinianism and Its Antecedents* (Cambridge, Mass., 1945); Roland H. Bainton, *The Travail of Religious Liberty* (Philadelphia, 1951); Joseph Lecler, *Toleration and the Reformation* (2 vols., New York, 1960); Stanislaw Kot, *Socinianism in Poland: The Social and Political Ideas of the Polish Antitrinitarians in the Sixteenth and Seventeenth Centuries* (Boston, 1957); Marc Lienhard, *Les Dissidents du XVIᵉ Siècle entre l'Humanisme et le Catholicisme* (Strasbourg, 1983), *Actes du Colloque de Strasbourg (5–6 février, 1982).*

Individual Biographies and Thought: David Steinmetz, *Reformers in the Wings* (Philadelphia, 1971); Will-Erich Peuckert, *Sebastian Franck ein deutscher Sucher* (Munich, 1943); Alfred Hegler, *Geist und Schrift bei Sebastien Franck: Eine Studie zur Geschichte des Spiritualismus in der Reformationszeit* (Freiburg, 1892); Paul Maier, *Caspar Schwenkfeld on the Person and Work of Christ* (Assen, 1959); Anne Jacobson Schutte, *Pier Paolo Vergerio: The Making of an Italian Reformer* (Geneva, 1977); Roland H. Bainton, *Hunted Heretic: The Life and Death of Michael Servetus 1511–1553* (Boston, 1953); Jerome Friedman, *Michael Servetus: A Case Study in Total Heresy* (Geneva, 1978); Werner Kaegi, *Castellio und die Anfänge der Tolerance* (Basel,

1953); Hans R. Guggisberg, *Sebastian Castellio im Urteil seiner Nachwelt vom Spät-humanismus bis zur Aufklärung* (Basel and Stuttgart, 1956).

Urban Reformation: To begin with, certain more general studies will be listed, as usual here in the general order of their utility to advanced students of history, and then various recent studies of the Reformation in the cities of the Empire, including Switzerland: Steven E. Ozment, *The Reformation in the Cities: The Appeal of Protestantism to Sixteenth-Century Germany and Switzerland* (New Haven, 1975); Alfred Schultze, *Stadtgemeinde und Reformation* (Tübingen, 1918), an older work illustrating that there is little novelty, despite the bravado of current historians, about "city reformation"; A. G. Dickens, *The German Nation and Martin Luther* (New York, 1974), chapters 7–9; Franz Lau, "Der Bauernkrieg und das Ange-bliche Ende der lutherischen Reformation als spontaner Volksbewegung," *Luther-Jahrbuch*, 26 (1959), 109–134; I. Bátori, ed., *Städtische Gesellschaft und Reformation* (Stuttgart, 1980); W. J. Mommsen et al., eds., *Stadtbürgertum und Adel in der Reformation / The Urban Classes, the Nobility and the Reformation* (*Publications of the German Historical Institute London*, 5) (Stuttgart, 1979); Bernd Moeller, *Imperial Cities and the Reformation: Three Essays*, trans. by Erik Midelfort and Mark U. Edwards, Jr. (Philadelphia, 1972).

Individual Cities: Gerald Strauss, *Nuremberg in the Sixteenth Century* (New York, 1966); Gottfried Seebass, "The Reformation in Nürnberg," in Jonathan W. Zophy and Lawrence P. Buck, eds., *The Social History of the Reformation* (Columbus, Ohio, 1972), pp. 17–40; Jackson Spielvogel, "Patricians in Dissension: A Case Study from Sixteenth Century Nürnberg," in ibid., pp. 73–92; Harold J. Grimm, *Lazarus Spengler: A Lay Leader of the Reformation* (Columbus, 1979); Rolf Kiessling, *Bürgerliche Gesellschaft und Kirche in Augsburg im Spätmittelalter: Ein Beitrag zur Strukturanalyse der oberdeutschen Reichsstadt* (Augsburg, 1971); Eberhard Naujoks, *Obrigkeitsgedanke, Zunftverfassung und Reformation: Studien zur Verfassungsgeschichte von Ulm, Esslingen und Schwäbisch Gmünd* (Stuttgart, 1958); Francis Rapp, *Réformes et Réformation à Strasbourg: Église et Société dans la diocèse (1450–1525)* (Paris, 1975); Miriam Usher Chrisman, *Strasbourg and the Reform: A Study in the Process of Change* (New Haven, 1967); Thomas A. Brady, Jr., *Ruling Class, Regime and Reformation at Strasbourg 1520–1555* (Leiden, 1978), stressing the disunity and factiousness of Reformation cities; Kaspar von Greyerz, *The Late City Reformation in Germany: The Case of Colmar 1522–1628* (Wiesbaden, 1980); Hans-Christoph Rublack, *Die Ein-führung der Reformation in Konstanz* (Gütersloh, 1971); Hans-Christoph Rublack, *Eine bürgerliche Reformation: Nördlingen (Quellen und Forschungen zur Reformationsges-chichte*, 51) (Gütersloh, 1982); Albert Schulze, *Bekenntnisbildung und Politik Lin-daus im Zeitalter der Reformation* (Nuremberg, 1971); Johannes Schildhauer, *Soziale, politische und religiöse Auseinandersetzungen in den Hansestädten Stralsund, Rostock und Wismar im ersten Drittel des XVI. Jahrhunderts* (Weimar, 1959); Georg Daur, *Von Predigern und Bürgern: Eine Hamburgische Kirchengeschichte von der Reformation bis zur*

Gegenwart (Hamburg, 1970); Heide Stratenwerth, *Die Reformation in der Stadt Osnabrück* (Wiesbaden, 1971); Johannes Hermann, "Reformation auf dem platten Lande," in Franz Lau, ed., *Das Hochstift Meissen: Aufsätze zur sächsischen Kirchengeschichte* (Berlin, 1973); Heinz Schilling, *Konfessionskonflikt und Staatsbildung: Eine Fallstudie über das Verhältnis von religiösem und sozialem Wandel in der Frühneuzeit am Beispiel der Grafschaft Lippe* (Gütersloh, 1981); Martin Schmidt, "Die Reformation im Freiberger Ländchen (im Albertinischen Sachsen) 1537 und ihre prototypische Bedeutung," in Lewis W. Spitz, ed., *Humanismus und Reformation als Kulturelle Kräfte in der deutschen Geschichte (Veröffentlichungen der Historischen Kommission zu Berlin,* 51) (Berlin and New York, 1981).

THE SECOND SURGE

General Situation: G. Baum and E. Cunitz, *Histoire ecclésiastique des églises réformées au Royaume de France: Édition nouvelle, avec commentaire, notice bibliographique et table de faits et des noms propres* (3 vols., Paris, 1883–1889); J. H. M. Salmon, *Society in Crisis: France in the Sixteenth Century* (London–Tonbridge, 1975); Jean Jacquart, *François Ier* (Paris, 1981), dividing Francis' life into four periods and integrating all recent research on France from 1515 to 1547; Nancy Roelker, *Queen of Navarre: Jeanne d'Albret, 1528–1572* (Cambridge, Mass., 1968); Victor Martin, *Les origines du gallicanisme* (2 vols., Paris, 1939); J. P. Massaut, *Critique et Tradition à la veille de la Réforme en France* (Paris, 1974).

Humanism in France: Augustin Renaudet, *Préréforme et Humanisme à Paris pendant les Premières Guerres de l'Italie, à 1495–1515* (2nd ed., Paris, 1953); A. H. Levi, *Humanism in France at the End of the Middle Ages* (New York, 1970); Franco Simone, *The French Renaissance* (London, 1969), tracing humanism through the fifteenth century and clarifying the relationship between sixteenth-century humanism and early trends in French culture; Lucien Febvre, *The Problem of Unbelief in the Sixteenth Century: The Religion of Rabelais* (Cambridge, Mass., 1982); G. Bedouelle, *Lefèvre d'Étaples et l'Intelligence des Écritures* (Geneva, 1975); Augustin Renaudet, "Un Problème historique: la Pensée religieuse de J. Lefèvre d'Étaples," in *Humanisme et Renaissance* (Geneva, 1958); Eugene Rice, *The Prefatory Epistles of Jacques Lefèvre d'Étaples and Related Texts* (New York, 1971); Arthur Tilley, author of two venerable volumes on the literature of the French Renaissance, has a chapter on humanism under Francis I in *Studies in the French Renaissance* (Cambridge, 1922); David O. McNeil, *Guillaume Budé and Humanism in the Reign of Francis I* (Geneva, 1975); D. F. Pelham, *Guillaume Budé's De Transitu Hellenismi ad Christianismus* (Ann Arbor, 1955); J. P. Maussaut, *Josse Clichtove* (2 vols., Paris, 1968).

Protestantism in France: Pierre Imbart de la Tour, *Les Origines de la Réforme* (2 vols., 2nd ed. Melun, 1948); Samuel Mours, *Le Protestantisme en France au XVIe siècle* (2 vols., Paris, 1959); still of value, J. Viénot, *Histoire de la Réforme française des origines à l'Édit de Nantes* (Paris, 1926); a classic statement on indigenous or imported reform, Lucien Febvre, "Une question mal posée: Les origines de la réforme française et le problème général des causes de la réforme," *Revue historique*, 161 (1929), 20ff.; W. G. Moore, *La réforme allemande et la littérature française: Récherches sur la notoriété de Luther en France* (Strasbourg, 1930); René Jacques Lovy, *Les origines de la Réforme française: Meaux, 1518–1546* (Paris, 1959); Jan Lavicka, "Les débuts de la Réforme en France, 1530–1540," *Bollettino della Societa di studi valdesi*, 99 (1979), 45–57, asserting that Calvin belonged to a secret Valdesian confraternity prior to his encounter with Lutheran evangelicalism in Paris; also still of value, Henri Hauser, *Études sur la Réforme française* (Paris, 1909), and *La Naissance du Protestantisme* (Paris, 1940; 2nd ed., 1963); and, finally, dealing with a problem analogous to the source of Lutheran preachers, H. Meylan, "Le recrutement et la formation des pasteurs dans les Églises reformées du XVIe siècle," *Miscellanea Historiae Ecclesiasticae,* III (Louvain, 1970), pp. 127–50.

French Reformation and Printing: Hans J. Hillerbrand, "The Spread of the Protestant Reformation of the Sixteenth Century: A Historical Case Study in the Transfer of Ideas," *The South Atlantic Quarterly,* 67, no. 2 (Spring 1968), 265–86; Anatole Claudin, *Histoire de l' imprimerie en France au XVe et au XVIe siècle* (4 vols., Paris 1900–1914); R. Doucet, *Les bibliothèques parisiennes au XVIe siècle* (Paris, 1956); Paul Chaix, *Recherches sur l'imprimerie à Genève de 1550 à 1564* (Geneva, 1954); Paul Chaix, Alain Dufour, and Gustav Moeckli, *Les livres imprimés à Genève de 1550 à 1600* (Geneva, 1966); Robert M. Kingdon, "The Flood Tide: Books from Geneva," in *Geneva and the Coming of the Wars of Religion in France, 1555–1563* (Geneva, 1956), chapter 9; Peter Bietenholz, *Basle and France in the Sixteenth Century: The Basle Humanists and Printers* (Toronto, 1971), and *Der italienische Humanismus und die Blütezeit des Buchdrucks in Basel* (Basel, 1959); J. Baudrier, *Bibliographie lyonnaise: Recherches sur les imprimeurs, libraires, relieurs et fondeurs de lettres de Lyon au XVIe siècle* (12 vols., Lyon and Paris, 1895–1921, reprint, 1964).

Calvin Bibliographies: Wilhelm Niesel, *Calvin-Bibliographie 1901–1959* (Munich, 1961); D. Kampff, *A Bibliography of Calviniana: 1959–1974* (Potchefstroom, 1975), continues Niesel's work; John T. McNeill, "Fifty Years of Calvin Study, 1918–1968," in Williston Walker, *John Calvin: The Organiser of Reformed Protestantism, 1509–1564* (New York, 1969, reprint of 1906 ed.), pp. xvii–lxxvii, best for beginners; Peter DeKlerk, "Calvin Bibliography," published annually in the *Calvin Theological Journal.*

Calvin's Works: *Joannis Calvini opera quae supersunt omnia,* vols. 29–87, *Corpus Reformatorum,* eds. G. Baum, E. Cunitz, E. Reuss, A. Erichson (Brunswick, 1863–1900); available in the Johnson Reprints Corporation edition (New York, 1964); *Opera Selecta,* eds. Petrus Barth and Guilelmus Niesel (5 vols., 1926–1957); the Edinburgh edition in English and the Grand Rapids reprint are well known and essential; *Institutes of the Christian Religion,* ed. John T. McNeill, trans. F. L. Battles (Philadelphia, 1960); *Commentary on Seneca's De clementia,* ed. and trans. Ford

Lewis Battles and André Malan Hugo (Leiden, 1969); J. D. Benoît, ed., *Institution de la religion chrétienne* (5 vols., 1957–1963), a fine critical edition; T. H. L. Parker, *Calvin's New Testament Commentaries* (London, 1971), a very valuable guide and interpretation of Calvin's exegetical writings on the New Testament; A. L. Herminjard (9 vols., 1878–1897) and J. Bonnet (4 vols., reprint, 1972–1973) are the most readily available sources for Calvin's correspondence; *Tracts and Treatises on the Reformation of the Church* (3 vols., Grand Rapids, Mich., 1958, reprint from the Edinburgh ed. of 1844), are valuable; plus *Calvin: Theological Treatises,* ed. J. K. S. Reid (*Library of Christian Classics,* 22) (Philadelphia, 1954).

Calvin's Biography: T. H. L. Parker, *John Calvin: A Biography* (Philadelphia, 1975), is the best biography, along with his *Portrait of Calvin* (Philadelphia, 1954), updating the standard Williston Walker cited above; Alexandre Ganoczy, *La jeune Calvin: Genèse et évolution de sa vocation réformatrice* (Wiesbaden, 1966), a detailed study; the old classic, Émile Doumerge, *Jean Calvin, les hommes et les choses de son temps* (7 vols., Lausanne, 1899–1927); Richard Stauffer, *The Humanness of Calvin* (Nashville, Tenn., 1971); Ford Lewis Battles, ed. and trans., *The Piety of John Calvin* (Grand Rapids, Mich., 1978), giving Calvin's autobiographical statements in verse form. For Calvin and humanism, see Josef Bohatec, *Budé und Calvin: Studien zur Gedankenwelt des französischen Frühhumanismus* (Graz, 1950); Quirinus Breen, *John Calvin: A Study in French Humanism* (2nd ed., Hamden, Conn, 1960); André Biéler, *The Social Humanism of Calvin* (Richmond, Va., 1964; French ed., 1961); Charles Partee, *Calvin and Classical Philosophy* (Leiden, 1977); Leroy Nixon, *John Calvin's Teachings on Human Reason* (New York, 1963). On Calvin and Luther: Charles Boyer, *Calvin et Luther: Accords et Différences* (Rome, 1973); Brian A. Gerrish, "The Pathfinder: Calvin's Image of Martin Luther," *The Old Protestantism and the New* (Chicago, 1982), pp. 27–48. Three recent books of essays add new material: Gervase E. Duffield, ed., *John Calvin* (Grand Rapids, Mich., 1966), with essays such as "Calvin the Letter Writer," "Calvin Against the Calvinists," and the like; Brian Gerrish, ed., *Reformatio Perennis: Essays on Calvin and the Reformation in Honor of Ford Lewis Battles* (Allison Park, Pa., 1981); and W. Stanford Reid, ed., *John Calvin: His Influence in the Western World* (Grand Rapids, Mich., 1982).

Calvin and Geneva: Robert M. Kingdon and J. F. Bergier, *Registres de la compagnie des pasteurs de Genève au temps de Calvin* (3 vols., Geneva, 1962–1969), and P. E. Hughes, ed. and trans., *The Register of the Company of Pastors in the Time of Calvin* (Grand Rapids, Mich., 1966), are important tools. The studies of E. William Monter are to be recommended, *Calvin's Geneva* (New York, 1967), *Studies in Genevan Government, 1536–1605* (Geneva, 1964), "Historical Demography and Religious History in Sixteenth Century Geneva," *Journal of Interdisciplinary History,* 9 (1979), 399–427, and others. Robert Kingdon, the distinguished editor of *The Sixteenth Century Journal* has done a number of studies on Geneva:

Geneva and the Coming of the Wars of Religion in France, 1555–1563 (Geneva, 1956), *Geneva and the Consolidation of the French Protestant Movement, 1564–1572* (Madison, 1967), "Was the Protestant Reformation a Revolution?: The Case of Geneva," in Kingdon, ed., *Transition and Revolution: Problems and Issues of European Renaissance and Reformation History* (Minneapolis, 1974), pp. 53–76, and others. See also W. Fred Graham, *The Constructive Revolutionary John Calvin and His Socio-economic Impact* (Richmond, Va., 1977) and *Calvin and His City: A Study of Human Seizure of Control* (Richmond, Va., 1970); Jeannine Fahsl Olson, "The *Bourse française:* Deacons and Social Welfare in Calvin's Geneva" (diss., Stanford, 1980); Eugène Choisy, *La Théocratie à Genève au temps de Calvin* (Geneva, 1897), was typical of the old view that Calvin virtually ran the city with autocratic powers; Jean François Bergier, *Genève et l'économie européenne de la Renaissance* (Paris, 1963); Henri Naef, *Les origines de la Réforme à Genève* (2 vols., Geneva, 1968); Alain Dufour, "Le mythe de Genève au temps de Calvin," in *Histoire politique et psychologie historique, suivie de deux essais sur humanisme et réformation et le mythe de Genève aux temps de Calvin* (Geneva, 1966), relating how religious refugees created myths about Geneva.

Calvin's Theology: Some excellent works on the religious thought and theology overall: François Wendel, *Calvin: The Origins and Development of His Religious Thought* (London, 1963), the best single volume survey; Lucien Joseph Richard, *The Spirituality of John Calvin* (Atlanta, 1974); Wilhelm Niesel, *The Theology of Calvin* (Philadelphia, 1956), stressing the importance of Christ in his theology; W. H. Neuser, *Calvinus Theologus* (Neukirchen, 1976), containing essays on topics such as Calvin as a Paulinist. On special aspects: Günter Gloede, *Theologia Naturalis bei Calvin* (Stuttgart, 1935); Edward D. Willis, *Calvin's Catholic Christology* (Leiden, 1966); E. A. Dowey, *The Knowledge of God in Calvin's Theology* (New York, 1952 and 1965); T. F. Torrance, *Calvin's Doctrine of Man* (Grand Rapids, 1957); Jean-Daniel Benoît, *Calvin: directeur d'âmes; contribution à l'histoire de la piété réformée* (Strasbourg, 1947); Jean Boisset, *Sagesse et Sainteté dans la pensée de Jean Calvin* (Paris, 1959); T. H. L. Parker, *Calvin's Doctrine of the Knowledge of God* (rev. ed., Grand Rapids, Mich., 1959); T. H. L. Parker, *The Oracles of God: An Introduction to the Preaching of John Calvin* (London, 1947); Richard Stauffer, *Dieu: La création et la providence dans la prédication de Calvin* (Bern, 1978); Luchesius Smits, *Saint Augustin dans l'oeuvre de Jean Calvin* (2 vols., Assen, 1957–1958); Henri Strohl, *La Pensée de la Réforme* (Neuchâtel, 1951); E. David Willis, *Calvin's Catholic Christology (Studies in the History of Christian Thought,* 1) (Leiden, 1966). On church and sacraments: Benjamin C. Milner, Jr., *Calvin's Doctrine of the Church* (Leiden, 1970); Kilian McDonnell, *John Calvin, the Church and the Eucharist* (Princeton, 1967); Ronald S. Wallace, *Calvin's Doctrine of the Word and Sacrament* (Edinburgh, 1953; Grand Rapids, Mich., 1957); H. Jackson Forstman, *Word and Spirit: Calvin's Doc-*

trine of Biblical Authority (Stanford, 1962); Richard A. Muller, *Christ and the Decree: Christology and Predestination in the Developing Soteriological Structure of Sixteenth Century Reformed Theology* (Durham, N.C., 1984); Alexandre Ganoczy, *Calvin, théologien de l'église et du ministère* (Paris, 1964). On history and eschatology: H. Quistorp, *Calvin's Doctrine of the Last Things* (London, 1955), and H. Berger, *Calvins Geschichtsauffassung* (Zurich, 1955).

Calvinism: John T. McNeill, *The History and Character of Calvinism* (New York, 1954); R. T. Kendall, *Calvin and English Calvinism to 1649* (Oxford, 1979); John H. Bratt, ed., *The Heritage of John Calvin* (The Heritage Hall Lectures 1960–1970) (Grand Rapids, Mich., 1973); Robert M. Kingdon and Robert D. Linder, eds., *Calvin and Calvinism: Sources of Democracy?* (Lexington, Mass., 1970). On Theodore Beza: John S. Bray, *Theodore Beza's Doctrine of Predestination* (Nieuwkoop, 1975); Paul F. Geisendorf, *Théodore de Bèze* (Geneva, 1949, and 1967); Walter Kickel, *Vernunft und Offenbarung bei Theodore Beza* (Neukirchen, 1967); Jill Raitt, *The Eucharistic Theology of Theodore Beza: Development of the Reformed Doctrine* (Chambersburg, Pa., 1972).

The Reformation in Italy, Spain, the Netherlands: Standard works include: Frederick C. Church, *The Italian Reformers, 1534–1564* (New York, 1932); Delio Cantimori, *Eretici italiani del Cinquecento: Ricerche storiche* (Florence, 1967, 1st ed., 1939); Emmanuel Pierre Rodocanacchi, *La Réforme en Italie* (2 vols., Paris, 1920–1921). See also Elisabeth G. Gleason, "On the Nature of Sixteenth Century Italian Evangelism: Scholarship, 1953–1978," *The Sixteenth Century Journal,* 9 (1978), 3–26; Antonio Rotondo, *Studi e Ricerche di Storia ereticale italiana del Cinquecento,* I (Turin, 1974); Paolo Simoncelli, *Evangelismo italiano del Cinquecento* (Rome, 1979); John A. Tedeschi, ed., *Italian Reformation Studies in Honor of Laelius Socinus* (Florence, 1965); Paolo Brezzi, *Le Origini del Protestantesimo* (Rome, 1961); Delio Cantimori, et al., eds., *Ginevra e l'Italia* (Florence, 1959); and Delio Cantimori, *Prospettive di Storia Ereticale Italiana del Cinquecento* (Bari, 1960). Individual Italian protestants: Salvatore Caponetto, *Aonio Paleario (1503–1570) e la Riforma Protestante in Toscana* (Torino, 1979); Anne Jacobson Schutte, *Pier Paolo Vergerio: The Making of an Italian Reformer* (Geneva, 1977); Joseph C. McLelland, *The Visible Words of God: An Exposition of the Sacramental Theology of Peter Martyr Vermigli, 1500–1562* (Edinburgh and London, 1957); J. P. Donnelly, *Calvinism and Scholasticism in Vermigli's Doctrine of Man* (Leiden, 1976); Robert M. Kingdon, *The Political Thought of Peter Martyr Vermigli: Selected Texts and Commentary* (Geneva, 1980); Philip McNair, *Peter Martyr in Italy: An Anatomy of Apostasy* (Oxford, 1967); Delio Cantimori, *Bernardino Ochino: Uomo del Rinascimento e Riformatore* (Pisa, 1929). For Spain: José C. Nieto, *Juan de Valdés and the Origins of the Spanish and Italian Reformation* (Geneva, 1970); John Edward Longhurst, *Luther and the Spanish Inquisition: The Case of Diego de Uceda 1528–1529* (Albuquerque, N.M., 1953), and *Luther's Ghost in Spain, 1517–1546* (Lawrence,

Kan., 1969). Netherlands: P. M. Crew, *Calvinist Preaching and Iconoclasm in the Netherlands, 1544–1569* (Cambridge, 1978).

THE REFORMATION IN ENGLAND

Popular Piety: Denys Hay, *Europe in the Fourteenth and Fifteenth Centuries* (New York, 1966), includes information on English lay protest against clerical abuses; Claire Cross, "Popular Piety and the Records of the Unestablished Churches, 1460–1660," in *The Materials, Sources and Methods of Ecclesiastical History, Studies in Church History*, 11, Derek Baker, ed. (New York, 1975), pp. 269–92; Claire Cross, *Church and People, 1450–1660: The Triumph of the Laity in the English Church* (Hassocks, Sussex, 1976); Peter Heath, *English Parish Clergy on the Eve of the Reformation* (London, 1969); Keith Wrightson and David Levine, *Poverty and Piety in an English Village: Terling, 1525–1700* (New York, 1979); Keith Thomas, *Religion and the Decline of Magic* (London, 1969); Irvin B. Horst, *The Radical Brethren: Anabaptism and the English Reformation to 1558* (Nieuwkoop, 1972). The Lollards: John A. F. Thomson, *The Later Lollards 1414–1520* (Oxford, 1965); A. G. Dickens, *Lollards and Protestants in the Diocese of York 1509–1558* (London, 1959); James Gairdner, *Lollardy and the Reformation in England* (4 vols., London, 1908–1913); Margaret Aston, "Lollardy and the Reformation: Survival or Revival," *History*, 49 (1964), 149–70.

Wolsey: Albert Frederick Pollard, *Wolsey* (London and New York, 1953; first pub., 1929); John Alexander Guy, *The Cardinal's Court: The Impact of Thomas Wolsey in Star Chamber* (Hassocks, 1977), a more positive view of Wolsey's achievement; Charles W. Ferguson, *Naked to Mine Enemies: The Life of Cardinal Wolsey* (Boston, 1958).

Colet: Frederic Seebohm, *The Oxford Reformers: John Colet, Erasmus and Thomas More* (London, 1896), an old classic still to be considered; John H. Lupton, *A Life of John Colet* (London, 1887); John H. Lupton, ed., *John Colet: Exposition of St. Paul's Epistle to the Romans* (2nd ed., Ridgewood, N.J., 1965); Ernest Hunt, *Dean Colet and His Theology* (London, 1956); Sears Jayne, *John Colet and Marsilio Ficino* (Oxford, 1963).

More: Reginald W. Gibson and J. Max Patrick, *St. Thomas More: A Preliminary Bibliography of His Works and of Moreana to the Year 1750* (New Haven, 1961); Constance Smith, *An Updating of R. W. Gibson's St. Thomas More, a Preliminary Bibliography* (*Sixteenth Century Bibliography*, 20) (St. Louis, 1981); *The Complete Works of St. Thomas More* (Yale Edition) is basic; R. W. Chambers, *Thomas More* (New York, 1935; reprint, Ann Arbor, Mich., 1958), stressing his medieval side; J. H. Hexter, *More's Utopia: The Biography of an Idea* (Princeton, 1952), a society designed to minimize basic vices; Russell Ames, *Citizen Thomas More and His Utopia* (Princeton, 1949); Karl Kautsky, *Thomas More and His Utopia* (New York, 1927), a socialist reading; Germain Marc'Hadour, *The Bible in the Works of Thomas More,*

1 (Nieuwkoop, 1969), by the editor of *Moreana*, published in Angers; James McConica, *Thomas More: A Short Biography* (London, 1977); E. E. Reynolds, *Thomas More and Erasmus* (New York, 1965); John Guy, *The Public Career of Sir Thomas More* (New Haven, 1980), showing More as tougher and less scrupulous as a politician than sometimes thought; Alistair Fox, *Thomas More: History and Providence* (Oxford, 1982); Rainer Pineas, *Thomas More and Tudor Polemics* (Bloomington, Ind., 1968), the less agreeable side of More; André Prévost, *Thomas More et la Crise de la Pensée Européene* (Lille, 1969).

Barnes and Tyndale: Neelak S. Tjernagel, *The Reformation Essays of Dr. Robert Barnes, Chaplain to Henry VIII* (London, 1963); James E. MacGoldrick, *Luther's English Connection: The Reformation Thought of Robert Barnes and William Tyndale* (Milwaukee, 1979), seeking to establish their Lutheran credentials; William A. Clebsch, *England's Earliest Protestants, 1520–1535* (New Haven, 1964), the best single volume on the Cambridge group and pioneers; James F. Mozley, *William Tyndale* (London and New York, 1937); G. E. Duffield, ed., *The Work of William Tyndale* (Philadelphia, 1965).

Economic Life: E. M. Carus-Wilson and O. Coleman, *England's Export Trade, 1275–1547* (Oxford, 1963); C. A. Challis, *The Tudor Coinage* (Manchester, 1977); Peter Ramsey, *Tudor Economic Problems* (London, 1963) and *The Price Revolution in Sixteenth Century England* (London, 1971); R. B. Outhwaite, *Inflation in Tudor and Early Stuart England* (London, 1969); J. E. Thorold Rogers, *A History of Agriculture and Prices in England* (7 vols., Oxford, 1866–1902) (vols. 3 and 4, 1401–1582); Joan Thirsk, ed., *The Agrarian History of England and Wales, 1500–1640* (Cambridge, 1967), gen. ed., H. P. R. Finberg; Eric Kerridge, *The Agrarian Problems in the Sixteenth Century and After* (London, 1969).

Social Conditions: Fritz Caspari, *Humanism and the Social Order in Tudor England* (Chicago, 1954); J. H. Hexter, "Storm over the Gentry," in *Reappraisals in History* (London, 1961; 2nd ed., Chicago, 1979); W. K. Jordan, *Philanthropy in England, 1480–1660* (New York, 1959), arguing that the Reformation produced a marked increase in charitable giving, redirecting it into secular channels; F. Heal and R. O'Day, eds., *Church and Society in England, Henry VIII to James I* (London, 1977), with essays on the economic problems of the clergy, popular culture, and the like; Lawrence Stone, *The Family, Sex and Marriage in England 1500–1800* (New York, 1977); M. E. James, *Family, Lineage and Civil Society: A Study of Society, Politics and Mentality in the Durham Region 1500–1640* (Oxford, 1974); Peter Clark, *English Provincial Society from the Reformation to the Revolution: Religion, Politics and Society in Kent, 1500–1640* (Hassocks, Sussex, 1977).

Secular and Ecclesiastical Government: Conyers Read, *The Tudors: Personalities and Practical Politics in Sixteenth Century England* (New York, 1936); John A. F. Thomson, *The Transformation of Medieval England, 1370–1529* (London and New York, 1983); Conrad Russell, *The Crisis of Parliaments, 1509–1660* (Oxford, 1971); James

McConica, *English Humanists and Reformation Politics under Henry VIII and Edward VI* (Oxford, 1965), stressing the role of Erasmians; G. R. Elton, *The Tudor Revolution in Government: Administrative Changes in the Reign of Henry VIII* (Cambridge, 1973); *Studies in Tudor and Stuart Politics and Government* (2 vols., Cambridge, 1974), a collection of papers; *The Tudor Constitution: Documents and Commentary* (Cambridge, 1960), a succinct account of institutions with good bibliography to 1959; *Reform and Reformation England, 1509–1558* (Cambridge, Mass., 1977), drawing together a quarter century of research. Church: Rosemary O'Day and Felicity Heal, *Princes and Paupers in the English Church 1500–1800* (Leicester, 1981), on revenues of bishops and clerical incomes, and *Continuity and Change: Personnel Administration of the Church of England 1500–1642* (Leicester, 1976), containing essays on subjects such as clerical tax collections; E. W. Ives, R. J. Knecht, and J. J. Scarisbrick, eds., *Wealth and Power in Tudor England* (London, 1978), with essays such as "Episcopal Palaces, 1535–1660," pp. 146–66; Lacey Baldwin Smith, *Tudor Prelates and Politics, 1536–1558* (Princeton, 1953); G. W. Child, *Church and State Under the Tudors* (London, 1950); Craig R. Thompson, *The English Church in the Sixteenth Century* (Washington, D.C., 1958); Felicity Heal, *Of Prelates and Princes: A Study of the Economic and Social Position of the Tudor Episcopate* (Cambridge and New York, 1980); Ralph A. Houlbrooke, *Church Courts and the People During the English Reformation, 1520–1570* (Oxford, 1979); David Knowles, *The Religious Orders in England* (3 vols., Cambridge, 1950–1959).

General Studies: Christopher W. Haigh, "Some Aspects of the Recent Historiography of the English Reformation," in W. J. Mommsen et al., eds., *Stadtbürgertum und Adel in der Reformation* (Stuttgart, 1979), pp. 88–106; A. G. Dickens, *The English Reformation* (London, 1964), the best account; David H. Pill, *The English Reformation 1529–58* (Totowa, N.J., 1973); Thomas Maynard Parker, *The English Reformation to 1558* (London, 1963); Maurice Powicke, *The Reformation in England* (London, 1941), still stressing the Reformation as an affair of state; Ernest Gordon Rupp, *Studies in the Making of the English Protestant Tradition* (Cambridge, 1947); Constantin Hopf, *Martin Bucer and the English Reformation* (Oxford, 1946); Leslie P. Fairfield, *John Bale: Mythmaker for the English Reformation* (Lafayette, Ind., 1976); Paul Christianson, *Reformers in Babylon: English Apocalyptic Visions from the Reformation to the Eve of the Civil War* (Toronto, 1978); K. R. Firth, *The Apocalyptic Tradition in Reformation Britain 1530–1695* (Oxford, 1979); A. G. Dickens and Dorothy Carr, eds., *Documents of Modern History: The Reformation in England to the Accession of Elizabeth I* (New York, 1968); John Davis, *Heresy and Reformation in the South-East of England 1520–1559* (London, 1983).

Henry VIII: J. J. Scarisbrick, *Henry VIII* (London, 1968), the best modern biography; Erwin Doernberg, *Henry VIII and Luther: An Account of Their Personal Relations* (Stanford, 1961); Neelak Tjernagel, *Henry VIII and the Lutherans* (St. Louis, 1965); H. A. Kelly, *The Matrimonial Trials of Henry VIII* (Stanford, 1976), good on canon law, less so on political and personal issues; Alan Kreider, *English Chantries: The Road to Dissolution* (Cambridge, Mass., 1979); Christopher Haigh, *Reformation and Resistance in Tudor Lancashire* (Cambridge, 1975); Stanford E. Lehmberg, *The Reformation Parliament, 1529–1536* (Cambridge, 1970) and *The Later Parliaments of Henry VIII, 1536–1547* (Cambridge, 1977).

Cromwell: The great Cromwell specialist is G. R. Elton, whose studies include: *Reform and Renewal: Thomas Cromwell and the Commonweal* (Cambridge, 1973), *Policy and Police: The Enforcement of the Reformation in the Age of Thomas Cromwell* (Cambridge, 1972), and "Reform and Reformation England and the Continent c. 1500–c. 1750," *Studies in Church History*, sub. 2, Derek Baker, ed. (Oxford, 1979), 1–16. See also A. G. Dickens, *Thomas Cromwell and the English Reformation* (London, 1959); Antonia Fraser, *Cromwell: Our Chief of Men* (London, 1973); B. W. Beckingsale, *Thomas Cromwell, Tudor Minister* (London, 1978), popular; R. B. Merriman, *Life and Letters of Thomas Cromwell* (2 vols., Oxford, 1902), good on letters, contains errors on life; A. J. Slavin, ed., *Thomas Cromwell on Church and Commonwealth* (New York, 1969), a newer selection of letters.

Edward VI: Wilbur K. Jordan, *Edward VI: The Young King* (2 vols., London, 1968, 1970); D. E. Hoak, *The King's Council in the Reign of Edward VI* (Cambridge, 1976); C. H. Smyth, *Cranmer and the Reformation Under Edward VI* (Cambridge, 1926), emphasizing the role of the Cambridge Protestants active as ministers under Edward VI and Elizabeth I.

Mary Tudor: Walter Cecil Richardson, *Mary Tudor: The White Queen* (London, 1970); Carolly Erickson, *Bloody Mary* (New York, 1978), popular; John Cedric H. Aveling, *The Handle and the Axe: The Catholic Recusants in England from the Reformation to the Emancipation* (London, 1976); James Oxley, *The Reformation in Essex to the Death of Mary* (Manchester, 1965); E. Harris Harbison, *Rival Ambassadors at the Court of Queen Mary* (Princeton, 1940); Edward J. Baskerville, *A Chronological Bibliography of Propaganda and Polemic Published in English Between 1553 and 1558, from the Death of Edward VI to the Death of Mary I* (*Memoirs of the American Philosophical Society*, 136) (Philadelphia, 1979); Frederic Youngs, *Proclamations of the Tudor Queens* (Cambridge, 1976).

Elizabethan Settlement: Carl S. Meyer, *Elizabeth I and the Religious Settlement of 1559* (St. Louis, 1960); Winthrop S. Hudson, *The Cambridge Connection and the Elizabethan Settlement of 1559* (Durham, N.C., 1980); Dewey D. Wallace, Jr., *Puritans and Predestination: Grace in English Protestant Theology, 1525–1695* (Chapel Hill, N.C., 1982).

Scotland: John Knox, *History of the Reformation in Scotland*, ed. W. C. Dickinson, taken from the works of Knox, I–II (1949); John H. S. Burleigh, *A Church History of Scotland* (2 vols., London, 1949); R. Nicholson, *Scotland: The Later Middle Ages* (Edinburgh, 1974), covering A.D. 1057–1603; Gordon Donaldsen, *The Scottish Reformation* (Cambridge, 1960); Richard L. Greaves, *Theology and Revolution in the*

Scottish Reformation: Studies in the Thought of John Knox (Grand Rapids, 1980), a collection of articles with substantial bibliography; Jasper Ridley, *John Knox* (New York, 1968); W. Stanford Reid, *Trumpeter of God: A Biography of John Knox* (New York, 1974); Duncan Shaw, ed., *John Knox: A Quartercentenary Reappraisal* (Edinburgh, 1975); Ian B. Cowan, *The Scottish Reformation. Church and Society in 16th Century Scotland* (New York, 1982).

Ireland: Brendan Bradshaw, *The Dissolution of the Religious Orders in Ireland under Henry VIII* (Cambridge, 1974); Nicholas Canny, "Why the Reformation Failed in Ireland: *Une Question Mal Posée,*" *Journal of Ecclesiastical History,* 30, no. 4 (October 1979), 423–50.

CATHOLIC RENEWAL AND RESPONSE

Sources and Bibliography: One of the more important more recent source publications is the *Acta Reformationis Catholicae Ecclesiam Germaniae Concernentia Saecula XVI. Die Reformverhandlungen des deutschen Episkopats von 1520 bis 1570,* edited by Georg Pfeilschifter, I, 1520–1532 (Regensburg, 1959), an ongoing series. The fourth volume of Hubert Jedin's *Handbuch der Kirchengeschichte, Reformation, Katholische Reform und Gegenreformation* (2nd ed., Freiburg im Breisgau, 1967), has been translated as volume 5 of Hubert Jedin and John Dolan's, *History of the Church, Reformation and Counter Reformation* (New York, 1980), with an extensive bibliography. Several studies offer up-to-date bibliographical material: Anne Jacobson Schutte, *Printed Italian Vernacular Religious Books 1465–1550: A Finding List* (Geneva, 1983); John W. O'Malley, "Recent Studies in Church History 1300–1600," *Catholic Historical Review,* 55 (1969), 394–437; Jean-François Gilmont, "La bibliographie de la controverse catholique au XVIe siècle," *Revue d'histoire ecclésiastique,* 74 (1979), 362–71; Eric Cochrane, "New Light on Post-Tridentine Italy: A Note on Recent Counter-Reformation Scholarship," *Catholic Historical Review,* 56 (1970), 291–319. Among the best works on the Catholic Reformation are Marvin R. O'Connell, *The Counter Reformation 1559–1610* (New York, 1974); Ernst Walter Zeeden, *Das Zeitalter der Gegenreformation* (Freiburg, 1967); A. G. Dickens, *The Counter-Reformation* (New York, 1969); Henry Outram Evennet, *The Spirit of the Counter-Reformation* (Cambridge, 1968); Karl Brandi, *Reformation und Gegenreformation, 2, Reformation und Religionskriege* (Leipzig, 1942); Heinrich Lutz, *Reformation und Gegenreformation* (Munich, 1979). Two Italian documents books are M. Marcocchi, *La Riforma Cattolica: Documenti e Testimonianze* (2 vols., Brescia, 1970), and M. Bendiscioli and M. Marcocchi, *Riforma Cattolica: Antologia di Documenti* (Rome, 1963). Other works and monographs of special interest include Francis Oakley, *The Western Church in the Later Middle Ages* (Ithaca, 1979); "Catholic Reformation," *Sixteenth Century Journal,* 11, no. 2 (Summer 1980), a collection of articles; Wilbirgis Klaiber, ed., *Katholische Kontroverstheologen und Reformer des 16. Jahrhunderts: Ein Werkverzeichnis* (Münster, 1978); Robert E.

McNally, *The Unreformed Church* (New York, 1965), an appraisal of Catholic reform; John W. O'Malley, *Praise and Blame in Renaissance Rome* (Durham, N.C., 1979); James Obelkevich, ed., *Religion and the People* (Chapel Hill, 1979), containing a chapter by Philip Benedict on "the Catholic response to Protestantism"; Marvin O'Connell, *Thomas Stapleton and the Counter-Reformation* (New Haven, 1964); Gerhard Bellinger, *Der Catechismus Romanus und die Reformation* (Paderborn, 1970); Michele Monaco, *Lo Stato della Chiesa*, I, *Dalla fine del Grande scisma alla Pace di Cateau-Cambrésis (1427-1559)* (Lecce, 1978).

Conciliarism and Reform Before Trent: Olivier de La Brosse, *Le Pape et le Concile: La comparaison de leurs pouvoirs à la veille de la Réforme* (Paris, 1965); Francis Oakley, "Conciliarism in the Sixteenth Century: Jacques Almain Again," *Archiv für Reformationsgeschichte*, 68 (1977), 111-32; P. Matheson, *Cardinal Contarini at Regensburg* (Oxford, 1971); John O'Malley, *Giles of Viterbo on Church and Reform: A Study in Renaissance Thought* (Leiden, 1968); Olivier de la Brosse, Joseph Lecler, et al., eds., *Lateran V und Trient* (Mainz, 1978). On evangelicalism: Elisabeth Gleason, *Reform Thought in Sixteenth Century Italy* (Chico, Ca., 1981); Eva-Marie Jung, "On the Nature of Evangelism in Sixteenth-Century Italy," *Journal of the History of Ideas*, 14 (1953), 511-27; Salvatore Caponetto, ed., *Il Beneficio di Cristo (Corpus Reformatorum Italicorum)* (Florence and Chicago, 1972), an excellent edition; Adriano Prosperi, *Tra Evangelismo e Controriforma: G. M. Giberti, 1495-1543* (Rome, 1969), the best biography of Giberti; Marcel Bataillon, *Érasme et l'Espagne: Recherches sur l'Histoire Spirituelle du XVIᵉ siècle* (Paris, 1937). Dennis Janz, ed., *Three Reformation Catechisms: Catholic, Anabaptist, Lutheran* (Lewiston, N.Y., 1982).

Popes and Prelates: In addition to the classical histories of the popes by Ludwig Pastor, Leopold von Ranke, and the like, a sample of the newer studies of the popes of the Catholic Reformation includes Cardinal van Roey, et al., *Adrien VI, le premier pape de la Contre-Réforme (Bibliotheca Ephemeridum Theologicarum Lovaniensium, 14)* (Gembloux, 1959); Ludwig Riess, *Die Politik Pauls IV. und seiner Nepoten* (Berlin, 1909, reprint Vaduz, 1965). Prelates: Walter Lipgens, *Kardinal Johannes Gropper* (Münster 1951); Lawrence G. Duggan, *Bishop and Chapter: The Governance of the Bishopric of Speyer to 1552* (New Brunswick, N.J., 1978); Richard M. Douglas, *Jacopo Sadoleto, 1477-1547: Humanist and Reformer* (Cambridge, Mass., 1959); Peter Matheson, *Cardinal Contarini at Regensburg* (Oxford, 1972); Hubert Jedin, *Papal Legate at the Council of Trent: Cardinal Seripando* (St. Louis, 1947; German, 2 vols. with documents, Würzburg, 1937); Paolo Simoncelli, *Il Caso Reginald Pole: Eresia e Santità nelle Polemiche Religiose del Cinquecento (Uomini e Dottrini, 23), Edizioni di Storia e Letteratura* (Rome, 1977); Dermot Fenlon, *Heresy and Obedience in Tridentine Italy: Cardinal Pole and the Counter Reformation* (Cambridge, 1972); Wilhelm Schenk, *Reginald Pole, Cardinal of England* (London, 1950), the standard biography with a good bibliography and notes; Joseph G. Dwyer, trans., *Pole's Defense of the Unity of the Church* (Westminster, Md., 1965); Roger Mols, "Saint Charles Borromée, pionnier de la pastorale moderne," *Nouvelle revue théologique,* 79 (1957), 600ff., an excellent article; and an exegetical study relevant to the papacy, John E. Bigane III, *Faith, Christ or Peter: Matthew 16:18 in Sixteenth Century Roman Catholic Exegesis* (Lanham, Md., 1981).

Counter-Reformation: Sacrae Congregationis de Propaganda Fide Memoria Rerum (3 vols., Rome, 1971–1976); Bartolomé Bennassar, *L'Inquisition espagnole (XVe–XVIe siècles)* (Paris, 1979); F. S. Betten, *The Roman Index of Forbidden Books* (Chicago, 1935); Paul J. Hauben, ed., *The Spanish Inquisition* (New York, 1969); Joseph Lecler, *Toleration and Reformation* (2 vols., London, 1960).

The Jesuits, Loyola, and Xavier: Heinrich Boehmer, *The Jesuits* (Philadelphia, 1928); James Brodrick, S.J., *The Economic Morals of the Jesuits* (London, 1934), *The Origin of the Jesuits* (London, 1940), and *The Progress of the Jesuits* (London, 1947); Maria Scaduto, S.J., *Storia della Campagnia di Gesù in Italia* (3 vols. to date, Rome, 1964); René Fülöp-Miller, *The Jesuits: A History of the Society of Jesus* (New York, 1963); Michael Foss, *The Founding of the Jesuits 1540* (London, 1969), pointing to the founding as the turning point in the Catholic Reformation; Joseph de Guibert, *The Jesuits: Their Spiritual Doctrine and Practice* (Chicago, 1964), emphasizing Loyola's key role; J. C. H. Aveling, *The Jesuits* (London, 1981); H. Fouqueray, *Histoire de la compagnie de Jésus en France des origines à la suppression, 1528–1762* (5 vols., Paris, 1910–1925); Pietro Tacchi Venturi, *Storia della Compagnia di Gesù in Italia* (2 vols., Rome, 1922–1931; rev. ed., 2 vols., Rome, 1930–1951). Loyola: *Autobiography of St. Ignatius Loyola,* John C. Olin, ed. (New York, 1974); James Brodrick, S.J., *Saint Ignatius Loyola: The Pilgrim Years 1491–1538* (New York, 1956); Heinrich Böhmer, *Ignatius von Loyola* (Stuttgart, 1951); Hugo Rahner, *Ignatius the Theologian* (New York, 1968), part of Rahner's longer study in German on Loyola's personality and theological development; Karl Rahner and Paul Imhoff, *Ignatius of Loyola* (London, 1979), an interpretive essay with splendid old engravings and color photos; Friedrich Wulf, ed., *Ignatius Loyola: His Personality and Spiritual Heritage, 1556–1956* (St. Louis, 1977), essays by Austrian and German scholars. Xavier: James Brodrick, S.J., *Saint Francis Xavier (1506–1552)* (London, 1952); Georg Schurhammer, *Francis Xavier: His Life, His Times* (4 vols., Rome, 1973–1981); and on Canisius, James Brodrick, S.J., *St. Peter Canisius* (London, 1935).

Council of Trent: Giuseppe Alberigo, *I vescovi italiani al Concilio di Trento (1545–1547)* (Florence, 1959); L. Cristiani, *L'Église à l'époque du Conseil de Trente* (Turin, 1948); H. O. Evennett, *The Cardinal of Lorraine and the Council of Trent* (Cambridge, 1940); Hubert Jedin, *A History of the Council of Trent* (London, 1957– ; German, 4 vols., Freiburg i. B., 1949–1975); Hubert Jedin, *Crisis and Closure of the Council of Trent: A Retrospective View from the Second Vatican Council* (London, 1967), a brief account of the final period; Henry J. Schroeder, ed., *Canons and Decrees of the Council of Trent* (St. Louis, 1941); Gordon Spykman, *Attrition and*

Contrition at the Council of Trent (Kampen, 1955); Léopold Willaert, S.J., *Après le Conseil de Trente: La restauration catholique, 1563-1648*, 18, *L'histoire de l'Église* (Tournai, 1960); Henry D. Wojtyska, *Cardinal Hosius, Legate to the Council of Trent* (Rome, 1967).

Post-Trent: Robert M. Kingdon, "Some French Reactions to the Council of Trent," *Church History*, 33 (1964), 149–55; Theodore Casteel, "Calvin and Trent," *Harvard Theological Review*, 63 (1970), 91–117; Oskar Garstein, *Rome and the Counter-Reformation in Scandinavia* (2 vols., New York, 1963–1980); Paul F. Grendler, *The Roman Inquisition and the Venetian Press, 1540-1605* (Princeton, 1977); Franz Ortner, *Reformation, Katholische Reform und Gegenreformation im Erzstift Salzburg* (Salzburg and Munich, 1981). Popular religion after Trent: William A. Christian, Jr., *Local Religion in Sixteenth Century Spain* (Princeton, 1981); A. N. Galpern, *The Religions of the People in Sixteenth Century Champagne* (Cambridge, Mass., 1976), on the widespread popular religious conservatism after Trent; John Bossy, "The Counter-Reformation and the People of Catholic Europe," *Past and Present*, 47 (1970), 51–70, and "The Counter-Reformation and the People of Catholic Ireland, 1596–1641," *Historical Studies*, 8 (1971), 155–69, argued for a deleterious effect of the enforcement of a code of religious observance on the natural family-related conservative Catholicism of areas safely Catholic, a controversial point of view.

EUROPE—EAST AND WEST

Diplomacy: Charles Howard Carter, *The Western European Powers, 1500–1700* (Ithaca, 1971), and "The Ambassadors of Early Modern Europe," in C. H. Carter, ed., *From the Renaissance to the Counter-Reformation: Essays in Honor of Garrett Mattingly* (New York, 1965); Garrett Mattingly, *Renaissance Diplomacy* (New York, 1954), indicating how Italian Renaissance diplomatic methods were adopted by the powers of western and southern Europe; Marie Alphonse René de Maulde-la-Clavière, *La diplomatie au temps de Machiavel* (3 vols., Paris, 1892–1893), a comprehensive classic; Henri Lapeyre, *Les monarchies européenes du XVI e siècle: Les relations internationales* (Paris, 1967), with an extensive bibliography of manuscript and printed sources; David Jayne Hill, *A History of Diplomacy in the International Development of Europe* (3 vols., New York, 1905–1914), a general survey.

France Under Francis I: R. J. Knecht, *Francis I* (Cambridge, 1982), the first scholarly account in English; Roland Mousnier, *Les XVIe et XVIIe Siècles* (Paris, 1953), quite sympathetic to Francis I; Henri Hauser and Augustin Renaudet, *Les Débuts de l'Âge Moderne: La renaissance et la réforme* (Paris, 1929; reprint, 1946); with a classical account of the reign; Anne Denieul-Cormier, *A Time of Glory: The Renaissance in France, 1488-1559* (Garden City, N.Y., 1968); Jean Zeller, *La diplomatie française vers le milieu du XVIe siècle d'après la correspondance de Guillaume*

Pellicier, évêque de Montpellier, ambassadeur de François Ier à Venise, 1539–1542 (Paris, 1881; reprint, Geneva, 1969), sound treatment of the Habsburg-Valois struggle; Ion Ursu, *La politique orientale de François Ier* (Paris, 1908).

Charles V, the Habsburgs and Spain: Gerhard Benecke, *Maximilian I. Analytical Biography* (London, 1982), containing much material that is not well integrated into a biography; Karl Brandi, *Kaiser Karl V.* (2 vols., Munich, 1937–1941), the second volume being sources; volume 1 trans. into English by C. V. Wedgwood (New York, 1939), the fullest modern biography of Charles; Jean Babelon, *Charles Quint* (Paris, 1947); Peter Rassow and Fritz Schalk, eds., *Karl V. Der Kaiser und seine Zeit* (Cologne, 1960); Peter Rassow, *Die KaiserIdee Karls V. dargestellt an der Politik der Jahre 1528–1540* (Berlin, 1932; reprint, Vaduz, 1965); Volker Press, *Kaiser Karl V., König Ferdinand und die Entstehung der Reichsritterschaft* (Wiesbaden, 1976), on the 1523 Knights' revolt; H. G. Koenigsberger, "The Empire of Charles V in Europe," in his *The Habsburgs and Europe, 1516–1660* (Ithaca, 1971, 1–62; Robert J. W. Evans, *The Making of the Habsburg Monarchy 1550–1700* (Oxford, 1979), good on the Counter-Reformation; John H. Elliott, *Imperial Spain, 1469–1716* (New York, 1963), a masterful work; Reginald Trevor Davies, *The Golden Century of Spain, 1501–1621* (London, 1937); John Lynch, *Spain under the Habsburgs* (2 vols., New York, 1964; 2nd ed., Oxford, 1981), the first volume covering 1516–1598; Bohdan Chuboda, *Spain and the Empire, 1519–1643* (Chicago, 1952); Peter Pierson, *Philip II of Spain* (Levittown, N.Y., 1975); John M. Headley, *The Emperor and His Chancellor: A Study of the Imperial Chancellery Under Gattinara* (Cambridge, 1982). On the Holy Roman Empire: Heinrich Lutz, *Christianitas Afflicta* (Göttingen, 1964), on Charles V's failure in Germany; Francis Ludwig Carsten, *Princes and Parliaments in Germany from the Fifteenth to the Eighteenth Century* (Oxford, 1959), and, finally, André Chastel, *The Sack of Rome 1527* (Princeton, 1982).

Ottoman Turks and Their Impact on Europe: Stanford Shaw, *History of the Ottoman Empire and Modern Turkey,* I, *Empire of the Gazis: The Rise and Decline of the Ottoman Empire, 1280–1808* (Cambridge, 1976), an excellent account; Wayne S. Vucinich, *The Ottoman Empire: Its Record and Legacy* (Princeton, 1965); W. E. D. Allen, *Problems of Turkish Power in the Sixteenth Century* (London, 1963); Donald F. Lach, *Asia in the Making of Europe* (2 vols., Chicago, 1965–1970), the first volume is on the century of discovery; Bernard Lewis, *Istanbul and the Civilization of the Ottoman Empire* (Norman, Okla., 1963); Paul Wittek, *The Rise of the Ottoman Empire* (London, 1938; reprint, 1966); Nicoară Beldiceanu, *Le Timar dans l'État Ottoman (début XIVe–début XVIe siècle* (Wiesbaden, 1980); Roger Bigelow Merriman, *Suleiman the Magnificent, 1520–1566* (Cambridge, Mass., 1944; New York, 1966), the standard biography; A. H. Lybyer, *The Government of the Ottoman Empire in the Time of Suleiman the Magnificent* (Cambridge, Mass., 1913; reprint, New York, 1966); Stephen A. Fischer-Galati, *Ottoman Imperialism and German Protestantism 1521–1555*

(Cambridge, Mass., 1959); Ernst Benz, *Wittenberg und Byzanz: Zur Begegnung und Auseinandersetzung der Reformation und der östlich-orthodoxen Kirche* (Marburg, 1949); Paul Coles, *The Ottoman Impact on Europe* (London and New York, 1968), a handy guide; H. A. R. Gibb and Harold Bowen, *Islamic Society and the West* (London and New York, 1950), on west European awareness of the Turks; Dorothy Margaret Vaughan, *Europe and the Turk: A Pattern of Alliances, 1350–1700* (Liverpool, 1954); *Cambridge History of Islam* (Cambridge, 1970).

Russia: J. L. I. Fennell, "Russia, 1462–1583," in G. R. Elton, ed., *The New Cambridge Modern History*, II, *The Reformation* (Cambridge, 1958), pp. 534–61; Nicholas V. Riasanovsky, *A History of Russia* (New York, 1963).

Exploration and Trade: Charles E. Nowell, "The Expansion of Europe," in *The American Historical Association Guide to Historical Literature* (New York, 1963), pp. 404–26; Charles E. Nowell, *The Great Discoveries and the First Colonial Empires* (Ithaca, 1954), a brief but useful introduction; John H. Elliott, *The Old World and the New, 1492–1650* (Cambridge, 1970); John H. Parry, *The Establishment of the European Hegemony, 1415–1715: Trade and Exploration in the Age of the Renaissance* (London, 1949), "The New World, 1521–1580," in *The New Cambridge Modern History*, II, *The Reformation*, pp. 562–90, *The Spanish Theory of Empire in the Sixteenth Century* (Cambridge, 1940), and Parry, ed., *The European Reconnaissance: Selected Documents* (New York, 1968); Boies Penrose, *Travel and Discovery in the Renaissance, 1420–1620* (Cambridge, Mass., 1952); Carlo M. Cipolla, *Guns, Sails, and Empires: Technological Innovation and the Early Phases of European Expansion, 1400–1700* (New York, 1965); Clarence H. Haring, *The Spanish Empire in America* (New York, 1947), and *Trade and Navigation Between Spain and the Indies* (Cambridge, Mass., 1918); Francis M. Rogers, *The Quest for Eastern Christians* (Minneapolis, 1962), on the role of religion in motivating exploration, especially the Portuguese interest in Asia and Africa; George A. Collier, Renato I. Rosaldo, and John D. Wirth, eds., *The Inca and Aztec States, 1400–1800* (New York, 1982), a collection of anthropological and historical essays; DeLamar Jensen, ed., *The Expansion of Europe: Motives, Methods, and Meanings* (Boston, 1967); Lewis Hanke, *The Spanish Struggle for Justice in the Conquest of America* (Philadelphia, 1949, and also 1959); Paul Gaffarel, *Histoire du Brésil français au XVIe siècle* (2 vols., Paris, 1878); Charles J. Boxer, *The Portuguese Seaborne Empire, 1415–1825* (London and New York, 1969).

SOCIETY AND CULTURE

Religious Change: Bernard M. G. Reardon, *Religious Thought in the Reformation* (London and New York, 1981), from Erasmus to Trent; Guy F. Lytle, ed., *Reform and Authority in the Medieval and Reformation Church* (Washington, D.C., 1981), a unique collection of independent essays; Heiko Augustinus Oberman, *Masters of the Reformation: The Emergence of a New Intellectual Climate in Europe* (Cambridge,

1981), translated from *Werden und Wertung der Reformation* with pruned notes and some rewritten passages, on the general academic thought from Tübingen out and its impact on later medieval thought to Luther and the urban Reformation; Joseph C. McLelland, *The Reformation and Its Significance Today* (Philadelphia, 1962); Brian Gerrish, *The Old Protestantism and the New: Essays on the Reformation Heritage* (Chicago, 1982); Wilhelm Pauck, *The Heritage of the Reformation* (Glencoe, Ill., 1961); Fred W. Meuser and Stanley D. Schneider, *Interpreting Luther's Legacy* (Minneapolis, 1969); Jill Raitt, ed., *Shapers of Religious Traditions in Germany, Switzerland, and Poland, 1560–1600* (New Haven, 1981), essays examining the careers of twelve prominent men shaping the post-Reformation church; Walther von Loewenich, *Luther und der Neuprotestantismus* (Witten, 1963); Jean Delumeau, *Catholicism Between Luther and Voltaire* (London, 1977).

Popular Culture and Social Change: Peter Burke, *Popular Culture in Early Modern Europe* (New York, 1978); A. N. Galpern, *The Religions of the People in Sixteenth-Century Champagne* (Cambridge, Mass., 1976); Lawrence P. Buck and Jonathan W. Zophy, eds., *The Social History of the Reformation* (Columbus, Ohio, 1972); Hugh Trevor-Roper, *Religion, the Reformation and Social Change* (London, 1967); Miriam Eliav-Feldon, *Realistic Utopias: The Ideal Imaginary Societies of the Renaissance, 1516–1630* (Oxford, 1982); Guy E. Swanson, *Religion and Regime: A Sociological Account of the Reformation* (Ann Arbor, 1967), seeking to correlate the political experience of various nations with their choice of religion and ecclesiastical governance; Natalie Zemon Davis, *Society and Culture in Early Modern France* (Stanford, 1975), brilliant and original, employing anthropological insights to good advantage; Norman Birnbaum, *Social Structure and the German Reformation* (New York, 1980). On monasticism and family life: Bernhard Lohse, *Mönchtum und Reformation: Luthers Auseinandersetzung mit dem Mönchsideal des Mittelalters* (Göttingen, 1963), arguing that the final break with celibate vows came with Luther's conviction that baptismal vows were absolutely final for all Christians; August Franzen, *Zölibat und Priesterehe in der Auseinandersetzung der Reformationszeit und der katholischen Reform des 16. Jahrhunderts* (Münster, 1969); Klaus Arnold, *Kind und Gesellschaft im Mittelalter und Renaissance: Beiträge und Texte zur Geschichte der Kindheit* (Paderborn, 1980), going farther back in time than Philippe Ariès; Steven Ozment, *When Fathers Ruled: Family Life in Reformation Europe* (Cambridge, Mass., 1983), a study of patriarchy, the extended family, and place of women in early modern times; Edward S. Morgan, *The Puritan Family* (Boston, 1944); A. D. J. Macfarlane, *The Origins of English Individualism: The Family, Property and Social Transition* (Oxford, 1978); Lawrence Stone, *The Family, Sex and Marriage in England 1500–1800* (New York, 1977), a monumental study. On cities: Peter Clark, ed., *The Early Modern Town: A Reader* (New York, 1976); F. Petri, ed., *Kirche und gesellschaftlicher Wandel in deutschen und niederländischen Städten der werdenden Neuzeit* (Cologne and Vienna, 1980). On poverty and crime: T. Fischer, *Städtische Armut und Armenfürsorge im 15.*

und 16. Jahrhundert (Göttingen, 1979); B. Lenman, G. Parker, and V. Gatrell, eds., *Crime and the Law: The Social History of Crime in Western Europe since 1500* (London, 1980); John Langbein, *Prosecuting Crime in the Renaissance, England, Germany, France* (Cambridge, Mass., 1974).

Women in the Reformation: Roland H. Bainton, *Women of the Reformation: In Germany and Italy* (Minneapolis, 1971), *Women of the Reformation: In France and England* (Boston, 1973), and *Women of the Reformation from Spain to Scandinavia* (Minneapolis, 1977); Derek Baker, ed., *Medieval Women: Studies in Church History, Sub.* 1 (Oxford, 1978), containing essays such as on women among the Lollards; Max Bauer, *Die deutsche Frau in der Vergangenheit* (Berlin, 1907), pp. 217–41 on the Reformation; Mary Beard, *Women as Force in History* (London and New York, 1946; reprint, New York, 1973); Barbara Becker-Cantarino, ed., *Die Frau von der Reformation zur Romantik: Die Situation der Frau vor dem Hintergrund der Literatur- und Sozialgeschichte* (Bonn, 1980); Susan Groag Bell, *Women from the Greeks to the French Revolution* (Belmont, Ca., 1973); André Biéler, *L'homme et la femme dans la morale calviniste* (Geneva, 1963); P. W. Bomli, *La femme dans l'Espagne du siècle d'or* (The Hague, 1950); Miriam Chrisman, "Women of the Reformation in Strasbourg 1490–1530," *Archiv für Reformationsgeschichte,* 63, 2 (1972), 143–67; Patrick Collinson, "The Role of Women in the English Reformation Illustrated by the Life and Friendships of Anne Locke," *Studies in Church History,* 2 (1965), 258–72; Natalie Zemon Davis, "City Women and Religious Change in Sixteenth Century France," in Dorothy Gies McGuigan, ed., *A Sampler of Women's Studies* (Ann Arbor, 1973), pp. 17–45; Pearl Hofgrefe, *Tudor Women: Commoners and Queens* (Ames, Iowa, 1975), and *Women of Action in Tudor England* (Ames, Iowa, 1977); Joyce L. Irwin, ed., *Womanhood in Radical Protestantism 1525–1675* (New York, 1979); Joan Kelly-Gadol, with Barbara Alpern Engel and Kathleen Casey, *Bibliography in the History of European Women* (4th rev. ed., Bronxville, New York, 1976); Patricia Labalme, ed., *Beyond Their Sex: Learned Women of the European Past* (New York, 1980), dealing with a limited group of exceptional women poets, scholars, historians, and patrons of the arts; Laure de Mandach, *Portraits de Femmes: Renaissance et Réforme* (Geneva, 1952); Francis Lee Utley, *The Crooked Rib: An Analytical Index to the Argument about Women in English and Scots Literature to the End of the Year 1568* (Columbus, Ohio, 1944; reprint, New York, 1970); Merry E. Wiesner, *Women in the 16th Century: A Bibliography (Sixteenth Century Bibliography,* 23) (St. Louis, 1983); Sherrin Marshall Wyntjes, "Women in the Reformation Era," in Renate Bridenthal and Claudia Koonz, eds., *Becoming Visible: Women in European History* (Boston, 1977), pp. 167–91.

The Jews: H. H. Ben-Sasson, *The Reformation in Contemporary Jewish Eyes* (Israel Academy of Sciences and Humanities Proceedings, iv, no. 12 (Jerusalem, 1970); W. Bienert, *Martin Luther und die Juden* (Frankfurt a. M., 1982), documents; Johannes Brosseder, *Luthers Stellung zu den Juden im Spiegel seiner Interpreten: Interpretation und*

Rezeption von Luthers Schriften und Aüsserungen zum Judentum im 19. und 20. Jahrhundert vor allem im deutschsprachigen Raum (Munich, 1972); Carl Cohen, "Die Juden und Luther," *Archiv für Reformationsgeschichte,* 54, 1 (1963), 38–51; Alfred Haverkamp, ed., *Zur Geschichte der Juden im Deutschland des späten Mittelalters und der frühen Neuzeit* (Stuttgart, 1981); Armas K. E. Holmio, *The Lutheran Reformation and the Jews* (Hancock, Michigan, 1949); Reinhold Levin, *Luthers Stellung zu den Juden* (Berlin, 1911); Simon Markish, *Érasme et les Juifs* (Lausanne, 1979), putting the texts and Erasmus in proper perspective; Heiko A. Oberman, *Wurzeln des Antisemitismus: Christenangst und Judenplage im Zeitalter von Humanismus und Reformation* (Berlin, 1981); Selma Stern, *Josef von Rosheim: Befehlshaber der Judenschaft im Heiligen Römischen Reich Deutscher Nation* (Stuttgart, 1959; English trans., The Jewish Publication Society of America, n.p., 1965);

Protestantism and Capitalism: Fernand Braudel, *The Structures of Everyday Life* (New York, 1982); R. W. Green, ed., *Protestantism and Capitalism: The Weber Thesis and Its Critics* (Lexington, Mass., 1973); R. H. Tawney, *Religion and the Rise of Capitalism* (New York, 1926); Max Weber, *The Protestant Ethic and the Spirit of Capitalism* (New York, 1950; 2nd ed., London, 1976); Schmuel Noah Eisenstadt, ed., *The Protestant Ethic and Modernization: A Comparative View* (New York, 1968); Benjamin N. Nelson, *The Idea of Usury from Tribal Brotherhood to Universal Otherhood* (Princeton, 1949), seeing the Reformation as a major force for political freedom and social justice at least up to 1525; F. C. Spooner, *L'économie mondiale et les frappes monétaires en France, 1493–1680* (Paris, 1956), arguing for a seesaw effect on the Reformation of monetary and economic developments.

Political Theory and Practice: J. W. Allen, *A History of Political Thought in the Sixteenth Century* (London, 1928), has held up well on the positions of the major reformers. It has overall been superseded, however, by Quentin Skinner, *The Foundations of Modern Political Thought* (2 vols., Cambridge, 1978). See also the following: W. D. J. Cargill-Thompson, "The 'Two Kingdoms' and the 'Two Regiments': Some Problems of Luther's 'Zwei-Reiche-Lehre,' " *Journal of Theological Studies,* 20 (1969), 164–85; F. Edward Cranz, *An Essay on the Development of Luther's Thought on Justice, Law, and Society* (Cambridge, Mass., 1959); J. Russell Major, *Representative Government in Early Modern France* (New Haven, 1980); John U. Nef, *Industry and Government in France and England, 1540–1640* (Ithaca, 1957; 1st ed., Philadelphia, 1940); Donald R. Kelley, *The Beginning of Ideology: Consciousness and Society in the French Reformation* (Cambridge, 1981); John Tonkin, *The Church and the Secular Order in Reformation Thought* (New York and London, 1971); Perez Zagorin, *Rebels and Rulers, 1500–1660* (2 vols., Cambridge, 1982); Franz Lau, *Luthers Lehre von den beiden Reichen* (Berlin, 1953); Lewis W. Spitz, "The Impact of the Reformation on Church-State Issues," in Albert Huegli, ed., *Church and State Under God* (St. Louis, 1964), pp. 59–112, 459–72.

Resistance Theory: Heinz Scheible, ed., *Das Widerstandsrecht als Problem der deutschen Protestanten* (Gütersloh, 1969); Eike Wolgast, *Die Religionsfrage als Problem des Widerstandsrechts im 16. Jahrhundert* (Heidelberg, 1980).

Art: Theodore Besterman, *Art and Architecture: A Bibliography of Bibliographies* (Totowa, N.J., 1971); Carl C. Christensen, *Art and the Reformation in Germany* (Columbus, Ohio, 1979); William H. Halewood, *Six Subjects of Reformation Art* (Toronto, 1982); Craig Harbison, *The Last Judgment in Sixteenth Century Northern Europe: A Study in the Relationship Between Art and the Reformation* (New York, 1976); Michael Baxandall, *The Limewood Sculptures of Renaissance Germany, 1475–1525* (New Haven and London, 1980); Christiane Andersson and Charles Talbot, *From a Mighty Fortress: Prints, Drawings and Books in the Age of Luther 1483–1546* (Detroit, 1983); Wolfgang Stechow, ed., *Northern Renaissance Art 1400–1600: Sources and Documents* (Englewood Cliffs, N.J., 1966). Iconoclasm: Hans Carl von Haebler, *Das Bild in der evangelischen Kirche* (Berlin, 1957); Phyllis Mack Crew, *Calvinist Preaching and Iconoclasm in the Netherlands 1544–1569* (Cambridge, 1978); Charles Garside, Jr., *Zwingli and the Arts* (New Haven, 1966); John Phillips, *The Reformation of Images: Destruction of Art in England, 1535–1660* (Berkeley, 1973). Cranach: Werner Schade, *Cranach: A Family of Master Painters* (New York, 1980; Dresden, 1974); Max J. Friedländer and Jakob Rosenberg, *The Paintings of Lucas Cranach* (rev. ed., Ithaca, 1978); Johannes Jahn, *Lucas Cranach d. Ä., 1472–1553: Das gesamte graphische Werk* (Munich, 1972); Christiane D. Andersson, "Religiöse Bilder Cranachs im Dienste der Reformation," in Lewis W. Spitz, ed., *Humanismus und Reformation als Kulturelle Kräfte in der deutschen Geschichte,* (Berlin and New York, 1981), pp. 43–79, 170–73; Oskar Thulin, *Cranach Altäre der Reformation* (Berlin, 1955). Dürer: Erwin Panofsky, *The Life and Art of Albrecht Dürer* (Princeton, 1955); Hans Rupprich, ed., *Dürer: Schriftlicher Nachlass* (3 vols., Berlin, 1956–1969); William Martin Conway, ed., *The Writings of Albrecht Dürer* (New York, 1958). Michelangelo: Romeo de Maio, *Michelangelo e la Controriforma* (Rome/Bari, 1978).

Music: Donald Jay Grout with Claude V. Palisca, *A History of Western Music* (3rd ed., New York, 1980); Paul Nettl, *Luther and Music* (Philadelphia, 1948; new ed., 1967); Charles Garside, Jr., *The Origins of Calvin's Theology of Music: 1536–1543* (Trans. of the Am. Phil. Soc., 69, part 4) (Philadelphia, 1979); John K. Harms, "Music of the Radical Reformation I: Thomas Muentzer and his Hymns and Liturgy," *Church Music,* 77, 49–57; Dietz-Rüdiger Moser, *Verkündigung durch Volksgesang: Studien zur Liedpropaganda und-Katechese der Gegenreformation* (Berlin, 1981).

Education: Gerald Strauss, *Luther's House of Learning: Indoctrination of the Young in the German Reformation* (Baltimore and London, 1978); Anton Schindling, *Humanistische Hochschule und Freie Reichstadt: Gymnasium und Akademie in Strassburg*

1538–1621 (Wiesbaden, 1977); Hellmuth Rössler and Günther Franz, *Universität und Gelehrtenstand 1400–1800* (Limburg/Lahn, 1970); Leif Grane, ed., *University and Reformation* (Leiden, 1981), containing essays on the Lutheran Reformation and the universities and Calvinism and the universities, and the like; Hugh Kearney, *Scholars and Gentlemen: Universities and Society in Pre-Industrial Britain, 1500–1700* (London, 1970); Kenneth Charlton, *Education in Renaissance England* (Routledge, 1965), skeptical about the efficacy of education; Joan Simon, *Education and Society in Tudor England* (Cambridge, 1966); Craig R. Thompson, *Universities in Tudor England* (Washington, D.C., 1959); David Cressy, *Literacy and the Social Order: Reading and Writing in Tudor and Stuart England* (Cambridge and New York, 1980), though his methodology has been questioned by G. R. Elton; Gabriel Codina Mir, *Aux Sources de la Pédagogie des Jésuites: Le 'Modus Parisiensis'* (Rome, 1968); Gian Paolo Brizzi, ed., *La "Ratio Studiorum": Modelli culturali e pratiche educative dei Gesuiti in Italia tra Cinque e Seicento* (Rome, 1981); Richard L. Kagan, *Students and Society in Early Modern Spain* (Baltimore and London, 1974), examining the dynamics of the relationship between universities and the bureaucracies of church and state.

Cultural Change: Richard H. Popkin, *The History of Skepticism from Erasmus to Descartes* (Assen, 1960); J. H. Hexter, *Reappraisals in History: New Views on History and Society in Early Modern Europe* (London, 1961; 2nd ed., Chicago, 1979); Paul Lawrence Rose, *Bodin and the Great God of Nature: The Moral and Religious Universe of a Judaiser* (Geneva, 1980, on his *Heptaplomeres,* and Rose, ed., *Jean Bodin. Selected Writings on Philosophy, Religion and Politics* (Geneva, 1980); Eric Cochrane, *Florence in the Forgotten Centuries, 1527–1800* (Chicago, 1973), and Cochrane, ed., *The Late Italian Renaissance, 1525–1630* (New York, 1970); Manfred P. Fleischer, *Späthumanismus in Schlesien: Ausgewählte Aufsätze* (Munich, 1984).

Machiavelli and Machiavellianism: J. H. Hexter, *The Vision of Politics on the Eve of the Reformation: More, Machiavelli, and Seyssel* (New York, 1973); Roberto Ridolfi, *The Life of Niccolò Machiavelli* (Chicago, 1963); Felix Gilbert, *Machiavelli and Guicciardini: Politics and History in Sixteenth Century Florence* (Princeton, 1965); Friedrich Meinecke, *Machiavellism: The Doctrine of Raison d'État and Its Place in Modern History* (New Haven, 1957); Rodolfo de De Mattei, *Dal premachiavellismo all'antimachiavellismo* (Florence, 1969); Hiram Haydn, *The Counter-Renaissance* (New York, 1950).

Occult Science: Carlo Ginzburg, "High and Low: The Theme of Forbidden Knowledge in the Sixteenth and Seventeenth Centuries," *Past and Present,* 73 (1976), 28–41; Wayne Shumaker, *The Occult Sciences in the Renaissance: A Study in Intellectual Patterns* (Berkeley, 1972); David P. Walker, *Spiritual and Demonic Magic from Ficino to Campanella* (London, 1958); Frances Amelia Yates, *Giordano Bruno and the Hermetic Tradition* (Chicago, 1964). Paracelsus: Robert-Henri Blaser, *Paracelsus et sa conception de la nature* (Geneva, 1950); Kurt Goldammer, ed., *Theologische und religionsphilosophische Schriften: Sämtliche Werke, 2. Abt.* (Wiesbaden, 1955–1961); *Paracelsus in der Tradition. Vorträge/Paracelsustag 1978,* ed., Internationale Paracelsusgesellschaft zu Salzburg (Vienna, 1980); Walter Pagel, *Paracelsus: An Introduction to Philosophical Medicine in the Era of the Renaissance* (Basel, 1958).

Witchcraft: Sydney Anglo, *The Damned Art: Essays in the Literature of Witchcraft* (London, 1977); Norman Cohn, *Europe's Inner Demons: An Enquiry Inspired by the Great Witch Hunt* (New York, 1975); H. R. Trevor-Roper, "The European Witch-Craze of the Sixteenth and Seventeenth Centuries," in his *The Crisis of the Seventeenth Century: Religion, the Reformation and Social Change* (New York, 1968), pp. 90–192; H. C. Eric Midelfort, *Witch Hunting in Southwestern Germany, 1562–1684: The Social and Intellectual Foundations* (Stanford, 1972); E. William Monter, *Witchcraft in France and Switzerland: The Borderlands During the Reformation* (Ithaca, 1976); Russell Zguta, "Witchcraft and Medicine in Pre-Petrine Russia," *The Russian Review,* 37 (1978), 438–48; Alan Macfarlane, *Witchcraft in Tudor and Stuart England* (London, 1970); Cécile Ernst, *Teufelaustreibungen: Die Praxis der katholischen Kirche im 16. und 17. Jahrhundert* (Bern, 1972); Brian Easlea, *Witch Hunting, Magic, and the New Philosophy: An Introduction to the Debates of the Scientific Revolution 1450–1750* (Brighton, 1980).

Scientific Revolution: Allen G. Debus, *Man and Nature in the Renaissance* (Cambridge, 1978), and *The Chemical Philosophy: Paracelsian Science and Medicine in the Sixteenth and Seventeenth Centuries* (New York, 1977); Alistair C. Crombie, *Medieval and Early Modern Science* (2 vols., 2nd ed., New York, 1959); Marie Boas, *The Scientific Renaissance, 1450–1630* (New York, 1962); Alexandre Koyré, *From the Closed World to the Infinite Universe* (Baltimore, 1957); Herbert Butterfield, *The Origins of Modern Science, 1300–1800* (London, 1957); Alfred Rupert Hall, *The Scientific Revolution, 1500–1800* (London and New York, 1954); Donald O'Malley, *Andreas Vesalius* (Berkeley, 1964); Paolo Rossi, *Francis Bacon: From Magic to Science* (London, 1968); John Dillenberger, *Protestant Thought and Natural Science* (New York, 1960); Brian Gerrish, "The Reformation and the Rise of Modern Science: Luther, Calvin, and Copernicus," in his *The Old Protestantism and the New: Essays on the Reformation Heritage* (Chicago, 1982), pp. 163–78.

"Every great book is an action,
and every great action is a book!"
—Martin Luther

INDEX